The Methodology and Practice of Econometrics

A Festschrift in Honour of David F. Hendry

Edited by

Jennifer L. Castle

and

Neil Shephard

OXFORD
UNIVERSITY PRESS

OXFORD
UNIVERSITY PRESS

Great Clarendon Street, Oxford, OX2 6DP,
United Kingdom

Oxford University Press is a department of the University of Oxford.
It furthers the University's objective of excellence in research, scholarship,
and education by publishing worldwide. Oxford is a registered trade mark of
Oxford University Press in the UK and in certain other countries

First published 2009
First published in paperback 2015

Published in the United States of America by Oxford University Press
198 Madison Avenue, New York, NY 10016, United States of America

British Library Cataloguing in Publication Data
Data available

Library of Congress Cataloging in Publication Data
Data available

ISBN 978–0–19–923719–7 (Hbk.)
ISBN 978–0–19–874378–1 (Pbk.)

Preface

This book collects a series of essays to celebrate the work of David Hendry: one of the most influential of all modern econometricians.

David's writing has covered many areas of modern econometrics, which brings together insights from economic theory, past empirical evidence, the power of modern computing, and rigorous statistical theory to try to build useful empirically appealing models. His work led to the blossoming of the use of error correction models in applied and theoretical work. The questions he asked about multivariate nonstationary time-series were the basis of Clive Granger's formalization of cointegration. His sustained research programme has led to a massive increase in the rigour with which many economists carry out applied work on economic time-series. He pioneered the development of strong econometric software (e.g. PcGive and PcGets) to allow applied researchers to use their time effectively and developed the general-to-specific approach to model selection. Throughout the period we have known him he has been the most intellectually generous colleague we have ever had. A brave searcher for truth and clarity, with broad and deep knowledge, he is, to us, what an academic should be.

The volume is a collection of original research in time-series econometrics, both theoretical and applied, and reflects David's interests in econometric methodology. The volume is broadly divided into five sections, including model selection, correlations, forecasting, methodology, and empirical applications, although the boundaries are certainly opaque. The first four chapters focus on issues of model selection, a topic that has received a revival of interest in the last decade, partly due to David's own writings on the subject. Johansen and Nielsen provide rigorous model selection theory by deriving an innovative estimator that is robust to outliers and structural breaks. Three further chapters consider more applied aspects of model selection, including Hoover, Demiralp, and Perez who use automatic causal search and selection search algorithms to identify structural VARs, White and Kennedy who develop methods for defining, identifying, and estimating causal effects, and Doornik who develops a new general-to-specific search algorithm, Autometrics.

The next two chapters focus on techniques for modelling financial data, with applications to equity and commodity prices. Engle proposes a new estimation method for Factor DCC models called the 'McGyver' method, and Trivedi and Zimmer consider the use of copula mixture models to test for dependence.

The third section focuses on economic forecasting, an area that David has been prolific in. Stock and Watson consider the performance of factor based macroeconomic forecasts under structural instability, Banerjee and Marcellino extend the dynamic factor model to incorporate error correction models, and Clements considers whether forecasters are consistent in making forecasts, enabling a test of forecaster rationality. The fourth section considers econometric methodology in the broad sense, commencing with Granger's appeal for pragmatic econometrics, embodying much of David's econometric philosophy. The question of how to undertake simulations in dynamic models is addressed by Abadir and Paruolo, both Dolado, Gonzalo, and Mayoral, and Davidson examine the order of integration of time-series data, either for fractionally integrated processes or stationary versus nonstationary processes, and finally Hendry, Lu, and Mizon, complete the section by considering model identification and the implications it has for model evaluation.

The final section of the volume consists of a range of empirical applications that implement much of the Hendry methodology. Beyer and Juselius consider the question of how to aggregate data, with an application to a small monetary model of the Euro-area, Bårdsen and Nymoen consider the US natural rate of unemployment, selecting between a Phillips curve and a wage equilibrium correction mechanism, and Ericsson and Kamin revisit a model of Argentine broad money demand using general-to-specific model selection algorithms. The contributions cover the full breadth of time-series econometrics but all with the overarching theme of congruent econometric modelling using the coherent and comprehensive methodology that David has pioneered.

The volume assimilates original scholarly work at the frontier of academic research, encapsulating the current thinking in modern day econometrics and reflecting the intellectual impact that David has had, and will continue to have, on the profession.

We are indebted to a great many referees for their hard work in ensuring a consistently high standard of essays. Furthermore, it is a great pleasure to acknowledge all who helped to organize the conference in honour of David, held in Oxford in August 2007. In particular, our thanks go to Maureen Baker, Ann Gibson, Carlos Santos, Bent Nielsen, Jurgen Doornik, and the staff at the Economics Department. The conference was generously supported by our sponsors including the Bank of England, ESRC, Journal of Applied

Econometrics, Oxford-Man Institute of Quantitative Finance, Oxford Economic Papers, Oxford University Press, Royal Economic Society, Timberlake Consultants, and Wiley-Blackwell Publishers, and we are delighted to record our gratitude to them. Finally, our thanks extend to David, whose interactions and discussions with all the authors in the volume have been the inspiration for the research in this collection.

Jennifer L. Castle
Neil Shephard

Contents

List of Contributors

Karim M. Abadir *Imperial College, London*

Anindya Banerjee *University of Birmingham*

Gunnar Bårdsen *The Norwegian University of Science and Technology*

Andreas Beyer *European Central Bank*

Michael P. Clements *University of Reading*

James Davidson *University of Exeter*

Selva Damiralp *Kǫc University*

Juan J. Dolado *Universidad Carlos III de Madrid*

Jurgen A. Doornik *University of Oxford*

Robert F. Engle *New York University*

Neil R. Ericsson *Board of Governors of the Federal Reserve System*

Jesus Gonzalo *Universidad Carlos III de Madrid*

Clive W. J. Granger

David F. Hendry *University of Oxford*

Kevin D. Hoover *Duke University*

Søren Johansen *University of Copenhagen, and CREATES, University of Aarhus*

Katarina Juselius *University of Copenhagen*

Steven B. Kamin *Board of Governors of the Federal Reserve System*

Pauline Kennedy *Bates White, LLC*

Maozu Lu *University of Southampton*

Massimiliano Marcellino *Bocconi University and European University Institute, Florence*

Laura Mayoral *Institute for Economic Analysis, Spain (CSIC)*

Grayham E. Mizon *University of Southampton*

Bent Nielsen *University of Oxford*

Ragnar Nymoen *University of Oslo*

Paolo Paruolo *University of Insubria*

Stephen J. Perez *California State University*

James H. Stock *Harvard University and the National Bureau of Economic Research*

Pravin K. Trivedi *Indiana University*

Mark W. Watson *Princeton University, and the National Bureau of Economic Research*

Halbert White

David H. Zimmer *Western Kentucky University*

1

An Analysis of the Indicator Saturation Estimator as a Robust Regression Estimator

*Søren Johansen and Bent Nielsen**

1.1 Introduction

In an analysis of US food expenditure Hendry (1999) used an indicator saturation approach. The annual data spanned the period 1931–1989 including the Great Depression, World War II, and the oil crises. These episodes, covering 25% of the sample, could potentially result in outliers. An indicator saturation approach was adopted by forming zero-one indicators for these observations. Condensing the outcome, this large number of indicators could be reduced to just two outliers with an institutional interpretation.

The suggestion for outlier detection divides the sample in two sets and saturates first one set and then the other with indicators. The indicators are tested for significance using the parameter estimates from the other set and the corresponding observation is deleted if the test statistic is significant. The estimator is the least squares estimator based upon the retained observations. A formal version of this estimator is the indicator saturation estimator. This was analysed recently by Hendry, Johansen, and Santos (2008), who derived the asymptotic distribution of the estimator of the mean in the case of i.i.d. observations.

The purpose of the present chapter is to analyse the indicator saturation algorithm as a special case of a general procedure considered in the literature of robust statistics. We consider the regression model $y_t = \beta' x_t + \varepsilon_t$ where ε_t

* The first author gratefully acknowledges support from Center for Research in Econometric Analysis of Time Series, CREATES, funded by the Danish National Research Foundation. The second author received financial support from ESRC grant RES-000-27-0179. The figure was constructed using R (R Development Core Team, 2006). The authors would like to thank David Cox and Mette Ejrnæs for some useful comments on an earlier version of the chapter.

are i.i.d. $(0, \sigma^2)$, and a preliminary estimator $(\hat{\beta}, \hat{\sigma}^2)$, which gives residuals $r_t = y_t - \hat{\beta}' x_t$. Let $\hat{\omega}_t^2$ be an estimate of the variance of r_t. Examples are $\hat{\omega}_t^2 = \hat{\sigma}^2$ which is constant in t and $\hat{\omega}_t^2 = \hat{\sigma}^2\{1 - x_t'(\sum_{s=1}^T x_s x_s')^{-1} x_t\}$ which varies with t. From this define the normalized residuals $v_t = r_t/\hat{\omega}_t$. The main result in Theorem 1.1 is an asymptotic expansion of the least squares estimator for (β, σ^2) based upon those observations for which $\underline{c} \leq v_t \leq \overline{c}$.

This expansion is then applied to find asymptotic distributions for various choices of preliminary estimator, like least squares and the split least squares considered in the indicator saturation approach. Asymptotic distributions are derived under stationary and trend stationary autoregressive processes and some results are given for unit root processes.

We do not give any results on the behaviour of the estimators in the presence of outliers, but refer to further work which we intend to do in the future.

1.1.1 *The Relation to the Literature on Robust Statistics*

Detections of outliers is generally achieved by robust statistics in the class of M-estimators, or L-estimators, see for instance Huber (1981). An M-estimator of the type considered here is found by solving

$$\sum_{t=1}^{T} (y_t - \beta' x_t) x_t' 1_{(\sigma \underline{c} \leq y_t - \beta' x_t \leq \sigma \overline{c})} = 0, \tag{1.1}$$

supplemented with an estimator of the variance of the residual. The objective function is known as Huber's skip function and has the property that it is not differentiable in β, σ^2. The solution may not be unique and the calculation can be difficult due to the lack of differentiability, see Koenker (2005). A more tractable one-step estimator can be found from a preliminary estimator $(\hat{\beta}, \hat{\sigma})$ and choice of $\hat{\omega}_t^2$, by solving

$$\sum_{t=1}^{T} (y_t - \beta' x_t) x_t' 1_{(\hat{\omega}_t \underline{c} \leq y_t - \hat{\beta}' x_t \leq \hat{\omega}_t \overline{c})} = 0, \tag{1.2}$$

which is just the least squares estimator where some observations are removed as outliers according to a test based on the preliminary estimator. Note that the choice of the quantiles requires that we know the density f of ε_t.

An alternative method is to order the residuals $r_t = y_t - \beta' x_t$ and eliminate the smallest $T\alpha_1$ and largest $T\alpha_2$ observations, and then use the remaining observations to calculate the least squares estimators. This is an L-estimator, based upon order statistics. A one-step estimator is easily calculated if a preliminary estimator is used to define the residuals. One can consider the M- and L-estimators as the estimators found by iterating the one step procedure described.

Rather than discarding outliers they could be capped at the quantile c as in the Winsorized least squares estimator solving $\sum_{t=1}^{T} r_t x_t' \min(1, c\hat{\omega}_t/|r_t|) = 0$, see Huber (1981, page 18). While the treatment of the outliers must depend on the substantive context, we focus on the skip estimator in this chapter. A related estimator is the least trimmed squares estimator by Rousseeuw (1984) which minimizes $\sum_{i=1}^{h} r_i^2$ after having discarded the largest $T - h = T(\alpha_1 + \alpha_2)$ values of r_i^2.

The estimator we consider in our main result is the estimator (1.2), and we apply the main result to get the asymptotic distribution of the estimators for stationary processes, trend stationary processes, and some unit root processes for different choices of preliminary estimator.

One-step estimators have been considered before. The paper by Bickel (1975) has a one-step M-estimator of a different kind as the minimization problem is approximated using a linearization of the derivative of the objective function around a preliminary estimator. The estimator considered by Ruppert and Carroll (1980), however, is a one-step estimator of the kind described above, although of the L-type, see also Yohai and Maronna (1976).

The focus in the robustness literature has been on deterministic regressors satisfying $T^{-1}\sum_{t=1}^{T} x_t x_t' \to \Sigma > 0$, whereas we prove results for stationary and trend stationary autoregressive processes. We also allow for a nonsymmetric error distribution.

We apply the theory of empirical processes using tightness arguments similar to Bickel (1975). The representation in our main result Theorem 1.1 generalizes the representations in Ruppert and Carroll (1980) to stochastic regressors needed for time-series analysis.

As an example of the relation between the one-step estimator we consider and the general theory of M-estimators, consider the representation we find in Theorem 1.1 for the special case of i.i.d. observations with a symmetric distribution with mean μ, so that $x_t = 1$. In this case we find

$$T^{1/2}(\breve{\mu} - \mu) = (1-\alpha)^{-1}\left\{T^{-1/2}\sum_{t=1}^{T} \varepsilon_t 1_{(\underline{c}\sigma \le \varepsilon_t \le \sigma\overline{c})} + 2c\mathsf{f}(c)T^{1/2}(\hat{\mu} - \mu)\right\} + \mathrm{o_P}(1).$$

If we iterate this procedure we could end up with an estimator, μ^*, which satisfies

$$T^{1/2}(\mu^* - \mu) = (1-\alpha)^{-1}\left\{T^{-1/2}\sum_{t=1}^{T} \varepsilon_t 1_{(\underline{c}\sigma \le \varepsilon_t \le \sigma\overline{c})} + 2c\mathsf{f}(c)T^{1/2}(\mu^* - \mu)\right\} + \mathrm{o_P}(1),$$

so that

$$\begin{aligned} T^{1/2}(\mu^* - \mu) &= \{1 - \alpha - 2c\mathsf{f}(c)\}^{-1} T^{-1/2}\sum_{t=1}^{T} \varepsilon_t 1_{(\underline{c}\sigma \le \varepsilon_t \le \sigma\overline{c})} + \mathrm{o_P}(1) \\ &\overset{\mathsf{D}}{\to} \mathsf{N}\left[0, \sigma^2 \frac{\tau_2^c}{\{1 - \alpha - 2c\mathsf{f}(c)\}^2}\right], \end{aligned}$$

which is the limit distribution conjectured by Huber (1964) for the M-estimator (1.1). It is also the asymptotic distribution of the least trimmed squares estimator, see Rousseeuw and Leroy (1987, p. 180), who rely on Yohai and Maronna (1976) for the i.i.d case.

1.1.2 *The Structure of the Chapter*

The one-step estimators are described in detail in section 1.2, and in section 1.3 we find the asymptotic expansion of the estimators under general assumptions on the regressor variables, but under the assumption that the data generating process is given by the regression model without indicators. The situation where the initial estimator is a least square estimator is analysed for stationary processes in section 1.4.1. The situation where the initial estimator is an indicator saturated estimator is then considered for stationary process in section 1.4.2 and for trend stationary autoregressive processes and unit root processes in section 1.5. Section 1.6 contains the proof of the main theorem, which involves techniques for empirical processes, whereas proofs for special cases are given in section 1.7. Finally, section 1.8 concludes.

1.2 The One-step *M*-estimators

First the statistical model is set up. Subsequently, the considered one-step estimators are introduced.

1.2.1 *The Regression Model*

As a statistical model consider the regression model

$$y_t = \beta' x_t + \sum_{i=1}^{T} \gamma_i 1_{(i=t)} + \varepsilon_t \qquad t = 1, \ldots, T, \tag{1.3}$$

where x_t is an m-dimensional vector of regressors and the conditional distribution of the errors, ε_t, given $(x_1, \ldots x_t, \varepsilon_1, \ldots, \varepsilon_{t-1})$ has density $\sigma^{-1}\mathsf{f}(\sigma^{-1}\varepsilon)$, so that $\sigma^{-1}\varepsilon_t$ are i.i.d. with density f. Thus, the density of y_t given the past should be a member of a location-scale family such as the family of univariate normal distributions. When working with other distributions, such as the t-distribution the degrees of freedom should be known. We denote expectation and variance given $(x_1, \ldots x_t, \varepsilon_1, \ldots, \varepsilon_{t-1})$ by E_{t-1} and Var_{t-1}.

The parameter space of the model is given by $\beta, (\gamma_1, \ldots, \gamma_T), \sigma^2 \in \mathbb{R}^m \times \mathbb{R}^T \times \mathbb{R}_+$. The number of parameters is therefore larger than the sample length. We want to make inference on the parameter of interest β in this regression problem with T observations and m regressors, where we consider the γ_is as nuisance parameters. The least squares estimator for β is contaminated by the γ_is and we therefore seek to robustify the estimator by introducing two critical values $\underline{c} < \overline{c}$ chosen so that

$$\tau_0^c = \int_{\underline{c}}^{\overline{c}} \mathsf{f}(v)dv = 1 - \alpha \quad \text{and} \quad \tau_1^c = \int_{\underline{c}}^{\overline{c}} v\mathsf{f}(v)dv = 0. \tag{1.4}$$

It is convenient to introduce as a general notation

$$\tau_n = \int_{\mathbb{R}} u^n \mathsf{f}(u)du, \qquad \tau_n^c = \int_{\underline{c}}^{\overline{c}} u^n \mathsf{f}(u)du, \tag{1.5}$$

for $n \in \mathbb{N}_0$, for the moments and truncated moments of f. A smoothness assumption to the density is needed.

Assumption A. *The density* f *has continuous derivative* f′ *and satisfies the condition*

$$\sup_{v\in\mathbb{R}}\{(1 + v^4)\mathsf{f}(v) + (1 + v^2)|\mathsf{f}'(v)|\} < \infty,$$

with moments $\tau_1 = 0$, $\tau_2 = 1$, $\tau_4 < \infty$.

1.2.2 *Two One-step M-estimators*

Two estimators are presented based on algorithms designed to eliminate observations with large values of $|\gamma_i|$. Both estimators are examples of one-step M-estimators. They differ in the choice of initial estimator. The first is based on a standard least squares estimator, while the second is based on the indicator saturation argument.

1.2.2.1 The Robustified Least Squares Estimator

The robustified least squares estimator is a one-step M-estimator with initial estimator given as the least squares estimator $(\hat{\beta}, \hat{\sigma}^2)$. From this, construct the t-ratios for testing $\gamma_t = 0$ as

$$v_t = (y_t - \hat{\beta}' x_t)/\hat{\omega}_t, \tag{1.6}$$

where $\hat{\omega}_t^2$ could simply be chosen as $\hat{\sigma}^2$ or as $\hat{\sigma}^2\{1 - x_t'(\sum_{s=1}^T x_s x_s')^{-1} x_t\}$ by following the usual finite sample formula for the distribution of residuals for fixed regressors.

We base the estimator on those observations that are judged insignificantly different from the predicted value $\hat{\beta}' x_t$, and define the robustified least squares estimator as the one-step M-estimator

$$\breve{\beta}_{LS} = \left\{ \sum_{t=1}^{T} x_t x_t' 1_{(\underline{c} \le v_t \le \overline{c})} \right\}^{-1} \sum_{t=1}^{T} x_t y_t 1_{(\underline{c} \le v_t \le \overline{c})}, \tag{1.7}$$

$$\breve{\sigma}_{LS}^2 = \left(\frac{\tau_2^c}{1-\alpha} \right)^{-1} \left\{ \sum_{t=1}^{T} 1_{(\underline{c} \le v_t \le \overline{c})} \right\}^{-1} \sum_{t=1}^{T} (y_t - \breve{\beta}_{LS}' x_t)^2 1_{(\underline{c} \le v_t \le \overline{c})}. \tag{1.8}$$

It will be shown that $\{\sum_{t=1}^{T} 1_{(\underline{c} \le v_t \le \overline{c})}\}^{-1} \sum_{t=1}^{T} (y_t - \breve{\beta}_{LS}' x_t)^2 1_{(\underline{c} \le v_t \le \overline{c})} \overset{\mathsf{P}}{\to} \sigma^2 \tau_2^c/(1-\alpha)$, which justifies the bias correction in the expression for $\breve{\sigma}_{LS}^2$.

Obviously the denominators can be zero, but in this case also the numerator is zero and we can define $\breve{\beta}_{LS} = 0$ and $\breve{\sigma}_{LS}^2 = 0$.

1.2.2.2 The Indicator Saturation Estimator

Based on the idea of Hendry (1999) the indicator saturated estimator is defined as follows:

1. We split the data in two sets $\mathcal{I}_1$ and $\mathcal{I}_2$ of T_1 and T_2 observations respectively, where $T_j T^{-1} \to \lambda_j > 0$ for $T \to \infty$.
2. We calculate the ordinary least squares estimator for (β, σ^2) based upon the sample $\mathcal{I}_j$

$$\hat{\beta}_j = \left(\sum_{t \in \mathcal{I}_j} x_t x_t' \right)^{-1} \sum_{t \in \mathcal{I}_j} x_t y_t, \qquad \hat{\sigma}_j^2 = \frac{1}{T_j} \sum_{t \in \mathcal{I}_j} (y_t - \hat{\beta}_j' x_t)^2, \tag{1.9}$$

   and define the t-ratios for testing $\gamma_t = 0$:

$$v_t = 1_{(t \in \mathcal{I}_2)} (y_t - \hat{\beta}_1' x_t)/\hat{\omega}_{t,1} + 1_{(t \in \mathcal{I}_1)} (y_t - \hat{\beta}_2' x_t)/\hat{\omega}_{t,2}, \tag{1.10}$$

   where $\hat{\omega}_{t,j}^2$ could be chosen as $\hat{\sigma}_j^2$ or $\hat{\sigma}_j^2\{1 + x_t'(\sum_{s \notin \mathcal{I}_j} x_s x_s')^{-1} x_t\}$ as for fixed regressors.
3. We then compute robustified least squares estimators $\tilde{\beta}$ and $\tilde{\sigma}^2$ by (1.7) and (1.8) based on v_t given by (1.10).
4. Based on the estimators $\tilde{\beta}$ and $\tilde{\sigma}^2$ define the t-ratios for testing $\gamma_t = 0$:

$$\tilde{v}_t = (y_t - \tilde{\beta}' x_t)/\tilde{\omega}_t, \tag{1.11}$$

   where $\tilde{\omega}_t^2$ could be chosen as $\tilde{\sigma}^2$. It is less obvious how to choose a finite sample correction since the second round initial estimator $(\tilde{\beta}, \tilde{\sigma}^2)$ is not based upon least squares.
5. Finally, compute the indicator saturated estimators $\breve{\beta}_{Sat}$ and $\breve{\sigma}_{Sat}^2$ as the robustified least squares estimators (1.7) and (1.8) based on $\tilde{v}_t$ given by (1.11).

1.3 The Main Asymptotic Result

Asymptotic distributions will be derived under the assumption that in (1.3) the indicators are not needed because $\gamma_i = 0$ for all i, that is, $(y_t - \beta' x_t)/\sigma$ are i.i.d. with density f. The main result, given here, shows that in the analysis of one-step M-estimators the indicators $1_{(\underline{c} \leq v_t \leq \overline{c})}$, based on the normalized residual $v_t = (y_t - \hat{\beta}' x_t)/\hat{\omega}_t$, can be replaced by $1_{(\underline{c}\sigma \leq \varepsilon_t < \overline{c}\sigma)}$ combined with correction terms. This shows how the limit distributions of the initial estimators $\hat{\beta}$ and $\hat{\sigma}^2$ influence the limit distribution of the robustified estimators. The result is the basis for any further asymptotic analysis and can be applied both for stationary and trend stationary regressors, and for unit root processes, but not for explosive processes.

It is convenient to define product moments of the retained observations for any two processes u_t and w_t as $S_{uw} = \sum_{t=1}^{T} u_t w_t' 1_{(\underline{c} \leq v_t \leq \overline{c})}$, so that the robustified estimators (1.7) and (1.8) become

$$\breve{\beta} = S_{xx}^{-1} S_{xy}, \tag{1.12}$$

$$\breve{\sigma}^2 = (1 - \alpha)(\tau_2^c S_{11})^{-1}(S_{yy} - S_{yx} S_{xx}^{-1} S_{xy}). \tag{1.13}$$

The estimator $\hat{\omega}_t^2$ for the variance of residual r_t can be chosen from a wide range of estimators including $\hat{\sigma}^2$ and $\hat{\sigma}^2\{1 - x_t'(\sum_{s=1}^{T} x_s x_s')^{-1} x_t\}$. These estimators do, however, have to satisfy the following condition.

Assumption B. *The estimator* $\hat{\omega}_t^2$ *is chosen so* $\max_{1 \leq t \leq T} T^{1/2} |\hat{\omega}_t^2 - \hat{\sigma}^2| = o_P(1)$.

We can now formulate the main result which shows how the product moments S_{uv} depend on the truncation points $\underline{c}$ and $\overline{c}$ and the initial estimators $\hat{\beta}$ and $\hat{\sigma}^2$.

Theorem 1.1. *Consider model (1.3), where* $\gamma_i = 0$ *for all i, and there exists some estimators* $(\hat{\beta}, \hat{\sigma}^2)$ *and nonstochastic normalization matrices* $N_T \to 0$, *so that*

(i) The initial estimators satisfy

(a) $T^{1/2}(\hat{\sigma}^2 - \sigma^2)$, $(N_T^{-1})'(\hat{\beta} - \beta) = O_P(1)$,

(b) $\hat{\omega}_t^2$ *satisfies Assumption B.*

(ii) The regressors satisfy, jointly,

(a) $N_T \sum_{t=1}^{T} x_t x_t' N_T' \overset{D}{\to} \Sigma \overset{a.s.}{>} 0$,

(b) $T^{-1/2} N_T \sum_{t=1}^{T} x_t \overset{D}{\to} \mu$,

(c) $\max_{t \leq T} \mathsf{E}|T^{1/2} N_T x_t|^4 = O(1)$.

(iii) *The density* f *satisfies Assumption A, and* $\underline{c}$ *and* $\overline{c}$ *are chosen so that* $\tau_1^c = 0$.

Then it holds

$$T^{-1}S_{11} \overset{\mathsf{P}}{\to} 1-\alpha, \tag{1.14}$$

$$N_T S_{xx} N_T' \overset{\mathsf{D}}{\to} (1-\alpha)\Sigma, \tag{1.15}$$

$$T^{-1/2} N_T S_{x1} \overset{\mathsf{D}}{\to} (1-\alpha)\mu. \tag{1.16}$$

For $\xi_n^c = (\overline{c})^n f(\overline{c}) - (\underline{c})^n f(\underline{c})$ *and* $\tau_2^c = \int_{\underline{c}}^{\overline{c}} v^2 \mathsf{f}(v)dv$ *we find the expansions*

$$N_T S_{x\varepsilon} = N_T \sum_{t=1}^{T} \left\{ x_t \varepsilon_t 1_{(\underline{c}\sigma \le \varepsilon_t \le \overline{c}\sigma)} + \xi_1^c x_t x_t'(\hat{\beta}-\beta) + \xi_2^c(\hat{\sigma}-\sigma)x_t \right\} + \mathrm{o_P}(1), \tag{1.17}$$

$$S_{\varepsilon\varepsilon} = \sum_{t=1}^{T} \left\{ \varepsilon_t^2 1_{(\underline{c}\sigma \le \varepsilon_t \le \overline{c}\sigma)} + \sigma\xi_2^c(\hat{\beta}-\beta)'x_t + \sigma\xi_3^c(\hat{\sigma}-\sigma) \right\} + \mathrm{o_P}\left(T^{1/2}\right), \tag{1.18}$$

$$S_{11} = \sum_{t=1}^{T} \left\{ 1_{(\underline{c}\sigma \le \varepsilon_t \le \overline{c}\sigma)} + \xi_0^c(\hat{\beta}-\beta)'x_t/\sigma + \xi_1^c(\hat{\sigma}/\sigma - 1) \right\} + \mathrm{o_P}\left(T^{1/2}\right). \tag{1.19}$$

Combining the expressions for the product moments gives expressions for the one-step *M*-estimators of the form (1.12), (1.13). The expressions give a linearization of these estimators in terms of the initial estimators. For particular initial estimators explicit expressions for the limiting distributions are then derived in the subsequent sections.

Corollary 1.2. *Suppose the assumptions of Theorem 1.1 are satisfied. Then*

$$(1-\alpha)\Sigma(N_T^{-1})'(\breve{\beta}-\beta) = N_T \sum_{t=1}^{T} x_t \varepsilon_t 1_{(\underline{c}\sigma \le \varepsilon_t \le \sigma\overline{c})}$$
$$+ \xi_1^c \Sigma(N_T^{-1})'(\hat{\beta}-\beta) + \xi_2^c T^{1/2}(\hat{\sigma}-\sigma)\mu + \mathrm{o_P}(1), \tag{1.20}$$

$$\tau_2^c T^{1/2}(\breve{\sigma}^2 - \sigma^2) = T^{-1/2} \sum_{t=1}^{T} \left(\varepsilon_t^2 - \sigma^2 \frac{\tau_2^c}{1-\alpha} \right) 1_{(\underline{c}\sigma \le \varepsilon_t \le \sigma\overline{c})}$$
$$+ \sigma\zeta_2^c \mu'(N_T^{-1})'(\hat{\beta}-\beta) + \sigma\zeta_3^c T^{1/2}(\hat{\sigma}-\sigma) + \mathrm{o_P}(1), \tag{1.21}$$

where $\zeta_n^c = \xi_n^c - \xi_{n-2}^c \tau_2^c/(1-\alpha)$. *It follows that*

$$\left\{ (N_T^{-1})'(\breve{\beta}-\beta), T^{1/2}(\breve{\sigma}^2 - \sigma^2) \right\} = \mathrm{O_P}(1), \tag{1.22}$$

so that $(\breve{\beta}, \breve{\sigma}^2) \overset{\mathsf{P}}{\to} (\beta, \sigma^2)$.

The proofs of Theorem 1.1 and Corollary 1.2 are given in section 1.6. It involves a series of steps. In section 1.6.1 a number of inequalities are given for the indicator functions appearing in S_{xx} and $S_{x\varepsilon}$, and in section 1.6.2 we show some limit results which take care of the remainder terms in the expansions.

The argument involves weighted empirical processes with weights $x_t x_t'$, $x_t\varepsilon_t$, ε_t^2 and 1 appearing in the numerator and denominators of $\breve{\beta}$ and $\breve{\sigma}^2$. Weighted empirical processes have been studied by Koul (2002), but with conditions on the weights that would be too restrictive for this study. Finally, the threads are pulled together in section 1.6.3.

The assumptions (ii,a) and (ii,b) are satisfied in a wide range of models. The assumption (ii,c) is slightly more restrictive: It permits classical stationary regressions as well as stationary autoregressions in which case $N_T = T^{-1/2}$ and trend stationary processes with a suitable choice of N_T. It also permits unit root processes where $N_T = T^{-1}$, as well as processes combining stationary and unit root phenomena. The assumption (ii,c) does, however, exclude exponentially growing regressors. As an example let $x_t = 2^t$. In that case $N_T = 2^{-T}$ and $\max_{t\leq T} T^{1/2}2^{-T}2^t = T^{1/2}$ diverges. Likewise, explosive autoregressions are excluded.

Similarly, the assumption (i,b), referring to Assumption B, is satisfied for a wide range of situations. If $\hat{\omega}_t^2 = \hat{\sigma}^2$ it is trivially satisfied. If $\hat{\omega}_t^2 = \hat{\sigma}^2\{1 - x_t'(\sum_{s=1}^T x_s x_s')^{-1}x_t\}$ as in the computation of the robustified least squares estimator the assumption is satisfied when the regressors x_t have stationary, unit root, or polynomial components, but not if the regressors are explosive. This is proved by first proving (ii,a,c) and then combining these conditions.

The assumption that $\tau_1^c = 0$ is important. If it had been different from zero then $\varepsilon_t 1_{(\underline{c}\sigma\leq\varepsilon\leq\sigma\overline{c})}$ would not have zero mean and the conclusion (1.22) would in general fail because $N_T S_{x\varepsilon}$ would diverge.

1.4 Asymptotic Distributions in the Stationary Case

We now apply Theorem 1.1 and Corollary 1.2 to the case of stationary regressors with finite fourth moment where we can choose $N_T = T^{-1/2}I_m$. With this choice the assumptions $(ii)(a,b,c)$ of Theorem 1.1 are satisfied by the Law of Large Numbers for stationary processes with finite fourth moments.

The stationary case covers a wide range of standard models:

(i) The classical regression model, where x_t is stationary with finite fourth moment.

(ii) Stationary autoregression of order k. We let $y_t = X_t$ and $x_t = (X_{t-1} \dots X_{t-k})'$. An intercept could, but need not, be included as in the equation

$$X_t = \sum_{j=1}^{k} \alpha_j X_{t-j} + \mu + \varepsilon_t.$$

(iii) Autoregressive distributed lag models of order k. For this purpose consider a p-dimensional stationary process X_t partitioned as $X_t = (y_t, z_t')'$.

This gives the model equation for y_t given the past $(X_s, s \leq t-1)$ and z_t

$$y_t = \sum_{j=1}^{k} \alpha'_j X_{t-j} + \beta' z_t + \mu_y + \varepsilon_t.$$

Here, the regressor z_t could be excluded to give the equation of a vector autoregression.

1.4.1 *Asymptotic Distribution of the Robustified Least Squares Estimator*

In this section we denote the least squares estimators by $(\hat{\beta}, \hat{\sigma}^2)$ and we let $(\breve{\beta}_{LS}, \breve{\sigma}^2_{LS})$ be the robustified least squares estimators based on these, as given by (1.6), (1.12), and (1.13). We find the asymptotic distribution of these estimators with a proof in section 1.7.

Theorem 1.3. *Consider model (1.3) with $\gamma_i = 0$ for all i. We assume that x_t is a stationary process with mean μ, variance Σ, and finite fourth moment so we can take $N_T = T^{-1/2} I_m$, and that $\hat{\omega}^2_t$ satisfies Assumption B. The density f satisfies Assumption A, and $\underline{c}$ and $\bar{c}$ are chosen so that $\tau^c_1 = 0$. Then*

$$T^{1/2} \begin{pmatrix} \breve{\beta}_{LS} - \beta \\ \breve{\sigma}^2_{LS} - \sigma^2 \end{pmatrix} \overset{D}{\to} \mathsf{N}_{m+1} \left\{ 0, \begin{pmatrix} \Omega_\beta & \Omega_c \\ \Omega'_c & \Omega_\sigma \end{pmatrix} \right\},$$

where

$$\Omega_\beta = \sigma^2 (\eta_\beta \Sigma^{-1} + \kappa_\beta \Sigma^{-1} \mu \mu' \Sigma^{-1}),$$

$$\Omega_c = \sigma^3 (\eta_c \Sigma^{-1} \mu + \kappa_c \Sigma^{-1} \mu \mu' \Sigma^{-1} \mu),$$

$$\Omega_\sigma = 2\sigma^4 (\eta_\sigma + \kappa_\sigma \mu' \Sigma^{-1} \mu),$$

and

$$(1-\alpha)^2 \eta_\beta = \tau^c_2 (1 + 2\xi^c_1) + (\xi^c_1)^2,$$

$$(1-\alpha)^2 \kappa_\beta = \xi^c_2 \left\{ \frac{1}{4} \xi^c_2 (\tau_4 - 1) + \xi^c_1 \tau_3 + \tau^c_3 \right\},$$

$$(1-\alpha)\tau^c_2 \eta_c = \zeta^c_2 (\tau^c_2 + \xi^c_1) + \frac{\xi^c_2}{2} \left\{ \tau^c_4 - \frac{(\tau^c_2)^2}{1-\alpha} \right\} + \frac{\xi^c_2 \zeta^c_3}{4} (\tau_4 - 1)$$
$$+ (1 + \xi^c_1) \tau^c_3 + \frac{\zeta^c_3}{2} (\tau^c_3 + \xi^c_1 \tau_3),$$

$$(1-\alpha)\tau^c_2 \kappa_c = \frac{(\zeta^c_2)^2}{2} \tau^c_3,$$

$$2(\tau^c_2)^2 \eta_\sigma = \left\{ \tau^c_4 - \frac{(\tau^c_2)^2}{1-\alpha} \right\} (1 + \zeta^c_3) + \frac{(\zeta^c_3)^2}{4} (\tau_4 - 1),$$

$$2(\tau^c_2)^2 \kappa_\sigma = \zeta^c_2 (\zeta^c_2 + 2\tau^c_3 + \zeta^c_3 \tau_3).$$

For a given f, α, $\underline{c}$, *and* $\bar{c}$, *the coefficients* η *and* κ *are known. The parameters* (σ^2,Σ,μ) *are estimated by* $\breve{\sigma}^2_{LS}$, *see (1.22),* $N_T S_{xx} N_T/(1-\alpha)$, *see (1.15), and* $T^{-1/2}N_T S_{x1}/(1-\alpha)$, *see (1.16), respectively, so that, for instance*

$$(\eta_\beta \breve{\Sigma}^{-1} + \kappa_\beta \breve{\Sigma}^{-1}\breve{\mu}\breve{\mu}'\breve{\Sigma}^{-1})^{-1/2}\breve{\sigma}^{-1}_{LS}T^{1/2}(\breve{\beta}_{LS}-\beta) \overset{\mathsf{D}}{\to} \mathsf{N}_m(0,I_m).$$

The case where f is symmetric is of special interest. The critical value is then $c = -\underline{c} = \bar{c}$ and $\tau_3 = \tau_3^c = 0$ and $\xi_0^c = \xi_2^c = 0$ so $\zeta_2^c = 0$, whereas $\xi_1^c = 2c\mathsf{f}(c)$ and $\xi_3^c = 2c^3\mathsf{f}(c)$ so $\zeta_3^c = \{c^2 - \tau_2^c/(1-\alpha)\}2c\mathsf{f}(c)$. It follows that $\kappa_\beta = \kappa_\sigma = \kappa_c = \eta_c = 0$. Theorem 1.3 then has the following Corollary.

Corollary 1.4. *If* f *is symmetric and the assumptions of Theorem 1.3 hold, then*

$$T^{1/2}\begin{pmatrix} \breve{\beta}_{LS} - \beta \\ \breve{\sigma}^2_{LS} - \sigma^2 \end{pmatrix} \overset{\mathsf{D}}{\to} \mathsf{N}_{m+1}\left\{0, \begin{pmatrix} \sigma^2\eta_\beta\Sigma^{-1} & 0 \\ 0 & 2\sigma^4\eta_\sigma \end{pmatrix}\right\},$$

where, with $\xi_1^c = 2c\mathsf{f}(c)$ *and* $\zeta_3^c = \{c^2 - \tau_2^c/(1-\alpha)\}2c\mathsf{f}(c)$, *it holds*

$$(1-\alpha)^2\eta_\beta = \tau_2^c\left(1 + 2\xi_1^c\right) + \left(\xi_1^c\right)^2,$$

$$2\left(\tau_2^c\right)^2\eta_\sigma = \{\tau_4^c - \frac{\left(\tau_2^c\right)^2}{1-\alpha}\}(1+\zeta_3^c) + \frac{\left(\zeta_3^c\right)^2}{4}(\tau_4 - 1).$$

Corollary 1.4 shows that the efficiency of the indicator saturated estimator $\breve{\beta}_{LS}$ with respect to the least squares estimator $\hat{\beta}$ is

$$\mathsf{efficiency}(\hat{\beta},\breve{\beta}_{LS}) = \{\mathsf{asVar}(\breve{\beta}_{LS})\}^{-1}\{\mathsf{asVar}(\hat{\beta})\} = \eta_\beta^{-1}.$$

Likewise the efficiency of $\breve{\sigma}_{LS}$ is $\mathsf{efficiency}(\hat{\sigma}^2,\breve{\sigma}^2_{LS}) = \eta_\sigma^{-1}$. In the symmetric case the efficiency coefficients do not depend on the parameters of the process, only on the reference density f and the chosen critical value $c = \bar{c} = -\underline{c}$. They are illustrated in Figure 1.1.

1.4.2 *The Indicator Saturated Estimator*

The indicator saturated estimator, $\breve{\beta}_{Sat}$, is a one-step M-estimator iterated twice. Its properties are derived from Theorem 1.1. We first prove two representations corresponding to (1.20) and (1.21) for the first round estimators $\tilde{\beta}$, $\tilde{\sigma}^2$ based on the least squares estimators $\hat{\beta}_j$ and $\hat{\sigma}_j$. Secondly, the limiting distributions of these first round estimators are found. Finally, the limiting distributions of the second round estimators $\breve{\beta}_{Sat}$, $\breve{\sigma}_{Sat}$ are found.

Theorem 1.5. *Suppose* $\gamma_i = 0$ *for all* i *in model (1.3), and that* x_t *is stationary with mean* μ, *variance* Σ, *and finite fourth moment, and that* $\hat{\omega}^2_{t,1}$ *and* $\hat{\omega}^2_{t,2}$ *satisfy Assumption B. The density* f *satisfies Assumption A, and* $\underline{c}$ *and* $\bar{c}$ *are chosen so*

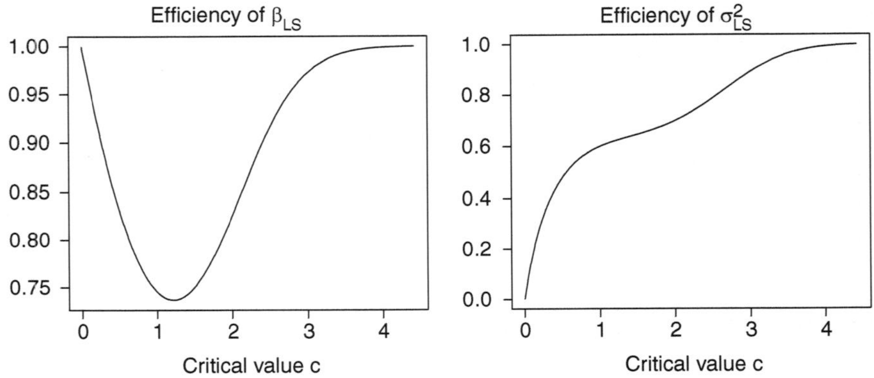

FIG. 1.1. The efficiency of the estimators $\breve{\beta}_{LS}$ and $\breve{\sigma}^2_{LS}$ with respect to the least squares estimators $\hat{\beta}$ and $\hat{\sigma}^2$, respectively, for f equal to the Gaussian density.

that $\tau_1^c = 0$. *Then, for* $j = 1,2$ *it holds, with* $\lambda_1 + \lambda_2 = 1$ *and* $\lambda_j > 0$, *that*

$$T^{-1}\sum_{t\in\mathcal{I}_j} x_t \overset{\mathsf{P}}{\to} \lambda_j\mu, \qquad T^{-1}\sum_{t\in\mathcal{I}_j} x_t x_t' \overset{\mathsf{P}}{\to} \lambda_j\Sigma. \tag{1.23}$$

Defining $\zeta_n^c = \xi_n^c - \xi_{n-2}^c\tau_2^c\sigma^2/(1-\alpha)$ *and the function* $h_t = (\lambda_1/\lambda_2)1_{\{t\in\mathcal{I}_2\}} + (\lambda_2/\lambda_1)1_{\{t\in\mathcal{I}_1\}}$. *Then it holds that*

$$(1-\alpha)\Sigma T^{1/2}(\tilde{\beta}-\beta) = T^{-1/2}\sum_{t=1}^{T}\left[x_t\{\varepsilon_t 1_{(\underline{c}\sigma\le\varepsilon_t\le\sigma\bar{c})} + h_t\xi_1^c\varepsilon_t\} + \frac{\xi_2^c}{2}\mu h_t(\varepsilon_t^2/\sigma-\sigma)\right] + \mathrm{o}_{\mathsf{P}}(1), \tag{1.24}$$

$$\tau_2^c T^{1/2}(\tilde{\sigma}^2-\sigma^2) = T^{-1/2}\sum_{t=1}^{T}\left\{\left(\varepsilon_t^2-\sigma^2\frac{\tau_2^c}{1-\alpha}\right)1_{(\underline{c}\sigma\le\varepsilon_t\le\sigma\bar{c})} + \sigma\zeta_2^c\mu'\Sigma^{-1}x_t\varepsilon_t h_t + \sigma\frac{\zeta_3^c}{2}(\varepsilon_t^2/\sigma-\sigma)h_t\right\} + \mathrm{o}_{\mathsf{P}}(1). \tag{1.25}$$

The asymptotic distribution of the first-round estimators $\tilde{\beta},\tilde{\sigma}^2$ can now be deduced. For simplicity only $\tilde{\beta}$ is considered.

Theorem 1.6. *Suppose* $\gamma_i = 0$ *for all i in model (1.3), and that* x_t *is stationary with mean* μ, *variance* Σ, *and finite fourth moment, and that* $\hat{\omega}^2_{t,1}$ *and* $\hat{\omega}^2_{t,2}$ *satisfy Assumption B. The density* f *satisfies Assumption A, and* $\underline{c}$ *and* $\bar{c}$ *are chosen so that* $\tau_1^c = 0$. *Then*

$$T^{1/2}(\tilde{\beta}-\beta) \overset{\mathsf{D}}{\to} \mathsf{N}_m\left\{0,\sigma^2(\eta\Sigma^{-1}+\kappa\Sigma^{-1}\mu\mu'\Sigma^{-1})\right\}, \tag{1.26}$$

where

$$(1-\alpha)^2\eta = \tau_2^c\left(1+2\xi_1^c\right) + \left(\xi_1^c\right)^2\left(\frac{\lambda_2^2}{\lambda_1} + \frac{\lambda_1^2}{\lambda_2}\right),$$

$$(1-\alpha)^2\kappa = \xi_2^c\left[\left\{\frac{1}{4}\xi_2^c(\tau_4-1) + \xi_1^c\tau_3\right\}\left(\frac{\lambda_2^2}{\lambda_1} + \frac{\lambda_1^2}{\lambda_2}\right) + \tau_3^c\right].$$

We note that the result of Hendry, Johansen, and Santos (2008) is a special case of Theorem 1.6. They were concerned with the situation of estimating the mean in an i.i.d. sequence where $\Sigma = 1$. Due to the relatively simple setup their proof could avoid the empirical process arguments used here.

In the special case where $\lambda_1 = \lambda_2 = 1/2$ then the limiting expression for $\tilde{\beta}$ is exactly the same as that for the robustified least squares estimator $\breve{\beta}_{LS}$, in that $\eta = \eta_\beta$ and $\kappa = \kappa_\beta$.

We finally analyse the situation where we first find the least squares estimators in the two subsets $\mathcal{I}_1$ and $\mathcal{I}_2$, then construct $\tilde{\beta}$ and finally find the robustified least squares estimator $\breve{\beta}_{Sat}$ based upon $\tilde{\beta}$. For simplicity we consider only the symmetric case.

Theorem 1.7. *Suppose $\gamma_t = 0$, $t = 1, \ldots, T$ in model (1.3), and that x_t is stationary with mean μ, variance Σ, and finite fourth moment, and that $\hat{\omega}_{t,j}^2$ and $\tilde{\omega}_t^2$ satisfy Assumption B. The symmetric density* f *satisfies Assumption A, and $\underline{c}$ and $\bar{c}$ are chosen so that $\tau_1^c = 0$. Then*

$$T^{1/2}(\breve{\beta}_{Sat} - \beta) \xrightarrow{D} \mathsf{N}_m(0, \sigma^2\Sigma^{-1}\eta_{Sat}),$$

where

$$(1-\alpha)^4\eta_{Sat} = \left(1-\alpha+\xi_1^c\right)\tau_2^c\left\{\left(1-\alpha+\xi_1^c\right) + 2\left(\xi_1^c\right)^2\right\} + \left(\xi_1^c\right)^4\left(\frac{\lambda_1^2}{\lambda_2} + \frac{\lambda_2^2}{\lambda_1}\right). \quad (1.27)$$

The assumption to the residual variance estimators is satisfied in a number of situations. If $\hat{\omega}_{t,j}^2 = \hat{\sigma}_j^2$ and $\tilde{\omega}_t^2 = \tilde{\sigma}^2$ then Assumption B is trivially satisfied. If $\hat{\omega}_{t,j}^2 = \hat{\sigma}_j^2\{1 + x_t'(\sum_{s\notin\mathcal{I}_j} x_s x_s')^{-1}x_t\}$ then Assumption B is satisfied due to the difference in the order of magnitude of x_t and $\sum_{s\notin\mathcal{I}_j} x_s x_s'$.

1.5 Asymptotic Distribution for Trending Autoregressive Processes

We first discuss the limit distribution of the least squares estimator in a trend stationary k-th order autoregression, and then apply the results to the indicator saturated estimator. Finally, the unit root case is discussed.

1.5.1 *Least Squares Estimation in an Autoregression*

The asymptotic distribution of the least squares estimator is derived for a trend stationary autoregression. Consider a time series $y_{1-k}, \ldots, y_T$. The model for y_t has a deterministic component d_t. These satisfy the autoregressive equations

$$
\begin{aligned}
y_t &= \sum_{i=1}^{k} \delta_i y_{t-i} + \varphi d_{t-1} + \varepsilon_t, \qquad (1.28)\\
d_t &= D d_{t-1},
\end{aligned}
$$

where $\varepsilon_t \in \mathbb{R}$ are independent, identically distributed with mean zero and variance σ^2, whereas $d_t \in \mathbb{R}^\ell$ are deterministic terms. The autoregression (1.28) is of the form (1.3) with $x_t' = (y_{t-1}, \ldots, y_{t-k}, d_t')$ and $\beta' = (\delta_1, \ldots, \delta_k, \phi)$, so $m = k + \ell$. The least squares estimator is denoted $(\hat{\beta}, \hat{\sigma}^2)$.

The deterministic terms are defined in terms of the matrix D which has characteristic roots on the complex unit circle, so d_t is a vector of terms such as a constant, a linear trend, or periodic functions like seasonal dummies. For example

$$
D = \begin{pmatrix} 1 & 0 \\ 0 & -1 \end{pmatrix} \qquad \text{with} \qquad d_0 = \begin{pmatrix} 1 \\ 1 \end{pmatrix}
$$

will generate a constant and a dummy for a bi-annual frequency. The deterministic term d_t is assumed to have linearly independent coordinates, which is formalized as follows.

Assumption C. $|\text{eigen}(D)| = 1$ *and* $\text{rank}(d_1, \ldots, d_\ell) = \ell$.

It is convenient to introduce the companion form

$$
Y_{t-1} = \begin{pmatrix} y_{t-1} \\ \vdots \\ y_{t-k} \end{pmatrix}, \quad A = \begin{Bmatrix} (\delta_1, \ldots, \delta_{k-1}) & \delta_k \\ I_{k-1} & 0 \end{Bmatrix}, \quad \Phi = \begin{pmatrix} \varphi \\ 0 \end{pmatrix}, \quad e_t = \begin{pmatrix} \varepsilon_t \\ 0 \end{pmatrix},
$$

so that $Y_t = AY_{t-1} + \Phi d_{t-1} + e_t$. Focusing on the stationary case where $|\text{eigen}(A)| < 1$ so A and D have no eigenvalues in common, Nielsen (2005, section 3) shows that

$$
Y_t = Y_t^* + \Psi d_t \qquad \text{where} \qquad Y_t^* = AY_{t-1}^* + e_t,
$$

and Ψ is the unique solution of the linear equation $\Phi = \Psi D - A\Psi$.

A normalization matrix N_T is needed. To construct this let

$$
M_T = \left(\sum_{t=1}^{T} d_{t-1} d_{t-1}' \right)^{-1/2},
$$

so that $M_T \sum_{t=1}^{T} d_{t-1} d_{t-1}' M_T' = I_\ell$. Equivalently, a block diagonal normalization, N_D, could be chosen if D, without loss of generality, were assumed to have a Jordan structure as in Nielsen (2005, section 4). Theorem 4.1 of that paper then implies that

$$T^{-1/2} M_T \sum_{t=1}^{T} d_{t-1} \to \mu_D,$$

for some vector μ_D. For the entire vector of regressors, $x_t = (Y_{t-1}', d_{t-1}')'$, define

$$N_T = \begin{pmatrix} T^{-1/2} & 0 \\ 0 & M_T \end{pmatrix} \begin{pmatrix} I_k & -\Psi \\ 0 & I_\ell \end{pmatrix}. \tag{1.29}$$

Theorem 1.8. *Let y_t be the trend stationary process given by (1.28) so $|\text{eigen}(A)| < 1$, with finite fourth moment and deterministic component satisfying Assumption C. Then, with $\Sigma_Y = \sum_{t=0}^{\infty} A^t \Omega (A^t)'$ and $\Sigma_D = I_\ell$ and $\mu_D = \lim_{T\to\infty} T^{-1/2} M_T \sum_{t=1}^{T} d_t$ it holds*

$$N_T \sum_{t=1}^{T} \begin{pmatrix} Y_{t-1} \\ d_{t-1} \end{pmatrix} \begin{pmatrix} Y_{t-1} \\ d_{t-1} \end{pmatrix}' N_T' \overset{\mathsf{P}}{\to} \Sigma \overset{\text{def}}{=} \begin{pmatrix} \Sigma_Y & 0 \\ 0 & \Sigma_D \end{pmatrix}, \tag{1.30}$$

$$T^{-1/2} N_T \sum_{t=1}^{T} \begin{pmatrix} Y_{t-1} \\ d_{t-1} \end{pmatrix} \overset{\mathsf{P}}{\to} \mu \overset{\text{def}}{=} \begin{pmatrix} 0 \\ \mu_D \end{pmatrix}, \tag{1.31}$$

$$\max_{1\le t\le T} |M_T d_t| = \mathrm{O}(T^{-1/2}), \tag{1.32}$$

$$N_T \sum_{t=1}^{T} \begin{pmatrix} Y_{t-1} \\ d_{t-1} \end{pmatrix} \varepsilon_t' \overset{\mathsf{D}}{\to} \mathsf{N}_m(0, \sigma^2 \Sigma). \tag{1.33}$$

In particular, it holds

$$(N_T^{-1})'(\hat\beta - \beta) \overset{\mathsf{D}}{\to} \mathsf{N}_m(0, \sigma^2 \Sigma^{-1}), \tag{1.34}$$

$$T^{1/2}(\hat\sigma^2 - \sigma^2) = T^{-1/2} \sum_{t=1}^{T} (\varepsilon_t^2 - \sigma^2) + \mathrm{o}_{\mathsf{P}}(1) = \mathrm{O}_{\mathsf{P}}(1). \tag{1.35}$$

A conclusion from the above analysis is that the normalization by N_T involving the parameter separates the asymptotic distribution into independent components. This will be exploited to simplify the analysis of the indicator saturated estimator below.

1.5.2 *Indicator Saturation in a Trend Stationary Autoregression*

We now turn to the indicator saturated estimator in the trend stationary autoregression, although only the first round estimator $\tilde\beta$ is considered. As before this estimator will consist of a numerator and a denominator term, each of which is a sum of two components. The main result in Theorem 1.1 can then be applied to each of these components.

Theorem 1.9. *Let y_t be the trend stationary process given by (1.28) so $|\text{eigen}(A)| < 1$, with finite fourth moment, deterministic component satisfying Assumption C, and $\hat{\omega}^2_{\xi,j}$ satisfies Assumption B. Suppose the density* f *satisfies Assumption A, and the truncation points are chosen so that $\tau_1^c = 0$. Finally, assume that*

$$\lim_{T\to\infty} M_T \sum_{t\in\mathcal{I}_j} d_t d_t' M_T = \Sigma_{D,j} > 0, \tag{1.36}$$

$$\lim_{T\to\infty} T^{-1/2} M_T \sum_{t\in\mathcal{I}_j} d_t = \mu_{D,j}, \tag{1.37}$$

where $\Sigma_{D,1} + \Sigma_{D,2} = I_m$ and $\mu_{D,1} + \mu_{D,2} = \mu$ and define

$$\mu_j = \begin{pmatrix} 0 \\ \mu_{D,j} \end{pmatrix}, \qquad \Sigma_j = \begin{pmatrix} \lambda_j \Sigma_Y & 0 \\ 0 & \Sigma_{D,j} \end{pmatrix}.$$

Then it holds

$$(N_T')^{-1}(\tilde{\beta} - \beta) \overset{D}{\to} \mathsf{N}_m(0, \sigma^2 \Sigma^{-1} \Phi \Sigma^{-1}), \tag{1.38}$$

where $\Sigma = \Sigma_1 + \Sigma_2$ and

$$\begin{aligned}(1-\alpha)^2\Phi = {} & \tau_2^c(1 + 2\xi_1^c)\Sigma + (\xi_1^c)^2(\Sigma_2\Sigma_1^{-1}\Sigma_2 + \Sigma_1\Sigma_2^{-1}\Sigma_1) \\ & + \tau_3^c \frac{\xi_2^c}{2}(\mu_2\mu_1' + \mu_1\mu_2')\left(\frac{1}{\lambda_1} + \frac{1}{\lambda_2}\right) + (\tau_4 - 1)\left(\frac{\xi_2^c}{2}\right)^2\left(\frac{\mu_2\mu_2'}{\lambda_1} + \frac{\mu_1\mu_1'}{\lambda_2}\right) \\ & + \tau_3 \frac{\xi_1^c\xi_2^c}{2}\left(\frac{\mu_2\mu_1'\Sigma_1^{-1}\Sigma_2 + \Sigma_2\Sigma_1^{-1}\mu_1\mu_2'}{\lambda_1} + \frac{\mu_1\mu_2'\Sigma_2^{-1}\Sigma_1 + \Sigma_1\Sigma_2^{-1}\mu_2\mu_1'}{\lambda_2}\right).\end{aligned}$$

A closer look at the expression for Φ shows that it is block diagonal. The variance for the autoregressive components is $(1-\alpha)^2\Phi_Y = \Sigma_Y\{\tau_2^c(1 + 2\xi_1^c) + (\xi_1^c)^2(\lambda_2^2\lambda_1^{-1} + \lambda_1^2\lambda_2^{-1})\}$. The somewhat complicated limiting covariance matrix for the deterministic terms, Φ_D, simplifies in two important special cases highlighted in the next Corollary. This covers the case where the reference density f is symmetric so $\xi_2^c = 0$ and the terms involving μ_j disappear. Alternatively, the proportionality $\Sigma_{D,j} = \lambda_j I_\ell$ and $\mu_{D,j} = \lambda_j \mu_D$ would also simplify the covariance. In section 1.5.3 it is shown how this proportionality can be achieved by choosing the index sets in a particular way.

Corollary 1.10. *If* f *is symmetric then $\xi_2^c = 0$ so*

$$(1-\alpha)^2\Phi = \tau_2^c(1 + 2\xi_1^c)\Sigma + (\xi_1^c)^2(\Sigma_2\Sigma_1^{-1}\Sigma_2 + \Sigma_1\Sigma_2^{-1}\Sigma_1).$$

If $\Sigma_{D,j} = \lambda_j I_\ell$ and $\mu_{D,j} = \lambda_j \mu_D$ then $\Sigma_j = \lambda_j \Sigma$ and $\mu_j = \lambda_j \mu$ so $\Phi = \eta_\beta \Sigma + \kappa_\beta \mu\mu'$, where the constants η_β, κ_β were defined in Theorem 1.3.

1.5.3 *Choice of Index Sets in the Nonstationary Case*

Corollary 1.10 showed that the limiting distribution for the trend stationary case reduces to that of the strictly stationary case in the presence of proportionality, that is, if $\Sigma_{D,j} = \lambda_j I_\ell$ and $\mu_{D,j} = \lambda_j \mu_D$. This can be achieved if the index sets are chosen carefully. The key is that the index sets are, up to an approximation, alternating and dense in [0,1], so that for any $0 \leq u \leq v \leq 1$

$$\frac{1}{T} \sum_{t \in \mathrm{int}(Tu)+1}^{\mathrm{int}(Tv)} 1_{(t \in \mathcal{I}_j)} \to \lambda_j (v - u), \tag{1.39}$$

where $\lambda_1 + \lambda_2 = 1$. The alternating nature of the sets allows information to be accumulated in a proportional fashion over the two sub-samples, even though the process at hand is trend stationary. Two schemes for choosing the index sets are considered. First, a random scheme which is, perhaps, most convenient in applications, and, secondly, a deterministic scheme. The random scheme is not far from what has been applied in some Monte Carlo simulation experiments made by David Hendry in similar situations.

1.5.3.1 RANDOM INDEX SETS

We will consider one particular index set which is alternating in a random way. Generate a series of independent Bernoulli variables, $s_1, \ldots, s_T$ taking the values 1 and 2 so that

$$\mathsf{P}(s_t = 1) = \lambda_1, \qquad \mathsf{P}(s_t = 2) = \lambda_2, \qquad \text{so} \qquad \lambda_1 + \lambda_2 = 1$$

for some $0 \leq \lambda_1, \lambda_2 \leq 1$. Then form the index sets

$$\mathcal{I}_1 = (t : s_t = 1) \qquad \text{and} \qquad \mathcal{I}_2 = (t : s_t = 2).$$

The index sequence has to be independent of the generating process for the data, so that the data can be analysed conditionally on the index sets. In the following we will comment on examples of deterministic processes and unit root processes.

Consider the trend stationary model in (1.28). Since the index sets are constructed by independent sampling then

$$\mathsf{E}\left(N_T \sum_{t \in \mathcal{I}_j} x_t x_t' N_T'\right) = \mathsf{E}\left\{N_T \sum_{t=1}^{T} (x_t x_t') N_T'\right\} \mathsf{E} 1_{(S_t = j)} = \mathsf{E}\left\{N_T \sum_{t=1}^{T} x_t x_t' N_T'\right\} \lambda_j \to \lambda_j \Sigma,$$

$$\mathsf{E}\left(T^{-1/2} N_T \sum_{t \in \mathcal{I}_j} x_t\right) = \mathsf{E}\left(T^{-1/2} N_T \sum_{t=1}^{T} x_t\right) \mathsf{E} 1_{(S_t = j)} = \mathsf{E}\left(T^{-1/2} N_T \sum_{t=1}^{T} x_t\right) \lambda_j \to \lambda_j \mu.$$

1.5.3.2 ALTERNATING INDEX SETS

It is instructive also to consider an index set, which is alternating in a deterministic way. That is

$$\mathcal{I}_1 = (t \text{ is odd}) \qquad \text{and} \qquad \mathcal{I}_2 = (t \text{ is even}).$$

This index set satisfies the property (1.39) with $\lambda_1 = \lambda_2 = 1/2$.

Consider the trend stationary model in (1.28) where the eigenvalues of the deterministic transition matrix D are all at one, so only polynomial trends are allowed. For simplicity restrict the calculations to a bivariate deterministic terms and let T be even, so with

$$d_t = \begin{pmatrix} 1 \\ t \end{pmatrix}, \qquad Q_T = \begin{pmatrix} 1 & 0 \\ 0 & T^{-1} \end{pmatrix},$$

the desired proportionality then follows, in that

$$T^{-1}Q_T \sum_{t\in\mathcal{I}_j} d_t d_t' Q_T = T^{-1}Q_T \sum_{t=0}^{T/2-1} d_{2t+j}d_{2t+j}' Q_T \to \frac{1}{2}\begin{pmatrix} 1 & 1/2 \\ 1/2 & 1/3 \end{pmatrix},$$

$$T^{-1}Q_T \sum_{t\in\mathcal{I}_j} d_t = T^{-1}Q_T \sum_{t=0}^{T/2-1} d_{2t+j} \to \frac{1}{2}\begin{pmatrix} 1 \\ 1/2 \end{pmatrix}.$$

The proportionality will, however, fail if the process has a seasonal component with the same frequency as the alternation scheme. If for instance $d_t = (-1)^t$ and T even then it holds that

$$\mu_{D,1} = T^{-1}\sum_{t\in\mathcal{I}_1}(-1)^t = -\frac{1}{2}, \quad \mu_{D,2} = T^{-1}\sum_{t\in\mathcal{I}_2}(-1)^t = \frac{1}{2}, \quad \mu = T^{-1}\sum_{t=1}^{T}(-1)^t = 0,$$

so $\mu_{D,j} \neq \lambda_j\mu$, and proportionality does not hold. The proportionality will only arise when information is accumulated proportionally over the two index sets, either by choosing them randomly or by constructing them to be out of sync with the seasonality, for instance by choosing the first index set as every third observation.

1.5.4 *A Few Results for Unit Root Processes*

Consider the first order autoregression

$$X_t = \beta X_{t-1} + \varepsilon_t, \tag{1.40}$$

where $\beta = 1$ gives the unit root situation, and we assume for simplicity that f is symmetric so $\xi_2^c = 0$ and the term involving k_t falls away. The Functional

Central Limit Theorem shows that

$$T^{-1/2}\sum_{t=1}^{\text{int}(Tu)}\left\{\begin{array}{c}\varepsilon_t 1_{(t\in\mathcal{I}_1)}\\ \varepsilon_t 1_{(t\in\mathcal{I}_2)}\\ \varepsilon_t 1_{(|\varepsilon_t|<c\sigma)}\end{array}\right\}\overset{\mathsf{D}}{\to}\begin{pmatrix}w_{1u}\\ w_{2u}\\ w_u^c\end{pmatrix}=W_u,$$

where W_u is a Brownian motion with variance matrix

$$\widetilde{\Omega}\overset{\text{def}}{=}\sigma^2\begin{pmatrix}\lambda_1 & 0 & \lambda_1\tau_2^c\\ 0 & \lambda_2 & \lambda_2\tau_2^c\\ \lambda_1\tau_2^c & \lambda_2\tau_2^c & \tau_2^c\end{pmatrix}.$$

From the decomposition

$$\sum_{t\in\mathcal{I}_j}X_{t-1}^2=\sum_{t=1}^{T}X_{t-1}^2 1_{(t\in\mathcal{I}_j)}=\sum_{t=1}^{T}X_{t-1}^2\lambda_j+\sum_{t=1}^{T}X_{t-1}^2\left\{1_{(t\in\mathcal{I}_j)}-\lambda_j\right\},$$

it is seen that the first term is of order T^2, whereas the second term has mean zero and variance $\lambda_1\lambda_2\mathsf{E}(\sum_{t=1}^{T}X_{t-1}^4)$; it is therefore of order $T^{3/2}$. It follows that

$$\frac{1}{T^2}\left(\sum_{t\in\mathcal{I}_1}X_{t-1}^2,\sum_{t\in\mathcal{I}_2}X_{t-1}^2,\sum_{t=1}^{T}X_{t-1}^2\right)\overset{\mathsf{D}}{\to}(\lambda_1,\lambda_2,1)\int_0^1 w_u^2du,$$

where $w_u=w_{1u}+w_{2u}$ is the Brownian motion generated by the cumulated ε_t. The information accumulated over each of the two sub-samples are therefore proportional to $\int_0^1 w_u^2du$. It follows from Corollary 1.2, that the first round indicator saturated estimator satisfies

$$T(\widetilde{\beta}-1)\overset{\mathsf{D}}{\to}\frac{\int_0^1 w_u d\left\{w_u^c+2\mathsf{c}f(c)\left(\lambda_1^{-1}\lambda_2 w_{1u}+\lambda_2^{-1}\lambda_1 w_{2u}\right)\right\}}{(1-\alpha)\int_0^1 w_u^2du}.$$

When $c\to\infty$ then $w_u^c\overset{\mathsf{D}}{\to}w_u$ while $\mathsf{c}f(c)\to 0$ and $\alpha\to 0$ giving the usual Dickey–Fuller distribution

$$T(\hat{\beta}-1)\overset{\mathsf{D}}{\to}\frac{\int_0^1 w_u dw_u}{\int_0^1 w_u^2du}.$$

While the limiting distribution is now different from the stationary case, the relevant modification corresponds to the usual modification of normal distributions into Dickey–Fuller-type distributions when moving from the stationary to the nonstationary case.

For the case of alternating index sets, nearly the same arguments apply as with random index sets. In this case the definition of the Brownian motions becomes

$$T^{-1/2}\sum_{t=1}^{\text{int}(Tu/2)}\left\{\begin{array}{c}\varepsilon_{2t-1}\\ \varepsilon_{2t}\\ \varepsilon_t 1_{(|\varepsilon_t|<c)}\end{array}\right\}\overset{\mathsf{D}}{\to}\begin{pmatrix}w_{1u}\\ w_{2u}\\ w_u^c\end{pmatrix}=W_u.$$

1.6 Proof of Main Result

The results of Theorem 1.1 concern the matrices

$$N_T S_{xx} N_T' = \sum_{t=1}^{T} N_T x_t x_t' N_T' 1_{(\underline{c} \le v_t \le \overline{c})}, \qquad N_T S_{x\varepsilon} = \sum_{t=1}^{T} N_T x_t \varepsilon_t 1_{(\underline{c} \le v_t \le \overline{c})}.$$

For $N_T S_{xx} N_T'$ the main idea in the proof is to approximate $\hat{\omega}_t v_t = \varepsilon_t - (\hat{\beta} - \beta)' x_t$ by ε_t and the indicator $1_{(\underline{c} \le v_t \le \overline{c})}$ by $1_{(\underline{c}\sigma \le \varepsilon_t \le \overline{c}\sigma)}$, because the limit of the approximation $\sum_{t=1}^{T} N_T x_t x_t' N_T' 1_{(\underline{c}\sigma \le \varepsilon_t \le \overline{c}\sigma)}$ is easy to find. It turns out that the approximation involves terms from the preliminary estimator of β and σ. In the proof of Theorem 1.1 this replacement is justified using techniques for empirical processes and in particular Koul (2002, Theorem 7.2.1, p. 298).

We define the normalized regressors $x_{Tt} = T^{1/2} N_T x_t$ and the estimation errors $\hat{a}_{Tt} = \hat{\omega}_t - \sigma$, $\hat{a}_T = \hat{\sigma} - \sigma$ and $\hat{b}_T = T^{-1/2}(N_T^{-1})'(\hat{\beta} - \beta)$. Then $T^{1/2}(\hat{a}_T, \hat{b}_T) = O_P(1)$ and $T^{1/2} \max_{1 \le t \le T} |\hat{a}_{Tt} - \hat{a}_T| = T^{1/2} \max_{1 \le t \le T} |\hat{\omega}_t - \hat{\sigma}| = o_P(1)$ by assumption (*i*) of Theorem 1.1. Note that

$$\hat{\omega}_t v_t = \varepsilon_t - (\hat{\beta} - \beta)' x_t = \varepsilon_t - \{T^{-1/2}(N_T^{-1})'(\hat{\beta} - \beta)\}'(T^{1/2} N_T x_t) = \varepsilon_t - \hat{b}_T' x_{Tt}, \quad (1.41)$$

so that

$$(\underline{c} \le v_t \le \overline{c}) = \{\underline{c}(\sigma + \hat{a}_{Tt}) \le \varepsilon_t - \hat{b}_T' x_{Tt} \le \overline{c}(\sigma + \hat{a}_{Tt})\}.$$

We define $u = (a, b')'$ and

$$I_t(u) = I_t(a, b) = 1_{\{\underline{c}(\sigma + a) \le \varepsilon_t - b' x_{Tt} \le \overline{c}(\sigma + a)\}} - 1_{(\underline{c}\sigma \le \varepsilon_t \le \overline{c}\sigma)}, \quad (1.42)$$

and find for the denominator $N_T S_{xx} N_T'$

$$N_T S_{xx} N_T' = T^{-1} \sum_{t=1}^{T} x_{Tt} x_{Tt}' 1_{(\underline{c} \le v_t \le \overline{c})} = T^{-1} \sum_{t=1}^{T} x_{Tt} x_{Tt}' 1_{(\underline{c}\sigma \le \varepsilon_t \le \overline{c}\sigma)} \quad (1.43)$$

$$+ T^{-1} \sum_{t=1}^{T} x_{Tt} x_{Tt}' \{I_t(\hat{a}_{Tt}, \hat{b}_T) - I_t(\hat{a}_T, \hat{b}_T)\} + T^{-1} \sum_{t=1}^{T} x_{Tt} x_{Tt}' I_t(\hat{a}_T, \hat{b}_T).$$

We then have to show that $\hat{a}_{Tt}$ is so close to $\hat{a}_T$ that the second term tends to zero, and if we can show that $T^{-1} \sum_{t=1}^{T} x_{Tt} x_{Tt}' I_t(a, b)$ is tight as a process in (a, b) and because $T^{-1} \sum_{t=1}^{T} x_{Tt} x_{Tt}' I_t(0, 0) = 0$, and $(\hat{a}_T, \hat{b}_T) = O_P(T^{1/2})$, we find that the last term tends to zero. Finally we find from the Law of Large Numbers the probability limit of the first term.

Similarly we find for $N_T S_{x\varepsilon}$

$$N_T S_{x\varepsilon} = T^{-1/2} \sum_{t=1}^{T} x_{Tt}\varepsilon_t 1_{(\underline{c} \le \upsilon_t \le \overline{c})} = T^{-1/2} \sum_{t=1}^{T} x_{Tt}\varepsilon_t 1_{(\underline{c}\sigma \le \varepsilon_t \le \overline{c}\sigma)}$$

$$+ T^{-1/2} \sum_{t=1}^{T} x_{Tt}\varepsilon_t \{ I_t(\hat{a}_{tT},\hat{b}_T) - I_t(\hat{a}_T,\hat{b}_T)\} + T^{-1/2} \sum_{t=1}^{T} x_{Tt}\varepsilon_t I_t(\hat{a}_T,\hat{b}_T).$$

The limit of the second term will be shown to be zero because $\hat{a}_{Tt}$ is very close to $\hat{a}_T$. We get a contribution from the third term, which we decompose at the point (a,b) as

$$T^{-1/2} \sum_{t=1}^{T} x_{Tt}\varepsilon_t I_t(a,b) = T^{-1/2} \sum_{t=1}^{T} x_{Tt}[\varepsilon_t I_t(a,b) - \mathsf{E}_{t-1}\{\varepsilon_t I_t(a,b)\}]$$

$$+ T^{-1/2} \sum_{t=1}^{T} x_{Tt} \mathsf{E}_{t-1}\{\varepsilon_t I_t(a,b)\}.$$

The first of these tends to zero, and for the second we find that a linear approximation to the smooth function $\mathsf{E}_{t-1}\{\varepsilon_t I_t(a,b)\}$ is $a\xi_2^c + b' x_{Tt}\xi_1^c$, and we therefore introduce the processes, for $\ell,m = 0,1,2$,

$$M_T^{\ell,m} = T^{-1/2} \sum_{t=1}^{T} g_m(x_{Tt})\, \varepsilon_t^{\ell} \{ I_t(\hat{a}_{Tt},\hat{b}_T) - I_t(\hat{a}_T,\hat{b}_T)\}, \tag{1.44}$$

$$W_T^{\ell,m}(a,b) = \frac{1}{T} \sum_{t=1}^{T} g_m(x_{Tt})\, \varepsilon_t^{\ell} I_t(a,b), \tag{1.45}$$

$$V_T^{\ell,m}(a,b) = \frac{1}{\sqrt{T}} \sum_{t=1}^{T} g_m(x_{Tt}) \left\{ \varepsilon_t^{\ell} I_t(a,b) - \sigma^{\ell-1}\left(a\xi_{\ell+1}^c + b' x_{Tt}\xi_{\ell}^c \right) \right\}, \tag{1.46}$$

where the function g_m is given as

$$g_0(x_{Tt}) = 1, \qquad g_1(x_{Tt}) = x_{Tt}, \qquad g_2(x_{Tt}) = x_{Tt}x_{Tt}'. \tag{1.47}$$

Lemma 1.14 below shows that $\sigma^{\ell-1}(a\xi_{\ell+1}^c + b' x_{Tt}\xi_{\ell}^c)$ is an approximation to the conditional mean of $\varepsilon_t^{\ell} I_t(a,b)$ given the past. Theorems 1.15, 1.16, and 1.17 below show that as $T \to \infty$ and if $T^{1/2}(\hat{a}_T,\hat{b}_T)$ is tight, then

$$M_T^{\ell,m} \overset{\mathsf{P}}{\to} 0, \qquad W_T^{\ell,m}(\hat{a}_T,\hat{b}_T) \overset{\mathsf{P}}{\to} 0 \qquad \text{and} \qquad V_T^{\ell,m}(\hat{a}_T,\hat{b}_T) \overset{\mathsf{P}}{\to} 0. \tag{1.48}$$

Some equalities and expansions are established initially in section 1.6.1. The remainder terms are analysed in section 1.6.2. Finally, the threads are pulled together in a proof of Theorem 1.1 in section 1.6.3.

1.6.1 *Some Initial Inequalities and Expansions*

We define the indicator function $1_{(e\leq\varepsilon\leq f)}$ as

$$1_{(e\leq\varepsilon\leq f)} = 1_{(e\leq f)}\{1_{(\varepsilon\leq f)} - 1_{(\varepsilon\leq e)}\}.$$

We first prove an inequality for differences of such indicator functions.

Lemma 1.11. *For $e < f$, $e_0 < f_0$, and $\zeta \geq \max(|e-e_0|,|f-f_0|)$ we have*

$$|1_{(e\leq\varepsilon\leq f)} - 1_{(e_0\leq\varepsilon\leq f_0)}| \leq 1_{(|\varepsilon-e_0|\leq\zeta)} + 1_{(|\varepsilon-f_0|\leq\zeta)}.$$

Proof of Lemma 1.11. From $e = e_0 + (e - e_0)$ and $|e - e_0| \leq \zeta$ we find $e_0 - \zeta \leq e \leq e_0 + \zeta$ and similarly $f_0 - \zeta \leq f \leq f_0 + \zeta$. Hence using the monotonicity in e and f, we find

$$1_{(e_0+\zeta\leq\varepsilon\leq f_0-\zeta)} \leq 1_{(e\leq\varepsilon\leq f)} \leq 1_{(e_0-\zeta\leq\varepsilon\leq f_0+\zeta)}.$$

Because the same inequalities hold for $1_{\{e_0\leq\varepsilon\leq f_0\}}$ we find

$$|1_{(e\leq\varepsilon\leq f)} - 1_{(e_0\leq\varepsilon\leq f_0)}| \leq 1_{(e_0-\zeta\leq\varepsilon\leq f_0+\zeta)} - 1_{(e_0+\zeta\leq\varepsilon\leq f_0-\zeta)} \leq 1_{(|\varepsilon-e_0|\leq\zeta)} + 1_{(|\varepsilon-f_0|\leq\zeta)},$$

where the last inequality is found by exploiting that $e_0 \leq f_0$ by assumption so

$$1_{(e_0-\zeta\leq\varepsilon\leq f_0+\zeta)} = 1_{(e_0-\zeta\leq f_0+\zeta)}\{1_{(\varepsilon\leq f_0+\zeta)} - 1_{(\varepsilon\leq e_0-\zeta}\} = 1_{(\varepsilon\leq f_0+\zeta)} - 1_{(\varepsilon\leq e_0-\zeta)},$$

whereas $1_{(e_0+\zeta> f_0-\zeta)}\{1_{(\varepsilon\leq e_0+\zeta)} - 1_{(\varepsilon\leq f_0-\zeta)}\} \geq 0$ so

$$-1_{(e_0+\zeta\leq\varepsilon\leq f_0-\zeta)} = 1_{(e_0+\zeta\leq f_0-\zeta)}\{1_{(\varepsilon\leq e_0+\zeta)} - 1_{(\varepsilon\leq f_0-\zeta)}\} \leq 1_{(\varepsilon\leq e_0+\zeta)} - 1_{(\varepsilon\leq f_0-\zeta)}.$$

Now, apply this result to the indicator function $I_t(u)$ introduced in (1.42). Note that $I_t(0) = 0$ and introduce the notation, for some $\delta > 0$, and $c = \max(|\underline{c}|,|\overline{c}|)$,

$$J_t(u,\delta) = 1_{\{|\varepsilon_t-\underline{c}(\sigma+a)-b'x_{Tt}|\leq\delta(c+|x_{Tt}|)\}} + 1_{\{|\varepsilon_t-\overline{c}(\sigma+a)-b'x_{Tt}|\leq\delta(c+|x_{Tt}|)\}}.$$

Lemma 1.12. *For $u = (a,b')'$, $u_0 = (a_0,b_0')'$ and $|u - u_0| \leq \delta$ we have*

$$|I_t(u) - I_t(u_0)| \leq J_t(u_0,\delta).$$

Proof of Lemma 1.12. The object of interest is

$$I_t(u) - I_t(u_0) = 1_{\{\underline{c}(\sigma+a)+b'x_{Tt}\leq\varepsilon_t\leq\overline{c}(\sigma+a)+b'x_{Tt}\}} - 1_{\{\underline{c}(\sigma+a_0)+b_0'x_{Tt}\leq\varepsilon_t\leq\overline{c}(\sigma+a_0)+b_0'x_{Tt}\}}.$$

The inequality follows from Lemma 1.11 by the choice $e = \underline{c}(\sigma + a) + b'x_{Tt}$, $e_0 = \underline{c}(\sigma + a_0) + b_0'x_{Tt}$, $f = \overline{c}(\sigma + a) + b'x_{Tt}$, $f_0 = \overline{c}(\sigma + a_0) + b_0'x_{Tt}$, and $\zeta = \delta(c + |x_{Tt}|)$.

Introduce the notation E_{t-1} for the expectation conditional on the information given by $(x_s,\varepsilon_s,s \leq t-1,x_t)$.

Lemma 1.13. *For $\ell \in \mathbb{N}_0$, let $u = (a,b')'$, $u_0 = (a_0,b_0')'$ be random and $\mathsf{E}|\varepsilon_t|^\ell < \infty$. Then it holds with $c = \max(|\underline{c}|,|\overline{c}|)$ that*

$$\mathsf{E}_{t-1}\{1_{(|u-u_0|\leq\delta)}|\varepsilon_t|^\ell|I_t(u) - I_t(u_0)|\} \leq \mathsf{E}_{t-1}|\varepsilon_t|^\ell J_t(u_0,\delta)$$
$$\leq 4\delta\sigma^{\ell-1}(c + |x_{Tt}|)\sup_{v\in\mathbb{R}}|v|^\ell \mathsf{f}(v).$$

Proof of Lemma 1.13. The first inequality follows from Lemma 1.12. The function $J_t(u_0,\delta)$ is nonzero on two intervals of total length $4\delta(c + |x_{Tt}|)$, and the integrand $|\varepsilon_t|^\ell \mathsf{f}(\varepsilon_t/\sigma)/\sigma$ is bounded by $\sigma^{\ell-1}\sup_{v\in\mathbb{R}}|v|^\ell \mathsf{f}(v)$, so that the second inequality holds.

Finally, an approximation to the conditional expectation of $\varepsilon_t I_t(u)$ follows.

Lemma 1.14. *Let* f *have derivative* f′. *For $u = (a,b')'$ and $|u| \leq \delta$ it holds for $\ell \in \mathbb{N}_0$*

$$\left|\mathsf{E}_{t-1}\left\{\varepsilon_t^\ell I_t(u)\right\} - \sigma^{\ell-1}(a\xi_{\ell+1}^c + b'x_{Tt}\xi_\ell^c)\right| \leq 2\delta^2\sup_{v\in\mathbb{R}}\{\ell|v|^{\ell-1}\mathsf{f}(v) + |v^\ell \mathsf{f}'(v)|\}(c^2 + |x_{Tt}|^2),$$

where $c = \max(|\underline{c}|,|\overline{c}|)$ and $\xi_\ell^c = (\overline{c})^\ell \mathsf{f}(\overline{c}) - (\underline{c})^\ell \mathsf{f}(\underline{c})$.

Proof of Lemma 1.14. Let $\psi(\varepsilon) = (\varepsilon/\sigma)^\ell \mathsf{f}(\varepsilon/\sigma)$. A second order Taylor expansion gives

$$\int_{c\sigma}^{c\sigma+h}\psi(\varepsilon)d\varepsilon = h\psi(c\sigma) + \frac{1}{2}h^2\psi'(\sigma c^*),$$

for c^* satisfying $|\sigma c - \sigma c^*| \leq h$. Thus

$$\sigma^{1-\ell}\mathsf{E}_{t-1}\left\{\varepsilon_t^\ell I_t(u)\right\} = \int_{\underline{c}(\sigma+a)+b'x_{Tt}}^{\overline{c}(\sigma+a)+b'x_{Tt}}\psi(\varepsilon)d\varepsilon - \int_{\underline{c}\sigma}^{\overline{c}\sigma}\psi(\varepsilon)d\varepsilon = \overline{S} - \underline{S},$$

where

$$\overline{S} = (\overline{c}a + b'x_{Tt})\psi(\overline{c}\sigma) + \frac{1}{2}(\overline{c}a + b'x_{Tt})^2\psi'(\sigma c_1^*),$$
$$\underline{S} = (\underline{c}a + b'x_{Tt})\psi(\underline{c}\sigma) + \frac{1}{2}(\underline{c}a + b'x_{Tt})^2\psi'(\sigma c_2^*).$$

Using $\psi(c\sigma) = c^\ell \mathsf{f}(c)$ the first order term of $\overline{S} - \underline{S}$ is

$$(\overline{c}a + b'x_{Tt})(\overline{c})^\ell \mathsf{f}(\overline{c}) - (\underline{c}a + b'x_{Tt})(\underline{c})^\ell \mathsf{f}(\underline{c}) = a\xi_{\ell+1}^c + b'x_{Tt}\xi_\ell^c.$$

Using $(|c|a + b'x_{Tt})^2 \leq 2\delta^2(c^2 + |x_{Tt}|^2)$ the second order term is bounded by

$$2\delta^2(c^2 + |x_{Tt}|^2)\sup_{v\in\mathbb{R}}\left|\psi'(v)\right| \leq 2\delta^2(c^2 + |x_{Tt}|^2)\sup_{v\in\mathbb{R}}\{\ell|v|^{\ell-1}\mathsf{f}(v) + |v^\ell \mathsf{f}'(v)|\}.$$

1.6.2 *Some Limit Results*

The first result on $M_T^{\ell,m}$ shows that we can replace the estimator, $\hat{\omega}_t^2$, of the variance of the residuals with $\hat{\sigma}^2$.

Theorem 1.15. *Let $\ell \in \mathbb{N}_0$ and $m \in \{0,1,2\}$. Suppose that*

(*i*) $\theta_T T^{1/2} \max_{1\leq t\leq T} |\hat{a}_{Tt} - \hat{a}_T| = \mathsf{O}_{\mathsf{P}}(1)$, *for some* $\theta_T \to \infty$,
(*ii*) $\max_{t\leq T} \mathsf{E}\,|x_{Tt}|^3 = \mathsf{O}(1)$,
(*iii*) $\sup_v |v|^\ell \mathsf{f}(v) < \infty$ *and* $\mathsf{E}|\varepsilon_t|^\ell < \infty$. *Then it holds for* $T \to \infty$ *that*

$$M_T^{\ell,m} = \frac{1}{T^{1/2}} \sum_{t=1}^{T} g_m(x_{Tt})\, \varepsilon_t^\ell \{I_t(\hat{a}_{Tt},\hat{b}_T) - I_t(\hat{a}_T,\hat{b}_T)\} \overset{\mathsf{P}}{\to} 0.$$

Proof of Theorem 1.15. Due to condition (*i*), for all $\zeta > 0$ there exists a $U > 0$ so that for large T then $\mathsf{P}(\theta_T T^{1/2} \max_{1\leq t\leq T} |\hat{a}_{Tt} - \hat{a}_T| \leq U) \geq 1 - \zeta$. Thus, with $\delta_T = UT^{-1/2}\theta_T^{-1}$, it suffices to show that $|M_T^{\ell,m}| 1_{(\max_{1\leq t\leq T} |\hat{a}_{Tt}-\hat{a}_T|\leq\delta_T)} \overset{\mathsf{P}}{\to} 0$, and in turn by the Markov inequality it suffices to show $S = \mathsf{E}|M_T^{\ell,m}| 1_{(\max_{1\leq t\leq T} |\hat{a}_{Tt}-\hat{a}_T|\leq\delta_T)} \to 0$.

Using the triangle inequality and taking iterated expectations it holds

$$S \leq \frac{1}{T^{1/2}} \sum_{t=1}^{T} \mathsf{E}|x_{Tt}|^m \mathsf{E}_{t-1}\{\varepsilon_t^\ell |I_t(\hat{a}_{Tt},\hat{b}_T) - I_t(\hat{a}_T,\hat{b}_T)| 1_{(\max_{1\leq t\leq T} |\hat{a}_{Tt}-\hat{a}_T|\leq\delta_T)}\}.$$

Lemma 1.12 then shows

$$S \leq 4\delta_T T^{1/2} \sigma^{\ell-1} \sup_{v\in\mathbb{R}}\{|v|^\ell \mathsf{f}(v)\} a^{-1} T^{-1} \mathsf{E} \sum_{t=1}^{T} |x_{Tt}|^m (c + |x_{Tt}|).$$

This vanishes since $\delta_T T^{1/2} \to 0$ and the other terms are bounded.

Theorem 1.16. *Let $\ell \in \mathbb{N}_0$ and $m \in \{0,1,2\}$. Suppose that*

(*i*) $(\hat{a}_T,\hat{b}_T) = \mathsf{O}_{\mathsf{P}}(T^{-1/2})$,
(*ii*) $\max_{t\leq T} \mathsf{E}\,|x_{Tt}|^{m+1} = \mathsf{O}(1)$,
(*iii*) $\sup_v |v|^\ell \mathsf{f}(v) < \infty$ *and* $\mathsf{E}|\varepsilon_t|^\ell < \infty$.

Then it holds for $T \to \infty$ *that*

$$W_T^{\ell,m}(\hat{a}_T,\hat{b}_T) = \frac{1}{T} \sum_{t=1}^{T} g_m(x_{Tt})\, \varepsilon_t^\ell I_t(\hat{a}_T,\hat{b}_T) \overset{\mathsf{P}}{\to} 0, \tag{1.49}$$

where g_m was defined in (1.47) as 1, x_{Tt}, $x_{Tt}x'_{Tt}$ for $m = 0,1,2$, so that $|g_m(x_{Tt})| \leq |x_{Tt}|^m$.

Proof of Theorem 1.16. Due to condition (*i*), for all $\zeta > 0$ there exists a $U > 0$ so that for large T then $\mathsf{P}\{|(\hat{a}_T,\hat{b}_T)| \leq T^{-1/2}U\} \geq 1 - \zeta$. Thus, it suffices to show that $\sup_{|u|\leq T^{-1/2}U} |W_T^{\ell,m}(u)| \overset{\mathsf{P}}{\to} 0$, and in turn by the Markov inequality it suffices to show that $\mathsf{E}\sup_{|u|\leq T^{-1/2}U} |W_T^{\ell,m}(u)| \to 0$.

Because $I_t(0) = 0$ then $I_t(u) = I_t(u) - I_t(0)$. Lemma 1.12 then shows $|I_t(u)| \leq J_t\left(0, T^{-1/2}U\right)$ for $|u| \leq T^{-1/2}U$. Thus, using the triangle inequality it holds

$$\sup_{|u| \leq T^{-1/2}U} |W_T^{\ell,m}(u)| \leq \frac{1}{T}\sum_{t=1}^{T} |x_{Tt}|^m |\varepsilon_t|^\ell J_t(0, T^{-1/2}U).$$

Then take iterated expectations

$$S = \mathsf{E}\{\sup_{|u| \leq T^{-1/2}U} |W_T^{\ell,m}(u)|\} \leq \mathsf{E}\frac{1}{T}\sum_{t=1}^{T} |x_{Tt}|^m \mathsf{E}_{t-1}|\varepsilon_t|^\ell J_t(0, T^{-1/2}U). \tag{1.50}$$

Apply Lemma 1.13 with $\delta = T^{-1/2}U$ and find

$$S \leq \mathsf{E}\frac{1}{T}\sum_{t=1}^{T} |x_{Tt}|^m \frac{4U\sigma^{\ell-1}}{T^{1/2}}(c + |x_{Tt}|) \sup_{v\in\mathbb{R}} |v|^\ell \mathsf{f}(v)$$

$$= 4U\sigma^{\ell-1} \sup_{v\in\mathbb{R}}\{|v|^\ell \mathsf{f}(v)\} \frac{1}{T^{3/2}}\sum_{t=1}^{T}\{c\mathsf{E}(|x_{Tt}|^m) + \mathsf{E}(|x_{Tt}|^{m+1})\},$$

which vanishes due to Assumptions *(ii)* and *(iii)*.

Theorem 1.17. *Let $\ell \in \mathbb{N}_0$ and $m \in \{0,1\}$. Suppose that*

(i) $(\hat{a}_T, \hat{b}_T) = \mathrm{O}_\mathsf{P}(T^{-1/2})$,

(ii) $\max_{t\leq T} \mathsf{E}|x_{Tt}|^3 = \mathrm{O}(1)$,

(iii) $\sup_{v\in\mathbb{R}}\left\{(\ell|v|^{\ell-1} + |v|^\ell + v^{2\ell})\mathsf{f}(v) + |v^\ell \mathsf{f}'(v)|\right\} < \infty$ *and* $\mathsf{E}|\varepsilon_t|^{2\ell} < \infty$.

Then it holds for $T \to \infty$ that

$$V_T^{\ell,m}(\hat{a}_T, \hat{b}_T) = \frac{1}{\sqrt{T}}\sum_{t=1}^{T} g_m(x_{Tt})\{\varepsilon_t^\ell I_t(\hat{a}_T, \hat{b}_T) - \sigma^{\ell-1}(\hat{a}_T\xi_{\ell+1}^c + \hat{b}_T' x_{Tt}\xi_\ell^c)\} \overset{\mathsf{P}}{\to} 0.$$

Proof of Theorem 1.17. As in the proof of Theorem 1.16, using condition *(i)*, it suffices to show that $\sup_{|u|\leq T^{-1/2}U} |V_T^{\ell,m}(u)| \overset{\mathsf{P}}{\to} 0$.

1. *Decompose* $V_T^{\ell,m}$ as a sum of martingale differences $\tilde{V}_T$ and a correction term $\overline{V}_T$ so $V_T^{\ell,m}(u) = \tilde{V}_T(u) + \overline{V}_T(u)$, where

$$\tilde{V}_T(u) = \frac{1}{\sqrt{T}}\sum_{t=1}^{T} g_m(x_{Tt})[\varepsilon_t^\ell I_t(u) - \mathsf{E}_{t-1}\{\varepsilon_t^\ell I_t(u)\}],$$

$$\overline{V}_T(u) = \frac{1}{\sqrt{T}}\sum_{t=1}^{T} g_m(x_{Tt})[\mathsf{E}_{t-1}\{\varepsilon_t^\ell I_t(u)\} - \sigma^{\ell-1}(\hat{a}_{Tt}\xi_{\ell+1}^c + \hat{b}_T' x_{Tt}\xi_\ell^c)].$$

It has to be shown that the supremum of each of these terms vanishes.

2. *The term* $\overline{V}_T(u)$. Using first the triangular inequality and then Lemma 1.14 with $\delta = T^{-1/2}U$ gives

$$\sup_{|u|\leq T^{-1/2}U} |\overline{V}_T(u)| \leq \sup_{|u|\leq T^{-1/2}U} \frac{1}{\sqrt{T}} \sum_{t=1}^{T} |x_{Tt}|^m \, |\mathsf{E}_{t-1}\{\varepsilon_t^\ell I_t(u)\} - \sigma^{\ell-1}(a\xi^c_{\ell+1} + b' x_{Tt}\xi^c_\ell)|$$

$$\leq 2U^2 \sup_{v\in\mathbb{R}}\{\ell|v|^{\ell-1}\mathsf{f}(v) + |v^\ell \mathsf{f}'(v)|\} \frac{1}{T^{3/2}} \sum_{t=1}^{T} |x_{Tt}|^m (c^2 + |x_{Tt}|^2)$$

$$= \mathrm{O}_{\mathsf{P}}(T^{-1/2}),$$

by Assumption *(ii)* and *(iii)*, because $\max_{t\leq T}(\mathsf{E}\,|x_{Tt}|^m, \mathsf{E}\,|x_{Tt}|^{m+2})$ is bounded.

3. *The term* $\tilde{V}_T(u)$. For a given χ, to be chosen later, choose $|u_k| \leq UT^{-1/2}$, $k = 1,\ldots,K$ and $B_k = (u : |u - u_k| \leq \chi T^{-1/2}, |u| \leq UT^{-1/2})T^{-1/2}$ as a finite cover of $(u : |u| \leq UT^{-1/2})$. Thus, for any u we have $u \in B_k$ for some k. In particular, it holds for $u \in B_k$

$$|\tilde{V}_T(u)| \leq |\tilde{V}_T(u_k)| + |\tilde{V}_T(u) - \tilde{V}_T(u_k)| \leq \max_k |\tilde{V}_T(u_k)|$$

$$+ \max_k \sup_{u\in B_k} |\tilde{V}_T(u) - \tilde{V}_T(u_k)|.$$

4. *The term* $\max_k |\tilde{V}_T(u_k)|$. Because $\tilde{V}_T$ is a sum of martingale differences then

$$\mathsf{Var}\{\tilde{V}_T(u_k)\} = \frac{1}{T}\mathsf{E}\sum_{t=1}^{T} \left[g_m(x_{Tt})g_m(x_{Tt})'\mathsf{Var}_{t-1}\{\varepsilon_t^\ell I_t(u_k)\}\right].$$

From Lemma 1.12 with $u_0 = 0$, $I_t(0) = 0$, and $|u_k| \leq UT^{-1/2}$ we have $\{\varepsilon_t^\ell I_t(u_k)\}^2 \leq \varepsilon_t^{2\ell} J_t^2(0,UT^{-1/2})$. Further, by the inequality $(a+b)^2 \leq 2(a^2 + b^2)$ we have $J_t^2(0,UT^{-1/2}) \leq 2J_t(0,UT^{-1/2})$, so that from Lemma 1.13 we find

$$\mathsf{E}_{t-1}\{\varepsilon_t^\ell I_t(u_k)\}^2 \leq 2\mathsf{E}_{t-1}\varepsilon_t^{2\ell} J_t(0,UT^{-1/2}) \leq 8\frac{U}{T^{1/2}}\sigma^{2\ell-1}(c + |x_{Tt}|) \sup_{v\in\mathbb{R}} |v|^{2\ell}\mathsf{f}(v). \tag{1.51}$$

Since $\mathsf{Var}_{t-1}\{\varepsilon_t^\ell I_t(u_k)\} \leq \mathsf{E}_{t-1}\{\varepsilon_t^\ell I_t(u_k)\}^2$ it then holds

$$\mathsf{Var}\{\tilde{V}_T(u_k)\} \leq \frac{8U\sigma^{2\ell-1}}{T^{3/2}} \sup_{v\in\mathbb{R}}\{v^{2\ell}\mathsf{f}(v)\} \sum_{t=1}^{T} \mathsf{E}\{|x_{Tt}|^{2m}(c + |x_{Tt}|)\} \leq \frac{c_0}{T^{1/2}},$$

because $\max_{t\leq T}(\mathsf{E}\,|x_{Tt}|^{2m}, \mathsf{E}\,|x_{Tt}|^{2m+1})$ is bounded. Using first Boole's inequality and then Chebychev's inequality it then holds for a $\zeta > 0$ to be chosen later

$$\mathsf{P}\{\max_k |\tilde{V}_T(u_k)| \geq \zeta\} = \mathsf{P}\bigcup_{k=1}^{K}\{|\tilde{V}_T(u_k)| \geq \zeta\} \leq \sum_{k=1}^{K}\mathsf{P}\{|\tilde{V}_T(u_k)| \geq \zeta\}$$

$$\leq \frac{1}{\zeta^2}\sum_{k=1}^{K}\mathsf{Var}\{\tilde{V}_T(u_k)\} \leq \frac{c_0 K}{T^{1/2}\zeta^2} \to 0, \qquad (1.52)$$

for fixed K (and χ) and $T \to \infty$.

5. *The term* $\max_k \sup_{u\in B_k} |\tilde{V}_T(u) - \tilde{V}_T(u_k)|$. The inequality in Lemma 1.12 shows

$$\sup_{u\in B_k} |\tilde{V}_T(u) - \tilde{V}_T(u_k)| \leq Z_T(k)$$

where

$$Z_T(k) = \frac{1}{T^{1/2}}\sum_{t=1}^{T}|x_{Tt}|^m\,[|\varepsilon_t|^\ell J_t(u_k, T^{-1/2}\chi) + \mathsf{E}_{t-1}\{|\varepsilon_t|^\ell J_t(u_k, T^{-1/2}\chi)\}],$$

because $|u - u_k| \leq T^{-1/2}\chi$. Again, write Z_T as a sum of martingale differences $\tilde{Z}_T$ and a correction term $\overline{Z}_T$ so $Z_T(k) = \tilde{Z}_T(k) + \overline{Z}_T(k)$ where

$$\tilde{Z}_T(k) = \frac{1}{T^{1/2}}\sum_{t=1}^{T}|x_{Tt}|^m\,[|\varepsilon_t|^\ell J_t(u_k, T^{-1/2}\chi) - \mathsf{E}_{t-1}\{|\varepsilon_t|^\ell J_t(u_k, T^{-1/2}\chi)\}],$$

$$\overline{Z}_T(k) = \frac{2}{T^{1/2}}\sum_{t=1}^{T}|x_{Tt}|^m\,\mathsf{E}_{t-1}\{|\varepsilon_t|^\ell J_t(u_k, T^{-1/2}\chi)\}.$$

6. *The term* $\max_k \overline{Z}_T(k)$. Lemma 1.13 shows

$$\max_k \overline{Z}_T(k) \leq 8\chi \sup_{v\in\mathbb{R}}\{|v|^\ell \mathsf{f}(v)\}\frac{1}{T}\sum_{t=1}^{T}|x_{Tt}|^m(c + |x_{Tt}|) = \mathrm{O}_{\mathsf{P}}(\chi), \qquad (1.53)$$

due to Assumptions *(ii)*, *(iii)*.

7. *The term* $\max_k \tilde{Z}_T(k)$. Since $\tilde{Z}_T(k)$ is a sum of martingale differences then

$$\mathsf{Var}\{\tilde{Z}_T(k)\} = \frac{1}{T}\sum_{t=1}^{T}\mathsf{E}[g_m(x_{Tt})g_m(x_{Tt})'\mathsf{Var}_{t-1}\{|\varepsilon_t|^\ell J_t(u_k, T^{-1/2}\chi)\}].$$

Since $\mathsf{Var}_{t-1}\{|\varepsilon_t|^\ell J_t(u_k, T^{-1/2}\chi)\} \leq \mathsf{E}_{t-1}\{|\varepsilon_t|^\ell J_t(u_k, T^{-1/2}\chi)\}^2$ then (1.51) shows

$$\mathsf{Var}\{\tilde{Z}_T(k)\} \leq 4\chi\sigma^{2\ell-1}\sup_{v\in\mathbb{R}}\{v^{2\ell}\mathsf{f}(v)\}\frac{1}{T^{3/2}}\sum_{t=1}^{T}\mathsf{E}\{|x_{Tt}|^{2m}(c + |x_{Tt}|)\} = \mathrm{O}(T^{-1/2}),$$

because $\max_{t \le T}(\mathsf{E}\,|x_{Tt}|^{2m},\ \mathsf{E}\,|x_{Tt}|^{2m+1})$ is bounded, using Assumptions (*ii*) and (*iii*). Then, like the evaluation (1.52), we find

$$\mathsf{P}\{\max_k |\widetilde{Z}_T(k)| \ge \zeta\} \le \frac{c_0 M}{T^{1/2}\zeta^2} \to 0.$$

8. The proof is now complete by noticing that for given $\zeta > 0$ and $\xi > 0$ we can first choose U so large that

$$\mathsf{P}\{T^{1/2}|(\hat{a}_T,\hat{b}_T)| \ge U\} \le \xi,$$

using condition (*i*). Next choose χ so small that (1.53) is small. Finally, choose T so large that the remaining terms are small.

1.6.3 *Proof of Main Result*

Proof of Theorem 1.1. We analyse the properties of the product moments:

$$S_{11} = \sum_{t=1}^{T} 1_{(\underline{c} \le v_t \le \overline{c})}, \quad S_{xx} = \sum_{t=1}^{T} x_t x_t' 1_{(\underline{c} \le v_t \le \overline{c})},$$

$$S_{x\varepsilon} = \sum_{t=1}^{T} x_t \varepsilon_t 1_{(\underline{c} \le v_t \le \overline{c})}, \quad S_{x1} = \sum_{t=1}^{T} x_t 1_{(\underline{c} \le v_t \le \overline{c})}.$$

We define $(\hat{a}_{tT},\hat{b}_T) = \{\hat{\omega}_t - \sigma,\ T^{-1/2}(N_T^{-1})'(\hat{\beta} - \beta)\}$, and note, see (1.43) that the definition of $W_T^{\ell,m}(a,b)$ and $M_T^{\ell,m}$ implies that

$$T^{-1}\sum_{t=1}^{T} g_m(x_{Tt})\,\varepsilon_t^{\ell} 1_{(\underline{c} \le v_t \le \overline{c})} = T^{-1}\sum_{t=1}^{T} g_m(x_{Tt})\,\varepsilon_t^{\ell} 1_{(\underline{c}\sigma \le \varepsilon_t \le \overline{c}\sigma)} + T^{-1/2}M_T^{\ell,m} + W_T^{\ell,m}(\hat{a}_T,\hat{b}_T),$$

and that for $x_{Tt} = T^{1/2}N_T x_t$, Theorem 1.16 implies that $W_T^{\ell,m}(\hat{a}_T,\hat{b}_T) = \mathrm{o}_{\mathsf{P}}(1)$ and Theorem 1.15 shows that $M_T^{\ell,m} = \mathrm{O}_{\mathsf{P}}(1)$.

The limits (1.14), (1.15), and (1.16). For $m = 2$, $\ell = 0$ we find

$$N_T S_{xx} N_T' = N_T \sum_{t=1}^{T} x_t x_t' 1_{(\underline{c}\sigma \le \varepsilon_t \le \overline{c}\sigma)} N_T' + \mathrm{o}_{\mathsf{P}}(1).$$

Note that $\mathsf{E}_{t-1}\{1_{(\underline{c}\sigma \le \varepsilon_t \le \overline{c}\sigma)}\} = 1 - \alpha$, so a martingale decomposition of the main term on the right hand side is

$$N_T \sum_{t=1}^{T} x_t x_t' \{1_{(\underline{c}\sigma \le \varepsilon_t \le \overline{c}\sigma)} - (1-\alpha)\} N_T' + N_T \sum_{t=1}^{T} x_t x_t' N_T' (1-\alpha).$$

The first term vanishes due to Chebychev's inequality and Assumption (*ii,c*). The second term converges in probability to $(1-\alpha)\Sigma$ due to Assumption (*ii,a*).

The limit of S_{x1} is found by a similar argument for $m = 1$, $\ell = 0$, which gives

$$T^{-1/2}N_T\sum_{t=1}^{T} x_t 1_{(\underline{c}\le v_t\le \overline{c})} = T^{-1/2}N_T\sum_{t=1}^{T} x_t 1_{(\underline{c}\sigma\le\varepsilon_t\le\overline{c}\sigma)} + \mathrm{o_P}(1).$$

A martingale decomposition of the main term on the right hand side is

$$T^{-1/2}N_T\sum_{t=1}^{T} x_t\{1_{(\underline{c}\sigma\le\varepsilon_t\le\overline{c}\sigma)} - (1-\alpha)\} + T^{-1/2}N_T\sum_{t=1}^{T} x_t(1-\alpha).$$

The first term vanishes due to Chebychev's inequality and Assumption *(ii,a)*. The second term converges to $(1-\alpha)\mu$ due to Assumption *(ii,b)*.

Finally for $m = \ell = 0$, we find

$$T^{-1}\sum_{t=1}^{T} 1_{(\underline{c}\le v_t\le \overline{c})} = T^{-1}\sum_{t=1}^{T} 1_{(\underline{c}\sigma\le\varepsilon_t\le\overline{c}\sigma)} + \mathrm{o_P}(1) \overset{\mathsf{P}}{\to} 1-\alpha.$$

The representations (1.17), (1.18), and (1.19). The definition of $V_T^{\ell,m}(\hat{a}_T,\hat{b}_T)$ implies that for $m = 0,1, \ell = 0,1,2$ we have the representation

$$T^{-1/2}\sum_{t=1}^{T} g_m(x_{Tt})\varepsilon_t^{\ell} 1_{\{\underline{c}\le v_t\le\overline{c}\}} = M_T^{\ell,m} + V_T^{\ell,m}(\hat{a}_T,\hat{b}_T) + T^{-1/2}\sum_{t=1}^{T} g_m(x_{Tt})[\varepsilon_t^{\ell} 1_{(\underline{c}\sigma\le\varepsilon_t\le\overline{c}\sigma)}$$

$$+ \sigma^{\ell-1}\{x_t'(\hat{\beta}-\beta)\xi_\ell^c + (\hat{\sigma}-\sigma)\xi_{\ell+1}^c\}],$$

and that for $x_{Tt} = T^{1/2}N_T x_t$, Theorem 1.17 implies that $V_T^{\ell,m}(\hat{a}_T,\hat{b}_T) = \mathrm{o_P}(1)$ and Theorem 1.15 shows that $M_T^{\ell,m} = \mathrm{o_P}(1)$.

The representation of S_{11} follows for $\ell = m = 0$. The representation of $N_T S_{x\varepsilon}$ follows for $\ell = m = 1$. Finally the representation of term $S_{\varepsilon\varepsilon}$ follows for $m = 0, \ell = 2$.

Proof of Corollary 1.2. *Representation of* $(N_T^{-1})'(\breve{\beta}-\beta)$: From (1.12) we have

$$(N_T^{-1})'(\breve{\beta}-\beta) = (N_T S_{xx} N_T')^{-1} N_T S_{x\varepsilon}.$$

Because $N_T S_{xx} N_T' \overset{\mathsf{P}}{\to} (1-\alpha)\Sigma > 0$ by (1.15), we see that $\breve{\beta}$ is defined with probability tending to one, and the representation (1.20) follows from (1.17).

The representation of $T^{1/2}(\breve{\sigma}^2 - \sigma^2)$: We use the expression, see (1.13), to show that

$$S_{11}^{-1}(S_{yy} - S_{yx}S_{xx}^{-1}S_{xy}) = S_{11}^{-1}\{S_{\varepsilon\varepsilon} + \mathrm{O_P}(1)\} \overset{P}{\to} \sigma^2\frac{\tau_2^c}{1-\alpha}.$$

This shows that we need to bias correct the empirical variance and therefore we consider

$$\breve{\sigma}^2 - \sigma^2 = (1-\alpha)(\tau_2^c)^{-1}S_{11}^{-1}(S_{yy} - S_{yx}S_{xx}^{-1}S_{xy}) - \sigma^2$$

$$= (1-\alpha)(\tau_2^c)^{-1}S_{11}^{-1}(S_{\varepsilon\varepsilon} - \sigma^2\frac{\tau_2^c}{1-\alpha}S_{11}) + O_p(T^{-1}),$$

and hence

$$\tau_2^c T^{1/2}(\breve{\sigma}^2 - \sigma^2) = T^{1/2}(S_{\varepsilon\varepsilon} - \sigma^2 \frac{\tau_2^c}{1-\alpha} S_{11}) + \mathrm{O_P}(T^{-1/2}).$$

From (1.18) and (1.19) we find the representation

$$\tau_2^c T^{1/2}(\breve{\sigma}^2 - \sigma^2) = \{T^{-1/2} \sum_{t=1}^{T} (\varepsilon_t^2 - \sigma^2 \frac{\tau_2^c}{1-\alpha}) 1_{(\sigma \underline{c} \leq \varepsilon_t \leq \sigma \overline{c})}$$
$$+ T^{1/2}\sigma(\hat{\sigma} - \sigma)\zeta_3^c + \sigma(\hat{\beta} - \beta)' N_T^{-1} T^{-1/2} N_T x_t \zeta_2^c)\} + \mathrm{o_P}(1),$$

which proves (1.21), because $T^{-1/2} N_T x_t \overset{\mathrm{P}}{\to} \mu$.

Consistency of the estimators: Finally it follows from the Assumption (*i*), (*ii,a*), (1.20), and (1.21) that $\{(N_T^{-1})'(\breve{\beta} - \beta), T^{1/2}(\breve{\sigma}^2 - \sigma^2)\} = \mathrm{O_P}(1)$, and $N_T \to 0$ and $T \to \infty$ then imply that $(\breve{\beta}, \breve{\sigma}^2) \overset{\mathrm{P}}{\to} (\beta, \sigma^2)$.

1.7 Proofs for Stationary and Trend Stationary Cases

The proofs relating to section 1.4 and section 1.5 follow.

Proof of Theorem 1.3. We apply Corollary 1.2, using $N_T = T^{-1/2} I_m$. The least squares estimator based on the full sample satisfies condition (*i,a*) : $T^{1/2}(\hat{\sigma} - \sigma, \hat{\beta} - \beta) = \mathrm{O_P}(1)$, and the stationarity of x_t shows that conditions (*ii,a,b,c*) hold.

For the numerator of the estimator $\breve{\beta}_{LS}$ we therefore consider

$$T^{-1/2} \sum_{t=1}^{T} x_t \varepsilon_t 1_{(\sigma \underline{c} \leq \varepsilon_t \leq \overline{c}\sigma)} + \xi_1^c \Sigma T^{1/2}(\hat{\beta} - \beta) + \xi_2^c T^{1/2}(\hat{\sigma} - \sigma)\mu,$$

and insert

$$T^{1/2}(\hat{\beta} - \beta) = \Sigma^{-1} T^{-1/2} \sum_{t=1}^{T} x_t \varepsilon_t + \mathrm{o_P}(1),$$

$$T^{1/2}(\hat{\sigma} - \sigma) = \frac{1}{2} T^{-1/2} \sum_{t=1}^{T} (\varepsilon_t^2/\sigma - \sigma) + \mathrm{o_P}(1).$$

This shows that $(1-\alpha)\Sigma T^{1/2}(\breve{\beta}_{LS} - \beta)$ has the same limit distribution as

$$T^{-1/2} \sum_{t=1}^{T} \{x_t(\varepsilon_t 1_{(\sigma \underline{c} \leq \varepsilon_t \leq \overline{c}\sigma)} + \xi_1^c \varepsilon_t) + \frac{\xi_2^c}{2}(\varepsilon_t^2/\sigma - \sigma)\mu\}, \qquad (1.54)$$

where the summand is a martingale difference sequence. The Central Limit Theorem for martingales shows that this expression is asymptotically

$N_m(0,\sigma^2\Phi_\beta)$. To find Φ_β we calculate the sum of the conditional variances

$$T^{-1}\sum_{t=1}^{T} x_t x_t'\{\tau_2^c + (\xi_1^c)^2 + 2\xi_1^c\tau_c^2\} + \mu\mu'\left(\frac{\xi_2^c}{2}\right)^2 T^{-1}\sum_{t=1}^{T}(\tau_4 - 1)$$

$$+T^{-1}\sum_{t=1}^{T}(x_t\mu' + \mu x_t')\frac{\xi_2^c}{2}(\tau_3^c + \xi_1^c\tau_3)$$

$$\overset{\mathsf{P}}{\to} \Sigma\{\tau_2^c + (\xi_1^c)^2 + 2\xi_1^2\tau_2^c\} + \mu\mu'\left\{\left(\frac{\xi_2^c}{2}\right)^2(\tau_4 - 1) + \xi_2^c(\tau_3^c + \xi_1^c\tau_3)\right\}.$$

Divide by $(1-\alpha)\Sigma$ from right and left to get the limiting variance for $T^{-1/2}(\breve{\beta}_{LS} - \beta)$.

For the estimator $\breve{\sigma}_{LS}$ the limiting distribution of $\tau_2^c T^{1/2}(\breve{\sigma}_{LS} - \sigma)$ is, in the same way, that of

$$T^{-1/2}\sum_{t=1}^{T}\left\{\left(\varepsilon_t^2 - \frac{\sigma^2\tau_2^c}{1-\alpha}\right)1_{(\sigma\underline{c}\le\varepsilon_t\le\overline{c}\sigma)} + \sigma\zeta_2^c\mu'\Sigma^{-1}x_t\varepsilon_t + \sigma\frac{\zeta_3^c}{2}(\varepsilon_t^2/\sigma - \sigma)\right\}. \quad (1.55)$$

This variable is asymptotically normal with variance gives by $\sigma^4\Phi_\sigma$ where

$$\Phi_\sigma = \tau_4^c - \frac{(\tau_2^c)^2}{1-\alpha} + (\zeta_2^c)^2\mu'\Sigma^{-1}\mu + \frac{(\zeta_3^c)^2}{4}(\tau_4 - 1)$$

$$+2\zeta_2^c\mu'\Sigma^{-1}\mu\tau_3^c + 2\frac{\zeta_3^c}{2}\left(\tau_4^c - \frac{(\tau_2^c)^2}{1-\alpha}\right) + 2\zeta_2^c\frac{\zeta_3^c}{2}\mu'\Sigma^{-1}\mu\tau_3.$$

Finally, the asymptotic covariance of the expressions (1.54), (1.55) is $\sigma^3\Phi_c$ where

$$\Phi_c = \mu(1 + \xi_1^c)\tau_3^c + \mu\zeta_2^c(\tau_2^c + \xi_1^c) + \mu\frac{\zeta_3^c}{2}(\tau_3^c + \xi_1^c\tau_3)$$

$$+\mu\frac{\xi_2^c}{2}\left\{\tau_4^c - \frac{(\tau_2^c)^2}{1-\alpha}\right\} + \mu\mu'\Sigma^{-1}\mu\frac{\xi_2^c\zeta_2^c}{2}\tau_3 + \mu\frac{\xi_2^c\zeta_3^c}{4}(\tau_4 - 1).$$

Proof of Theorem 1.5. We want to apply Theorem 1.1 to the contributions for the two subsets $\mathcal{I}_1$ and $\mathcal{I}_2$. The least squares estimator based on the full sample satisfies condition (i,a) : $T^{1/2}(\hat{\sigma}_j - \sigma, \hat{\beta}_j - \beta) = O_P(1)$, and the stationarity of x_t shows that conditions (ii,a,b,c) hold. Thus, define the product moments

$$S_{uv} = \sum_{t=1}^{T} u_t w_t' 1_{\{\underline{c}\le v_t\le\overline{c}\}} = \sum_{t\in\mathcal{I}_1} u_t w_t' 1_{\{\underline{c}\le v_t\le\overline{c}\}} + \sum_{t\in\mathcal{I}_2} u_t w_t' 1_{\{\underline{c}\le v_t\le\overline{c}\}} = S_{uw}^1 + S_{uw}^2.$$

The stationarity of x_t implies that (1.23) holds. Considering the term S_{xx} apply (1.15) of Theorem 1.1 to get

$$T_1^{-1}S_{xx}^j \overset{\mathsf{P}}{\to} \lambda_j(1-\alpha)\Sigma \qquad \text{so} \qquad T^{-1}S_{xx} \overset{\mathsf{P}}{\to} (1-\alpha)\Sigma, \tag{1.56}$$

since $T_j/T \to \lambda_j$.

Representation of $T^{1/2}(\tilde{\beta}-\beta)$: the estimator $\tilde{\beta}$ satisfies

$$\tilde{\beta}-\beta = S_{xx}^{-1}S_{x\varepsilon} = S_{xx}^{-1}\{S_{xx}^1(\tilde{\beta}^1-\beta)+S_{xx}^2(\tilde{\beta}^2-\beta)\},$$

where $\tilde{\beta}^j-\beta=(S_{xx}^j)^{-1}S_{x\varepsilon}^j$ is the contribution from $\mathcal{I}_j$. Due to (1.56) we then find

$$\tilde{\beta}-\beta = \lambda_1(\tilde{\beta}^1-\beta)+\lambda_2(\tilde{\beta}^2-\beta)+\mathrm{o_P}(1). \tag{1.57}$$

Turning to the individual contributions $\tilde{\beta}^j$, Theorem 1.1 shows

$$\{(1-\alpha)\Sigma\}(\tilde{\beta}^1-\beta) = T_1^{-1}\sum_{t\in\mathcal{I}_1} x_t\varepsilon_t 1_{(\underline{c}\sigma\le\varepsilon_t\le\sigma\overline{c})} + \xi_1^c\Sigma(\hat{\beta}_2-\beta)+\xi_2^c(\hat{\sigma}_2-\sigma)\mu+\mathrm{o_P}(T_1^{-1/2}),$$

where $\hat{\beta}_2,\hat{\sigma}_2$ are the initial least squares estimators satisfying

$$\hat{\beta}_2-\beta = \Sigma^{-1}T_2^{-1}\sum_{t\in\mathcal{I}_2} x_t\varepsilon_t + \mathrm{o_P}(1),$$

$$\hat{\sigma}_2-\sigma = \frac{1}{2}T_2^{-1}\sum_{t\in\mathcal{I}_2}(\varepsilon_t^2/\sigma-\sigma)+\mathrm{o_P}(1).$$

Inserting these in the expression for $\tilde{\beta}^1$ then gives

$$\begin{aligned}&\{(1-\alpha)\Sigma\}(\tilde{\beta}^1-\beta)\\ &= T_1^{-1}\sum_{t\in\mathcal{I}_1} x_t\varepsilon_t 1_{(\underline{c}\sigma\le\varepsilon_t\le\sigma\overline{c})} + \xi_1^c T_2^{-1}\sum_{t\in\mathcal{I}_2} x_t\varepsilon_t + \frac{1}{2}\xi_2^c\mu T_2^{-1}\sum_{t\in\mathcal{I}_2}(\varepsilon_t^2/\sigma-\sigma)+\mathrm{o_P}\left(T^{-1/2}\right).\end{aligned}$$

Interchanging the role of the indices 1, 2 gives a similar expression for $\tilde{\beta}^2-\beta$. Combining these expressions according to (1.57) then proves (1.24).

Representation of $T^{1/2}(\tilde{\sigma}^2-\sigma^2)$: we use the expression (1.13) showing

$$\begin{aligned}\tilde{\sigma}^2 &= (1-\alpha)(\tau_2^c S_{11})^{-1}(S_{yy}-S_{yx}S_{xx}^{-1}S_{xy})\\ &= (1-\alpha)(\tau_2^c S_{11})^{-1}\{S_{\varepsilon\varepsilon}-(\tilde{\beta}-\beta)'S_{xx}(\tilde{\beta}-\beta)\}.\end{aligned}$$

Since (1.24) implies $\tilde{\beta}-\beta=\mathrm{O_P}\left(T^{-1/2}\right)$ while $S_{xx}=\mathrm{O_P}(T)$ by (1.56) then

$$\tilde{\sigma}^2 = (1-\alpha)(\tau_2^c S_{11})^{-1}\{S_{\varepsilon\varepsilon}+\mathrm{O_P}(1)\},$$

so that, using $T^{-1}S_{11}\overset{\mathsf{P}}{\to} 1-\alpha$,

$$\tau_2^c T^{1/2}(\tilde{\sigma}^2-\sigma^2) = T^{-1/2}\left(S_{\varepsilon\varepsilon}-\sigma^2\frac{\tau_2^c}{1-\alpha}S_{11}\right)+\mathrm{o_P}(1).$$

We apply (1.18) and (1.19) and find that the contribution from $\mathcal{I}_1$ is

$$T^{-1/2}\sum_{t\in\mathcal{I}_1}\left[\left(\varepsilon_t^2-\sigma^2\frac{\tau_2^c}{1-\alpha}\right)1_{(\underline{c}\sigma\le\varepsilon_t\le\overline{c}\sigma)}\right.$$

$$\left.+\sigma\frac{\lambda_1}{\lambda_2}\left\{\zeta_2^c\mu'\Sigma^{-1}T^{-1/2}\sum_{t\in\mathcal{I}_2}x_t\varepsilon_t+\frac{\zeta_3^c}{2}T^{-1/2}\sum_{\mathcal{I}_2}(\varepsilon_t^2/\sigma-\sigma)\right\}\right]+\mathrm{O_P}\left(T^{1/2}\right),$$

which together with an expression for the contribution from $\mathcal{I}_2$ shows (1.25).

Proof of Theorem 1.6. We apply (1.24) where the summands on the right hand side is a martingale difference sequence and we apply the Central Limit Theorem for martingales to show that $T^{1/2}(\tilde{\beta}-\beta)\overset{\mathrm{D}}{\to}\mathrm{N}_m(0,\Phi)$. In order to find Φ we calculate the sum of the conditional variances and find

$$T^{-1}\sum_{t=1}^{T}x_tx_t'\{\tau_2^c+h_t^2(\xi_1^c)^2+2h_t\xi_1^c\tau_2^c\}+\mu\mu'\left(\frac{\xi_2^c}{2}\right)^2h_t^2(\tau_4-1)$$

$$+T^{-1}\sum_{t=1}^{T}(x_t\mu'+\mu x_t')\frac{\xi_2^c}{2}(h_t\tau_3^c+h_t^2\xi_1^c\tau_3).$$

Using the relations

$$T^{-1}\sum_{t=1}^{T}h_t=1 \qquad T^{-1}\sum_{t=1}^{T}h_t^2=\frac{\lambda_1^2}{\lambda_2}+\frac{\lambda_2^2}{\lambda_1},$$

$$T^{-1}\sum_{t=1}^{T}x_th_t\overset{\mathrm{P}}{\to}\mu \qquad T^{-1}\sum_{t=1}^{T}x_th_t^2\overset{\mathrm{P}}{\to}\mu\left(\frac{\lambda_1^2}{\lambda_2}+\frac{\lambda_2^2}{\lambda_1}\right),$$

$$T^{-1}\sum_{t=1}^{T}x_tx_t'h_t\overset{\mathrm{P}}{\to}\Sigma, \qquad T^{-1}\sum_{t=1}^{T}x_tx_t'h_t^2\overset{\mathrm{P}}{\to}\Sigma\left(\frac{\lambda_1^2}{\lambda_2}+\frac{\lambda_2^2}{\lambda_1}\right), \tag{1.58}$$

we find the limit (1.26).

Proof of Theorem 1.7. We apply Theorem 1.1 and Corollary 1.2. The initial estimators $\tilde{\beta}$ and $\tilde{\sigma}^2$ satisfy condition (i,a), and the stationarity implies conditions (ii,a,b,c). We therefore get that $T^{-1}S_{xx}\overset{\mathrm{P}}{\to}(1-\alpha)\Sigma$, and $T^{-1}S_{x1}\overset{\mathrm{P}}{\to}(1-\alpha)\mu$. Finally we find from (1.20), that, when the density is symmetric so that $\xi_2^c=0$,

$$(1-\alpha)\Sigma T^{1/2}(\breve{\beta}_{Sat}-\beta)=T^{-1/2}\sum_{t=1}^{T}x_t\varepsilon_t1_{(\underline{c}\sigma\le\varepsilon_t\le\sigma\overline{c})}+\xi_1^c\Sigma T^{1/2}(\tilde{\beta}-\beta)+\mathrm{o_P}(1),$$

Now insert the expression for $\tilde{\beta}$ in (1.24) with $\xi_2^c=0$, which is

$$(1-\alpha)\Sigma T^{1/2}(\tilde{\beta}-\beta)=T^{-1/2}\sum_{t=1}^{T}x_t\{\varepsilon_t1_{(\underline{c}\sigma\le\varepsilon_t\le\sigma\overline{c})}+\xi_1^c\varepsilon_th_t\}+\mathrm{o_P}(1)$$

and we find

$$(1-\alpha)\Sigma T^{1/2}(\breve{\beta}_{Sat}-\beta)$$

$$= T^{-1/2}\sum_{t=1}^{T} x_t\left\{\left(1+\frac{\xi_1^c}{1-\alpha}\right)\varepsilon_t 1_{(\underline{c}\sigma\le\varepsilon_t\le\sigma\overline{c})}+\varepsilon_t\frac{(\xi_1^c)^2}{1-\alpha}h_t\right\}+\mathrm{o_P}(1).$$

Again the summands form a martingale difference sequence and the Central Limit Theorem for martingales shows that $T^{1/2}(\breve{\beta}-\beta)\overset{\mathsf{D}}{\to}N(0,\Phi)$. We calculate the sum of the conditional variances

$$\sigma^2 T^{-1}\sum_{t=1}^{T}x_t x_t'\left\{\left(1+\frac{\xi_1^c}{1-\alpha}\right)^2\tau_2^c+h_t^2\frac{(\xi_1^c)^4}{(1-\alpha)^2}+2\left(1+\frac{\xi_1^c}{1-\alpha}\right)\frac{(\xi_1^c)^2}{1-\alpha}h_t\tau_2^c\right\},$$

which converges in probability towards

$$\frac{\sigma^2}{(1-\alpha)^2}\Sigma\left\{(1-\alpha+\xi_1^c)^2\tau_2^c+2(1-\alpha+\xi_1^c)(\xi_1^c)^2\tau_2^c+\left(\frac{\lambda_1^2}{\lambda_2}+\frac{\lambda_2^2}{\lambda_1}\right)(\xi_1^c)^4\right\},$$

which gives the expression (1.27) after dividing by $(1-\alpha)^2\Sigma^2$.

Proof of Theorem 1.8. The results (1.30), (1.31), (1.32): Note that it can be assumed without loss of generality that D has the Jordan form of Nielsen (2005, Section 4). Using the normalization N_D suggested in that paper it follows that $T^{-1}N_D'\sum_{t=1}^{T}d_t d_t' N_D$ converges. The results then follow from Nielsen (2005, Theorem 4.1, 6.2, 6.4).

The result (1.33) follows from the Central Limit Theorem for martingales noting that the Lindeberg conditions hold

$$T^{-1}\sum_{t=1}^{T}\mathsf{E}|(Y_{t-1}-\Psi d_{t-1})\varepsilon_t'|^2 1_{\{|(Y_{t-1}-\Psi d_{t-1})\varepsilon_t'|\ge T^{1/2}a\}}\to 0,$$

$$\sum_{t=1}^{T}\mathsf{E}|M_T d_t\varepsilon_t'|^2 1_{(|M_T d_{t-1}\varepsilon_t'|\ge T^{1/2}a)}\le c\frac{1}{T}\sum_{t=1}^{T}|M_T d_t|^4\to 0.$$

Finally, (1.34), (1.35) follow by combining (1.30) and (1.33).

Proof of Theorem 1.9. We can mimic the steps of the proof of Theorem 1.8 for the sums over the subsets $t\in\mathcal{I}_j$ rather than $t\in\mathcal{I}_1\cup\mathcal{I}_2$. Thus, the assumptions of Theorem 1.1 are satisfied for each subset. In particular, it holds

$$(N_T^{-1})'(\hat{\beta}_j-\beta)=\Sigma_j^{-1}N_T\sum_{t\in\mathcal{I}_j}x_t\varepsilon_t+\mathrm{o_P}(1), \tag{1.59}$$

$$T^{1/2}(\hat{\sigma}_j-\sigma)=(2\sigma\lambda_j)^{-1}T^{-1/2}\sum_{t\in\mathcal{I}_j}\left(\varepsilon^2-\sigma^2\right)+\mathrm{o_P}(1). \tag{1.60}$$

We can now apply Theorem 1.1 to the estimator

$$(N_T^{-1})'(\tilde{\beta} - \beta) = (N_T S_{xx} N_T')^{-1} N_T S_{x\varepsilon}.$$

Apply (1.15), (1.16), (1.17) of Theorem 1.1 to each component to get

$$N_T S_{xx} N_T' \xrightarrow{\mathsf{P}} (1-\alpha)(\Sigma_1 + \Sigma_2) = (1-\alpha)\Sigma,$$

$$T^{-1/2} N_T S_{x1} \xrightarrow{\mathsf{P}} (1-\alpha)(\mu_1 + \mu_2) = (1-\alpha)\mu,$$

$$N_T S_{x\varepsilon} = N_T \sum_{j=1}^{2} \sum_{t \notin \mathcal{I}_j} \{x_t \varepsilon_t 1_{(\underline{c}\sigma < \varepsilon_t < \overline{c}\sigma)} + \xi_1^c x_t x_t' (\hat{\beta}_j - \beta) + \xi_2^c x_t (\hat{\sigma}_j - \sigma)\} + \mathrm{o_P}(1).$$

For $S_{x\varepsilon}$ insert the expressions (1.59), (1.60) for the estimators to get the expression

$$\sum_{t=1}^{T} N_T x_t \varepsilon_t 1_{(\underline{c}\sigma < \varepsilon_t < \overline{c}\sigma)} + \xi_1^c \sum_{t=1}^{T} H_t N_T x_t \varepsilon_t + \frac{\xi_2^c}{2\sigma} T^{-1/2} \sum_{t=1}^{T} K_t (\varepsilon^2 - \sigma^2) + \mathrm{o_P}(1),$$

where

$$H_t = \Sigma_2 \Sigma_1^{-1} 1_{(t \in \mathcal{I}_1)} + \Sigma_1 \Sigma_2^{-1} 1_{(t \in \mathcal{I}_2)},$$

$$K_t = \mu_2 \lambda_1^{-1} 1_{(t \in \mathcal{I}_1)} + \mu_1 \lambda_2^{-1} 1_{(t \in \mathcal{I}_2)}.$$

This expression is a sum of a martingale difference sequence and we therefore apply the Central Limit Theorem for martingales. We calculate the sum of the conditional variances to be

$$\sum_{t=1}^{T} N_T x_t x_t' N_T' \sigma^2 \tau_2^c + \sigma^2 (\xi_1^c)^2 \sum_{t=1}^{T} H_t N_T x_t x_t' N_T' H_t' + \left(\frac{\xi_2^c}{2}\right)^2 T^{-1} \sum_{t=1}^{T} K_t K_t (\tau_4 - 1)$$

$$+ \sigma^2 \xi_1^c \tau_2^c \sum_{t=1}^{T} (N_T x_t x_t' N_T' H_t' + H_t N_T x_t x_t' N_T')$$

$$+ \sigma^2 \tau_3 \frac{\xi_2^c}{2} \xi_1^c T^{-1/2} \sum_{t=1}^{T} (H_t N_T x_t K_t' + K_t x_t' N_T' H_t') + \sigma^2 \frac{\xi_2^c}{2} \tau_3^c T^{-1/2} \sum_{t=1}^{T} (N_T x_t K_t' + K_t x_t' N_T').$$

Now we apply the results that

$$\sum_{t=1}^{T} N_T x_t x_t' N_T' \xrightarrow{\mathsf{P}} \Sigma, \quad T^{-1} \sum_{t=1}^{T} K_t K_t' \to \frac{\mu_2 \mu_2'}{\lambda_1} + \frac{\mu_1 \mu_1'}{\lambda_2},$$

$$\sum_{t=1}^{T} H_t N_T x_t x_t' N_T' H_t' \xrightarrow{\mathsf{P}} \Sigma_2 \Sigma_1^{-1} \Sigma_2 + \Sigma_1 \Sigma_2^{-1} \Sigma_1, \quad T^{-1/2} \sum_{t=1}^{T} N_T x_t K_t' \xrightarrow{\mathsf{P}} \mu_1 \mu_2' + \mu_2 \mu_1',$$

$$\sum_{t=1}^{T} N_T x_t x_t' N_T' H_t' \xrightarrow{\mathsf{P}} \Sigma, \quad T^{-1/2} \sum_{t=1}^{T} H_t N_T x_t K_t' \xrightarrow{\mathsf{P}} \Sigma_2 \Sigma_1^{-1} \mu_1 \mu_2' \lambda_1^{-1} + \Sigma_1 \Sigma_2^{-1} \mu_2 \mu_1' \lambda_2^{-1},$$

which give the result.

1.8 Conclusion

Various robust regression estimators were analysed including a robustified least squares estimator and a dummy saturated estimator. These estimators are examples of one-step M-estimators involving Huber's skip function. The main result, Theorem 1.1, permits analysis of such estimators in a time-series context in the situation where there are no outliers. In future work it would be of interest to investigate the properties of the estimators when outliers are present and to clarify the properties of estimators found by iterating one-step M-estimators.

References

Bickel, P. J. (1975). One step Huber estimates in the linear model. *Journal of the American Statistical Association*, **70**, 428–434.

Hendry, D. F. (1999). An econometric analysis of US food expenditure, 1931–1989. In Magnus, J. R. and Morgan, M. S. (eds.), *Methodology and Tacit Knowledge: Two Experiments in Econometrics*, pp. 341–361. New York: Wiley.

——Johansen, S., and Santos, C. (2008). Automatic selection of indicators in a fully saturated regression. *Computational Statistics*, **23**, 317–335 and Erratum 337–339.

Huber, P. (1964). Robust estimation of location parameter. *Annals of Mathematical Statistics*, **35**, 73–101.

——(1981). *Robust Statistics*. New York: Wiley.

Koenker, R. (2005). *Quantile Regression*. Cambridge: Cambridge University Press.

Koul, H. L. (2002). *Weighted Empirical Processes in Dynamic Nonlinear Models*, 2nd edition. New York: Springer.

Nielsen, B. (2005). Strong consistency results for least squares estimators in general vector autoregressions with deterministic terms. *Econometric Theory*, **21**, 534–561.

R Development Core Team (2006). *R: A Language and Environment for Statistical Computing*. Vienna: R Foundation for Statistical Computing.

Rousseeuw, P. J. (1984). Least median of squares regression. *Journal of the American Statistical Association*, **79**, 871–880.

——and Leroy, A. M. (1987). *Robust Regression and Outlier Detection*. New York: Wiley.

Ruppert, D. and Carroll, R. J. (1980). Trimmed least squares estimation in the linear model. *Journal of the American Statistical Association*, **75**, 828–838.

Yohai V. and Maronna, R. (1976). Location estimators based on linear combinations of modified order statistics. *Communications in Statistics Theory and Methods*, **5**, 481–486.

2

Empirical Identification of the Vector Autoregression: The Causes and Effects of US M2

*Kevin D. Hoover, Selva Demiralp, and Stephen J. Perez**

A commonplace in economics is that theory and empirics stand in a position of mutual support.[1] But there can be little doubt that for some time theory has had the upper hand. We see this in the widespread view that it is only through a priori theory that a system of equations can be identified, and we see it in the equally widespread view that data-mining—that is, using empirical data to shape the formulation of an econometric model—is, in all of its forms, an unequivocally bad thing. We are left with the odd view that theory proposes and data disposes. On this principle, empirical evidence is, at best, destructive, but cannot be constructive. In reality we find it hard to live up to such fine principles, but the economics profession naturally tries its best to hide (or disguise) its apostacy.

David Hendry belongs to the minority camp that embraces the notion that empirical investigation plays a *constructive* role in developing our understanding of the economy. In his inaugural address at the London School of Economics, 'Econometrics: Alchemy or Science?' (1980), Hendry cogently made the case for constructive econometrics—a chemistry, not an alchemy. Hendry and the so-called LSE school (Gilbert, 1986; Mizon, 1995) recognize that, for many important economic problems, economic theory is too weak—and absent learning more about the facts on the ground—always will be too

* The authors thank Søren Johansen for valuable econometric advice.

[1] Kant is frequently quoted in support without a specific reference as: 'Theory without empirics is empty. Empirics without theory is blind.' or 'Experience without theory is blind, but theory without experience is mere intellectual play.' Both seem to be overly free translations of '*Gedanken ohne Inhalt sind leer, Anschauungen ohne Begriffe sind blind*' ('Thoughts without contents are empty; opinions without concepts are blind'—Hoover translation); Kant (1787, part 2, section 1).

weak to fulfill the dominant role that the reigning ideology of economics assigns it. If one wants to know the truth about the economy, one often has to grub through the data with economic theory providing—at most—broad guidance and not detailed specifications. In his vital work on encompassing and general-to-specific specification search, culminating in his work on automatic model selection (particularly, in the PcGets software—see Hendry and Krolzig 1999, 2001; Krolzig and Hendry, 2001), Hendry grasps the nettle. Rather than hiding constructive econometrics to suit the prejudices of the profession, he asks sensibly, how should it be done well.

We have long taken Hendry's side of the debate. And indeed, we have contributed something to automatic model selection in the spirit of the LSE school (Hoover and Perez 1999, 2004). We have also long been interested in what, at first, might seem an orthogonal concern: causality in economics (Perez, 1998; Hoover, 2001; Demiralp and Hoover, 2003).[2] We believe that there is an important complementarity, which has yet to be fully exploited, between Hendry's general-to-specific approach and recent work on the graph-theoretic approach to causal modelling (Spirtes, Glymour, and Scheines, 2001; Pearl, 2000; Swanson and Granger, 1997; Demiralp and Hoover, 2003; Hoover, 2005). Krolzig (2003) demonstrates that PcGets is effective at recovering the dynamic structure of a system of equations (a structural vector autoregression or SVAR), provided that one starts with a diagonal covariance matrix—in other words, provided that one knows the contemporaneous causal order of the SVAR. Graph-theoretic causal-search algorithms can aid in the discovery of that causal order, so that, together with a general-to-specific search algorithm, we have some hope of identifying the structure of the SVAR empirically. (Instead of PcGets, we in fact use Autometrics—see the chapter by Doornik in this volume for description of the algorithm.)

In this chapter we provide a concrete illustration of the complementary use of graph-theoretic causal modelling and automated general-to-specific specification search. Our problem is to identify the factors determining the US M2 monetary aggregate and its role in the transmission of monetary policy—a problem for which economic theory provides only the broadest guidance.

2.1 Understanding M2

M2 consists of liquid deposits, small time deposits, retail money funds, and currency in circulation. Even though, owing to the widespread use of alternative financial market instruments, the relationship between monetary

[2] And on which Hendry might be seen as somewhat sceptical—see Hendry *et al.* (1990), p. 184.

aggregates and income growth has loosened over the last decade, the Federal Reserve still regards the pattern of M2 growth as providing information about the conditions of aggregate demand. M2 growth is monitored by the Monetary and Reserve Analysis Section of the Division of Monetary Affairs of the Board of Governors of the Federal Reserve System.[3] Although the Section implicitly assumes a relatively rich causal structure in explaining the process of M2 growth, there are no formal studies (inside or outside the Federal Reserve) that analyse M2 growth analytically. The Federal Reserve's econometric models do forecast M2 growth, but these models are mostly driven by the quantity theory of money, and omit many of the implicit structural considerations that the Section regards as important.

Before each meeting of the Federal Open Market Committee (FOMC), the Section prepares a contribution to the briefing document, known as the 'Bluebook', in which it analyses the growth of M2 in relation to a number of factors that have not yet been investigated structurally. The economic theory used is fairly broad brush. According to the quantity theory of money, the growth rate of money should equal the growth rate of nominal income, adjusting for the trend in velocity. The Section's analysis, therefore, starts by anchoring the underlying growth rate of M2 to the growth rate of GDP, and then considers 'special factors' that may cause deviations of M2 growth rate from that of GDP. These special factors comprise:

i) Interest rate effects: changes in the Federal funds rate target lead to subsequent changes in the opportunity cost of holding M2 type of assets.
ii) Equity market effects: high volatility and downwards revisions to the expectations of earnings on equities earnings *ceteris paribus* boost M2 as investors substitute away from the stock market and into safe and liquid M2-type assets.
iii) Other special factors including: activity in *mortgage-backed securities*, as mortgage servicers temporarily accumulate the proceeds of pre-paid mortgages in the liquid-deposits component of M2; *tax effects*, which influence the money-market-deposit-account (MMDA) component of liquid deposits as people pay their taxes out of their savings accounts; and *currency shipments abroad*.

To illustrate, Table 2.1 shows the growth rates of the components of M2 as of December 2004. Comparing the second and the seventh columns shows to that in the second quarter of 2004 M2 growth exceeded that of GDP growth (row 1), whereas in the third quarter it fell behind (row 2). The Section attributed the accelerated pace in the second quarter to: (i) mortgage

[3] This chapter was conceived while Demiralp was employed as a staff economist in the Monetary and Reserve Analysis Section.

Table 2.1. Growth rates of M2 and its major components (percent per annum)

	M2	Liquid Deposits	Small Time Deposits	M2 Money Funds	Currency	Nominal GDP	Inflation[1]
2004:2	9.7	17.1	−4.6	−7.2	4.0	6.6	4.7
2004:3	2.7	4.5	1.8	−11.3	9.3	5.1	6.2
October 2004	2.5	6.1	3.3	−20.2	4.2		
November 2004	6.3	8.0	5.1	−5.7	9.9		

Source: Board of Governors of the Federal Reserve System and Bureau of Economic Analysis.

[1] Measured by the personal consumption expenditure deflator.

refinancing activity in April (which was boosted by a decline in mortgage interest rates), and (ii) inflows from equity and bond funds as well as increased deposits of tax refunds in May. Meanwhile the slowdown in the third quarter was mostly explained by the rising opportunity cost in the face of a series of steps to tighten monetary policy. In each case, the largest component of M2, liquid deposits, accounts for most of the overall growth rate (see Table 2.2).

Liquid Deposits, which constitute about 65% of M2, comprise *demand deposit accounts* (DDAs), *other certificates of deposits* (OCDs), and *savings deposits* (including MMDAs). DDAs and OCDs are the most liquid of the components of liquid deposits, and appear to respond to changes in the opportunity cost of holding M2 and similar assets. In addition to this opportunity-cost channel, running from changes in the Federal funds rate to the opportunity cost of M2 to liquid deposits, a decline in the Federal-funds-rate target may also lead to a decline in mortgage rates, a consequent rise in the mortgage refinancing, and a rise in liquid deposits to meet the temporary need of mortgage servicers to park funds for several weeks until the mortgage-backed securities are redeemed. Other transitory changes in the holdings of liquid deposits may be related to tax payments, influencing especially DDAs and OCDs. The MMDA component of liquid deposits is a close substitute for stock

Table 2.2. Contributions of M2 components to M2 growth

	2004:2	2003:3	October 2004	November 2004
M2	9.7	2.7	2.5	6.3
Liquid Deposits	10.8	2.9	4.0	5.2
MMMF	−0.9	−1.4	−2.3	−0.6
Small Time	−0.6	0.2	0.4	0.6
Currency	0.4	1.0	0.5	1.1

Source: Board of Governors of the Federal Reserve System.

Components may not sum to total because traveller's cheques are not shown.

mutual funds and may, therefore, display sensitivity to the performance of the stock market. Events, such as domestic or international political crises, also boost the demand for safe and liquid M2 components. On the other hand, steepening of the yield curve, because of an increase in long-term yields or a looser monetary policy, may reduce the growth of liquid deposits as investors substitute into longer-term assets.

After a brief detour to set out the strategy of empirical investigation, we will in sections 2.3 through 2.6 investigate to what degree the data support qualitatively and quantitatively the Monetary and Reserve Analysis Section's informal understanding of the role of M2 in the transmission of monetary policy.

2.2 Empirical Identification

Our approach will be to specify a structural vector autoregression as far as possible using the tools of graph-theoretic causal-search algorithms and Doornik and Hendry's Autometrics software. Autometrics is sufficiently well described (Doornik, this volume) that we need not spend time on explaining the principles of its operation. Although the same is not true of the graph-theoretic causal-search algorithms, we nonetheless will give only an informal sketch and refer the reader to the fuller descriptions cited in the introduction.

The SVAR can be written as:

$$\mathbf{A}_0\mathbf{Y}_t = \mathbf{A}(L)\mathbf{Y}_{t-1} + \mathbf{E}_t, \tag{2.1}$$

where $\mathbf{Y}_t$ is an $n \times 1$ vector of contemporaneous variables, $\mathbf{A}_0$ is a full rank $n \times n$ matrix with ones on the main diagonal and possibly non-zero off-diagonal elements; $\mathbf{A}(L)$ is a polynomial in the lag operator, L; and $\mathbf{E}_t$ is an identical independent normal $n \times 1$ vector of error terms $\mathbf{E}_t \sim N(0, \mathbf{\Sigma})$. Let $\mathbf{E} = [\mathbf{E}_t]$, $t = 1, 2, \ldots, T$, then the covariance matrix $\mathbf{\Sigma} = \mathrm{E}(\mathbf{EE}')$ is diagonal. The individual error terms (shocks) can be assigned unequivocally to particular equations because $\mathbf{\Sigma}$ is diagonal. The matrix $\mathbf{A}_0$ defines the causal interrelationships among the contemporaneous variables. The system is identified provided that there are $n(n-1)/2$ zero restrictions on $\mathbf{A}_0$. For any just-identified system, $\mathbf{A}_0$ can be rendered lower triangular by selecting the appropriate order of the variables $\mathbf{Y}$ along with the conformable order the rows of $\mathbf{A}_0$. This is the *recursive* (or *Wold causal*) *order*.

Starting with the SVAR as the data-generating process (DGP), premultiplying by $\mathbf{A}_0^{-1}$ yields the reduced-form or ordinary vector autoregression (VAR):[4]

$$\mathbf{Y}_t = \mathbf{A}_0^{-1}\mathbf{A}(L)\mathbf{Y}_{t-1} + \mathbf{A}_0^{-1}\mathbf{E}_t = \mathbf{B}(L)\mathbf{Y}_{t-1} + \mathbf{U}_t. \tag{2.2}$$

[4] This and the next six paragraphs are closely based on Hoover (2005).

The transformed error terms are $\mathbf{U} = [\mathbf{U}_t]$, $t = 1, 2, \ldots, T$. And, in general, $\boldsymbol{\Omega} = E(\mathbf{UU}')$ is, unlike $\boldsymbol{\Sigma}$, not diagonal. If we *knew* $\mathbf{A}_0$, then recovery of the SVAR (equation 2.1) from the easily estimated VAR (equation 2.2) would be straightforward. There are, however, a large number of $n \times n$ matrices, $\mathbf{P}_i$ that may be used to premultiply equation (2.2) such that the covariance matrix $\boldsymbol{\Omega} = E(\mathbf{P}_i\mathbf{U}(\mathbf{P}_i\mathbf{U})')$ is diagonal. The central identification problem for SVARs is to choose the one member of $\mathbf{P}_i$ that corresponds to the data-generating process, that is to find $\mathbf{P}_i = \mathbf{A}_0$, when $\mathbf{A}_0$ is unknown.

Identification requires at least $n(n-1)/2$ restrictions on $\mathbf{P}_i$. If we restrict ourselves to zero restrictions on recursive systems, then any just-identified $\mathbf{P}_i$ can be arranged in the form of one of the $n!$ Choleski orderings (or decompositions) corresponding to each of the possible permutations of the variables in $\mathbf{Y}$. For any given permutation, there is a unique lower triangular $\mathbf{P}_i$ such that $\mathbf{P}_i\,\boldsymbol{\Omega}\,\mathbf{P}_i'$ is diagonal. The just-identified SVARs specified by each of the Choleski orderings is observationally equivalent in the sense that they each have the same likelihood. Yet, the different orderings have different consequences for the dynamics of the SVAR.

On what basis, then, should we choose? If we are restricted to just-identified SVARs, then we have little choice but to appeal to economic theory to tell us what the causal order should be. This is, in fact, what almost all practitioners of VAR methodologies profess to do. Unfortunately, formal economic theory is rarely decisive about causal order. So, VAR practitioners either choose the order arbitrarily, sometimes with an accompanying claim that their results are robust to alternative causal orderings—apparently unaware that such robustness arises in just those cases that the contemporaneous terms are unimportant. Or they appeal, not so much to theory, as to 'just so' stories: intuition or commonsense tells them that, say, financial markets adjust more quickly than goods markets, so that interest rates, for instance, ought to be causally ordered ahead of real GDP. It is usually easy, however, to tell a 'just so' story to justify almost any order—the time order of variables that are contemporaneously related at the given frequency of observation being especially unreliable. There is a special irony that this strategy should be so commonly accepted among VAR practitioners. After all, Sims's (1980) motivation in initiating the VAR program was to avoid the need to appeal to 'incredible' identifying restrictions.

If, however, the true SVAR is overidentified, then we have another option. Graph-theoretic causal search provides a method of choosing $\mathbf{P}_i$, very much in the spirit of Hendry's general-to-specific model selection. In a causal graph, arrows connecting causal variables to their effects represent causal relationships. Spirtes *et al.* (2001) and Pearl (2000) show that there are isomorphisms between graphs and the probability distributions of variables. In particular, certain graphical patterns imply certain relationships of conditional independence and dependence among the variables. The graph of the DGP can also be represented through the restrictions on $\mathbf{A}_0$. Working backwards from statistical measures of conditional independence and dependence, it is possible to infer the class of graphs compatible with the data. Sometimes that class has only a single member, and then $\mathbf{A}_0$ can be identified statistically.

The key ideas of the graph-theoretic approach are simple. Suppose that $A \rightarrow B \rightarrow C$ (that is, A causes B causes C). A and C would be dependent, but conditional on B, they would be independent. Similarly for $A \leftarrow B \leftarrow C$. In each case, B is said to *screen* A from C. Suppose that $A \leftarrow B \rightarrow C$. Then, once again A and C would be dependent, but conditional on B, they would be independent. B is said to be the *common cause* of A and C. Now suppose that A and B are independent conditional on sets of variables that exclude C or its descendants, and $A \rightarrow C \leftarrow B$, and none of the variables that cause A or B directly causes C. Then, conditional on C, A and B are dependent. C is called an *unshielded collider* on the path ACB. (A *shielded collider* would have a direct link between A and B.)

Causal search algorithms use a statistical measure of independence, commonly a measure of conditional correlation, to check systematically the patterns of conditional independence and dependence and to work backwards to the class of admissible causal structures. In this chapter, we use the PC algorithm, the most common of the causal-search algorithms (Spirtes *et al.*, 2001, pp. 84–85; Pearl, 2000, pp. 49–51; Cooper, 1999, p. 45, Figure 22). It assumes that graphs are *acylical* or strictly recursive—that is, loops in which $A \rightarrow B \rightarrow C \rightarrow A$ are ruled out. Naturally, acyclicality also rules out simultaneity—that is, a very tight loop in which $A \rightarrow B \rightarrow A$ (or $A \leftrightarrow B$). While the assumption of acyclicality is restrictive, it is nonetheless more general than limiting SVARs to Choleski orders, which remain the default in most VAR studies.

The details of the PC algorithm are described in Demiralp and Hoover (2003). Essentially, it begins with the complete set of variables in the VAR densely connected by undirected edges, represented as lines in a graph without arrowheads. It then tests for unconditional correlations and removes any uncorrelated edges. It then tests for correlations conditional on one other variable, again removing edges for which correlations vanish on conditioning. It then proceeds to conditioning on two, three, ... variables. The result is an undirected *skeleton*. The algorithm begins orienting edges by seeking triples of linked variables (A—B—C) in which the variables on the endpoints (A and C) are independent on some conditioning set, but become dependent when conditioning on the intermediate variable (B). This is the pattern of an unshielded collider, and the edges are then oriented ($A \rightarrow B \leftarrow C$). Some edges may be oriented *logically* (rather than statistically), based on maintaining the assumption of acyclicality and avoiding implying the existence of unshielded colliders not identified statistically.

Not all causal graphs are recoverable from the probability distribution. Graphs that have the same unshielded colliders and the same skeleton are observationally equivalent (Pearl, 2000, p. 19). If the true graph is a member of an observationally equivalent set, the algorithm will not orient the edges that distinguish one member of the set from another. In these cases, unoriented edges can be oriented in either direction without changing the likelihood, provided that no new unshielded colliders or cyclicality is introduced. Also, the maintained assumption of acyclicality notwithstanding, the algorithm will sometimes identify edges as bidirectional as a result of either ambiguity in the statistical test because of small samples or omitted latent variables.

Following Swanson and Granger (1997), we treat the estimated errors ($\hat{\mathbf{U}}_t$) from the VAR in equation (2.2) as the original data purged of their dynamics. The covariance matrix of these transformed data ($\hat{\boldsymbol{\Omega}}$) provides the necessary data for computing the various conditional correlations required by the PC algorithm. The algorithm selects a graph that best represents the causal order, and this graph in turn corresponds to particular zeros in (and overidentifying restrictions on) $\mathbf{A}_0$.

Demiralp and Hoover (2003) provide Monte Carlo evidence that shows that the PC algorithm is highly effective at recovering the skeleton of the DGP graph and moderately effective at recovering the directions of individual links, provided that signal-to-noise ratios are high enough. Demiralp, Hoover, and Perez (2008) develop and validate a bootstrap procedure to assess the effectiveness of the closely related SGS algorithm. The procedure constructs many simulations of the VAR, equation (2.2), based on the actual coefficient estimates ($\hat{\mathbf{B}}(L)$) and resampling of the columns of $\hat{\mathbf{U}}_t$, runs the search algorithm, and keeps track of the distribution of edges in the resulting graphs. The bootstrap method is essentially heuristic and provides guidance for more formal investigation of the overidentifying restrictions on $\mathbf{A}_0$.

Once we have selected $\mathbf{A}_0$ as the orthogonalizing transformation to transform the VAR, equation (2.2), into the SVAR, equation (2.1), then we can appeal to Krolzig's (2003) evidence for the effectiveness of PcGets at locating the true restrictions on the lagged coefficients—that is, the placement of zeros in the matrix $\mathbf{A}(L)$.

2.3 Data

The data consist of eleven monthly series that run from 1990:02 to 2005:03. Sources and details are provided in Appendix A.[5] Our main interest is in M2 and its role in the transmission mechanism. M2 is represented by its active component, (the logarithm of) liquid deposits (*LIQDEP*). Following

[5] The data are available from http://www.econ.duke.edu/~kdh9/research.html.

the considerations of the Monetary and Reserve Analysis Section discussed in section 2.1, the principal factors related to liquid deposits are core CPI inflation (*COREINF*) and a monthly proxy for real GDP, (the logarithm of) industrial production (*IP*). The additional considerations of the equity market are represented by (the logarithm of) the S&P 500 stock market index (*SP500*), its price–earnings ratio (*SPPE*), and stock market volatility (*VOL*). Mortgage activity is represented by (the logarithm of) an index of mortgage refinancing (*REFI*) and the interest rate on 30-year fixed-rate mortgages (*MORG30*). Monetary policy is represented by the Federal funds rate (*FF*). The Section also monitors the opportunity cost of M2 (*M2OC*), which is constructed from the 3-month Treasury bill rate (*TBILL3*) and the own-rate on *M2* (*M2OWN*). One question to be addressed is whether the two interest rates from which the opportunity cost of M2 is constructed enter only through *M2OC* or in fact have differential effects on other variables. The interest rates in the data set are rich enough to allow us to assess the interest-rate channel and the role of the yield curve in the transmission mechanism for monetary policy.[6]

As a preliminary, the data were graphed and tested for nonstationarity. Dickey–Fuller tests (with a constant and a trend), indicate that each of the series is very likely I(1), although for industrial production the test was borderline, and the series may even be better described as I(2).

2.4 Contemporaneous Causal Order

In order to test whether the opportunity cost of M2 is a satisfactory summary of the effects of its component rates, we test the restriction that the 10-variable VAR using *M2OC* is a valid restriction of the 11-variable VAR using *M2OWN* and *TBILL3*. The test is a likelihood ratio test with 40 restrictions: $\chi^2(40) = 476$, where the critical value $\chi^2_{0.05} = 56$. The 10-variable VAR is decisively rejected, and we analyse the 11-variable VAR hereafter.

Our first task in establishing the contemporaneous causal order among our variables is to estimate the unrestricted VAR—that is, equation (2.2), where $\mathbf{Y}_t$ = [*COREINF, FF, IP, SPPE, M2OWN, LIQDEP, SP500, REFI, MORG30, VOL, TBILL3*]′. The corrected Akaike Information Criterion of Hurwich and Tsai (1991), which seems well-adapted to this problem, selects a lag length of one. Both the Hannan–Quinn and Schwarz criteria also select only a single lag. However, all of these tests impose the same lag length on all equations. And, since in a later step, we intend to search for parsimonious, variable-specific dynamics, we should not be too restrictive at this stage. Therefore, we set

[6] We have restricted ourselves to factors considered by the Section. There are other possible channels of monetary transmission. These are to some extent captured by *LIQDEP*, which is linked to the balance sheets of banks. A richer specification of the SVAR is possible, but it is beyond the scope of the present chapter.

the lag length to four, which will allow three lagged differences when we later construct error-correction specifications. We estimate the VAR and obtain the covariance matrix of $\hat{\mathbf{U}}_t$, using it as the input into the PC algorithm, with a critical value of 10% for tests of conditional correlation. This is the critical value suggested on the basis of Monte Carlo studies by Spirtes *et al.* (1994, pp. 103–107) for the number of available observations (178 after accounting for lags). A critical value higher than the more common 5% is also justified by our concern not to restrict the specification too much (that is, we choose a 'liberal' strategy that shifts the balance somewhat towards the avoidance of type 2 error).

The algorithm selects the graph in Figure 2.1. While one should not read too much into the contemporaneous structure, since many important causal channels may operate with a lag, the graph is striking in that the variables are distinctly grouped: 1) the various interest rates are ordered as block recursively above the financial-asset variables; 2) core inflation is isolated contemporaneously from all other variables; and 3) mortgage refinancing is causally connected to the 30-year mortgage rate, but the direction of causation is

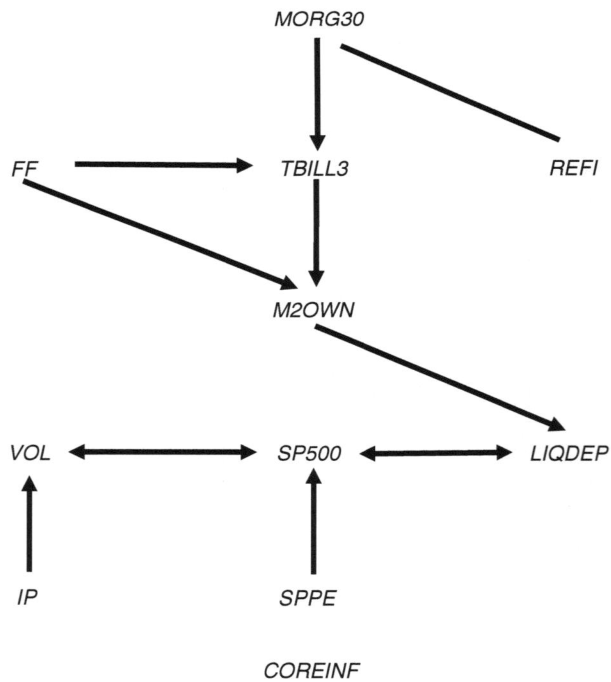

FIG. 2.1. Initial contemporaneous causal graph.

unresolved. Note the bidirectional edges between *VOL* and *SP500* and between *SP500* and *LIQDEP*.

How reliable is the identified graph? To evaluate it, we apply the bootstrap procedure of Demiralp, Hoover, and Perez (2008) with 10,000 replications. The results are shown in Table 2.3. There are 55 possible edges among eleven variables. The first three columns show the results of the PC algorithm for 16 of them—the 10 selected by the algorithm and 6 more that are selected in 10% or more of the bootstrap replications. The next five columns show the actual distribution of edges from the bootstrap. The last three columns present summary statistics: *exists* is the fraction of replications in which some edge is found (= 100 – *no edge*); *directed* is the percentage of edges discovered that have a definite direction; *net direction* is the difference between the percentage of edges directed rightward (→) and edges directed leftward (←).

The bootstrap presents strong evidence in favour of the existence of the first six edges in Table 2.3 (*exists* greater than 95%). In four of the six cases, the bootstrap favours the direction selected by the PC algorithm. One edge is undirected (*REFI* — *MORG30*). The bootstrap directs it only 35% of the time

Table 2.3. Bootstrap evaluation of the causal graph

Causal Order Selected by the PC Algorithm[1]			Edge Identification (percent of bootstrap realizations)[2]					Summary Statistics for Bootstrap Distribution[3]		
			—	←	no edge	→	↔	exists	directed	net direction
REFI	—	*MORG30*	65	22	0	11	3	100	35	−11
SP500	←	*SPPE*	17	52	0	11	20	100	83	−41
FF	→	*M2OWN*	47	14	0	38	1	100	53	25
FF	→	*TBILL3*	7	5	1	79	8	99	93	73
VOL	↔	*SP500*	8	20	5	28	39	95	92	8
MORG30	→	*TBILL3*	7	3	5	75	10	95	93	72
LIQDEP	↔	*SP500*	0	0	45	30	24	55	100	30
IP	→	*VOL*	2	1	47	37	14	53	97	37
M2OWN	←	*TBILL3*	0	10	64	16	10	36	99	6
LIQDEP	←	*M2OWN*	2	8	72	7	12	28	94	−1
REFI	no edge	*TBILL3*	0	0	82	15	3	18	98	14
REFI	no edge	*M2OWN*	3	6	83	3	4	17	80	−3
IP	no edge	*SPPE*	1	0	85	7	7	15	94	7
SP500	no edge	*M2OWN*	1	4	86	1	9	14	95	−3
COREINF	no edge	*SP500*	1	0	87	10	2	13	95	10
IP	no edge	*M2OWN*	0	0	88	5	7	12	99	5

[1] 16 of 55 candidate edges; only edges that are identified as existing in 12% or more of the bootstrap replications are shown.

[2] Values indicate percentage of 10,000 bootstrap replications in which each type of edge is found. Based on the procedure in Demiralp, Hoover, and Perez (2007) with critical value of 2.5% for tests of conditional correlation (corresponding to the 10% critical value used in the PC algorithm).

[3] *exists* = the percentage of bootstrap replications in which an edge is selected (= 100 – no edge); *directed* = edges directed as a percentage of edges selected; *net direction* = difference between edges directed right (→) and left (←).

with an 11-point preference for the order *REFI* ← *MORG30*. Another one of the six, *VOL* ↔ *SP500* is bidirected. The bootstrap finds bidirectional edge in a plurality of cases, while in the others directs it *VOL* → *SP500* with an 8-point preference. The remainder of the edges chosen by the PC algorithm are less well supported by the bootstrap. The weakest case is for the edge *LIQDEP* ← *M2OWN* with *exists* only registering at 28%. However, in all but one case, *net direction* agrees with the selected order. The exception is *M2OWN* ← *TBILL3* for which the bootstrap would direct the edge in the opposite direction 6 points more frequently. We explore the problematic edges identified by the bootstrap more fully below.

A causal graph corresponds to a set of over-identifying restrictions (zero restrictions on $\mathbf{A}_0$), which can be tested. The graph in Figure 2.1, however, cannot be tested as is, since it contains an undirected edge. There is, then, a two-member equivalence class one in which *REFI* → *MORG30*, the other in which *REFI* ← *MORG30*. The overidentifying assumptions implied by the graph can be tested with either ordering of this edge; and, because they define an equivalence class, the result will be the same. The likelihood-ratio test of the overidentifying restrictions for the graph strongly rejects the restrictions (p-value of 0.002).

Since the risk, we believe, is greater of too tightly restricting the causal order, we investigate the graph further through an informal general-to-specific procedure. In Table 2.4, we investigate two search paths, one for each of the graphs in the equivalence class. Search I, with *REFI* → *MORG30*, adds to the graph all of the edges that the bootstrap finds in 12% or more replications, directed as indicated by *net direction* in Table 2.3. As shown in Table 2.4, this model (General Model I) cannot be rejected against a just-identified SVAR (p-value = 0.14). The table also reports a sequence of tests in which successive edges are removed, starting with the edge with the lowest t-statistic when the SVAR based on the ordering starting with the general model is estimated. Each time an edge is removed, the p-value of the likelihood ratio test against the just-identified model is calculated. Test 1 results in a failure of the estimates to converges, so the edge (*LIQDEP* ← *SP500*) is restored and the edge with the next lowest t-statistic is removed. (*LIQDEP* ← *SP500* is again removed with no converge problem in test 3.) In the end, six edges are removed, generating a sequence of specifications that cannot be rejected at a 10% critical value against the just-identified SVAR. Only the test 7 (omit *REFI* → *TBILL3*) rejects. The remaining edges all correspond to statistically significant t-statistics. And the likelihood ratio test for the final graph against the just-identified SVAR cannot be rejected (p = 0.102).

Search II takes the graph selected by the PC algorithm with the undirected edge oriented as *REFI* ← *MORG30*. When supplemented with additional edges, using the same criterion as in Search I, it is easily rejected against the just-identified SVAR. Adding even more edges—all those found to exist in 5% or

Table 2.4. Contemporaneous causal structure: Specification search

	Specification	Likelihood Ratio Test against the Just-Identified Model (*p-value*)
Search I		
Initial Model	Graph in Figure 1 modified with *REFI* → *MORG30*	0.002
General Model I	As above, plus: *REFI* → *TBILL3*; *REFI* ← *M2OWN*; *IP* → *SPPE*; *M2OWN* → *SP500*; *IP* → *M2OWN*; *COREINF* → *REFI*	0.140
Tests of Restrictions		
1	omit *LIQDEP* ← *SP500*	no convergence
2	restore *LIQDEP* ← *SP500*; omit *VOL* → *SP500*	0.163
3	omit *LIQDEP* ← *SP500*	0.185
4	omit *IP* → *SPPE*	0.166
5	omit *M2OWN* ← *TBILL3*	0.146
6	omit *COREINF* → *SP500*	0.123
7	omit *IP* → *M2OWN*	0.102
8	omit *REFI* → *TBILL3*	0.068
Search II		
Initial Model	Graph in Figure 1 modified with *REFI* ← *MORG30*	0.002
General Model II	As above, plus: all edges that appeared in more than 2.5% of bootstrap replications	0.069

even 2.5% of the bootstrap replications—still results in strong rejection of the specification. As a result, we discontinued further specification search for this graph and accepted the graph selected in Search I as our final graph.

Figure 2.2 shows the final graph. Notice that, compared to the initial graph (Figure 2.1), as well as orienting the undirected edge, it adds two edges (*REFI* ← *M2OWN* and *M2OWN* → *SP500*); it removes one edge (*M2OWN* ← *TBILL3*); and it turns the two bidirectional edges (*VOL* ↔ *SP500* and between *SP500* ↔ *LIQDEP*) into unidirectional edges.

2.5 The Lag Structure

Most VAR analysis would content itself with having established the contemporaneous causal order, which is all that is needed to identify independent shocks to the various equations in the SVAR, and then proceed to compute impulse-response functions and variance decompositions. We believe, however, that more is to be learned about the dynamic causal structure about

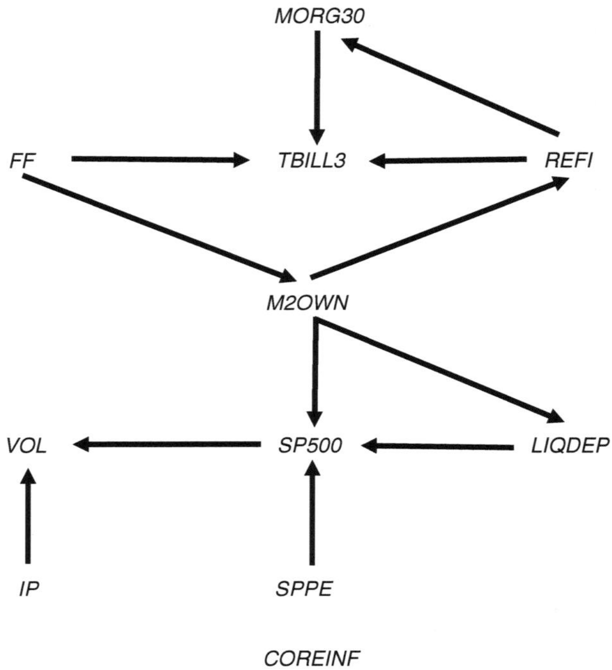

FIG. 2.2. Final contemporaneous causal graph.

which factors are truly important. And we believe that a more careful specification of the dynamics will deliver more precise estimates of the standard errors of impulse-response functions.

Our strategy is to follow the strategy outlined in Krolzig (2003) in which a general-to-specific search algorithm is used to select the lag structure of the model conditional on the contemporaneous causal structure. The initial selection of the contemporaneous causal structure is important, since equation-by-equation automated searches must start with a valid general unrestricted model in which the independent variables are either not the effects of the dependent variable or in which they are properly instrumented. The graph in Figure 2.2 gives just the needed information and allows us to specify which contemporaneous variables should appear in each equation.

While Krolzig (2003) used PcGets, we use the closely related search algorithm Autometrics, which is a package within the PcGive version 12 econometrics package (Doornik's chapter in this volume; Doornik and Hendry, 2007).

Since the data are all nonstationary, we reparameterize the SVAR with unrestricted lags in a vector-error-correction form:

$$\mathbf{A}_0 \Delta \mathbf{Y}_t = \mathbf{A}_1(L)\Delta \mathbf{Y}_{t-1} + \mathbf{A}_2 \mathbf{Y}_{t-1} + \mathbf{E}_t. \tag{2.3}$$

$\mathbf{A}_0$ is specified according to Figure 2.2 and is held fixed though all searches.

As $\Delta\mathbf{Y}_{t-1}$ is stationary, the estimates of the elements of $\mathbf{A}_1$ have standard distributions; while, since $\mathbf{Y}_{t-1}$ is nonstationary, the estimates of the elements of $\mathbf{A}_2$ have nonstandard distributions and critical values need to be inflated in the direction of those provided by Dickey and Fuller (1979). PcGets does not allow the different critical values for different types of variables. Our strategy will be to conduct two ordinary-least-squares searches for each separate equation of the SVAR, using 5% and 1% critical values. Since these correspond to the default 'liberal' and 'conservative' settings that were built into PcGets, we continue to use that terminology. The critical values for these tests assume a normal distribution. The conservative setting is used here as an *ad hoc* method of mimicking the higher critical values of the nonstandard distributions appropriate for nonstationary variables. Each of our two searches has two stages:

1. (i) A liberal search in which the contemporaneous variables and the lagged levels are held fixed; (ii) followed by a conservative search in which the contemporaneous variables and the short-term dynamics selected in stage (i) and indicated by the specification of $\mathbf{A}_1$—the placement of zeros in the matrix, but not the estimates of the elements—are held fixed, while a search is conducted over the lagged level terms.
2. (i) A conservative search in which only contemporaneous variables (identified by the nonzero elements of $\mathbf{A}_0$) and the lagged differences are held fixed; (ii) followed by a liberal search in which the contemporaneous variables and the long-term dynamics selected in stage (i) and indicated by the specification of $\mathbf{A}_2$—the placement of zeros in the matrix, but not the estimates of the elements—are held fixed, while a search is conducted over the lagged differences.

The specification with the lowest Schwarz information criterion is chosen.

The detailed specification of the SVAR is estimated as a system by maximum likelihood. (While we do not report the detailed estimates here, they are available from the authors.)[7]/ The complete causal order is summarized in Table 2.5. To get an idea of how much detail about the causal process our investigation has uncovered, how parsimonious our final specification is, consider what Table 2.5 would look like for any typical Choleski ordering: every cell on the main-diagonal and above would be filled in as light grey (indicating the presence of lagged variables) and every cell below the main diagonal in black (indicating the presence of contemporaneous and lagged

[7] Estimates are available at http://www.econ.duke.edu/~kdh9/research.html.

Table 2.5. The causal structure of the SVAR

	Causes										
Effects	COREINF	FF	IP	SPPE	M2OWN	LIQDEP	SP500	REFI	MORG30	VOL	TBILL3
COREINF	lagged	lagged			lagged	lagged	lagged			lagged	
FF		lagged	lagged			lagged	lagged				lagged
IP		lagged	lagged		lagged	lagged	lagged	lagged			
SPPE			lagged	lagged	lagged		lagged			lagged	
M2OWN		lagged and contemporaneous		lagged	lagged		lagged	lagged			lagged
LIQDEP		lagged		lagged	lagged and contemporaneous		lagged	lagged	lagged	lagged	lagged
SP500	lagged			lagged and contemporaneous	lagged and contemporaneous	contemporaneous	lagged	lagged		lagged	lagged
REFI					lagged and contemporaneous	lagged			lagged		
MORG30		lagged		lagged	lagged			lagged and contemporaneous	lagged	lagged	
VOL			lagged and contemporaneous	lagged	lagged	lagged	lagged and contemporaneous			lagged	
TBILL3		lagged and contemporaneous				lagged	lagged	lagged and contemporaneous	contemporaneous	lagged	lagged

Key:
= lagged causes only
= contemporaneous causes only
= lagged and contemporaneous causes

variables). The overall lighter tone, especially the white (empty) cells, reveals that we have stripped away large numbers of redundant regressors.

2.6 The Role of M2 in the Monetary Transmission Process

We are now in a position to return to the business of the Monetary and Reserve Analysis Section. Table 2.5 is concerned with direct effects or proximate causes. The discussion in section 2.1 suggests that the entire *LIQDEP* row should be filled, indicating that each of the other variables is either a contemporaneous or lagged cause of *LIQDEP*. Most of the variables do cause *LIQDEP*; but the ones that do not are a surprise: neither the central quantity-theoretic variables, *COREINF* and *IP*, nor lagged *LIQDEP* itself causes *LIQDEP*. The 'special factors' are all selected as direct causes of *LIQDEP*. A pitfall of many statistical studies is to mistake causation for correlation. The pit is quite deep here, as *LIQDEP* is identified as a direct cause of each of the other variables except for *SPPE, M2OWN*, and *MORG30*.

Another pitfall of single-equation and correlational studies is the mixing of direct and indirect causes. Indirect causes can be investigated through impulse-response functions. In the interest of conserving space, we omit most impulse-response functions and focus on the ones most relevant to the role of M2 in the transmission of monetary policy.[8]

While most of the considerations concerning the relationship of M2 to other variables in section 2.1 are discussed from the point of view of the demand for money, the real importance of M2 to the Federal Reserve is found in its place in the transmission mechanism for monetary policy, in which M2 is a cause rather than an effect. Table 2.5 indicates that *LIQDEP* (and, therefore, M2) is a cause of both industrial production (*IP*), representing the real economy, and of core inflation (*COREINF*). But how important is this relationship in the transmission of monetary policy? This is difficult to quantify with the usual impulse-response functions, since there is no natural metric on which to compare the different effects of *LIQDEP*. In order to get a better handle on the role of *LIQDEP* in the transmission mechanism, we concentrate on the effects of a shock to the Federal funds rate (*FF*), the Federal Reserve's main policy variable. We consider a permanent, 25-basis-point shock, since this is by far the Federal Reserve's most common monetary policy action in practice.[9] And since the Fed is principally concerned with the effects of its policies on growth and inflation, we focus on responses of core inflation (*COREINF*) and industrial production (*IP*) to the monetary-policy shock. Figure 2.3 displays the ordinary impulse-response functions, as well as impulse-response functions where *LIQDEP* has been shut down by setting its value to zero in all equations and all periods. The difference between these two impulse-response functions is a measure of the role of *LIQDEP* in the transmission mechanism.

The evidence of Figure 2.3 is that M2 (or *LIQDEP*) plays an almost immeasurably small role in the transmission mechanism. The effect of the increase in the Federal funds rate on core inflation (Figure 2.3) is not even statistically significantly different from zero except in period 4. The maximum difference between the impulse-response functions for *COREINF* occurs at period 3 and is less that a tenth of percentage point on the inflation rate. And the two impulse-response functions are nowhere statistically distinguishable in the sense that both lie within the standard-error bands for the function with *LIQDEP*. The differences between the two impulse-response functions for *IP* (Figure 2.3B) are similarly small, at most less than one-tenth of a percentage point on the growth rate of industrial production.

[8] All of the impulse-responses of each of the other variables to *LIQDEP* and of *LIQDEP* to each of the other variables are available on Kevin Hoover's website (see footnote 7).

[9] A permanent shock in the VECM form is a positive shock in the first period with no shocks in subsequent periods.

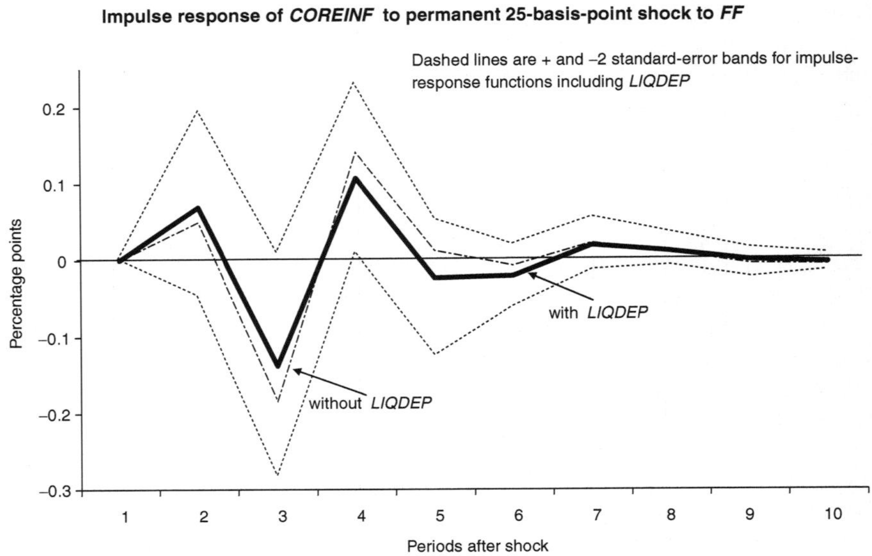

(A)

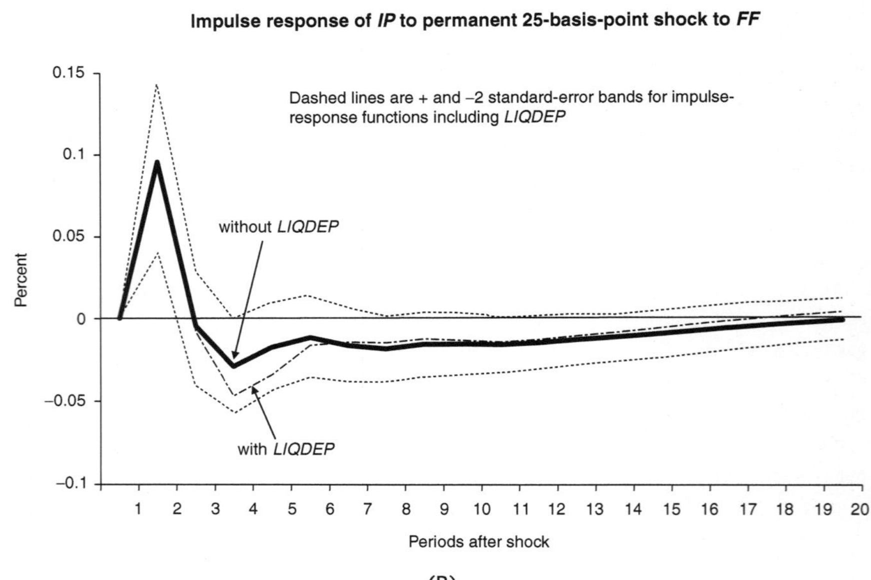

(B)

FIG. 2.3. The importance of *LIQDEP* in the transmission of monetary policy.

2.7 Conclusions

Our investigation is both methodological and substantial. Methodologically, it provides a concrete illustration of how to coordinate the graph-theoretic causal-search algorithms, previously applied to vector autoregressions by a number of investigators, with David Hendry's general-to-specific search methodology, embodied in PcGets and Autometrics, to identify empirically a structural econometric model in a case in which theory is relatively weak and not a reliable source of identifying restrictions. Typically, investigators use the PC algorithm or one of its relatives to select a contemporaneous causal graph. We showed how to use the bootstrap techniques developed by Demiralp, Hoover, and Perez to assess the uncertainties associated with selecting such a graph. These techniques proved invaluable guiding an informal general-to-specific search using test of overidentifying restrictions to select a contemporaneous causal order for the SVAR in which we could have reasonable confidence. One avenue for future development would be to provide a more formally developed search procedure along these lines. In applying Autometrics to nonstationary data, we adopted what we believe to be an effective, though *ad hoc*, procedure to ensure that appropriate selection criteria were applied to the I(1) as well as the I(0) terms. Another future development would be to extend Autometrics to do this automatically.

On the substantial side, we were able to provide a carefully tested fully identified model of the role of M2 in the transmission mechanism in which the informal assumptions of the Federal Reserve's Monetary and Reserve Analysis Section could be assessed. On the positive side, the evidence supports the section's identification of particular 'special factors' connected to the behaviour of M2. On the negative side, the quantity-theoretic core of their analysis seems to be largely at odds with the data. What is more, the rationale for focusing attention on M2 is undermined by evidence that it plays an insignificant role in the transmission of monetary policy. This is in keeping with other recent findings about M2 (Hale and Jordá, 2007). Some economists have argued that, while M2 has only a small role in the substantive transmission of monetary policy, it nonetheless conveys significant information about the state of the monetary economy in much the same way that a barometer, while not a causal linkage in weather systems, nonetheless provides useful information (see Dotsey and Otrok, 1994, for a survey of views). Our conclusions are different. Once we have such a detailed causal identification, we can see that M2 does play a real causal role (*LIQDEP* is identified as a cause of six of nine nonpolicy variables (other than itself) in our system). Its role is, nonetheless, a practically insignificant one. Our identified model conveys fuller information—and serves as a better barometer—than M2 can.

Appendix A. Data

All data are monthly. If a Haver series code is given, the data were downloaded from Haver Analytics *United States Economic Statistics* database, version date 3 June 2005. Natural logarithms indicated by 'log'.

COREINF = 1200[log($corecpi_t$) – log($corecpi_{t-1}$)], where *corecpi* = Consumer Price Index less Food and Energy. Source: Bureau of Labor Statistics [Haver: *pcuslfe*]. Units: Index 1982–84 = 100; seasonally adjusted.

FF = Effective Federal Funds Rate. Source: Federal Reserve [Haver: *ffed*]. Units: annual yield to maturity (percent per annum).

IP = log(*industrial production index*). Source: Federal Reserve [Haver: *ip*]. Units: index 1997 = 100; seasonally adjusted.

LIQDEP = log(*liquid deposits*), *liquid deposits* = Demand Deposits + Other Checkable Deposits + Savings Deposits. Source: Federal Reserve. Units: millions of dollars; seasonally adjusted.

M2OC = Opportunity Cost of Holding M2 = *TBILL3* – *M2OWN*. Source: Federal Reserve (Division of Monetary Affairs, Reserve Analysis Division).

M2OWN = Own Yield on M2 = weighted average of yields on deposits. Federal Reserve (Division of Monetary Affairs, Reserve Analysis Division); source for underlying yields: *Bank Rate Monitor*.

MORG30 = Interest Rate on 30-year Mortgages. Source: Federal Mortgage Acceptance Corporation, Primary Market Survey: 30-year Fixed Rate Mortgages [Haver: *frm30*]. Units: annual yield to maturity (percent per annum).

REFI = log(*mortage refinance*). Source: Mortgage Banker's Association. Units: index 1990 = 100.

SVOL = log(*volatility*), where *volatility* = VIX (up to August 2003), renamed VXO thereafter (both are measure of implied volatility based on the S&P 100 Index (OEX) option prices). Source: Chicago Board Options Exchange Units: percent.

SP500 = log(*s&p 500 stock index*). Source: *Wall Street Journal* [Haver: *sp500*]. Units: index 1941–43 = 10.

SPPE = S&P 500 Price–Earnings Ratio. Source: Standard & Poors (http://www2.standardandpoors.com/spf/xls/ondex/SP500EPSEST.XLS) Units: ratio.

TBILL3 = Yield on 3-month Treasury bills. Source: Federal Reserve.

References

Cooper, G. F. (1999). An overview of the representation and discovery of causal relationships using Bayesian networks. In Clark Glymour and Gregory F. Cooper (eds.), *Computation, Causation, and Discovery*, pp. 3–64. Menlo Park, CA and MIT Press, Cambridge, MA: American Association for Artificial Intelligence.

Demiralp, S. and Hoover, K. D. (2003). Searching for the causal structure of a vector autoregression. *Oxford Bulletin of Economics and Statistics*, **65** (Supplement), 745–767.

——— and Perez, S. J. (2008). A bootstrap method for identifying and evaluating a structural vector autoregression. *Oxford Bulletin of Economics and Statistics*, **70**, 509–533.

Dickey, D. A. and Fuller, W. A. (1979). Distribution of the estimators for autoregressive time series with a unit root. *Journal of the American Statistical Association*, **74**(2), 427–431.

Doornik, J. A. and Hendry, D. F. (2007). *PcGive Professional 12*, Vols. 1–3 and accompanying *PcGive*, version 12 software. London: Timberlake Consultants.

Dotsey, M. and Otrok, C. (1994). M2 and monetary policy: A critical review of the recent debate. Federal Reserve Bank of Richmond, *Economic Quarterly*, **80**(1), 41–49.

Gilbert, C. L. (1986). Professor Hendry's econometric methodology. *Oxford Bulletin of Economics and Statistics*, **48**(3), 283–307.

Hale, G. and Jordá, O. (2007). Do monetary aggregates help forecast inflation? *Federal Reserve Bank of San Francisco Economic Letter* 2007–10, 13 April.

Hendry, D. F. (1980). Econometrics: Alchemy or science? *Economica*, **47**(188), 387–406.

—— and Krolzig, H.-M. (1999). Improving on 'Data Mining Reconsidered', by K. D. Hoover and S. J. Perez. *Econometrics Journal*, **2**, pp. 202–218.

——— (2001). *Automatic Econometric Model Selection Using PcGets 1.0* and accompanying *PcGets*, version 1.0 software. London: Timberlake Consultants.

—— Leamer, E. E. and Poirier, D. J. (1990). The *ET* dialogue: A conversation on econometric methodology. *Econometric Theory*, **6**(2), 171–261.

Hoover, K. D. (2001). *Causality in Macroeconomics*. Cambridge: Cambridge University Press.

—— (2005). Automatic inference of contemporaneous causal order of a system of equations. *Econometric Theory*, **21**(1), 69–77.

—— and Perez, S. J. (1999). Data mining reconsidered: Encompassing and the general-to-specific approach to specification search. *Econometrics Journal*, **2**(2), 167–191.

——— (2004). Truth and robustness in cross country growth regressions. *Oxford Bulletin of Economics and Statistics*, **66**(5), 765–798.

Hurvich, C. M. and Tsai, C.-L. (1991). Bias of the corrected AIC criterion for underfitted regression and time series models. *Biometrika*, **86**(3), 499–509.

Kant, I. (1787). *Kritik der reinen Vernunft*, 2nd edition.

Krolzig, H.-M. (2003). General to specific model selection procedures for structural autoregressions. Working Paper, Department of Economics and Nuffield College Oxford, March.

—— and Hendry, D. F. (2001). Computer automation of general-to-specific model selection procedures. *Journal of Economic Dynamics and Control*, **25**(6–7), 831–866.

Mizon, G. E. (1995). Progressive modelling of economic time series: The LSE methodology. In Hoover, K. D. (ed.), *Macroeconometrics: Developments, Tensions and Prospects*, pp. 107–170. Boston: Kluwer.

Pearl, J. (2000). *Causality: Models, Reasoning, and Inference*. Cambridge: Cambridge University Press.

Perez, S. J. (1998). Causal ordering and the 'bank lending channel'. *Journal of Applied Econometrics*, **13**(6), 613–626.

Sims, C. A. (1980). Macroeconomics and reality. *Econometrica*, **48**(1), 1–48.

Spirtes, P., Clark Glymour, C., and Scheines, R. (2001). *Causation, Prediction, and Search*, 2nd edition. Cambridge, MA: MIT Press.

—— Scheines, R., Meek, C. and Glymour, C. (1994). *Tetrad II: Tools for Causal Modeling: User's Manual*.

Swanson, N. R. and Granger, C. W. J. (1997). Impulse response functions based on a causal approach to residual orthogonalization in vector autoregressions. *Journal of the American Statistical Association*, **92**, 357–367.

3

Retrospective Estimation of Causal Effects Through Time

*Halbert White and Pauline Kennedy**

3.1 Introduction

This chapter studies methods for retrospectively estimating the causal effects of arbitrary interventions to dynamic economic systems, extending the work of White (2006), where the focus was on methods for estimating the effects of natural experiments, e.g. a regime shift.

In pursuing this goal, we blend a number of research themes that have been of central interest to David Hendry throughout his prolific and influential career: *policy analysis* (e.g. Favero and Hendry, 1992; Banerjee, Hendry, and Mizon, 1996; Ericsson, Hendry, and Mizon, 1998; Hendry, 2000; Hendry and Mizon, 2000; Hendry, 2002); *dynamic modelling* (e.g. Hendry, 1974; Hendry and Richard, 1982; Hendry, Pagan, and Sargan, 1984; Hendry, 1995c; Hendry, 1996); *forecasting* (e.g. Clements and Hendry, 1996; Clements and Hendry, 1998a, b; Clements and Hendry, 1999; Hendry and Ericsson, 2001; Clements and Hendry, 2002a, b; Clements and Hendry, 2003; Hendry, 2003; Chevillon and Hendry, 2005); *forecast failure* (e.g. Clements and Hendry, 2002a; Hendry, 2002); *notions of exogeneity and their relation to causality* (e.g. Engle, Hendry, and Richard, 1983 (EHR); Engle and Hendry, 1993; Hendry, 1995a; Hendry and Mizon, 1998, 1999; Hendry, 2004); *the links between economics and econometrics* (e.g. Hendry, 1980; Hendry, 1995b; Hendry and Wallis, 1984; Hendry, 1993; Hendry, 2001; Hendry, 2005); *cointegration* (e.g. Hendry, 1986; Banerjee and Hendry, 1992); and *automatic modelling* (e.g. Hendry, 2001). Other areas where David Hendry has made seminal contributions, such as *encompassing* (e.g. Hendry and

* We would like to thank Rob Engle, Clive Granger, Jim Hamilton, Òscar Jordà, Xun Lu, Jim Stock, and Scott Thompson for their very helpful comments and suggestions. Any errors are the authors' sole responsibility.

Richard, 1982), are also relevant to our present subject, but are not directly touched on here. These references to Hendry's work are illustrative only. A fuller listing and discussion would leave little space for presenting our own results.

The plan of the chapter is as follows. In section 3.2, we posit a general dynamic data generating process (DGP), suitable for defining, identifying, and estimating well-defined causal effects. We do not require our dynamic structure to be separable between observable and non-observable variables of the system, nor do we impose other structure, such as linearity or monotonicity. The unobservable determinants of the dependent variable may be countably infinite in dimension. Our framework thus permits analysis of general dynamic treatment effects. These have been considered in depth for panel data in work of Robins (1997) and Abbring and Heckman (2007), among others. In the pure time-series setting considered here, cross-section variation is absent, necessitating the use of methods specific to time-series data.

In section 3.3, we define certain *retrospective* covariate-conditioned average effects. Retrospective conditioning makes use of all available relevant information in the past, relative to the present (time T). This creates the novel opportunity to improve predictions for a particular past period ($t < T$) using covariate information from the future relative to that period ($t + \tau, \tau > 0$). We see that structural identification of the effects of interest is ensured by *conditional exogeneity*, a generalization of strict exogeneity, distinct from the notions of weak, strong, and super-exogeneity of EHR, and an extension of the CIPP condition introduced by White (2006).

Section 3.3 also provides definitions of retrospective covariate-conditioned quantile responses and effects, together with point bands and path bands based on these quantile measures. We discuss how path bands can be used to test hypotheses about the effects of specific interventions.

In section 3.4 we propose estimation methods for the effects defined in section 3.3. Our estimators belong to a particular class of state-space filters, where counterfactual outcomes central to the definition of the effects of interest play the role of unobservable system states. Section 3.5 illustrates, with an application to the effects of crude oil prices on gasoline prices. Section 3.6 contains a summary and concluding remarks.

3.2 DGP: A Dynamic Structural System

Let y_t denote the values of a $k_y \times 1$ vector (k_y a finite integer) of *responses of interest*, let d_t represent a $k_d \times 1$ vector (k_d a finite integer) of values of response-determining variables whose effects on the response are of primary interest (*causes of interest*), and let υ_t and z_t represent countable vectors of values of other response-determining variables (*ancillary causes*). Below we distinguish further between v_t and z_t. We consider a system of structural equations in which the values y_t are generated dynamically as

$$y_t \overset{c}{=} q_t(y^{t-1},d^t,v^t,z^t), \quad t = 1,2,\ldots, \tag{3.1}$$

where q_t is an unknown $\mathbb{R}^{k_y}$-valued function (the *response function*), $y^{t-1} \equiv (y_0,y_1,\ldots,y_{t-1})$ denotes the $(t-1)$-*history* of the sequence $\{y_t\}$, and $d^t \equiv (d_0,d_1,\ldots,d_t)$, $v^t \equiv (v_0, v_1,\ldots,v_t)$, and $z^t \equiv (z_0, z_1,\ldots,z_t)$ similarly denote the t-histories of $\{d_t\}$,$\{v_t\}$, and $\{z_t\}$ respectively.

We enforce the causal direction of time by requiring that only the past and present of the referenced variables determine the time t response. We follow Chalak and White (2007) and White and Chalak (2007a) (WC) in using the notation $\overset{c}{=}$ to emphasize that the structural equations (3.1) represent directional causal links (Goldberger, 1972, p. 979), in which manipulations of elements of y^{t-1},d^t,v^t,z^t result in differing values for y_t, as in Strotz and Wold (1960) and Fisher (1966, 1970). Leading examples of such structures are those that arise from the dynamic optimization behaviour of economic agents and/or interactions among such agents. (See Chow, 1997, for numerous examples.)

Below, we assume that we can observe histories of y_t and d_t, but that we only observe the history of some finitely dimensioned subvectors $\tilde{v}_t$ and $\tilde{z}_t$ of v_t and z_t.

We seek to evaluate certain effects of the causes of interest viewed retrospectively, that is, from the present, time T. Specifying these effects requires special care. Following WC, we define effects in terms of interventions, that is, pairs of alternate values for arguments of the response function. We consider only interventions to the causes of interest. As we take a retrospective view, we focus solely on the effects of *retrospective interventions*, $d^T \to d^{*T} \equiv (d^T, d^{*T})$.

A consequence of the explicit dynamics (lagged y_t's) in equation (3.1) is that the effects of interventions can linger, that is, they can propagate through time. To handle this, we can use an alternate implicit dynamic representation. Recursive substitution gives

$$\begin{aligned}
y_1 &\overset{c}{=} q_1(y_0,d^1,v^1,z^1)\\
y_2 &\overset{c}{=} q_2(y_0,q_1(y_0,d^1,v^1,z^1),d^2,v^2,z^2)\\
&\vdots\\
y_t &\overset{c}{=} r_t(y_0,d^t,v^t,z^t) \qquad t = 1,2,\ldots,
\end{aligned}$$

say, where r_t is an unknown $\mathbb{R}^{k_y}$-valued function that expresses the response value y_t purely in terms of initial values y_0 and the history (d^t,v^t,z^t). We distinguish between q_t and r_t by calling q_t the *explicit* dynamic response function and r_t the *implicit* dynamic response function. With no dynamics, the two are identical.

Analogous to White (2006), we define the *time t ceteris paribus effect of the intervention* $d^T \to d^{*T}$ *at* (y_0,υ^t,z^t) to be

$$\Delta r_t(y_0,d^t,d^{*t},\upsilon^t,z^t) \equiv r_t(y_0,d^{*t},\upsilon^t,z^t) - r_t(y_0,d^t,\upsilon^t,z^t), \qquad t = 1,\ldots,T.$$

Because this effect involves the implicit dynamic response function, it fully accounts for any time propagation of effects. Significantly, this effect depends not only on d^t and d^{*t} but also y_0,υ^t, and z^t. These values are fixed, consistent with the notion of a *ceteris paribus* effect. Although this defines the effect of $d^T \to d^{*T}$ at time t, only the t-histories d^t,d^{*t},υ^t, and z^t matter, as the elements of d^T,d^{*T},υ^T, and z^T for dates later than t do not determine time t responses.

We ensure that $\Delta r_t(y_0,d^t,d^{*t},\upsilon^t,z^t)$ is the *total effect* of the intervention $d^T \to d^{*T}$ by requiring the system to have the property that y_0,υ^t, and z^t do not respond to interventions to d^T. (One can also define and study direct effects and various kinds of indirect effects by imposing other suitable structure (see Chalak and White, 2008, 2007b). For conciseness, we focus here solely on total effects.)

Equation (3.1) does not specify how y_0 is generated; we adopt the convention that y_0 is generated outside the system as the realization of a random vector Y_0. More elaborate conventions are possible. For example, take υ_0,z_0 as given, and require that interventions $d^T \to d^{*T}$ satisfy $d_0 = d_0^*$. Or replace d^t,υ^t, and z^t in equation (3.1) with d^{t-1},υ^{t-1}, and z^{t-1}, enforcing a stronger restriction on the operation of causes in time (as advocated by Granger, 1969). Our notation permits flexibility: if contemporaneous effects are allowed, then d_t,υ_t, and z_t are observed at time t. If not, then d_t,υ_t, and z_t are observed at time $t-1$. The specifics of any given application often dictate which is more suitable. In any case, we do not permit (d_0, υ_0, z_0) to respond to y_0.

For the ancillary causes, we require that υ_t and z_t do not vary in response to the histories of d_t or y_t, so that interventions $d^T \to d^{*T}$ have neither direct nor indirect effects on υ_t and z_t. If, contrary to this requirement, the dynamic response function is formulated initially in a way that includes ancillary causes that respond to histories of d_t or y_t, one can generally perform substitutions that deliver a system in which this response is absent. Specifically, one can generally express the original 'responding' ancillary causes as functions of histories of d_t or y_t and other ancillary causes that do not respond to these histories. With these substitutions, our requirement holds, ensuring that $\Delta r_t(y_0,d^t,d^{*t},\upsilon^t,z^t)$ gives the total effect of the intervention $d^T \to d^{*T}$. When ancillary causes respond to histories of the responses or causes of interest, the system is vulnerable to the Lucas critique (Lucas, 1976). Enforcing the requirement that these dependencies are absent ensures that our system properly captures effects of policy changes represented by interventions.

We enforce these properties by specifying a particular recursive dynamic structure in which "predecessors" structurally determine "successors," but not vice versa. We write $y \Leftarrow d$ to denote that d precedes y (y succeeds d). In particular, future variables (e.g., $d_t + 1$) cannot precede present or past variables (e.g., y_t). Necessarily, successors cannot determine predecessors. Predecessors may but do not necessarily cause successors, in the sense defined below. In particular, we specify that

$$
\begin{aligned}
d_t &\Leftarrow (d^{t-1}, v^t, w^t, z^t) \\
w_t &\Leftarrow (w^{t-1}, v^t, z^t) \\
v_t &\Leftarrow (v^{t-1}, z^t), \qquad\qquad t = 1, 2, \ldots
\end{aligned}
\tag{3.2}
$$

Here, we introduce w_t, a finitely dimensioned vector whose t-history may help determine d_t, but not y_t. We thus say that w_t is *structurally irrelevant* for the response of interest. As for y_t and d_t, we observe all elements of w_t. Note that z_t has no predecessors. Thus, we view $\{z_t\}$ as being generated *outside* the system, as the realization of a stochastic process $\{Z_t\}$ with whatever properties may be appropriate for a given application. White and Chalak (2007b) refer to such structurally exogenous variables as *fundamental variables*.

The distinction between v_t and z_t should now be clear: whereas v_t represents ancillary causes determined within the structural system, z_t represents ancillary causes determined outside the structural system.

We formalize the structure developed above as follows:

Assumption A.1. (a) Let $(\Omega, \mathbb{F}, P)$ be a complete probability space, on which are defined random vectors (D_0, V_0, W_0, Y_0) and the stochastic process $\{Z_t\}$, where D_0, V_0, W_0, Y_0, and Z_t take values in $\mathbb{R}^{k_d}, \mathbb{R}^{k_v}, \mathbb{R}^{k_w}, \mathbb{R}^{k_y}$, and $\mathbb{R}^{k_z}$, respectively, where k_v and k_z are countably valued integers and k_d, k_w, and k_y are finite integers, with $k_d, k_y > 0$, such that $Y_0 \Leftarrow (D_0, V_0, W_0, Z_0)$ and $D_0 \Leftarrow (V_0, W_0, Z_0)$. Further, let $\{D_t, V_t, W_t, Y_t\}$ be a sequence of random vectors generated as

$$
\begin{aligned}
V_t &\Leftarrow (V^{t-1}, Z^t) \\
W_t &\Leftarrow (W^{t-1}, V^t, Z^t) \\
D_t &\Leftarrow (D^{t-1}, V^t, W^t, Z^t) \\
Y_t &\stackrel{c}{=} q_t(Y^{t-1}, D^t, V^t, Z^t), \qquad t = 1, 2, \ldots,
\end{aligned}
$$

where $b_{0,t}$, $b_{1,t}$, $b_{2,t}$, and q_t is an unknown measurable function taking values in $\mathbb{R}^{k_y}$, and $E(Y_t) < \infty$.

(b) For $t = 0, 1, \ldots, V_t \equiv (\tilde{V}_t, \ddot{V}_t)$ and $Z_t \equiv (\tilde{Z}_t, \ddot{Z}_t)$, where $\tilde{V}_t$ and $\tilde{Z}_t$ take values in $\mathbb{R}^{k_{\tilde{v}}}$ and $\mathbb{R}^{k_{\tilde{z}}}$ respectively, and $k_{\tilde{v}}$ and $k_{\tilde{z}}$ are finite integers. Realizations of $Y_t, D_t, \tilde{V}_t, W_t$, and $\tilde{Z}_t$ are observed; realizations of $\ddot{V}_t$ and $\ddot{Z}_t$ are not observed.

This dynamic structure is quite flexible, as few restrictions are imposed. In particular, we do not require the structural reflections to be linear, separable, or monotonic in any of their arguments. Further flexibility can be gained by letting the dimensions of (D_0, V_0, W_0, Y_0) differ from those of $(D_t, V_t, W_t, Y_t), t > 0$. For simplicity, we leave this implicit.

In A.1(a), the referenced measurability refers to measurability-$\mathscr{B}^{\ell_t}/\mathscr{B}^{k_y}$, where $\mathscr{B}^{\ell_t}$ and $\mathscr{B}^{k_y}$ are σ–fields associated with the domain ($\mathbb{R}^{\ell_t}$) and range ($\mathbb{R}^{k_y}$) of q_t. With k_y (resp. ℓ_t) finite, the σ–field $\mathscr{B}^{k_y}$ (resp. $\mathscr{B}^{\ell_t}$) is the Borel σ–field generated by the open sets of $\mathbb{R}^{k_y}$ (resp. $\mathbb{R}^{\ell_t}$). Otherwise, the σ–field is that generated by the relevant Borel-measurable finite dimensional product cylinders (see, e.g. White, 2001, pp. 39–41).

In A.1(b), we specify that V_t and Z_t may not be fully observable. Instead, we observe realizations of finitely dimensioned sub-vectors $\widetilde{V}_t$ and $\widetilde{Z}_t$, respectively.

The response function q_t contains explicit dynamics. Recursive substitutions give a response with implicit dynamics as

$$Y_t \stackrel{c}{=} r_t(Y_0, D^t, V^t, Z^t) \qquad t = 1,2,\ldots$$

The measurability of r_t is ensured by the fact that compositions of measurable functions are again measurable.

3.3 Defining and Identifying Retrospective Effects

3.3.1 *Average Effects*

A key feature of the effect $\Delta r_t(y_0, d^t, d^{*t}, v^t, z^t)$ is that it is empirically inaccessible. That is, we cannot evaluate this effect, even if r_t were known, as not all elements of v_t, z_t are observed. Further, r_t is generally unknown. Nevertheless, it may be possible to estimate useful expected values of the effects of interventions. For this, we introduce some notation. First, let $X_t \equiv (\widetilde{V}_t, W_t, \widetilde{Z}_t)$ represent the *covariates*; these are observable. We call $U_t \equiv (\ddot{V}_t, \ddot{Z}_t)$ *unobserved causes* and let $U^t \equiv (\ddot{V}^t, \ddot{Z}^t)$ be the *t*-history of unobserved causes. We write realizations of X^T and U^t as x^T and u^t respectively.

When $E(r_t(Y_0, d^t, V^t, Z^t))$ is finite for each d^t in the support of D^t, we define the *retrospective counterfactual conditional expectation*

$$\rho_{t,T}(d^t \mid y_0, x^T) \equiv E(\, r_t(Y_0, d^t, V^t, Z^t) \mid Y_0 = y_0, X^T = x^T)$$

$$= \int r_t(y_0, d^t, v^t, z^t)\; dG_{t,T}(u^t \mid y_0, x^T).$$

The conditional expectation is 'retrospective', as $t \leq T$. We call this expectation 'counterfactual' to emphasize that we are *not* conditioning on $D^t = d^t$, as

$D^t = d^t$ does not appear in the list of conditioning arguments; we condition only on $(Y_0,X^T) = (y_0,x^T)$. Instead, we view d^t as *set* by some manipulation. The representation of the arguments of $\rho_{t,T}$ is intended to emphasize this distinction. The structure imposed in A.1(a) further ensures that d^t and (y_0,x^T) are variation free: different settings for d^t do not necessitate different values for (y_0,x^T), as (y_0,x^T) is functionally independent of d^t. Thus, $\rho_{t,T}(d^t \mid y_0,x^T)$ gives the expected response conditional on $(Y_0,X^T) = (y_0,x^T)$ for any value of d^t, in particular, for counterfactual values. The integral representation holds under A.1(a), provided $dG_{t,T}(u^t \mid y_0,x^T)$, the *retrospective conditional density of* U^t *given* $(Y_0,X^T) = (y_0,x^T)$, is regular (Dudley, 2002, Ch. 10.2). Throughout, we assume that any referenced conditional density is regular.

A noteworthy aspect of $\rho_{t,T}(d^t \mid y_0,x^T)$ is its explicit dependence on 'leads' of the covariates, that is, covariate values that occur in the future, relative to the response of interest. For example, if interest attaches to a response at time t, then whenever $t < T$, the expected response $\rho_{t,T}(d^t \mid y_0,x^T)$ can depend on x_{t+1}. Although leads have not received much attention in structural modelling, there is nothing inappropriate about their presence here; indeed, their presence is natural and helpful. Covariate leads do not violate the causal direction of time, as the covariates do not play a causal (structural) role in determining the expected response. They are instead predictive (in the back-casting sense), serving as proxies for unobservable structurally relevant but ancillary causes, U^t. Natural choices for such proxies, as discussed by White (2006), are observed responses $\tilde{V}_t, W_t$, to unobserved ancillary causes U_t of Y_t, observed drivers $\tilde{V}_t, W_t, \tilde{Z}_t$ of D_t, and observed responses $\tilde{V}_t, W_t$ to unobserved causes U_t of D_t. (See equation (3.2) above.) The presence of dynamics and resultant lingering effects makes it natural that one or more leads of the covariates may be driven by $\ddot{V}_t$ and/or $\ddot{Z}_t$. These leads are thus useful for backcasting U_t.

We use $\rho_{t,T}$ to define the *retrospective covariate-conditioned average effect of intervention* $d^T \to d^{*T}$ as

$$\begin{aligned}\Delta\rho_{t,T}(d^t,d^{*t} \mid y_0,x^T) &\equiv \rho_{t,T}(d^{*t} \mid y_0,x^T) - \rho_{t,T}(d^t \mid y_0,x^T)\\ &= \int \Delta r_t(y_0,d^t,d^{*t},v^t,z^t)\, dG_{t,T}(u^t \mid y_0,x^T)\\ &= E(\Delta r_t(Y_0,d^t,d^{*t},V^t,Z^t) \mid Y_0 = y_0, X^T = x^T).\end{aligned}$$

By the optimality property of conditional expectation, we see that $\Delta\rho_{t,T}$ $(d^t,d^{*t}|y_0,x^T)$ gives a mean squared error-optimal prediction of Δr_t (Y_0,d^t,d^{*t},V^t,Z^t), the effect of interest, conditional on the specified information $(Y_0 = y_0, X^T = x^T)$. Observe that the ancillary causes v^t,z^t are not held constant here, as they are in $\Delta r_t(y_0,d^t,d^{*t},v^t,z^t)$. Rather, we *average* over the t-history of unobserved causes U^t, *conditional* on initial values $Y_0 = y_0$ and a T-history of covariates $X^T = x^T$.

There may nevertheless be *ceteris paribus* aspects of $\Delta\rho_{t,T}(d^t,d^{*t} \mid y_0,x^T)$. Specifically, the intervention may hold certain components of the causes of interest constant. For example, if d_t is two dimensional, $d_t = (d_{t1},d_{t2})$, and we hold d_2^T constant (put $d_2^{*T} = d_2^T$), then $\Delta\rho_{t,T}(d^t,d^{*t} \mid y_0,x^T)$ represents the time t average effect of an intervention to d_1^T ($d_1^T \to d_1^{*T}$) holding d_2^T constant, averaged over the unobserved causes U^t, conditional on the given initial values and the T-history of covariates, y_0,x^T. Besides averages, other aspects of the retrospective conditional distribution of effects can be similarly defined. We discuss some of these in the next subsection.

Although $\rho_{t,T}(d^t \mid y_0,x^T)$ provides the basis for an effect measure whose arguments do not involve unknown quantities, it is nevertheless empirically inaccessible, because it is the conditional expectation of $r_t(Y_0,d^t,V^t,Z^t)$ for counterfactual values d^t, and we have no way to observe $r_t(Y_0,d^t,V^t,Z^t)$. An empirically accessible analog is the *retrospective conditional expectation*

$$\begin{aligned}\mu_{t,T}(y_0,d^t,x^T) &\equiv E(Y_t \mid Y_0 = y_0, D^t = d^t, X^T = x^T)\\ &= \int r_t(y_0,d^t,v^t,z^t)\, dG_{t,T}(u^t \mid y_0,d^t,x^T),\end{aligned}$$

where $dG_{t,T}(u^t \mid y_0,d^t,x^T)$ is the *retrospective conditional density of* U^t, *given* $(Y_0,D^t,X^T) = (y_0,d^t,x^T)$, viewing y_0,d^t, and x^T as realizations of random variables Y_0,D^t, and X^T, generated according to Assumption A.1(a). Because this quantity is defined as a functional of the joint distribution of observable variables only, it is empirically accessible, as it can be consistently estimated from a sample of observables under typically mild conditions.

Without further conditions, $\mu_{t,T}$ is purely a stochastic object, providing no information about causal effects. Nevertheless, the equality above shows that the underlying structure embodied in r_t helps determine the properties of $\mu_{t,T}$.

Inspecting $\rho_{t,T}$ and the structural representation for $\mu_{t,T}$, we see that the key difference between them is that $dG_{t,T}(u^t \mid y_0,x^T)$ appears in $\rho_{t,T}$, whereas $dG_{t,T}(u^t \mid y_0,d^t,x^T)$ appears in $\mu_{t,T}$. It follows that if $dG_{t,T}(u^t \mid y_0,d^t,x^T) = dG_{t,T}(u^t \mid y_0,x^T)$ for all u^t,y_0,d^t, and x^T, then $\mu_{t,T} = \rho_{t,T}$. This equality ensures that $\mu_{t,T}$ is not just a stochastic object but also provides structural/causal information. In this case, we say that $\mu_{t,T}$ is *structurally identified.* Similarly, $\rho_{t,T}$ is identified with a stochastic object; we thus say that $\rho_{t,T}$ is *stochastically identified.* When stochastic identification holds uniquely with a representation solely in terms of observable variables, we say that both $\mu_{t,T}$ and $\rho_{t,T}$ are *fully identified* (cf. WC).

The condition $dG_{t,T}(u^t \mid y_0,d^t,x^T) = dG_{t,T}(u^t \mid y_0,x^T)$ for all u^t,y_0,d^t, and x^T is a conditional independence requirement: D^t and U^t are independent given Y_0 and X^T. We express this as

$$D^t \perp U^t \mid Y_0,X^T, \tag{3.3}$$

following Dawid (1979) (hereafter designated 'D'). Because of the similarity to the concept of strict exogeneity (here, $D^t \perp U^t | Y_0$) and the central role played by this condition in identifying causal effects, we introduce the following definition.

Definition 3.1. *For given t and T, $t \leq T$, suppose that $D^t \perp U^t | Y_0, X^T$. Then we say that D^t is* conditionally exogenous with respect to U^t given (Y_0, X^T).

For brevity, we may just say that D^t is 'conditionally exogenous'. Conditional exogeneity contains strict exogeneity as the special case in which $X_t \equiv 1$. This concept involves only the DGP and does not involve any parametric model. It is thus distinct from notions of weak, strong, or super-exogeneity of Engle, Hendry, and Richard (1983), as these are defined in terms of the properties of correctly specified parametric models and have primary consequences for estimator efficiency. Although conditional exogeneity may have implications for estimator efficiency, its primary role is to facilitate identification of causal effects.

The plausibility of conditional exogeneity depends on the structure generating D_t. For example, suppose $D_t \overset{c}{=} c_t(D^{t-1}, X^t, \tilde{U}^t)$, with $(D_0, \tilde{U}^t) \perp U^t \mid Y_0, X^T$, where $\{\tilde{U}_t\}$ is a sequence of unobserved causes of $\{D_t\}$. Then conditional exogeneity holds as a consequence of D, lemmas 4.1 and 4.2.

To proceed, we impose conditional exogeneity.

Assumption A.2. For given T, D^t is conditionally exogenous with respect to U^t given $(Y_0, X^T), t = 1, \ldots, T$.

Our discussion above establishes the following identification result. For this, we let supp(Y_0, X^T) denote the support of (Y_0, X^T), that is, the smallest smallest set containing (Y_0, X^T) with probability one, and let supp$(D^t \mid y_0, x^T)$ denote the support of D^t given that $Y_0 = y_0, X^T = x^T$.

Proposition 3.2. *Suppose Assumptions A.1(a) and A.2 hold. Then $\mu_{t,T}(y_0, d^t, x^T) = \rho_{t,T}(d^t \mid y_0, x^T)$ for all $(y_0, x^T) \in$ supp(Y_0, X^T) and $d^t \in$ supp$(D^t \mid y_0, x^T)$. Thus, $\mu_{t,T}$ is structurally identified, and $\rho_{t,T}$ is stochastically identified. Further, $\Delta\mu_{t,T} = \Delta\rho_{t,T}$, so $\Delta\mu_{t,T}$ is structurally identified and $\Delta\rho_{t,T}$ is stochastically identified, where*

$$\Delta\mu_{t,T}(y_0, d^t, d^{*t}, x^T) \equiv \mu_{t,T}(y_0, d^{*t}, x^T) - \mu_{t,T}(y_0, d^t, x^T).$$

If Assumption A.1(b) also holds, then $\mu_{t,T}$ and $\rho_{t,T}$ are fully identified.

A measure of effect related to $\Delta\rho_{t,T}$ that is often of interest in applications is

$$y_t - \rho_{t,T}(d^t \mid y_0, x^T),$$

where $y_t = r_t(y_0, d^{*t}, v^t, z^t)$ is the factually observed response value associated with the factual initial value y_0, factual cause histories d^{*t}, v^t, z^t, and factual covariate history x^T; and d^t is a counterfactual scenario of interest. For example, when one is interested in retrospectively measuring the effect of a cartel, y_t represents the price actually generated by the cartel in a particular period t, and d^{*t} is a history representing the operation of the cartel, e.g. $d^*_\tau = 1$ if the cartel operates in period τ and $d^*_\tau = 0$ otherwise. The counterfactual $\rho_{t,T}(d^t \mid y_0,x^T)$ represents the price expected but for the operation of the cartel, under the identical market conditions otherwise. In this case, d^t represents a history in which the cartel did not operate, ie, a vector of zeros. We call $y_t - \rho_{t,T}(d^t \mid y_0,x^T)$ a 'but-for' average effect. Formally, we have

Corollary 3.3. *Given Assumptions A.1 and A.2, $y_t - \mu_{t,T}(y_0,d^t,x^T)$ and $y_t - \rho_{t,T}(d^t \mid y_0,x^T)$ are fully identified.*

3.3.2 *Quantile Responses, Quantile Effects, and Point Bands*

In applications, effects on aspects of the response distribution other than the average are often of interest. Here we also consider effects defined in terms of *retrospective counterfactual conditional quantiles* for scalar Y_t. (We ensure no loss of generality by letting Y_0 remain a vector.) We begin by defining the *retrospective counterfactual conditional distribution functions*

$$\mathcal{F}_{t,T}(y,d^t \mid y_0,x^T) \equiv P[r_t(Y_0,d^t,V^t,Z^t) \leq y \mid \; Y_0 = y_0, X^T = x^T]$$

$$= \int 1[r_t(y_0,d^t,v^t,z^t) \leq y] \; dG_{t,T}(u^t \mid y_0,x^T), \quad y \in \text{supp}(Y_t \mid y_0,x^T).$$

The *retrospective counterfactual conditional α–quantiles* are then given by

$$\mathcal{Q}_{t,T}(\alpha,d^t \mid y_0,x^T) \equiv \inf\{y : \alpha < \mathcal{F}_{t,T}(y,d^t \mid y_0,x^T)\}, \quad 0 < \alpha < 1.$$

The *retrospective covariate-conditioned α–quantile effect of intervention $d^T \to d^{*T}$* is defined by

$$\Delta\mathcal{Q}_{t,T}(\alpha,d^t,d^{*t} \mid y_0,x^T) \equiv \mathcal{Q}_{t,T}(\alpha,d^{*t} \mid y_0,x^T) - \mathcal{Q}_{t,T}(\alpha,d^t \mid y_0,x^T).$$

This measures the impact of the intervention $d^T \to d^{*T}$ on the retrospective conditional α–quantile of the response, a version of the covariate-conditioned quantile effect defined by WC, and the unconditional quantile effects of Lehmann (1974), also studied by Abadie, Angrist, and Imbens (2002) and Imbens and Newey (2003).

Observe that $\Delta\mathcal{Q}_{t,T}$ represents a *quantile effect*. The retrospective *effect quantile*, defined as the functional inverse of

$$P[\Delta r_t(Y_0,d^t,d^{*t},V^t,Z^t) \leq y \mid \; Y_0 = y_0, X^T = x^T],$$

although certainly of interest, is much more complicated to analyse, as it involves the difficult-to-access conditional joint distribution of the responses $r_t(Y_0,d^t,V^t,Z^t)$ and $r_t(Y_0,d^{*t},V^t,Z^t)$. A detailed consideration of the issues involved for dynamic treatment effect distributions in panel data is given by Abbring and Heckman (2007). Because of the challenges presented by these effects, we leave their consideration aside here. Nevertheless, we consider a related and more tractable measure of effect quantiles below.

The quantile function $\mathcal{Q}_{t,T}$ can be used to define other useful counterfactual objects of interest. For example, for a given time t, the interval

$$[\mathcal{Q}_{t,T}(\alpha/2,d^t \mid y_0,x^T),\ \mathcal{Q}_{t,T}(1-\alpha/2,d^t \mid y_0,x^T)]$$

is a *retrospective counterfactual conditional* $(1-\alpha)\times 100\%$ *confidence interval* for the response under the history d^T. (This is a symmetric interval. Asymmetric intervals can be analogously defined. These may be shorter; we discuss symmetric intervals to keep the notation simple.)

We also call such an interval a $(1-\alpha)$ 'point band' for the response at time t, as this interval represents a band of possible responses for a particular point in time having probability $(1-\alpha)$ of containing the true response with history d^T, given $Y_0 = y_0, X^T = x^T$.

Analogous to the but-for average effect measure $y_t - \rho_{t,T}(d^t \mid y_0,x^T)$ introduced above, we can also consider the but-for effect interval

$$[y_t - \mathcal{Q}_{t,T}(1-\alpha/2,d^t \mid y_0,x^T),\ y_t - \mathcal{Q}_{t,T}(\alpha/2,d^t \mid y_0,x^T)],$$

where y_t is the factually observed response value associated with factual initial value y_0, factual cause histories d^{*t},v^t,z^t, and factual covariate history x^T; and d^t is a counterfactual scenario whose effects are of interest. In the cartel example discussed above, where y_t represents the time t actual cartel price and d^t represents a history in which the cartel did not operate, this interval represents a range of price outcomes that would have been realized under identical market conditions, but for the operation of the cartel. This range is constructed so as to contain the true but-for outcome with probability $1-\alpha$. In this case, it is possible to measure the effect quantiles, because y_t is set to the actual value.

Stochastic objects analogous to the counterfactual objects just discussed are *retrospective conditional distribution functions*

$$\begin{aligned} F_{t,T}(y \mid y_0,d^t,x^T) &\equiv P[Y_t \le y \mid Y_0 = y_0, D^t = d^t, X^T = x^T] \\ &= \int 1[r_t(y_0,d^t,v^t,z^t) \le y]\, dG_{t,T}(u^t \mid y_0,d^t,x^T), \quad y \in \text{supp}(Y_t \mid y_0,d^t,x^T), \end{aligned}$$

and *retrospective conditional* α*–quantiles,*

$$Q_{t,T}(\alpha \mid y_0,d^t,x^T) \equiv \inf\{y : \alpha < F_{t,T}(y \mid y_0,d^t,x^T)\}, \quad 0<\alpha<1.$$

It is now a straightforward exercise to verify

Proposition 3.4. *Suppose Assumptions A.1(a) and A.2 hold. Then* $F_{t,T}(\cdot|y_0,d^t,x^T) = \mathcal{F}_{t,T}(\cdot,d^t|y_0,x^T)$ *and* $Q_{t,T}(\cdot|y_0,d^t,x^T) = \mathcal{Q}_{t,T}(\cdot,d^t|y_0,x^T)$ *for all* $(y_0,x^T) \in$

$\text{supp}(Y_0,X^T)$ and $d^t \in \text{supp}(D^t|y_0,x^T)$, so $F_{t,T}$ and $Q_{t,T}$ are structurally identified, and $\mathcal{F}_{t,T}$ and $\mathcal{Q}_{t,T}$ are stochastically identified.

Further, $\Delta Q_{t,T} = \Delta\mathcal{Q}_{t,T}$, so $\Delta Q_{t,T}$ is structurally identified, with

$$\Delta Q_{t,T}(\alpha \mid y_0,d^t,d^{*t},x^T) \equiv Q_{t,T}(\alpha \mid y_0,d^{*t},x^T) - Q_{t,T}(\alpha \mid y_0,d^t,x^T),$$

as are the point bands $[Q_{t,T}(\alpha/2 \mid y_0,d^tx^T),\ Q_{t,T}(1-\alpha/2|y_0,d^tx^T)]$ and $[y_t - Q_{t,T}(1-\alpha/2 \mid y_0,d^t,x^T),\ y_t - Q_{t,T}(\alpha/2 \mid y_0,d^t,x^T)]$. In addition, the counterfactual objects $\Delta\mathcal{Q}_{t,T}$, $[\mathcal{Q}_{t,T}(\alpha/2,d^t \mid y_0,x^T),\ \mathcal{Q}_{t,T}(1-\alpha/2,d^t \mid y_0,x^T)]$, and $[y_t - \mathcal{Q}_{t,T}(1-\alpha/2,d^t \mid y_0,x^T),\ y_t - \mathcal{Q}_{t,T}(\alpha/2,d^t \mid y_0,x^T)]$ are stochastically identified.

If Assumption A.1(b) also holds, then $F_{t,T}$, $Q_{t,T}$, $\Delta Q_{t,T}$, $\mathcal{F}_{t,T}$, $\mathcal{Q}_{t,T}$, and $\Delta\mathcal{Q}_{t,T}$ are fully identified, as are the corresponding point bands.

3.3.3 *Path Bands*

The point bands introduced above can be used to construct *path bands*, that is sequences of pairs of elements of supp (Y_t) such that a random sequence of responses, actual or counterfactual, for a given history of causes of interest exits the band defined by the pairs with a specified probability. These path bands are of interest in their own right, as they represent confidence intervals for the response path under the history d^T. Path bands can also be used to test the null hypothesis of the absence of effects for various interventions. They are analogs of the uniform confidence bands for nonparametric regression discussed by Härdle (1990); Jordà and Marcellino (2007) analyse related path bands for prospective forecasts. See also Jordà (2007). To keep the notation simple, we define symmetric path bands; asymmetric path bands can be analogously defined.

Definition 3.5. *A* retrospective covariate-conditioned $(1-\alpha)$-path band for $\{r_t(Y_0,d^t,V^t,Z^t)\}$ over $[\tau_1,\tau_2]$ *is a sequence of point bands*

$$\{[\mathcal{Q}_{t,T}(\alpha^*/2,d^t \mid y_0,x^T),\ \mathcal{Q}_{t,T}(1-\alpha^*/2,d^t \mid y_0,x^T)]\}_{t=\tau_1}^{\tau_2}, \tag{3.4}$$

where α^* is a function of α,τ_1,τ_2 such that

$$P\left[\prod_{t=\tau_1}^{\tau_2} 1\{\mathcal{Q}_{t,T}(\alpha^*/2,d^t \mid y_0,x^T) \le r_t(Y_0,d^t,V^t,Z^t) \le \mathcal{Q}_{t,T}(1-\alpha^*/2,d^t \mid y_0,x^T)\}\right.$$
$$\left. = 1 \mid Y_0 = y_0, X^T = x^T\right] = 1-\alpha.$$

Although the mathematical expression for this definition is somewhat cumbersome, the basic idea is straightforward: the path band is a sequence of point bands, where the point band coverage, $(1-\alpha^*)$, is chosen so that over the time interval $[\tau_1,\tau_2]$, the path bands contain 100 $(1-\alpha)$% of the realized response paths $\{r_t(Y_0,d^t,V^t,Z^t)\}$ generated by d^T, given $Y_0 = y_0$ and $X^T = x^T$. Below, we describe how to estimate $\alpha^* = \alpha^*(\alpha;\tau_1,\tau_2)$.

Equivalently, the (conditional) probability is α that the sequence of responses $\{r_t(Y_0,d^t,V^t,Z^t)\}$ exits the band at any point during the time interval $[\tau_1,\tau_2]$. Thus, one can use the path bands to test the hypothesis

$$H_o : d^T \rightarrow d^{*T} \text{ has no effect over the time interval } [\tau_1,\tau_2],$$

where the 'effect' is understood to be the effect of the intervention $d^T \rightarrow d^{*T}$ on the response of interest, conditional on $Y_0 = y_0$, $X^T = x^T$. To implement the test, one computes the path bands of equation (3.4) associated with the 'benchmark' history, d^T, for a given level, α. Then one inspects the path of $\{r_t(Y_0,d^{*t},V^t,Z^t)\}$ to see if it exits the band at any point during the interval $[\tau_1,\tau_2]$. If so, one rejects H_o at level α. Otherwise, one fails to reject H_o. The test relies on the fact that H_o is true if and only if $\{r_t(Y_0,d^{*t},V^t,Z^t)\}$ has the same conditional distribution (given $Y_0 = y_0$, $X^T = x^T$) on $[\tau_1,\tau_2]$ as $\{r_t(Y_0,d^t,V^t,Z^t)\}$.

In most applications, $\{r_t(Y_0,d^{*t},V^t,Z^t)\}$ will correspond to an observed response history $\{Y_t\}$ generated by the underlying natural data generating process (subject to the actual history d^{*T}), as the generation of other response histories will require knowledge of the history of the unobserved causes, U^T, as well as knowledge of $\{r_t\}$. Thus, for example, one can test whether a cartel had any effect on prices by comparing the price history generated by the cartel to the path bands generated by the counterfactual history d^T designating the absence of the cartel.

Such tests complement methods of Angrist and Kuersteiner (2004), who propose tests for the presence of causal effects associated with recurring interventions, such as the monetary policy interventions studied by Romer and Romer (1989). The Angrist and Kuersteiner tests make use of the 'policy propensity score', rather than directly estimating the effect of the intervention.

3.4 Estimating Retrospective Effects

When $\rho_{t,T}$ is fully identified, we can estimate $\rho_{t,T}$ by estimating $\mu_{t,T}$. For this, a useful representation of $\mu_{t,T}$ is

$$\mu_{t,T}(y_0,d^t,x^T) = \int y_t \, dF_{t,T}(y_t \mid y_0,d^t,x^T),$$

where $dF_{t,T}(y_t \mid y_0,d^t,x^T)$ defines the conditional density of Y_t given $(Y_0,D^t,X^T) = (y_0,d^t,x^T)$. There are many ways to proceed, but a particularly useful approach is based on estimating $dF_{t,T}(y_t \mid y_0,d^t,x^T)$, as this affords a complete characterization of the conditional stochastic behaviour of Y_t. This not only yields estimates of mean effects but also other effects of interest, such as quantile effects or path bands. As $dF_{t,T}$ involves only observable random variables, it can be estimated with suitable data.

Although sample values for Y_t are observable, our interest in counterfactual (thus unobservable) response values under interventions makes it natural to treat the response vector as the state vector for a dynamic state-space system with specific properties appropriate to the present context. This not only permits us to readily develop useful representations for the objects of interest, but also allows us to draw on appropriate segments of the extensive dynamic state-space systems literature.

Viewing Y_t as a state vector, we have the prediction density equation

$$dF_{t+1,T}(y_{t+1} \mid y_0,d^{t+1},x^T) = \int dF_{t+1,T}(y_{t+1} \mid y_t,y_0,d^{t+1},x^T)\, dF_{t,T}(y_t \mid y_0,d^{t+1},x^T). \tag{3.5}$$

The 'filtering' or 'updating' density is given by Bayes theorem as

$$dF_{t,T}(y_t \mid y_0,d^{t+1},x^T) = \frac{dF_{t+1,T}(d_{t+1} \mid y_t,y_0,d^t,x^T)\, dF_{t,T}(y_t \mid y_0,d^t,x^T)}{dF_{t+1,T}(d_{t+1} \mid y_0,d^t,x^T)}. \tag{3.6}$$

Our assumed DGP permits convenient simplifications. Specifically

$$dF_{t+1,T}(d_{t+1} \mid y_t,y_0,d^t,x^T) = dF_{t+1,T}(d_{t+1} \mid y_0,d^t,x^T). \tag{3.7}$$

Equivalently, this condition states that $D_{t+1} \perp Y_t \mid Y_0,D^t,X^T$; this also directly yields

$$dF_{t,T}(y_t \mid y_0,d^{t+1},x^T) = dF_{t,T}(y_t \mid y_0,d^t,x^T). \tag{3.8}$$

Formally, we have

Proposition 3.6. *Suppose Assumptions A.1(a) and A.2 hold. Then $D_{t+1} \perp Y_t \mid Y_0,D^t,X^T$, ie equations (3.7) and (3.8) hold.*

Proof: By A.2, $D^{t+1} \perp U^{t+1} \mid Y_0,X^T$. By D lemma 4.2(ii) (following Dawid, 1979), $D^{t+1} \perp U^{t+1} \mid Y_0,D^t,X^T$. D lemma 4.1 then gives $D^{t+1},Y_0,X^T \perp U^{t+1},Y_0,D^t,X^T \mid Y_0,D^t,X^T$. Given A.1(a), we have $Y_t \overset{c}{=} r_t(Y_0,D^t,V^t,Z^t)$, so D lemma 4.2(i) gives $D^{t+1},Y_0,X^T \perp Y_t \mid Y_0,D^t,X^T$. Applying D lemma 4.2(i) once more gives $D_{t+1} \perp Y_t \mid Y_0,D^t, X^T$.

The prediction density simplifies under plausible memory restrictions. For concreteness and simplicity, we exploit a 'first order' memory condition on the evolution of Y_t,

$$dF_{t,T}(y_t \mid y_{t-1},y_0,d^t,x^T) = dF_{t,T}(y_t \mid y_{t-1},d_t,x^T), \tag{3.9}$$

where the argument lists identify the relevant random variables in the obvious way. Other finite order memory conditions will yield results similar to what follows. We interpret the appearance on the right of d_t in place of d^t as requiring that only D_t has direct predictive relevance for Y_t, given (Y_{t-1},X^T). Also note that y_0 is absent on the right. Thus, any predictive impact of Y_0 or of past values D^{t-1} is indirect, through Y_{t-1}. (Note that although we permit the effect of D_t to be contemporaneous, this is not necessary, as D_t may be observed in period $t-1$, as mentioned above.)

The next result provides a restriction on the dynamic structure sufficient for equation (3.9).

Proposition 3.7. *Suppose Assumption A.1(a) holds, that* $U_t \perp Y_0 \mid Y_{t-1},D^t,X^T$ *and* $U_t \perp D^{t-1} \mid Y_{t-1},D_t,X^T$ *hold, and that*

$$Y_t \stackrel{c}{=} q_t(Y_{t-1},D_t,V_t,Z_t). \tag{3.10}$$

Then $Y_t \perp D^{t-1},Y_0 \mid Y_{t-1},D_t,X^T$, *i.e. equation (3.9) holds.*

Proof:

By D lemma 4.3, $U_t \perp Y_0 \mid Y_{t-1},D^t,X^T$ and $U_t \perp D^{t-1} \mid Y_{t-1},D_t,X^T$ imply $U_t \perp Y_0,D^{t-1} \mid Y_{t-1},D_t,X^T$. Eq. (3.10) and D lemmas 4.1 and 4.2 then give the result. ■

Substituting equation (3.9) into equation (3.5) gives

$$dF_{t+1,T}(y_{t+1} \mid y_0,d^{t+1},x^T) = \int dF_{t+1,T}(y_{t+1} \mid y_t,d_{t+1},x^T)\, dF_{t,T}(y_t \mid y_0,d^{t+1},x^T). \tag{3.11}$$

By equation (3.8), $dF_{t,T}(y_t \mid y_0,d^{t+1},x^T) = dF_{t,T}(y_t \mid y_0,d^t,x^T)$. Substituting this into equation (3.11) then gives

$$dF_{t+1,T}(y_{t+1} \mid y_0,d^{t+1},x^T) = \int dF_{t+1,T}(y_{t+1} \mid y_t,d_{t+1},x^T) dF_{t,T}(y_t \mid y_0,d^t,x^T),$$

which provides a recursion useful for estimating $dF_{t,T}(y_t \mid y_0,d^t,x^T)$. To apply this recursion, we seek an estimate of $dF_{t+1,T}(y_{t+1} \mid y_t,d_{t+1},x^T)$ for suitable values of t.

Estimation of these densities becomes especially tractable if for given T, there exists a finite non-negative integer τ such that for all $t \leq T-\tau$,

$$dF_{t,T}(y_t \mid y_{t-1},d_t,x^T) = dF_\tau(y_t \mid y_{t-1},d_t,x_{t-\tau}^{t+\tau}), \tag{3.12}$$

where $dF_\tau(y_t \mid y_{t-1},d_t,x_{t-\tau}^{t+\tau})$ defines the conditional density of Y_t given $Y_{t-1} = y_{t-1},D_t = d_t$, and $X_{t-\tau}^{t+\tau} = x_{t-\tau}^{t+\tau}$, where $X_{t-\tau}^{t+\tau} \equiv (X_{t-\tau},\ldots,X_{t+\tau})$ is the (τ−) *near history of* X_t. This combines a memory condition with a conditional stationarity assumption. Conditional stationarity holds because dF_τ does not depend on t. The memory condition says that given Y_{t-1} and D_t, only the near history of the covariates is useful in predicting Y_t. This is often plausible, as the memory of U_t contained in the covariates (and the memory of the covariates contained in U_t) will generally fade as time passes. Thus, we impose

Assumption A.3. For given T, there exists a finite non-negative integer τ and a conditional density dF_τ such that for all $t \le T - \tau$, and for all argument values

$$dF_{t,T}(y_t \mid y_{t-1}, d_t, x^T) = dF_\tau(y_t \mid y_{t-1}, d_t, x_{t-\tau}^{t+\tau}).$$

Combining our results and the above development of the prediction and filtering equations provides the basis for feasible estimation.

Proposition 3.8. *Suppose Assumption A.1(a) holds with equation (3.10), and that A.2 and A.3 hold. Then* $dF_{1,T}(y_1 \mid y_0, d^1, x^T) = dF_\tau(y_1 \mid y_0, d_1, x_{1-\tau}^{1+\tau})$ *and for* $t = 1, \ldots, T - \tau - 1$

$$dF_{t+1,T}(y_{t+1} \mid y_0, d^{t+1}, x^T) = \int dF_\tau(y_{t+1} \mid y_t, d_{t+1}, x_{t+1-\tau}^{t+1+\tau})\, dF_{t,T}(y_t \mid y_0, d^t, x^T).$$

This result makes it straightforward to estimate $dF_{t,T}(y_t \mid y_0, d^t, x^T)$ using sample data when A.1(b) holds. Using that estimate, we can then estimate any desired aspect of the distribution, in particular the means or quantiles that have been our focus here.

From Proposition 3.8, we see that the key to estimating $dF_{t,T}$ is the estimation of dF_τ. Let $d\hat{F}_\tau$ denote any suitable estimator for dF_τ. Depending on the context, one may use either parametric, semi-parametric, or nonparametric estimators $d\hat{F}_\tau$. For example, Li and Racine (2007, Ch. 5) provide nonparametric methods for conditional density estimation in the empirically relevant 'mixed data' case, in which the variables involved may be either continuously or discretely distributed. Given $d\hat{F}_\tau$, we can recursively construct estimators of $dF_{t,T}$ using the structure provided by Proposition 3.8. Specifically, we compute

$$d\hat{F}_{1,T}(y_1 \mid y_0, d^1, x^T) = d\hat{F}_\tau(y_1 \mid y_0, d_1, x_{1-\tau}^{1+\tau}) \qquad (t = 0)$$

$$d\hat{F}_{t+1,T}(y_{t+1} \mid y_0, d^{t+1}, x^T) = \int d\hat{F}_\tau(y_{t+1} \mid y_t, d_{t+1}, x_{t+1-\tau}^{t+1+\tau})\, d\hat{F}_{t,T}(y_t \mid y_0, d^t, x^T),$$

$$t = 1, \ldots, T - \tau - 1. \qquad (3.13)$$

In writing these recursions, we adopt the convention that covariate values for negative time indexes ($t = 1 - \tau, \ldots, -1$) are observable. (Now $X^T \equiv (X_{1-\tau}, \ldots, X_T)$.) This enables us to maintain our conventions regarding the starting and ending observation indexes for the other variables. It further implies that we can use sample observations $t = 1, \ldots, T - \tau$ to estimate dF_τ. The recursions above stop τ periods before the end of the sample to accommodate the covariate leads. If it is important to estimate response distributions in periods after $T - \tau$ (e.g., $dF_{T,T}(y_T \mid y_0,d^T,x^T)$), one can modify the procedures above to estimate these.

Using $d\hat{F}_{t,T}$, we estimate $\mu_{t,T}(y_0,d^t,x^T)$ and $\Delta\mu_{t,T}(y_0,d^t,d^{*t},x^T)$ as

$$\hat{\mu}_{t,T}(y_0,d^t,x^T) = \int y_t \, d\hat{F}_{t,T}(y_t \mid y_0,d^t,x^T)$$

$$\Delta\hat{\mu}_{t,T}(y_0,d^t,d^{*t},x^T) = \hat{\mu}_{t,T}(y_0,d^{*t},x^T) - \hat{\mu}_{t,T}(y_0,d^t,x^T), \quad t = 1,\ldots,T-\tau.$$

Under structural identification, these are also our estimators of $\rho_{t,T}(d^t \mid y_0,x^T)$ and $\Delta\rho_{t,T}(d^t,d^{*t} \mid y_0,x^T)$. The but-for average effect estimator is

$$y_t - \hat{\mu}_{t,T}(y_0,d^t,x^T).$$

To estimate $F_{t,T}$ and $Q_{t,T}$, we can use $d\hat{F}_{t,T}$ to compute

$$\hat{F}_{t,T}(y \mid y_0,d^t,x^T) \equiv \int 1[y_t \leq y] \, d\hat{F}_{t,T}(y_t \mid y_0,d^t,x^T)$$

$$\hat{Q}_{t,T}(\alpha \mid y_0,d^t,x^T) \equiv \inf\{y : \alpha < \hat{F}_{t,T}(y \mid y_0,d^t,x^T)\}, \quad 0 < \alpha < 1.$$

Under structural identification, we can thus estimate $\mathcal{F}_{t,T}$ using $\hat{F}_{t,T}$ and $\mathcal{Q}_{t,T}$ using $\hat{Q}_{t,T}$. The retrospective covariate-conditioned α–quantile effect estimator is

$$\Delta\hat{\mathcal{Q}}_{t,T}(\alpha,d^t,d^{*t} \mid y_0,x^T) = \hat{Q}_{t,T}(\alpha \mid y_0,d^{*t},x^T) - \hat{Q}_{t,T}(\alpha \mid y_0,d^t,x^T).$$

Similarly, the $1-\alpha$ counterfactual point bands can be estimated as

$$[\hat{Q}_{t,T}(\alpha/2 \mid y_0,d^t,x^T), \hat{Q}_{t,T}(1-\alpha/2 \mid y_0,d^t,x^T)],$$

and the but-for effect intervals can be estimated as

$$[y_t - \hat{Q}_{t,T}(1-\alpha/2 \mid y_0,d^t,x^T), y_t - \hat{Q}_{t,T}(\alpha/2 \mid y_0,d^t,x^T)].$$

To estimate the path bands, it suffices to construct a consistent estimate $\hat{\alpha}^*$ of $\alpha^*(\alpha;\tau_1,\tau_2)$; the path bands are then given by

$$\{[\hat{Q}_{t,T}(\hat{\alpha}^*/2 \mid y_0,d^t,x^T), \hat{Q}_{t,T}(1-\hat{\alpha}^*/2 \mid y_0,d^t,x^T)]\}_{t=\tau_1}^{\tau_2}.$$

To construct $\hat{\alpha}^*$, one can use the sequence $\{d\hat{F}_\tau\}$ to generate a large number, say N, of independent and identically distributed (i.i.d.) simulated response paths $\{\hat{Y}_{t,i}\}_{t=\tau_1}^{\tau_2}, i = 1,\ldots,N$, such that for each t and i, $\hat{Y}_{t,i}$ has density $d\hat{F}_\tau(\cdot \mid \hat{Y}_{t-1,i},d_t,x_{t-\tau}^{t+\tau})$. It is then a straightforward numerical exercise to choose $\hat{\alpha}^*$ to solve the problem

$$\min_{\alpha^*} |(1-\alpha) - N^{-1}\sum_{i=1}^{N}\prod_{t=\tau_1}^{\tau_2} 1\{\hat{Q}_{t,T}(\alpha^*/2 \mid y_0,d^t,x^T) \leq \hat{Y}_{t,i}$$
$$\leq \hat{Q}_{t,T}(1-\alpha^*/2 \mid y_0,d^t,x^T)\}|.$$

Space is not available here to undertake a formal analysis of the properties of these estimators. Because of the close similarity of the estimating equations (3.13) for $dF_{t,T}$ to those arising in the estimation of state-space models, one may bring the rich array of techniques of that literature to bear in implementing and analysing the estimators $\{d\hat{F}_{t,T}\}$. Specifically, methods of particle filtering (e.g. Crisan and Doucet, 2002), auxiliary particle filtering (Pitt and Shephard, 1999), or their extensions (e.g. Doucet and Tadić, 2003; Tadić and Doucet, 2002; DeJong, Hariharan, Liesenfeld, and Richard, 2007) are directly relevant.

3.5 An Illustrative Application

We illustrate the methods described in the previous section by constructing retrospective conditional means, point bands, and path bands useful for examining the impact of crude oil prices on gasoline prices at the monthly frequency. In particular, we study the effects of the Cushing OK WTI spot crude oil price (D_t) on the next month's spot price for US Gulf Coast conventional gasoline (Y_t).

3.5.1 *Gasoline Price Determination*

In the present framework, modelling proceeds by identifying the relevant variables of the DGP and then specifying a method for constructing the estimators $\{d\hat{F}_{t,T}\}$. We have already specified Y_t and D_t, so it remains to specify V_t, W_t, and Z_t. As the choice of W_t is primarily informed by that of (V_t, Z_t), we focus first on specifying these variables, the other drivers of gasoline price.

Economic theory says that gasoline prices are determined by the costs of producing gasoline, by demand for gasoline, and by the nature of the conduct among gasoline market participants. For the market and time period we examine (January 1994 through April 2006), we suppose that this conduct is relatively stable. Consequently, we will not include variables to proxy for this conduct. Nevertheless, we can and will use our methods to assess the validity of this assumption. It remains to specify the relevant cost and demand factors.

Crude oil prices are the main driver of gasoline cost, and it is the effect of crude prices on gasoline that is of interest here. To measure the total effect of interest, we thus must omit from consideration cost variables driving gasoline prices that are themselves driven by the crude oil price. This includes such things as crude oil inventories, refining capacity and utilization rates, or diesel fuel prices. Cost factors that may be much less strongly driven by crude oil prices are refinery worker wages, natural gas prices, and interest rates. We treat cost shifters other than crude oil prices as unobservable, belonging to U_t. Thus, we seek proxies for these.

Demand factors not driven by the price of crude oil are regional temperatures and seasonal factors. Income and population are also plausibly only weakly driven by crude oil prices in the short run, so we shall treat these also as elements of (V_t, Z_t). Prices of other goods may in principle impact gasoline demand, but for simplicity we assume here that the effects of other prices on gasoline demand are negligible. We thus do not consider these further. We do not assume we can measure the true demand drivers, so we assign these to U_t and seek suitable proxies. Thus, $(\widetilde{V}_t, \widetilde{Z}_t)$ has zero dimension here.

We also identify drivers of crude oil prices that do not drive gasoline prices and that are not themselves driven by crude oil prices. Such variables are things like exchange rates and industrial production for countries whose growth is not highly dependent on crude oil prices. As for the drivers of gasoline prices, we do not assume these are observable, so we assign them to U_t and seek suitable proxies.

These considerations lead us to select as covariates X_t the following cost and demand proxies W_t: (i) Texas Initial and Continuing Unemployment Claims (taken from State Weekly Claims for Unemployment Insurance Data, Not Seasonally Adjusted); (ii) Houston temperature; (iii) a Winter dummy for January, February, and March; (iv) a Summer dummy for June, July, and August; (v) the 3-Month T-Bill (Secondary Market Rate) (TB3MS); (vi) the US Bureau of Labor Statistics Natural Gas price index; (vii) the US Bureau of Labor Statistics Electricity price index; and (ix) the Yen–US dollar and British pound–US dollar exchange rates.

Our response variable Y_t is the US Gulf Coast Conventional Gasoline, Regular Spot Price (FOB), measured in cents per gallon; D_t is the previous month's Cushing, OK WTI Crude Oil Spot Price (FOB), measured in dollars per barrel.

3.5.2 *Estimation*

Figure 3.1 displays plots of the natural logarithm of gasoline and crude oil prices, together with the change in the natural logarithm of crude oil prices. As expected, gasoline and crude oil prices appear cointegrated. The stochastic trend of oil prices also exhibits an apparent change in January 2002. A test of the null of no change in the mean of the log crude oil price differences before and after January 2002 soundly rejects the null hypothesis of no change. This shift is plausibly thought to be driven by strong growth in demand in East Asia, especially China and India. We examine whether this shift is associated with any corresponding change in the relation between crude oil and gasoline prices. We also examine a counterfactual scenario in which this trend shift is absent.

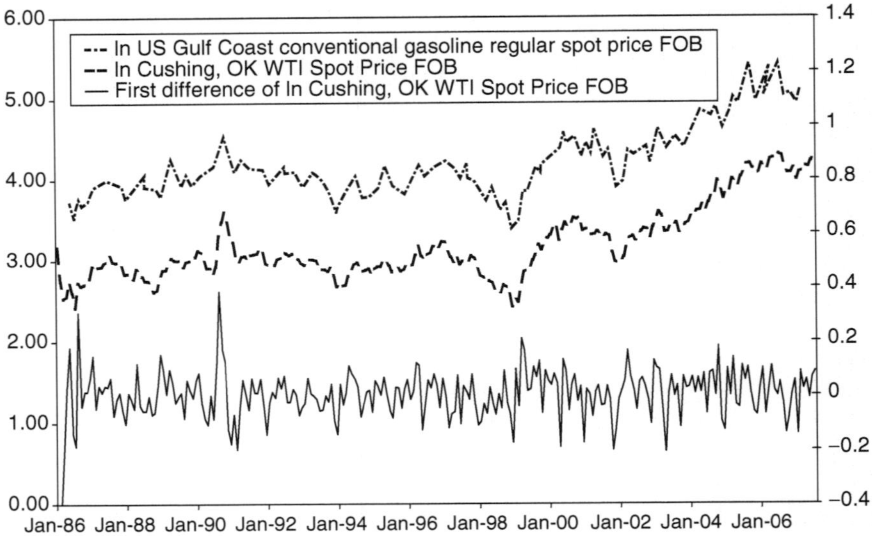

FIG. 3.1. Natural logarithm of crude oil and gasoline prices.

Accordingly, in a first step, we test for cointegration between these two variables over the period January 1994–December 2001 using the method of Johansen (1991). Finding that these series are cointegrated we estimate a regression model in differences (ΔY_t) by ridge regression. Our regression includes the error correction term and ΔD_t, together with optional lags of the dependent variable and ΔD_t, plus leads and lags of the covariates X_t, transformed to stationarity when appropriate. We explicitly allow changes in crude oil prices to have asymmetric directional impacts. We select variables for the final prediction equation using an automated selection algorithm that implements a general to specific search followed by a specific to general search. At each stage, variables are included or excluded so as to minimize the cross-validated root mean square error (CVRMSE). We also choose the optimal ridge parameter to minimize CVRMSE.

To generate counterfactual retrospective histories, we apply the method of White (2006), in which an initial counterfactual value of d_t is used to generate an initial counterfactual value for Y_t. For successive periods, counterfactual values of d_t are used together with lagged counterfactual values of Y_t to roll forward succeeding counterfactual values of Y_t. In each period, we introduce prediction errors drawn from a normal distribution with standard error equal to the CVRMSE for the estimated prediction equation. This generates a realization of a counterfactual history. Repeating this a large number of times yields conditional means and point bands. We construct path bands from the point bands, as described above. This corresponds to specifying that F_T is a conditional normal density with conditionally varying mean and conditional homoskedasticity. Other specifications are certainly of interest. We adopt the present specification for simplicity in conducting our illustration.

3.5.3 *Results*

First, we construct path bands for the period starting in January 2002 using the actual history of crude oil prices. (Note that these bands are for a period outside the estimation sample.) By comparing actual prices to these path bands, we can test the null hypothesis that there has not been a change in the process generating gasoline prices after 2001 (the 'test period'). Among other things, this tests for forecast failure and provides insight into the validity of the market stability assumption introduced above. Figure 3.2 plots the 5th and 95th percentile path bands around the retrospective dynamic forecast (conditional mean) starting in January 2002. Observed gasoline prices fall within these path bands throughout the entire test period. We thus fail to reject the null hypothesis of stability at the 10% level.

Next, we study crude oil price effects using two alternative counterfactual paths for crude oil prices. Our first counterfactual series is motivated by the

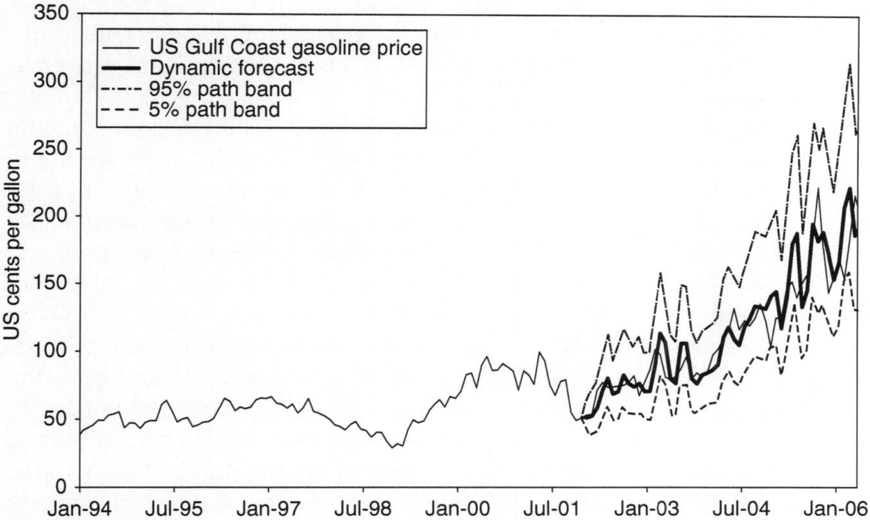

FIG. 3.2. Dynamic forecast of US Gulf Coast conventional gasoline from January 2002.

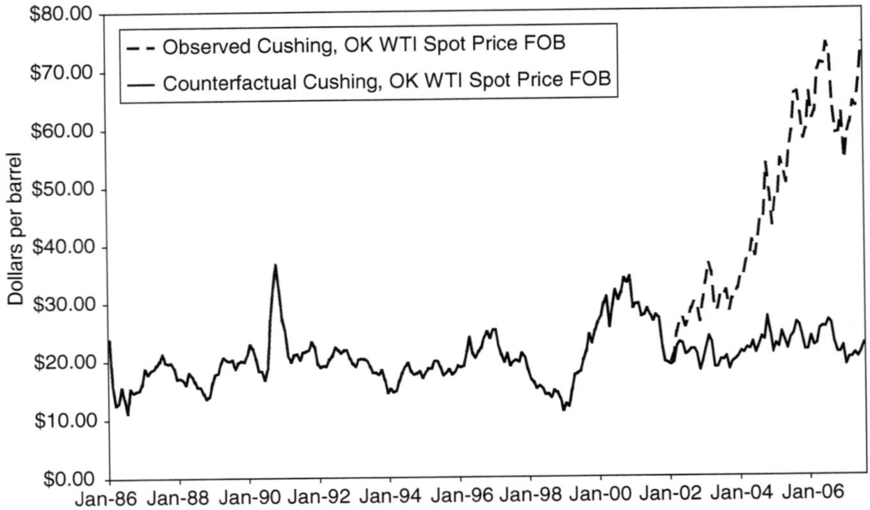

FIG. 3.3. Counterfactual of crude oil prices in the absence of a structural break.

apparent structural break in the mean log-difference of crude oil prices. We construct an alternative crude oil series in which no such break occurred by adjusting the post-2001 crude oil price series so that the month-to-month changes in natural logarithms have the same mean as that for the period prior to 2002. Figure 3.3 shows the actual and resulting counterfactual price series. (The series are constructed using natural log differences and converted to levels for plotting.)

Figure 3.4 displays 90% path bands for this first counterfactual scenario. Not surprisingly, we see that the actual price exits the path bands, leading to rejection of the null hypothesis of no effect of the change in crude oil price structure on gasoline prices. On average, prices were 54 cents per gallon higher in the period beginning in 2002 than they would otherwise have been, and the gap continues to widen.

Our second counterfactual series is motivated by the disruption to petroleum markets associated with hurricanes Katrina and Rita of 2005. (Katrina reached peak strength on 28 August 2005. We call September 2005 and after the 'Katrina period'.) We construct an alternative crude oil series representing price behaviour plausible in the absence of Katrina and Rita by applying to the Katrina period average month-specific changes for crude oil price in the periods prior to the hurricanes. Figure 3.5 displays the actual and resulting counterfactual price series. Figure 3.6 shows what happens when we estimate the model using data through July 2005 and then use this to generate counterfactual 90% path bands for the Katrina period. The actual price path begins by

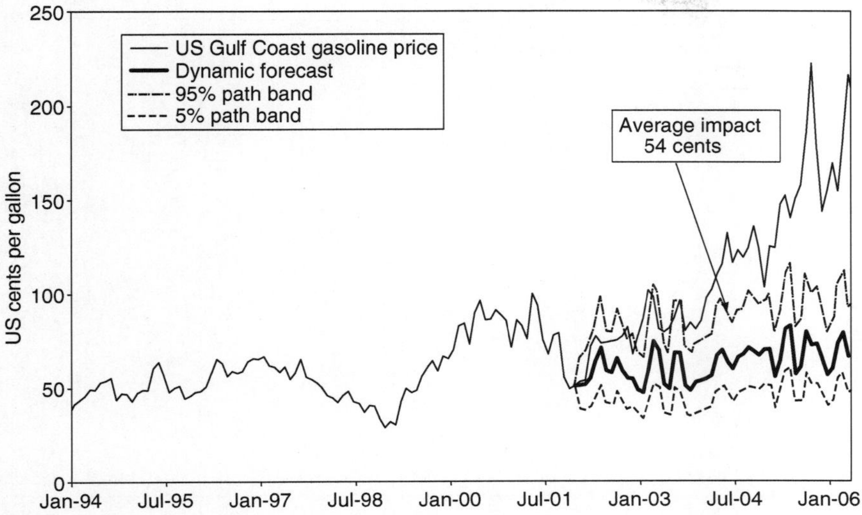

FIG. **3.4.** Dynamic forecast using counterfactual (no structural break) crude oil prices.

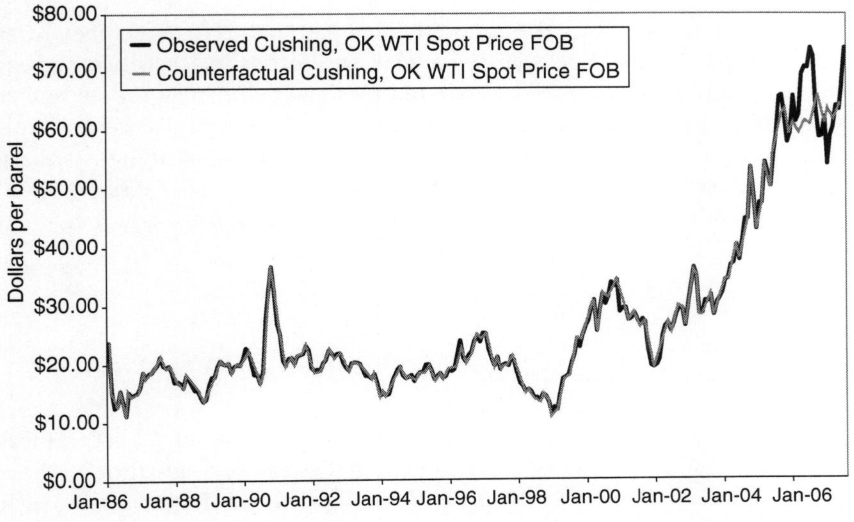

FIG. **3.5.** Counterfactual crude oil prices in the absence of hurricanes Rita and Katrina.

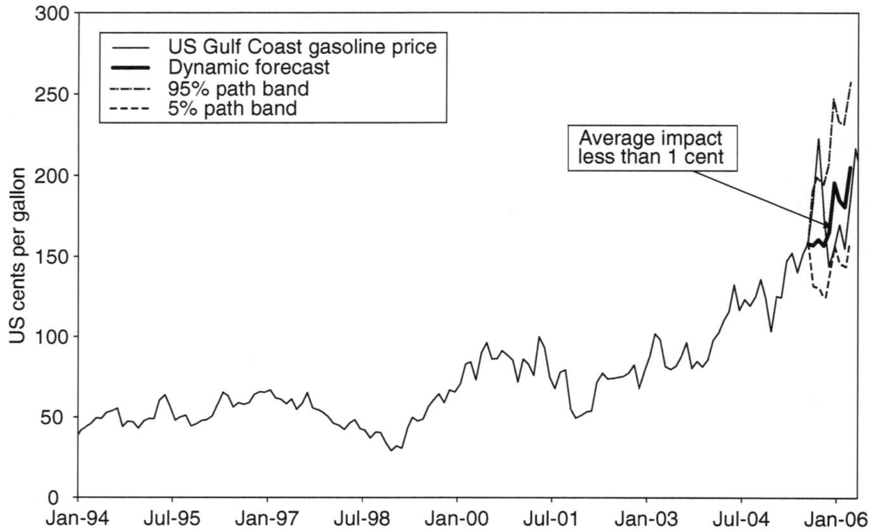

FIG. 3.6. Dynamic forecast based on observed and counterfactual (no hurricanes).

spiking up sharply, exiting the counterfactual path bands in September. After the initial price spike, however, the actual price drops to levels below what we would otherwise expect. An expected seasonal price spike for December is absent. Moreover, while gasoline prices are approximately 6 cents above what they would otherwise have been from August 1995 through January 2006, the average impact drops to less than one cent by February 2006, and actual prices are lower than we would expect under our counterfactual scenario.

3.6 Summary and Conclusion

This chapter provides methods for estimating a variety of retrospective measures of causal effects in systems of dynamic structural equations. These equations need not be linear or separable, or possess other properties such as monotonicity. Structural identification of effects of interest is ensured by certain conditional exogeneity conditions, an extension of the notion of strict exogeneity. The variables of the system can be characterized according to their role as responses of interest, causes of interest, ancillary causes, or proxies for unobserved drivers of the responses of interest and the causes of interest. The observed ancillary causes and proxies serve as covariates, playing a supporting role that is predictive rather than causal. Because this predictive role admits back-casting, not only lags but also leads of the covariates may be usefully employed.

We emphasize that only the effects of the causes of interest are informatively measured using our methods. They do not identify effects of observed ancillary causes or the structural dynamics associated with the lags of the dependent variable. Instead, observed ancillary causes and lagged dependent variables form part of the predictive support structure that serves to identify effects of causes of interest.

We pay particular attention to covariate-conditioned average and quantile effects, together with counterfactual objects that are associated with these, such as point bands and path bands. The latter are useful for constructing confidence intervals and testing hypotheses. We show how these objects can be estimated using state-space methods. We illustrate our methods with a study of the impact of crude oil prices on gasoline prices.

There are many interesting topics for further research beyond the scope of this chapter. One task is to provide formal conditions ensuring consistency, rates, and/or asymptotic distributions for the estimators proposed here. Another task is to study tests for conditional exogeneity appropriate to the present framework, e.g. extensions of tests proposed by White (2006), so that one can subject hypothesized structures to falsification. The present DGP, with its recursive structure, is only one of a variety of structures in which causal effects can be defined and identified, along the lines of the discussion in Chalak and White (2007); an interesting area for future work is the analysis of identification and estimation of effects in possibly non-recursive systems. Finally, the effects studied here are retrospective; the study of *prospective* effects is also of interest, especially for policy applications. Prospective effects present a variety of interesting analytical challenges distinct from those arising here. Nevertheless, many of the ideas developed here should also prove useful in that study.

References

Abadie, K., Angrist, J., and Imbens, G. (2002). Instrumental variables estimates of the effects of subsidized training on the quantiles of trainee earnings. *Econometrica*, **70**, 91–117.

Abbring, J. and Heckman, J. (2007). Econometric evaluation of social programs, part III: Distributional treatment effects, dynamic treatment effects, dynamic discrete choice, and general equilibrium policy evaluation. In Heckman, J. and

Leamer, E. (eds.), *Handbook of Econometrics*, vol 6B, pp. 5145–5303. Amsterdam: Elsevier.

Angrist, J. and Kuersteiner, G. (2004). Semiparametric causality tests using the policy propensity score. MIT Department of Economics Working Paper.

Banerjee, A. and Hendry, D. F. (1992). Testing integration and cointegration: An overview. *Oxford Bulletin of Economics and Statistics*, **54**, 225–255.

——— and Mizon, G.E. (1996). The econometric analysis of economic policy. *Oxford Bulletin of Economics and Statistics*, **58**, 573–600.

Chalak, K. and White, H. (2007). An extended class of instrumental variables for the estimation of causal effects. UCSD Department of Economics Discussion Paper.

——— (2008). Independence and conditional independence in structural systems. UCSD Department of Economics Discussion Paper.

Chevillon, G. and Hendry, D. F. (2005). Non-parametric direct multi-step estimation for forecasting economic processes. *International Journal of Forecasting*, **21**, 201–218.

Chow, G. (1997). *Dynamic Economics: Optimization by the Lagrange Method*. Oxford: Oxford University Press.

Clements, M.P. and Hendry, D. F. (1996). Multi-step estimation for forecasting. *Oxford Bulletin of Economics and Statistics*, **58**, 657–684.

——— (1998a). Forecasting economic processes. *International Journal of Forecasting*, **14**, 111–131.

——— (1998b). *Forecasting Economic Time Series*. Cambridge: Cambridge University Press.

——— (1999). *Forecasting Non-stationary Economic Time Series*. Cambridge, MA: MIT Press.

——— (2002a). Modelling methodology and forecast failure. *The Econometrics Journal*, **5**, 319–344.

——— (2002b). *A Companion to Economic Forecasting*. Oxford: Blackwell Publishers.

——— (2003). Economic forecasting: Some lessons from recent research. *Economic Modelling*, **20**, 301–329.

Crisan, D. and Doucet, A. (2002). A survey of results on particle filtering methods for practitioners. *IEEE Transactions on Signal Processing*, **50**, 736–746.

Dawid, A. P. (1979). Conditional independence in statistical theory. *Journal of the Royal Statistical Society, Series B*, **41**, 1–31.

DeJong, D., Hariharan, D., Liesenfeld, R., and Richard, J.-F. (2007). An efficient filtering approach to likelihood approximation for state-space representations. University of Pittsburgh Department of Economics Discussion Paper.

Doucet, A. and Tadić, V. (2003). Parameter estimation in general state-space models using particle methods. *Annals of the Institute of Statistical Mathematics*, **55**, 409–422.

Dudley, R. M. (2002). *Real Analysis and Probability*. New York: Cambridge University Press.

Engle, R. F. and Hendry, D. F. (1993). Testing super exogeneity and invariance in regression models. *Journal of Econometrics*, **56**, 119–139.

——— and Richard, J.-F. (1983). Exogeneity. *Econometrica*, **51**, 277–304.

Ericsson, N. R., Hendry, D. F., and Mizon, G. E. (1998). Exogeneity, cointegration and economic policy analysis. *Journal of Business and Economic Statistics*, **16**, 1–18.

Favero, C. and Hendry, D. F. (1992). Testing the Lucas critique: A review. *Econometric Reviews*, **11**, 265–306.

Fisher, F. (1966). *The Identification Problem in Econometrics*. New York: McGraw-Hill.

——(1970). A correspondence principle for simultaneous equations models. *Econometrica*, **38**, 73–92.

Goldberger, A. (1972). Structural equation methods in the social sciences. *Econometrica*, **40**, 979–1001.

Granger, C. W. J. (1969). Investigating causal relations by econometric and cross-spectral methods. *Econometrica*, **37**, 424–438.

Härdle, W. (1990). *Applied Nonparametric Regression*. Cambridge: Cambridge University Press.

Hendry, D. F. (1974). Stochastic specification in an aggregate demand model of the United Kingdom. *Econometrica*, **42**, 559–578.

——(1980). Econometrics: Alchemy or science? *Economica*, **47**, 387–406.

——(1986). Econometric modelling with cointegrated variables: An overview. *Oxford Bulletin of Economics and Statistics*, **48**, 201–212.

——(1993). *Econometrics: Alchemy or Science?* Oxford: Oxford University Press.

——(1995a). On the interactions of unit roots and exogeneity. *Econometric Reviews*, **14**, 383–419.

——(1995b). The role of econometrics in scientific economics. In d'Autume, A. and Cartelier, J. (eds.), *L'Economie Devient-elle une Science Dure?*, pp. 172–196. Paris. Reprinted in English as: *Is Economics Becoming a Hard Science?* Edward Elgar, 1997.

——(1995c). *Dynamic Econometrics*. Oxford: Oxford University Press.

——(1996). Typologies of linear dynamic systems and models. *Journal of Statistical Planning and Inference*, **49**, 177–201.

——(2000). Does money determine UK inflation over the long run? In Backhouse, R. and Salanti, A. (eds.), *Macroeconomics and the Real World*. Oxford: Oxford University Press.

——(2001). *Econometrics: Alchemy or Science?* 2nd edition. Oxford: Oxford University Press.

——(2002). Forecast failure, expectations formation, and the Lucas critique. Econometrics of Policy Evaluation, Special Issue of *Annales d'Economie et de Statistique*, **66–67**, 21–40.

——(2003). Forecasting pitfalls. *Bulletin of EU and US Inflation and Macroeconomic Analysis*, **100**, 65–82.

Hendry, D. F. (2004). Exogeneity and causality in non-stationary economic processes. In Welfe, A. (ed.), *New Directions in Macromodelling*, pp. 21–48. Amsterdam: North Holland.

——(2005). Bridging the gap: Linking economics and econometrics. In Diebolt, C. and Kyrtsou, C. (eds.), *New Trends in Macroeconomics*. Berlin: Springer Verlag.

——and Ericsson, N. R. (2001). *Understanding Economic Forecasts*. Cambridge, MA: MIT Press.

Hendry, D. F., and Krolzig, H.-M. (2001). *Automatic Econometric Model Selection*. London: Timberlake Consultants Press.

——and Mizon, G. E. (1998). Exogeneity, causality, and co-breaking in economic policy analysis of a small econometric model of money in the UK. *Empirical Economics*, **23**, 267–294.

——and Mizon, G. E. (1999). The pervasiveness of Granger causality in econometrics. In Engle, R. F. and White, H. (eds.), *Cointegration, Causality and Forecasting*, pp. 102–134. Oxford: Oxford University Press.

————(2000). On selecting policy analysis models by forecast accuracy. In Atkinson, A. B. Glennerster, H. and Stern, N. H. (eds.), *Putting Economics to Work: Volume in Honour of Michio Morishima*. London School of Economics: STICERD.

——and Wallis, K. F. (eds.) (1984). *Econometrics and Quantitative Economics*. Oxford: Basil Blackwell.

——Pagan, A. R., and Sargan, J. D. (1984). Dynamic specification. In Griliches, Z. and Intriligator, M. D. (eds.), *Handbook of Econometrics*, Volume 2–3, Chapter 18. Amsterdam: North-Holland.

——and Richard, J.-F. (1982). On the formulation of empirical models in dynamic econometrics. *Journal of Econometrics*, **20**, 3–33.

Imbens, G. and Newey, W. (2003). Identification and estimation of triangular simultaneous equations models without additivity. MIT Department of Economics Working Paper.

Johansen, S. (1991). Estimation and hypothesis testing of cointegration vectors in Gaussian vector autoregressive models. *Econometrica*, **59**, 1551–1580.

Jordà, Ò. (2007). Simultaneous confidence regions for impulse responses. UC Davis Department of Economics Working Paper.

——and Marcellino, M. (2007). Path forecast evaluation. UC Davis Department of Economics Working Paper.

Lehmann, E. (1974). *Nonparametrics: Statistical Methods Based on Ranks*. San Francisco: Holden-Day.

Li, Q. and Racine, J. (2007). *Nonparametric Econometrics: Theory and Practice*. Princeton, NJ: Princeton University Press.

Lucas, R. (1976). Econometric policy evaluation: A critique. *Carnegie-Rochester Conference Series on Public Policy*, **1**, 19–46.

Pitt, M. and Shephard, N. (1999). Filtering via simulation: Auxiliary particle filters. *Journal of the American Statistical Association*, **94**, 590–599.

Robins, J. (1997). Causal inference from complex longitudinal data. In Berkane, M. (ed.), *Latent Variable Modeling and Applications to Causality*, pp. 69–117. New York: Springer-Verlag.

Romer, C. and Romer, D. (1989). Does monetary policy matter? *NBER Macroeconomics Annual*, 121–170.

Strotz, R. and Wold, H. (1960). Recursive vs. nonrecursive systems: An attempt at synthesis. *Econometrica*, **28**, 417–427.

Tadić, V. and Doucet, A. (2002). Exponential forgetting and geometric ergodicity in state-space models. *Proceedings of the 41st IEEE Conference on Decision and Control*. IEEE Press.

White, H. (2001). *Asymptotic Theory for Econometricians*. New York: Academic Press.

——(2006). Time-series estimation of the effects of natural experiments. *Journal of Econometrics*, **135**, 527–566.
——and Chalak, K. (2007a). Identifying effects of endogenous causes in nonseparable systems using covariates. UCSD Department of Economics Discussion Paper.
————(2007b). Settable systems: An extension of Pearl's causal model with optimization, equilibrium, and learning. UCSD Department of Economics Discussion Paper.

4

Autometrics

*Jurgen A. Doornik**

4.1 Introduction

David Hendry has developed and advocated the use of general-to-specific procedures for model selection over many years, see the collection of his earlier papers in 'Econometrics: Alchemy or Science?', Hendry (2000). As a result of this, the 'battery of diagnostic tests' has become a salient feature of econometric software. Nonetheless, many practitioners found the application of the 'LSE' or 'Hendry' methodology quite difficult. On top of this, 'data-mining' had become a pejorative term in econometrics, partially as a result of the experiments by Lovell (1983).[1]

A sea change has followed the work by Hoover and Perez (1999). They revisited the experiments of Lovell (1983), and, helped by a 1000-fold increase in computational power, implemented an automated version of the approach advocated by David Hendry. To their surpise, the artificial practitioner adopting the general-to-specific (GETS) procedure did very well.

As could be expected, David Hendry was greatly interested in these results, and, together with Hans-Martin Krolzig, immediately set about replicating the results. Hendry and Krolzig proposed some improvements to the algorithm of Hoover and Perez (Hendry and Krolzig, 1999; Hendry and Krolzig, 2005), and considered the theoretical aspects of model selection in several papers, see Hendry and Krolzig (2005) in particular. In addition, they created PcGets, a user-friendly computer program aimed at the empirical modeller, see Hendry and Krolzig (2001).

In this chapter, I introduce Autometrics, a third implementation of GETS model selection. Because Autometrics is based on the same principles, it

* This research was supported by ESRC grant RES-062-23-0061. Helpful comments and suggestions from David Hendry and Bert Nielsen are gratefully acknowledged.

[1] Despite the fact that Lovell only considered three simple search methods: forward selection (a form of stepwise regression), maximum $\bar{R}^2$, and max-min t, on a very small annual data set (at least from a current perspective).

has much in common with the approaches of Hoover–Perez and Hendry–Krolzig. In particular, the general properties should remain valid (Hendry and Krolzig, 2005). There are also some differences, as discussed below, which result in somewhat improved operational characteristics.

PcGets has many control parameters that need calibration, documented in Hendry and Krolzig (2003), resulting in a 'liberal' and 'conservative' strategy.[2] Autometrics does not have quite as many, but still needs extensive testing to set default choices for parameters, and to assess its practical operation. Reporting on these experiments is the second objective of this chapter.

4.2 Main Aspects of the Automated GETS Algorithms

There are five main ingredients in the algorithm proposed by Hoover and Perez (1999):

1. General unrestricted model. The GUM[3] is the starting point for the model reduction procedure, and provides the initial information set. The GUM must be relevant, that is, provide sufficient information on the process that is modelled, and statistically well-behaved. The latter property is checked with a set of diagnostic tests. The objective is to create a 'congruent' initial model, see Hendry and Nielsen (2007, Ch. 20).

2. Multiple path search. Each insignificant variable in the GUM defines a reduction path. The first path is entered by deleting the most insignificant variable (that is, the one with the lowest absolute t-value). This path continues by deleting the most insignificant variable, each time re-estimating the model. The path terminates when all variables are significant. But note that other criteria will be used as well. With k insignificant variables, there are k paths. Hoover–Perez decided to follow 10 paths at most.[4]

3. Encompassing test. A second criteria for a model reduction to fail is when the current model fails to encompass the GUM. The model is always nested in the GUM, and this test is implemented as a simple F-test on the removed variables. In that case, the variable is kept in the model (despite being insignificant), and the next variable in line is considered. I shall refer to this specific encompassing test as: 'backtesting with respect to the GUM'. The current reduction is not allowed to fail the backtesting criteria. Since such backtesting is at a user-defined level, this stage is intended to limit the loss of information (relative to the GUM) that is tolerated in the reduction.

2 Although it was found that many of these were off-setting.

3 This terminology was introduced by Hendry–Krolzig.

4 Their motivation was to mimic the empirical modeller adopting GETS, rather than trying to improve on this using computer automation.

4. Diagnostic testing. In addition, every estimated model is subjected to a battery of diagnostic tests. When any test fails, the current reduction is rejected, and the next in line considered. Hoover–Perez use tests for normality, residual correlation, residual ARCH, as well as an in-sample Chow test. There is also an out-of-sample Chow test, which requires that some data is held back (10% here).

5. Tiebreaker. It is possible that every path reduces to the same terminal model. In this case there is a unique final model, at the cost of much redundant computation. In general, though, there can be multiple terminal models, all of which are valid reductions of the GUM. The user may have economic or aesthetic justifications to prefer one terminal over another. A fully automated procedure must decide on a final model; Hoover and Perez (1999) adopt the best fitting terminal model, while Hoover and Perez (2004) use the minimum Schwarz Criterion.

Hendry and Krolzig (1999) and Hendry and Krolzig (2001) extend the algorithm in three principal directions:

1. Presearch. Five types of presearches are added to reduce the computational effort as well as the empirical size: two on lags, one on variables (that is, the same variable at different lag lengths) and two more on groups of insignificant coefficients.

2. Multiple-path search. Hendry–Krolzig follow all paths, rather than the first 10. They also create additional search paths by working on blocks of regressors, selecting all whose individual insignificance exceeds a certain level. Hendry–Krolzig choose 6 levels for the 'liberal' (5%) strategy, adding 6 search paths, and 5 for the conservative (1%) strategy.

3. Iteration. Hoover–Perez perform one round of multiple-path searches. Hendry–Krolzig propose an iterative procedure as follows: form the union of the terminal candidate models after the first round, delete any model that is an invalid reduction of this union (an encompassing test), if necessary form the union again and run the encompassing tests again, until no further terminals are deleted. This union of surviving terminals makes a new 'GUM'[5] which is the starting point for a completely new run of the whole algorithm. This process is iterated until convergence (the new GUM is the same as the previous GUM), after which the tiebreaker chooses a final model.

Hendry and Krolzig modify three additional aspects:

1. Tiebreaker. The minimum Schwarz Criterion as used as the default tiebreaker, with AIC and Hannan-Quinn as an option.

2. Out-of-sample testing. There is a trade-off between holding data back for out-of-sample testing, and using a larger sample for model estimation.

[5] Perhaps it would be better to call it a SUM: specific unrestricted model.

Lynch and Vital-Ahuja (1998) study this in more detail, and conclude that the latter is preferable. Hendry and Krolzig (2004) revisit this within the context of model selection, reaching a similar conclusion: holding data back reduces the extent to which wrong variables are selected, but at the same time makes it harder to find those that matter. In the methods that we consider this trade-off can be controlled directly through the significance levels that are chosen. Then, split sample methods provide a less transparent mechanism, which tend to cost more than they gain (also see Hoover and Perez, 2004 footnote 12).

3. Invalid GUM. Hoover–Perez remove replications for which the GUM fails two or more diagnostic tests from their simulation experiments; if only one test fails, it is removed from the criterion set. Hendry–Krolzig retain all such cases, adjusting the level of diagnostic testing instead. If the GUM fails one or more test at p-value p_d (with a default of $p_d = 0.01$), then each failed test is made less strict by raising its p_d to a point where the test passes. The new level is then maintained throughout.

This approach allows model selection to work with an invalid GUM. But it should be noted that it invalidates a fundamental assumption of the method.

The Autometrics algorithm follows on from the Hendry–Krolzig algorithm, aiming to improve on the implementations by Hoover–Perez and Hendry–Krolzig (as envisaged by Hoover and Perez, 2004, p. 790):

1. Presearch. The presearch is an ad hoc addition to the algorithm, which has been getting more complex over time. This is particularly true for variable-based presearch. The automated GETS algorithms are so involved because they are designed to handle complex correlations between (sets of) variables. The candidate sets for the presearches are constructed in simplistic ways, and once a variable is removed, it cannot reappear. This works well when the DGP consists of only a few highly significant variables, because the power is hardly affected and the size improves. Or when the DGP consists of orthogonal variables, when it is much easier to construct the relevant sets. However, in general we don't know the state of nature. This argument applies more weakly to lag-length reduction, because most modellers tend to have a preference for shorter over longer lags.

The objective of Autometrics is to create an algorithm that can function without (but may still be improved somewhat by a presearch).

2. Search paths. The multiple-path search is an unstructured way of searching the model space (that is, all possible sets of the variables in the GUM): many paths may turn out to be the same, while other paths are left unsearched. Hoover–Perez motivate this approach by wanting to de-emphasize the mechanical nature of the search. However, this is one aspect at which computers are much better than humans. Autometrics considers the whole search space from the outset, but may discard parts in a systematic way. This tree-search method is considered in section 4.3.1.

3. Scope. The algorithm can have wider use than regression models only, therefore Autometrics is implemented entirely within the likelihood framework (of which regression is a special case).[6]

4. Efficiency. The aim of Autometrics is to improve computational efficiency, for example by avoiding repeated estimation of the same model, delayed diagnostic testing, and remembering terminals between iterations.

The next section considers these aspects in more detail. Readers who are not interested in these details, or in the calibration experiments (section 4.4, 4.5), can jump straight to the comparison with Hoover–Perez and PcGets (section 4.6) or a practical illustration (section 4.7).

4.3 The Autometrics Algorithm

4.3.1 *Tree Search*

The starting point for Autometrics is the whole space of models generated by the variables in the initial model. At every node in this tree is a unique model which can be estimated. Then, the subnodes on the next level can be ordered according to increasing significance of the variables in the model.

Figure 4.1 provides an example. With four variables ABCD in the GUM, there are 4! possible unique models (the ordering of variables within a model is irrelevant), represented by solid dots in the figure. The GUM is at the root, the next model is obtained by removing A, then removing AB, etc.[7] However, models are invariant to the ordering of the variables they consist of. The redundant models are represented by an open circle; the first open circle in the rightmost column would be D. Only the unique 2^4 models are labelled in Figure 4.1.

The root node in Figure 4.1 is the GUM, model ABCD. With A the most insignificant variable in the GUM, the next model would be without A, which is model BCD. This is followed by CD, when B is the most insignificant in BCD. If, on the other hand, D would be most insignificant in model BCD, then D would be the first candidate for removal. In that case we would need to change the labelling in the graph of the tree. Within the regression context, the significance of each variable in a model is based on the individual t-value.

[6] This is for future research: different model types have their own relevant tests, and may have different categories of parameters. For example, in an ARFIMA model with regressors the ARFIMA parameters may need to be treated separately.

[7] Figure 4.1 is a tree that lies on its side. We move through this representation of the tree from left to right and top to bottom starting at the root (skipping through the nodes in parentheses): ABCD, BCD, CD, D, (CD), C, (BCD), BD, B, (BCD), BC, (ABCD), ACD, ...

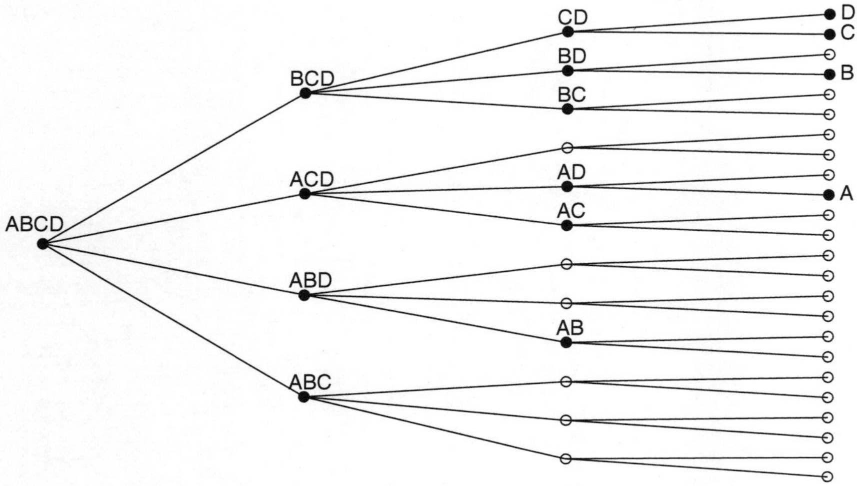

FIG. 4.1. Search tree: All unique models starting from a GUM with variables ABCD.

Once the complete branch that started with deleting A has finished, we can continue with the next major branch that starts from the GUM by deleting variable B. Note that variable A is always part of the models in this branch: ACD, AD, A, AC.

The resulting tree of Figure 4.1 is a unique representation of the model space, and, if we move through it from left to right and top to bottom all possible models will be estimated.[8]

The Hoover–Perez and Hendry–Krolzig multiple-path search is depicted in Figure 4.2, assuming that the ordering always stays the same. The first path in the Autometrics search corresponds to the first of the paths considered by Hoover–Perez and Hendry–Krolzig, but after that the methods diverge.

4.3.2 *Efficient Tree Search*

For k insignificant variables, there are 2^k models, so visiting each node is not feasible in practice. Autometrics implements several strategies to skip nodes and move efficiently through the tree. Figure 4.3 shows the order in which the nodes are visited.[9] Remember that, at each node, the subnodes are reordered with the most insignificant variable first. This is not visible in the graph, unless we allow the letters to refer to different variables (so, as depicted here, in the model CD, C is the most insignificant variable).

[8] Of course, other orderings of the tree are feasible. When all regressors are orthogonal, this ordering is most likely to yield the final model first.

[9] Strictly speaking, the tree contains the empty model after node 4, which is omitted from the graph.

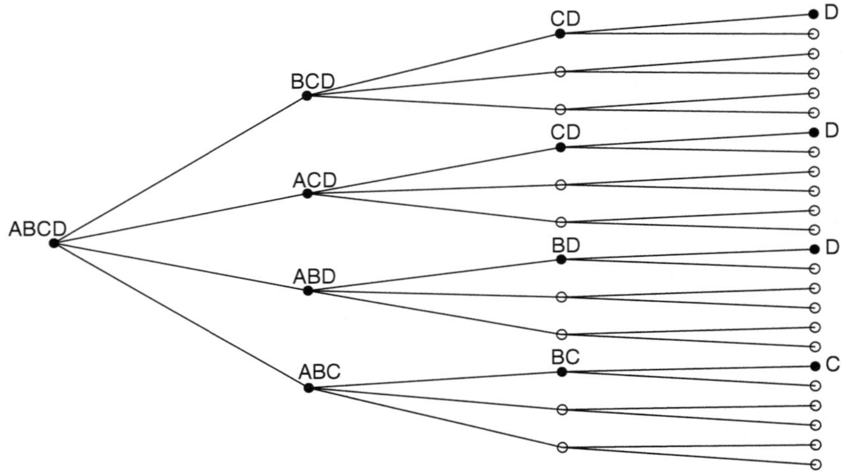

FIG. **4.2.** Multiple-path search: Representation for a GUM with variables ABCD.

Also note that the relevant information is the reduction path from the GUM: for model 12, AC, this is $1 \to 9 \to 12$. The search algorithm can be designed in such a way that we always have the path back to the GUM in memory, *k* models at most, rather than the full tree.

Autometrics uses the following principles to advance the tree search:

Pruning. By default, every reduction involves removing one variable. The first and most obvious principle is that, if a deletion fails or the reduced model fails (on backtesting or diagnostic testing), the node is invalid. Then all subsequent subbranches of the tree can be pruned (ignored).

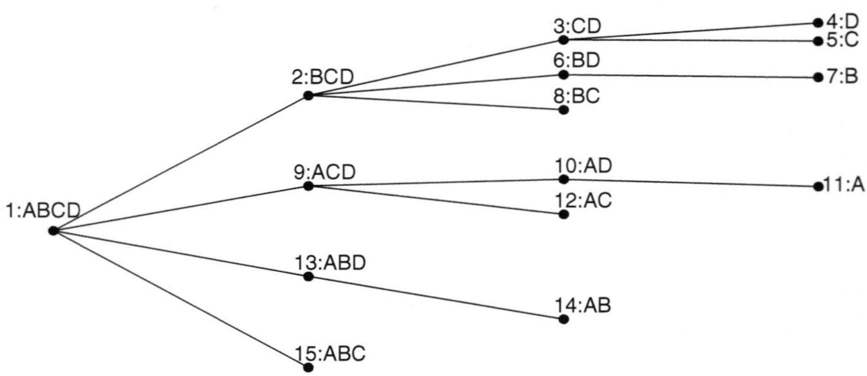

FIG. **4.3.** Search tree: All unique models starting from a GUM with variables ABCD, numbered according to the order in which the search algorithm considers them.

Starting from model BCD of Figure 4.3: if the variable B cannot be removed, there is no need to consider models CD, D, or C. As another example, if model CD fails on the backtest with respect to the GUM, subnodes of CD need not be considered, and we can fall through to the next node at the same level, BD.

This pruning is governed by the main Autometrics p-value p_a, which determines the significance level below which a variable cannot be deleted from the model. Ideally, p_a defines the empirical behaviour of the procedure: the fraction of irrelevant variables retained (the 'size') is close to p_a.

Bunching. Instead of always removing a single variable at a time, it can be useful to consider groups. In other words, a bunch of branches. Bunching works as follows: from the current node, along the generated search path, variables are grouped together provided their individual insignificance merits this. Deletion is then tried as a block. If successful, we can jump straight ahead, thus replacing several separate steps with a single blocked step. If deletion fails, the algorithm backtracks until a bunch is found that can be deleted—if necessary, to a bunch of size one.

As an illustration, assume that in the second node of Figure 4.3, model BCD, the variables BC are both insignificant enough to be bunching candidates. Then we start with an F-test on BC jointly. If successful, this gives us the next node D directly. Otherwise we backtrack to deleting B only (ie model CD).

The significance test of the bunch is done at p_a, while the p-value p_b determines the amount of bunching, as described in section 4.4.3. If p_b is too high, there will be excessive backtracking, which is costly. Also, terms that may matter can then hide between insignificant ones. Setting it too low effectively switches bunching off, at some computational cost. By default $p_b = \max\{\frac{1}{2}p_a^{1/2}, p_a^{3/4}\}$, see section 4.4.2.

Chopping. Chopping refers to the permanent removal of a 'highly' insignificant variable from the branches of the model. When a bunch is insignificant enough, the whole bunch could get the chop. Chopping saves on computation, but could possibly mean that some combinations of variables are missed.

Continuing the example for node BCD. If B is insignificant enough to be considered for chopping, then, after visiting CD, D, and C, we don't consider any nested model with B in it. In other words, after C we fall through to node ACD. If, on the other hand, BC can be chopped from BCD, then we only visit model D before falling through to node ACD.

The p-value p_c determines whether chopping is applied. By default $p_c = p_b$, see section 4.4.2.

Model contrasts. A terminal candidate model ('terminal') is a model that cannot be reduced any further on the adopted criteria. When a terminal has been found, there is no need to find the same model again. Because the tree is uniquely ordered, we can determine the minimal bunch along the current trajectory which must be deleted to give a different model. We can use this to our advantage to move more efficiently through the tree.

Suppose, for example, that model D was found as a terminal candidate, and the search has taken us to model 9:ACD. Whether A is significant or not, it is always kept in the models that originate from ACD; C and D are the 'free' variables. Model ACD nests D, and it is of no interest when D is already a terminal. Instead, at least CD has to be removed to find a different terminal, so this bunch can be tested immediately through an F-test at p_a.

Although the principles underlying pruning, chopping, and bunching are quite simple, implementing them in software involves some fairly complex administrative code.

The combination of bunching and chopping can be seen as a form of embedded presearch. However, here it is an integral part of the structure of the search procedure.

There is one fundamental aspect of the tree search which is very different from the multiple-path search. In the latter, all terminal candidate models have no insignificant variables left, unless further reduction failed because of diagnostic testing or backtesting with respect to the GUM. In the tree search, branches maintain insignificant variables by design. For example, any branch starting from model 13:ABD has AB in, which may or may not be significant. Therefore, we denote such a terminal candidate with insignificant variables as a 'semiterminal'. Only further refinement will turn a semiterminal into a proper terminal, which cannot be reduced any further. This is one of the issues considered in the next section.

4.3.3 *Further Details of the Autometrics Algorithm*

Several aspects are not yet specified, or handled differently in Autometrics:

Backtracking on diagnostic failure. Unlike the algorithms of Hoover–Perez and Hendry–Krolzig, diagnostic checking is not performed when the reduction is in progress. Instead, the diagnostic tests are only evaluated when a terminal is reached. Upon failure, we backtrack until a valid model is found. This is feasible because the path back to the GUM is available. There are two benefits to this approach. First, diagnostic testing is relatively costly (roughly five times more than model estimation). Second, diagnostic failure could be a temporary blockage on a reduction path: it is possible (and indeed happens in practice) that only some intermediate models fail.

Diagnostic failure of the GUM. The execution of diagnostic testing follows Hendry–Krolzig: if at the GUM one or more tests fail at p_d (with a default of $p_d = 0.01$), the significance level of those tests is made less strict. Autometrics differs in that it tries to restore diagnostic validity along the way. When there are multiple terminal candidates and some pass at the original levels, then only the successful terminals are kept, and the p-values reset to the original level.

Root branches. The GUM is the root model, and the root branches are the models with just one variable deleted (BCD, ACD, ABD, ABC in Figures 4.1 and 4.3; these are also the starting point for the multiple-path searches of Hoover–Perez and Hendry–Krolzig). By default Autometrics starts applying the bunching and chopping only from a root branch, not directly from the root. This means that each variable is used as a 'pivot' for entering the tree search. As a consequence, each variable will have an opportunity to enter the set of final models.

Model contrasts. There are two ways in which model contrasts are used in Autometrics. *Union contrast* determines the contrasting bunch with respect to the union of the current set of terminal candidates. Union contrast is used while the current GUM (the new union of the set of terminals) still changes between iterations: there is no need yet to find all possible models—our primary interest is to find variables that should be in the GUM. *Terminal contrast* determines the smallest bunch that would yield a model that is different from any of the current terminals. This mode is used at the end when the current GUM is fixed.

Branches with nested terminals. A branch has a nested terminal if any restriction on that branch (possibly invalid) could yield that terminal candidate. Autometrics search is split in two parts. Paths with nested terminals are skipped in the first round. The second round then follows all root paths with nested terminals using union contrast (or terminal contrast at the end) to jump ahead in the branches.

Insignificant variables. All but one of the root branches start with keeping one or more insignificant variable in the model. Some of these may still be insignificant in the terminal candidate models that were found, that is they are semiterminals, as discussed in section 4.3.2. To turn these into terminal candidates, the tree search reduction procedure is applied to it (but without using root branches). Another potential source of semiterminals is the backtracking from diagnostic failure. Such semiterminals are refined in the same way, until they are proper terminals.

Any irreduceable terminal candidate model can still have insignificant variables from failure in backtesting against the GUM or diagnostic failure.

Presearch. Only a presearch on lag length is switched on by default. The method used is the so-called extended lag reduction, see section 4.4.5.

4.3.4 *Iterative Search*

The following steps describe the iterative procedure as used in Autometrics. The steps that involve the tree search are labelled in bold.

0.0 Estimate the initial GUM.
This initializes the search procedure.

0.1 (optional) Add dummy variables for outliers.
If any are detected, the expanded model becomes the initial GUM.

0.2 (optional) Lag-length pre-search.

0.3 Test all regressors at a loose significance level.
If passed, accept the empty model as the final model, provided diagnostic testing is satisfied, then stop.

1.0 Set $i = 0$.
The starting point for the current iteration is GUM 0 (this may be the same as the initial GUM), which has k free regressors.

1.1 (convergence) If all regressors in the GUM are significant then stop.
This is at a slightly more stringent p-value to allow for 'squeezing', §4.5.2.

1.2 Update the diagnostic p-values.
Ideally, the user ensures that the initial GUM passes the diagnostic tests. However, when this is not the case, the p-value for each failed test statistic is increased. Subsequently, the p-values are adjusted downwards again if possible.

1.3 **Run reduction over the root branches**.
Terminal candidate models ('terminals') are collected as the search progresses. Any subtree that has a previously found terminal nested in it is skipped to speed up the search. This will result in one or more terminal.

1.4 **Run reduction to search for nested terminals**.
Revisit the subtrees that were skipped before. At each point it is possible to compute the minimal contrast with a known terminal to jump ahead to a possible new (non-nested) terminal. If the union of terminals after the previous step 1.3 is smaller than the union from the previous iteration, then use union contrast, otherwise use terminal contrast.

1.5 Remove terminals that fail diagnostics.
If the p-values p_d for diagnostic testing had to be adjusted downwards, and there are some terminals that pass at the original p-value, then keep only those terminal models which pass and reset p_d to the original value.

1.6 Form the union of the terminal models.
The union is called the *current GUM* or GUM $i + 1$.

1.7 Remove terminals that fail backtesting.
When using the default Autometrics settings, this step is skipped, because backtesting with respect to GUM 0 has already been done as an integral part of the tree search: there are no terminals that fail.
Optionally, the PcGets default of backtesting with respect to the current GUM can be adopted instead. In that case, there may be terminals that fail the encompassing test against the new GUM.

1.8 Remove terminals with insignificant variables.
When using the default Autometrics settings, this step is skipped, because a terminal remains a terminal candidate for subsequent iterations.
However, this step is relevant when the PcGets default is used in 1.7: backtesting is with respect to the current GUM, which changes between iterations. So a terminal candidate with insignificant variables may not be a terminal next time.

1.9 Increment i and continue to step 1.1.
GUM i (determined at 1.6, but now i has been incremented), is the new base for the search. Note that steps 1.7 and 1.8 (when they are not skipped) remove terminals but do not modify the GUM. This is different from the PcGets implementation.

In addition to the tree search, notable differences with PcGets are: reduced presearch, an attempt to restore original diagnostic p-values during the iteration, use of GUM 0 for backtesting, a different way (more gentle) of constructing the new GUM for the next iteration, and survival of terminals between iterations.

4.4 Calibration

In addition to the choice of p-value, p_a, at which the Autometrics reduction is executed, there are some design parameters of the algorithm which can be changed. We run calibration experiments to find a balanced default setting for these, as well as design strategies that focus on different goals.

Table 4.1. Design aspects that are determined through calibration

Bunch and chop factor	
1	bunching and chopping is done at p_a, the deletion p-value;
a	bunching and chopping is done at $a p_a$, $a = 2,4,6,9$.
Tree search method	
1	prune only—delete one variable at a time;
2	prune & chop—delete one variable at a time and allow for chopping the deleted variable;
3	prune & bunch—delete one or more variable at a time, the criterion for addition becomes more stringent as the bunch grows;
4	prune & bunch & chop—as above, allowing for chopping of the bunch;
5	prune & bunch & chop aggressively—as above, but keeping the p-value for extending the bunch fixed.
Backtesting	
0	none;
1	initial GUM backtest;
2	GUM0 backtest (same as initial GUM when there is no presearch);
3	current GUM backtest.
Presearch	
0	none;
1	lag reduction;
2	lag reduction followed by variable reduction.

In the evaluation, we define the 'size' of the experiments as the proportion of irrelevant variables that survives the reduction process. If we start with n_1 irrelevant regressors, and are left with $\hat{n}_1$, the size is $\hat{n}_1/n_1$.[10] Ideally, this is roughly equal to p_a. 'Power'[11] reflects the success of the reduction: the proportion of relevant variables that is retained. This can be written as $\hat{n}_0/n_0$, where n_0 is the number of regressors in the DGP, and $\hat{n}_0$ the (subset) of those that are in the final model. In our experiments the GUM always nests the DGP.

In most cases there is a trade-off between size and power: a gain in power is achieved at a cost in size (ie both increase). Then it can be difficult to make a choice. Only rarely is it possible to decrease size and increase power simultaneously.

Table 4.1 summarizes the parameters that are to be determined, while Table 4.2 indicates which aspects are kept fixed. Throughout, the calibration experiments are run at several reduction p-values p_a.

4.4.1 *Experimental Design*

The experimental design closely resembles some of the experiments reported in Hendry and Krolzig (2005). The first three, labelled *static GUM* in Table 4.3,

[10] Hoover and Perez (1999) define size as the proportion of *significant* irrelevant variables: $\hat{n}_1^*/n_1$, which is smaller or equal to $\hat{n}_1/n_1$.

[11] Power and size are used somewhat differently here than in statistical testing. More recently we have started to experiment with the terms *potency* and *gauge* to avoid confusion.

Table 4.2. Design aspects that are kept fixed during calibration

Outlier detection	switched off,
Pretest on all variables jointly	at* $p_p = f(p_a^{0.8},5) \approx 5p_a^{0.8}$,
Squeezing	at $p_s = f(p_a,0.2) \approx p_a/5$,
Diagnostic testing	at $p_d = 0.01$,
Tiebreaker	Schwarz criterion (SC),
Iteration	until new GUM does not reduce any further,
Maximum terminals	20,
Diagnostic test set	Normality, AR(2), ARCH(2), Chow(50%), Hetero, see Hendry and Doornik (2007).

* $f(p,\alpha) = \alpha p$ if $0.94 \leq 1 + p(\alpha - 1) \leq 1.06$; $f(p,\alpha) = \frac{\alpha p}{1+p(\alpha-1)}$ otherwise.

correspond to Hendry and Krolzig's S_2, S_3, and S_4: the DGP has 8 regressors (all t-values are 2 in experiment 1, $t = 3$ in experiment 2, and $t = 4$ in experiment 3), while the GUM contains the DGP variables and an additional 22 irrelevant regressors; all regressors are generated as i.i.d standard normals.

The next three experiments (*dynamic GUM* in Table 4.3) correspond to those labelled JEDC in Hendry and Krolzig (2005), but with a larger GUM. The DGP has 5 variables at lag 0, with t-values 8,6,4,3,2 respectively; the GUM also includes the (irrelevant) first lag of these 5, plus lags zero and one of 7 irrelevant variables, as well as y_{t-1}. In this case, the regressors are created with autocorrelation, as a way to introduce correlation between regressors.

Table 4.3. Experimental design

DGP

$$y_t = \sum_{i=1}^{k_0} \beta_j x_{i,t} + u_t, \qquad u_t \sim \text{IN}[0,1],$$

$$x_{i,t} = \rho x_{i,t-1} + \upsilon_{i,t}, x_{i,0} = 0, i = 1,\ldots,k_0 + k_1 \qquad \upsilon_{i,t} \sim \text{IN}[0,(1-\rho)^2].$$

GUM

$$y_t = \gamma_0 + \delta_0 y_{t-1} + \sum_{i=1}^{k_0+k_1} \left(\gamma_j x_{i,t} + \delta_j x_{i,t-1}\right) + \epsilon_t, \quad \epsilon_t \sim \text{IN}[0,\sigma_\epsilon^2].$$

Experiments* 1,2,3 (*static GUM*)
$DGP: k_0 = 8, t_{\beta_1} = \ldots = t_{\beta_8} = \{2,3,4\}, \rho = 0,$
$GUM: \delta_i = 0, k_1 = 26$: 26 irrelevant regressors.

Experiments* 4,5,6 (*dynamic GUM*)
$DGP: k_0 = 5, t_{\beta_1}, \ldots, t_{\beta_5} = (8,6,4,3,2), \rho = \{0, 0.4, 0.8\},$
$GUM: k_1 = 7$: 20 irrelevant regressors (12 at lag 1).

Experiments* 7,8 (*small and large dynamic GUM*)
$DGP: k_0 = 5, t_{\beta_1}, \ldots, t_{\beta_5} = (2,3,4,6,8), \rho = 0,$
$GUM: k_1 = \{1,19\}$: 8 or 44 irrelevant regressors respectively.

* All regressions include a constant.

The final two experiments are a smaller and larger version of experiments 4–6, but with i.i.d. regressors.

$M = 1{,}000$ Monte Carlo replications are used throughout for sample sizes $T = 60,100,250$. The reduction p-values p_a are chosen as 0.001, 0.01, 0.05, 0.1, each requiring a separate run of the experiment. So the 8 experiments are run 12 times (3 sample size at 4 nominal p-values). The graphs show the result separated by sample size: 32 outcomes along each vertical line (8 experiments at 4 p-values). At each sample size, the experiments use exactly the same artificial data. The outcomes at $p_a = 0.1$ are shown as a circle, and their averages as a solid line; those at $p_a = 0.05$ are shown as a plus symbol, and their average as a dashed line; etc.

All simulations were implemented in Ox version 5, see Doornik (2007). Where timings are reported, it is relevant to know that the programs were run in single-threaded mode (`-rp1` command line switch) on a PC with a Core 2 Duo Q6600 running at 2.4 Ghz.

4.4.2 *Bunch and Chop Factor*

First we consider how the bunch and chop factor impacts on the algorithm. For this we keep the remainder of Table 4.1 fixed: the tree search method is 4 (prune & bunch & chop, these were introduced in section 4.3.2; additional detail is given in the next section), and backtesting is against GUM 0. Presearch is switched off until section 4.4.5. The p-value at which we bunch and chop is αp_a, with α displayed on the horizontal axis in Figure 4.4. So, for example, when $p_a = 0.05$, the bunching and chopping is at p-values 0.05,0.1, …,0.45.

Figure 4.4 shows that the choice of α has almost no impact on power (the middle three graphs, for sample sizes $T = 60,100,250$) for $p_a = 0.1$, but somewhat more as p_a falls. The size plots (top three) follow a similar pattern. There is a clearer pattern in terms of the time it takes to run a reduction: for $p_a = 0.1,0.05$ it slopes upwards, even at $T = 250$. But for the smallest p-value there is almost no impact.

The default value of α is chosen from these experiments as close to 2 for larger p-values, and much larger as the p-values get very small:

$$p_b = p_c = \max\left\{\frac{1}{2}p_a^{1/2}, p_a^{3/4}\right\}. \tag{4.1}$$

The following table shows which values of α are implied by (4.1):

p_a	0.25	0.1	0.05	0.01	0.001	0.0001
$p_b(= p_c)$	0.354	0.178	0.112	0.050	0.016	0.005
implicit $\alpha(= p_b/p_a)$	1.414	1.778	2.236	5.000	15.811	50.000

4.4.3 *Tree Search Method*

Although the bunching and chopping factor was chosen to balance time against the power/size performance, its overall impact is small. We now turn to the question of whether these operations matter at all.

We consider the 5 settings for the tree search method listed in Table 4.1. The first (*prune* = 1) is pruning only, which coincides with setting $p_b = p_c = 1$. In this case, a regressor is considered for deletion if its p-value is above p_a.

The remainder uses the default determined in (4.1). The second (*prune* = 2) is chopping only: one regressor at a time is considered for deletion (at p_a) and removed permanently from the search procedure when its significance is above p_c. The next case (*prune* = 3) is bunching only: regressors are grouped for deletion, if the whole group fails jointly, it is shrunk until the remaining group succeeds. The fourth case extends this by permanent removal (chopping) if the group's significance is above p_c. The aggressive case (*prune* = 5) differs from cases 3 and 4 in how the inital candidate group is determined.

The bunching in cases 3 and 4 works as follows. If a regressor's p-value is above p_a, it is considered for deletion. If it also is above $p_b \equiv p_b^*(1)$, bunching is started, adding variables as long as the *smallest p-value in the bunch* is above $p_b^*(k_b)$:

$$p_b^*(k_b) = p_b^{1/2}\left[1 - \left(1 - p_b^{1/2}\right)^{k_b}\right],$$

with k_b the size of the bunch. The following table gives some numerical examples:

p_a	0.25	0.1	0.05	0.01	0.001
$p_b = p_b^*(1) = p_c$	0.353	0.178	0.112	0.050	0.016
$p_b^*(2)$	0.497	0.281	0.186	0.089	0.030
$p_b^*(3)$	0.555	0.340	0.236	0.119	0.042
$p_b^*(5)$	0.588	0.394	0.291	0.161	0.062
$p_b^*(10)$	0.595	0.420	0.329	0.206	0.093

Of course, for the actual bunch to be deleted, its joint p-value must be above p_a (in addition to satisfying backtesting and diagnostic testing conditions).

In the aggressive case variables are added to the bunch as long as their individual significance is above p_b. The bunches are therefore allowed to be larger.

Figure 4.5 shows that pruning values 1–4 are almost identical in terms of size and power. There is a considerable difference in speed: *prune* = 4 takes about 2/3 of the time of single step deletion (*prune* = 1). Only at $T = 60$ is this

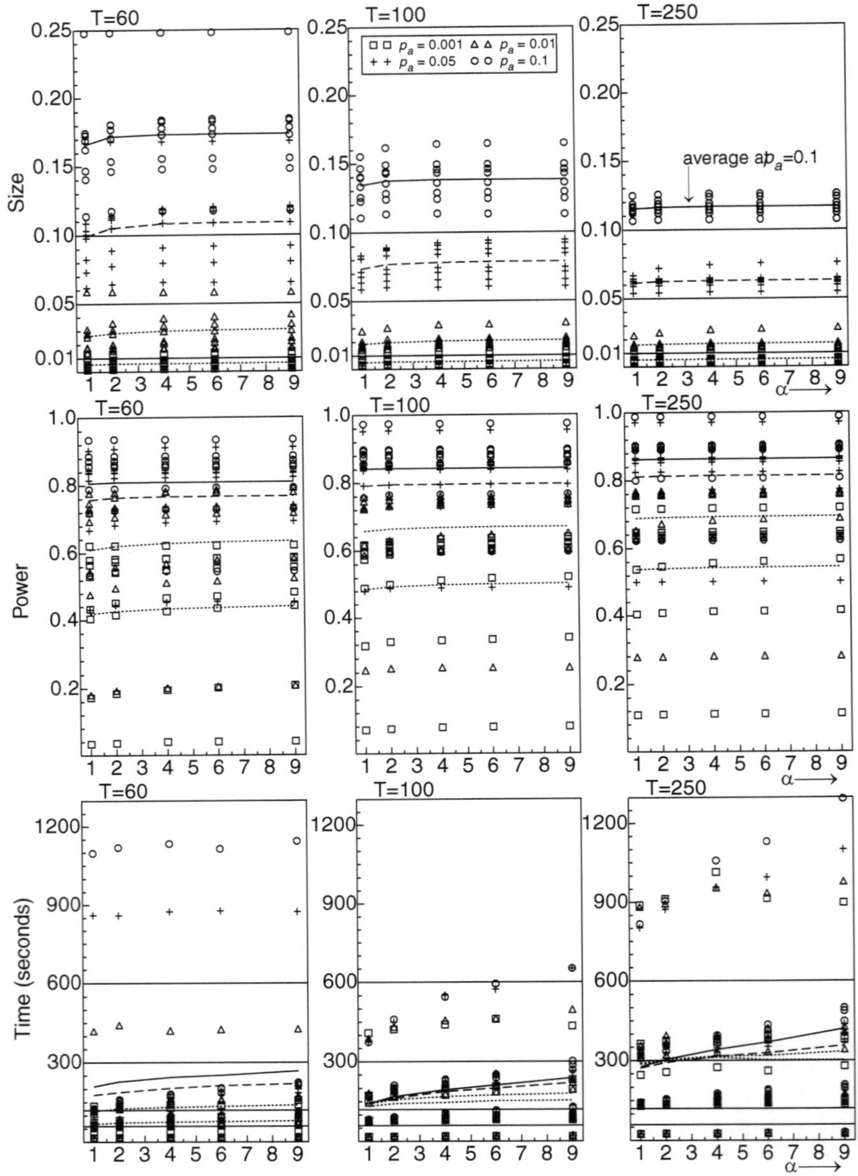

FIG. **4.4.** Chop & bunch factor: size (top three), power (middle three), and time (bottom three; in seconds for $M = 1{,}000$ replications) for chopping and bunching at αp_a: individual results and averages for each p_a (squares for $p_a = 0.001$, triangles for $p_a = 0.01$, plusses for $p_a = 0.05$, circles for $p_a = 0.1$).

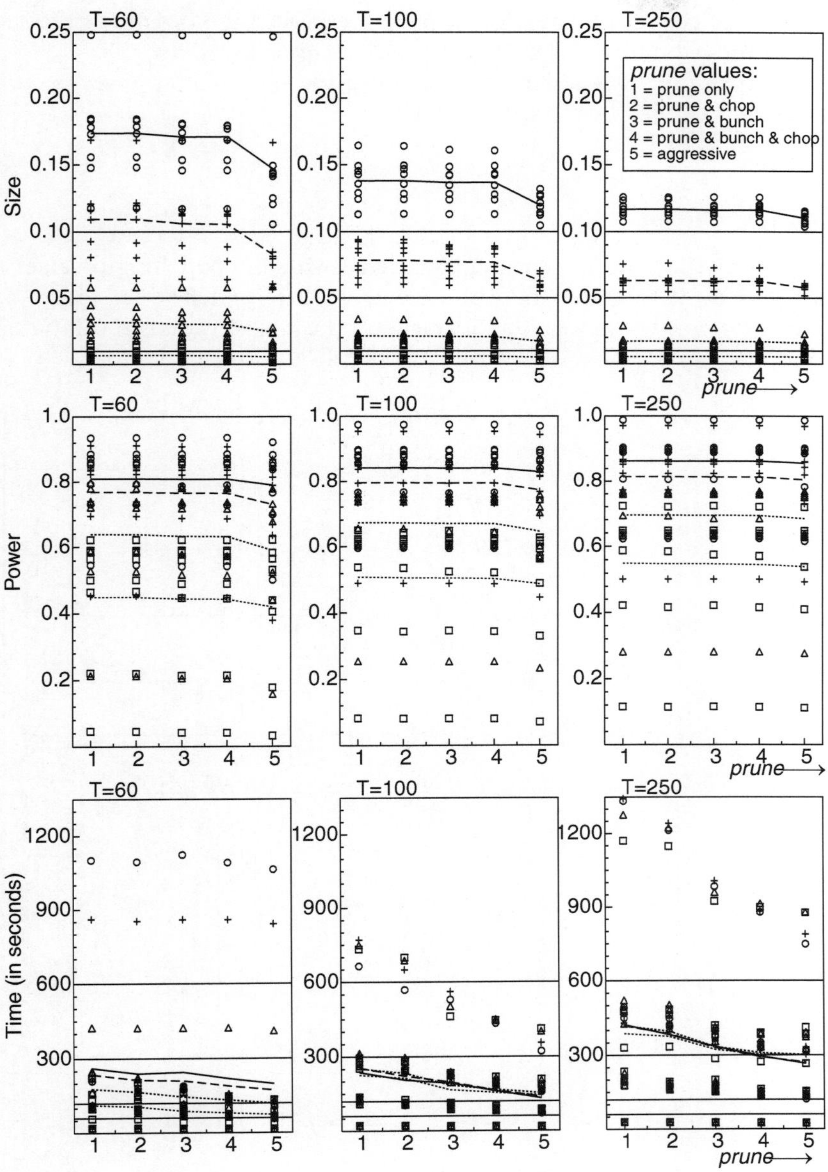

FIG. **4.5.** Tree search method: size (top three), power (middle three), and time (bottom three) for five pruning methods: individual results and averages for each p_a (squares for $p_a = 0.001$, triangles for $p_a = 0.01$, plusses for $p_a = 0.05$, circles for $p_a = 0.1$). Method 1: prune only, 2: prune & chop, 3: prune & bunch, 4: prune & bunch & chop, 5: aggressive.

less pronounced, mainly because the largest experiment is not much affected. Among these, we have a clear preference for *prune* = 4.

Aggressive pruning provides an additional speed-up, but at lower size and power. This will not be chosen as default.

4.4.4 *Backtesting*

The three backtesting modes are considered with the bunching p-value set according to (4.1), and *prune* = 4, the defaults determined so far. Figure 4.6 shows that no backtesting at all (value 0 on the x-axis) is disastrous: the size

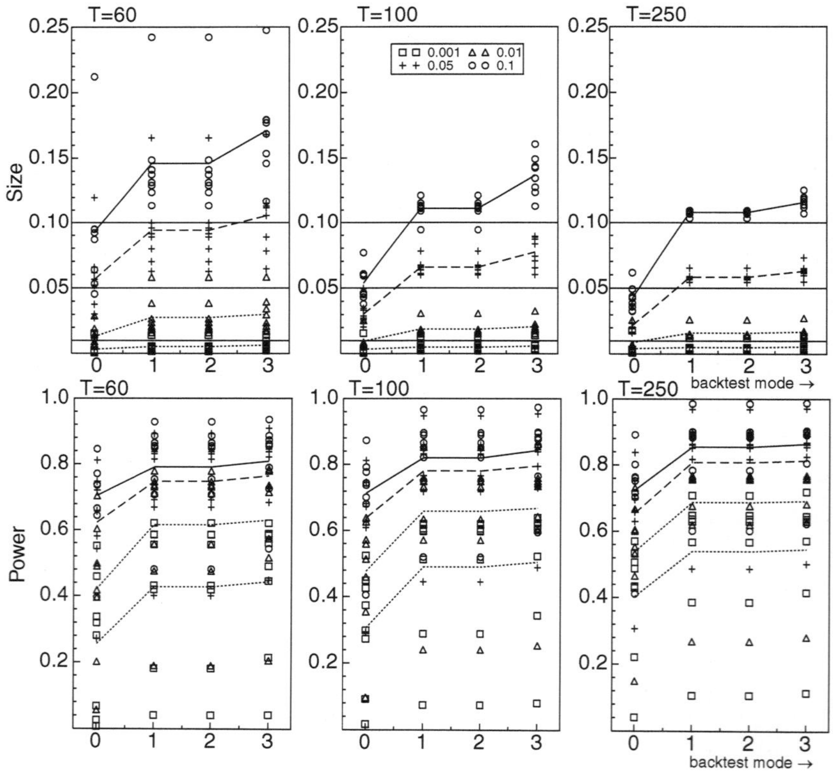

FIG. 4.6. Backtesting: size (top three) and power (bottom three) for three backtesting methods: individual results and averages for each p_a (squares for $p_a = 0.001$, triangles for $p_a = 0.01$, plusses for $p_a = 0.05$, circles for $p_a = 0.1$). Backtest mode 0: none, 1: w.r.t. initial GUM, 2: w.r.t. GUM0, 3: w.r.t. current GUM.

collapses as the sample size grows, while the power is much lower too. This applies *a fortiori* to backwards selection, also see Doornik (2008).

The other backtesting modes are: (1) backtesting with respect to the original GUM (value 1 on the x-axis) and (3) backtesting with respect to the most recent GUM. Surprisingly, this makes a difference in terms of size, but perhaps less so in terms of power, at least at the smaller sample sizes. Backtesting w.r.t. the original GUM also results in smaller dispersion of size between experiments. The timings of the experiments are unaffected by the choice of backtesting.

At this stage, backtesting modes 2 and 3 are identical. However, presearch adds another possible mode of backtesting.

4.4.5 *Presearch*

Presearch adds a new GUM before the tree search algorithm commences. The initial GUM is the GUM before any presearch is performed. GUM 0 is the GUM after the presearch.

Lag reduction groups the regressors by lag. Any variables that have no lags at all are excluded in the Autometrics implementation, while seasonals are not considered to be lagged. So, for example, constant, trend, and seasonals are not part of the regressors that are tested at lag zero. Also, lag presearch is skipped altogether if there are no lags in the model.

Three methods of presearch lag reduction and one method of variable reduction are considered:

- *Closed lag reduction* tests lags from the largest lag downwards, stopping as soon as a lag cannot be deleted. The following steps are taken:
  Collect all regressors at lag m, then if:

  1. no individual p-value is below $\max\{p^*_{p,1}(k_p), p_s\}$, with p_s defined in Table 4.2,
  $$p^*_{p,1}(k_p) = 1 - \left(1 - p_{p,1}\right)^{k_p}, \tag{4.2}$$
  and where k_p is the number of regressors involved (so the marginal p-value decreases as k_p grows), and
  2. their joint p-value in the most recent model is above p_p, and
  3. backtesting with respect to initial GUM and diagnostic testing conditions are satisfied,

  then delete all these regressors, set this to the current model, and continue with lag $m - 1$.
- *Common lag reduction* tests all remaining lags starting from the least significant.

Determine the joint significance of each lag in the starting model (ie the model after common lag reduction), and order the lags with the most insignificant first. Then if:

1. their joint p-value in the starting model is above p_p, and
2. no individual p-value is below $\max\{p^*_{p,1}(k_p), p_s\}$, and
3. their joint p-value in the most recent model is above p_p, and
4. backtesting with respect to initial GUM and diagnostic testing conditions are satisfied,

then delete all these regressors, set this to the current model, and continue with the next lag.

- *Common X-lag reduction* is the same as the previous method, but now the lagged dependent variables are excluded from the lag reduction.
- *Variable reduction* is similar to common lag reduction, but focusing on variables rather than lags:
Determine the joint significance of variable in the starting model (ie the model after lag presearch), and order the variables with the most insignificant first. Then if:

1. the joint p-value in the starting model is above p_p,
2. no individual p-value is below $\max\{p^*_{p,1}(k_p), p_s\}$, and
3. backtesting with respect to initial GUM and diagnostic testing conditions are satisfied,

then delete all the regressors belonging to this variable.

Four levels of presearches are considered in the simulations:

0 no presearch,

1 lag reduction (closed followed by common lag reduction),

a 'Model' 1 is determined by two lag presearches, first closed, then common.

b 'Model' 2 is determined by running the two lag presearches in opposite order.

c Remove any failed model.

d Form the union of the remaining models (usually both survive the previous step), which is now GUM 0.

2 extended lag reduction (closed followed by two passes of common lag reduction),

a 'Model' 1 is determined by three lag presearches, first closed, then common, then common on X's only.

b 'Model' 2 is determined by running the three lag presearches in opposite order.

c Remove any failed model.

d Form the union of the two models, which is now GUM 0.

3 lag reduction (closed, common) followed by variable reduction.

a 'Model' 1 is determined by two lag presearches, first closed, then common, followed by variable reduction.

b 'Model' 2 is determined by running variable presearch, common, and closed lag presearches.

c Remove any failed model.

d Form the union of the two models, which is now GUM 0.

The presearch cut-off p-value are set to $p_{p,1} = p_c$ and $p_p = f(p_a^{0.8}, 5) \approx 5p_a^{0.8}$:

p_a	0.25	0.1	0.05	0.01	0.001
p_p	0.711	0.485	0.334	0.114	0.020
$p^*_{p,1}(1) = p_c$	0.353	0.178	0.112	0.050	0.016

These were chosen to be conservative with presearch removal, and no other values were tried (but could lead to better or worse results).

Figure 4.7 gives the results for the four presearch settings. Note that 3 out of 8 experiments are static, and are unaffected by the presearch lag reduction. Lag reduction is beneficial here: the size is reduced at no cost in power, while time is also substantially reduced.

Subsequent variable reduction is less clear cut, because, while power improves, the size also deteriorates. These effects are offsetting. For example, comparing presearch methods 2 and 3 at $T = 250$, the average size at $p_a = 0.001$ is halfway between the average sizes for $p_a = 0.001$ and 0.01 using method 2. But so is the power: the same power gain can be achieved using method 2 by raising p_a. Note also that the size dispersion increases. At $T = 250$ and $p_a = 0.01$ the size for lag presearch ranges from around 0.010 to 0.017 for methods 1 and 2, but increases to 0.018–0.057 when variable presearch is used.

To study the effect of lag presearch more closely, we repeat experiments 4–8 (see Table 4.3), but now adding all variables up to lag 2 in the GUM. Denoting the new experiments with an asterisk, then experiments 4*,5*,6* have 33 irrelevant variables, and 7* has 15. Finally, 8* has 64 irrelevant variables, so we omit $T = 60$. The results for these extended experiments are in Figure 4.8. The advantages of lag presearch are accentuated. Subsequent variable reduction is again ineffective, although the increase in size dispersion is now only visible at $T = 100$.

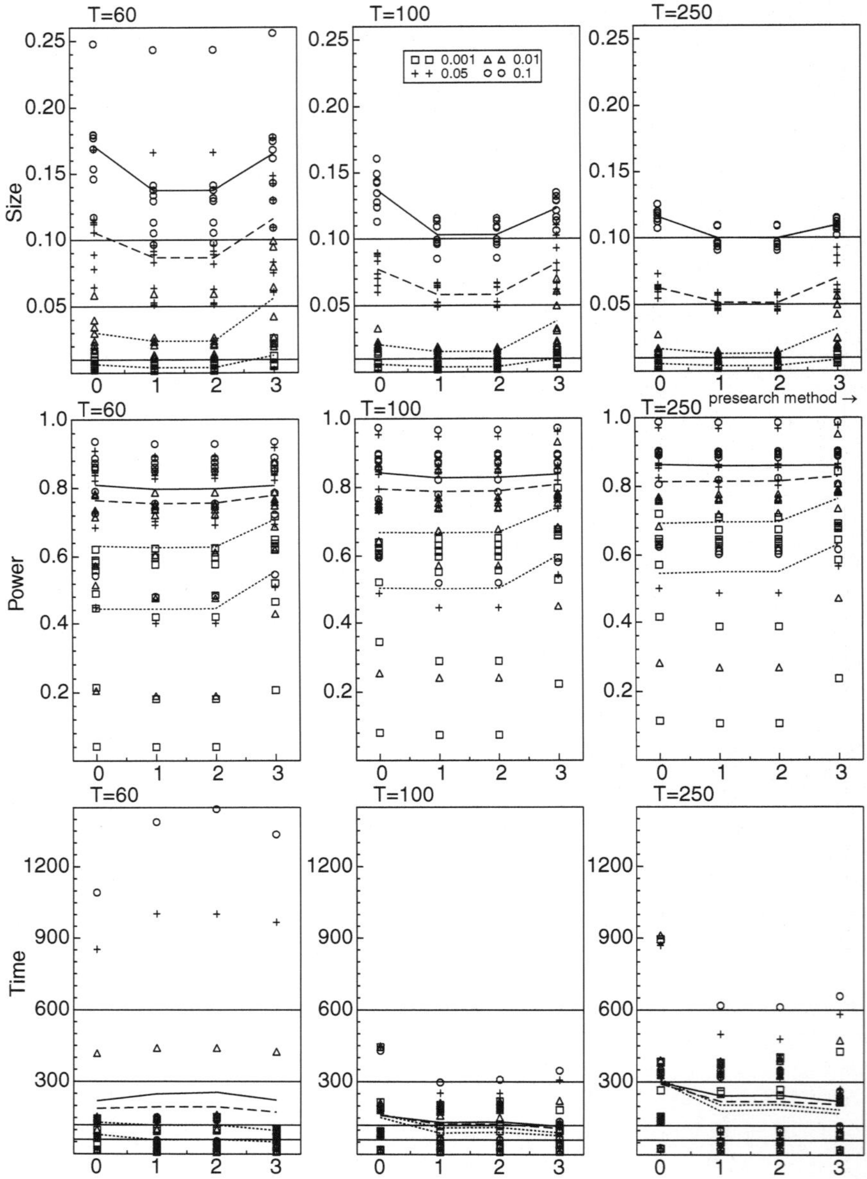

FIG. 4.7. Presearch: size (top three), power (middle three), and time (bottom three) for three presearch settings: individual results and averages for each p_a (squares for $p_a = 0.001$, triangles for $p_a = 0.01$, plusses for $p_a = 0.05$, circles for $p_a = 0.1$). Presearch method 0: none, 1: lags (two passes), 2: lags (three passes), 3: lags and variables.

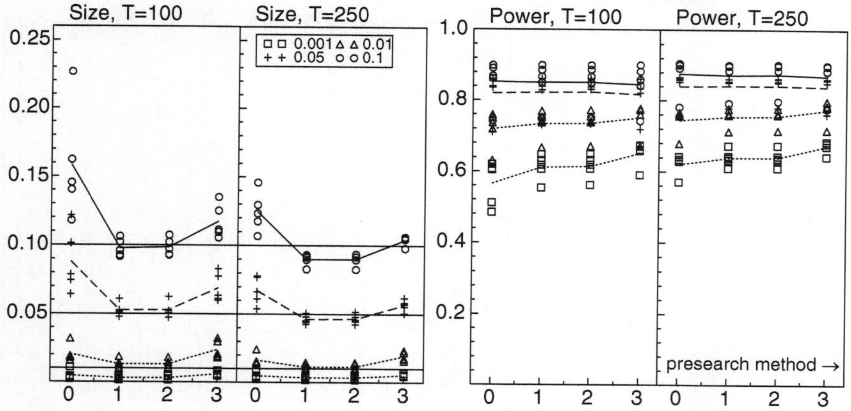

FIG. **4.8.** Presearch*: size (left), power (right) for three presearch settings in extended experiments: individual results and averages for each p_a (squares for $p_a = 0.001$, triangles for $p_a = 0.01$, plusses for $p_a = 0.05$, circles for $p_a = 0.1$). Presearch method 0: none, 1: lags (two passes), 2: lags (three passes), 3: lags and variables.

The conclusion is that presearch lag reduction is beneficial and should be switched on by default (Autometrics adopts method 2, which uses three passes of lag reduction). Variable reduction, on the other hand, is ambiguous at best (but other methods of presearch variable reduction may behave better).

4.4.6 *Backtesting after Presearch*

When presearch is used, three GUMs could be used for backtesting:

1 initial GUM, prior to presearch,

2 GUM 0, after presearch but before further reduction,

3 current GUM, the union of final models after a reduction pass.

The additional mode 3 is investigated in the larger experiments 4* to 8*, which have all variables up to lag 2 in the GUM. Figure 4.9 shows that it is almost identical to backtesting with respect to GUM 0. Otherwise, mode 1 leads again to lower and more concentrated size for roughly the same power.

The conclusions related to backtesting remain unaffected by the presearch: the lower, less dispersed size, with small impact on power, leads us to prefer backtesting with respect to GUM 0.

4.4.7 *Defaults after Calibration*

Table 4.4 summarizes the default settings for the Autometrics algorithm that were inferred from the simulation results in this section.

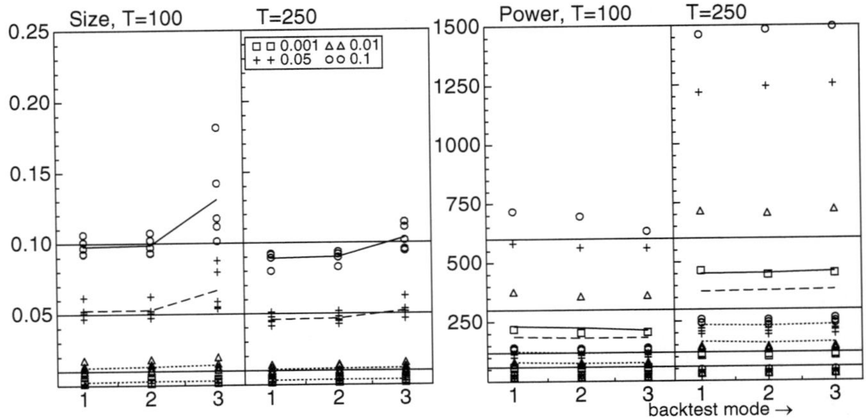

FIG. 4.9. Backtesting after presearch*: size (left), power (right) for two backtest settings after presearch lag reduction: individual results and averages for each p_a (squares for $p_a = 0.001$, triangles for $p_a = 0.01$, plusses for $p_a = 0.05$, circles for $p_a = 0.1$). Backtest mode 1: with respect to initial GUM, 2: with respect to GUM0, 3: with respect to current GUM.

4.5 Impact of Other Design Aspects

4.5.1 *Termination: Iteration and Tiebreaker*

Autometrics finishes iterating when the new GUM (ie the union of the final models) is the same as the previous GUM. It is common at that stage to find multiple final candidate models. These models are all valid reductions of the initial GUM, and any could be chosen by the modeller. In an automated setting, as well as Monte Carlo experiments, a choice must be made by the program. Following PcGets, the default is the Schwarz criterion, but other choices can be made. This ranges from the best fitting model, via AIC, HQ, SC to the smallest model; we label these 2,…,6, where the ordering is in increasing penalty of model size, as in Table 4.5. There may well be multiple smallest models among the final candidates, but ties among the other criteria are exceedingly unlikely.

Table 4.4. Design aspects that are determined through calibration

Bunch and chop factor	α	$\alpha = \max\left\{\frac{1}{2}p_a^{1/2}, p_a^{3/4}\right\}/p_a$ see (1).
Tree search method	4	prune & bunch & chop;
Backtesting	2	GUM0 backtest;
Presearch	2	extended lag reduction.

Table 4.5. GUM and tiebreaker modes used in Figure 4.10

0	GUM 1 (ie GUM after one iteration of the algorithm)
1	Final GUM
2	Best fitting final model (highest likelihood)
3	Final model with smallest AIC (Akaike Information Criterion)
4	Final model with smallest HQ (Hannan–Quinn Information Criterion)
5	Final model with smallest SC (Schwarz Criterion)
6	Smallest final model (best fitting smallest if there is more than one)

Figure 4.10 plots size and power for the standard set of experiments of the previous section. It also includes the first GUM of the reduction (ie the union of models after one round), labelled 0, and the final GUM, labelled 1. The initial GUM has a size close to one, and a power of one. Figure 4.10 shows the progress made from that starting point via the first GUM to the final GUM. Because backtesting is with respect to GUM 0, there is no difference between GUM 1 and the final GUM: terminal candidates remain unchanged after GUM 1 because the backtesting criteria are unchanged (but additional terminal candidates may still be found).

The final GUM is always oversized, remaining so at $T = 250$ (but not asymptotically). The tiebreakers are ordered in decreasing model size, with the best fit being the least stringent. Choosing the best fitting terminal model has roughly a similar impact on size and power. But then, moving from best fit to SC, the size keeps going down with little impact on power, motivating our choice of SC as the default tiebreaker (although, when forecasting is the main objective, another choice may be preferred). Choosing the smallest model impacts power as well as size. These are largely small sample issues, as the plots suggest.

4.5.2 *Squeezing*

Squeezing allows for a single reduction to be tried at a smaller p-value than p_a. The subsequent branch is accepted only if, jointly with one or more subsequent variables, the reduction is valid at p_a. So squeezing will not result in an invalid reduction, but allows for the case when two or more variables are highly correlated so that they are jointly insignificant, even though the individual terms appear significant. Whether squeezing is on or off has no impact on any of the simulations in this chapter.

4.5.3 *Diagnostic Testing*

Diagnostic testing has no effect on size and power in these sets of experiments. We need to find a different set of experiments to show the impact of diagnostic testing. However, in terms of speed, the effect is dramatic: delayed diagnostic

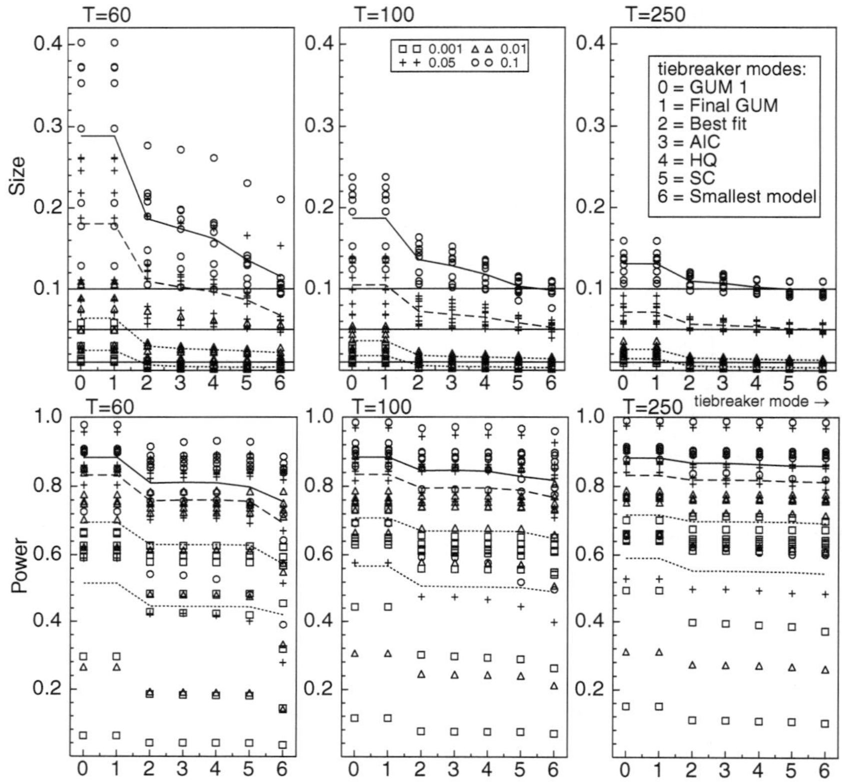

FIG. **4.10.** Tiebreaker: size (top three), power (bottom three) for the first GUM, the final GUM, and 5 tiebreaker settings: individual results and averages for each p_a (squares for $p_a = 0.001$, triangles for $p_a = 0.01$, plusses for $p_a = 0.05$, circles for $p_a = 0.1$). Tiebreaker modes listed in Table 4.5.

testing is 2.5 times faster than always diagnostic testing (in experiment 2 of Table 4.3, where the t-value is 3, using $T = 100$ and $T = 250$).

4.6 Comparison to Hoover–Perez and PcGets

Hendry and Krolzig (2003) discuss the shortcomings of some of the experiments used by Hoover and Perez (1999) (denoted HP1 to HP9, *op.cit.*, Table 3). In particular, the variables that matter are either highly significant (t-values of 5,8,10,12), or insignificant (t-value less than 1). The former are perhaps too easy, while the latter are almost impossible to detect on statistical grounds. Indeed, in some experiments stepwise regression fares just as well as PcGets or Autometrics. The exception is experiment HP8, where stepwise regression is dramatically worse. As pointed out by Hendry and Krolzig (2003), in most of these experiments it is beneficial to set the size very tightly. This will not affect power much, but greatly help with finding the DGP.

Here we focus on HP2, HP7, HP8, and HP9. Hendry and Krolzig (2003) choose HP2 and HP7 because all relevant variables are significant.[12] We add HP9 because of the size problems reported by Hoover and Perez (1999).

Note again that Hoover and Perez (1999) define the size of the Monte Carlo experiments in relation to *significant* variables only: the rate at which falsely significant variables are retained in the final model. I follow Hendry and Krolzig (1999) in defining the size for *all* falsely included variables, which is always higher than the Hoover and Perez (1999) definition.

Table 4.6 compares the Hoover and Perez (1999) and PcGets results with Autometrics. The former are taken from their published tables, so use their definition of size. All other results report size over all irelevant variables; this slightly favours Hoover and Perez (1999). Also note that in the Hoover and Perez (1999) results the constant is always included in the model, but excluded from the evaluation. In the PcGets and Autometrics experiments the constant is kept free, and treated as the other variables. Again the difference is small. Because Hoover and Perez (1999) do not implement a presearch, the PcGets and Autometrics results in Table 4.6 do not either. The PcGets results are for an older version of the software, but, because almost all later changes are in the presearch, these results are still deemed relevant. Autometrics is run without presearch, and with pruning set to 1 (so no bunching and chopping—the latter could be seen as a form of embedded presearch).

Table 4.6 shows that the tree search of Autometrics improves on the multiple-path search algorithms: it is able to deliver consistent performance across experiments without presearch. Although somewhat oversized, the empirical size is closer to the nominal size. At first sight, Autometrics does not do as well in finding the DGP in HP8, but this is entirely a result of the larger empirical size, as discussed above.[13]

Table 4.7 shows the results with presearch switched on, using the default settings for PcGets and Autometrics. It includes the Autometrics results using 'quick mode' (aggressive bunching and reduced effort). The presearch in PcGets has a much more dramatic effect than with Autometrics. The lower score of Autometrics in terms of the percentage of experiments in which the

[12] Hendry and Krolzig (2003) should also have included HP8. There is a mistake in Table 3 of Hoover and Perez (1999): the coefficient on $x3$ of model 8′ should be 0.0345 (computed as 0.75×0.046). Model 7′ also has a mistake: 6.73 should be 6.44. The code of Hoover and Perez (1999) shows that they used the version with autoregressive errors in the simulations, which are therefore unaffected by these typos.

[13] And as Autometrics quick reduction and default presearch confirms, see Table 4.7.

Table 4.6. Comparision of three model selection algorithms without presearch

	HP2			HP7			HP8		HP9		
	HP	PcGets*	Auto*	HP	PcGets*	Auto*	HP	Auto*	HP	PcGets*	Auto*
1% nominal size											
Size (%)	5.7	2.4	2.0	3.0	2.4	2.1	0.9	2.1	3.2	2.5	2.1
Power (%)	100.0	100.0	100.0	94.0	99.9	99.8	99.9	100.0	57.3	61.9	60.9
DGP (%)	0.8	60.2	62.0	24.6	59.0	61.7	78.0	63.8	0.8	0.0	0.1
5% nominal size											
Size (%)	10.7	10.7	6.3	8.2	10.2	6.6	3.7	6.5	8.5	10.4	6.5
Power (%)	100.0	100.0	100.0	96.7	99.9	99.9	100.0	100.0	60.4	66.2	63.0
DGP (%)	0.0	8.4	11.9	4.0	4.0	11.1	31.6	13.0	1.2	0.0	0.5
10% nominal size											
Size (%)	16.2	—	10.0	14.2	—	10.1	10.6	10.0	14.1	—	10.1
Power (%)	100.0	—	100.0	96.9	—	99.9	100.0	100.0	62.5	—	64.6
DGP (%)	0.0	—	2.3	0.2	—	1.8	7.6	1.8	0.4	—	0.0

Source HP: Hoover and Perez (1999) Tables 4,6,7.
Source PcGets*: Hendry and Krolzig (1999) Table 2, no presearch.
Auto*: Autometrics using default settings, but with presearch, bunching and chopping switched off.
DGP is % of experiments in which the DGP is exactly found.
Size HP: % falsely significant variables; others: % falsely included variables.
Power: % of DGP variables included.

DGP is found is commensurate with the higher empirical size. The exception is HP2 at 5%, where PcGets has higher size and a higher score on DGP found.

Next, we consider a set of experiments with a better range of t-values, namely those reported under section 5.1 of Hendry and Krolzig (2005). These are smaller versions of experiments 4,5, and 6 in Table 4.3. Now the constant is

Table 4.7. Comparision of two model selection algorithms with presearch

	HP2			HP7			HP8		HP9
	PcGets	Auto	Quick	PcGets	Auto	Quick	Auto	Quick	Auto
1% nominal size									
Size (%)	0.9	1.3	0.9	1.0	1.7	1.0	1.6	0.8	1.7
Power (%)	100.0	100.0	100.0	99.8	99.3	99.2	100.0	100.0	60.4
DGP (%)	81.0	75.0	81.1	80.8	67.3	80.8	69.8	82.5	0.1
5% nominal size									
Size (%)	5.5	5.2	3.9	5.4	6.0	4.2	5.9	3.9	6.1
Power (%)	100.0	100.0	100.0	99.8	99.8	99.6	100.0	100.0	62.6
DGP (%)	34.5	27.2	39.8	34.7	15.6	39.5	18.6	41.3	0.5

Source PcGets: Hendry and Krolzig (2003) Table 6.
Auto: Autometrics using default settings.
Quick: Autometrics using quick reduction which is more aggressive.
Additional notes, see Table 4.6.

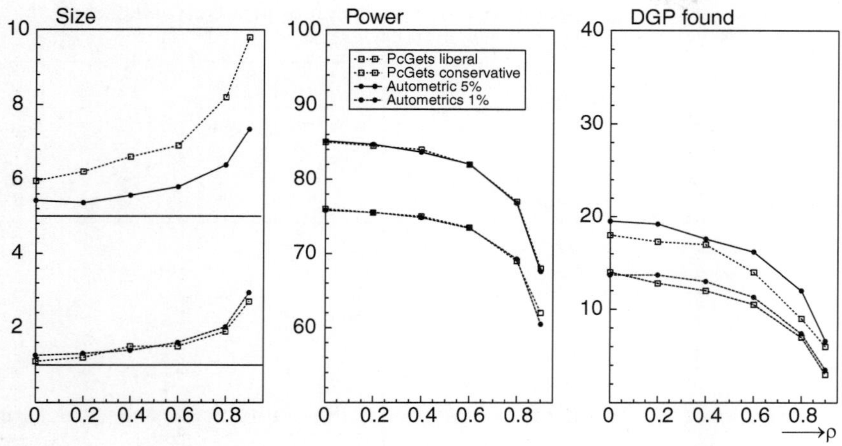

FIG. 4.11. Comparison of PcGets (dotted lines) and Autometrics (solid lines). Horizontal axis: ρ ranging from 0 to 0.9; percentages on vertical axis.

free and $k_1 = 5$, so there are 22 regressors of which 17 are irrelevant. Figure 4.11 gives the results (the PcGets outcomes have been taken from Figure 10 of Hendry and Krolzig, 2005). Remember that the liberal strategy of PcGets is aimed at 5% and conservative at 1%. The figure shows that the size behaviour of Autometrics is similar at 1% and 5%, the size is less sensitive to ρ, and closer to the nominal size at 5%.

Castle and Hendry (2007) run a most interesting experiment to study colinearity caused by nonlinear transformations of the data (such as using age and age-squared in a regression). They find that, with a nonzero mean, the colinearity can be substantial. The DGP is as follows (now using N to denote the sample size in this cross-section example):

$$\begin{aligned} y_i &= \beta x_i + u_i, \; \beta = N^{-1/2}5, u_i \sim IN(0,1), \\ x_i &= \mu + v_i, \quad v_i \sim IN(0,1), \end{aligned}$$

with β chosen to give x_i a t-value of 5 in the DGP. The GUM contains three variables, two of which are nuisance:

$$y_i = \alpha_0 + \alpha_1 x_i + \alpha_2 x_i^2 + \varepsilon_i, \; \varepsilon_i \sim IN(0,\sigma_\varepsilon^2).$$

Two values of μ are used (0 and 10) at two sample sizes (100 and 1,000). Table 4.8 compares PcGets and Autometrics for this experiment, showing that Autometrics does dramatically better. Some closer investigation with PcGets shows that it seems to be that its presearch gets in the way.

Table 4.8. Comparision of two model selection algorithms in a cross-section case, $M = 10\,000$ at a 1% nominal size (conservative strategy).

	$\mu = 0, N = 100$		$\mu = 10, N = 100$		$\mu = 0, N = 1000$		$\mu = 10, N = 1000$	
	PcGets	Auto	PcGets	Auto	PcGets	Auto	PcGets	Auto
Size (%)	2	2	43	5	2	2	43	2
Power (%)	98	99	58	97	98	99	58	98

Source PcGets: Castle and Hendry (2007) Figure 1.
Auto: Autometrics using default settings.

4.7 BHS revisited (again)

The empirical application of Autometrics is illustrated using the model for real US money demand of Baba *et al.* (1992). Hendry and Krolzig (1999) tabulate the GUM, which has 38 coefficients: real money in logs, $m - p$, up to lag 6, GNP in logs, y, up to lag 6, 3 interest rates up to lag 1 (20-year treasury bills, R_{20}, 1-month bills, R_1, and M2 instruments, R_{ma}), 2 current account rates up to lag 2 (R_{na}, R_{sna}), a volatility measure up to lag 1 (V), and an interaction between volatility and the interest spread up to lag 2 (SV). Finally, there is a dummy which is 1 in 1980(2) and −1 in 1980(3) and an intercept.

Following Hendry and Krolzig (1999), the selection is run at $p_a = 0.01$. The Autometrics presearch on lags removes only three variables: $y_{t-5}, \Delta p_{t-5}, y_{t-6}$. This gives a GUM 0 with 35 coefficients. The first search through the model space is in branches that do not already have a terminal, yielding 4 terminal candidate models (including the final model). Next the union contrast yields another 6 terminals (the number is restricted). GUM 1 is the union of these 10 terminals with 29 coefficients.

In the next round, Autometrics finds an additional 8 contrasting terminals, taking the total to 18. PcGets is reported to have found only 2 terminals, illustrating how different the search procedures can be.[14] The first terminal found by Autometrics is the final model selected by PcGets. However, Autometrics chooses the second terminal because it has a smaller SC (and a better fit, because it also has 16 coefficients), see Table 4.9. The difference is very small though. The final model has one insignificant coefficient, which survives because of backtesting against GUM 0.

[14] Hendry and Krolzig (1999) use an early version of PcGets. The presearch removes 16 variables from the initial GUM, leaving 11 insignificant in GUM 0, and 11 paths to explore. A more recent PcGets (version 1.12 from 2002) has the more elaborate 5-step presearch. This removes 20 variables, leaving 18 significant variables (at 1%) in GUM 0. As a consequence, there are no paths to explore. So GUM 0 is the final model, corresponding to terminal 5 of Autometrics. This happens to be the terminal with the lowest AIC and HQ.

Table 4.9. GUM 1 and first two terminals found by Autometrics

	GUM 1	Terminal 1			Terminal 2		
	p-value	coeff.	(s.e.)	p-value	coeff.	(s.e.)	p-value
$(m-p)_{t-1}$	0.0000	1.115	(0.056)	0.0000	1.259	(0.063)	0.0000
$(m-p)_{t-2}$	0.0026	−0.419	(0.062)	0.0000	−0.564	(0.069)	0.0000
$(m-p)_{t-3}$	0.9531	—	—	—	—	—	—
$(m-p)_{t-4}$	0.2143	—	—	—	—	—	—
$(m-p)_{t-5}$	0.0000	0.260	(0.061)	0.0000	0.294	(0.062)	0.0000
$(m-p)_{t-6}$	0.0022	−0.134	(0.052)	0.0121	−0.148	(0.053)	0.0060
y_t	0.0000	0.113	(0.008)	0.0000	0.103	(0.009)	0.0000
y_{t-3}	0.0101	—	—	—	—	—	—
y_{t-4}	0.0522	—	—	—	—	—	—
Δp_t	0.0000	−0.845	(0.105)	0.0000	−0.842	(0.111)	0.0000
Δp_{t-1}	0.2905	—	—	—	0.250	(0.128)	0.0534
Δp_{t-2}	0.0038	−0.408	(0.112)	0.0005	−0.411	(0.114)	0.0005
Δp_{t-3}	0.0246	−0.335	(0.114)	0.0042	−0.406	(0.114)	0.0006
Δp_{t-4}	0.0378	—	—	—	—	—	—
V_t	0.1430	0.701	(0.080)	0.0000	—	—	—
V_{t-1}	0.5509	—	—	—	0.663	(0.080)	0.0000
R_{20}	0.0000	−0.751	(0.065)	0.0000	−0.830	(0.083)	0.0000
$R_{20,t-1}$	0.0083	—	—	—	—	—	—
$R_{1,t}$	0.0038	—	—	—	—	—	—
$R_{ma,t}$	0.0032	—	—	—	—	—	—
$R_{ma,t-1}$	0.0005	—	—	—	0.134	(0.048)	0.0064
$R_{na,t}$	0.0189	1.187	(0.384)	0.0026	0.241	(0.070)	0.0008
$R_{na,t-1}$	0.0330	−1.857	(0.660)	0.0059	—	—	—
$R_{na,t-2}$	0.0521	0.902	(0.349)	0.0111	—	—	—
$R_{sna,t}$	0.1502	—	—	—	—	—	—
$D80_t$	0.0001	0.017	(0.003)	0.0000	0.019	(0.003)	0.0000
SV_{t-1}	0.0286	—	—	—	—	—	—
SV_{t-2}	0.0000	−13.03	(1.705)	0.0000	−11.74	(1.825)	0.0000
1	0.0000	0.240	(0.022)	0.0000	0.214	(0.020)	0.0000
$\hat{\sigma}$		0.4319%			0.4316%		
SC	−7.3415	−7.5347			−7.5361		

The content of all 18 terminals is represented in Table 4.10. The remaining terminals differ largely in which lags of m_p, y, Δp, V, and SV enter the model. In addition, they illustrate that it is difficult to distinguish between the many interest rate variables (and their lags). This is probably no surprise, but no previous technology revealed this so clearly to the empirical modeller.

4.8 Conclusions

Autometrics is a new algorithm for model selection within the general-to-specific framework. It follows on the work by Hoover and Perez (1999) and Hendry and Krolzig (2005). The multiple path search is replaced by a tree search, which improves the small sample behaviour considerably without

Table 4.10. Eighteen terminals found by Autometrics; in the last column ++ denotes a variable in all terminals, + in twelve or more terminals

	1	2	3	4	5	6	7	8	9	10	11	12	13	14	15	16	17	18	All
$(m-p)_{t-1}$	*	*	*	*	*	*	*	*	*	*	*	*	*	*	*	*	*	*	++
$(m-p)_{t-2}$	*	*	*	*	*	*	—	—	*	*	—	*	*	*	*	*	*	*	+
$(m-p)_{t-3}$	—	—	—	—	—	—	*	*	—	—	*	—	*	—	*	—	—	*	
$(m-p)_{t-4}$	—	—	—	*	—	—	—	—	—	—	—	—	*	—	*	*	*	—	
$(m-p)_{t-5}$	*	*	*	*	*	*	*	*	*	*	*	*	*	*	*	*	*	*	++
$(m-p)_{t-6}$	*	*	*	*	—	—	—	*	*	—	*	*	*	*	*	*	*	*	+
y_t	*	*	*	*	*	*	*	*	*	*	*	*	*	*	*	*	*	*	++
y_{t-3}	—	—	—	—	—	—	—	—	*	—	—	—	*	—	*	—	—	—	
y_{t-4}	—	—	—	—	—	—	—	—	*	—	—	—	*	—	*	—	—	—	
Δp_t	*	*	*	*	*	*	*	*	*	*	*	*	*	*	*	*	*	*	++
Δp_{t-1}	—	*	—	—	—	—	—	—	—	—	—	*	*	—	*	—	—	—	
Δp_{t-2}	*	*	*	*	*	*	—	—	*	*	*	*	*	*	*	*	*	*	+
Δp_{t-3}	*	*	*	—	*	*	*	*	*	*	*	*	—	—	—	—	—	*	+
Δp_{t-4}	—	—	—	*	—	—	*	—	—	—	—	—	—	—	*	—	—	*	
V_t	*	—	*	*	*	*	*	*	—	—	*	—	—	*	*	*	*	—	+
V_{t-1}	—	*	—	—	—	—	—	—	*	*	—	*	*	—	—	—	—	*	
R_{20}	*	*	*	*	*	*	*	*	*	*	*	*	*	*	*	*	*	*	++
$R_{20,t-1}$	—	—	*	—	*	*	*	*	—	*	*	—	—	*	—	—	*	—	
$R_{1,t}$	—	—	*	—	*	*	*	*	—	*	*	*	*	*	*	—	*	—	+
$R_{ma,t}$	—	—	*	—	*	*	*	*	—	—	—	*	*	*	*	—	*	—	
$R_{ma,t-1}$	—	*	*	—	*	*	*	*	—	*	*	*	*	*	*	*	*	—	+
$R_{na,t}$	*	*	—	*	—	*	*	*	*	*	*	—	—	*	.	*	—	*	+
$R_{na,t-1}$	*	—	—	*	—	—	*	*	*	*	*	—	—	—	—	*	—	*	
$R_{na,t-2}$	*	—	—	*	*	—	*	*	*	*	*	*	*	—	—	*	*	*	+
$R_{sna,t}$	—	—	*	—	—	—	—	—	—	—	—	—	—	*	*	—	—	—	
$D80_t$	*	*	*	*	*	*	*	*	*	*	*	*	*	*	*	*	*	*	++
SV_{t-1}	—	—	*	—	*	*	*	*	—	—	*	—	—	*	—	—	*	—	
SV_{t-2}	*	*	*	*	*	*	*	*	*	*	*	*	*	*	*	*	*	*	++
1	*	*	*	*	*	*	*	*	*	*	*	*	*	*	*	*	*	*	++
k	16	16	19	17	18	18	20	20	18	18	20	18	21	19	22	17	19	18	

requiring the addition of presearches to the algorithm. Additional proposed improvements include delayed diagnostic testing, and using the unique tree representation to implement union and terminal contrasts. Another interesting finding is the somewhat better performance of backtesting with respect to the initial GUM (or the GUM after presearch), thus effectively removing the encompassing step from the iterations (because it already takes place inside the tree search).

References

Baba, Y., Hendry, D. F., and Starr, R. M. (1992). The demand for M1 in the U.S.A., 1960–1988. *Review of Economic Studies*, **59**, 25–61.

Castle, J. L. and Hendry, D. F. (2007). Extending the boundaries of automatic selection: Non-linear models. Mimeo, Department of Economics, Oxford University.

Doornik, J. A. (2007). *Object-Oriented Matrix Programming Using Ox*, 6th edition. London: Timberlake Consultants Press.

——(2008). Encompassing and automatic model selection. Oxford Bulletin of Economics and Statistics, **70**, 915–925.

Hendry, D. F. (2000). *Econometrics: Alchemy or Science?* Oxford: Oxford University Press.

——and Doornik, J. A. (2007). *Empirical Econometric Modelling Using PcGive: Volume I*, 5th edition. London: Timberlake Consultants Press.

——and Krolzig, H.-M. (1999). Improving on 'Data mining reconsidered' by K. D. Hoover and S. J. Perez. *Econometrics Journal*, **2**, 202–219.

————(2001). *Automatic Econometric Model Selection*. London: Timberlake Consultants Press.

————(2003). New developments in automatic general-to-specific modelling. In Stigum, B. P. (ed.), *Econometrics and the Philosophy of Economics*, pp. 379–419. Princeton: Princeton University Press.

————(2004). Sub-sample model selection procedures in general-to-specific modelling. In Becker, R. and Hurn, S. (eds.), *Contemporary Issues in Economics and Econometrics: Theory and Application*, pp. 53–74. Cheltenham: Edward Elgar.

————(2005). The properties of automatic Gets modelling. *Economic Journal*, **115**, C32–C61.

——and Nielsen, B. (2007). *Econometric Modeling: A Likelihood Approach*. Princeton: Princeton University Press.

Hoover, K. D. and Perez, S. J. (1999). Data mining reconsidered: Encompassing and the general-to-specific approach to specification search. *Econometrics Journal*, **2**, 167–191.

Hoover, K. D. and Perez, S. J. (2004). Truth and robustness in cross-country growth regressions. *Oxford Bulletin of Economics and Statistics*, **66**, 765–798.

Lovell, M. C. (1983). Data mining. *Review of Economics and Statistics*, **65**, 1–12.

Lynch, A. W. and Vital-Ahuja, T. (1998). Can subsample evidence alleviate the data-snooping problem? A comparison to the maximal R^2 cutoff test. Discussion Paper, Stern Business School, New York University.

5

High Dimension Dynamic Correlations

Robert F. Engle

5.1 Introduction

David Hendry is perhaps the best. When the debate over general to simple specification searches gets most heated, the approach is often called the Hendry method. Critics say that only David can really do this. Everyone agrees that in his hands, economic time-series yield up reasonable models that are coherent with both data and theory. To quiet the critics, much of David's recent research has been to automate the methodology so that even a computer can do it. Econometricians might be sceptical of such methods, yet their practical relevance for empirical work is hard to dismiss.

At the same time, David has carefully described what he calls 'predictive failure' of economic time-series models. Even the best models appear to frequently have forecast errors larger than can be expected. Perhaps the economy is not as stationary as we think. Perhaps there are 'Black Swans' everywhere, to use a recent metaphor by Taleb (2007) which refers to the observation that since every swan seen in Europe was white, there was no way statistically to be prepared for the fact that there were black swans in Australia. This tension between model selection and predictive failure lies at the heart of all empirical econometrics.

Nowhere is this tension more apparent than in Finance where large sums are invested on the assumption that history will repeat itself in some fashion. Many such investments are well rewarded until there is some unexpected event where they go rapidly in the wrong direction. The summer of 2007 was such an event and it will be interesting to look back at it. An extension of this analysis to a dataset through January 2008 is included in Engle (2008).

Many financial models are designed to measure risks. Once risks are measured, then investments can be structured to maximize predicted return and minimize risk. However, if the risks are not well represented by historical experience, then it will turn out that investors frequently take risks they did not realize they were taking and consequently have, on average, inferior outcomes.

The goal of this chapter is to develop time-series measures of risks in a highly multivariate framework. In this multidimensional context, the risk is often summarized not only by the volatility of the components but also the correlation among them. Since the world is hopelessly multidimensional, the forecasting of correlations is a central feature of financial planning. The dynamics must quickly adapt to new types of risks yet be unresponsive to random shocks. The structure must evolve but still allow the possibility of 'Black Swan' events without letting such events have undue effect on the performance. This is very similar to the model selection vs predictive failure dichotomy emphasized by David Hendry.

In this chapter I will take a forecasting point of view in modelling correlations between asset returns. The chapter will discuss the Dynamic Conditional Correlation (DCC) model and its general approach to estimating correlations. For large systems, a new improved estimation method will be presented, called the MacGyver method. Then to increase accuracy, a factor structure will be incorporated into the DCC model. This chapter will introduce the FACTOR DCC model that has the potential to forecast correlations in high dimensional systems of asset returns.

5.2 Dynamic Conditional Correlation

The search for multivariate models that can effectively estimate volatilities and correlations for a large class of assets has continued for more than 20 years. The menu of choices is immense and has been surveyed recently by Bauwens, Laurent and Rambouts (2006) and Silvennoinen and Teräsvirta (2008) and less recently by Bollerslev, Engle, and Nelson (1994). Only a few of these models are amenable to estimating correlations for more than half a dozen assets.

One of the most practical and simple is the Dynamic Conditional Correlation (DCC) model introduced by Engle (2002). This model uses a sequential estimation scheme and a very parsimonious parametrization to enable it to estimate models with 50 or more assets rather easily. It is a simple generalization of Bollerslev's Constant Conditional Correlation (CCC) model, Bollerslev (1990). Alternatives to this approach have been introduced by Tse and Tsui (2002), Ledoit, Santa Clara, and Wolf (2003), Alexander (2002), Chib, Nardari, and Shephard (2006), Audrino and Barone-Adesi (2006), He and Teräsvirta (2004), Hafner, Van Dijk, and Franses (2006), and Palandri (2005). It has been applied in many studies; see *inter alia* Engle and Sheppard (2005b), Chan, Lim, and McAleer (2005), Bautista (2003), Kim and Wu (2006), Lee (2006), Engle and Colacito (2006), Cappiello, Engle, and Sheppard (2007), Billio, Caporin, and Gobbo (2006), and Pelletier (2006).

Consider an $n \times 1$ vector of returns, r_t, with conditional covariance matrix H_t. The conditional covariance matrix must be positive definite if there are no redundant assets. Such a covariance matrix can always be decomposed into a diagonal matrix D_t which has the conditional standard deviation of each asset along the main diagonal, and a correlation matrix R_t which has ones on the diagonal and correlations off the diagonal.

$$V_{t-1}(r_t) = H_t = D_t R_t D_t, \quad D_t \sim diagonal, \quad R_t \sim correlation \tag{5.1}$$

Clearly, the correlation matrix is the same as the covariance matrix of standardized returns, s_t.

$$s_t \equiv D_t^{-1} r_t, \quad V_{t-1}(s_t) = R_t \tag{5.2}$$

Hence models to estimate the conditional correlations would naturally use standardized returns as inputs. These standardized returns are sometimes called volatility adjusted returns or standardized residuals. As residuals will have a slightly different meaning in the factor model, I will use the expression standardized returns.

The heart of the DCC model is the parametrization of the equation for updating or forecasting correlations. The correlation matrix is expressed as a function of past observables and this matrix must indeed be a correlation matrix, that is be positive definite and have ones on the diagonal. Two versions can be presented simply while many others are obvious generalizations. The two are called 'integrated' and 'mean reverting'. They are defined more precisely by

$$R_t = diag(Q_t)^{-1/2} Q_t \, diag(Q_t)^{-1/2} \tag{5.3}$$

where Q is defined either by the integrated model

$$Q_t = (1 - \lambda) s_{t-1} s_{t-1}' + \lambda Q_{t-1} \tag{5.4}$$

or the mean reverting model

$$Q_t = \Omega + \alpha s_{t-1} s_{t-1}' + \beta Q_{t-1}. \tag{5.5}$$

There are advantages and disadvantages of each specification. Both (5.4) and (5.5) will generate Q matrices that are positive definite as long as the initial condition is positive definite and the matrix intercept of (5.5) is positive definite. If Q is positive definite, then R will be a correlation matrix. The integrated model assumes all changes in correlations to be permanent. This may be a reasonable assumption, although it appears that many correlation processes are mean reverting. The integrated model is not a satisfactory description of the data in another way. It implies that asymptotically correlations go to plus or minus one. This can be verified by simulating

(5.2), (5.3), and (5.4). Nevertheless, it may be a good filter in the sense of Nelson and Foster (1994).

The mean reverting model assumes that all changes in correlations are transitory although they can last quite a long time if the sum of alpha and beta is close to unity. This model has $n(n-1)/2+2$ parameters while the integrated model has only 1. The solution to this set of extra parameters is to introduce another set of estimating equations. These equations are moment conditions that can be used with the FOC of the likelihood function. Letting the sample correlation of the standardized returns be $\bar{R}$, a second relation can be obtained among the unknowns

$$\bar{R} = \frac{1}{T}\sum_{t=1}^{T} s_t s_t', \quad \bar{Q} = \frac{1}{T}\sum_{t=1}^{T} Q_t \cong \Omega + \alpha\bar{R} + \beta\bar{Q} \tag{5.6}$$

Finally, adding the assumption that on average, $\bar{Q} = \bar{R}$, the intercept can be expressed as

$$\Omega = (1 - \alpha - \beta)\,\bar{R} \tag{5.7}$$

and equation (5.5) can be rewritten as

$$Q_t = \bar{R} + \alpha\left(s_{t-1}s_{t-1}' - \bar{R}\right) + \beta\left(Q_{t-1} - \bar{R}\right) \tag{5.8}$$

Hence, Q is mean reverting to the average correlation. Equation (5.8) only has two parameters no matter how big the system is. The assumption (5.7) is called 'correlation targeting' and is an estimator of the omega parameters that is different from maximum likelihood. As a consequence, this is necessarily an asymptotically inefficient estimator although it may be relatively robust to some forms of misspecification. This is a generalization of the 'variance targeting' approach of Engle and Mezrich (1996). It has been analysed both theoretically and empirically in Engle and Sheppard (2005a).

Many other specifications have been introduced for DCC models. Asymmetric correlation models were introduced in Cappiello, Engle, and Sheppard (2007) who find that correlations become larger when two returns are both negative than if they are equally positive and all other factors are the same. They and Hafner and Franses (2003) also introduce a more generous parametrization of the DCC process called Generalized DCC. Engle (2002) and Engle and Sheppard (2005b) discuss additional lags. Billio, Caporin, and Gobbo (2006) explore a block DCC structure and Pelletier (2006) allows regime shifts. Many formulations are included in Engle (2008).

Maximum likelihood estimation of such systems must include a distributional assumption and multivariate normality is common although not very accurate. Fortunately, estimation of most multivariate GARCH models by maximizing the Gaussian likelihood is consistent as long as the covariance equations are correctly specified, even if the normality assumption is incorrect. See, for example, Bollerslev and Wooldridge (1992) for proof of the consistency of such QMLE estimators.

Assuming multivariate normality, the average log likelihood function plus some unimportant constants, becomes

$$L = -\frac{1}{2T}\sum_{t=1}^{T}\left[\log|H_t| + r_t' H_t^{-1} r_t\right]$$

$$= -\frac{1}{2T}\sum_{t=1}^{T}\left[2\log|D_t| + r_t' D_t^{-2} r_t\right] - \frac{1}{2T}\sum_{t=1}^{T}\left[\log|R_t| + s_t' R_t^{-1} s_t\right] + \frac{1}{2T}\sum_{t=1}^{T} s_t' s_t \tag{5.9}$$

This log likelihood can be maximized with respect to all the parameters in the volatilities, which are inside the matrices D_t, and correlations which are inside R_t. This means simply maximizing the first line of (5.9). Alternatively, the likelihood can be approximately maximized by finding the maximum of the first square bracket terms with respect to the volatility parameters, and then the maximum of the second square bracket terms with respect to the correlation parameters. The first problem gives a consistent estimate of the volatility parameters and, consequently, the maximum of the second part will be consistent under standard regularity conditions and the third term will converge to a constant. Engle and Sheppard (2005a) give this argument in more detail. The log likelihood for the correlation estimation is called L_2 and is given by

$$L_2 = -\frac{1}{2}\sum_{t=1}^{T}\left[\log|R_t| + s_t' R_t^{-1} s_t\right] \tag{5.10}$$

This two step estimation method is very appealing. Univariate models are estimated for each of the volatilities and typically these are simple GARCH models. They can be estimated separately, giving consistent estimates. Then the correlations are estimated by MLE where the data are the standardized returns. In the two cases discussed above there are only one or two parameters respectively in this estimation stage, regardless of n. Thus a very parsimonious parametrization can be used to estimate arbitrarily large systems.

5.3 The MacGyver Method

The estimation of correlation matrices for large systems might appear solved from the previous section. However, there are three reasons to believe that this is not a full solution. First, the evaluation of the log likelihood function requires inversion of matrices R_t, which are full $n \times n$ matrices, for each observation. To maximize the likelihood function, it is necessary to evaluate the log likelihood for many parameter values and consequently invert a great many $n \times n$ matrices. These numerical problems can surely be alleviated, but ultimately for very large n, the numerical issues will dominate. Second, Engle and Sheppard (2005a) show that in correctly specified models with simulated data, there is a finite sample, large n downward bias in α. Thus the correlations are estimated to be smoother and less variable when a large number of assets are considered than when a small number of assets are considered. Third, there may be structure in correlations which is not incorporated in this specification. This of course depends upon the economics of the data in question but the introduction of the FACTOR DCC model in section 5.4 is a response to this issue.

In this section I will introduce a new estimation method which is designed to solve the first two problems and a few others as well. I call this a MacGyver method after the old TV show, which showed MacGyver using whatever was at hand to cleverly solve his problem. The show was a triumph of brain over brawn.

The MacGyver method is based on bivariate estimation of correlations. It assumes that the selected DCC model is correctly specified between every pair of assets i and j. Hence the correlation process is simply

$$\rho_{i,j,t} = \frac{q_{i,j,t}}{\sqrt{q_{i,i,t}q_{j,j,t}}}$$

$$q_{i,j,t} = \bar{R}_{i,j}(1 - \alpha - \beta) + \alpha s_{i,t-1}s_{j,t-1} + \beta q_{i,j,t-1}, \tag{5.11}$$

and the log likelihood function for this pair of assets is simply extracted from (5.10). It is given by

$$L_{2,i,j} = -\frac{1}{2}\sum_t \left(\log\left[1 - \rho_{i,j,t}^2\right] + \frac{s_{i,t}^2 + s_{j,t}^2 - 2\rho_{i,j,t}s_{i,t}s_{j.t}}{\left[1 - \rho_{i,j,t}^2\right]} \right) \tag{5.12}$$

More precisely, the MacGyver method is defined below.

Definition 5.1. *The log of the joint density of an* $n \times 1$ *vector* $\{s_t\}$ *for* $t = 1, \ldots, T$ *is* $L_T(s^T, \theta)$ *for* $\theta \in \Theta$ *and the log of the joint density of the (i,j) element of* $\{s_t\}$ *for* $t = 1$ *to* T *is* $L_{i,j,T}(s^T, \theta)$. *Let* $\hat{\theta}_{i,j} = \underset{\theta \in \Theta}{\arg\max}\ L_{i,j,T}(s^T, \theta)$. *The MacGyver estimator is a blend of these bivariate estimates given by a blend function* $\hat{\theta} = b(\hat{\theta}_{1,2}, \hat{\theta}_{1,3}, \ldots, \hat{\theta}_{1,n}, \hat{\theta}_{2,3}, \ldots, \hat{\theta}_{n-1,n})$. *The blend function must have the property that* $b(\theta, \ldots, \theta) = \theta$ *for any* $\theta \in \Theta$.

A variety of different blend functions could be used. A natural choice would be the mean although, as will be shown below, this is dominated by the median. The consistency of a MacGyver estimator is easily established in two steps for fixed n as $T \to \infty$. First, the bivariate estimates are consistent because they are MLEs of correctly specified bivariate log likelihoods. Second, the blend function of consistent estimates will be a consistent estimate of the true parameter vector.

In the DCC case, the high dimension model and the bivariate model have the same form and the same parameters. Under standard regularity conditions, the consistency of the bivariate MLE is easily established. The asymptotic efficiency of different blend functions could be compared but it is unlikely that analytical expressions can be found to solve this problem. This is particularly complex because the bivariate data are dependent and the bivariate parameter estimates are dependent. The construction of standard errors for MacGyver estimators remains unsolved.

Obviously, however, information is being ignored that could yield more efficient estimates. A MacGyver estimator will not be asymptotically efficient. The efficiency loss relative to full MLE in using such an estimation method is not clear. However, as the number of variables becomes large, the precision of estimation of the small number of parameters should become very great even for inefficient methods. There is no reason to expect precision to increase as $n \to \infty$ but instead it should plateau.

In this chapter, I will seek optimal blend functions based on Monte Carlo performance. A variety of simulation environments is postulated. In each case all bivariate pairs are estimated and then simple aggregation procedures such as means or medians are applied. Several issues immediately arise. What should be done about cases where the estimation does not converge or where it converges to a value outside the region of stationarity? When averaging parameters that have constrained ranges, it is easy to introduce bias.

Six estimators will be considered consisting of three blend functions and two forms of MLE. These are shown in Table 5.1 below.

The trimmed means are computed by deleting the largest and smallest 5% of the estimates and then taking the mean of the remaining ones. The unrestricted MLE simply maximizes the log likelihood (5.12) without restriction. If it does not converge in a finite number of iterations, then the final value of the estimate is taken. Obviously, this estimation can and does occasionally lead to some very bizarre parameter estimates. The restricted MLE reparametrizes the log likelihood using a logistic functional form so that both

Table 5.1. MacGyver estimators

Blend Function	Unrestricted MLE	Restricted MLE
Mean	MEAN	_R MEAN
Median	MED	_R MED
5%Trimmed Mean	MEANT05	_R MEANT05

parameters must lie in the interval (0,1). Their sum was not restricted in this case. The model is expressed as

$$q_{i,j,t} = \bar{R}_{i,j} + \frac{e^{\theta}}{1+e^{\theta}}\left(s_{i,t-1}s_{j,t-1} - \bar{R}_{i,j}\right) + \frac{e^{\phi}}{1+e^{\phi}}\left(q_{i,j,t-1} - \bar{R}_{i,j}\right) \quad (5.13)$$

The optimizer chooses (θ,ϕ) but the estimated values of (α,β) are passed back to be averaged across bivariate pairs.

Ten experiments are run with various parameter values and dimensions. All have a time-series sample size of 1,000 observations and 100 replications of each experiment. The dimensions range from $n = 3$ to $n = 50$. The ten experiments are defined in Table A1 in the Appendix. The true correlation matrix has all correlations equal to Rhobar. In each case the parameters are estimated by bivariate MLE or restricted bivariate MLE and then the summary measures are computed according to each expression in Table 5.1. The ultimate result is a table of root mean squared errors and a table of biases across the simulations for each of the two parameters, alpha and beta.

The tables of RMS errors and biases are presented in the Appendix as Tables A2 and A3. The net result is that the smallest errors are achieved by the median estimator. For beta the best estimator for each experiment is either the median or the median of the restricted estimator. On average the median of the unrestricted estimator is the smallest. For alpha, the medians are best in most experiments and the median of the unrestricted parameter estimates has the smallest RMS error. This estimator effectively ignores all the non-convergent and non-stationary solutions and gives parameter estimates which are very close to the true value.

The biases of these estimators are also of interest. In all experiments the bias in beta is negative and the bias in alpha is positive. This is not surprising in a context where the beta is truncated from above (at one) while alpha is truncated below (at zero). Notice however that this bias is in the opposite direction from the bias observed by Engle and Sheppard (2005a) who found alpha too small and beta too big for large systems. Notice also that the bias is very small. On average over the experiments the bias in alpha is 0.001 and the bias in beta is −0.008. Since these biases result from bivariate estimation, there is no large system bias as there is for MLE estimation of DCC. In fact, the RMSEs are smallest for the largest systems.

In addition to the computational simplification and bias reduction, there are several other advantages to this MacGyver method of estimating a DCC model. When there are 50 assets, there are 1,225 bivariate pairs. When there are 100 assets, there are 4,950 asset pairs. Hence the number of bivariate estimations increases as well. However, since only the median of all these estimations is needed, there is little loss of efficiency if some are not run. This opens the possibility of estimating a subset of the bivariate pairs. While it is not clear how to select a good subset, it is clear that there is little advantage to doing all of them. When new assets are added to the collection, it may not be necessary to reestimate at all if the investigator is confident that the specification is adequate.

A second advantage is that the data sets for each bivariate pair need not be of the same length. Thus, an asset with only a short history can be added to the system without requiring the shortening of all other series. This is particularly important when examining large asset classes and cross country correlations as there are many assets which are newly issued, merged, or otherwise associated with short time histories.

A potential third advantage which will not be explored in this chapter, is that there may be evidence in these bivariate parameter estimates that the selected DCC model is not correctly specified. Presumably, the bivariate models would show less dispersion if the model is correctly specified than if it is incorrect.

5.4 FACTOR DCC

The most popular approach to estimating large covariance matrices in finance is the use of factor models. By specifying a small number of factors that summarize all the dependence between returns, a complete matrix of correlations can be estimated. This is a simple strategy in principle, but in practice it is difficult to select factors and difficult to estimate the factor loadings and other parameters of the process. Nevertheless, this class of models can incorporate directly some effects which the DCC model can only indirectly replicate. Factor models have been at the heart of asset pricing since the monumental work of Sharpe (1964) and Ross (1976) among so many others.

Consider first the very simple static one factor model that is the centrepiece of the Capital Asset Pricing Model or CAPM. Measuring returns in excess of the risk free rate and letting r_m be the market return, the model is most simply expressed as

$$r_{i,t} = \alpha_i + \beta_i r_{m,t} + \varepsilon_{i,t} \tag{5.14}$$

From theoretical arguments, we expect the alphas to be zero in an efficient market and we expect the idiosyncratic returns to be uncorrelated across assets. Hence

$$\begin{aligned} V(r_{i,t}) &= \beta_i^2 V(r_{m,t}) + V(\varepsilon_{i,t}) \\ Cov\left(r_{i,t}, r_{j,t}\right) &= \beta_i \beta_j V(r_{m,t}) \end{aligned} \tag{5.15}$$

Thus the correlation between two assets can be expressed as

$$\rho_{i,j} = \frac{\beta_i \beta_j V(r_{m,t})}{\sqrt{\left(\beta_i^2 V(r_{m,t}) + V(\varepsilon_{i,t})\right)\left(\beta_j^2 V(r_{m,t}) + V\left(\varepsilon_{j,t}\right)\right)}} \tag{5.16}$$

These expressions ensure that the correlation matrix will be positive definite. They however do not provide any measures of time varying variances, covariances, or correlations.

The simplest approach to formulating a dynamic version of this one factor model is to follow Engle, Ng, and Rothschild (1990, 1992). In this case the factor has time varying volatility and can be modelled with some form of ARCH model. Consequently, the expressions in (5.15) and (5.16) can be rewritten in terms of conditional variances. The conditional correlation then becomes

$$\rho_{i,j,t} = \frac{\beta_i \beta_j V_{t-1}(r_{m,t})}{\sqrt{\left(\beta_i^2 V_{t-1}(r_{m,t}) + V_{t-1}(\varepsilon_{i,t})\right)\left(\beta_j^2 V_{t-1}(r_{m,t}) + V_{t-1}(\varepsilon_{j,t})\right)}} \tag{5.17}$$

The model used by ENR assumed that the idiosyncratic volatilities were not changing over time. They called this the FACTOR ARCH model and I will use that name here. Letting β, and r_t be $n \times 1$ vectors, the statistical specification is

$$V_{t-1}\begin{pmatrix} r_t \\ r_{m,t} \end{pmatrix} = \begin{pmatrix} \beta\beta' h_{m,t} + D^2 & \beta h_{m,t} \\ \beta' h_{m,t} & h_{m,t} \end{pmatrix}, \quad D \sim diagonal \tag{5.18}$$

The conditional correlation between each pair of assets would be time varying only because the market volatility is changing. From an examination of (5.17) it is clear that the conditional correlation in this model is a monotonic function of market volatility ranging in absolute value from zero to one as market volatility ranges from zero to infinity.

In the ENR or FACTOR ARCH model, there would always be portfolios of assets which would have no ARCH. Engle and Susmel (1993) looked for such portfolios and found in an international context that they are uncommon. Almost all portfolios have time varying volatility, even if they have a zero beta on the market. Hence, there must either be more factors or time varying idiosyncratic volatility.

The natural extension of this model is to allow the idiosyncrasies to follow a GARCH process as well as the market return. This model can simply be estimated by regressing each asset return on the market return with OLS, and then estimating the market volatility with GARCH. It is not an example of a factor ARCH model as in ENR. The system has $n+1$ observables and $n+1$ factors hence it is related to the extended CCC model of He and Teräsvirta (2004) or the Full Factor model of Vrontos *et al.* (2003) or OGARCH model of Alexander (2002). However, it differs from these in specifying a particular relation between the individual GARCH random variables, suggested by finance theory.

Thus there are two GARCH processes for an asset. For convenience we will call this model a FACTOR DOUBLE ARCH. The model is expressed as

$$V_{t-1}\begin{pmatrix} r_t \\ r_{m,t} \end{pmatrix} = \begin{pmatrix} \beta\beta' h_{m,t} + D_t^2 & \beta h_{m,t} \\ \beta' h_{m,t} & h_{m,t} \end{pmatrix}, \quad D_t \sim diagonal\{garch\ std\} \tag{5.19}$$

Where D_t is a diagonal matrix with GARCH standard deviations on the diagonal.

Assuming conditionally normal returns this can be rewritten as

$$r_t \left| r_{m,t}, \mathrm{F}_{t-1} \sim N\left(\beta r_{m,t}, D_t^2\right), \quad r_{m,t} \right| \mathrm{F}_{t-1} \sim N\left(0, h_{m,t}\right) \tag{5.20}$$

This model is still easy to estimate by MLE. The return on an asset is regressed on the market return with disturbances that follow a GARCH. Then the GARCH for the market is only estimated once. To see that this two step estimator is MLE, express the likelihood for this problem as the density of asset returns conditional on the market return times the marginal density of market returns. Ignoring irrelevant constants, the log likelihood is

$$L\left(r, r_m\right) = -\sum_{t=1}^{T} \log\left|D_t\right| - \frac{1}{2}\sum_{t=1}^{T}\left(r_t - \beta r_{m,t}\right) D_t^{-2}\left(r_t - \beta r_{m,t}\right) - \frac{1}{2}\sum_{t=1}^{T}\left[\log\left(h_t\right) + \frac{r_{m,t}^2}{h_t}\right] \tag{5.21}$$

This model satisfies the weak exogeneity conditions of Engle, Hendry, and Richard (1983) which allow for separate estimation of the conditional and marginal models. As long as the parameters are distinct or *variation free* so that no information from the marginal model would affect inference in the conditional model, then market returns can be considered weakly exogenous and the MLE of the system is the same as the MLE done in two steps.

There are many reasons to believe that the ONE FACTOR DOUBLE ARCH model just described will still be too simple to accurately forecast correlations. The correlations between stock returns in the same industry are typically higher than for stocks across industries and these correlations will rise if the industry volatility rises. These are essentially additional factors with impacts on correlations that vary over time. Even more interesting are factors that have zero variance some of the time and a large variance other times. Energy prices might be in this category. It would be impossible to identify this factor until it is active, but then it may be too late to add another factor. Finally, the model assumes that the factor loadings or betas are constant over time, yet whenever a firm changes its line of business, its sensitivity to various factors will naturally change.

Ideally, the model should allow correlations among idiosyncrasies and between idiosyncrasies and market shocks and these correlations should be time varying. In this way the statistical model will recognize the changing correlation structure when a new factor emerges or factor loadings change.

The FACTOR DCC model is designed to do just this. It proceeds exactly as described above for the FACTOR DOUBLE ARCH and then estimates a DCC model on the residuals. More precisely, the FACTOR DCC model has the specification

$$r_t = \beta r_{m,t} + D_t \varepsilon_t, \quad r_{m,t} = \sqrt{h_t}\varepsilon_{m,t}, \quad \begin{pmatrix} \varepsilon_t \\ \varepsilon_{m,t} \end{pmatrix} \sim N(0, R_t) \tag{5.22}$$

The specification of the correlation matrix can be the same as (5.3) coupled with either (5.4) or (5.5) or more general versions of DCC. It might be sensible to allow the correlations between market innovations and idiosyncracies to have a different dynamic from those between idiosyncratic errors, but that has not been allowed here. Partitioning the $(n+1) \times (n+1)$ correlation matrix into its conformal parts as

$$R_t = \begin{pmatrix} R_{11,t} & R_{1,m,t} \\ R_{m,1,t} & 1 \end{pmatrix} \tag{5.23}$$

the covariance matrix of returns is given by

$$V_{t-1}\begin{pmatrix} r_t \\ r_{m,t} \end{pmatrix} = \begin{pmatrix} \beta\beta' h_{m,t} + D_t R_{1,1,t} D_t + \sqrt{h_{m,t}}\beta R_{m,1,t} D_t + \sqrt{h_{m,t}} D_t R_{1,m,t}\beta' & \beta h_{m,t} + \sqrt{h_{m,t}} D_t R_{1,m,t} \\ \beta' h_{m,t} + \sqrt{h_{m,t}} R_{m,1,t} D_t & h_{m,t} \end{pmatrix} \tag{5.24}$$

The covariances between asset returns are given by the upper left block which now has four terms. The first term is the same as for the FACTOR ARCH. The second term allows for new factors through changes in correlations between the idiosyncrasies. The third and fourth terms allow correlations between market innovations and idiosyncrasies reflecting time variations in conditional betas.

The model in equation (5.22) is only a small generalization of the basic DCC model. The data in this case are not just standardized returns but standardized idiosyncratic returns. If either the FACTOR ARCH or the FACTOR DOUBLE ARCH are correctly specified, then the DCC should find zero correlations both conditionally and unconditionally. Estimation is naturally done in two steps again where the first step estimates both the static factor loading and the idiosyncratic GARCH. The second step estimates the DCC parameters. Here joint estimation is possible or the MacGyver method can be used. In this chapter the MacGyver method will be employed.

The conditional correlations are again defined as the conditional covariance divided by the product of the conditional standard deviations, using the expression for the conditional covariance matrix of returns in (5.24). In each case there are now four terms and the last three depend upon the DCC estimated correlations.

5.5 Performance

To examine the properties of these correlation estimators a set of 18 daily US large cap equity returns will be examined. The data range from 1994 through 2004 for 2,771 observations. The tickers are {aa, axp, ba, cat, dd, dis, ge, gm, ibm, ip, jnj, jpm, ko, mcd, mmm, mo, mrk, msft} which are all components of the Dow. The S&P500 is taken as the market return.

5.5.1 *MacGyver Estimates*

The MacGyver method is applied to this data set to estimate all the correlations with DCC. Although it is not necessary to use the same GARCH model for each series, in this investigation I do. To account for the asymmetry in volatility, the GJR or Threshold GARCH model is used. It is specified by

$$r_{i,t} = \sqrt{h_{i,t}}\varepsilon_{i,t}, \quad h_{i,t} = \omega_i + \theta_i r_{i,t-1}^2 + \gamma_i r_{i,t-1}^2 I_{r_{i,t-1}<0} + \phi h_{i,t-1} \tag{5.25}$$

The standardized returns from these models are saved and used as inputs for the DCC estimation by MacGyver. For 18 returns there are $18 \times 17/2 = 153$ bivariate models. For most of these, the results are quite standard. For a few, they are completely unsatisfactory. For example, all of the alphas are estimated to be between zero and 0.05 except for one that is just over 2. Similarly, most of the betas are less than 1 but for the same bivariate estimate, beta is over 4,000. A few of the betas are quite small or negative. Nevertheless, the medians are very close to general experience. The median for alpha is 0.0157 and the median for beta is 0.9755 so that the sum is just over 0.99 leading to a good degree of persistence in correlations. The actual plots are given in the appendix.

The DCC estimation produces 153 time-series of correlations based on these two parameters and the unconditional correlations. It is difficult to examine so many time-series at once. Some clear patterns can easily be seen by looking at the average correlations. These will establish the stylized facts of correlations in the US equity market. In Figure 5.1, the mean correlation is plotted from the 100-day historical method and the DCC method with TARCH volatilities.

The historical correlations and the DCC correlations trace out very much the same pattern. The range of the historical correlations is a little greater, but this may be a result of the choice of smoothing. A 200-day correlation would move substantially less. The historical correlations also have wider peaks making the correlation estimate somewhat slower to respond to news. A plot of

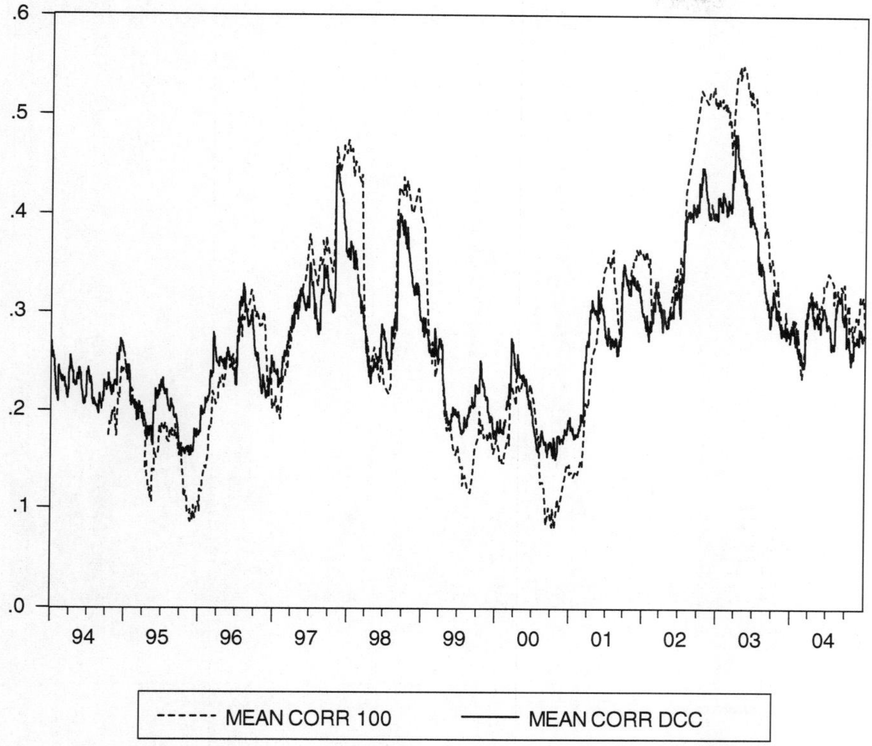

FIG. 5.1. Mean historical and DCC correlations.

the cross-sectional standard deviation of the 153 bivariate correlations reveals that the historical correlations are more varied across pairs than the DCC.

It is clear that these correlations have changed substantially over the 10-year period. The highest correlations are during the recession in 2002 and the first part of 2003. Correlations are low during the Internet bubble and its subsequent bursting. They rise in 2001 and abruptly increase further after 9/11. In 2003 correlations fall as the economy and stock market recover. There are two episodes of spiking correlations in the late 1990s which can be associated with the LTCM/Russian Default and the Asian currency crisis. In fact the proximate cause of the second spike is the 'Anniversary Crash' on 27 October 1997 when the market fell 7% and then recovered 5% the next day. These events are plotted with the correlations in Figure 5.2.[1] It certainly appears that economic crises lead to rising correlations.

[1] The LTCM dummy is defined for August 1998 through 25 September 1998, the Asia Crisis dummy is defined for 14 May 1997 through 31 July 1997, the Anniversary Crash dummy is defined for 27 and 28 October 1997.

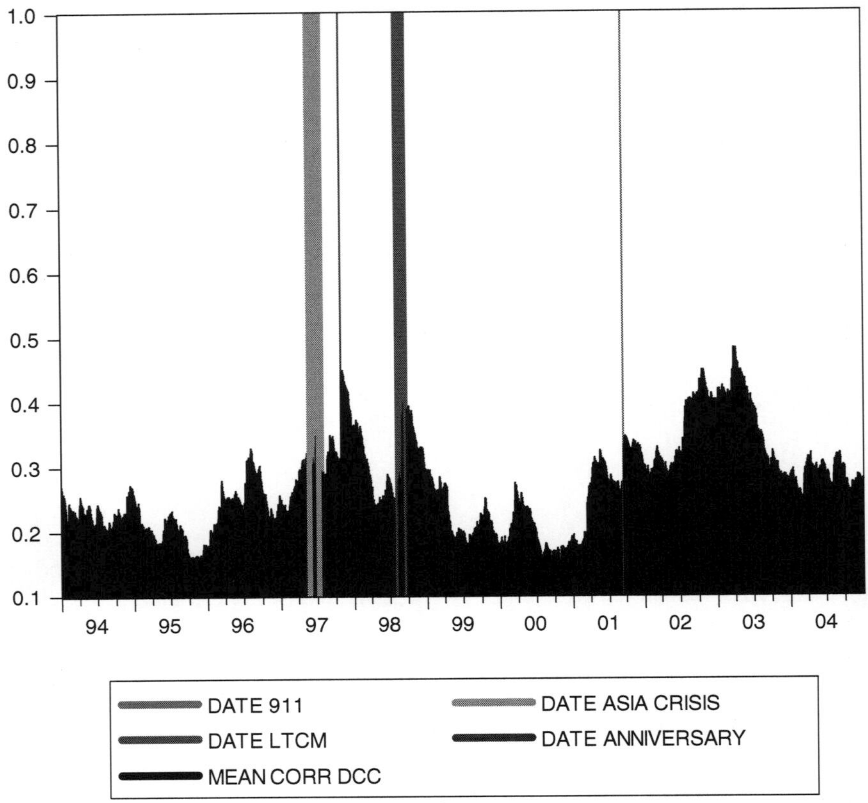

FIG. 5.2. Mean correlations and significant dates.

5.5.2 *Factor Arch, Factor Double Arch*

The sharp movements in correlations that are associated with movements in the S&P itself suggest the usefulness of a factor model. The FACTOR ARCH and the FACTOR DOUBLE ARCH are now calculated. They follow the specification (5.18) and (5.19). The betas are estimated by OLS for the FACTOR ARCH and by GLS with GARCH errors for the FACTOR DOUBLE ARCH and consequently are slightly different. These differences are small for all 18 stocks.

The correlations from each of these models can be calculated using (5.17). The average across all pairs is again a useful measure. This is shown in Figure 5.3. The average correlation from the FACTOR DOUBLE ARCH model is very similar in level to the average DCC. It differs primarily in that the FACTOR DOUBLE ARCH correlations are more volatile. When the correlations

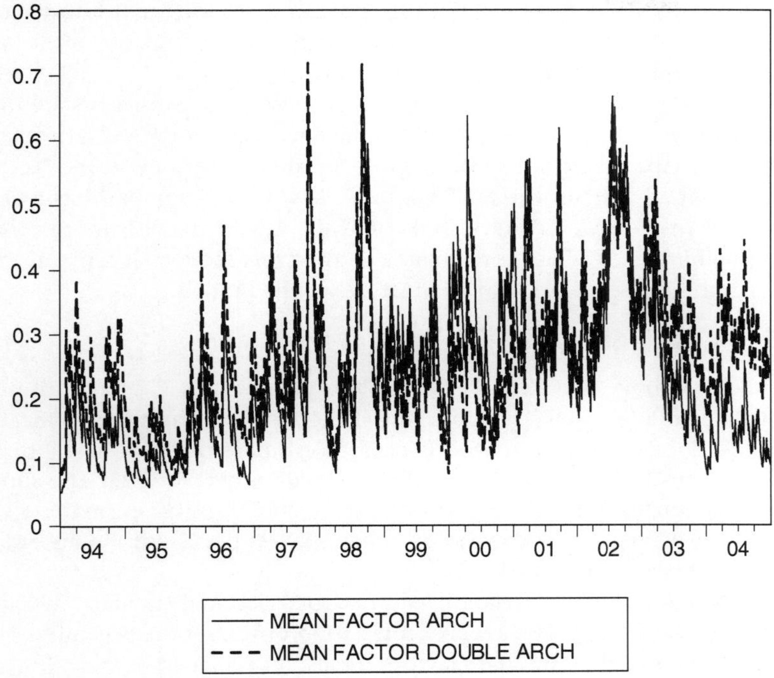

FIG. 5.3. Mean correlations of FACTOR MODELS.

spike up because of some market event, they rise up to 0.7 in several cases, and when the correlations fall, they fall further. It is not clear whether the higher volatility is a good or bad aspect of this estimator as we do not know what the true conditional correlations are at any point in time.

The patterns of the FACTOR ARCH are, however, different in several important ways. Over the last two years of the sample, the FACTOR ARCH correlations fall much lower than any of the other correlation estimators. This is also the case in the mid-1990s. The opposite, however, occurs in 1999 and 2000 when the FACTOR ARCH correlations are higher than DCC and FACTOR DOUBLE ARCH. These differences are easy to understand. The monotonic relation between average correlation and market volatility in the FACTOR ARCH model implies that the correlations should be at their lowest in the mid-1990s and since 2003 since market volatility is lowest then. However, the idiosyncratic volatilities also change in much the same direction so that the more accurately estimated correlations either from the DCC or the FACTOR DOUBLE ARCH model mitigate these movements. For the Internet bubble, the opposite effect is observed. The market volatility is high but so are idiosyncratic volatilities so the correlations are low. The FACTOR ARCH model cannot do this. The observation of Campbell *et al.* (2001), that idiosyncratic volatilities are rising, should not be interpreted as a trend but rather as a process that ultimately reverses in about 2002.

The cross-sectional standard deviations of these three estimators are interesting. DCC has correlations that differ more across pairs than the two factor models. Perhaps this is not surprising as the component due to the factor is the same for all pairs in the FACTOR models, whereas each pair has its own time-series in the DCC. The FACTOR DOUBLE ARCH model is more volatile over time but the DCC is more volatile in the cross-section. It remains to be seen whether these are good or bad features of the models.

5.5.3 *FACTOR DCC*

As discussed above, FACTOR DCC simply estimates a DCC model from the residuals of the FACTOR DOUBLE ARCH model following the specification in (5.22). The MacGyver method is used to estimate the parameters of this DCC. The median alpha = 0.009 while the median beta = 0.925. The sum of these two numbers is much further from unity than the DCC estimates on the simple returns; hence the correlation process is less persistent. Because alpha is smaller, it is also less volatile.

The average residual correlation and its cross-sectional standard deviation can now be computed. The average correlation of the residuals is quite small as would be implied by standard factor models. It averages 0.01 over time and cross-sectional pairs. It does rise in 2000 and 2001 but only to 0.04. The cross-sectional standard deviation is, however, of the same order of magnitude as the cross-sectional standard deviation of the DCC. Thus the average correlation among the idiosyncrasies is small but it has substantial cross-sectional variability. Many of these are of course negative.

When these residual correlations are incorporated into the calculation of the conditional correlations, the result is a substantial change for some pairs and very little for many others. In fact, the average correlation looks almost identical to the FACTOR DOUBLE ARCH. However the cross-sectional dispersion is now greater. The cross-sectional standard deviation of FACTOR DCC is almost as high as the DCC itself and is quite similar to the DCC at the end of the sample.

The reasons for these differences are easily seen in a few examples shown in the appendix. Stocks in the same industry have idiosyncratic shocks that are correlated. The FACTOR DCC method incorporates these idiosyncratic correlations into the correlation estimates. If these residual correlations are constant, the correction is static, but if it is dynamic, then a time varying correction is automatically generated by the FACTOR DCC method. The appendix shows the correlations estimated between International Paper and Caterpillar, between Merck and Johnson and Johnson, and between Coke and Phillip Morris.

5.5.4 *Hedging Experiment*

To establish which of these models does a better job of forecasting correlations, an economic criterion is desirable since we never know what the correlations truly were. A natural criterion is based on portfolio optimization or hedging. This is an example of the methodology introduced by Engle and Colacito (2006). The optimal portfolio of two stocks with equal expected return, is to choose the minimum variance combination. For example, the minimum variance combination of assets (i, j) is given by

$$r_{port,t} = w_t r_{i,t} + (1 - w_t) r_{j,t}$$
$$w_t = \frac{h_{j,j,t} - h_{i,j,t}}{h_{i,i,t} + h_{j,j,t} - 2h_{i,j,t}}, \quad V_{t-1}(r_t) = H_t \tag{5.26}$$

Thus the optimal proportion of each asset to hold is changing over time based on the forecast of the covariance matrix. To achieve this optimal holding, the investor would forecast the next day covariance matrix just before the close and then adjust his portfolio to have the weights given in (5.26). The criterion for success is that the portfolio indeed has a smaller variance than if the weights had not been changed. More generally, this benefit should cover transaction costs. For the purpose here, we simply want to know which method of forecasting the covariance matrix achieves the lowest variance.

A closely related problem is holding a position in one stock because it has an abnormal expected return and hedging the position with a second stock. Typically this would mean shorting either the first or second stock to obtain a hedge portfolio with the minimum variance. Although the problem is different, the same approach can be used to solve it. The optimal hedge is given by

$$r_{port,t} = r_{i,t} - \beta_{i,j,t} r_{j,t}, \quad \beta_{i,j,t} = h_{i,j,t}/h_{j,j,t} \tag{5.27}$$

The criterion for success again is simply the smallest variance of the portfolio.

These two criteria are applied for each of the models we have discussed, to all the pairs of stocks in the data set, and on all the dates in the data set. The average volatility for each pair over time is averaged over all pairs to obtain a single number for the performance of a particular correlation estimator. The results are in Table 5.2 and two figures in the appendix.

Table 5.2. Average volatility of optimized portfolios

	CONST	HIST100	DCC	FACTOR ARCH	DOUBLE ARCH	FACTOR DCC
Min Variance	0.015764	0.015889	0.015632	0.015743	0.015628	**0.015604**
Hedge	0.018989	0.019072	0.018844	0.019026	0.018883	**0.018804**

The results show that for both criteria, the FACTOR DCC model produces the best hedge portfolio. For the hedging problem, the DCC is next followed by the FACTOR DOUBLE ARCH while for the minimum variance criterion, the order is the opposite. All except the 100-day historical volatility outperform the optimal constant set of weights and in the hedging problem, the FACTOR ARCH. The differences are however very small. It appears that the gains from a better model may only be 1% reduction in volatility. This does not however mean that for other problems the gains will also be small. See, for example, Engle and Colacito (2006) for discussion of this.

To determine whether these differences are systematic or not, I looked at how many of the pairs preferred one estimator to another. These winning percentages tell a much stronger story. In the appendix, Tables A2 and A3 show the fraction of times the row method beats the column method. The best method has the largest fractions in the labelled row. For example, in hedging, the FACTOR DCC is superior to a constant hedge for 88% of the pairs, and superior to the DCC for 74%. It beats the historical hedge 98%, the FACTOR ARCH 99% and the DOUBLE ARCH 91%. In conclusion, although the differences are small, they are systematic.

Engle (2008) has extended this study through January 2008. He used the parameter estimates from this study which ended in 2004 and updated the volatilities and correlations daily using each of the models. Repeating the hedging and minimum variance portfolio problems gives very similar results with a slight improvement of DCC relative to FACTOR DCC.

5.6 Conclusion

Forecasts of correlations are of prime importance for financial decision making. This chapter has introduced several new models and compared them with existing models. The use of FACTOR models combined with time-series methods such as ARCH/GARCH and DCC provides a rich class of estimators that can approximate a flexible correlation structure. Models called FACTOR ARCH, FACTOR DOUBLE ARCH, and FACTOR DCC are introduced and compared. The chapter discusses estimation of these models in the context of large systems. A new method for estimating DCC models in large systems is called the MacGyver method. It first estimates all the bivariate models and then selects the median of all these parameter estimates to use in creating and forecasting correlations.

An economic loss function is used to compare these models on a data set of large cap US stocks. Dynamic portfolio strategies designed to create minimum variance portfolios from pairs of stocks, have different performance depending on what model is used for correlations. By averaging over time and pairs of stocks, it is found that the FACTOR DCC method has the best performance. This is followed either by the DCC or the FACTOR DOUBLE ARCH in different circumstances. The standard one factor model FACTOR ARCH is not as good and a 100-day historical correlation is worse than a constant hedge.

Appendix

Table A1. Experiments for MacGyver simulation

	Number	Alpha	Beta	Rhobar
Exp1	3.00	0.05	0.90	0.50
Exp2	5.00	0.05	0.90	0.50
Exp3	10.00	0.05	0.90	0.50
Exp4	20.00	0.05	0.90	0.50
Exp5	30.00	0.05	0.90	0.50
Exp6	50.00	0.05	0.90	0.50
Exp7	10.00	0.05	0.94	0.50
Exp8	10.00	0.02	0.97	0.50
Exp9	10.00	0.05	0.90	0.20
Exp10	10.00	0.05	0.90	0.80

Table A2. RMS errors from MacGyver method

	Alpha					
	amean	a_rmean	ameant05	a_rmeant05	amed	a_rmed
exp1	**0.01092**	0.01233	0.01150	0.01386	0.01150	0.01386
exp2	0.00720	0.00807	0.00710	0.00854	**0.00682**	0.00843
exp3	0.02550	0.00543	0.00528	0.00504	**0.00491**	0.00510
exp4	0.01509	0.00419	0.00438	0.00383	0.00410	**0.00357**
exp5	5.63324	0.00403	0.00389	0.00361	0.00358	**0.00321**
exp6	0.01088	0.00352	0.00301	0.00308	**0.00274**	0.00275
exp7	0.00578	0.00380	0.00430	**0.00371**	0.00424	0.00379
exp8	471.66375	0.00552	0.00377	0.00391	**0.00283**	0.00295
exp9	10.58470	0.00469	0.00424	0.00432	**0.00402**	0.00441
exp10	0.00554	0.00498	0.00542	**0.00483**	0.00539	0.00516
average	48.79626	0.00566	0.00529	0.00547	**0.00501**	0.00532

	Beta					
	bmean	b_rmean	bmeant05	b_rmeant05	bmed	b_rmed
exp1	0.03743	0.05134	0.03417	0.03584	**0.03417**	0.03584
exp2	0.03693	0.03630	0.02716	0.02910	**0.02186**	0.02438
exp3	1.20351	0.02736	0.02080	0.02040	0.01629	**0.01515**
exp4	0.21512	0.02543	0.01796	0.01729	0.01289	**0.01179**
exp5	0.07398	0.02388	0.01542	0.01592	**0.01041**	0.01047
exp6	0.14473	0.02400	0.01490	0.01578	**0.00969**	0.01022
exp7	0.01311	0.00819	0.00705	0.00747	**0.00578**	0.00703
exp8	88.71563	0.05939	0.06618	0.03728	**0.01015**	0.01178
exp9	15.72034	0.03100	0.02297	0.02220	0.01510	**0.01449**
exp10	0.02063	0.01894	0.01585	0.01453	0.01361	**0.01177**
average	10.61814	0.03058	0.02425	0.02158	**0.01499**	0.01529

Table A3. Bias from MacGyver method

	Alpha					
	amean	a_rmean	ameant05	a_rmeant05	amed	a_rmed
exp1	0.00071	0.00110	0.00024	0.00094	0.00024	0.00094
exp2	0.00124	0.00285	0.00077	0.00210	0.00079	0.00153
exp3	−0.00036	0.00261	0.00184	0.00195	0.00082	0.00106
exp4	0.00352	0.00254	0.00222	0.00188	0.00142	0.00088
exp5	−0.55754	0.00248	0.00183	0.00180	0.00099	0.00095
exp6	0.00096	0.00224	0.00152	0.00152	0.00071	0.00067
exp7	0.00272	0.00158	0.00214	0.00134	0.00134	0.00092
exp8	−48.11060	0.00428	0.00158	0.00298	0.00142	0.00174
exp9	−1.05017	0.00251	0.00208	0.00192	0.00072	0.00113
exp10	0.00247	0.00233	0.00215	0.00196	0.00183	0.00170
average	−4.97070	0.00245	0.00164	0.00184	**0.00103**	0.00115
	Beta					
	bmean	b_rmean	bmeant05	b_rmeant05	bmed	b_rmed
exp1	−0.01710	−0.02087	−0.01165	−0.01022	−0.01165	−0.01022
exp2	−0.01945	−0.02216	−0.01450	−0.01674	−0.00942	−0.01079
exp3	0.09886	−0.02275	−0.01615	−0.01605	−0.01036	−0.00933
exp4	−0.01104	−0.02333	−0.01524	−0.01518	−0.00951	−0.00900
exp5	−0.02231	−0.02257	−0.01333	−0.01429	−0.00741	−0.00811
exp6	−0.00020	−0.02264	−0.01344	−0.01414	−0.00765	−0.00789
exp7	0.00175	−0.00661	−0.00062	−0.00577	−0.00252	−0.00479
exp8	11.18001	−0.05195	−0.01487	−0.02937	−0.00859	−0.00998
exp9	1.54597	−0.02653	−0.01931	−0.01814	−0.01033	−0.00994
exp10	−0.01524	−0.01525	−0.01106	−0.01087	−0.00803	−0.00666
average	1.27412	−0.02347	−0.01302	−0.01508	**−0.00855**	−0.00867

Table A4. Fraction of minimum variance portfolios where row beats column

	CONST	HIST 100	DCC	FACTOR ARCH	DOUBLE ARCH	FACTOR DCC
CONST	0.000	0.778	0.235	0.451	0.196	0.163
HIST 100	0.222	0.000	0.000	0.196	0.013	0.007
DCC	0.765	1.000	0.000	0.791	0.464	0.261
FACTOR ARCH	0.549	0.804	0.209	0.000	0.137	0.137
DOUBLE ARCH	0.804	0.987	0.536	0.863	0.000	0.183
FACTOR DCC	0.837	0.993	0.739	0.863	0.817	0.000

Table A5. Fraction of hedges where row beats column

	CONST	HIST 100	DCC	FACTOR ARCH	DOUBLE ARCH	FACTOR DCC
CONST	0.000	0.660	0.154	0.634	0.258	0.114
HIST 100	0.340	0.000	0.013	0.379	0.121	0.013
DCC	0.846	0.987	0.000	0.899	0.569	0.255
FACTOR ARCH	0.366	0.621	0.101	0.000	0.059	0.007
DOUBLE ARCH	0.742	0.879	0.431	0.941	0.000	0.088
FACTOR DCC	0.886	0.987	0.745	0.993	0.912	0.000

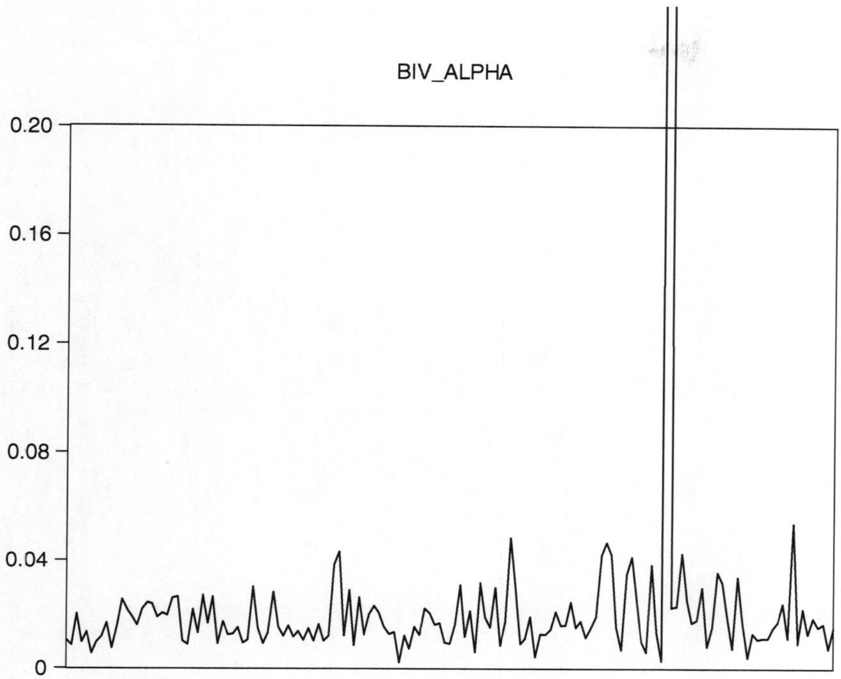

FIG. A1. Estimated alphas from bivariate estimates in MacGyver method.

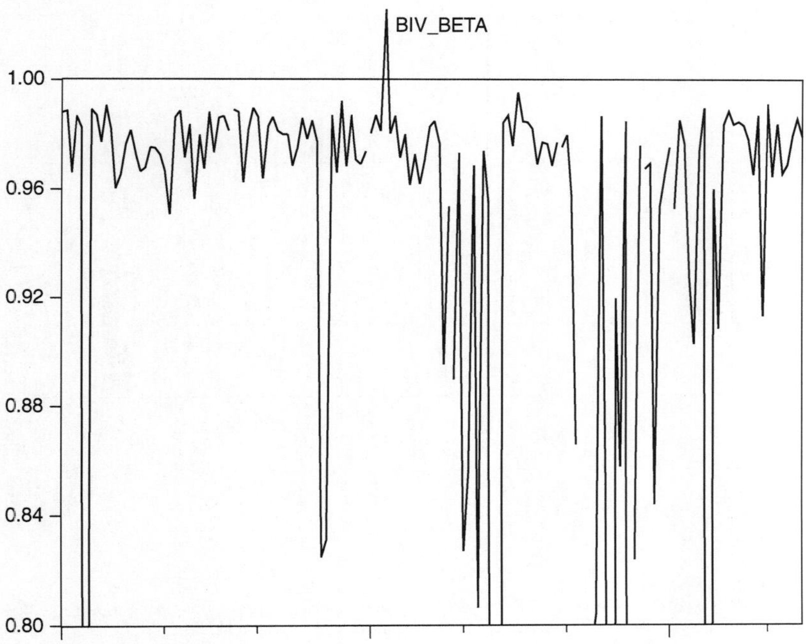

FIG. A2. Estimated betas from bivariate estimates in MacGyver method.

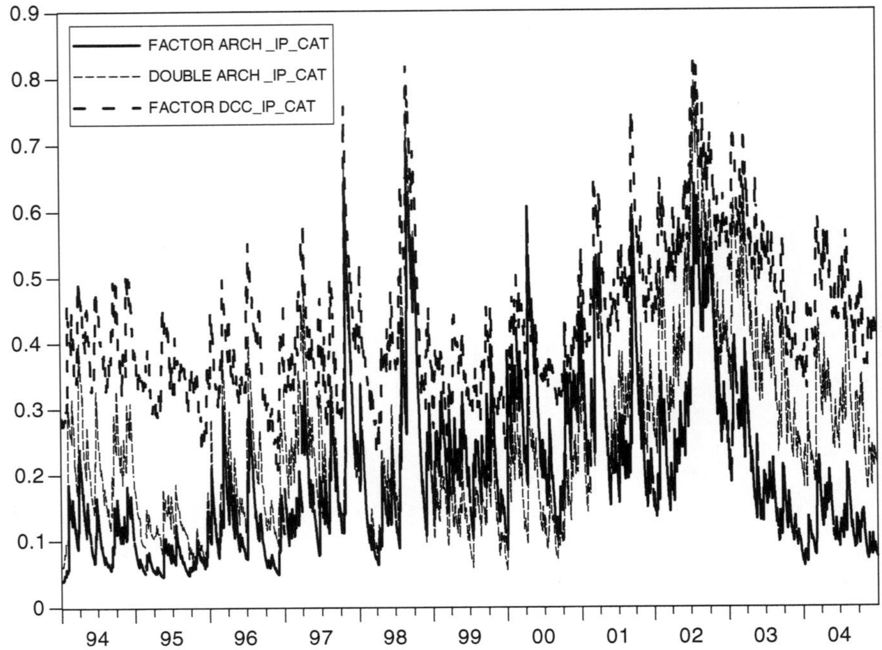

FIG. A3. Correlations between International Paper Caterpillar by several methods.

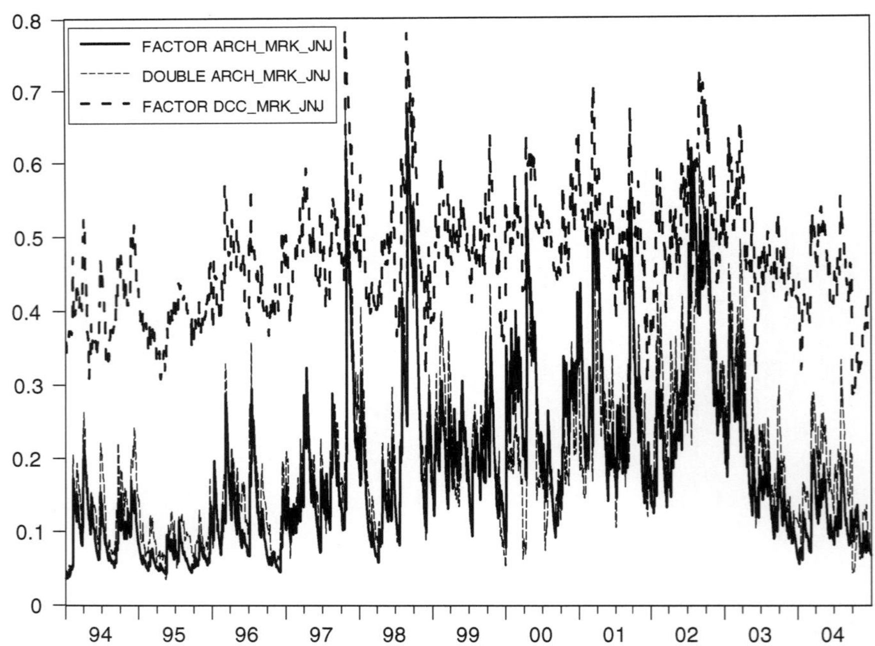

FIG. A4. Correlations between Merck and Johnson and Johnson by various methods.

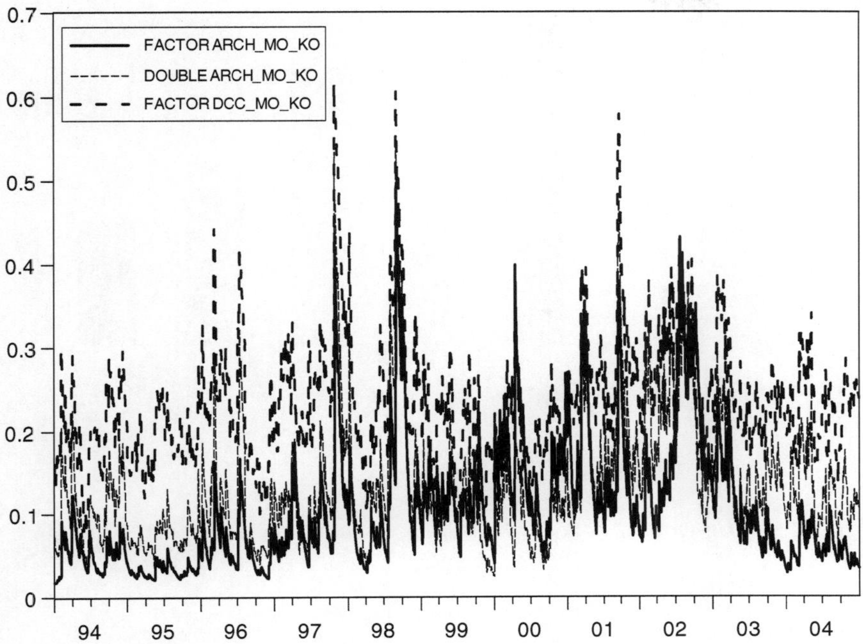

FIG. A5. Correlations between Phillip Morris and Coca Cola by various methods.

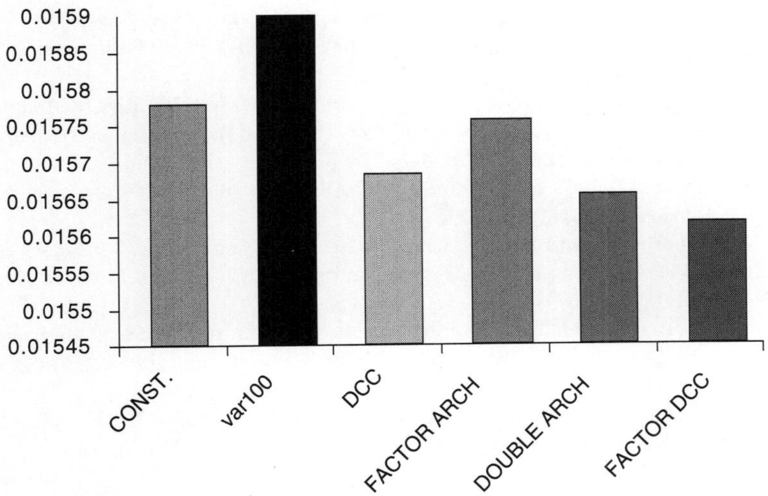

FIG. A6. Average performance of minimum variance portfolios.

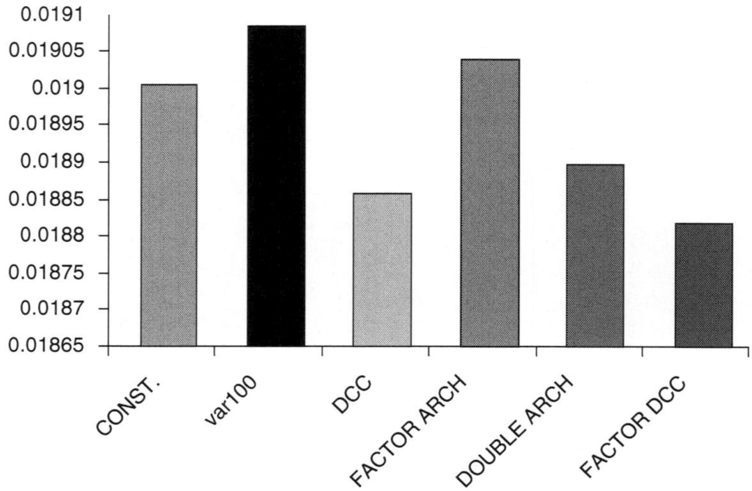

FIG. A7. Average volatility of optimal hedge portfolios.

References

Alexander, C. (2002). Principal compenent models for generating large GARCH covariance matrices. *Economic Notes*, **23**, 337–359.

Audrino, F. and Giovanni, B.-A. (2006). Average conditional correlation and tree structures for multivariate GARCH models. *Journal of Forecasting*, **25**(8), 579–600.

Bautista, C. C. (2003). Interest rate–exchange rate dynamics in the Philippines: a DCC analysis. *Applied Economics Letters*, **10**(2), 107–111.

Bauwens L. Laurent S. (2005). A new class of multivariate skew densities (with application to generalized autoregressive conditional heteroscedasticity models). *Journal of Business & Economic Statistics*, **23**(3), 346–354.

——— and Rombouts, J. (2006). Multivariate GARCH models: A survey. *Journal of Applied Econometrics*, **21**(1), 79–109.

Billio, M., Caporin, M., and Gobbo, M. (2006). Flexible dynamic conditional correlation multivariate GARCH models for asset allocation. *Applied Financial Economics Letters*, **2**(2), 123–130.

Bollerslev, T. (1990). Modelling the coherence in short-run nominal exchange rates: A multivariate generalized ARCH model. *Review of Economics and Statistics*, **72**(3), 498–505.

—— Engle, R., and Nelson, D. (1994). ARCH models. In Engle, R. and McFadden, D. (eds.), *Handbook of Econometrics, Volume IV*, pp. 2959–3038. Amsterdam: North-Holland.

—— and Wooldridge, J. F. (1992). Quasi-maximum likelihood estimation and inference in dynamic models with time varying covariances. *Econometric Reviews*, **11**(2), 143–172.

Campbell, J., Lettau, M., Malkiel, B., and Xu, Y. (2001). Have individual stocks become more volatile? An empirical exploration of idiosyncratic risk. *Journal of Finance*, **LVI**(1), 1–43.

Cappiello, L., Engle, R., and Sheppard, K. (2007). Asymmetric dynamics in the correlations of global equity and bond returns. *Journal of Financial Econometrics*, **4**(4), 537–572.

Chan, F., Lim, C., and McAleer, M. (2005). Modeling multivariate international tourism demand and volatility. *Tourism Management*, **26**(3), 459–471.

Chib, S., Nardari, F., and Shephard, N. (2006). Analysis of high dimensional multivariate stochastic volatility models. *Journal of Econometrics*, **134**(2), 341–371.

Engle, R. (2002). Dynamic conditional correlation—A simple class of mltivariate GARCH models. *Journal of Business and Economic Statistics*, **20**(3), 339–350.

——(2009). *Anticipating Correlations*. Princeton: Princeton University Press.

——and Colacito, R. (2006). Testing and valuing dynamic correlations for asset allocation. *Journal of Business and Economic Statistics*, **24**(2), 238–253.

——Hendry, D. F., and Richard, J.-F. (1983). Exogeneity, *Econometrica*, **51**, 277–304.

——and Kroner, K. (1995). Multivariate simultaneous GARCH. *Econometric Theory*, **11**, 122–150.

——and Mezrich, J. (1996). GARCH for groups. *Risk*, **9**(8), 36–40.

—— Ng, V., and Rothschild, M. (1990). Asset pricing with a factor ARCH covariance structure: Empirical estimates for treasury bills. *Journal of Econometrics*, **45**(1/2), 213–237.

——————(1992). A multi-dynamic factor model for stock returns. *Journal of Econometrics*, **52**(1–2), 245–266.

————(1993). Time varying volatility and the dynamic behavior of the term structure. *Journal of Money, Credit and Banking*, **25**, 336–349.

——and Sheppard, K. (2005a). Theoretical properties of dynamic conditional correlation multivariate GARCH. Manuscript.

————(2005b). Evaluating the specification of covariance models for large portfolios. Manuscript.

——and Susmel, R. (1993). Common volatility in international equity markets. *Journal of Business and Economic Statistics*, **11**(2), 167–176.

Hafner, C. M. and Franses, P. H. (2003). A generalized dynamic conditional correlation model for many assets. *Econometric Institute Report No. 18*, Erasmus University Rotterdam.

——van Dijk, D., and Franses, P. H. (2006). Semi-parametric modelling of correlation dynamics. In Terrell, D. and Fomby, T. B. (eds.), *Econometric Analysis of Financial and Economic Time Series*, Part A. Advances in Econometrices, volume 20, pp. 59–103. Elsevier.

He, C. L. and Teräsvirta, T. (2004). An extended constant conditional correlation GARCH model and its fourth-moment structure. *Econometric Theory*, **20**(5), 904–926.

Kim, S. J., Moshirian, F., and Wu, E. (2006). Evolution of international stock and bond market integration: Influence of the European Monetary Union. *Journal of Banking & Finance*, **30**(5), 1507–1534.

Ledoit, O., Santa-Clara, P., and Wolf, M. (2003). Flexible multivariate GARCH modeling with an application to international stock markets. *Review of Economics and Statistics*, **85**(3), 735–747.

Lee, J. (2006). The comovement between output and prices: Evidence from a dynamic conditional correlation GARCH model. *Economics Letters*, **91**(1), 110–116.

Nelson, D. and Foster, D. (1994). Asymptotic Filtering theory for univariate ARCH models. *Econometrica*, **62**(2), 1–41.

Pelletier, D. (2006). Regime switching for dynamic correlations. *Journal of Econometrics*, **127**(1–2), 445–473.

Palandri, A. (2005). Sequential conditional correlations: Inference and evaluation. Working Paper, SSRN.

Ross, S. (1976). The Arbitrage theory of capital asset pricing. *Journal of Economic Theory*, **13**, 341–360.

Sharpe, W. (1964). Capital asset prices: A theory of market equilibrium under conditions of risk. *Journal of Finance*, **19**, 425–442.

Silvennoinen, A. and Teräsvirta, T. (2008). Multivariate GARCH models. In Andersen, T. W., Davis, R. A., Kreiss, J. P., and Mikosch, T. *Handbook of Financial Time Series*. Springer Verlag.

Taleb, N. (2007). *The Black Swan: The Impact of the Highly Improbable*. Random House Publishing Group.

Tse, Y. K. and Tsui, A. K. C. (2002). A multivariate generalized autoregressive conditional heteroscedasticity model with time-varying correlations. *Journal of Business and Economic Statistics, American Statistical Association*, **20**(3), 351–362.

Vrontos, I. D., Dellaportas, P., and Politis, D. N. (2003). A full-factor multivariate GARCH model. *Econometrics Journal*, **6**, 311–333.

6

Pitfalls in Modelling Dependence Structures: Explorations with Copulas

*Pravin K. Trivedi and David M. Zimmer**

6.1 Introduction

This chapter proposes a modelling approach for testing hypotheses about general forms of stochastic dependence between variables, eg, asset prices, whose marginal distributions display strong nonnormal features such as skewness and/or leptokurticity. The suggested approach exploits the recently developed copula approach that separates inference about marginals and inference about dependence. Additional flexibility results from our use of finite mixture of copulas that reduce both the risk and effects of misspecification. Our analysis is in the spirit of other recent copula-based research on dependence between asset prices, exchange rates, and so forth. In financial econometrics and time-series analysis, the copula approach has attracted considerable attention recently.[1] A central topic in empirical applications concerns the nature of dependence and the interpretation of a copula as a dependence function.

To illustrate the main ideas of this chapter we revisit the problem of testing for (excess) co-movements in commodity prices, previously analysed in Pindyck and Rotemberg (1990) and Deb, Trivedi, and Varangis (1996). The *excess* co-movement (ECM) hypothesis concerns the presence and interpretation of stochastic dependence between price movements of different commodities, even after controlling for the impact of exogenous variables. Such excess co-movement has been interpreted in the literature as casting doubt

* We thank Andrew Patton for helpful comments and suggestions for improving the original draft, and Partha Deb for helpful discussions pertaining to multivariate GARCH Models. All errors are our own.

[1] See Bouyé *et al.* (2000) and Cherubini *et al.* (2004) where many issues of specific relevance to financial applications are covered. See Breymann *et al.* (2003), Chen and Fan (2006), and Patton (2006) for applications that specifically deal with time-series data.

on the efficiency of commodity markets and on the standard competitive commodity price models. Excess co-movements, it has been argued, could reflect a 'herd' or 'fad' mentality on the part of traders that is unrelated to market fundamentals. In a similar spirit, Kyle and Xiong (2001) find that seemingly unrelated assets might exhibit correlation through the people who trade them. Their paper demonstrates that when a certain type of trader loses money, he liquidates assets across other markets generating dependence between unrelated assets. Pindyck and Rotemberg (1990) show, in a linear regression framework, that monthly price changes of a number of *unrelated* commodities displayed the property of co-movements, after accounting for the common effects of observable macroeconomic shocks. Deb *et al.* (1996) show that such evidence was very weak if the modelling and tests of co-movements accommodate both the structural breaks in time-series and certain well-known nonnormal features of commodity prices.[2] Although the two modelling approaches differ substantially, both used linear correlation concepts in examining these hypotheses. In this chapter we propose an alternative and more flexible approach for testing for co-movements.

The main empirical focus in this chapter is modelling co-movements rather than excess co-movements in prices of unrelated commodities. The goal is *not* to link excess co-movements in commodities to 'irrational behaviour' of traders. Because that was the focus in some previous studies, attention was focused on conditional correlation in price changes of commodities that are unrelated in either production or consumption. In this chapter, however, the main interest is in different ways of modelling conditional dependence in commodity price changes, regardless of how the commodities may be related. Studies of commodity prices have often noted the tendency of many commodity prices to rise or fall synchronously, especially when commodity prices are generally high (see Cooper and Lawrence, 1975; Cashin *et al.*, 1999). The literature leaves open the possibility that dependence may be asymmetric and nonlinear rather than symmetric and linear; hence this is the topic of main interest here. Analogously, there are claims in the financial literature that dependence between stock markets may increase during financial crises.

The concept of stochastic dependence is broader than the conventional linear correlation measures typically used in tests of dependence. Therefore, more general approaches are inherently attractive alternatives. Approaches based on copulas can potentially support broader concepts of dependence and thereby allow for a relatively more complete exploration of dependence. Our exploration is confined to the study of commodity price co-movements, but methodological issues that arise have wider relevance and significance.

[2] See Deaton and Laroque (1992) and Deb *et al.* (1996) for a discussion of why commodity prices display strong nonnormal features. See Cashin *et al.* (1999) and Ai *et al.* (2006) for evidence againt the ECM hypothesis.

An important methodological theme that runs through many published works of David Hendry, as well as those of his co-authors and students, is the desirability of a 'general-to-specific' modelling approach, also referred to as 'the LSE approach'. In a series of papers, Hendry and Mizon have developed the idea of 'encompassing' that is closely related to this approach.[3] Hoover and Perez (1999) provide a convenient short characterization of the general-to-specific modelling approach:

> ... a sufficiently complicated model can, in principle, describe the salient features of the economic world. Any more parsimonious model is an improvement on such a complicated model if it conveys all of the same information in a simpler, more compact form. ... The art of model specification in the LSE framework is to seek out models that are valid parsimonious restrictions of the completely general model. ... The name 'general-to-specific' itself implies the contrasting methodology. The LSE school stigmatizes much of common econometric practice as specific-to-general. Here one starts with a simple model, perhaps derived from a simplified (or highly restricted) theory.

Many methodological discussions concerning desirable modelling strategies have been carried out in the context of simple linear dynamic models in which there is local uncertainty about specification. In contrast, this chapter explores types of misspecification that are potentially more severe. We attempt to demonstrate that in studies of dependence between pairs of commodity prices, it is relatively easy to misinterpret dependence as linear and symmetric when in fact dependence is far more complex, and its investigation calls for more complicated models. The reason that dependence is easy to misinterpret in simple linear models is because results often look reasonable at first glance, with no obvious 'red flags' denoting specification problems.

This discussion might appear to suggest that an appropriate remedy is to start with a sufficiently parameterized model capable of handling complex dependence structures. Yet, in the context of modelling heterogeneous data generated by nonlinear models, successful implementation of either the 'general-to-specific' or 'specific-to-general' strategies faces major challenges. To address them adequately requires us to expand the space of models and to include models that go considerably beyond local variants of the initial model.

The purpose of this chapter is not to endorse either of the two approaches as a general modelling strategy. Rather, this chapter is a note of caution that when misspecification is potentially more than a local departure, more effort should be invested into determining the source and nature of dependence. Specifically, we demonstrate how copulas can help determine whether dependence arises from single bivariate distributions or from mixtures of different distributions.

[3] See Mizon and Hendry (1990), Mizon (1995), and Hendry (1997) for some examples.

6.2 Modelling Co-movements

Three approaches for modelling co-movements in commodity prices will be considered. The first, and statistically the simplest and the crudest, is linear regression. The second is based on the 1990s' variants of the multivariate GARCH model. The third, based on copulas, is relatively new in applied econometrics.

6.2.1 *Linear Regression*

Consider the following linear regression model for price changes with a common set of macroeconomic variables, denoted $\mathbf{X}$, used to filter out the linear influence of common observable (macro) shocks.[4] The system of commodity price equations for a set of M 'seemingly unrelated' commodities is given by

$$\Delta p_{it} = \sum_{j=0}^{J} \alpha_{ij} \Delta \mathbf{X}_{t-j} + \rho_i \Delta p_{i,t-1} + \varepsilon_{it}; \; i = 1, \ldots, M, \; t = 1, \ldots, T \tag{6.1}$$

where Δ is the difference operator, and Δp_i denotes the difference in the logarithm of the price of the i-th commodity, and $\mathbf{X}$ is a vector of variables that are weakly exogenous with respect to the individual commodity prices.

In this case tests of conditional dependence are based on whether there is significant correlation between ε_{it} and ε_{jt}, $i = 1, \ldots, M$; $j = 1, \ldots, M$, denoted ρ_{ij}.

6.2.2 *Multivariate GARCH*

The GARCH framework, which allows the conditional distribution of ε_{it} to be time-varying, is an attractive starting point for a modelling exercise; see Engle (2002) and Bauwens *et al.* (2006). Let $\varepsilon_{it} = \eta_{it}\sqrt{h_{it}}$, where h_{it} is the conditional variance at time t and $\Omega_{t-1} = \{\varepsilon_{it-1}, \varepsilon_{it-2}, \ldots\}$ is the conditioning information set indexed at $t-1$ and $\eta_{it} \sim D(0,1)$, a distribution with zero mean and unit variance. Popular choices for D are the normal and the Student $t(\nu)$ distributions; the latter is a priori more attractive when the data display excess kurtosis.

In the multivariate GARCH (M-GARCH) model, the M-element residual vector ε_t is specified as follows:

$$\varepsilon_t \mid \Omega_{t-1} \sim \mathcal{N}(\mathbf{0}, \mathbf{H}_t) \tag{6.2}$$

where $\mathbf{H}_t : (M \times M)$ is the time-varying conditional covariance matrix. Hypotheses about co-movements translate into restrictions on the $\mathbf{H}$

[4] The macroeconomic variables are logarithms of the CPI, industrial production, exchange rate, a stock price, money stock, and interest rate (not in logs). See Deb *et al.* (1996).

matrix. For example, diagonality implies an absence of co-movements. The restrictions depend upon the specification of $\mathbf{H}_t$ and there are several alternatives including (i) the diagonal vech GARCH form, (ii) the positive definite GARCH form, and (iii) the generalized positive definite GARCH form.

We choose to work with the alternative (iii) because it is parsimonious and has a potentially appealing property that each element of $\mathbf{H}_t$ is a function of only its own past history. But this variant does not guarantee positive definiteness of $\mathbf{H}_t$ for all realizations of ε_t. In the Engle–Kroner generalized positive definite form, the conditional covariance matrix for a GARCH (p,q) process is given by:

$$\mathbf{H}_t = \mathbf{C}^* + \sum_{k=1}^{K}\sum_{i=1}^{q} \mathbf{A}_{ik}^{'}\varepsilon_{t-i}\varepsilon_{t-i}^{'}\mathbf{A}_{ik} + \sum_{k=1}^{K}\sum_{i=1}^{p} \mathbf{G}_{ik}^{'}\mathbf{H}_{t-i}\mathbf{G}_{ik}. \tag{6.3}$$

Two alternative factorizations of $\mathbf{C}^*$ are possible (Engle and Kroner, 1995); a symmetric factorization which we use in which $\mathbf{C}^* = \mathbf{C}'\mathbf{C}$ and $\mathbf{C}$ is a symmetric matrix with the ij^{th} element c_{ij} and positive diagonal elements, and a triangular factorization $\mathbf{C}^* = \mathbf{T}'\mathbf{T}$ where $\mathbf{T} = [t_{ij}]$ is an upper triangular matrix. Under the restriction that the diagonal elements of $\mathbf{T}$ are positive, t_{ij} are locally identified. In contrast, the elements c_{ij} are not identified; but some functions of c_{ij}, e.g. c_{ij}^*, are identified, and hence it is valid to compare models with restricted and unrestricted values of $\mathbf{C}^*$.

The number K determines the generality of the process. If $K = 1$, one obtains the positive definite GARCH formulation that has been utilized in a number of applications. This specification is not suitable here because it does not permit tests of diagonality of the $\mathbf{H}_t$ matrix without imposing additional unacceptable restrictions on the parameter matrices, $\mathbf{A}_i$ and $\mathbf{G}_i$.

We use a form of the generalized positive definite GARCH model that sets $K = M$ and imposes restrictions on $\mathbf{A}_{ik}$ and $\mathbf{G}_{ik}$ so that it mimics the diagonal vech formulation. Now it is feasible to test the diagonality of the $\mathbf{H}_t$ matrix without imposing extraneous restrictions on $\mathbf{A}_{ik}$ and $\mathbf{G}_{ik}$. In order to establish the connection between this special case of the generalized positive definite form and the diagonal vech form consider the GARCH(1,1) case with $M = 2$. Then $K = 2$ and

$$\mathbf{H}_t = \mathbf{C}^* + \sum_{k=1}^{K} \mathbf{A}_{k}^{'}\varepsilon_{t-1}\varepsilon_{t-1}^{'}\mathbf{A}_{k} + \sum_{k=1}^{K} \mathbf{G}_{k}^{'}\mathbf{H}_{t-1}\mathbf{G}_{k}. \tag{6.4}$$

Let

$$\mathbf{A}_1^* = \begin{bmatrix} a_{1,11} & 0 \\ 0 & a_{1,22} \end{bmatrix}, \mathbf{A}_2^* = \begin{bmatrix} 0 & 0 \\ 0 & a_{2,22} \end{bmatrix},$$

$$\mathbf{G}_1^* = \begin{bmatrix} g_{1,11} & 0 \\ 0 & g_{1,22} \end{bmatrix}, \mathbf{G}_2^* = \begin{bmatrix} 0 & 0 \\ 0 & g_{2,22} \end{bmatrix}.$$

Then

$$h_{11,t} = c_{11}^2 + c_{12}^2 + a_{1,11}^2 \varepsilon_{1,t-1}^2 + g_{1,11}^2 h_{11,t-1}^2$$
$$h_{12,t} = c_{12}(c_{11} + c_{22}) + a_{1,11}a_{1,22}\varepsilon_{1,t-1}\varepsilon_{2,t-1} + g_{1,11}g_{1,22}h_{12,t-1}.$$
$$h_{22,t} = c_{22}^2 + c_{12}^2 + (a_{1,22}^2 + a_{2,22}^2)\varepsilon_{2,t-1}^2 + (g_{1,22}^2 + g_{2,22}^2)h_{22,t-1}^2$$

The unconditional covariance is defined as

$$\mathrm{E}[\varepsilon_{1t}\varepsilon_{2t}] = \mathrm{E}(h_{12,t}) = \frac{c_{12}(c_{11} + c_{22})}{1 - a_{1,11}a_{1,22} - g_{1,11}g_{1,22}}$$

where the last line is derived using covariance stationarity.

6.2.3 *Interpreting Dependence*

The M-GARCH framework is difficult to implement without simplifying assumptions. Even if such assumptions are accepted, there remains a crucial limitation of the proposed tests of co-movements that they are all tests of *linear dependence* only. Of course, under the normality assumption these are also tests of independence, but normality is a tenuous assumption for commodity price data, which are famously leptokurtic. For an arbitrary pair (X,Y), zero correlation only requires $\mathrm{cov}[X,Y] = 0$, whereas zero dependence requires $\mathrm{cov}[\phi_1(X),\phi_2(Y)] = 0$ for any functions ϕ_1 and ϕ_2. This represents a weakness of correlation as a measure of dependence.

Second, correlation is not defined for some heavy-tailed distributions whose second moments do not exist, eg some members of the stable class and the Student $t(\nu)$ distribution with $\nu \leq 2$. Many commodity prices and financial time-series display the distributional property of heavy tails and nonexistence of higher moments; see, for example, Cont (2001). Boyer, Gibson, and Loretan (1999) found that correlation measures were not sufficiently informative in the presence of asymmetric dependence.[5]

Third, correlation is not invariant under strictly increasing nonlinear transformations, ie, $\rho[T(X),T(Y)] \neq \rho_{XY}$ for $T : \Re \rightarrow \Re$.

Fourth, attainable values of the correlation coefficient within the interval $[-1, +1]$ between a pair of variables depend upon their respective marginal distributions, denoted F_1 and F_2, that place bounds on the value, see Joe (1997, section 3.1). These limitations motivate an alternative measure of dependence, rank correlation.

6.2.3.1 RANK CORRELATION

Similar to linear correlation measures, Spearman and Kendall's rank correlation measures, denoted respectively by $\rho_S(X, Y)$ and $\rho_\tau(X,Y)$, have the property

[5] This paper, which studies 'correlation breakdown', states that in financial applications 'correlations computed separately for ordinary and stressful market conditions differ considerably'.

of symmetry in that $\rho(X,Y) = \rho(Y,X)$. However, in contrast to linear measures, the rank correlation measures have the properties of normalization, co- and countermonotonicity, and assume the value zero under independence.[6] A disadvantage is that although the rank correlation measures have the property of invariance under monotonic transformations and can capture perfect dependence, they are not simple functions of moments and hence computation is more involved. However, for specific parametric copulas the rank correlation can be calculated from the dependence parameter.

6.2.3.2 TAIL DEPENDENCE

Although linear correlation is by far the most widely used measure of dependence in applied econometrics, in some cases the concordance between extreme (tail) values of random variables is often of major interest; see Breymann *et al.* (2003) for a financial application. Other measures of dependence include quadrant dependence and tail dependence. Here we concentrate on tail dependence. Suppose one is interested in the probability that two variables exceed (or fall below) given levels. This requires a dependence measure for upper and lower tails of the distribution. Such a dependence measure is essentially related to the conditional probability that one index exceeds some value given that another exceeds some value. If such a conditional probability measure is a function of the copula, then it too will be invariant under strictly increasing transformations.

Let $F_1(X)$ and $F_2(Y)$ denote the marginal cumulative distribution functions (cdf) of random variables X and Y, respectively. Let $U_1 = F_1^{-1}(X)$ and $U_2 = F_2^{-1}(Y)$ be two random variables with uniform [0,1] distributions. Then $S(u_1,u_2) = \Pr[U_1 > u_1, U_2 > u_2]$ represents the joint survival function. Given the joint survival function $S(u_1,u_2)$ for standard uniform random variables u_1 and u_2, lower and upper tail dependence measures are defined, respectively, by

$$\lambda_L = \lim_{v \to 0^+} \frac{C(v,v)}{v}, \tag{6.5}$$

$$\lambda_U = \lim_{v \to 1^-} \frac{S(v,v)}{1-v}. \tag{6.6}$$

The upper tail dependence measure λ_U is the limiting value of $S(v,v)/(1-v)$, which is the conditional probability $\Pr[U_1 > v | U_2 > v]$ $(= \Pr[U_2 > v | U_1 > v])$; the lower tail dependence measure λ_L is the limiting value of the conditional probability $C(v,v)/v$, which is the conditional probability $\Pr[U_1 < v | U_2 < v]$ $(= \Pr[U_2 < v | U_1 < v])$. The measure λ_U is widely used in actuarial applications

[6] For any (x_j,y_j) and (x_k,y_k), a co-monotonic set is that for which $\{x_j \le y_j, x_k \le y_k\}$ or $\{x_j \ge y_j, x_k \ge y_k\}$. A countermonotonic set is that for which $\{x_j \le y_j, x_k \ge y_k\}$ or $\{x_j \ge y_j, x_k \le y_k\}$. Normalization means that rank correlation measures lie in the interval $[-1,1]$.

of extreme value theory to handle the probability that one event is extreme conditional on another extreme event.

6.3 Copulas

This section presents an approach for testing for dependence using copulas. Hypotheses regarding co-movements can be expressed in terms of restrictions on joint distributions. But the parametric functional forms of joint distributions themselves place restrictions on the nature of dependence that is supported. In this context copulas are useful because, first, they represent a method for deriving alternative functional forms of joint distributions given fixed marginals that can be chosen separately; see Trivedi and Zimmer (2007), Zimmer and Trivedi (2006). Further, in a bivariate context, copulas can be used to define nonparametric measures of dependence for pairs of random variables that can capture asymmetric (tail) dependence as well as correlation or linear association.

6.3.1 *Background*

It is useful to begin with some definitions and background before proceeding to characterization and estimation of dependence parameters. An m-copula is an m-dimensional cdf whose support is contained in $[0,1]^m$ and whose one-dimensional margins are uniform on $[0,1]$. In other words, an m-copula is an m-dimensional distribution function with all m univariate margins being $U(0,1)$. To see the relationship between distribution functions and copulas, consider a continuous m-variate distribution function $F(y_1,\ldots y_m)$ with univariate marginal distributions $F_1(y_1), \ldots, F_m(y_m)$ and inverse probability transforms (quantile functions) $F_1^{-1}, \ldots, F_m^{-1}$. Then $y_1 = F_1^{-1}(u_1) \sim F_1, \ldots, y_m = F_m^{-1}(u_m) \sim F_m$ where $u_1, \ldots, u_m$ are uniformly distributed variates. Copulas are expressed in terms of marginal c.d.f., meaning that $F_1,\ldots,F_m$ are cumulative distribution functions rather than probability density (or mass) functions. The transforms of uniform variates are distributed as $F_i (i = 1,\ldots,m)$. Hence

$$F(y_1,\ldots,y_m) = F(F_1^{-1}(u_1),\ldots,F_m^{-1}(u_m)) = C(u_1,\ldots,u_m), \tag{6.7}$$

is the unique copula associated with the distribution function. By Sklar's (1973) theorem, the copula parameterizes a multivariate distribution in terms of its marginals. For an m-variate distribution F, the copula satisfies

$$F(y_1,\ldots,y_m) = C(F_1(y_1),\ldots,F_m(y_m);\theta), \tag{6.8}$$

where θ is usually a scalar-valued dependence parameter. Like all multivariate distributions, copulas are bounded below and above by the Fréchet lower and upper bounds (see Joe, 1997, Ch. 3). However, the functional form of some copulas might place restrictions on the dependence parameter such that one or both Fréchet bounds are not included in the permissible range.

6.3.2 *Dependence*

In the present context, the dependence parameter is the focus of estimation. Because the marginal distributions may be freely chosen, copulas provide a method for generating joint distributions by combining given marginal distributions using a known copula. This construction allows researchers to consider marginal distributions and dependence as two separate issues.

The functional form of a copula places restrictions on the dependence structure; for example it may only support positive dependence. Therefore, a pivotal modelling problem is to choose a copula that adequately captures dependence structures of the data without sacrificing attractive properties of the marginals.

An important advantage of copulas is that they generate more general measures of dependence than the correlation coefficient. Correlation is a symmetric measure of linear dependence, bounded between +1 and −1, and invariant with respect to only linear transformations of the variables. By contrast, copulas have an attractive invariance property: the dependence captured by a copula is invariant with respect to increasing and continuous transformations of the marginal distributions. The same copula may be used for, say, the joint distribution of (Y_1, Y_2) as $(\exp(Y_1), \exp(Y_2))$.

Measures of dependence based on concordance, such as Spearman's rank correlation (ρ) and Kendall's τ, overcome limitations of the correlation coefficient. In some cases the concordance between extreme (tail) values of random variables is of interest. For example, one may be interested in the probability of the event that price changes of gold and oil exceed (or fall below) given levels. This requires a dependence measure for upper and lower tails of the distribution, rather than a linear correlation measure. Measures of lower and upper tail dependence can be readily derived for a stated copula. The copula dependence parameter θ can be converted to measures of concordance such as Spearman's ρ and Kendall's τ (Nelsen, 2006).

Copulas are also useful for examining issues regarding tail dependence. For copulas with simple analytical expressions, the computation of λ_U can be straightforward, being a simple function of the dependence parameter. For example, for the Gumbel copula λ_U equals $2 - 2^{\theta}$. In cases where the copula's analytical expression is not available, the tail dependence measure can be calculated using the conditional probability representation.

6.3.3 *Selected Copulas*

Standard works on copulas, eg Nelsen (2006), provide extensive tabulations of copulas. The main points of this chapter can be made using a handful of these, so four copulas, as well as other mixture copulas generated from them, will be used.

6.3.3.1 GAUSSIAN (NORMAL) COPULA

The normal copula takes the form

$$C(u_1,u_2;\theta) = \Phi_G\left(\Phi^{-1}(u_1),\Phi^{-1}(u_2);\theta\right), \tag{6.9}$$

$$= \int_{-\infty}^{\Phi^{-1}(u_1)} \int_{-\infty}^{\Phi^{-1}(u_2)} \frac{1}{2\pi(1-\theta^2)^{1/2}} \left\{ \frac{-(s^2 - 2\theta st + t^2}{2(1-\theta^2)} \right\} dsdt$$

where Φ is the cdf of the standard normal distribution, and $\Phi_G(u_1,u_2)$ is the standard bivariate normal distribution with correlation parameter θ restricted to the interval $(-1,1)$. The normal copula is flexible in that it allows for equal degrees of positive and negative dependence and includes both Fréchet bounds in its permissible range.

The bivariate Gaussian copula has the property of asymptotic independence. Embrechts *et al.* (2002) remark: 'Regardless of how high a correlation we choose, if we go far enough into the tail, extreme events appear to occur independently in each margin.' In contrast, the bivariate *t*-distribution displays asymptotic upper tail dependence even for negative and zero correlations, with dependence rising as the degrees-of-freedom parameter decreases and the marginal distributions become heavy-tailed; see Table 1 in Embrechts *et al.* (2002).

6.3.3.2 STUDENT *T*-COPULA

An example of a copula with two dependence parameters is that for the bivariate *t*-distribution with ν degrees of freedom and correlation θ,

$$C^t(u_1,u_2;\nu,\theta) = \int_{-\infty}^{t_\nu^{-1}(u_1)} \int_{-\infty}^{t_\nu^{-1}(u_2)} \frac{1}{2\pi(1-\theta^2)^{1/2}} \tag{6.10}$$

$$\times \left\{ 1 + \frac{(s^2 - 2\theta st + t^2}{\nu(1-\theta^2)} \right\}^{-(\nu+2)/2} dsdt$$

where $t_\nu^{-1}(u_1)$ denotes the inverse of the cdf of the standard univariate *t*-distribution with ν degrees of freedom. The two dependence parameters are (ν,θ). The parameter ν controls the heaviness of the tails. For $\nu < 3$, the variance does not exist, for $\nu < 5$, the fourth moment does not exist. As $\nu \to \infty$, $C^t(u_1,u_2;\nu,\theta) \to \Phi_G(u_1,u_2;\theta)$. This copula permits symmetric tail dependence.

6.3.3.3 CLAYTON COPULA

The Clayton (1978) copula takes the form

$$C(u_1,u_2;\theta) = (u_1^{-\theta} + u_2^{-\theta} - 1)^{-1/\theta} \tag{6.11}$$

with the dependence parameter θ restricted on the region $(0,\infty)$. As θ approaches zero, the marginals become independent. As θ approaches infinity, the copula attains the Fréchet upper bound, but for no value does it attain the Fréchet lower bound. The Clayton copula exhibits asymmetric dependence in that dependence in the lower tail is stronger than in the upper tail, but the Clayton copula cannot account for negative dependence.

6.3.3.4 GUMBEL COPULA

The Gumbel (1960) copula takes the form

$$C(u_1,u_2;\theta) = \exp\left(-(\tilde{u}_1^{\theta} + \tilde{u}_2^{\theta})^{1/\theta}\right) \tag{6.12}$$

where $\tilde{u}_j = -\log u_j$. The dependence parameter is restricted to the interval $[1,\infty)$. Values of 1 and ∞ correspond to independence and the Fréchet upper bound, but this copula does not attain the Fréchet lower bound for any value of θ. Similar to the Clayton copula, Gumbel does not allow negative dependence, but in contrast to Clayton, Gumbel exhibits strong upper tail dependence and relatively weak lower tail dependence.[7]

The table below summarizes the main features of the four copulas.

Table 6.1. Some standard copula functions

Copula type	Function $C(u_1,u_2)$	θ-domain	Kendall's τ	Spearman's ρ
Gaussian	$\Phi_G[\Phi_G^{-1}(u_1)\Phi_G^{-1}(u_2);\theta]$	$-1<\theta<+1$	$\frac{2}{\pi}\arcsin(\theta)$	$\frac{6}{\pi}\arcsin(\frac{\theta}{2})$
Student's t	$\int_{-\infty}^{t_\nu^{-1}(u_1)}\int_{-\infty}^{t_\nu^{-1}(u_2)}\frac{1}{2\pi(1-\theta^2)^{1/2}} \times \left\{1+\frac{(s^2-2\theta st+t^2)}{\nu(1-\theta^2)}\right\}^{-(\nu+2)/2} dsdt$	$-1<\theta<+1$	$\frac{2}{\pi}\arcsin(\theta)$	Not available
Clayton	$(u_1^{-\theta}+u_2^{-\theta}-1)^{-1/\theta}$	$(0,\infty)$	$\theta/(\theta+2)$	Complicated
Gumbel	$\exp\left(-(\tilde{u}_1^{\theta}+\tilde{u}_2^{\theta})^{1/\theta}\right)$, $\tilde{u}_j=-\log u_j$	$[1,\infty)$	$1-\frac{1}{\theta}$	No closed form

[7] The dependence characteristics of the Clayton and Gumbel copulas suggest that Clayton (Gumbel) is an appropriate choice when dependence is expected to be strongest in the lower (upper) tail. However, there are other options. Patton (2004) finds that the survival Gumbel fits stock returns with lower tail dependence better than the Clayton. In a later article (Patton, 2006), he takes a more agnostic approach in using a 'symmetrized Joe-Clayton' copula that can flexibly handle both lower and upper tail dependence.

6.3.4 *Mixtures of Copulas*

As mentioned above, parametric copulas place restrictions on the dependence parameter. When the process generating data is heterogenous, it is desirable to have additional flexibility in modelling dependence. Finite mixtures of copulas can provide such flexibility. For example, consider a finite mixture with three bivariate component copulas (Gaussian (C_{Ga}), Gumbel (C_{Gu}), and Clayton (C_C)), each with different dependence properties:

$$C_{mix}(u_1,u_2;\rho,\alpha,\theta) = \pi_1 C_{Ga}(u_1,u_2;\rho) + \pi_2 C_{Gu}(u_2,u_2;\alpha) + (1-\pi_1-\pi_2)C_C(u_1,u_2;\theta), \tag{6.13}$$

$0 < \pi_j < 1$, $\sum \pi_j = 1$, and π_1 and π_2 may be interpreted as population weights of the Gaussian and Gumbel copulas, respectively. Such a mixture allows one to capture left and/or right tail dependence. The Clayton component can model lower tail dependence that depends upon θ, the Gumbel component can model upper tail dependence, and the Gaussian component can model linear dependence.[8]

The cost of additional flexibility of functional form is the added complexity of estimation and inference. These issues are covered in section 6.4.

6.3.5 *Two Monte Carlo Experiments*

As discussed above, linear correlation is the most widely used dependence concept in econometrics, but for many financial applications linear measures of correlation might fail to capture potentially strong concordance between extreme (tail) values. Linear correlation measures are especially problematic when two random variables exhibit asymmetric tail dependence. For example, prices of two different commodities, say, cotton and gold, might be mostly unrelated, and consequently the time-series of prices might exhibit almost zero linear correlation. But when the price of gold increases by a large amount, cotton prices might also increase dramatically, as prices of both commodities partly depend on economy-wide phenomena. Linear measures of correlation are poorly suited for capturing this type of asymmetric tail dependence.

This section presents and discusses results of two Monte Carlo experiments. The experiments attempt to generate data that are similar to those used in financial empirical applications. The purpose of the experiments is to demonstrate the shortcomings of models that are typically used to model financial data; these models usually rely on symmetric measures of linear correlation to capture dependence.

[8] Hu (2004) studies the dependence of monthly returns between four stock indexes: S&P 500, FTSE, Nikkei, and Hang Seng. She models dependence on a pair-wise basis using a finite mixture of three copulas (Gaussian (C_G), Gumbel (C_{Gumbel}) and Gumbel-Survival (C_{GS})).

We attempt to demonstrate three specific conclusions. First, linear correlation measures are not sufficiently informative when dependence is asymmetric. This finding corroborates the conclusions of Boyer, Gibson, and Loretan (1999). Second, linear correlation measures tend to underestimate the magnitude of dependence in the presence of asymmetric dependence. Although Student t-copula is a slight improvement due to its ability to accommodate tail dependence, it also underestimates dependence when dependence is not symmetric. Third, when dependence arises from a mixture of different data generating processes, no single copula is able to accurately estimate dependence, not even copulas that account for asymmetric tail dependence, such as the Gumbel copula. Rather, the results indicate that finite mixtures of copulas significantly improve accuracy in estimating dependence.

6.3.5.1 EXPERIMENT 1

The first experiment investigates the implications of pairs of random variables that exhibit weak dependence throughout the middle of the distribution and strong upper tail dependence. The experiment uses 4,000 pairs of randomly drawn observations, of which 3,600 (90%) are generated by a Gaussian copula with standard normal marginals and dependence parameter set equal to 0.05. The remaining 400 (10%) observations are drawn from the Gumbel copula with standard normal marginals and dependence parameter equal to 3.33. (The Gumbel dependence parameter of 3.33 translates to a Kendall's τ value of 0.7.) The sample is intended to mimic the dependence characteristic of many commodity price pairs that exhibit mostly weak dependence in the middle and lower parts of bivariate distributions but strong dependence in the upper tails.

The Monte Carlo experiment is conducted as follows. First, 4,000 pairs of observations are randomly drawn as described in the previous paragraph. Second, three different copula models are estimated: (1) Gaussian with standard normal marginals, (2) Student $t(5)$-copula, with standard normal marginals, and (3) a finite mixture of Gaussian and Gumbel copulas, both with standard normal marginals. We refer to Models (1) and (2) as '1-component' and Model (3) as '2-component'. The number of Monte Carlo replications is 1,000.

A priori, Model (1) is expected to understate the magnitude of dependence, as the Gaussian copula cannot accommodate symmetric or asymmetric tail dependence. Model (2) should offer a small improvement, as the Student t-copula can capture tail dependence, but it should also understate the magnitude of dependence, because similar to the Gaussian copula, the $t(\nu)$-copula imposes symmetric dependence. On the other hand, Model (3) should accurately estimate all parameters, as this is consistent with the true data generating process.

Medians, means, and standard deviations of the estimates across the 1,000 replications from Experiment 1 are reported in Table 6.2. Figure 6.1 shows

Table 6.2. Summary statistics for Monte Carlo Experiment 1

Copula specification	Median	Mean	St. Dev.	True values
2-component				
Gaussian	0.05	0.05	0.02	0.05
Gumbel	3.34	3.41	0.71	3.33
$\pi_{Gaussian}$	0.90	0.90	0.04	0.90
1-component				
Gaussian	0.13	0.13	0.02	na
Student's $t(5)$	0.13	0.13	0.02	na

the smoothed kernel distribution of the dependence parameters obtained in the Monte Carlo experiment. In the correctly specified 2-component case the dependence parameter for the Gaussian component has a symmetric distribution centred on the true value, but the parameter of the Gumbel component appears upward biased, albeit with a large standard deviation. Its Monte Carlo distribution also does not seem symmetric. The latter may reflect the difficulty of pinning down accurately the existence of tail dependence in what may be effectively a 'small sample'.

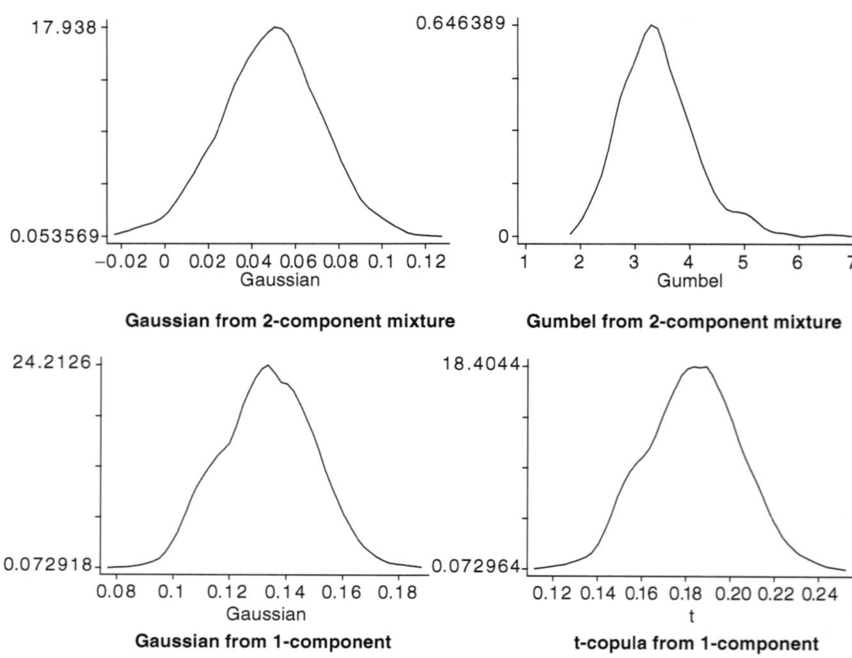

FIG. 6.1. Monte Carlo distribution of $\hat{\theta}$ in Experiment 1.

In contrast, the two 1-component (misspecified) models would suggest symmetric dependence structures. On average both specifications overestimate the symmetric dependence parameter. The Gaussian one-component model 'hides' the dependence between extreme values in the upper tail of the distribution because it cannot support tail dependence. In theory, the Student $t(5)$ should provide a better specification because it is consistent with the presence of *symmetric* tail dependence.[9] If similar results were found in an empirical study, potentially misleading conclusions might be drawn.

6.3.5.2 EXPERIMENT 2

The DGP in Experiment 2 uses a 3-component mixture of Gaussian (80%), Gumbel (10%), and Clayton (10%). The total sample size is 4,000 observations; the Gumbel dependence parameter is set to 1.50, the Clayton dependence parameter is set to 0.80, and the Gaussian dependence parameter is set to 0.10. The dependence parameters for Gumbel and Clayton translate to Kendall's τ values of 0.33 and 0.29, respectively. All marginals are standard normal. Compared to the data generating process Experiment 1, dependence is greater in the middle of the distribution and smaller but more symmetric in the tails, as Gumbel imposes upper tail dependence while Clayton imposes lower tail dependence. The purpose of the experiment is to examine how well any of the 1- or 2-component misspecified models perform.

For each replication, nine different models are estimated. The first five are 1-component models: (1) Gaussian, (2) Clayton, (3) Gumbel, (4) Student $t(5)$, and (5) Student $t(3)$. The first three are expected to perform poorly, as the Gaussian does not account for tail dependence, while Clayton and Gumbel account only for lower and upper tail dependence, respectively. The Student t-copula might provide better fit than the Gaussian. The next three models are 2-component mixtures: (6) Gaussian–Clayton, (7) Gaussian–Gumbel, and (8) Clayton–Gumbel. The final model is a 3-component mixture consistent with the true data generating process: (9) Gauss–Clayton–Gumbel.

Results from 1,000 replications are reported in Table 6.3 and Figure 6.2. Results for model 9, the correctly specified 3-component mixture, show that all dependence parameters have a positive bias. Further, the Clayton and Gumbel parameters have right-skewed sampling distributions that are inconsistent with asymptotic normality.

In the case of the three variants of the 2-component misspecified mixture models, the most seriously misspecified is the Clayton–Gumbel mixture as it lacks the Gaussian component that accounts for 80% of the observations.

[9] In preliminary work, a similar experiment was conducted where the data generating process drew 3,600 observations from Student's $t(\nu)$-copula and dependence parameter equal to 0.05, and the remaining 400 observations were drawn from the Gumbel copula with dependence parameter equal to 3.33. Results were similar to those reported in Experiment 1.

Table 6.3. Summary statistics for Monte Carlo Experiment 2

Copula specification	Median	Mean	St. Dev.	True values
	3-component mixture			
Gaussian	0.11	0.14	0.16	0.10
Clayton	0.77	0.94	0.95	0.80
Gumbel	1.45	1.78	1.19	1.50
π_{Ga}	0.76	0.69	0.24	0.80
π_{Gu}	0.11	0.18	0.22	0.10
	2-component mixtures			
Gaussian	0.18	0.18	0.17	
Clayton	1.54	1.54	1.87	
π_{Ga}	0.92	0.87	0.20	
Gaussian	0.14	0.14	0.04	
Gumbel	2.23	2.56	1.31	
π_{Ga}	0.95	0.93	0.07	
Clayton	0.29	0.40	0.29	
Gumbel	1.10	1.19	0.23	
π_{Cl}	0.44	0.46	0.23	
	1-component copulas			
Gaussian	0.17	0.17	0.02	na
Clayton	—	—	—	—
Gumbel	1.10	1.10	0.04	—
Student's $t(3)$	0.15	0.15	0.02	—
Student's $t(5)$	0.16	0.16	0.02	

In this case, the true tail dependence coefficients are

$$\tau^L = 0.10 \times 2^{-1/0.8} + 0.80 \times 0 + 0.10 \times 0 = 0.042,$$

$$\tau^U = 0.10 \times 0 + 0.80 \times 0 + 0.10 \times (2 - 2^{1/1.5}) = 0.0413,$$

whereas the estimated tail dependence coefficients from the Clayton–Gumbel mixture are

$$\hat{\tau}^L = 0.46 \times 2^{-1/0.40} + 0.54 \times 0 = 0.0813,$$

$$\hat{\tau}^U = 0.46 \times 0 + 0.54 \times (2 - 2^{1/1.19}) = 0.1131.$$

So tail dependence is exaggerated. In general, it is important to exercise care when discussing dependence because the evaluation will depend on which measure of dependence one uses.

Finally, consider the five specifications of 1-component models. Of these the Clayton model is found to be the least satisfactory as it fails to converge in a large number of the cases; the results for this case are not included. The performance of the Gaussian and Student $t(\nu)$ specifications is very similar. Here the dependence parameter is overestimated. The Gumbel model, by contrast, underestimates upper tail dependence. None of the copulas is informative about the dependence structure, although all capture some aspect of

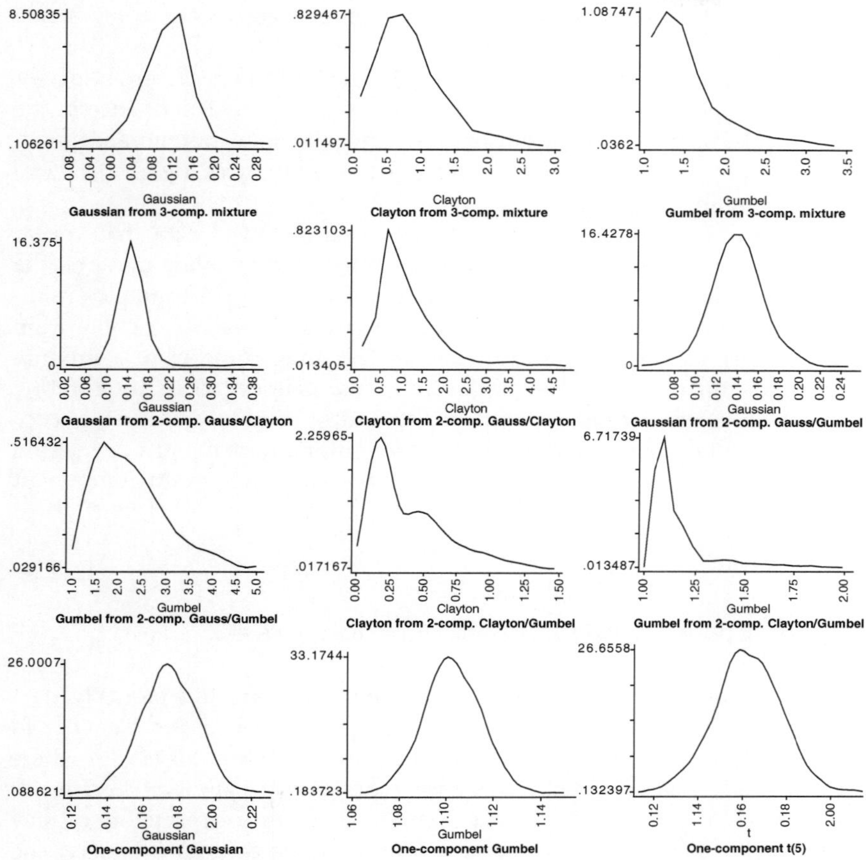

FIG. 6.2. Monte Carlo distribution of $\hat{\theta}$ in Experiment 2.

dependence in the true specification. It is interesting that in all four cases the sampling distribution of the dependence parameter is symmetric.

6.3.5.3 IMPLICATIONS FOR MODELLING STRATEGIES

The results of this sampling experiment suggest that identification of dependence parameters of a mixture copula is quite difficult even in a relatively simple setting. More research is needed to determine the source of biases that have been observed. The development of a robust general-to-specific modelling strategy in such a setting is also far from obvious.

The DGP in the two experiments above have dependence characteristics that are frequently expected in applied econometrics. These are tail dependence and switching regimes that justify the mixture specification.

Yet empirical workers typically favour homogeneous (one-component) models with symmetric dependence.

For highly skewed data, the Monte Carlo results of Experiment 1 suggest that one-component symmetric models will overestimate dependence in the middle of the distribution but substantially underestimate (or ignore) dependence between extreme values. This could be a potentially costly misspecification for commodity traders.

Results from Experiment 2 are also discouraging. Given data that appear symmetrically distributed but actually generated by a bivariate mixture, the results of 1-component models can be quite misleading. For example, a simple scatter plot might lead one to conclude that the variables come from a bivariate spherical distribution when in fact they come from a mixture of bivariate distributions. Hence one must use caution when interpreting results from overly simplified models. Estimation of finite mixtures of copulas is a useful (albeit a potentially computationally demanding) method for checking whether dependence is consistent with multi-component mixing.

6.4 An Application to Monthly Commodity Prices

In this section, we estimate bivariate copula models using monthly data from 1974–92 period on four commodities—corn, cotton, crude oil, and gold. These data are a subset of the data used in Deb *et al.* (1996) where they are described in detail. Here three commodity pairs will be considered: corn–cotton; oil–gold; gold–cotton. The first pair is expected to display co-movement because the commodities are both agricultural products. The second pair might be expected to exhibit co-movement, as global prices of oil and gold are expressed in US dollars and thus both are dependent on US monetary policy. However, the third pair is expected to display less co-movement.

For each pair several copulas are estimated. Estimation of a copula requires specification of the marginal distributions and of the copula. In all three cases the marginal distribution of the errors is assumed to follow the Student $t(5)$ distribution. Four specifications of copulas were considered: Gaussian, Student $t(\nu)$ with ν free or fixed at 5, Clayton, and Gumbel. The Gaussian copula does not display tail dependence, but the Student t potentially does. Both can be used to model either positive or negative association. The Clayton copula can capture only positive lower tail dependence, and the Gumbel copula can capture positive upper tail dependence. The choice of copulas is influenced by the expectation of positive association predicted by the co-movement hypothesis.

6.4.1 *Copula Estimation*

A two-step maximum likelihood method is used that separates the estimation of the marginals from that of the dependence parameter. Consider a bivariate copula. The first stage of estimation, described below, generates residuals that are treated as realizations of i.i.d. random variables. After applying a probability integral transformation, whose form is determined by the assumption about the parametric marginal distribution, one obtains observations that are treated as realizations of uniform random variables u_1 and u_2, respectively. Given the realizations $\{\hat{u}_{1t}, \hat{u}_{2t}, t = 1, \ldots, T\}$, and a copula density $c(F_1(u_1),\ F_2(u_2)) = dC(F_1(u_1), F_2(u_2))/dy_2dy_1. = C_{12}(F_1(u_1), F_2(u_2))\, f_1(\cdot)\, f_2(\cdot)$, the dependence parameter θ can be estimated as follows:

$$\hat{\theta}_{TSML} = \arg\max_{\theta} \sum_{t=1}^{T} \ln c_t(\hat{u}_{1t}, \hat{u}_{2t}; \theta). \tag{6.14}$$

Inference on $\hat{\theta}_{TSML}$ can be carried out using standard quasi-maximum likelihood theory.

The estimation procedure is similar to the approach of Chen and Fan (2006) for estimating semiparametric copula-based multivariate dynamic (SCOMDY) models, eg, the generalized autoregressive conditional heteroskedastic (GARCH) model.[10] In the first step of our approach, univariate GARCH(1,1) AR(6) models are estimated for each commodity, and standardized residuals are calculated from these regressions.[11] The purpose of the first step is to filter out any volatility and autoregressive behaviour that might contaminate estimation of dependence in the second stage. Let the first stage estimated residuals be denoted $\hat{\varepsilon}_{jt}$ for commodity j at time t. At the second stage the likelihood based on a specified copula density $c(F_1(\hat{\varepsilon}_{1t}), \ldots, F_M(\hat{\varepsilon}_{Mt}); \theta)$ is maximized to estimate the dependence parameters θ. A Gaussian copula has been used by Hull and White (1998) and is a special case of model in Engle (2002); Student t and Clayton copulas are used in Breymann (2003) and mixture copulas are used in Dias and Embrechts (2004).

6.4.2 *Results from Copula Models*

The main focus in the results is on the nature of dependence between commodity pairs. If the dependence is nonlinear and mainly in the lower or upper tails of the joint distribution, we would expect Clayton or Gumbel copulas to

[10] Chen and Fan establish the asymptotic distribution of the dependence parameter and provide an estimation procedure for the variances under possible misspecification of the parametric copula. One interesting result they obtain is that the asymptotic distribution of the dependence parameters is not affected by the estimation of the first stage parameters.

[11] The first stage models were estimated with and without exogenous explanatory variables with similar results. Estimates presented below do not include explanatory variables.

Table 6.4. Estimates of dependence parameters of bivariate models of commodity prices

	Dependence parameter and standard error								
	Gold–crude oil			Commodity pairs corn–cotton			Gold–cotton		
Copula	Est.	Std. err.	Log-lik	Est.	Std. err	Log-lik	Est.	Std. err	Log-lik
Gauss	0.237	0.151	−377.4	0.250	0.109	−645.5	0.061	0.123	−657.2
Student $t(5)$	0.219	0.124	−375.4	0.241	0.097	−642.1	0.049	0.105	−653.5
Student $t(\nu) : \hat{\theta}$	0.183	0.108	−372.2	0.194	0.088	−637.6	0.043	0.088	−647.5
Student $t(\nu) : \hat{\nu}$	13.110	7.80	—	11.581	4.75	—	15.882	6.39	—
Clayton	0.286	0.217	−377.5	0.362	0.139	−644.7	nc	nc	nc
Gumbel	1.196	0.107	−376.2	1.189	0.085	−644.8	1.097	0.060	−655.4
Copula mixture									
Mix(2):CGu									
C	1.467	0.980	−376.0	7.434	8.117	−643.5	nc	nc	nc
Gu	1.144	0.146	—	1.122	0.102	—	nc	nc	—
π_C	0.141	0.215		0.086	0.082		nc	nc	—
Mix(2):GaC									
Ga	−0.042	0.508	−376.6	−0.796	0.422	−643.4	−0.450	0.256	−656.3
C	1.342	1.212		0.514	0.234		0.551	0.667	
π_{Ga}	0.669	0.461		0.109	0.149		0.384	0.338	
Mix(2):GaGu									
Ga	−0.340	0.191	−374.6	−0.612	0.206	−642.5	−0.414	0.161	−652.3
Gu	1.824	0.371		1.415	0.200		1.555	0.504	
π_{Ga}	0.504	0.167		0.225	0.151		0.545	0.250	
Mix(3):CGaGu									
Ga	−0.398	0.153	−374.5	−0.691	0.250	−641.3	nc	nc	nc
C	0.459	0.468		0.359	0.233		nc	nc	
Gu	1.809	0.363		2.180	1.186		nc	nc	
π_{Ga}	0.394	0.258		0.163	0.140		nc	nc	
π_C	0.169	0.401		0.576	0.308		nc	nc	

provide better fits. For Clayton the measure of lower tail dependence is $2^{-1/\theta}$ and for Gumbel the measure of upper tail dependence is $2 - 2^{\theta}$. Therefore, for small values of θ, there would be little lower tail dependence. For $\theta \simeq 1$, Gumbel copula would indicate no right tail dependence. If dependence is mostly linear, then the Gaussian copula should fit well. If tail dependence is symmetric, then the Student $t(\nu)$ copula is a suitable choice. The degrees-of-freedom parameter ν can be constrained or left free. As $\nu \to \infty$, tail dependence will disappear. Both alternatives will be considered. Whether we can discriminate between the alternative specifications is an empirical question.

The results are given in Table 6.4. They indicate positive dependence in all three cases, though it is weak for the gold–cotton pair, as expected. The highest log-likelihood value is obtained for the Student t copula with two dependence parameters, though the 2-standard error confidence interval around $\hat{\nu}$ is quite wide. Nevertheless the likelihood ratio test of $H_0 : \nu = 5$ vs. $H_1 : \nu \neq 5$ rejects the null at 5% in all three cases. However, for the Student $t(5)$ copula the log-likelihood is larger than for the remaining competing alternatives.

The log-likelihood of the Gumbel and Clayton copulas is similar and slightly better than that of the Gaussian copula. While the dependence parameter for the Clayton model is positive it is quite imprecisely estimated and implies negligible lower tail dependence. The Gumbel results, on the other hand, suggest some upper tail dependence. In sum, discrimination between the copulas is not at all sharp.

The results for the cotton–corn pair are somewhat clearer. All copulas provide evidence of positive dependence, and there is also evidence from Clayton and Gumbel estimates that support both lower and upper tail dependence, respectively. Consistent with this interpretation is the result that the Student $t(5)$ model fits the data best, a result that suggests that tail dependence is a feature of the data and that the Gaussian copula fails to capture this dependence.

The results for the gold–cotton pair overall suggest, as expected, zero dependence. For this pair the maximization of likelihood of the Clayton model fails to converge.

6.4.3 *Results from Copula Mixtures*

Commodity prices are known at times to move in highly nonlinear fashion; see Deaton and Laroque (1992) for an explanation of such nonlinearities. If co-movements are associated with such sharp movements, rather than with smooth small changes, then mixture models seem to offer the flexibility needed for modelling such data. We therefore test the copula specification against a mixture alternative.

The most general of the mixture specifications considered here is (6.13), a 3-component mixture whose special cases are the Clayton, Gumbel, and Gaussian copulas. The essential idea is that such a specification can potentially capture all types of dependences—positive, negative, and asymmetric tail dependence—that may occur in a heterogeneous sample. Additional special cases can be generated using four 2-component mixtures, each generated using components selected from the three previously mentioned copulas. The four mixture models were estimated using the two-step procedure, the first step having been implemented exactly as described for the case of non-mixture copula models.

The results obtained are generally unsatisfactory. In the case of the gold–cotton pair estimation does not converge in two of the four cases. In the other two cases the improvement in log-likelihood is small, as was expected. It is likely that the effective number of observations required for identifying the mixture components is considerably larger than the available sample.

Mixture models for the remaining two pairs are also difficult to interpret. The mixture proportions (π's) are estimated with very large variances, which means that the results are consistent with the specification of a single component model. The dependence parameters are also estimated with a large variance. Again, one interpretation of these results is that the mixture models are hard to identify empirically because the sample data do not have sufficient variability that is needed for identifying the more highly parameterized mixture model.

6.5 Discussion and Concluding Remarks

The objective of this chapter was to study co-movements using a bivariate statistical model capable of capturing different types of nonlinear dependence. A priori considerations suggest that mixture copulas are a promising approach and potentially less restrictive than other competing models. However, our experience with Monte Carlo experiments suggests that identification of such models is difficult and requires samples that are sufficiently large in the relevant sense. Our experience with models of commodity prices also carries a similar message.

Monte Carlo experiments suggest that restrictive one-component models might be inferior to more complex multi-component mixtures in the presence of nonlinear asymmetric dependence. On the other hand, multi-component mixtures from the commodity price example were not satisfactory. These models were plagued with convergence problems, large variances in estimates, and minuscule improvements in fit compared to more parsimonious models.

Although the poor performance of the multi-component mixtures for commodity prices suggests starting with mixture models and working backward, mixture models require delicate handling. The difficultly these models sometimes encounter in achieving convergence suggests that a single component Student $t(\nu)$ copula with symmetric tail dependence might be a good starting point. However, as the Monte Carlo experiments reveal, starting with a simple model and working forward puts the researcher at risk of stopping too soon and misinterpreting dependence.

This modelling dilemma is related to David Hendry's research on 'general-to-specific' modelling. A general conclusion from this chapter is that whether one follows a general-to-specific approach or the opposite, the initial starting point of the model search may turn out to be a pivotal step. Thus, when misspecification is more than a local deviation from the true specification, we appear stuck in limbo between general-to-specific and specific-to-general approaches. This deduction was succinctly noted by Granger and Timmermann (2000) in their comment on Hoover and Perez (1999):

> Uncovering the true model from a set of possibly non-linear candidate models is a far more difficult task than the equivalent exercise of finding the true model when this is known to be linear. Parameters governing non-linear dynamics are often determined

from a few episodes and the effective sample sizes used to identify such parameters tend to be very small. The likelihood of overfitting the data-generating process is much higher with flexible modeling approaches such as neural networks, which at least opens the possibility that the results overstate the degree of success of the general-to-specific approach when adopted in a more general setting.

A modelling approach that is directed by a sound understanding of the economic context and properties of the available data has much to recommend it.

References

Ai, C., Chatrath, A., and Song, F. M. (2006). On the comovement of commodity prices. *American Journal of Agricultural Economics*, **88**(3) 574–588.

Bauwens, L., Laurent, S., and Rombouts, J. (2006). Multivariate GARCH models: A survey. *Journal of Applied Econometrics*, **21**, 79–110.

Bouyé, E., Durrleman, V., Nikeghbali, A., Ribouletm, G., and Roncalli, T. (2000). Copulas for finance: A reading guide and some applications. Unpublished Manuscript, Financial Econometrics Research Centre, City University Business School: London.

Boyer, B. H., Gibson, M. S., and Loretan, M. (1999). Pitfalls in tests for changes in correlations. Federal Reserve Board, IFS Discussion Paper No. 597R.

Breusch, T. and Pagan, A. R. (1980). The Lagrange multiplier test and its application to model specification in econometrics. *Review of Economic Studies*, **47**, 239–253.

Breymann, W., Dias, A., and Embrechts, P. (2003). Dependence structures for multivariate high-frequency data in finance. *Quantitative Finance*, **3**(1), 1–14.

Cashin, P., McDermott, C. J., and Scott, A. (1999). The myth of co-moving commodity prices. Reserve Bank of New Zealand Discussion Paper G99/9.

Chen, X. and Fan, Y. (2006). Estimation and model selection of semiparametric copula-based multivariate dynamic models under copula misspecification. *Journal of Econometrics*, **135**(1–2), 125–154.

Cherubini, U., Luciano, E., and Vecchiato, W. (2004). *Copula Methods in Finance*. New York: John Wiley.

Clayton, D. G. (1978). A model for association in bivariate life tables and its application in epidemiological studies of familial tendency in chronic disease incidence. *Biometrika*, **65**, 141–151.

Cont, R. (2001). Empirical properties of asset returns: Stylized facts and statistical issues. *Quantitative Finance*, **1**, 223–236.

Cooper, R. N. and Lawrence, R. Z. (1975). The 1972–75 commodity boom. *Brookings Papers in Economic Activity*, 671–715 (716–723).

Deaton, A. and Laroque, G. (1992). On the behavior of commodity prices. *Review of Economic Studies*, **59**, 1–23.

Deb, P., Trivedi, P. K., and Varangis, P. (1996). Excess co-movement in commodity prices reconsidered. *Journal of Applied Econometrics*, **11**, 275–291.

Dias, A. and Embrechts, P. (2004). Dynamic copula models for multivariate high-frequency data in finance. Manuscript, ETH Zurich.

Embrechts, P., McNeil, A., and Straumann, D. (2002). Correlation and dependence in risk management: Properties and pitfalls. In Dempster, M. A. H. (ed.) *Risk Management: Value at Risk and Beyond*, pp. 176–223. Cambridge, Cambridge University Press.

Engle, R. (2002). Dynamic conditional correlation—a simple class of multivariate GARCH models. *Journal of Business and Economic Statistics*, **20**(3), 339–350.

——and Kroner, K. (1995). Multivariate simultaneous generalized ARCH. *Econometric Theory*, **11**(1), 122.

Fang, K.-T. and Zhang, Y. T. (1990). *Generalized Multivariate Analysis*. Berlin and New York: Springer-Verlag.

Granger, C. W. J. and Timmermann, A. (2000). Data mining with local model specification uncertainty: A discussion of Hoover and Perez. *Econometrics Journal*, **2**, 220–225.

Gumbel, E. J. (1960). Distributions des valeurs extremes en plusieurs dimensions. *Publications de l'Institute de Statistique de l'Universite de Paris*, **9**, 171–173.

Hendry, D. F. (1997). On congruent econometric relations: A comment. *Carnegie-Rochester Conference Series on Public Policy*, **47**, 163–190.

Hoover, K. D. and Perez, S. J. (1999). Data mining reconsidered: Encompassing and generel-to-specific approach to specification search. *Econometrics Journal*, **2**, 167–191.

Hu, L. (2004). Dependence patterns across financial markets: A mixed copula approach. The Ohio State University, working Paper.

Hull, J. and White, A. (1998). Value at risk when daily changes in market variables are not normally distributed. *Journal of Derivatives*, **5**, 9–19.

Joe, H. (1997). *Multivariate Models and Dependence Concepts*. London: Chapman & Hall.

Kyle, A. and Xiong, W. (2001). Contagion as a wealth effect. *Journal of Finance*, **LVI**, 1401–1440.

Mizon, G. E. (1995). Progressive modelling of macroeconomic time series: The LSE methodology. In Hoover, K. D. (ed.), *Macroeconometrics: Developments, Tensions and Prospects*, pp. 107–70. Boston: Kluwer.

——and Hendry, D. F. (1990). Procrustean econometrics: Or stretching and squeezing data. In Granger, C. W. J. (ed.), *Modelling Economic Series: Readings in Econometric Methodology*, pp. 121–36. Oxford: Clarendon Press.

Nelsen, R. B. (2006). *An Introduction to Copulas*, 2nd edition. New York: Springer.

Patton, A. (2004). On the out-of-sample importance of skewness and asymmetric dependence for asset allocation. *Journal of Finacial Econometrics*, **2**, 130–168.

——(2006). Modelling asymmetric exchange rate dependence. *International Economic Review*, **47**(2), 527–556.

Pindyck, R. S. and Rotemberg, J. J. (1990). The excess co-movement of commodity prices. *Economic Journal*, **100**, 1173–1189.

Sklar, A. (1973). Random variables, joint distributions, and copulas. *Kybernetica*, **9**, 449–460.

Trivedi, P. K. and Zimmer, D. M. (2007). Copula modeling: An introduction for practitioners. *Foundations and Trends in Econometrics*, **1**(1), 1–110.

Zimmer, D. M. and Trivedi, P. K. (2006). Using trivariate copulas to model sample selection and treatment effects: Application to family health care demand. *Journal of Business and Economic Statistics*, **24**, 63–76.

7

Forecasting in Dynamic Factor Models Subject to Structural Instability

*James H. Stock and Mark W. Watson**

7.1 Introduction

An ongoing theme in David Hendry's work has been concern about detecting and avoiding forecast breakdowns that arise because of structural instability. Parameter instability can arise for various reasons, including structural breaks in the economy (for example, changes in technology), policy regime shifts, or changes in the survey instruments from which the time-series are constructed. Hendry and coauthors have argued that such instability, whatever its source, often manifests itself as breaks in time-series forecasting relations, and moreover that such breaks constitute one of the primary reasons for forecast failures in practice (see for example Clements and Hendry, 1999, 2002; Hendry and Clements, 2002; Hendry, 2005; and Hendry and Mizon, 2005). One line of Hendry's research has been to develop and to analyse non-structural forecasting methods for their potential robustness to parameter instability, including error correction models, overdifferencing, intercept shift methods, and—closest to the focus of this chapter—forecast pooling (Hendry and Clements, 2002).

This chapter continues this line of inquiry, in which forecasting methods are examined for their reliability in the face of structural breaks. We focus here on forecasts constructed using dynamic factor models (DFMs) (Geweke, 1977; Sargent and Sims, 1977). In DFMs, the comovements of the observable time-series are characterized by latent dynamic factors. Over the past decade, work on DFMs has focused on high-dimensional systems in which very many series depend on a handful of factors (Forni, Lippi, Hallin, and Reichlin, 2000; Stock and Watson, 2002a, 2002b; and many others; for a survey, see Stock and Watson, 2006). These factor-based forecasts have had notable

* This research was funded in part by NSF grant SBR-0617811.

empirical forecasting successes. Yet, there has been little work to date on the performance of factor-based macroeconomic forecasts under structural instability (exceptions are Stock and Watson, 1998, 2002b and Banerjee, Marcellino, and Masten, 2007, which are discussed below).

Despite the limited research on the effect of structural instability on forecasting using factor models, it is plausible that factor-based forecasts might be robust to certain types of structural instability, for reasons akin to those discussed in Hendry and Clements (2002) in the context of forecast pooling. Hendry and Clements (2002) consider forecast breakdowns arising from intercept shifts, which in turn arise from shifts in the means of omitted variables. These intercept breaks doom the forecasting regression in which they arise, but if one averages forecasts over many forecasting regressions, and if the intercept shifts are sufficiently uncorrelated across the different regressions, then the intercept shifts average out and the pooled forecast is relatively more robust to this source of structural instability than any of the constituent forecasting regressions. In factor models, a similar logic could apply: even if factor loadings are unstable, if the instability is sufficiently independent across series then using many series to estimate the factors could play the same 'averaging' role as the pooling of forecasts, and the estimated factors could be well estimated even if individual relations between the observable series and the factors are unstable. Given well-estimated factors, forecasts can be made by standard time-varying parameter or rolling regression methods.

This chapter provides empirical results concerning the estimation of dynamic factors and their use for forecasting when there is structural instability in the underlying factor model. Section 7.2 lays out the time-varying DFM and categorizes the implications for forecasting when the model is subject to different types of structural instability (breaks in the factor loadings, in the factor dynamics, or in the idiosyncratic dynamics). Section 7.2 also reviews what little is known about factor estimation and forecasting with structural instabilities.

We then turn to an empirical examination of instability in DFMs using a new data set consisting of 144 quarterly macroeconomic time-series for the United States, spanning 1959–2006. This data set, which is described in section 7.3, improves upon earlier versions of the Stock–Watson US quarterly data set by having more complete and consistent tiers of disaggregation. Motivated by the literature on the Great Moderation, we consider split-sample instability with a single break in 1984. Our forecast comparisons focus on the performance of different ways of handling this break, relative to standard full-sample factor-based forecasts (there have been numerous studies comparing full-sample factor-based forecasts to other forecasting methods and we do not repeat those exercises here, see Stock and Watson (2006) for a review). The results are summarized in section 7.4. We find considerable instability in the factor loadings around the 1984 break date, but despite this instability principal components provides stable estimates of the factors. In consequence, the best factor-based forecasts of individual variables use full-sample estimates of the factors but use subsample (or time-varying) estimates of the regression coefficients.

The chapter most closely related to this are Stock and Watson (1998, 2002b), Banerjee, Marcellino, and Masten (2007), and Del Negro and Otrok (2008). Stock and Watson (2002b) provide some theoretical results concerning factor estimation (but not forecasting) with time variation. Stock and Watson (1998) and Banerjee, Marcellino, and Masten (2007) provide Monte Carlo results about, respectively, nonparametric principle components estimation of factors and factor-based forecasting with instability. Banerjee, Marcellino, and Masten (2007) also report an application to data from the EU and from Slovenia, which investigates split-sample instability in the factor forecasts (but not the factor estimates themselves). Del Negro and Otrok (2008) investigate a parametric DFM estimated on G-7 data using Bayer methods. Relative to these papers, the contribution here is first to lay out the implications for forecasting of different types of structural instability in DFMs, second to provide a new empirical investigation using US data of factor-based forecasting with potential instability, and third to investigate separately the effects of structural change on the estimation of the factors and on the use of those factors for forecasting. An additional contribution is the compilation of the new quarterly data set, which is available on Watson's website.

7.2 The Time-Varying Dynamic Factor Model and Implications for Factor-Based Forecasts

This section sets out the time-varying dynamic factor model and examines the separate implications for forecasting of structural breaks in the factor loadings, in the factor dynamics, and in the idiosyncratic dynamics.

7.2.1 *The Time-Varying Factor Model*

We work with the static representation of the dynamic factor model

$$X_t = \Lambda_t F_t + e_t, \tag{7.1}$$

where $X_t = (X_{1t}, \ldots, X_{nt})'$, F_t is a r-vector of static factors, Λ_t is a $n \times r$ matrix of factor loadings, and $e_t = (e_{1t}, \ldots, e_{nt})'$ is a n-vector of idiosyncratic disturbances. The difference between (7.1) and standard formulations of the DFM is that (7.1) allows for the possibility that the factor loadings can change over time.

Although parametric specifications for the factor and idiosyncratic dynamics are not needed to estimate the factors, such parametric specifications are useful when discussing forecasts using the factors. Accordingly, we specify finite-order autoregressive dynamics for the factors and idiosyncratic term

$$F_t = \Phi_t F_{t-1} + \eta_t \tag{7.2}$$

$$e_{it} = a_{it}(\mathrm{L})e_{it-1} + \varepsilon_{it},\ i = 1,\ldots,n, \tag{7.3}$$

where η_t is a r-vector of factor innovations with $\mathrm{E}(\eta_t|F_{t-1},F_{t-2},\ldots,X_{it-1},X_{it-2},\ldots) = 0$. The static factor model (7.1)–(7.3) can be derived from the dynamic factor model assuming finite lag lengths and VAR factor dynamics in the dynamic factor model, in which case F_t contains lags of the dynamic factors and Φ_t is a companion matrix so that the static factor dynamics are first order.

7.2.2 *Time-Varying Forecast Functions with Split-Sample Time Variation*

For the discussion in this subsection, suppose that $E(\varepsilon_{is}|F_t, F_{t-1},\ldots,X_{it},X_{it-1},\ldots) = 0$ and $E(\eta_s|F_t,F_{t-1},\ldots,X_{it},X_{it-1},\ldots) = 0$ for $s > t$, and that the idiosyncratic errors $\{\varepsilon_{it}\}$ are uncorrelated with the factor disturbances $\{\eta_t\}$ at all leads and lags. Then, given the data and factors through date t, and assuming the potentially time varying parameters are known, the h-step ahead conditional expectation of X_{it+h} is

$$\begin{aligned} X_{it+h|t} &= E(X_{it+h}|F_t,F_{t-1},\ldots,X_{it},X_{it-1},\ldots) \\ &= E(\Lambda_{t+h}F_{t+h} + e_{t+h}|F_t,F_{t-1},\ldots,X_{it},X_{it-1},\ldots) \\ &= \beta_{it}^{h\prime} F_t + a_{it}^h(\mathrm{L})e_{it}, \end{aligned} \tag{7.4}$$

where $\beta_{it}^{h\prime} = \Lambda_{it+h} \prod_{s=t+1}^{t+h} \Phi_s$ and $a_{it}^h(\mathrm{L})e_{it}' = E[a_{it+h}(\mathrm{L})e_{t+h-1}|F_t,F_{t-1},\ldots,X_{it},X_{it-1},\ldots] = E[e_{it+h}|e_{it},e_{it-1},\ldots]$, where the final equality obtains by using the factor model assumption that $\{e_{it}\}$ and $\{\eta_t\}$ are independent and by modelling expectations as linear.

Looking ahead to the empirical analysis, we consider the case of a single break at known date $t = \tau$, and consider three special cases of interest, respectively corresponding to a break in Λ, Φ, and $a_{it}(\mathrm{L})$.

(a) *Forecast function with a single break in* Λ. In this case, $\Lambda_{it} = \Lambda_{i1}$, $t < \tau$, and $\Lambda_{it} = \Lambda_{i2}$, $t \geq \tau$, so (7.4) becomes

$$X_{it+h|t} = \begin{cases} \beta_{i1}^{h\prime} F_t + a_i^h(\mathrm{L})e_{it},\ t < \tau - h, & \text{where } \beta_{i1}^{h\prime} = \Lambda_{i1}\Phi^h \\ \beta_{i2}^{h\prime} F_t + a_i^h(\mathrm{L})e_{it},\ t \geq \tau, & \text{where } \beta_{i2}^{h\prime} = \Lambda_{i2}\Phi^h \end{cases} \tag{7.5}$$

If the only break is in the factor loadings, then coefficients on F_t, but not those on e_{it} and its lags, change.

(b) Forecast function when only Φ is time-varying. In this case, $\Phi_t = \Phi_1$, $t < \tau$, and $\Phi_t = \Phi_2$, $t \geq \tau$, so (7.4) becomes

$$X_{it+h|t} = \begin{cases} \beta_{i1}^{h\,\prime} F_t + a_i^h(\mathrm{L})e_{it}, \; t < \tau - h, & \text{where } \beta_{i1}^{h\,\prime} = \Lambda_i \Phi_1^h \\ \beta_{i2}^{h\,\prime} F_t + a_i^h(\mathrm{L})e_{it}, \; t \geq \tau, & \text{where } \beta_{i2}^{h\,\prime} = \Lambda_i \Phi_2^h \end{cases} \tag{7.6}$$

If the only break is in the factor dynamics, then only the coefficients on F_t change.

(c) Forecast function when only a_{it} is time-varying. In this case, $a_{it}(\mathrm{L}) = a_{i1}(\mathrm{L})$, $t < \tau$, and $a_{it}(\mathrm{L}) = a_{i2}(\mathrm{L})$, $t \geq \tau$, so (7.4) becomes

$$X_{it+h|t} = \begin{cases} \beta_i^{h\prime} F_t + a_{i1}^h(\mathrm{L})e_{it}, \; t < \tau - h \\ \beta_i^{h\prime} F_t + a_{i2}^h(\mathrm{L})e_{it}, \; t \geq \tau \end{cases} \tag{7.7}$$

where $\beta_i^{h\prime} = \Lambda_i \Phi^h$. If the only break is in the idiosyncratic dynamics, then only coefficients on e_{it} and its lags change.

In certain circumstances these expressions can tell a researcher what sort of forecast instability to expect. For example, a revision of the survey used to construct a particular series X_{it} generally would result in different dynamics for the idiosyncratic term (case (c)) and possibly a change in the factor loadings (case (a)), but not a change in the factor dynamics. Although the origin of the instability is not in general known a priori, by working backwards, these three cases can help to identify the nature of an observed structural break. Stable factor loadings in (7.1), combined with a break in the coefficient on F_t in (7.4), point to a break in the factor dynamics. Similarly, a break in the coefficients on lagged e_{it} in (7.4) points to a break in the idiosyncratic dynamics.

7.2.3 *Estimation of Static Factors in the Presence of Time Variation*

The only theoretical result concerning factor estimation under model instability of which we are aware is Stock and Watson (2002b), theorem 3. That result states that the factor space can be consistently estimated if there is time variation in the factor loadings, as long as that time variation is relatively small in magnitude. Monte Carlo results in Stock and Watson (1998) support this theoretical result, in fact even with quite large time variation in the factor loadings the Stock–Watson (1998) Monte Carlo experiments suggest that the factors are well estimated using principal components. That paper does not, however, consider time variation in the factor transition equation itself (Φ_t).

As the cases considered in section 7.2.2 make clear, robust estimation of the factors under time variation does not imply that factor-based forecasts will be robust to time variation because of implied instability in the forecast function. This deterioration of factor-based forecasts (in contrast to the estimation of the factors themselves) is evident in Banerjee, Marcellino, and Masten's (2007)

Monte Carlo results. This dichotomy—potential stability of factor estimates but instability of factor-based forecasts—is the main focus of the empirical application in section 7.4.

7.3 The Quarterly US Data Set

The empirical work employs a newly compiled data set consisting of 144 quarterly time series for the United States, spanning 1959:I–2006:IV. The variables, sources, and transformations are listed in Appendix Table A.1. The first two quarters were used for initial values when computing first and second differences, so the data available for analysis span 1959:III–2006:IV, for a total of $T = 190$ quarterly observations.

The main change in the new data set, relative to the quarterly data sets we have used in previous work, is a more complete treatment of disaggregation. The full data set contains both aggregate and subaggregate series. By construction, the idiosyncratic term of aggregate series (eg nonresidential investment) will be correlated with the idiosyncratic term of lower-level subaggregates (eg nonresidential investment—structures), and the inclusion of series related by identities (an aggregate being the sum of the subaggregates) does not provide additional information useful for factor estimation. For this reason, the factor estimates were computed using the subset of 109 series that excludes higher level aggregates related by identities to the lower level subaggregates (the series used to estimate the factors are indicated in Table A.1). This represents a departure from the approach in some previous work (e.g. Stock and Watson, 2002a, 2005) in which both aggregates and subaggregates are used to estimate the factors. The data set here includes more subaggregates than the quarterly data set in Stock and Watson (2005).

The series were transformed as needed to eliminate trends by first or second differencing (in many cases after taking logarithms); see Table A.1 for specifics.

7.4 Empirical Results

The empirical analysis focuses on instability around a single break in 1984:I. The reason for the 1984 break date is that 1984 (more generally, the mid-1980s) has been identified as an important break date associated with the so-called Great Moderation of output (Kim and Nelson, 1999; McConnell and Perez-Quiros, 2000), and there have been shifts in other properties of time-series such as the inflation–output relation that can be dated to the mid- to late-1980s (cf. Stock and Watson, 2007).

Our analysis of forecasting stability focuses on four-quarter ahead prediction. For real activity variables, the four-quarter object of interest, $X_{it+4}^{(4)}$, corresponds to growth over the next four quarters; for inflation measures, $X^{(4)}_{it+4}$ is average quarterly inflation over the next four quarters, minus inflation last quarter; and for variables entered in levels such as the capacity utilization rate, it is the value of that variable four quarters hence. Specifics are given in the appendix.

All forecasts are direct, specifically, forecasts of $X^{(4)}_{it+4}$ are obtained by regressing $X^{(4)}_{it+4}$ on variables dated t and earlier using the forecasting regression,

$$X^{(4)}_{it+4} = \mu_i + \beta_i' \hat{F}_t + \sum_{j=0}^{p-1} a^4_{ij} \hat{e}_{it-j} + \text{error}. \tag{7.8}$$

For comparability of results across series, $p = 4$ lags of $\hat{e}_{it}$ were used for all forecasts.

7.4.1 *The Number and Stability of the Factors*

Estimates of the number of factors. Table 7.1 presents estimates of the number of factors, computed using criteria proposed by Bai and Ng (2002), for the full sample and the two subsamples. The results are not sharp and depend on which criterion is used. For the purposes of forecasting, 10 factors (the *ICP3* estimate) introduces a large number of parameters in the forecasting regressions so we focus on numbers of factors towards the lower end of the range in Table 7.1, three to five factors.

Comparison of full-sample and subsample estimated factors. Theorem 3 in Stock and Watson (2002b) suggests that, despite possible time variation in the factor loadings, full- and subsample estimates of the factors could well be close, in the sense that the subsample estimates of the factor space is nearly spanned by the full-sample estimate of the factor space. This possibility is examined in Table 7.2, which presents the squared canonical correlations, computed over the two subsamples, between the factors estimated over the full sample and the factors estimated over the subsample. The factors were estimated by principal components over the full sample or subsample as appropriate, always using the 109 variable data set of subaggregates indicated

Table 7.1. Number of factors estimated using Bai–Ng (2002) criteria

Sample	Dates	No. Obs	Estimated number of factors based on:		
			ICP1	ICP2	ICP3
Full	1959:III–2006:IV	190	4	2	10
Pre-84	1959:III–1983:IV	98	3	2	10
Post-84	1984:I–2006:IV	92	3	2	10

Note: All estimates use $N = 109$ series.

Table 7.2. Canonical correlations between subsample and full-sample estimates of the factors

Estimated number of factors		Squared canonical correlations between full- and subsample factors:									
Full sample	Subsample	Pre-84					Post-84				
		1	2	3	4	5	1	2	3	4	5
3	3	1.00	0.99	0.03			0.99	0.91	0.84		
4	3	1.00	0.99	0.92			0.99	0.92	0.91		
4	4	1.00	0.99	0.94	0.33		1.00	0.93	0.92	0.65	
5	4	1.00	0.99	0.94	0.89		1.00	0.97	0.92	0.74	
5	5	1.00	1.00	0.94	0.90	0.49	1.00	0.97	0.93	0.79	0.11

Notes: The entries are the squared canonical correlations between the estimated factors in the indicated subsample and the factors estimated over the full-sample. Factors are estimated using principal components.

in the Appendix. Canonical correlations close to one indicate that the full-sample and subsample factors span nearly the same spaces.

The results in Table 7.2 are consistent with there being four full-sample factors and three or four factors in each subsample. If there were only two full- and subsample factors (as suggested by the ICP2 results in Table 7.1), then one would expect the third and fourth estimated factors to have little relation to each other over the two subsamples (they would be noise), so the third canonical correlation would be low in both samples. But this is not the case, suggesting that there are at least three factors in each subsample. When four factors are estimated in both the full sample and the subsamples, the fourth canonical correlation is small in the first subsample; this is consistent with the space of three first subsample factors being spanned by the four full-sample factors, and the fourth subsample factor being noise. The moderate fourth canonical correlation in the second subsample in the case of four full- and four subsample factors leads to some ambiguity, and raises the possibility that there are four factors in the second subsample, which in turn would be consistent with four factors in the full sample.

We interpret the results in Tables 7.1 and 7.2, taken together, as being consistent with there being four factors in the full sample and three factors in each subsample. The large squared canonical correlations in Table 7.2 for four full-sample and three subsample factors indicate that the full-sample estimated factors span the space of the three estimated factors in each subsample. Accordingly, the base case for our empirical analysis (the case used to compute all subsequent tables and figures) has four full-sample factors and three subsample factors. Still, the statistics in Table 7.2 alternatively could be interpreted as being consistent with other numbers of factors in the full sample and subsamples. As a robustness check, results therefore were also computed for 4 full/4 subsample, 5 full/4 subsample, and 5 full/5 subsample factors; these results are discussed briefly at the end of this section.

7.4.2 *Stability of Factor Loadings and Forecasting Regression Coefficients*

Stability of factor loadings. The stability of the factor loadings are examined in the first numeric column Table 7.3, which reports Chow statistics testing the hypothesis that the factor loadings are the same in the two subsamples, computed by regressing each variable onto the four full-sample estimated factors, allowing for a break in 1984:1 and using the Newey–West (1987) variance estimator (four lags). There is evidence of some instability in the factor loadings: 41% of these Chow statistics reject at the 5% significance level, and 23% reject at the 1% significance level. If one compares the results across classes of series, there are relatively fewer rejections of the stability of the factor loadings for output, employment, and inflation, and relatively more for exchange rates, term spreads, and stock returns.

Figures 7.1–7.4 focus on the stability of the estimated factors and the factor loadings for four series: real GDP growth, temporally aggregated to be the four-quarter average of the quarterly growth rates (Figure 7.1); the change in core PCE inflation, temporally aggregated to be the four-quarter change in inflation (Figure 7.2); the quarterly change in the Federal Funds rate (not temporally aggregated, Figure 7.3); and the term spread between the one-year and 3-month Treasury rates (not temporally aggregated, Figure 7.4). Part (a) of each figure presents the series, the common component computed using factors estimated from the full sample with split-sample estimates of the factor loadings (the 'full–split' estimate), and the common component computed using split-sample estimates of the factors and split-sample estimates of the factor loadings ('split–split'). Part (b) presents the series, the full–split estimate of the common component, and the common component computed using factors estimated from the full sample and full-sample estimates of the factor loadings ('full–full').

In all four figures, the full–split and split–split common components (part (a)) are quite similar, consistent with the full-sample factor estimates spanning the spaces of the subsample factor estimates. There are, however, two different patterns evident in part (b) of the figures. For GDP, core PCE, and the Federal Funds rate, the full–split and full–full are similar, indicating that for those series there is little time variation in the factor loadings. This is consistent with the failure of the Chow statistic to reject the hypothesis of stable Λ's for those three series in Table 7.3. In contrast, stability of the factor loadings is rejected at the 1% significance level for the term spread, and the common components computed using the full-sample factors differ greatly depending on whether the factor loadings are estimated over the full sample or the subsample.

Stability of forecasting regressions. The remaining numeric columns of Table 7.3 examine the stability of the coefficients in the forecasting regression (7.8). Specifically, (7.8) was estimated by OLS using 4 lags ($p = 4$ in (7.8)), where $\hat{e}_{it}$ in (7.8) was computed as the residual from the regression of X_{it} onto

Table 7.3. Chow statistics testing the stability of the factor loadings and the 4-step ahead forecasting equations, 4-factor model

Factor loading null regression: $X_{it} = \Lambda_i' \hat{F}_t + e_{it}$

Forecasting null regression: $X^{(4)}_{i,t+4} = \mu_i + \beta_i' \hat{F}_t + \sum_{j=0}^{3} a_{ij}\hat{e}_{it-j} + \text{error}$,

where $\hat{F}_t$ are the full-sample factors estimated using principal components, $\hat{e}_{it}$ is the residual from the factor loading regression and $X^{(4)}_{i,t}$ is the 4-quarter variable to be forecast.

Series	Split-sample Chow statistics testing the stability of:			
	Factor loadings (Λ_i)	4-step ahead forecasting regressions:		
		All coefficients	Coefficients on on F_t	Intercept & coefficients on u_{it-1}
RGDP	5.8	36.1**	11.6*	5.8
Cons	11.1*	50.5**	18.0**	2.5
Cons-Dur	12.6*	60.2**	22.3**	3.4
Cons-NonDur	9.9*	22.5**	10.2*	8.3
Cons-Serv	5.1	69.0**	10.5*	33.8**
GPDInv	1.6	25.1**	10.2*	7.3
FixedInv	6.9	46.6**	28.6**	8.9
NonResInv	5.0	27.4**	20.9**	5.2
NonResInv-struct	5.6	17.9*	12.0*	5.4
NonResInv-Bequip	5.9	46.0**	29.4**	12.5*
Res.Inv	3.2	64.1**	12.5*	36.8**
Exports	10.6*	25.8**	4.5	18.6**
Imports	3.4	23.3**	12.2*	3.5
Gov	7.9	7.8	3.7	3.9
Gov Fed	12.8*	8.9	5.0	3.6
Gov State/Loc	4.7	13.4	1.9	11.7*
IP: total	10.7*	32.3**	12.8*	4.4
IP: products	6.2	31.1**	11.8*	7.5
IP: final przod	5.6	29.6**	12.3*	7.5
IP: cons gds	11.3*	55.4**	15.3**	19.4**
IP: cons dble	9.3	20.2*	9.0	2.1
iIP: cons nondble	6.0	65.6**	18.8**	13.0*
IP: bus eqpt	5.5	34.4**	21.2**	1.3
IP: matls	9.5*	28.5**	14.4**	7.1
IP: dble mats	8.7	28.1**	15.7**	11.5*
IP: nondble mats	9.1	71.5**	11.0*	26.8**
IP: mfg	9.5	33.4**	12.3*	3.7
IP: fuels	4.1	10.3	3.4	3.7
NAPM prodn	21.9**	36.4**	7.3	14.3*
Capacity Util	13.0*	43.9**	26.7**	11.0
Emp: total	25.3**	48.9**	20.9**	9.9
Emp: gds prod	17.7**	71.8**	23.8**	21.1**
Emp: mining	2.4	17.2*	8.7	9.4
Emp: const	14.3**	56.9**	45.7**	16.0**
Emp: mfg	22.4**	67.5**	21.0**	22.1**
Emp: dble gds	21.5**	75.4**	26.2**	16.8**
Emp: nondbles	7.0	79.4**	11.8*	60.1**
Emp: services	10.5*	54.0**	20.4**	15.6**
Emp: TTU	28.0**	80.1**	34.8**	24.6**

Table 7.3. (*Continued*)

Series	Split-sample Chow statistics testing the stability of:			
	Factor loadings (Λ_i)	4-step ahead forecasting regressions:		
		All coefficients	Coefficients on on F_t	Intercept & coefficients on u_{it-1}
Emp: wholesale	29.2**	76.9**	35.1**	22.4**
Emp: retail	11.8*	170.6**	48.1**	58.5**
Emp: FIRE	16.2**	99.5**	31.9**	38.9**
Emp: Govt	31.0**	30.3**	11.1*	23.0**
Help wanted indx	14.3**	55.7**	7.5	26.8**
Help wanted/emp	1.4	24.8**	7.4	12.0*
Emp CPS total	12.4*	27.2**	14.6**	13.1*
Emp CPS nonag	6.4	34.2**	11.2*	17.8**
Emp. Hours	28.1**	69.8**	31.9**	9.4
Avg hrs	6.6	89.4**	9.1	70.0**
Overtime: mfg	2.1	20.9*	3.0	8.3
U: all	10.6*	26.3**	22.5**	2.5
U: mean duration	5.6	55.7**	15.2**	27.4**
U < 5 wks	16.1**	13.7	10.7*	2.7
U 5–14 wks	5.5	17.5*	15.6**	0.9
U 15+ wks	1.5	27.2**	18.1**	11.3*
U 15–26 wks	3.1	27.5**	14.9**	12.0*
U 27+ wks	0.4	32.1**	15.8**	18.1**
HStarts: Total	11.2*	35.9**	8.7	14.2*
BuildPermits	9.9*	25.0**	9.8*	6.0
HStarts: NE	1.7	42.2**	9.3	25.7**
HStarts: MW	23.4**	20.2*	10.5*	5.2
HStarts: South	18.1**	29.6**	19.6**	8.0
HStarts: West	7.7	26.5**	18.0**	4.1
PMI	24.9**	31.6**	8.9	13.6*
NAPM new ordrs	40.7**	28.3**	4.8	16.1**
NAPM vendor del	14.0**	17.5*	12.1*	6.0
NAPM Invent	18.1**	75.8**	16.8**	50.8**
Orders (Cons-Goods)	11.7*	38.9**	14.0**	12.8*
Orders (NDCap-Goods)	6.1	33.3**	23.5**	6.2
PGDP	9.8*	32.4**	26.5**	1.0
PCED	2.0	23.8**	18.8**	3.6
CPI-All	7.5	32.9**	22.0**	5.4
PCED-Core	6.7	29.5**	24.0**	5.6
CPI-Core	19.3**	14.1	9.9*	5.4
PCED-Dur	2.2	17.2*	11.6*	2.8
PCED-motorveh	2.5	9.2	6.7	3.3

Table 7.3. (*Continued*)

Series	Split-sample Chow statistics testing the stability of:			
	Factor loadings (Λ_i)	4-step ahead forecasting regressions:		
		All coefficients	Coefficients on on F_t	Intercept & coefficients on u_{it-1}
PCED-hhequip	9.0	71.9**	61.2**	14.2*
PCED-oth dur	3.2	25.1**	13.4**	16.3**
PCED-nondur	2.8	23.2**	10.6*	2.9
PCED-food	5.3	34.6**	22.7**	5.9
PCED-clothing	2.1	10.1	4.4	3.9
PCED-energy	7.7	44.7**	26.5**	4.0
PCED-oth nondur	5.9	17.8*	2.2	14.5*
PCED-services	4.6	57.7**	45.8**	4.3
PCED-housing	2.6	5.7	4.1	2.7
PCED-hhops	4.5	13.0	8.7	4.1
PCED-elect & gas	4.8	9.7	3.9	3.1
PCED-oth hhops	2.2	12.3	3.1	4.9
PCED-transport	9.5	76.2**	16.4**	44.9**
PCED-medical	24.2**	34.3**	11.8*	12.7*
PCED-recreation	5.8	14.5	8.0	8.0
PCED-oth serv	8.6	25.5**	9.3	7.3
PGPDI	8.4	21.4*	16.6**	2.8
PFI	5.9	27.3**	15.8**	7.4
PFI-nonres	4.5	32.1**	12.9*	20.2**
PFI-nonres struc	6.2	14.2	6.1	9.0
PFI-nonres equip	3.6	13.9	10.8*	2.3
PFI-resdidential	4.7	59.5**	21.3**	10.5
PEXP	5.1	23.8**	11.4*	14.3*
PIMP	4.3	27.1**	16.2**	1.3
PGOV	3.0	22.6**	16.8**	7.0
PGOV-Federal	1.6	23.6**	6.1	5.5
PGOV-St & loc	3.3	28.6**	24.0**	4.6
Com: spot price (real)	8.1	30.1**	15.3**	10.0
OilPrice (Real)	26.9**	24.6**	12.9*	11.5*
NAPM com price	8.7	104.0**	22.2**	62.0**
Real AHE: goods	5.0	58.0**	11.9*	36.1**
Real AHE: const	13.3**	38.5**	22.6**	6.2
Real AHE: mfg	8.0	54.8**	9.4	27.1**
Labor Prod	10.6*	8.4	5.0	1.7

Table 7.3. (*Continued*)

Series	Split-sample Chow statistics testing the stability of:			
	Factor loadings (Λ_i)	4-step ahead forecasting regressions:		
		All coefficients	Coefficients on on F_t	Intercept & coefficients on u_{it-1}
Real Comp/Hour	12.5*	8.7	5.1	4.0
Unit Labor Cost	18.3**	45.4**	9.0	37.7**
FedFunds	8.6	48.5**	33.1**	12.6*
3 mo T-bill	4.7	43.7**	32.4**	11.5*
6 mo T-bill	15.4**	32.6**	16.8**	12.7*
1 yr T-bond	14.8**	22.8**	12.0*	12.2*
5 yr T-bond	8.2	9.9	1.4	7.5
10 yr T-bond	6.1	13.4	1.1	7.2
Aaabond	9.6*	14.4	4.3	6.3
Baa bond	11.3*	17.6*	7.7	5.1
fygm6-fygm3	22.7**	34.6**	4.2	24.5**
fygt1-fygm3	23.2**	55.7**	25.7**	14.1*
fygt10-fygm3	17.4**	26.4**	9.7*	7.5
fyaaac-fygt10	4.9	60.4**	11.7*	35.5**
fybaac-fygt10	15.2**	57.5**	33.5**	11.6*
M1	2.5	11.6	2.8	4.6
MZM	5.3	13.2	7.1	4.0
M2	13.0*	55.5**	40.3**	6.7
MB	8.1	34.4**	12.2*	21.5**
Reserves tot	4.6	49.2**	9.2	22.4**
Reserves nonbor	8.7	16.1	12.1*	5.7
Bus loans	3.2	38.0**	15.3**	10.7
Cons credit	3.3	20.5*	15.9**	2.6
Ex rate: avg	26.8**	21.0*	11.0*	4.1
Ex rate: Switz	9.6*	17.0*	8.0	9.7
Ex rate: Japan	6.4	26.0**	9.6*	10.0
Ex rate: UK	6.4	43.4**	13.5**	10.6
EX rate: Canada	6.4	26.5**	19.3**	6.2
S&P 500	11.0*	22.2**	12.4*	6.1
S&P: indust	11.1*	22.7**	13.3*	5.7
S&P div yield	11.3*	21.8**	15.2**	5.5
S&P PE ratio	18.6**	56.6**	37.1**	7.3
DJIA	6.8	33.0**	14.3**	15.4**
Consumer expect	23.5**	38.0**	18.4**	10.2

Notes: Entries are chi-squared Chow statistics computed using Newey–West (1987) standard errors with 4 lags (numeric column 1) and 5 lags (numeric columns 2–4). Asterisks indicate that the Chow statistics exceed standard *5% and **1% critical values.

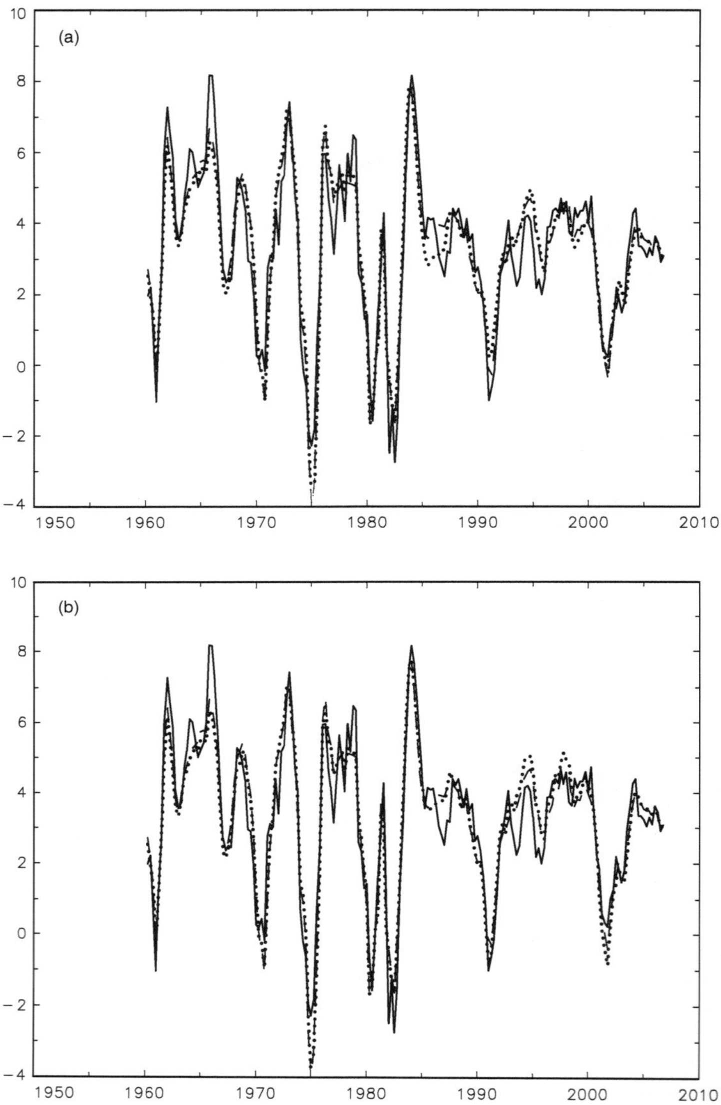

FIG. 7.1. Four-quarter real GDP growth (solid line) and three estimates of its common component: split sample factors, split sample factor loadings (split–split); full sample factors, split sample factor loadings (full–split); and full sample factors, full sample factor loadings (full–full).
(a) full–split (dashes) and split–split (dots)
(b) full–split (dashes) and full–full (dots)

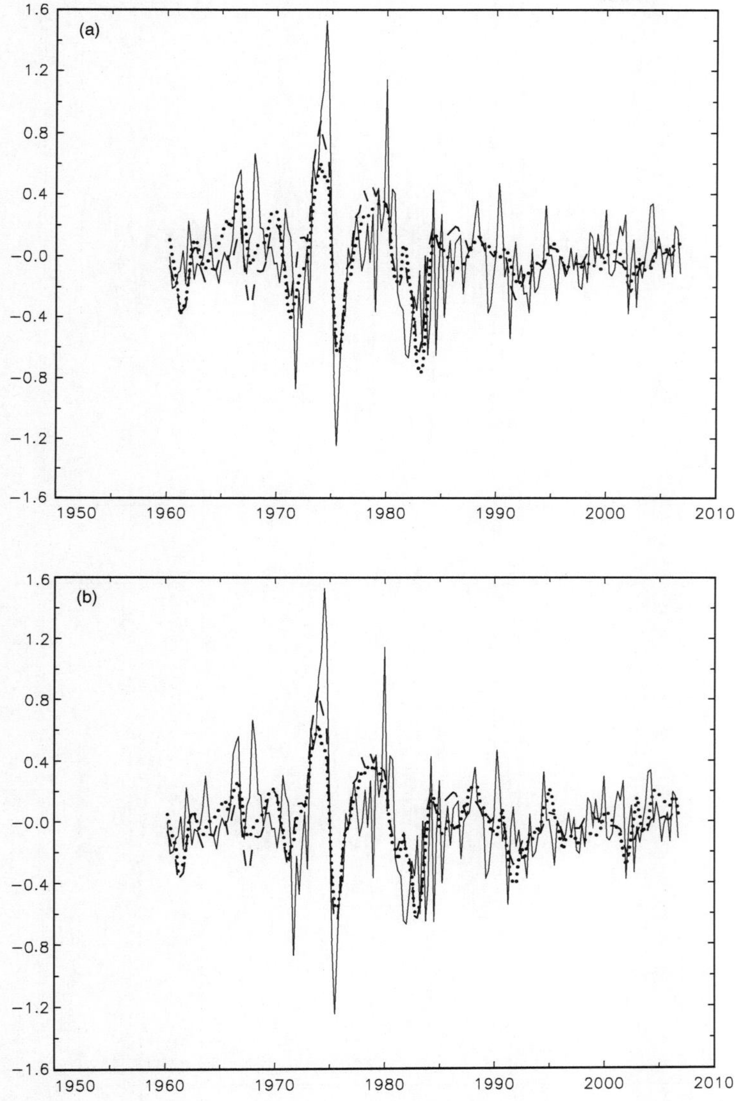

FIG. 7.2. Four-quarter change in core PCE inflation (solid line) and three estimates of its common component.
(a) full–split (dashes) and split–split (dots)
(b) full–split (dashes) and full–full (dots)

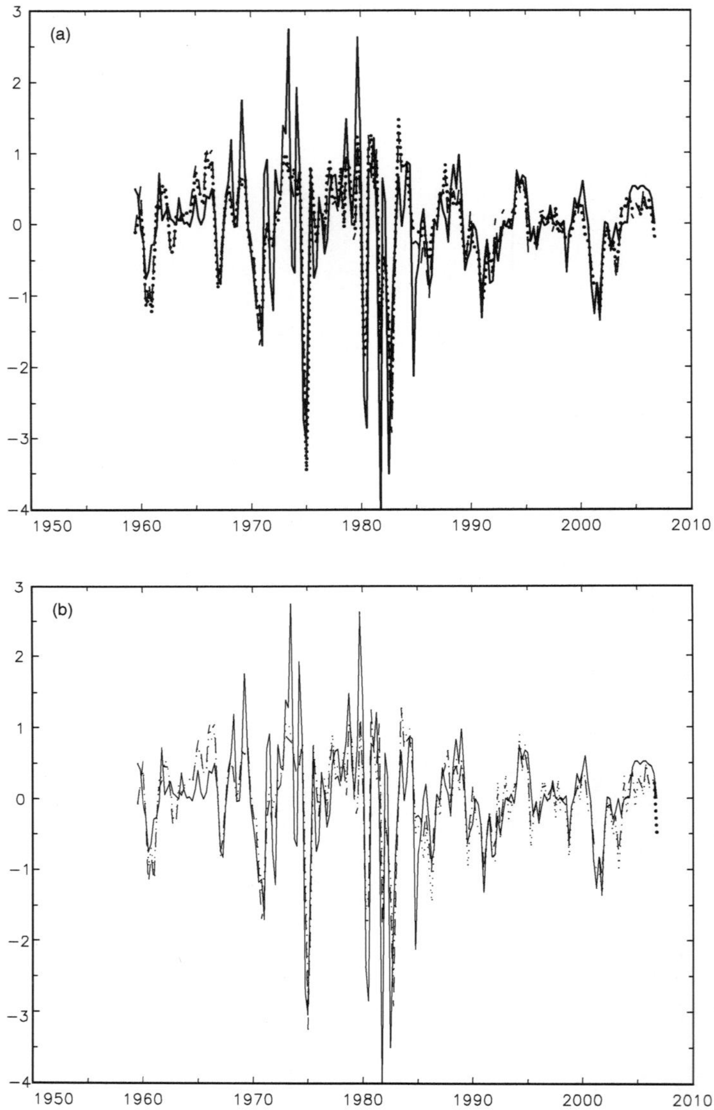

FIG. **7.3.** The Federal Funds rate (solid line) and three estimates of its common component.
(a) full–split (dashes) and split–split (dots)
(b) full–split (dashes) and full–full (dots)

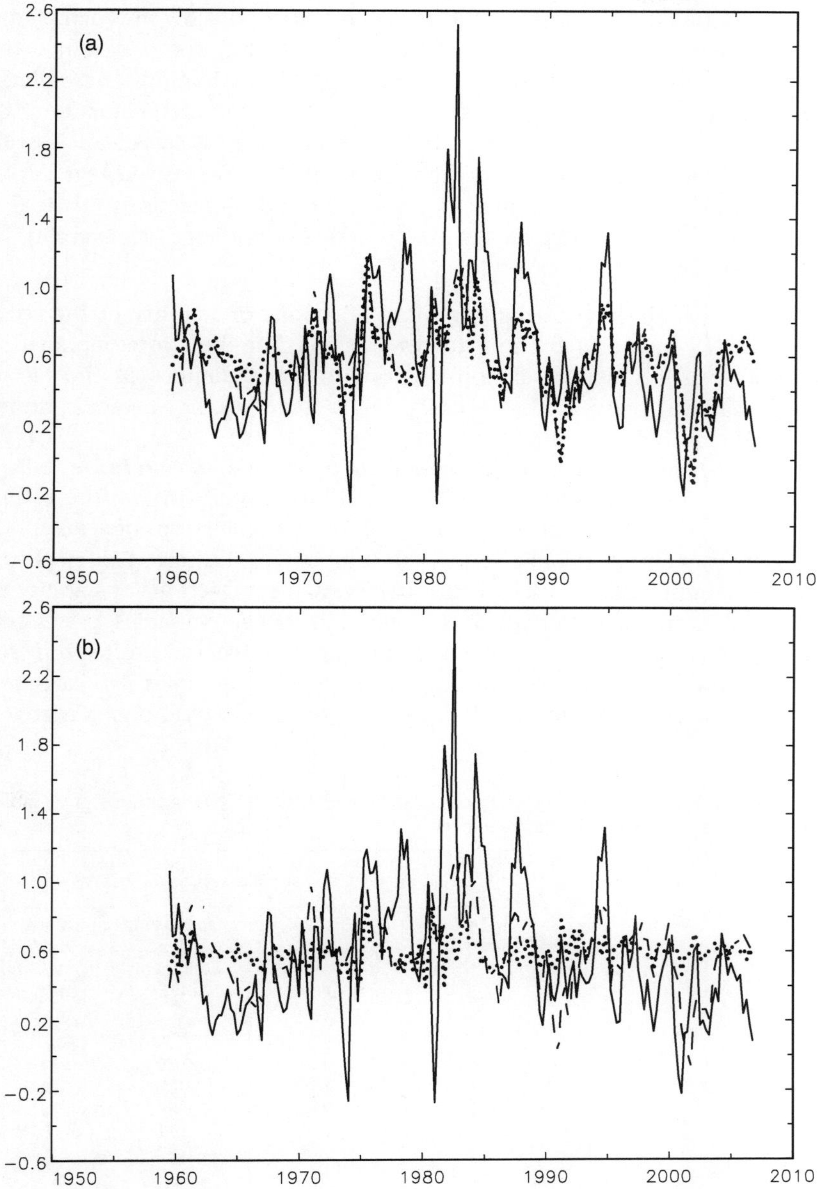

FIG. **7.4.** The one-year/3-month Treasury term spread (solid line) and three estimates of its common component.
(a) full–split (dashes) and split–split (dots)
(b) full–split (dashes) and full–full (dots)

the full-sample factors and interactions were included to allow the coefficients to differ in the two subsamples. There is considerably more evidence for instability in the forecasting regression than in the factor loadings themselves: 84% of the Chow statistics testing the stability of all the coefficients in (7.8) reject at the 5% significance level, and 74% reject at the 1% significance level. If we focus on the coefficients on the factors in the forecasting regression, there is again widespread evidence of instability (72% rejections at the 5% level, 47% rejections at the 1% level). There is also evidence of instability in the idiosyncratic dynamics.

The fact that there are strikingly more rejections of stability of the coefficients on $\hat{F}_t$ in the forecasting regressions than in the contemporaneous (factor-loading) regressions is consistent with the dynamics of the factor process changing between the two subsamples, see (7.6), however additional analysis is required to confirm this conjecture.

Stability of forecasting regressions by category of variable being forecasted. One possibility is that the instability evident in the forecasting equations seen in Table 7.3 is concentrated in a few categories of series. This possibility is explored in Table 7.4, which summarizes the Table 7.3 rejections (at the 5% significance level) by category of variable. Rejections of stability of the factor loadings are relatively less frequent for output variables, prices and wages, and money and credit variables, and are relatively more frequent for consumption, labour market, housing, and financial variables. No category, however, is immune from instability in the forecasting equations. Moreover,

Table 7.4. Summary of Chow tests by category of variable: Fraction rejections of variables within category at the 5% significance level

Category	Number of series	Split-sample Chow statistics testing the stability of:			
		Factor loadings (Λ_i)	4-step ahead forecasting regressions:		
			All coefficients	Coefficients on F_t	Intercept & coefficients on u_{it-1}
Output	14	0.29	0.93	0.79	0.36
Consumption	4	0.75	1.00	1.00	0.25
Labour market	27	0.59	0.96	0.81	0.74
Housing	7	0.57	1.00	0.71	0.43
Investment, inventories, & orders	11	0.45	1.00	0.82	0.45
Prices & wages	42	0.17	0.74	0.67	0.29
Financial variables	23	0.61	0.87	0.74	0.39
Money & credit	8	0.13	0.63	0.63	0.25
Other	8	0.63	0.50	0.38	0.25
All	144	0.41	0.84	0.72	0.41

for all categories the instability arises more commonly from instability in the coefficients on the factors, which in turn points to instability in the dynamics of the factor process.

7.4.3 *Subsample v. Full-Sample Forecasting Regressions*

We now turn to a comparison of three different direct four-quarter ahead forecasting methods: 'full–full' (that is, full-sample estimates of the factors and full-sample estimates of the forecasting regression (7.8), with $\hat{e}_{it}$ the residual from the full-sample regression of X_{it} onto the four full-sample factors), 'full–split' (full-sample estimates of the four full-sample factors and split-sample estimates of (7.8), with $\hat{e}_{it}$ the residual from the split-sample regression of X_{it} onto the four full-sample factors), and 'split–split' (split-sample estimates of the three split-sample factors and split-sample estimates of (7.8), with $\hat{e}_{it}$ the residual from the split-sample regression of X_{it} onto the three split-sample factors). In each case, $p = 4$ in (7.8).

These comparisons are summarized in Table 7.5. Of particular interest are the relative MSEs of the three different methods, which are presented in the third and fourth columns for the pre-84 sample and in the seventh and eighth columns for the post-84 sample. Note that the relative MSEs are computed using the residuals from various fitted regressions, that is, these are in-sample not pseudo out-of-sample estimates; also note that the method of construction of $\hat{e}_{it}$ and the lag specification in (7.8) implies that the MSE of the full–full forecast can be less than the MSE of the full–split forecast.

The relative MSEs in Table 7.5 are summarized in Figure 7.5(**a**) (pre-84 sample) and Figure 7.6(**a**) (post-84 sample). Part (a) of each figure is a histogram of the MSE of the full–split forecasts to the full–full forecasts. Part (b) is a histogram of the MSE of the split–split forecast to the full–split, so values exceeding 1.0 indicate that the full–split forecast outperforms the split–split forecast.

The hypothesis tests in Table 7.3 examined direct forecasting equations using the full-sample factors, in which the coefficients are allowed to change between the two samples; the finding from Table 7.3, summarized in the second column ('all coefficients') of Table 7.4, is that for most of the series the change in the coefficients in (7.8) is statistically significant. The magnitude of this improvement, measured by relative MSEs, is quantified in the 'full–split to full–full' column of Table 7.5. As can be seen in Figures 7.5(**a**)(a) and 7.6(**a**)(a), allowing the forecasting coefficients to change, while using the full-sample factors, typically produces modest improvements in fit in the pre-84 sample but very substantial improvements in fit in the post-84 sample.

Given this large and statistically significant change in the forecasting coefficients using the full-sample estimates of the factors, it is natural to wonder whether one might further improve the forecasts using split-sample estimates

Table 7.5. In-sample root mean square errors (RMSEs) and relative MSEs of 4-step ahead forecasting regressions: 4 full-sample factors, 3 subsample factors

The forecasting regressions (specification (7.8)) are estimated using:
(a) full-sample factor estimates and full-sample coefficients ('full–full')
(b) full-sample factor estimates and split-sample coefficients ('full–split')
(c) split-sample factor estimates and split-sample coefficients ('split–split')

Series (X_{it})	Pre-84 Sample				Post-84 Sample			
	Std dev of $X_{it}^{(4)}$	RMSE, full–full	MSE ratio		Std dev of $X_{it}^{(4)}$	RMSE, full–full	MSE ratio	
			full–split to full–full	split–split to full–split			full–split to full–full	split–split to full–split
RGDP	2.73	2.13	0.94	0.99	1.29	1.23	0.69	1.17
Cons	2.16	1.80	0.95	0.99	1.11	1.08	0.71	1.16
Cons-Dur	7.59	5.71	0.94	0.99	4.42	4.47	0.83	1.05
Cons-NonDur	2.01	1.75	0.88	1.10	1.18	1.18	0.77	1.14
Cons-Serv	1.26	1.17	0.90	0.98	0.86	0.84	0.54	1.29
GPDInv	11.97	8.28	0.90	1.01	6.72	6.27	0.80	1.07
FixedInv	7.85	5.73	0.89	1.00	5.10	4.60	0.69	1.04
NonResInv	7.47	5.43	0.87	1.03	6.14	4.87	0.76	0.99
NonResInv-struct	7.65	6.62	0.87	1.00	7.71	6.17	0.80	1.01
NonResInv-Bequip	8.33	5.80	0.86	1.04	6.09	5.07	0.72	1.01
Res.Inv	16.88	12.11	0.95	1.00	7.25	7.20	0.62	1.18
Exports	6.76	5.34	0.92	0.98	5.27	5.09	0.88	1.01
Imports	8.63	5.81	0.96	1.03	4.56	3.97	0.86	1.04
Gov	2.85	2.48	1.00	1.00	1.77	1.49	0.93	0.99
Gov Fed	5.07	4.34	1.00	1.00	3.54	2.87	0.90	0.94
Gov State/Loc	2.51	2.08	0.99	1.00	1.61	1.32	0.82	1.05
IP: total	5.37	3.68	0.93	1.00	2.80	2.56	0.76	1.05
IP: products	4.58	3.25	0.92	0.99	2.46	2.23	0.74	1.09
IP: final prod	4.50	3.26	0.91	1.00	2.42	2.25	0.73	1.06
IP: cons gds	4.05	2.62	0.96	1.02	1.70	1.88	0.56	1.18
IP: cons dble	9.46	6.63	0.97	0.99	4.80	4.49	0.85	1.08
IP: cons nondble	2.38	2.01	0.88	1.12	1.40	1.62	0.51	1.20
IP: bus eqpt	8.29	5.34	0.89	1.03	5.88	4.84	0.86	1.01
IP: matls	6.48	4.41	0.93	0.98	3.42	3.25	0.75	0.99
IP: dble mats	9.70	6.43	0.93	1.01	5.52	5.09	0.73	1.03
IP: nondble mats	5.91	4.48	0.85	1.02	2.91	3.19	0.60	1.13
IP: mfg	6.00	4.08	0.93	0.99	3.18	2.84	0.78	1.06
IP: fuels	5.19	5.05	0.96	1.00	3.52	3.41	0.81	1.06
NAPM prodn	8.00	6.97	0.96	0.98	5.56	5.27	0.80	1.20
Capacity Util	5.35	3.01	0.90	1.00	3.19	2.15	0.73	1.12
Emp: total	2.36	1.61	0.89	0.96	1.53	1.00	0.61	1.15
Emp: gds prod	4.20	2.78	0.90	0.97	2.44	1.79	0.58	1.13
Emp: mining	6.69	6.33	0.93	1.01	6.41	5.50	0.83	1.03
Emp: const	5.45	3.99	0.92	0.98	3.89	2.87	0.70	1.09
Emp: mfg	4.26	2.97	0.86	0.98	2.48	2.03	0.49	1.11
Emp: dble gds	5.48	3.75	0.87	0.99	3.11	2.42	0.56	1.07
Emp: nondbles	2.57	2.03	0.74	1.04	1.90	1.47	0.53	1.08
Emp: services	1.33	0.87	0.87	0.98	1.13	0.68	0.70	1.15
Emp: TTU	1.78	1.26	0.81	0.99	1.59	1.06	0.62	1.19
Emp: wholesale	1.88	1.44	0.71	1.04	1.86	1.29	0.71	1.10
Emp: retail	1.74	1.28	0.79	1.01	1.64	1.21	0.58	1.19

Table 7.5. (*Continued*)

Series (X_{it})	Pre-84 Sample				Post-84 Sample			
	Std dev of $X_{it}^{(4)}$	RMSE, full–full	MSE ratio		Std dev of $X_{it}^{(4)}$	RMSE, full–full	MSE ratio	
			full–split to full–full	split–split to full–split			full–split to full–full	split–split to full–split
Emp: FIRE	1.29	0.88	0.85	1.01	1.63	1.19	0.75	1.12
Emp: Govt	1.93	1.25	0.94	1.02	0.80	0.85	0.65	1.00
Help wanted indx	3.46	2.68	0.84	1.01	2.44	1.87	0.81	1.13
Help wanted/emp	0.09	0.07	0.97	1.01	0.04	0.04	0.71	1.07
Emp CPS total	1.55	1.15	0.86	0.99	0.98	0.78	0.65	1.38
Emp CPS nonag	1.58	1.16	0.84	0.98	1.03	0.83	0.64	1.38
Emp. Hours	2.70	1.92	0.85	0.98	1.98	1.61	0.68	1.08
Avg hrs	0.50	0.35	0.98	0.98	0.42	0.31	0.89	0.99
Overtime: mfg	0.12	0.08	0.93	1.00	0.08	0.07	0.91	1.06
U: all	0.30	0.20	0.95	1.01	0.16	0.12	0.71	1.23
U: mean duration	0.55	0.29	0.92	1.03	0.43	0.25	0.68	1.17
U < 5 wks	9.85	8.13	0.93	1.02	6.50	6.14	0.85	1.10
U 5–14 wks	21.00	15.44	0.96	1.01	11.52	9.60	0.76	1.24
U 15+ wks	38.50	23.62	0.93	1.00	22.77	15.14	0.65	1.18
U 15–26wks	34.09	22.62	0.94	1.00	19.93	15.23	0.68	1.24
U 27+wks	46.91	27.03	0.95	1.02	27.70	16.88	0.67	1.23
HStarts: Total	0.23	0.19	0.94	1.01	0.18	0.12	0.78	0.99
BuildPermits	0.26	0.21	0.98	0.98	0.21	0.13	0.77	0.98
HStarts: NE	0.30	0.21	0.96	0.97	0.27	0.15	0.79	1.10
HStarts: MW	0.32	0.25	1.00	1.00	0.14	0.11	0.98	1.08
HStarts: South	0.26	0.19	0.97	0.92	0.23	0.13	0.76	1.03
HStarts: West	0.33	0.24	0.99	1.00	0.20	0.14	0.84	1.03
PMI	7.82	6.70	0.93	0.94	4.66	4.55	0.73	1.22
NAPM new ordrs	8.58	7.38	0.98	0.99	5.85	5.43	0.80	1.23
NAPM vendor del	13.51	11.12	0.95	0.97	4.66	5.17	0.56	1.18
NAPM Invent	7.68	6.39	0.84	0.90	3.15	3.59	0.42	1.22
Orders (ConsGoods)	8.51	6.34	0.87	0.96	3.49	3.61	0.68	1.06
Orders (NDCapGoods)	15.02	10.98	0.89	1.01	9.89	8.66	0.78	1.00
PGDP	1.43	0.99	0.96	0.99	0.73	0.59	0.63	1.13
PCED	1.49	1.17	0.97	0.98	0.99	0.80	0.69	1.10
CPI-All	1.98	1.33	0.95	1.00	1.39	1.14	0.70	1.02
PCED-Core	1.24	0.98	0.98	1.01	0.60	0.49	0.60	1.16
CPI-Core	1.99	1.74	0.98	1.04	0.55	0.56	0.54	1.07
PCED-Dur	2.50	1.81	0.95	1.05	1.33	1.26	0.63	1.19
PCED-motorveh	4.17	2.86	0.98	1.02	2.30	1.89	0.83	1.04
PCED-hhequip	1.92	1.44	0.91	1.08	1.82	1.47	0.59	1.15
PCED-oth dur	2.87	2.36	0.96	1.02	2.00	1.34	0.72	1.28
PCED-nondur	2.59	1.99	0.95	0.95	2.95	1.99	0.90	1.03
PCED-food	3.28	2.33	1.00	0.98	1.24	0.99	0.75	1.16
PCED-clothing	2.14	1.58	0.95	1.07	3.03	1.78	0.87	1.08
PCED-energy	14.29	11.06	0.83	0.99	27.93	18.87	1.01	0.93
PCED-oth nondur	2.49	1.91	0.91	1.04	1.59	1.19	0.75	1.09
PCED-services	1.21	0.91	0.98	0.97	0.82	0.55	0.76	1.00
PCED-housing	1.22	0.97	0.98	0.98	0.81	0.63	0.90	1.04
PCED-hhops	2.40	1.82	0.92	0.98	3.50	2.31	0.94	1.07

Table 7.5. (*Continued*)

Series (X_{it})	Pre-84 Sample				Post-84 Sample			
	Std dev of $X_{it}^{(4)}$	RMSE, full–full	MSE ratio		Std dev of $X_{it}^{(4)}$	RMSE, full–full	MSE ratio	
			full–split to full–full	split–split to full–split			full–split to full–full	split–split to full–split
PCED-elect & gas	3.78	2.90	0.70	1.02	7.30	5.90	0.92	1.01
PCED-oth hhops	2.74	2.23	0.97	1.01	1.72	1.19	0.78	1.16
PCED-transport	6.80	5.04	0.57	1.07	6.60	7.15	0.71	0.99
PCED-medical	1.80	1.42	0.93	1.00	0.94	0.97	0.71	1.01
PCED-recreation	1.72	1.13	1.03	0.97	1.10	0.77	0.87	1.08
PCED-oth serv	2.59	2.13	0.96	1.00	2.71	1.97	0.76	0.84
PGPDI	2.63	1.72	0.95	1.08	1.25	1.19	0.54	1.13
PFI	2.66	1.75	0.94	1.06	1.29	1.20	0.55	1.11
PFI-nonres	2.60	1.89	0.91	1.07	1.32	1.23	0.59	1.08
PFI-nonres struc	3.68	2.90	0.96	1.01	2.12	1.81	0.73	1.08
PFI-nonres equip	2.74	1.92	0.90	1.09	1.62	1.46	0.66	1.06
PFI-resdidential	4.53	4.08	0.98	1.00	2.21	1.94	0.43	1.01
PEXP	5.17	3.93	0.97	0.95	2.38	2.19	0.69	1.11
PIMP	8.49	7.55	0.95	0.96	6.58	4.79	0.83	1.00
PGOV	2.29	1.34	0.89	1.00	1.62	1.11	0.71	1.02
PGOV-Federal	3.89	1.86	0.95	1.01	2.72	1.25	0.87	0.99
PGOV-St & loc	1.94	1.40	0.89	0.97	1.55	1.27	0.68	1.06
Com: spot price (real)	12.85	9.93	0.88	1.06	9.21	8.58	0.77	1.06
OilPrice (Real)	11.51	11.16	0.72	1.00	24.19	21.91	0.82	1.01
NAPM com price	12.95	11.27	0.86	0.94	13.22	13.50	0.66	1.14
Real AHE: goods	1.49	1.37	0.91	1.06	1.16	0.86	0.74	1.09
Real AHE: const	2.60	1.93	0.98	1.02	1.43	1.20	0.80	0.97
Real AHE: mfg	1.40	1.36	0.87	1.04	1.07	0.92	0.72	1.09
Labor Prod	1.95	1.76	0.95	1.03	1.28	1.17	0.84	1.00
Real Comp/Hour	1.24	1.11	0.93	1.07	1.58	1.53	0.96	1.01
Unit Labor Cost	3.74	2.43	1.01	0.94	1.38	1.54	0.59	1.05
FedFunds	0.63	0.44	0.89	0.97	0.38	0.32	0.66	1.03
3 mo T-bill	0.45	0.33	0.87	0.99	0.35	0.31	0.71	1.03
6 mo T-bill	0.45	0.37	0.88	1.06	0.35	0.32	0.72	1.06
1 yr T-bond	0.46	0.39	0.89	1.08	0.36	0.33	0.79	1.07
5 yr T-bond	0.34	0.31	0.93	1.04	0.30	0.30	0.89	0.94
10 yr T-bond	0.29	0.28	0.92	1.02	0.27	0.27	0.86	0.92
Aaabond	0.26	0.24	0.93	1.03	0.21	0.22	0.86	0.92
Baa bond	0.30	0.26	0.92	1.03	0.21	0.21	0.86	0.93
fygm6-fygm3	0.22	0.21	0.95	1.01	0.14	0.14	0.73	1.12
fygt1-fygm3	0.46	0.40	0.85	1.08	0.31	0.33	0.70	1.09
fygt10-fygm3	1.20	0.93	0.95	1.01	1.12	0.83	0.70	0.99
fyaaac-fygt10	0.34	0.30	0.81	1.04	0.40	0.32	0.88	1.02
fybaac-fygt10	0.72	0.47	0.89	0.99	0.50	0.41	0.84	1.02
M1	3.16	2.08	0.87	1.01	4.40	3.77	0.94	0.84
MZM	5.97	5.29	0.96	0.96	5.08	4.61	0.81	0.81
M2	3.09	2.23	0.87	1.03	2.49	2.23	0.71	0.84
MB	1.82	1.41	0.81	0.98	2.94	2.73	0.96	0.97
Reserves tot	5.25	4.02	0.60	0.98	8.64	7.43	0.84	0.98
Reserves nonbor	12.74	12.73	0.77	1.08	14.49	13.04	0.76	1.03

Table 7.5. (*Continued*)

Series (X_{it})	Pre-84 Sample				Post-84 Sample			
	Std dev of $X_{it}^{(4)}$	RMSE, full–full	MSE ratio		Std dev of $X_{it}^{(4)}$	RMSE, full–full	MSE ratio	
			full–split to full–full	split–split to full–split			full–split to full–full	split–split to full–split
Bus loans	6.71	4.90	0.91	1.03	4.91	4.07	0.79	1.08
Cons credit	4.23	3.07	0.87	1.03	3.48	3.37	0.84	1.01
Ex rate: avg	5.00	4.51	0.86	0.97	7.62	6.97	0.90	1.14
Ex rate: Switz	9.70	9.13	0.90	1.05	12.49	11.69	0.89	1.05
Ex rate: Japan	8.71	7.93	0.87	1.13	12.59	11.72	0.92	1.06
Ex rate: UK	9.05	8.29	0.78	1.01	9.12	8.99	0.77	1.22
EX rate: Canada	3.37	3.69	0.75	1.04	5.58	4.55	0.93	0.96
S&P 500	14.28	12.57	0.79	1.05	14.21	14.72	0.74	1.00
S&P: indust	14.66	13.04	0.80	1.05	15.08	15.34	0.76	1.02
S&P div yield	0.17	0.12	0.90	1.12	0.09	0.10	0.61	0.99
S&P PE ratio	0.68	0.54	0.69	1.12	1.27	1.07	0.79	1.01
DJIA	14.09	11.83	0.78	1.03	13.06	14.01	0.67	1.00
Consumer expect	2.92	2.12	0.83	1.01	2.46	2.52	0.69	1.01

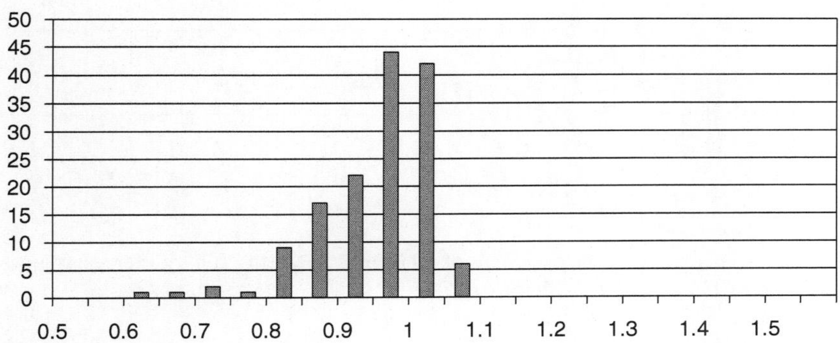

FIG. **7.5(a).** Histogram of relative MSEs of full–split forecasts to full–full forecasts, pre-1984 sample (mean = 0.91, median = 0.92).

of the factors. This possibility is examined in the 'split–split to full–split' columns of Table 7.5 and in Figures 7.5(**a**)(b) and 7.6(b). In the pre-84 sample, there is little difference on average across the series between using the full- and split-sample factors. In contrast, in the post-84 sample there is noticeable deterioration on average, and substantial degradation for many individual series, when forecasts are made using the split-sample factors. Strikingly, despite the evidence of some instability in the factor loadings, it is best to

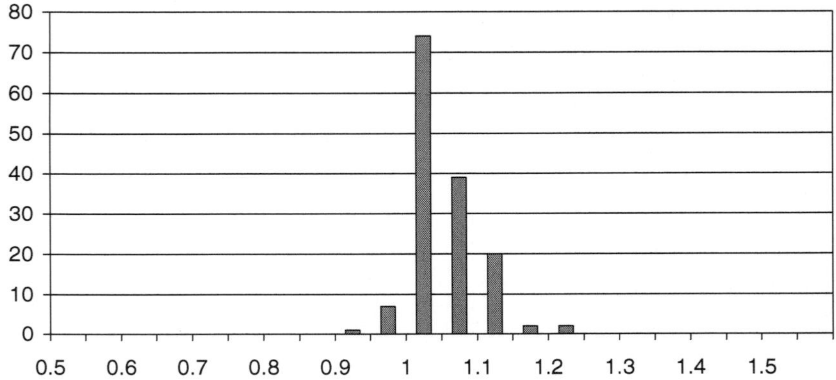

FIG. 7.5(b). Histogram of relative MSEs of split–split forecasts to full–split forecasts, pre-1984 sample (mean = 1.01, median = 1.00).

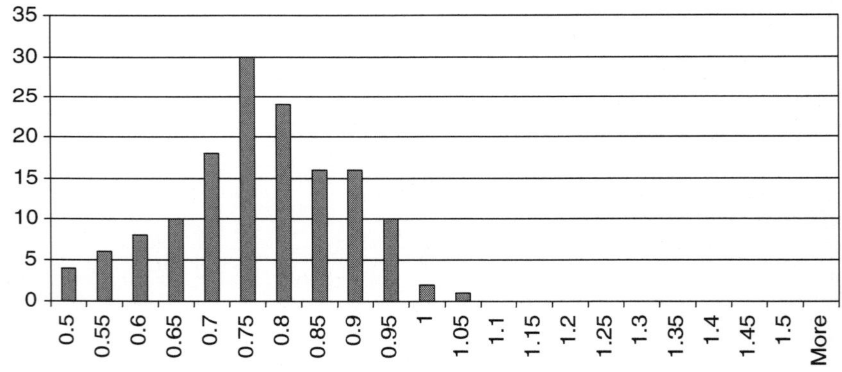

FIG. 7.6(a). Histogram of relative MSEs of full–split forecasts to full–full forecasts, post-1984 sample (mean = 0.75, median = 0.75).

use all the data to estimate the factors, but to allow the coefficients of the forecasting regressions to change.

As mentioned above, there is ambiguity concerning the number of factors, and the computations underlying Tables 7.3–7.5 were repeated for various numbers of full-sample factors and subsample factors (specifically, 4 and 4, 5 and 4, and 5 and 5, respectively). The main findings stated above are robust to these changes in the estimated factors. The results for 4 and 4, 5 and 4, and 5 and 5 factors, like those in Table 7.4 for 4 and 3 factors, are also consistent with the full-sample factor estimates spanning the space of the subsample factor estimates, but the predictive regressions having coefficients which are unstable across subsamples.

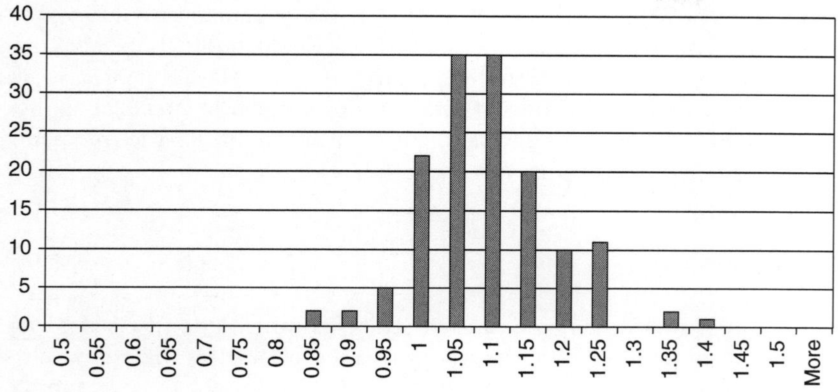

FIG. **7.6(b).** Histogram of relative MSEs of split–split forecasts to full–split forecasts, post-1984 sample (mean = 1.07, median = 1.06).

7.5 Discussion and Conclusions

Several caveats are in order concerning the empirical results. The empirical investigation has focused on the single-break model, and multiple breaks and continuous parameter evolution have been ignored. The break date, 1984, has been treated as known a priori, however it was chosen because of a number of interesting macroeconomic transitions that have been noticed around 1984 and thus the break date should in fact be thought of as estimated (although not on the basis of breaks in a factor model). The forecasting regressions examined here are all in-sample estimates and might not reflect out-of-sample performance. Finally, the formal theoretical justification for some of this work is limited. In particular, Stock and Watson (2002b), theorem 3, only states that the space of the factors will be consistently estimated, and it does not formally justify the application of the Bai–Ng (2002) criteria or the use of the factors as regressors (existing proofs of these have time-invariant factor loadings, eg Bai and Ng, 2006). These extensions of Stock and Watson (2002b), theorem 3, remain a topic of ongoing research.

Despite these caveats, the results suggest three interesting conclusions. First, there is considerable evidence of instability in the factor model; the indirect evidence suggests instability in all elements (the factor loadings, the factor dynamics, and the idiosyncratic dynamics). Second, despite this instability, the factors seem to be well estimated using the full sample: the full-sample estimates of the factors span the space of the split-sample factor estimates. Third, we have the striking finding that forecasting equations estimated using full-sample estimates of the factors and subsample estimates of the coefficients fit better than equations estimated using subsample estimates of both the factors and coefficients. This final finding is rather remarkable and is consistent with the theoretical results and Monte Carlo findings in Stock and Watson (1998, 2002b) and Banerjeee, Marcellino, and Masten (2007). It also suggests that when factor forecasts start to break down in practical applications, attention should initially be focused on instability of the forecasting equation instead of problems with the estimates of the factors.

Data Appendix

Table A.1 lists the short name of each series, its mnemonic (the series label used in the source database), the transformation applied to the series, and a brief data description. All series are from the Global Insight Basic Economics Database, unless the source is listed (in parentheses) as TCB (The Conference Board's Indicators Database) or AC (author's calculation based on Global Insight or TCB data). The binary entry in Table A.1 the column labelled 'E.F.?' indicates whether that variable was used to estimate the factors. For series available monthly, quarterly values were computed by averaging (in native units) the monthly values over the quarter. There are no missing observations.

The transformation codes in the third column of Table A.1 are defined in the subsequent table, along with the *h*-period ahead version of the variable used in the direct forecasting regressions. In this table, Y_{it} denotes the original (native) untransformed quarterly series.

Table A1. Data sources, transformations, and definitions

Short name	Mnemonic	Trans. Code	E.F.?	Description
RGDP	GDP251	5	0	Real gross domestic product, quantity index (2,000 = 100), saar
Cons	GDP252	5	0	Real personal consumption expenditures, quantity index (2,000 = 100), saar
Cons-Dur	GDP253	5	1	Real personal consumption expenditures - durable goods, quantity index (2,000 = 100), saar
Cons-NonDur	GDP254	5	1	Real personal consumption expenditures - nondurable goods, quantity index (2,000 = 100), saar
Cons-Serv	GDP255	5	1	Real personal consumption expenditures - services, quantity index (2,000 = 100), saar
GPDInv	GDP256	5	0	Real gross private domestic investment, quantity index (2,000 = 100), saar
FixedInv	GDP257	5	0	Real gross private domestic investment - fixed investment, quantity index (2,000 = 100), saar
NonResInv	GDP258	5	0	Real gross private domestic investment - nonresidential, quantity index (2,000 = 100), saar
NonResInv-struct	GDP259	5	1	Real gross private domestic investment - nonresidential - structures, quantity
NonResInv-Bequip	GDP260	5	1	Real gross private domestic investment - nonresidential - equipment & software
Res.Inv	GDP261	5	1	Real gross private domestic investment - residential, quantity index (2,000 = 100), saar
Exports	GDP263	5	1	Real exports, quantity index (2,000 = 100), saar
Imports	GDP264	5	1	Real imports, quantity index (2,000 = 100), saar
Gov	GDP265	5	0	Real government consumption expenditures & gross investment, quantity index (2,000 = 100), saar
Gov Fed	GDP266	5	1	Real government consumption expenditures & gross investment - federal, quantity
Gov State/Loc	GDP267	5	1	Real government consumption expenditures & gross investment - state & local, quantity
IP: total	IPS10	5	0	Industrial production index - total index
IP: products	IPS11	5	0	Industrial production index - products, total
IP: final prod	IPS299	5	0	Industrial production index - final products
IP: cons gds	IPS12	5	0	Industrial production index - consumer goods
IP: cons dble	IPS13	5	1	Industrial production index - durable consumer goods
IP: cons nondble	IPS18	5	1	Industrial production index - nondurable consumer goods
IP: bus eqpt	IPS25	5	1	Industrial production index - business equipment
IP: matls	IPS32	5	0	Industrial production index - materials

Table A1. *(Continued)*

Short name	Mnemonic	Trans. Code	E.F.?	Description
IP: dble mats	IPS34	5	1	Industrial production index - durable goods materials
IP: nondble mats	IPS38	5	1	Industrial production index - nondurable goods materials
IP: mfg	IPS43	5	1	Industrial production index - manufacturing (sic)
IP: fuels	IPS306	5	1	Industrial production index - fuels
NAPM prodn	PMP	1	1	Napm production index (percent)
Capacity Util	UTL11	1	1	Capacity utilization - manufacturing (sic)
Emp: total	CES002	5	0	Employees, nonfarm - total private
Emp: gds prod	CES003	5	0	Employees, nonfarm - goods-producing
Emp: mining	CES006	5	1	Employees, nonfarm - mining
Emp: const	CES011	5	1	Employees, nonfarm - construction
Emp: mfg	CES015	5	0	Employees, nonfarm - mfg
Emp: dble gds	CES017	5	1	Employees, nonfarm - durable goods
Emp: nondbles	CES033	5	1	Employees, nonfarm - nondurable goods
Emp: services	CES046	5	1	Employees, nonfarm - service-providing
Emp: TTU	CES048	5	1	Employees, nonfarm - trade, transport, utilities
Emp: wholesale	CES049	5	1	Employees, nonfarm - wholesale trade
Emp: retail	CES053	5	1	Employees, nonfarm - retail trade
Emp: FIRE	CES088	5	1	Employees, nonfarm - financial activities
Emp: Govt	CES140	5	1	Employees, nonfarm - government
Help wanted indx	LHEL	2	1	Index of help-wanted advertising in newspapers (1967 = 100; sa)
Help wanted/emp	LHELX	2	1	Employment: ratio; help-wanted ads:no. Unemployed clf
Emp CPS total	LHEM	5	0	Civilian labor force: employed, total (thous.,sa)
Emp CPS nonag	LHNAG	5	1	Civilian labor force: employed, nonagric.industries (thous.,sa)
Emp. Hours	LBMNU	5	1	Hours of all persons: nonfarm business sec (1982 = 100,sa)
Avg hrs	CES151	1	1	Avg wkly hours, prod wrkrs, nonfarm - goods-producing
Overtime: mfg	CES155	2	1	Avg wkly overtime hours, prod wrkrs, nonfarm - mfg
U: all	LHUR	2	1	Unemployment rate: all workers, 16 years & over (%,sa)
U: mean duration	LHU680	2	1	Unemploy.by duration: average(mean)duration in weeks (sa)
U < 5 wks	LHU5	5	1	Unemploy.by duration: persons unempl.less than 5 wks (thous.,sa)
U 5–14 wks	LHU14	5	1	Unemploy.by duration: persons unempl.5 to 14 wks (thous.,sa)
U 15 + wks	LHU15	5	1	Unemploy.by duration: persons unempl. 15 wks+ (thous.,sa)
U 15–26 wks	LHU26	5	1	Unemploy.by duration: persons unempl.15 to 26 wks (thous.,sa)
U 27 + wks	LHU27	5	1	Unemploy.by duration: persons unempl. 27 wks+ (thous,sa)
HStarts: Total	HSFR	4	0	Housing starts: nonfarm(1947–58); total farm&nonfarm(1959-) (thous.,sa)

Table A1. (*Continued*)

Short name	Mnemonic	Trans. Code	E.F.?	Description
BuildPermits	HSBR	4	0	Housing authorized: total new priv housing units (thous., saar)
HStarts: NE	HSNE	4	1	Housing starts:northeast (thous.u.), sa
HStarts: MW	HSMW	4	1	Housing starts:midwest (thous.u.), sa
HStarts: South	HSSOU	4	1	Housing starts:south (thous.u.), sa
HStarts: West	HSWST	4	1	Housing starts:west (thous.u.), sa
PMI	PMI	1	1	Purchasing managers' index (sa)
NAPM new ordrs	PMNO	1	1	Napm new orders index (percent)
NAPM vendor del	PMDEL	1	1	Napm vendor deliveries index (percent)
NAPM Invent	PMNV	1	1	Napm inventories index (percent)
Orders (ConsGoods)	MOCMQ	5	1	New orders (net) - consumer goods & materials, 1996 dollars (bci)
Orders (NDCapGoods)	MSONDQ	5	1	New orders, nondefense capital goods, in 1996 dollars (bci)
PGDP	GDP272A	6	0	Gross domestic product price index
PCED	GDP273A	6	0	Personal consumption expenditures price index
CPI-All	CPIAUCSL	6	0	CPI all items (sa) fred
PCED-Core	PCEPILFE	6	0	PCE price index less food and energy (sa) (FRED)
CPI-Core	CPILFESL	6	0	CPI less food and energy (sa) (FRED)
PCED-Dur	GDP274A	6	0	Durable goods price index
PCED-motorveh	GDP274_1	6	1	Motor vehicles and parts price index
PCED-hhequip	GDP274_2	6	1	Furniture and household equipment price index
PCED-oth dur	GDP274_3	6	1	Other durable price index
PCED-nondur	GDP275A	6	0	Nondurable goods price index
PCED-food	GDP275_1	6	1	Food price index
PCED-clothing	GDP275_2	6	1	Clothing and shoes price index
PCED-energy	GDP275_3	6	1	Gasoline, fuel oil, and other energy goods price index
PCED-oth nondur	GDP275_4	6	1	Other nondorable price index
PCED-services	GDP276A	6	0	Services price index
PCED-housing	GDP276_1	6	1	Housing price index
PCED-hhops	GDP276_2	6	0	Household operation price index
PCED-elect & gas	GDP276_3	6	1	Electricity and gas price index
PCED-oth hhops	GDP276_4	6	1	Other household operation price index
PCED-transport	GDP276_5	6	1	Transportation price index
PCED-medical	GDP276_6	6	1	Medical care price index
PCED-recreation	GDP276_7	6	1	Recreation price index
PCED-oth serv	GDP276_8	6	1	Other service price index
PGPDI	GDP277A	6	0	Gross private domestic investment price index
PFI	GDP278A	6	0	Fixed investment price index
PFI-nonres	GDP279A	6	0	Nonresidential price index
PFI-nonres struc	GDP280A	6	1	Structures
PFI-nonres equip	GDP281A	6	1	Equipment and software price index
PFI-resdidential	GDP282A	6	1	Residential price index
PEXP	GDP284A	6	1	Exports price index
PIMP	GDP285A	6	1	Imports price index
PGOV	GDP286A	6	0	Government consumption expenditures and gross investment price index

Table A1. (*Continued*)

Short name	Mnemonic	Trans. Code	E.F.?	Description
PGOV-Federal	GDP287A	6	1	Federal price index
PGOV-St & loc	GDP288A	6	1	State and local price index
Com: spot price (real)	PSCCOMR	5	1	Real spot market price index:bls & crb: all commodities (1967 = 100) (psccom/PCEpilfe)
OilPrice (Real)	PW561R	5	1	Ppi crude (relative to core PCE) (pw561/PCEpilfe)
NAPM com price	PMCP	1	1	Napm commodity prices index (percent)
Real AHE: goods	CES275R	5	0	Real avg hrly earnings, prod wrkrs, nonfarm - goods-producing (ces275/pi071)
Real AHE: const	CES277R	5	1	Real avg hrly earnings, prod wrkrs, nonfarm - construction (ces277/pi071)
Real AHE: mfg	CES278 R	5	1	Real avg hrly earnings, prod wrkrs, nonfarm - mfg (ces278/pi071)
Labor Prod	LBOUT	5	1	Output per hour all persons: business sec (1982 = 100,sa)
Real Comp/Hour	LBPUR7	5	1	Real compensation per hour,employees:nonfarm business (82 = 100,sa)
Unit Labor Cost	LBLCPU	5	1	Unit labor cost: nonfarm business sec (1982 = 100,sa)
FedFunds	FYFF	2	1	Interest rate: federal funds (effective) (% per annum,nsa)
3 mo T-bill	FYGM3	2	1	Interest rate: u.s.treasury bills,sec mkt,3-mo.(% per ann,nsa)
6 mo T-bill	FYGM6	2	0	Interest rate: u.s.treasury bills,sec mkt,6-mo.(% per ann,nsa)
1 yr T-bond	FYGT1	2	1	Interest rate: u.s.treasury const maturities,1-yr.(% per ann,nsa)
5 yr T-bond	FYGT5	2	0	Interest rate: u.s.treasury const maturities,5-yr.(% per ann,nsa)
10 yr T-bond	FYGT10	2	1	Interest rate: u.s.treasury const maturities,10-yr.(% per ann,nsa)
Aaabond	FYAAAC	2	0	Bond yield: moody's aaa corporate (% per annum)
Baa bond	FYBAAC	2	0	Bond yield: moody's baa corporate (% per annum)
fygm6-fygm3	SFYGM6	1	1	fygm6-fygm3
fygt1-fygm3	SFYGT1	1	1	fygt1-fygm3
fygt10-fygm3	SFYGT10	1	1	fygt10-fygm3
fyaaac-fygt10	SFYAAAC	1	1	fyaaac-fygt10
fybaac-fygt10	SFYBAAC	1	1	fybaac-fygt10
M1	FM1	6	1	Money stock: m1 (curr, trav.cks, dem dep, other ck'able dep) (bil$,sa)
MZM	MZMSL	6	1	Mzm (sa) frb st. Louis
M2	FM2	6	1	Money stock:m2 (m1+o'nite rps, euro$, g/p&b/d mmmfs&sav&sm time dep (bil$,sa)
MB	FMFBA	6	1	Monetary base, adj for reserve requirement changes (mil$,sa)
Reserves tot	FMRRA	6	1	Depository inst reserves:total,adj for reserve req chgs (mil$,sa)

Table A1. (*Continued*)

Short name	Mnemonic	Trans. Code	E.F.?	Description
Reserves nonbor	FMRNBA	6	1	Depository inst reserves:nonborrowed,adj res req chgs (mil$,sa)
Bus loans	BUSLOANS	6	1	Commercial and industrial loans at all commercial banks (FRED) billions $ (sa)
Cons credit	CCINRV	6	1	Consumer credit outstanding – nonrevolving (g19)
Ex rate: avg	EXRUS	5	1	United States;effective exchange rate(merm) (index no.)
Ex rate: Switz	EXRSW	5	1	Foreign exchange rate: Switzerland (Swiss franc per u.s. $)
Ex rate: Japan	EXRJAN	5	1	Foreign exchange rate: Japan (yen per u.s. $)
Ex rate: UK	EXRUK	5	1	Foreign exchange rate: United Kingdom (cents per pound)
EX rate: Canada	EXRCAN	5	1	Foreign exchange rate: Canada (Canadian $ per u.s. $)
S&P 500	FSPCOM	5	1	S&P's common stock price index: composite (1941–43 = 10)
S&P: indust	FSPIN	5	1	S&P's common stock price index: industrials (1941–43 = 10)
S&P div yield	FSDXP	2	1	S&P's composite common stock: dividend yield (% per annum)
S&P PE ratio	FSPXE	2	1	S&P's composite common stock: price-earnings ratio (%, nsa)
DJIA	FSDJ	5	1	Common stock prices: Dow Jones industrial average
Consumer expect	HHSNTN	2	1	U. of Mich. index of consumer expectations (bcd-83)

Code	Transformation (X_{it})	h-quarter ahead variable $X_{it}^{(h)}$
1	$X_{it} = Y_{it}$	$X_{it}^{(h)} = Y_{it+h}$
2	$X_{it} = \Delta Y_{it}$	$X_{it}^{(h)} = Y_{it+h} - Y_{it}$
3	$X_{it} = \Delta^2 Y_{it}$	$X_{it}^{(h)} = h^{-1}\sum_{j=1}^{h} \Delta Y_{i,t+h-j} - \Delta Y_{it}$
4	$X_{it} = \ln Y_{it}$	$X_{it}^{(h)} = \ln Y_{it+h}$
5	$X_{it} = \Delta \ln Y_{it}$	$X_{it}^{(h)} = \ln Y_{it+h} - \ln Y_{it}$
6	$X_{it} = \Delta^2 \ln Y_{it}$	$X_{it}^{(h)} = h^{-1}\sum_{j=1}^{h} \Delta \ln Y_{i,t+h-j} - \Delta \ln Y_{it}$

References

Bai, J. and Ng, S. (2002). Determining the number of factors in approximate factor models. *Econometrica*, **70**, 191–221.

——— (2006). Confidence intervals for diffusion index forecasts and inference for factor-augmented regressions. *Econometrica*, **74**, 1133–1150

Banerjee, A., Marcellino, M. and Masten, I. (2007). Forecasting macroeconomic variables using diffusion indexes in short samples with structural change, forthcoming in *Forecasting in the Presence of Structural Breaks and Model Uncertainty*, edited by D. Rapach and M. Wohar, Elsevier.

Chamberlain, G. and Rothschild, M. (1983). Arbitrage factor stucture, and mean-variance analysis of large asset markets. *Econometrica*, **51**, 1281–1304.

Clements, M. P. and Hendry, D. F. (1999). *Forecasting Non-stationary Economic Time Series*. Cambridge, Mass: MIT Press.

——— (2002). Modeling methodology and forecast failure. *Econometrics Journal*, **5**, 319–344.

Del Negro, M. and Otrok, C. (2008). Dynamic factor models with time-varying parameters: Measuring changes in international business cycles. Federal Reserve Bank of New York Staff Report No. 326.

Forni, M., Hallin, M., Lippi, M. and Reichlin, L. (2000). The generalized factor model: Identification and estimation, *The Review of Economics and Statistics*, **82**, 540–554.

Geweke, J. (1977). The dynamic factor analysis of economic time series. In Aigner, D. J. and Goldberger, A. S. (eds.) *Latent Variables in Socio-Economic Models*. Amsterdam: North-Holland.

Hendry, D. F. (2005). Unpredictability and the foundations of economic forecasting. Nuffield Economics Working Paper 2004–W15.

—— and Clements, M. P. (2002). Pooling of forecasts. *Econometrics Journal*, **5**, 1–26.

—— and Mizon, G. E. (2005). Forecasting in the presence of structural breaks and policy regime shifts. Ch. 20 in Stock, J. H. and Andrews, D. W. K. (eds.), *Identification and Inference for Econometric Models: Essays in Honor of Thomas J. Rothenberg*, pp. 481–502. Cambridge: Cambridge University Press.

Kim, C. -J. and Nelson, C. R. (1999). Has the U.S. economy become more stable? A Bayesian approach based on a Markov-switching model of the business cycle. *The Review of Economics and Statistics*, **81**, 608–616.

McConnell, M. M. and Perez-Quiros, G. (2000). Output fluctuations in the United States: What has changed since the early 1980's. *American Economic Review*, **90**(5), 1464–1476.

Newey, W. K. and West, K. D. (1987). A simple positive semi-definite, heteroskedasticity and autocorrelation consistent covariance matrix. *Econometrica*, **55**, 703–708.

Sargent, T. J. (1989). Two models of measurements and the investment accelerator. *The Journal of Political Economy*, **97**, 251–287.

—— and Sims, C. A. (1977). Business cycle modeling without pretending to have too much a-priori economic theory. In Sims, C. *et al.*, (eds.), *New Methods in Business Cycle Research*. Minneapolis: Federal Reserve Bank of Minneapolis.

Stock, J. H. and Watson, M. W. (1998). Diffusion indexes manuscript, Harvard University.

———(2002a). Macroeconomic forecasting using diffusion indexes. *Journal of Business and Economic Statistics*, **20**, 147–162.
———(2002b). Forecasting using principal components from a large number of predictors. *Journal of the American Statistical Association*, **97**, 1167–1179.
———(2005). Implications of dynamic factor models for VAR analysis, Manuscript.
———(2006). Forecasting with many predictors, Ch. 6 in Elliott, G., Granger, C. W. J. and Timmermann, A. (eds.), *Handbook of Economic Forecasting*, pp. 515–554, Elsevier.
———(2007). Why has inflation become harder to forecast?. *Journal of Money, Credit, and Banking*, **39**, 3–34.

8

Internal Consistency of Survey Respondents' Forecasts: Evidence Based on the Survey of Professional Forecasters

*Michael P. Clements**

8.1 Introduction

There is a large literature addressing the rationality, efficiency, and accuracy of various types of forecasts. In the economics sphere point forecasts of the conditional mean or some other measure of the central tendency have been the main focus (see, e.g., Mincer and Zarnowitz, 1969; Figlewski and Wachtel, 1981; Zarnowitz, 1985; Chong and Hendry, 1986; Keane and Runkle, 1990; Clements and Hendry, 1993; Davies and Lahiri, 1995; Clements and Hendry, 1998, 1999; and Stekler, 2002), but there has also been research on the evaluation of probability distributions (e.g., Diebold, Gunther, and Tay, 1998; Diebold, Hahn, and Tay, 1999a; Berkowitz, 2001; Thompson, 2002; and Corradi and Swanson, 2006), interval and quantile forecasts (Granger, White, and Kamstra, 1989; Baillie and Bollerslev, 1992; McNees, 1995; Christoffersen, 1998; and Giacomini and Komunjer, 2005), volatility forecasts (Andersen and Bollerslev, 1998; Andersen, Bollerslev, Diebold, and Labys, 2003), and event and probability forecasts (e.g., Granger and Pesaran, 2000a, 2000b; and Clements and Harvey, 2006, drawing on the meteorological literature: see Dawid, 1986; for a review).

All of these papers evaluate series of forecasts of the same type. The forecasts are tested for biasedness, or efficiency, often in the context of addressing the validity of expectations formation mechanisms, such as rational expectations.

* Computations were performed using code written in the Gauss Programming Language. Paul Söderlind kindly made available some of the code used in Giordani and Söderlind (2003).

The novel aspect of our chapter is that we consider forecaster rationality in terms of the internal consistency of the different types of forecasts simultaneously made by individual forecasters. This is an area which appears to have gone largely unresearched, but offers an alternative angle on the notion of individual forecaster rationality, and complements the standard approaches in the literature. Our source of forecasts is the SPF survey data. The SPF is a quarterly survey of macroeconomic forecasters of the US economy that began in 1968, administered by the American Statistical Association (ASA) and the National Bureau of Economic Research (NBER). Since June 1990 it has been run by the Philadelphia Fed, renamed as the Survey of Professional Forecasters (SPF): see Zarnowitz (1969) and Croushore (1993). This is a unique resource, in that it allows us to derive matched point, probability, and probability distribution forecasts for individual forecasters. Put simply, suppose a forecaster reports point forecasts x, probability forecasts p (of the event that $X < 0$, say) and probability distributions f_X. Internal consistency places restrictions on the values that these forecasts would be expected to take. In this chapter we consider whether forecasters' point forecasts are consistent with the central tendencies of their reported probability distributions, and whether their reported probability forecasts of a decline in output are consistent with their probability distributions.

Because the SPF respondents report their probability distributions as histograms, a difficulty is inferring the measures of central tendency from the histograms. To compare the point forecasts and the histograms, we follow Engelberg, Manski, and Williams (2009) in calculating bounds on the moments. We then adapt their idea in a simple way to calculate bounds on the probabilities of decline from the histograms. The point and probability forecasts are then compared to the relevant bounds. Focusing on the conditional mean, our findings for point forecasts match those of Engelberg *et al.* (2009), in that most, but not all, point forecasts lie within the bounds on the histogram means, and violations that exceed the upper bound are more common than those in the other direction. Our results for the probability forecasts show a far greater proportion of violations even though the bounds are often wide (in a sense explained below). Nevertheless, the probability forecasts follow the point forecasts in that they also tend to be favourable, in the sense that the forecast probabilities of decline tend to understate the probabilities derived from the histograms.

We then consider a leading explanation for these findings: that forecasters' loss functions are asymmetric. If this is the case, rationality does not preempt the forecaster reporting as a point forecast a quantile of their probability distribution that is arbitrarily far from the central tendency for a high enough degree of asymmetry: see e.g., Elliott, Komunjer, and Timmermann (2008) and Patton and Timmermann (2007). As individuals may have loss functions with different degrees of asymmetry, this line of investigation leads to a consideration of forecasts at an individual level, even though the nature of the SPF data set is such that the number of observations for a specific individual may be relatively small. We consider an approach to testing for rationality allowing for asymmetric loss based on the difference between an individual's conditional mean and point forecast, rather than actual forecast errors. As our test is based on OLS, it may be more robust for small data samples than methods such as Elliott, Komunjer, and Timmermann (2005) based on GMM, although the informational requirements of our method will limit its general applicability.

The plan of the rest of the chapter is as follows. Section 8.2 discusses the different types of forecast of output reported in the SPF. Section 8.3 reports the comparison of the histograms and point forecasts across all forecasters using the Engelberg *et al.* (2009) nonparametric bounds approach. Section 8.4 reports an extension of this approach to the comparison of the histograms and probabilities of decline. We also consider whether favourable point and probability forecasts tend to be issued simultaneously by an individual. Section 8.5 reports the individual-level analysis of the hypothesis that forecasters have asymmetric loss functions, as a possible explanation of the discrepancies between individuals' point forecasts and histograms. We propose a test of rationality allowing for asymmetric loss based on the difference between an individual's conditional mean and point forecast, and also report results for tests based on realised forecast errors. In section 8.6 a further analysis of forecast errors complements the evidence in section 8.5 concerning the hypothesis of asymmetric loss. Section 8.7 provides some concluding remarks.

8.2 The Survey of Professional Forecasters (SPF)

The SPF quarterly survey runs from 1968:4 to the present day. The survey questions elicit information from the respondents on their point forecasts for a number of variables; their histograms for output growth and inflation; and the probabilities they attach to declines in real output. We analyse the forecasts of real output, as for this variable alone we have point and probability forecasts as well as histograms. The SPF point forecasts and histograms have been widely analysed in separate exercises (see, for example, Zarnowitz, 1985; Keane and Runkle, 1990; Davies and Lahiri, 1999, for the former, and Diebold, Tay, and Wallis, 1999b; Giordani and Söderlind, 2003; and Clements, 2006, for the latter). The probability forecasts (of the event that output will decline) have received relatively little attention, although the Philadelphia Fed produces an 'anxious index' by averaging the SPF respondents' probabilities.

We use data from 1981:3 to 2005:1, as prior to 1981:3 the histograms for output growth referred to nominal output, and point forecasts for real GDP (GNP) were not recorded. For these surveys, we have individual respondents' point forecasts for the level of output in the current year, as well as for the previous quarter, for the current quarter, the next four quarters, and for the current year. From the annual forecasts we construct forecasts of the annual growth rate using values of output for the previous year taken from the Real Time Data Set for Macroeconomists (RTDSM) maintained by the Federal Reserve Bank of Philadelphia (see Croushore and Stark, 2001). The RTDSMs contain the values of output that would have been available at the time the forecast was made, as subsequent revisions, base-year and other definitional changes that occurred after the reference date are omitted.

For the probabilities of declines in real GDP, respondents give probabilities of a decline in the current quarter (the survey date quarter) relative to the previous quarter, for the next quarter relative to the current quarter, and so on up to the same quarter a year ahead relative to three quarters ahead. The probability distributions refer to the annual change from the previous year to the year of the survey, as well as of the survey year to the following year, and we use only the former. Therefore, the Q1 surveys provide four-quarter ahead probability distribution forecasts (as histograms) of the annual change in the current year over the previous year, which can be matched to the annual output growth point forecasts. The Q2 surveys provide three-quarter ahead forecasts, down to one-quarter ahead forecasts from the Q4 surveys. Thus we obtain a matched pair of point and histogram forecasts of a single horizon from each survey.

The total number of usable point and probability forecasts across all surveys and respondents is 2462. These forecasts come from the 95 quarterly surveys from 1981:3 to 2005:1, and from 181 different respondents. We only include 'regular forecasters'—those who have responded to more than 12 surveys. This gives 73 respondents, who account for 1969 forecasts, some 80% of the total.

8.3 Consistency of the Point Forecasts and Histograms

Establishing whether the point forecasts and probability distributions are consistent is complicated by it being unclear whether the point forecasts should be interpreted as the means, modes, or even medians of the probability distributions. One possibility is to calculate nonparametric bounds for these measures of central tendency for the histograms, following Engelberg *et al.* (2009), and then to see whether the point forecasts fall within the bounds. Engelberg *et al.* (2009) calculate bounds for the three measures of central tendency, and obtain similar results, so that for brevity we focus on the mean. Our analysis of consistency using bounds replicates that of Engelberg *et al.* (2009), but uses an additional decade of quarterly surveys. Engelberg *et al.* (2009) restrict their start period to 1992:1, in part because it is not clear whether prior to this period respondents were always provided with the previous year's level of output. There is therefore uncertainty over the previous year's value of output that the forecaster had in mind when reporting their current year forecast level. We choose to use the data from the 1981:3 to 1991:4 surveys and construct the previous years' output levels using the RTDSMs.

Possible methods of calculating means from histograms include assuming that the probability mass is uniform within a bin (eg, Diebold *et al.*, 1999b, make this assumption in the context of calculating probability integral transforms), and fitting a parametric distribution such as the normal (eg, Giordani and Söderlind, 2003, p. 1044) or the unimodal generalized beta distribution (Engelberg *et al.* 2009). Using the assumption of uniform mass within a bin, and approximating the histogram by a normal density, results in the correlations between the annual growth point forecasts and the histogram means recorded in Table 8.1.

The crude correlations are high, between 0.92 and 0.96, and the results indicate little difference between the two methods of calculating histogram means that we consider. Nevertheless, it is difficult to infer much about the consistency of the probability distributions and the point forecasts from these correlations. The bounds approach allows us to compare the point forecasts and histogram means without making any assumptions about the distribution of probability mass—albeit at the cost of an upper and lower bound on the mean rather than a point estimate. The lower (upper) bound is calculated by assuming that all the probability lies at the lower (upper) limit of the histogram bin or interval. The last three columns of the table present the percentage of point forecasts that lie within, below, and above, the bounds respectively. The Q1 figure of 74.7 indicates that about three-quarters of all

Table 8.1. The point forecasts and the means of the probability distributions (histograms)

Survey quarter	# of forecasts	Hist.^{1}	Hist.^{n}	% within mean bounds	% below mean bounds	% above mean bounds
Q1	451	0.92	0.93	74.7	4.8	20.4
Q2	487	0.94	0.95	80.9	3.7	15.4
Q3	439	0.92	0.93	81.8	3.6	14.6
Q4	408	0.95	0.96	89.7	3.4	6.9

The columns headed Hist.^{1} and Hist.^{n} report correlations between the annual growth point forecasts and the means either calculated directly from the histograms (Hist.^{1}), or using a normal approximation to the histogram (Hist.^{n}).

The Q1 surveys of 1985 and 1986 are excluded as the Philadelphia Fed has documented possible problems with the forecast distributions in these surveys.

The point forecasts of the growth rate are calculated using the actual data for the previous year from the RTDSM available in the quarter of the survey. The one exception is that the RTDSM for 1996Q1 is missing the value for 1995Q4. In constructing the year-on-year point forecast growth rates for the respondents to the 1996Q1 survey we use the previous-quarter forecasts (of 1995Q4).

first-quarter survey point forecasts of annual growth lie within the bounds on the histogram mean. Alternatively, one quarter of point forecasts are not consistent with the histogram means. Of this quarter, approximately 80% exceed the upper limit, indicating a preponderance of 'favourable' point forecasts. We find that the proportion which are consistent increases with the survey quarter, corresponding to a shortening horizon, although the tendency to report favourable point forecasts persists. These results are qualitatively similar to those obtained by Engelberg *et al.* (2009) on a shorter sample of surveys. Before investigating a possible explanation for this finding, the next section analyses the consistency of the histograms and the probability forecasts.

8.4 Consistency of the Probability Forecasts and Histograms

For the Q4 surveys we calculate the current-quarter probabilities of decline implied by the histograms, and compare these to the directly-reported current-quarter forecast probabilities of decline. For other survey quarters there is insufficient information to infer the probability of decline from the histogram. The Q4 survey histograms relate to annual growth in the current year, but as the only unknown is the value of output in the current (fourth) quarter, the probability of a decline in output relative to the previous quarter can be calculated. Given the realized values of output in the seven quarters to the fourth quarter (taken from the appropriate RTDSM), we can infer the year-on-year rate of growth that equates the Q4 level of output with that of the preceding quarter. The implied probability of decline is then the probability that year-on-year output growth will not exceed this rate. As in the case of calculating means from the histograms, the required calculation could be performed by assuming uniformity of the probability mass within intervals, or by approximating the histograms by parametric densities. Rather than using either of these, we adapt the bounds approach of Engelberg *et al.* (2009) in a straightforward fashion to give an upper and lower bound on the histogram probability of a decline. This avoids making an assumption about precisely how the histogram reflects the respondents' actual beliefs.

The calculation of the bounds is best described by example. Suppose the forecaster attaches probabilities of 0.1, 0.5, and 0.4 to the intervals or bins [3,4), [4,5), and [5,6), with all other bins having zero probabilities. Suppose output will decline in Q4 relative to Q3 if the rate of output growth for the year is less than $y = 4.2$. An upper bound on the probability (when all mass in the [4,5) interval is less than 4.2) is $0.1 + 0.5 = 0.6$, and the lower bound is 0.1, when all mass in the [4,5] interval is greater than 4.2. Thus the lower bound sums the probabilities of all intervals whose upper bounds are less than y, and the upper bound includes in this sum the probability attached to the interval containing y. So the size of the bound is the probability attached to

Table 8.2. Bounds on histogram probabilities of decline and directly-reported probabilities

Survey quarter	# of forecasts	% within bounds	% below bounds	% above bounds
Q4	408	56.1	42.2	1.7

the interval containing the value, and may as a consequence be large. At the extremes, suppose y lies below the lowest interval. Then the upper and lower bounds on probability coincide at zero. If y lies above the highest interval, both bounds are 1. Note we are assuming that the upper and lower histogram bins are closed, with the upper limit to the upper bin, and the lower limit to the lower bin, set so that the bin widths are the same as those of interior bins. Bounds calculated in this way satisfy $u,l \in [0,1]$, and $u - l \in [0,1]$, where u and l are the upper and lower bounds on the probability.

The findings in Table 8.2 indicate that only just over a half of all probability forecasts of a decline in output in quarter 4 relative to quarter 3 are consistent with the bounds on this probablity calculated from the histograms. As for the point forecasts, respondents as a whole report more favourable probability assessments (that is, a lower probability of a decline in output) than is suggested by their histograms. Here the results are more stark—virtually all forecasts outside the bounds suggest more favourable assessments. The average width of the bands is 0.69.

Also of interest is whether there is a match between the favourable point and probability forecasts: is it the case that when a favourable point forecast is issued, this tends to be matched by a favourable probability forecast? Table 8.3 provides this information. The first row takes all the point forecasts that fell below the lower mean bound, and reports the percentage of times the corresponding probability forecasts fell below, within, and above the bounds on the probability of decline calculated from the probability distributions. Similarly for the next two rows, which condition on the point forecasts being within, and above, the bounds, respectively. The principal finding is that over

Table 8.3. Coincidence of favourable and unfavourable point and probability forecasts

	Percentage of probability forecasts corresponding to each category of point forecast		
	below	within	above
below	5.9	58.8	35.3
within	40.5	59.0	0.5
above	82.4	17.6	0.0

four fifths (82.4%) of favourable point forecasts (recall this is shorthand for forecasts above the upper band) are simultaneously reported with favourable (below the bound) probability forecasts, so that for the most part forecasters are consistent in reporting favourable assessments on both fronts.

To make further progress, in the next section we consider the empirical relationships between two of the different types of forecasts at an individual level: the point forecasts and histograms. We have so far considered the totality of forecasts, discriminated by survey quarter (or forecast horizon) but not by individual respondent. We will consider whether there are individual level effects, such as asymmetries in individual loss functions, which can account for these findings.

8.5 Individual Level Analysis of Point Forecasts and Histograms

An explanation of the tendency to report favourable point forecasts relative to the histogram mean is that forecasters' loss functions are asymmetric, and that greater costs attach to under-predictions compared to over-predictions. If one takes the view that loss is likely to be asymmetric (as in the recent literature, e.g., Elliott and Timmermann, 2004, p. 48), then it is likely that the number of violations of the bounds reported in Table 8.1 will understate the evidence against quadratic loss, as a forecaster's point forecast may satisfy asymmetric loss but still fall within the mean bounds if the forecast uncertainty at that point is low, or if the degree of asymmetry is low, or if the bounds are wide. These comments are motivated by the literature on the properties of optimal forecasts under asymmetric loss (see, *inter alia*, Granger, 1969; Zellner, 1986; Christoffersen and Diebold, 1997), and are developed more formally below.

The maintained assumption in the literature on testing for rationality allowing asymmetric loss is that the degree of asymmetry of the loss function is constant for a given individual over time, but may vary across individuals. This suggests an individual-level analysis, using all the forecasts made by a particular respondent. For the statistical tests described below, we need a point estimate of the individual's conditional expectation rather than a bound, so that the sharp results we obtain are at the cost of the assumption we make about the relationship between the histogram and the individual's underlying probability distribution. The results in this section are based on calculating conditional means directly from the histograms. The estimates of the conditional variances used in the tests are also calculated directly from the histograms (following Lahiri, Teigland, and Zaporowski, 1988, for example).

Much of the recent literature has sought to test whether forecasts are rational once we allow forecasters to have asymmetric loss functions: see, for example, Elliott *et al.* (2008, 2008) and Patton and Timmermann (2007).

We consider whether asymmetric loss can account for 'favourable' point forecasts of output growth (relative to conditional means). One advantage of the approach we propose for testing for rationality allowing asymmetric loss is that we do not require that individuals make use of all available information.

To motivate our approach to testing for rationality allowing for asymmetric loss, we make use of the results in Patton and Timmermann (2007) which require only weak restrictions on the form of the loss function and the data generating process. The only requirement of the data generating process is that the variable of interest is conditionally location-scale distributed, and the only requirement of the loss function is that it is homogeneous in the forecast error. Letting $E_t(y_{t+h}) \equiv E(y_{t+h} \mid \Omega_t)$, and $V_t(y_{t+h}) \equiv Var(y_{t+h} \mid \Omega_t)$, and $e_{t+h,t}$ denote the h-step ahead forecast error, then formally we are assuming that

$$y_{t+h} \mid \Omega_t \sim D(E_t[y_{t+h}], V_t[y_{t+h}]),$$

for some constant distribution function D, and

$$L(a \cdot e_{t+h,t}) = g(a) L(e_{t+h,t}),$$

for some positive function g, and all $a \neq 0$. Patton and Timmermann (2007, Proposition 2) show that the optimal forecast is given by

$$f^*_{t+h,t} = E_t(y_{t+h}) + \phi^*_h \cdot \sqrt{V_t(y_{t+h})}$$

where ϕ^*_h is a constant that depends only on the form of D and L. $\phi^*_h < 0$ when over-predictions ($e_{t+h,t} < 0$) are penalized more heavily than under-predictions, and vice versa. The deviation between the optimal point forecast and the conditional mean depends on the conditional standard deviation. Intuitively, the more costly over-predictions relative to under-predictions, say, and the more likely both over- and under-predictions (because the more uncertain the outlook), then the more the forecaster will aim to under-predict on average. Under the assumptions we have made, the bias of a rational forecaster should depend on the forecast standard deviation but should not be systematically related to other variables known at time t

$$\begin{aligned} E\left(y_{t+h} - f^*_{t+h,t} \mid \Omega_t\right) &= E\left(y_{t+h} - \left(E_t(y_{t+h}) + \phi^*_h \cdot \sqrt{V_t(y_{t+h})}\right) \mid \Omega_t\right) \\ &= -\phi^*_h \cdot \sqrt{V_t(y_{t+h})} \end{aligned}$$

This motivates the suggestion of Pesaran and Weale (2006) to test for rational expectations with asymmetric losses by running a regression such as

$$e_{t+h,t} \equiv y_{t+h} - f_{t+h,t} = \zeta_1 \sqrt{V_t(y_{t+h})} + \zeta_2' Z_t + \epsilon_{t+h} \tag{8.1}$$

where under the null we would expect to find $\zeta_2 = 0$, but $\zeta_1 \neq 0$ if loss is asymmetric. In this regression, we have replaced the optimal forecast by the reported forecast $f_{t+h,t}$ to allow for reporting errors etc, but provided the two differ by an error that is a zero-mean innovation on Ω_t this switch is innocuous.

In the above the forecasts and information set are not indexed by the individual, and so has the interpretation that it applies to individuals who have identical loss functions and information sets. Consider now the case of heterogeneous information sets and individual-specific ϕ values, ϕ_i (where we drop the subscript h denoting the dependence on the horizon, and the superscript '*' for notational convenience). Suppose forecaster i's information set is $\Omega_{t,i} \neq \Omega_t$, then for individual i, $y_{t+h} \mid \Omega_{t,i} \sim D_i\left(E_{t,i}\left(y_{t+h}\right), V_{t,i}\left(y_{t+h}\right)\right)$, where $E_{t,i}\left(y_{t+h}\right) \equiv E\left(y_{t+h} \mid \Omega_{t,i}\right)$, and $V_{t,i}\left(y_{t+h}\right) \equiv Var\left(y_{t+h} \mid \Omega_{t,i}\right)$. Then $f^*_{t+h,t,i} = E_{t,i}\left(y_{t+h}\right) + \phi_i \sqrt{V_{t,i}\left(y_{t+h}\right)}$. The bias conditional on $\Omega_{t,i}$ is:

$$E\left(y_{t+h} - f^*_{t+h,t,i} \mid \Omega_{t,i}\right) = E\left(y_{t+h} - \left(E_{t,i}\left(y_{t+h}\right) + \phi_i \sqrt{V_{t,i}\left(y_{t+h}\right)}\right) \mid \Omega_{t,i}\right)$$
$$= -\phi_i \sqrt{V_{t,i}\left(y_{t+h}\right)}.$$

We can test for efficient use of the individual's information set $\Omega_{t,i}$, assuming asymmetric loss, via a regression such as (8.1)

$$e_{t+h,t,i} \equiv y_{t+h} - f_{t+h,t,i} = \zeta_{1,i} \sqrt{V_{t,i}\left(y_{t+h}\right)} + \zeta_{2,i}' Z_{t,i} + \epsilon_{t+h,i} \tag{8.2}$$

where $Z_{t,i} \in \Omega_{t,i}$, and $\zeta_{2,i} = 0$ indicates an efficient use of information. But note that the bias conditional on Ω_t is given by

$$E\left(y_{t+h} - f^*_{t+h,t,i} \mid \Omega_t\right) = E\left(y_{t+h} - \left(E_{t,i}\left(y_{t+h}\right) + \phi_i \sqrt{V_{t,i}\left(y_{t+h}\right)}\right) \mid \Omega_t\right) \tag{8.3}$$
$$= E\left(y_{t+h} - E_{t,i}\left(y_{t+h}\right) \mid \Omega_t\right) - \phi_i E\left(\sqrt{V_{t,i}\left(y_{t+h}\right)} \mid \Omega_t\right).$$

Let $\xi_{t+h,i} = y_{t+h} - E_{t,i}\left(y_{t+h}\right)$. Then $E\left(\xi_{t+h,i} \mid \Omega_t\right) = 0$ when $\Omega_{t,i}$ contains Ω_t, ie, $\Omega_t \subseteq \Omega_{t,i}$, as required by Muthian rationality, but not otherwise. When the individual's information set does not include all relevant information, $\Omega_t \nsubseteq \Omega_{t,i}$, their forecast error can be written as the sum of three components (under asymmetric loss)

$$e_{t+h,t,i} = -\phi_i E\left(\sqrt{V_{t,i}\left(y_{t+h}\right)} \mid \Omega_t\right) + \xi_{t+h,i} + \varepsilon_{t+h,i}$$

where $\varepsilon_{t+h,i}$ is an innovation error relative to Ω_t, $E\left(\varepsilon_{t+h,i} \mid \Omega_t\right) = 0$, but in general $E\left(\xi_{t+h,i} \mid \Omega_t\right) \neq 0$. We assume that $E\left(\sqrt{V_{t,i}\left(y_{t+h}\right)} \mid \Omega_t\right) = \sqrt{V_{t,i}\left(y_{t+h}\right)}$, which requires that $\Omega_{t,i} \subseteq \Omega_t$—the individual's information set is a subset of all the relevant information. Then in the regression

$$y_{t+h} - f_{t+h,t,i} = \zeta_{1,i} \sqrt{V_{t,i}\left(y_{t+h}\right)} + \zeta_{2,i}' Z_t + \epsilon_{t+h,i} \tag{8.4}$$

the population value $\zeta_{2,i} \neq 0$ whenever Z_t is correlated with the omitted variable, $\xi_{t+h,i}$. In order for Z_t and $\xi_{t+h,i}$ to be correlated it must be the case that $Z_t \in \Omega_t$ but $Z_t \notin \Omega_{t,i}$. Tests based on (8.4) will find against rationality (assuming asymmetric loss) when information is used efficiently but is incomplete.

A test of the efficient use of the individual's information set can be constructed as follows. From rearranging (8.3) we obtain

$$E\left[\left(y_{t+h} - f^{*}_{t+h,t,i}\right) - \left(y_{t+h} - E_{t,i}\left(y_{t+h}\right)\right) \mid \Omega_t\right] = E\left(E_{t,i}\left(y_{t+h}\right) - f^{*}_{t+h,t,i} \mid \Omega_t\right)$$
$$= -\phi_i E\left(\sqrt{V_{t,i}(y_{t+h})} \mid \Omega_t\right)$$

which implies that $E_{t,i}\left(y_{t+h}\right) - f^{*}_{t+h,t,i}$ (or $E_{t,i}\left(y_{t+h}\right) - f_{t+h,t,i}$) should be related to the forecast standard deviation but should not vary systematically with any variables in Ω_t, irrespective of whether or not they are in the individual's information set. This suggests the following regression

$$E_{t,i}\left(y_{t+h}\right) - f_{t+h,t,i} = \delta_{1,i}\sqrt{V_{t,i}\left(y_{t+h}\right)} + \delta'_{2,i} Z_t + v_{t+h,i}. \tag{8.5}$$

The null of rationality and quadratic loss for individual i is that $\delta_{1,i} = 0$ and $\delta'_{2,i} = 0$, against the alternative that any of these coefficients are nonzero. A rejection of the null due to $\delta_{1,i} \neq 0$, with $\delta'_{2,i} = 0$, indicates asymmetry (and rationality), while $\delta'_{2,i} \neq 0$ indicates irrationality (conditional on the assumed form of the loss function). In order to carry out these tests, as well as the point forecasts we require the individual's predictive distributions $P_{t+h,t,i}(y) = \Pr_i\left(Y_{t+h} < y \mid \Omega_{t,i}\right)$ so that $E_{t,i}\left(Y_{t+h}\right)$ and $V_{t,i}\left(Y_{t+h}\right)$ can be derived (or that these conditional moments are available directly). Estimates of these distributions are available in the SPF in the form of histograms.

We test the SPF forecasts for rationality allowing for asymmetric loss using both (8.5) and (8.4). In general there are two advantages to using (8.5). The first is that we are able to test for an efficient use of the individual's information set, and will not reject rationality because this is incomplete. The second advantage comes from noticing that the dependent variable in (8.4) is a noisy measure of the dependent variable in (8.5), because $e_{t+h,i} = E_{t,i}\left(y_{t+h}\right) - f_{t+h,t,i} + \xi_{t+h,i}$, where $\xi_{t+h,i}$ is the measurement error. Standard analysis suggests that even if $E\left(\xi_{t+h,i} \mid \Omega_t\right) = 0$, so that $\xi_{t+h,i}$ is uncorrelated with any variables that might be included as explanatory variables in the regression (Z_t), then inference based on (8.4) is less precise. The disadvantage of (8.5) is that the SPF does not provide a direct measure of $E_{t,i}\left(y_{t+h}\right)$ needed to construct the dependent variable in (8.5). The need to estimate the conditional means from the histograms gives rise to a potential source of error, and for this reason we compare the results based on (8.5) with those based on actual forecast errors using (8.4), as a check on the robustness of our findings.

We estimate both (8.5) and (8.4) for each individual respondent and for each forecast horizon. For the regression given by (8.4) two versions are estimated—one with the actual values used to construct the forecast errors taken as the real-time estimates, and one using latest release values. See section 8.6 for further discussion of the actual values. As there are not many obervations per respondent by forecast horizon, we set the lower limit to ten observations, and we also restricted Z_t to a constant. When Z_t is simply a constant the possibility of the Z_t variables and $\xi_{t+h,i}$ being correlated does not arise, so that any rejections based on (8.4) do not result from the use of incomplete information. For each regression, we recorded the following information: whether the null that $\delta_{2,i} = 0$ was rejected at the 10% level when the forecast standard deviation was omitted from the regression; whether the null that $\delta_{2,i} = 0$ was rejected at the 10% level (when the standard deviation was included); and whether the null that $\delta_{2,i} = 0$ was not rejected and the null that $\delta_{1,i} = 0$ was rejected, ie, that only the forecast standard deviation was significant. We then aggregated this information over all individuals for a given horizon. This summary of our findings is recorded in Table 8.4.

First, consider the results based on (8.5), where the dependent variable is the conditional mean less the point forecast. The results for the three hypotheses set out above are recorded in columns 3, 6, and 9 of the table. The results indicate that in roughly 40% of the cases rationality is rejected if we assume quadratic loss (column 3), and in all these cases the estimated coefficients on the constant term (δ_{2i}) are negative (not shown), in line with the finding of the favourable reporting of point forecasts. If we test for rationality allowing for asymmetric loss (column 6), then for all quarters taken together we find that in roughly 25% of the cases rationality is rejected. Only for 7 of the 57 regressions is the variance term significant and the constant insignificant (column 9). This last finding in particular suggests that asymmetry is not an important feature of the loss function behind these forecasts. Second, compare the results of testing the same hypotheses using forecast errors as the dependent variable (regression (8.4)) constructed using real-time actuals (columns 4, 7, and 10) or last vintage values (columns 5, 8, and 11). The results corroborate the conclusion that asymmetry plays only a minor

Table 8.4. Testing for rationality and asymmetric loss

	Total # regressions	# rejecting rationality, assuming quadratic loss			# rejecting rationality, assuming asymmetry			# standard deviation significant, constant not significant		
		Eq.(8.5)	Eq.$(8.4)_{rt}$	Eq.(8.4)	Eq.(8.5)	Eq.$(8.4)_{rt}$	Eq.(8.4)	Eq.(8.5)	Eq.$(8.4)_{rt}$	Eq.(8.4)
		3.	4.	5.	6.	7.	8.	9.	10.	11.
All qtrs	57	22	8	12	14	16	7	7	2	3
Q1	16	10	6	4	3	7	2	3	0	0
Q2	16	6	2	4	4	4	2	1	0	0
Q3	12	5	0	2	3	3	3	2	1	1
Q4	13	1	0	2	4	2	0	1	1	2

Notes. Columns 3, 4, and 5 report the number of individual regressions for which we reject $\delta_{2,i} = 0$ at the 10% level with the variance term omitted. Column 3 is based on eq. (8.5), and columns 4 and 5 on eq. (8.4) with real-time and last-vintage data, respectively. Columns 6, 7, and 8 report rejections of $\delta_{2,i} = 0$ at the 10% level with the variance term included. Columns 9, 10, and 11 report the number of instances when we fail to reject the null that $\delta_{2,i} = 0$ and reject the null that $\delta_{1,i} = 0$. The White (1980) heteroscedasticity-consistent estimator of the covariance matrix of the parameter estimates is used.

role—in even fewer instances is the forecast standard deviation significant and the constant equal to zero (columns 10 and 11). Interestingly, there are more rejections of rationality assuming symmetric loss based on (8.5) compared to (8.4), which is consistent with measurement error in (8.4). The increase in the number of rejections of rationality using (8.4) with real-time actuals when asymmetry is allowed (cf. columns 4 and 7) does not occur when final-vintage values are used to calculate forecast errors (cf. columns 5 and 8).

8.6 Comparison of Forecasts to Outturns

In section 8.5 we presented evidence to suggest that asymmetric loss is not able to explain the tendency to report favourable forecasts of output. In this section we present additional evidence on the rationality and asymmetry hypotheses. We exploit the fact that the expected squared error of a point forecast must be at least as large as the expected squared error of the conditional mean. This is because the conditional mean minimizes the expected squared error amongst all possible forecasts. The expected squared error of the point forecast will equal that of the conditional mean when loss is quadratic, when the optimal point forecast is the conditional mean, but for asymmetric loss the squared-error loss of the optimal point forecast should exceed that of the conditional mean.

The problem with using outcomes is that it is unclear whether forecasters seek to forecast the first announcements of the data, or the second, or some later revision. We encountered this problem in section 8.5 when actual values were required to calculate forecast errors for the results reported in Table 8.4 based on equation (8.4). We countered the uncertainty as to what should constitute the actual values by assessing the sensitivity of the results to using two vintages of data—the second data release (following Romer and Romer, 2000 and Patton and Timmermann, 2007) and the latest release (2006Q1). We proceed in the same way in this section. As Figure 8.1 indicates, the latest vintage data suggest higher growth rates for much of the period up to 2000, after which growth rates have been revised down relative to the real-time series. The differences between the two series are persistent and at times substantial. Individual forecasters may be trying to forecast either of these two series, or another vintage altogether, so the strategy of reporting results for two vintages is at best a partial solution to the problem of not knowing what it is that the forecasters are attempting to forecast.

The results of calculating mean squared errors (MSFEs) for the forecasts are displayed in the first three columns of Table 8.5. The MSFE is the empirical estimate of the expected squared error, calculated as the mean of the

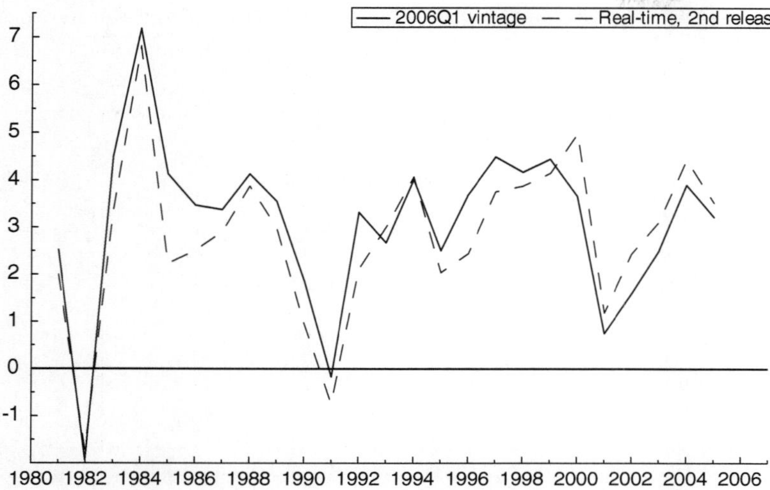

FIG. **8.1.** Annual real output growth 1981 to 2005 using the latest data vintage (2006:Q1) and the second release vintage ('real-time').

sample of observed squared forecast errors, by quarter. The MSFEs for the conditional expectation measured as either the directly-calculated mean of the histogram (Hist^1), or the mean based on a normal approximation to the histogram (Hist^n), are markedly higher than the MSFE for the point forecast, for both sets of outcomes. The MSFEs when the outcomes are taken to be the real-time series are lower than when latest vintage actuals are used, but the relative ranking across forecasts is the same. This is clearly at odds with the explanation of the discrepancies between the histogram means and point forecasts based on asymmetric loss, and is also evidence against rationality, as the expected squared error loss of the conditional mean should be no larger than that of the point forecast whatever the loss function. The possibility remains that we have not accurately captured individuals' means by either calculating the means directly from the histogram or assuming normality. Of interest is whether we still find against rationality if we calculate the conditional mean in a way that is most favourable to the asymmetry hypothesis, subject to the conditional mean remaining within the bounds of section 8.3. This is accomplished by setting the estimate of the histogram mean equal to the outcome, when the outcome falls within the bound; to the lower bound, when the outcome is less than the lower bound; and to the upper bound, when the outcome exceeds the upper bound. This will give a lower bound to the value of the MSFE for the histogram means. As the MSFE for the histogram mean calculated in this way is zero for the set of outcomes within the bounds, we report in Table 8.5 the percentage of the total number

Table 8.5. Forecast accuracy of point forecasts and histogram means

	MSFEs			Using bounds			
	Hist[1]	Hist[n]	Point forecasts	% below	MSFE ratio[1]	% above	MSFE ratio[2]
			Latest vintage data (2006Q1)				
Q1	1.98	1.99	1.72	18.9	0.30	49.0	0.67
Q2	1.16	1.19	1.04	21.8	0.32	45.2	0.49
Q3	1.04	1.08	0.88	19.1	0.40	43.3	0.55
Q4	1.00	0.99	0.73	24.0	0.52	39.7	0.52
			Real-time actuals (second-release)				
Q1	1.36	1.35	1.08	13.3	0.27	53.8	0.65
Q2	0.58	0.58	0.43	13.5	0.31	32.8	0.67
Q3	0.42	0.42	0.28	7.7	0.81	30.5	0.93
Q4	0.41	0.37	0.16	11.0	0.59	22.1	1.69

Hist.[1] denotes the means are calculated directly from the histograms. Hist.[n] denotes the means are calculated from the histogram using a normal approximation to the histogram. The columns headed % below and % above give the percentage of forecasts for which the outcome is below and above the bounds on the histogram mean. The MSFE ratios in the adjacent columns, MSFE ratio[1] and MSFE ratio[2], report the ratio of the MSFEs for the most favourable histogram mean to the point forecasts, for the forecasts corresponding to actuals that fall below and above the bounds.

of forecasts (by quarter) for which the actual falls below the bound, and above the bound. For these two sets of forecasts and observations, we calculate the ratio of the MSFE for the conditional expectation (equal to the lower, and upper, bounds, respectively) to the MSFE for the point forecasts. Based on this most favourable scenario for the asymmetry hypothesis, we no longer find that the point forecasts have smaller MSFEs: the aforementioned ratios are less than unity for all but the Q4 forecasts when the actuals are above the bound. By adopting a conservative approach, finding against the rationality hypothesis (or rationality and asymmetry) would have constituted strong evidence that it is false, but failure to find against it in these circumstances offers it little support. The fact that the actuals lie above the histogram bounds at least twice as often as they lie below (and four times as often for Q1 forecasts, using real-time data) is consistent with the evidence in the first three columns that favours the point forecasts on MSFE over the estimates of the conditional mean in scenarios other than that which is most favourable to the latter.

Finally, rather than comparing the accuracy of the point forecasts against (estimates of) the histogram means, we compare the overall accuracy of point forecasts that lie within the bounds against the accuracy of point forecasts that are outside the bounds. The finding that the latter are less accurate may indicate some element of strategic behaviour—when forecasters issue point forecasts and histograms which are inconsistent, forecasters may be pursuing

Table 8.6. Forecast accuracy (MSFE) of point forecasts by whether they are consistent or inconsistent with bounds on histogram means

	Relationship of point forecasts to bounds			
	Real-time actuals		Latest vintage actuals	
	Outside	Within	Outside	Within
Q1	1.048	1.093	1.701	1.731
Q2	0.538	0.403	1.057	1.032
Q3	0.682	0.189	1.090	0.831
Q4	0.137	0.167	0.784	0.723

some objective other than minimizing squared-error loss. Alternatively, no systematic differences between the two sets of point forecasts in terms of accuracy would indicate that the inconsistencies between the point forecasts and histograms may be more due to the histograms being out of synch with the point forecasts, than vice versa. This would appear to be at odds with the assumption that the histograms are an accurate representation of beliefs, in the sense that they are not intentionally biased and do not reflect strategic concerns.

The results in Table 8.6 do not present a clear picture: the relative accuracy of the two sets of point forecasts depends on the quarter and in part on what we take as the actual values to calculate forecast errors.

8.7 Conclusions

We have investigated whether the different types of forecasts simultaneously made by individual forecasters are consistent with one another. Our main focus is on whether forecasters' point forecasts are consistent with the central tendencies of their reported histograms, and whether their reported probability forecasts of a decline are consistent with their histograms. The main difficulty we face in addressing these questions is that the reported histograms do not uniquely reveal the individual's underlying probability distributions. We begin by constructing bounds on the permissible range of values for the conditional mean from the histogram. These bounds make no assumptions about the distribution of probability mass within the histogram intervals (except that the lower and upper intervals are closed). We then apply the spirit of this bounds approach of Engelberg *et al.* (2009) to the comparison of the histograms and probabilities of decline. We find that a proportion of point forecasts of output growth are not compatible with their being the conditional mean, and in the majority of these instances the point forecasts are too favourable in that they lie above the upper bound. The bounds analysis of the reported probabilities of decline and the histograms suggests a similar picture:

respondents as a whole report more favourable probability assessments (that is, a lower probability of a decline in output) than is suggested by their histograms. Virtually all probability forecasts outside the bounds suggest more favourable assessments, notwithstanding that the form of the histograms gives rise to wide average bounds in probability. Moreover, we find that the reporting of favourable point forecasts and probability forecasts are correlated: for the most part forecasters are consistent in reporting favourable assessments on both fronts.

A leading explanation for the tendency to report favourable point and probability forecasts is that forecasters' loss functions are asymmetric. Patton and Timmermann (2007) have shown that if this is the case, rationality does not pre-empt the forecaster reporting as a point forecast a quantile of their probability distribution other than the central tendency. We examine this as a possible explanation of the discrepancy between the point forecasts and histogram means. We do so at an individual level as some may weigh the costs of over-prediction more heavily than the costs of under-prediction, and vice versa. Because we have both the individuals' point forecasts and (estimates of) their conditional means, we can test the asymmetry hypothesis directly for each individual without needing to use outcomes. Our testing approach has the further advantage that we do not require that the forecasts efficiently use all available information. Consider a standard way of testing for asymmetry. This regresses the forecast error (constructed from the outcomes and point forecasts) on variables known at the time the forecast was made, and the conditional standard deviation of the forecasts. Suppose that, relative to an individual's information set, there are a series of negative shocks to output growth over the sample period, so that the individual's point forecasts tend to be too favourable—this could be taken as evidence that the individual has asymmetric loss such that over-predictions are less costly than under-predictions. Our test considers the deviation between the point forecast and the conditional mean, rather than the point forecast and the outcome. In the above example, the conditional mean would control for the negative shocks—it would be higher than warranted based on an information set that includes the shocks, but under the asymmetry hypothesis the deviation between the conditional mean and the point forecast should only depend on the conditional standard deviation of the forecast. Under quadratic loss this deviation should not differ systematically from zero and should not be related to any variables known at the time the forecasts are made.

Our tests of the asymmetry hypothesis require that the histograms accurately reflect the individuals' true beliefs, and that our methods of calculating the point estimates of the mean are consistent with these beliefs. In interpreting the tests of whether the point forecasts are unbiased or not, we have implicitly assumed that the histograms are not an intentionally 'biased' representation of the individuals' probability assessments. In principle one might test whether the histograms are correctly calibrated (see e.g., Dawid, 1984; Kling and Bessler, 1989), but the small number of observations available at an individual level rule this out in practice. Conditional on these assumptions, we find that asymmetry can explain only a relatively minor part of the favourable aspect of the point forecasts. Additional evidence can be brought to bear if we are prepared to take a stance on what the outcomes are against which the forecasts should be evaluated. Under asymmetric loss the point forecasts should have higher expected squared errors than the conditional expectations. This is the case if we take the scenario most favourable to the asymmetry hypothesis, but not if we calculate the conditional expectation directly from the histograms or via a normal approximation, so the evidence is inconclusive.

A possibility that we have briefly touched on is that forecasters may face economic incentives not to report their true beliefs: see, e.g., Ehrbeck and Waldmann (1996), Laster, Bennett, and Geoum (1999), and Ottaviani and Sorensen (2006). Forecasters may act strategically in the sense that they balance their goal of minimizing forecast errors against conflicting aims, such as convincing the market that they are well-informed, or of attracting media attention. It might be argued that the anonymity of the SPF respondents removes the incentives for the pursuance of strategic motives, although if the respondents report the same forecasts to the SPF as they make public these issues remain. Typically empirical evidence of strategic behaviour is based on an analysis of series of point forecasts and outcomes, whereas the existence of point forecasts and estimates of conditional expectations in the SPF makes it ideal for testing the asymmetry hypothesis. It may also be of interest to consider whether the literature on bounded rationality and learning (see, e.g., Evans and Honkapohja, 2001; Mankiw and Reis, 2002; and Carroll, 2003) can help explain our findings.

Our overall finding is that individuals' point and probability forecasts tend to present a rosier picture of the prospects for output growth than is implicit in their probability distributions, reported as histograms. It appears that endowing the respondents with asymmetric loss functions does not explain this puzzle.

References

Andersen, T. G. and Bollerslev, T. (1998). Answering the skeptics: Yes, standard volatility models do provide accuate forecasts. *International Economic Review*, **39**, 885–905.

Andersen, T. G., Bollerslev, T., Diebold, F. X., and Labys, P. (2003). Modelling and forecasting realized volatility. *Econometrica*, **71**, 579–625.

Baillie, R. T. and Bollerslev, T. (1992). Prediction in dynamic models with time-dependent conditional variances. *Journal of Econometrics*, **52**, 91–113.

Berkowitz, J. (2001). Testing density forecasts, with applications to risk management. *Journal of Business and Economic Statistics*, **19**, 465–474.

Carroll, C. D. (2003). Macroeconomic expectations of households and professional forecasters. *Quarterly Journal of Economics,* **118**, 269–298.

Chong, Y. Y. and Hendry, D. F. (1986). Econometric evaluation of linear macro-economic models. *Review of Economic Studies,* **53**, 671–690. Reprinted in Granger, C. W. J. (ed.) (1990), *Modelling Economic Series.* Oxford: Clarendon Press.

Christoffersen, P. F. (1998). Evaluating interval forecasts. *International Economic Review,* **39**, 841–862.

——and Diebold, F. X. (1997). Optimal prediction under asymmetric loss. *Econometric Theory,* **13**, 808–817.

Clements, M. P. (2006). Evaluating the Survey of Professional Forecasters probability distributions of expected inflation based on derived event probability forecasts. *Empirical Economics,* **31**(1), 49–64.

——and Harvey, D. I. (2006). Forecast encompassing tests and probability forecasts. Working paper, Department of Economics, University of Warwick.

——and Hendry, D. F. (1993). On the limitations of comparing mean squared forecast errors. *Journal of Forecasting,* **12**, 617–637. With discussion. Reprinted in Mills, T. C. (ed.) (1999), *Economic Forecasting. The International Library of Critical Writings in Economics.* Cheltenham: Edward Elgar.

————(1998). *Forecasting Economic Time Series.* Cambridge: Cambridge University Press. The Marshall Lectures on Economic Forecasting.

————(1999). *Forecasting Non-Stationary Economic Time Series.* Cambridge, Mass.: MIT Press. The Zeuthen Lectures on Economic Forecasting.

Corradi, V. and Swanson, N. R. (2006). Predictive density evaluation. In Elliott, G., Granger, C., and Timmermann, A. (eds.), *Handbook of Economic Forecasting, Volume 1. Handbook of Economics 24,* pp. 197–284. North-Holland: Elsevier.

Croushore, D. (1993). Introducing: The Survey of Professional Forecasters. *Federal Reserve Bank of Philadelphia Business Review,* November/December, 3–13.

——and Stark, T. (2001). A real-time data set for macroeconomists. *Journal of Econometrics,* **105**, 111–130.

Davies, A. and Lahiri, K. (1995). A new framework for analyzing survey forecasts using three-dimensional panel data. *Journal of Econometrics,* **68**, 205–227.

————(1999). Re-examining the rational expectations hypothesis using panel data on multi-period forecasts. In Hsiao, C., Lahiri, K., Lee, L. F., and Pesaran, M. H. (eds.), *Analysis of Panels and Limited Dependent Variable Models,* pp. 226–254. Cambridge: Cambridge University Press.

Dawid, A. P. (1984). Statistical theory: The prequential approach. *Journal of The Royal Statistical Society, ser. A,* **147**, 278–292.

——(1986). Probability forecasting. In Kotz, S., Johnson, N. L., and Read, C. B. (eds.), *Encyclopedia of Statistical Sciences, vol. 7,* pp. 210–218. New York: John Wiley.

Diebold, F. X., Gunther, T. A., and Tay, A. S. (1998). Evaluating density forecasts: With applications to financial risk management. *International Economic Review,* **39**, 863–883.

——Hahn, J. Y., and Tay, A. S. (1999a). Multivariate density forecast evaluation and calibration in financial risk management: High frequency returns on foreign exchange. *Review of Economics and Statistics,* **81**, 661–673.

——Tay, A. S., and Wallis, K. F. (1999b). Evaluating density forecasts of inflation: The Survey of Professional Forecasters. In Engle, R. F. and White, H. (eds.), *Cointegration,*

Causality and Forecasting: A Festschrift in Honour of Clive Granger, pp. 76–90. Oxford: Oxford University Press.
Ehrbeck, T. and Waldmann, R. (1996). Why are professional forecasters biased? Agency versus behavioral explanations. *The Quarterly Journal of Economics*, **111**(1), 21–40.
Elliott, G., and Timmermann, A. (2004). Optimal forecast combinations under general loss functions and forecast error distributions. *Journal of Econometrics*, **122**, 47–79.
——Komunjer, I., and Timmermann, A. (2005). Estimation and testing of forecast rationality under flexible loss. *Review of Economic Studies*, **72**, 1107–1125.
————(2008). Biases in macroeconomic forecasts: Irrationality or asymmetric loss. *Journal of the European Economic Association*, **6**, 122–157.
Engelberg, J., Manski, C. F., and Williams, J. (2009). Comparing the point predictions and subjective probability distributions of professional forecasters. *Journal of Business and Economic Statistics*. Forthcoming.
Evans, G. W. and Honkapohja, S. (2001). *Learning and Expectations in Macroeconomics*. Princeton: Princeton University Press.
Figlewski, S. and Wachtel, P. (1981). The formation of inflationary expectations. *Review of Economics and Statistics*, **63**, 1–10.
Giacomini, R. and Komunjer, I. (2005). Evaluation and Combination of Conditional Quantile Forecasts. *Journal of Business and Economic Statistics*, **23**, 416–431.
Giordani, P. and Söderlind, P. (2003). Inflation forecast uncertainty. *European Economic Review*, **74**, 1037–1060.
Granger, C. W. J. (1969). Prediction with a generalized cost of error function. *Operations Research Quarterly*, **20**, 199–207.
——and Pesaran, M. H. (2000a). A decision-based approach to forecast evaluation. In Chan, W. S., Li, W. K., and Tong, H. (eds.), *Statistics and Finance: An Interface*, pp. 261–278. London: Imperial College Press.
————(2000b). Economic and statistical measures of forecast accuracy. *Journal of Forecasting*, **19**, 537–560.
——White, H., and Kamstra, M. (1989). Interval forecasting: An analysis based upon ARCH-quantile estimators. *Journal of Econometrics*, **40**, 87–96.
Keane, M. P. and Runkle, D. E. (1990). Testing the rationality of price forecasts: New evidence from panel data. *American Economic Review*, **80**, 714–735.
Kling, J. L. and Bessler, D. A. (1989). Calibration-based predictive distributions: An application of prequential analysis to interest rates, money, prices and output. *Journal of Business*, **62**, 477–499.
Lahiri, K., Teigland, C., and Zaporowski, M. (1988). Interest rates and the subjective probability distribution of inflation forecasts. *Journal of Money, Credit and Banking*, **20**, 233–248.
Laster, D., Bennett, P., and Geoum, I. S. (1999). Rational bias in macroeconomic forecasts. *The Quarterly Journal of Economics*, **114**(1), 293–318.
Mankiw, N. G. and Reis, R. (2002). Sticky information versus sticky prices: A proposal to replace the new Keynesian Phillips curve. *Quarterly Journal of Economics*, **117**, 1295–1328.
McNees, S. K. (1995). Forecast uncertainty: Can it be measured? Federal Reserve Bank of New York Discussion Paper.

Mincer, J. and Zarnowitz, V. (1969). The evaluation of economic forecasts. In Mincer, J. (ed.), *Economic Forecasts and Expectations*. New York: National Bureau of Economic Research.

Ottaviani, M. and Sorensen, P. N. (2006). The strategy of professional forecasting. *Journal of Financial Economics*, **81**, 441–466.

Patton, A. J. and Timmermann, A. (2007). Testing forecast optimality under unknown loss. *Journal of the American Statistical Association*, **102**, 1172–1184.

Pesaran, M. H. and Weale, M. (2006). Survey expectations. In Elliott, G., Granger, C., and Timmermann, A. (eds.), *Handbook of Economic Forecasting, Volume 1. Handbook of Economics 24*, pp. 715–776. North-Holland: Elsevier.

Romer, C. D. and Romer, D. H. (2000). Federal Reserve information and the behaviour of interest rates. *American Economic Review*, **90**, 429–457.

Stekler, H. O. (2002). The rationality and efficiency of individuals' forecasts. In Clements, M. P. and Hendry, D. F. (eds.), *A Companion to Economic Forecasting*, pp. 222–240. Oxford: Blackwells.

Thompson, S. B. (2002). Evaluating the goodness of fit of conditional distributions, with an application to affine term structure models. Manuscript, Harvard University.

White, H. (1980). A heteroskedastic-consistent covariance matrix estimator and a direct test for heteroskedasticity. *Econometrica*, **48**, 817–838.

Zarnowitz, V. (1969). The new ASA-NBER Survey of Forecasts by Economic Statisticians. *The American Statistician*, **23**(1), 12–16.

Zarnowitz, V. (1985). Rational expectations and macroeconomic forecasts. *Journal of Business and Economic Statistics*, **3**, 293–311.

Zellner, A. (1986). Biased predictors, rationality and the evaluation of forecasts. *Economics Letters*, **21**, 45–48.

9

Factor-augmented Error Correction Models

*Anindya Banerjee and Massimiliano Marcellino**

9.1 Introduction

Our chapter is an exploration of a few of the many themes studied by David Hendry, whom this conference volume honours. Starting at least with Davidson, Hendry, Srba, and Yeo (1978), Hendry has argued in favour of the powerful role of error-correction mechanisms (ECM) in modelling macroeconomic data. While originally undertaken in an environment with supposedly stationary data, the subsequent development of cointegration served to renew emphasis on the long-run co-movement of macroeconomic variables. Models lacking such information are likely to be misspecified both within-sample and out-of-sample (or forecasting context).

Breaks in the structure of models pose additional challenges for forecasting since models well specified within sample may not provide any guide for the forecasting performance of such models. Key references for this observation include Clements and Hendry (1995) where an interesting finding is that including reduced-rank or cointegrating information may not have beneficial effects on the forecasting performance of models except in small sample sizes. However, unrestricted vector autoregressions will be dominated by models which incorporate cointegration restrictions for larger systems of equations where cointegration relations impose a large number of restrictions. This is important background for the analysis conducted here, since we focus

* We thank the Research Council of the European University Institute (EUI) for supporting this research. We also thank Igor Masten for many useful discussions and help with the simulations reported in this chapter. Katarzyna Maciejowska provided excellent research assistance. We are also grateful to Luca Sala and James Stock for helpful comments. Responsibility for any errors remains with us.

precisely and very largely on the implications of modelling cointegration in very large systems of equations.

Yet more pertinently from the point of view of our analysis, the fact that in large data sets much of the cointegration information may be unknown or difficult to model, will lead to a dependence of the performance of the macroeconomic models on exactly how successfully the cointegration information is extracted from the data. This is by no means a trivial problem, especially if the dimension of the system N is large. Clements and Hendry (1995) explore this issue using alternative criteria for assessing forecasting accuracy including the trace mean squared forecast error criterion (TMSFE) and their preferred invariant generalized forecast error second moment (GFESM) criterion. More recent analysis by Hendry (2006) has argued in favour of using a differenced vector error correction model (DVECM) which introduces error-correction information into a double-differenced-VAR (DDVAR). Particularly in an environment with structural change, a DVECM retains information relating to the change in the equilibrium in the system.

The main contributions of our chapter are (a) to bring together two important recent strands of econometric literature on modelling co-movement that have a common origin but, in their implementations, have remained apart, namely, cointegration and dynamic factor models[1] and (b) to evaluate the role of incorporating long-run information in modelling, within the framework of both simulation exercises (where the emphasis is on evaluating efficiency within-sample) and empirical examples (where we look at both within-sample and out-of sample performance). It is important, in our view, to consider factor models since a significant issue, as in Clements and Hendry (1995), is the modelling of large systems of equations in which the complete cointegrating space may either be difficult to identify or it may not be necessary to do so since we may be interested in only a sub-system as our variables of interest. In such circumstances, as we shall see, proxying for the missing cointegrating information, may turn out to be extremely useful.

Our evaluations are based both on in-sample measures of model fit, including R^2 and adjusted-R^2 (which, in our simulation exercises, is equivalent to the one-step ahead mean squared forecast error (MSFE) since here the models may be taken to be correctly specified and the fitted value of the modelled variable can be interpreted as its forecast), as well as on a number of other criteria such as AIC and BIC, in circumstances (such as in our empirical

[1] Our focus here is on the widespread application of these methods in econometrics to model macroeconomic variables. Factor models have of course been used in a large number of other contexts for a much longer period.

examples) where the cointegrating information needs to be estimated and correct specification can therefore no longer be assumed to hold.

Our attempt here is to develop a manageable approach to the problems posed by large data sets where there is cointegration and where such cointegration should be taken into account in modelling the data. In particular, in this chapter we study the relationship between dynamic factor models and error correction models. We introduce the Factor-augmented Error Correction Model (FECM), where the factors extracted from a dynamic factor model for a large set of variables in levels are jointly modelled with a limited set of economic variables of main interest.

The FECM represents an improvement with respect to the standard ECM for the subset of variables, since it protects, at least in part, from omitted variable bias and the dependence of cointegration analysis on the specific limited set of variables under analysis. The FECM is also a refinement of dynamic factor models, since it allows us to include the error correction terms into the equations for the key variables under analysis, preventing the errors from being non-invertible MA processes. The FECM can also be considered as a natural generalization of factor-augmented VARs (FAVAR) considered by Bernanke, Boivin, and Eliasz (2005), Favero, Marcellino, and Neglia (2005), and Stock and Watson (2005). The FAVARs in all of these papers are specified in first differences, so that they are misspecified in the presence of cointegration.

The FECM may be expected to have a vast range of applicability. Therefore, in order to evaluate its relative merits in small, medium, and large samples, we conduct a set of Monte Carlo experiments, while to illustrate its use in practice we present two empirical applications with economic data. The first empirical example studies the relationships among four US interest rate series (at different maturities), and proceeds to analyse the relationships among these interest rate series and other macroeconomic variables. The second example reconsiders the famous article by King, Plosser, Stock, and Watson (1991) on stochastic trends and economic fluctuations in the US economy. In both examples, the factors are estimated from a large set of 110 monthly US macroeconomic variables, extracted from the data set in Stock and Watson (2005).

The simulation and empirical results show systematic gains in terms of explanatory power from the use of the FECM with respect to both an ECM and a FAVAR model.

The rest of the chapter is organized as follows. In section 9.2 we introduce the FECM. In section 9.3 we discuss a simple analytical example. In section 9.4 we present the design and results of the Monte Carlo experiments to evaluate the finite sample performance of the FECM. In section 9.5 we discuss the empirical examples. Finally, in section 9.6 we summarize and conclude.

9.2 The Factor-augmented Error Correction Model

Let us assume that the N $I(1)$ variables x_t evolve according to the $VAR(p)$ model

$$x_t = \Pi_1 x_{t-1} + \ldots + \Pi_p x_{t-p} + \epsilon_t, \tag{9.1}$$

where ϵ_t is i.i.d. $(0,\Omega)$ and, for simplicity, the starting values are fixed and equal to zero.

The $VAR(p)$ can be reparametrized into the Error Correction Model (ECM)

$$\Delta x_t = \alpha\beta' x_{t-1} + v_t, \tag{9.2}$$

or in the so-called common trend specification

$$x_t = \Psi f_t + u_t, \tag{9.3}$$

see, eg, Johansen (1995, p. 49). In particular,

$$\Pi = \sum_{s=1}^{p} \Pi_s - I_N = \underset{N\times N-r}{\alpha} \underset{N-r\times N}{\beta'},$$

$$v_t = \Gamma_1 \Delta x_{t-1} + \ldots + \Gamma_{p-1}\Delta x_{t-p+1} + \epsilon_t, \quad \Gamma_i = -\sum_{s=i+1}^{p} \Pi_s, \quad \Gamma = I_N - \sum_{i=1}^{p-1}\Gamma_i,$$

$$\underset{N\times r}{\Psi} = \beta_\perp(\alpha'_\perp \Gamma \beta_\perp)^{-1}, \quad \underset{r\times 1}{f_t} = \alpha'_\perp \sum_{s=1}^{t} \epsilon_s, \quad u_t = C(L)\epsilon_t.$$

β' is the $N-r \times N$ matrix of cointegrating vectors with rank $N-r$, where $N-r$ is the number of cointegrating vectors. r is therefore the number of $I(1)$ common stochastic trends (or factors), $0 < r \leq N$, gathered in the $r \times 1$ vector f_t and the matrix $\alpha'_\perp \Gamma\beta_\perp$ is invertible since each variable is $I(1)$. α is the so-called loading matrix, which also has reduced rank $N-r$ and determines how the cointegrating vectors enter into each individual element x_{it} of the $N \times 1$ vector x_t.[2] u_t is an N-dimensional vector of stationary errors. We also assume that there are no common cycles in the sense of Engle and Kozicki (1993), ie, no linear combinations of the first differences of the variables that are correlated of lower order than each of the variables (in first differences), although adding such cycles (as in the analytical example below) poses no significant complications and is assumed here only for convenience.[3]

[2] Note that as $N \to \infty$, and the number of factors r remains fixed, the number of cointegrating relations $N-r \to \infty$.

[3] Common cycles are associated with reduced rank of (some of) the coefficient matrices in $C(L)$, where we remember that the errors in the stochastic trend representation (9.3) are $u_t = C(L)\epsilon_t$. Therefore, the presence of common cycles is associated with stationary common factors driving x_t, in addition to the I(1) factors.

From equation (9.3), it is possible to write the model for the first differences of x_t, Δx_t, as

$$\Delta x_t = \Psi \Delta f_t + \Delta u_t, \tag{9.4}$$

where Δu_t and ν_t can be correlated over time and across variables.

The literature on dynamic factor models has relied on a specification similar to (9.4) and has focused on the properties of the estimators of the common factors Δf_t, or of the common components $\Psi \Delta f_t$, under certain assumptions on the idiosyncratic errors, when the number of variables N becomes large. See, for example, Stock and Watson (2002a, 2002b) and Forni, Hallin, Lippi, and Reichlin (2000). A few papers have also analysed the model in (9.3) for the divergent N case, most notably Bai and Ng (2004) and Bai (2004).[4] We shall make use of both specification (9.3) and (9.4) when discussing factor models in what follows.

By contrast, the literature on cointegration has focused on (9.2) and has studied the properties of tests for the cointegrating rank ($N - r$) and estimators of the cointegrating vectors (β'), see e.g. Engle and Granger (1987) or Johansen (1995). A few papers have attempted to extend the analysis to the large N case, generating the so-called panel cointegration tests, where a factor structure is employed to explore issues relating to the dependence across the variables. See e.g. Banerjee, Marcellino, and Osbat (2004) and Banerjee and Carrion-i-Silvestre (2007), where the latter paper uses techniques used by Bai and Ng (2004) in developing their PANIC tests for unit roots in panels.[5] The extension of PANIC techniques to study cointegration is complicated by the curse of dimensionality which makes the modelling of cointegration—particularly when N is large and there are multiple cointegrating vectors, ie $N - r > 1$—extremely difficult and often subject to criticism.

To continue with our analysis, let us impose, without any loss of generality, the identifying condition

$$\underset{N-r\times N}{\beta'} = \left(\underset{N-r\times r}{\beta^{*'}} : \underset{N-r\times N-r}{I} \right).$$

This is standard practice in this literature, as also implemented by Clements and Hendry (1995, p. 129, lines 1–5) and ensures that the transformation from the levels x_t which are $I(1)$ to $I(0)$-space (involving taking the cointegrated combinations and the differences of the $I(1)$ variables) is scale preserving.

[4] Bai and Ng (2004) also allow for the possibility that some elements of the idiosyncratic error u_t are I(1). We will not consider this case and assume instead that all the variables under analysis are cointegrated, perhaps after pre-selection. We feel that this is a sensible assumption from an economic point of view.

[5] Other papers in this area include Breitung and Das (2005, 2008), Pesaran (2006), Bai, Kao, and Ng (2007).

From (9.3), partitioning u_t into

$$u_t = \begin{pmatrix} \underset{r\times 1}{u_{1t}} \\ \underset{N-r\times 1}{u_{2t}} \end{pmatrix},$$

the model for the error correction terms can be written as

$$\beta' x_t = \beta' u_t = \beta^{*'} u_{1t} + u_{2t}. \tag{9.5}$$

In this model each of the $N-r$ error correction terms depends on a common component that is a function of only r shocks, u_{1t}, and on an idiosyncratic component, u_{2t}. Different normalizations of the cointegrating vectors change the exact shocks that influence each error correction term, but its decomposition into a common component driven by r shocks and an idiosyncratic component remains valid. This is also in line with the stochastic trend representation in (9.3), where the levels of the variables are driven by r common trends.

Let us now partition the N variables in x_t into the N_A of major interest, x_{At}, and the $N_B = N - N_A$ remaining ones, x_{Bt}. We can partition the common trends model in (9.3) accordingly as

$$\begin{pmatrix} x_{At} \\ x_{Bt} \end{pmatrix} = \begin{pmatrix} \Psi_A \\ \Psi_B \end{pmatrix} f_t + \begin{pmatrix} u_{At} \\ u_{Bt} \end{pmatrix}, \tag{9.6}$$

where Ψ_A is of dimension $N_A \times r$ and Ψ_B is $N_B \times r$. Notice that when the number of variables N increases, the dimension of Ψ_A is fixed, while the number of rows of Ψ_B increases correspondingly. Therefore, for (9.6) to preserve a factor structure asymptotically, driven by r common factors, it is necessary that the rank of Ψ_B remains equal to r. Instead, the rank of Ψ_A can be smaller than r, ie, x_{At} can be driven by a smaller number of trends, say $r_A \leq r$.

From the specification in (9.6), it is evident that x_{At} and f_t are cointegrated, while from (9.3) the f_t are uncorrelated random walks. Therefore, from the Granger representation theorem, there must exist an error correction specification of the type

$$\begin{pmatrix} \Delta x_{At} \\ \Delta f_t \end{pmatrix} = \begin{pmatrix} \gamma_A \\ \gamma \end{pmatrix} \delta' \begin{pmatrix} x_{At-1} \\ f_{t-1} \end{pmatrix} + \begin{pmatrix} e_{At} \\ e_t \end{pmatrix}. \tag{9.7}$$

In practice, correlation in the errors of (9.7) is handled by adding additional lags of the differenced dependent variables, so that the model becomes

$$\begin{pmatrix} \Delta x_{At} \\ \Delta f_t \end{pmatrix} = \begin{pmatrix} \gamma_A \\ \gamma \end{pmatrix} \delta' \begin{pmatrix} x_{At-1} \\ f_{t-1} \end{pmatrix} + A_1 \begin{pmatrix} \Delta x_{At-1} \\ \Delta f_{t-1} \end{pmatrix} + \ldots + A_q \begin{pmatrix} \Delta x_{At-q} \\ \Delta f_{t-q} \end{pmatrix} + \begin{pmatrix} \epsilon_{At} \\ \epsilon_t \end{pmatrix}. \tag{9.8}$$

We label (9.8) as a Factor-augmented Error Correction Model (FECM).

Since there are $N_A + r$ dependent variables in the FECM model (9.8), x_{At} is driven by f_t or a subset of them, and the f_t are uncorrelated random walks, there must be N_A cointegrating relationships in (9.8). Moreover, since Ψ_A is of dimension $N_A \times r$ but can have reduced rank r_A, there are $N_A - r_A$ cointegrating relationships that involve the x_A variables only, say $\delta'_A x_{At-1}$, and the remaining r_A cointegrating relationships involve x_A and the factors f.

The cointegrating relationships $\delta'_A x_{At-1}$ would also emerge in a standard ECM for Δx_{At} only, say

$$\Delta x_{At} = \alpha_A \delta'_A x_{At-1} + \upsilon_{At}. \tag{9.9}$$

However, in addition to these $N_A - r_A$ relationships, in the FECM there are r_A cointegrating relationships that involve x_{At} and f_t, and that proxy for the potentially omitted $N - N_A$ cointegrating relationships in (9.9) with respect to the equations for Δx_{At} in the full ECM in (9.2).[6] Moreover, in the FECM there appear lags of Δf_t as regressors in the equations for Δx_{At}, that proxy for the potentially omitted lags of Δx_{Bt} in the standard ECM for Δx_{At} in (9.9). Therefore, the FECM provides an improved representation for the variables of interest x_{At}, in terms of modelling both the long-run and short-run evolution of these variables.

It is also important to point out that in the dynamic factor models à la Stock and Watson (2002a, 2002b) and in FAVAR specifications the error correction terms never appear, ie, $\gamma_A = 0$ is imposed in (9.8). Therefore, the FECM also represents an improvement for the specification of dynamic factor models and FAVAR models. Moreover, in our context where the data generating process is the common trends specification in (9.3), standard factor and FAVAR models have two additional substantial problems. First, the error process Δu_t in (9.4) has a non-invertible moving average component that prevents, from a theoretical point of view, the approximation of each equation of the model in (9.4) with an AR model augmented with lags of the factors. Second, and perhaps even more problematically, in (9.4) Δf_t and Δu_t are in general not orthogonal to each other, and in fact they can be highly correlated. This feature disrupts the factor structure and, from an empirical point of view, can require a large number of factors to summarize the information contained in Δx_t.

Notice that if the starting model is given by (9.3) but the shocks driving the integrated factors are orthogonal to u_t, so that Δf_t and Δu_t are also orthogonal, then the model in (9.4) is a proper factor model, but with a non-invertible moving average component. This feature does not pose any

[6] In the full ECM model (9.2), there would be up to $N - r_A$ cointegrating relationships in the equations for Δx_{At}, while in (9.9) there are only $N_A - r_A$ cointegrating relationships, so that there are $N - N_A$ potentially omitted long-run relationships in the ECM for Δx_{At} only.

additional complications for the estimation of the common component $\Psi\Delta f_t$ either with the static principal component approach of Stock and Watson (2002a, 2002b) or with the dynamic principal component method of Forni *et al.* (2000, 2005). However, the presence of a unit root in the moving average component still prevents the approximation of each equation of the model in (9.4) with an AR model augmented with lags of the factors, while factor augmented AR models have become a standard tool for forecasting.

The FECM also has its problems. In particular, the approach may find it difficult to handle situations where there is a large number of error correction terms affecting each equation, or when the cointegrating relationships include all the variables in x_t and not just the subset x_{At}.

An additional complication for the FECM is that in practice the common stochastic (integrated) factors, f_t, are not known. However, the principal components of x_t are a consistent estimator for (the space spanned by) f_t when N diverges, see e.g. Stock and Watson (1988) and Bai (2004). Moreover, Bai (2004) and Bai and Ng (2006) have shown that, when $\sqrt{T}/N$ is $o_p(1)$, the estimated factors can be used in subsequent analyses without creating any generated regressors problems. Therefore, the estimated factors can be used in the FECM instead of the true factors, assuming that the available data set is large enough to satisfy the condition $\sqrt{T}/N$ is $o_p(1)$. The role of the use of estimated versus true factors in finite sample is one of the issues explored in the simulation exercise.

9.3 An Analytical Example

Before proceeding to the simulations, we first consider a simple analytical example to illustrate the relationships between the ECM representation, the FECM, and the FAVAR. Let us assume that the N variables are generated by the ECM model

$$\Delta x_t = \alpha\beta' x_{t-1} + \epsilon_t, \tag{9.10}$$

with $\epsilon_t \sim i.i.d.(0,I_N)$, one common stochastic trend ($r = 1$), and

$$\beta' = \begin{pmatrix} -1 & 1 & 0 & 0 & \dots & 0 & 0 \\ -1 & 0 & 1 & 0 & \dots & 0 & 0 \\ -1 & 0 & 0 & 1 & & & \\ \dots & & & & & & \\ -1 & 0 & 0 & 0 & \dots & 0 & 1 \end{pmatrix}, \quad \alpha = \begin{pmatrix} 0 & 0 & 0 & \dots & 0 \\ -1 & 0 & 0 & \dots & 0 \\ -1 & -1 & 0 & \dots & 0 \\ -1 & 0 & -1 & & \\ \dots & & & & \\ -1 & 0 & 0 & \dots & -1 \end{pmatrix}.$$

Therefore, the equations of the ECM are

$$\begin{aligned}
\Delta x_{1t} &= \epsilon_{1t} \\
\Delta x_{2t} &= -(-x_{1t-1} + x_{2t-1}) + \epsilon_{2t} \\
\Delta x_{3t} &= -(-x_{1t-1} + x_{2t-1}) - (-x_{1t-1} + x_{3t-1}) + \epsilon_{3t} \\
\Delta x_{4t} &= -(-x_{1t-1} + x_{2t-1}) - (-x_{1t-1} + x_{4t-1}) + \epsilon_{4t} \\
&\dots \\
\Delta x_{Nt} &= -(-x_{1t-1} + x_{2t-1}) - (-x_{1t-1} + x_{Nt-1}) + \epsilon_{Nt}.
\end{aligned} \tag{9.11}$$

The stochastic trend representation becomes

$$\begin{aligned}
x_{1t} &= \sum_{s=1}^{t} \epsilon_{1s} \\
x_{2t} &= x_{1t-1} + \epsilon_{2t} \\
x_{3t} &= x_{1t-1} - \epsilon_{2t-1} + \epsilon_{1t-1} + \epsilon_{3t} \\
x_{4t} &= x_{1t-1} - \epsilon_{2t-1} + \epsilon_{1t-1} + \epsilon_{4t} \\
&\dots \\
x_{Nt} &= x_{1t-1} - \epsilon_{2t-1} + \epsilon_{1t-1} + \epsilon_{Nt}.
\end{aligned} \tag{9.12}$$

From this representation it clearly emerges that the variables are driven by an I(1) common factor, $\sum_{s=1}^{t} \epsilon_{1s}$, and by an I(0) common factor, $\epsilon_{1t} - \epsilon_{2t}$. If we write the model in (9.12) in a compact notation as

$$x_t = \nu \sum_{s=1}^{t-1} \epsilon_{1s} + \epsilon_t + C_1 \epsilon_{t-1},$$

where $\nu = (1, 1, \dots, 1)'$, it clearly emerges that C_1 has reduced rank (equal to one), ie, there are common cycles in the sense of Engle and Kozicki (1993).

From the stochastic trend representation in (9.12), we can easily derive that the specification for the error correction terms (cointegrating relationships) $\beta' x_{t-1}$ is given by

$$\begin{aligned}
x_{2t} - x_{1t} &= -(\epsilon_{1t} - \epsilon_{2t}) \\
x_{3t} - x_{1t} &= \epsilon_{1t-1} - \epsilon_{2t-1} - \epsilon_{1t} + \epsilon_{3t} \\
x_{4t} - x_{1t} &= \epsilon_{1t-1} - \epsilon_{2t-1} - \epsilon_{1t} + \epsilon_{4t} \\
&\dots \\
x_{Nt} - x_{1t} &= \epsilon_{1t-1} - \epsilon_{2t-1} - \epsilon_{1t} + \epsilon_{Nt}.
\end{aligned} \tag{9.13}$$

Therefore, the error correction terms are driven by two common I(0) factors, one is the same as for the levels of the variables, $\epsilon_{1t} - \epsilon_{2t}$, the other is the first difference of the common I(1) factor, $\Delta \sum_{s=1}^{t} \epsilon_{1s} = \epsilon_{1t}$.

Substituting the expression in (9.13) for $\beta' x_{t-1}$ into the ECM in (9.10), the representation for Δx_t corresponding to (9.4) is

$$\begin{aligned} \Delta x_{1t} &= \epsilon_{1t} \\ \Delta x_{2t} &= \epsilon_{1t-1} - \epsilon_{2t-1} + \epsilon_{2t} \\ \Delta x_{3t} &= \epsilon_{1t-1} - \epsilon_{2t-1} - (\epsilon_{1t-2} - \epsilon_{2t-2}) + \epsilon_{1t-1} + \epsilon_{3t} - \epsilon_{3t-1} \\ \Delta x_{4t} &= \epsilon_{1t-1} - \epsilon_{2t-1} - (\epsilon_{1t-2} - \epsilon_{2t-2}) + \epsilon_{1t-1} + \epsilon_{4t} - \epsilon_{4t-1} \\ &\dots \\ \Delta x_{Nt} &= \epsilon_{1t-1} - \epsilon_{2t-1} - (\epsilon_{1t-2} - \epsilon_{2t-2}) + \epsilon_{1t-1} + \epsilon_{Nt} - \epsilon_{Nt-1}. \end{aligned} \tag{9.14}$$

A few features of the model in (9.14) are worth noting. First, the common factors are the same as those in the model for $\beta' x_{t-1}$, namely, $\epsilon_{1t} - \epsilon_{2t}$ and ϵ_{1t}. Second, the common factors have a dynamic impact on the variables. Therefore, the number of static factors à la Stock and Watson (2002a, 2002b) in (9.14) would be larger than that of dynamic factors à la Forni *et al.* (2000, 2005). The difference can be substantial in models with more dynamics. Third, the idiosyncratic errors are non-invertible MA(1) in almost all the equations, given by $\epsilon_{it} - \epsilon_{it-1}$. This feature remains valid in models with more complex dynamics and suggests, as mentioned previously, that AR approximations to the equations of (9.14), namely FAVAR models, are inappropriate, at least from a theoretical point of view, when the factor model structure is (at least in part) due to cointegration. Finally, in this example the common factors driving the error correction terms, namely $\epsilon_{1t} - \epsilon_{2t}$ and ϵ_{1t}, are orthogonal to most of the errors $\epsilon_{1t}, \epsilon_{2t}, \dots, \epsilon_{Nt}$, which makes (9.14) a proper factor model. However, as mentioned in the previous section, typically the model for Δx_t no longer has a factor structure due to correlation between the driving forces of the error correction terms and the errors in the equations for the components of Δx_t.

Let us now assume that we are particularly interested in $x_{At} = (x_{2t}, x_{3t}, x_{4t})'$ and derive the subset ECM model for Δx_{At}. Since the three variables are driven by one stochastic trend, there will be two cointegrating relationships, whose parameters can be set equal to

$$\beta_A' = \begin{pmatrix} -1 & 1 & 0 \\ -1 & 0 & 1 \end{pmatrix}.$$

It can be shown that the pseudo-true values of the loadings of the cointegrating relationships are

$$\alpha_A = \begin{pmatrix} -1/7 & -1/7 \\ 6/7 & -1/7 \\ -1/7 & 6/7 \end{pmatrix}.$$

Hence, the ECM for Δx_{At} is

$$\Delta x_{At} = \alpha_A \beta_A' x_{t-1} + u_t, \tag{9.15}$$

where the errors follow a complex MA(2) process. Therefore, with respect to the equations for Δx_{At} in the ECM (9.11) for the whole vector Δx_t, there is a bias both in the long-run and short-run dynamics.

The FECM in this context requires modelling the variables $x_{ft} = (f_{1t}, x_{2t}, x_{3t}, x_{4t})'$, where the stochastic trend model in (9.12) implies that $f_{1t} = x_{1t-1}$. Therefore, the relevant equations of the FECM are

$$\begin{aligned} \Delta x_{2t} &= -(-f_{1t-1} + x_{2t-1}) + \epsilon_{2t} + \epsilon_{1t-1} \qquad (9.16) \\ \Delta x_{3t} &= -(-f_{1t-1} + x_{2t-1}) - (-f_{1t-1} + x_{3t-1}) + \epsilon_{3t} + 2\epsilon_{1t-1} \\ \Delta x_{4t} &= -(-f_{1t-1} + x_{2t-1}) - (-f_{1t-1} + x_{4t-1}) + \epsilon_{4t} + 2\epsilon_{1t-1}. \end{aligned}$$

Comparing (9.16) with the subset of equations for Δx_{At} in the ECM (9.11), we see that α and β are unaffected, and the errors remain uncorrelated over time. It is worth recalling that both these properties no longer necessarily hold in more complex specifications, eg, if the variables in x_{At} depend on several cointegrating relationships not modelled here or on the lags of other variables in x_t. Moreover, the standard deviation of the errors in (9.16) increases with respect to (9.11), and the errors become correlated across equations. With respect to the corresponding equations in (9.14), the standard deviation of the errors is larger for Δx_{3t} and Δx_{4t}. It can instead be shown that the standard deviation of the errors of the FECM is smaller than that of the subset ECM in (9.15).

Finally, it is worth considering the equation for Δf_{1t}. From, (9.10), it can be written as either

$$\Delta f_{1t} = \epsilon_{1t-1}, \tag{9.17}$$

or

$$\Delta f_{1t} = -(-f_{1t-1} + x_{2t-1}) - \epsilon_{2t-1}. \tag{9.18}$$

The two representations are observationally equivalent. The former is in line with the theoretical model (9.7), and indicates that the changes in the factors should be weakly exogenous for the parameters of the cointegration relationships. However, standard econometric packages for VAR and cointegration analysis will use the latter representation, where Δf_{1t} is instead affected by the error correction term.

9.4 Monte Carlo Experiments

In this section we conduct a set of simulation experiments to evaluate in finite samples the performance of the FECM, relative to that of an ECM and a FAVAR for the same small subset of variables of interest. An important feature to consider in the Monte Carlo design, is the way in which error-correcting or cointegrating information enters into the system for the variables of interest, ie whether the cointegrating vectors are common to each variable, or are idiosyncratic, or are a combination of the two. Another important aspect to bear in mind is how much cointegrating information needs to be incorporated, when looking at a sub-system of interest, from outside this sub-system. In the terminology established above, FECM should not in theory be able to handle well situations where there is a large number of error correction terms affecting each equation, or when the cointegrating relationships include all the variables in x_t and not just the subset x_{At}. However, in these cases, which are likely encountered in practical empirical situations, ECM and FAVAR would also experience serious problems. It is therefore worthwhile studying the performance of the alternative estimation methods using both simulations and empirical examples.

9.4.1 *Design of the Monte Carlo*

The basic data generating process (DGP) is the error correction mechanism

$$\Delta x_t = \alpha\beta' x_{t-1} + \epsilon_t, \tag{9.19}$$

where x_t is N-dimensional, α and β are of dimension $N \times N-r$, r is the number of common stochastic trends, and $\epsilon_t \sim N(0,I)$. We fix $r = 1$, set the cointegrating vectors equal to

$$\beta' = \begin{pmatrix} -1 & 1 & 0 & 0 & \dots & 0 & 0 \\ -1 & 0 & 1 & 0 & \dots & 0 & 0 \\ -1 & 0 & 0 & 1 & & & \\ \dots & & & & & & \\ -1 & 0 & 0 & 0 & \dots & 0 & 1 \end{pmatrix},$$

and assume that we are particularly interested in the variables $x_{At} = (x_{2t}, x_{3t}, x_{4t})'$.

We then consider three versions of this DGP, which differ according to the shape of the matrix of loadings, α. In DGP1, α is given by

$$\alpha = \begin{pmatrix} 0 & 0 & 0 & \dots & 0 \\ -1 & 0 & 0 & \dots & 0 \\ 0 & -1 & 0 & \dots & 0 \\ \dots & & & & \\ 0 & 0 & 0 & \dots & -1 \end{pmatrix},$$

so that each cointegrating relationship affects a single variable. This is a simplified version of the analytical example in the previous section. Using techniques similar to those used in the analytical example, it can be shown that the subset ECM for x_{At} leads to biases in α and β, and to correlated errors with a larger variance than those from the FECM. The ranking of the FAVAR and of the FECM should also favour the latter, since the model for Δx_t has a proper factor structure but the errors are non-invertible processes.

The loading matrix for DGP2 is

$$\alpha = \begin{pmatrix} 0 & 0 & 0 & \dots & 0 \\ -1 & 0 & 0 & \dots & 0 \\ -1 & -1 & 0 & \dots & 0 \\ -1 & 0 & -1 & & \\ \dots & & & & \\ -1 & 0 & 0 & \dots & -1 \end{pmatrix},$$

as in the analytical example in the previous section, so that one cointegrating relationship is common while the remaining $N-2$ relationships are idiosyncratic.

Finally, in DGP3 we set

$$\alpha = \begin{pmatrix} 0 & 0 & 0 & \dots & \dots & \dots & \dots & \dots & 0 & 0 \\ -1 & -1 & -1 & -1 & 0 & 0 & 0 & \dots & 0 & 0 \\ 0 & -1 & -1 & -1 & -1 & -1 & 0 & \dots & \dots & 0 \\ 0 & 0 & -1 & -1 & -1 & -1 & 0 & 0 & \dots & 0 \\ 0 & 0 & 0 & -1 & 0 & 0 & 0 & 0 & \dots & 0 \\ 0 & 0 & 0 & 0 & -1 & 0 & 0 & 0 & \dots & 0 \\ . & . & . & . & . & . & . & . & . & \\ . & . & . & . & . & . & . & . & . & \\ 0 & 0 & 0 & 0 & 0 & 0 & 0 & 0 & \dots & -1 \end{pmatrix}.$$

This is a case where the ranking of the ECM and FECM is less clear-cut for two reasons. First, the FECM equations should depend on as many error correction terms as modelled variables, four, while at most three error correction terms can be included in the FECM. Second, some of the error correction terms depend on variables not modelled in the FECM, such as x_5 and x_6.

For all three DGPs, we consider the following configurations for T and N: $T \in (50,100,200,500)$ and $N \in (50,100,200)$.

The comparisons between ECM, FECM, and FAVAR are based on the residual variances for each estimated equation/variable in x_{At} normalized on the variance obtained from estimating the ECM. The residual variances reported in the tables below are computed using the sample size T as the scaling term for the sum of squared residuals. We also have results, not reported here, where the residual variances are computed using a degrees-of-freedom correction for the number of parameters estimated under each method. While these results, available from us upon request, are quantitatively altered, the relative rankings of ECM versus FECM versus FAVAR are not. Rankings based on the adjusted-R^2 of each equation are also qualitatively similar and not reported to save space.

As discussed above, under correct specification as in most of our simulation experiments, the residual variance criterion yields a ranking equivalent to that resulting from a comparison of one-step ahead MSFEs. Instead, the equivalence does not necessarily hold in empirical applications, and therefore we also report the one-step-ahead MSFEs in our empirical examples in section 9.5.

In the FECM, the number of cointegrating relationships is taken as given, although the cointegrating vectors and the loading matrix are estimated using maximum likelihood, see Johansen (1995). The factors are estimated from the levels of the data using the methods proposed by Bai (2004). His information criterion IPC_2 is used to select the number of factors.

In the ECM, the number of cointegrating relationships is taken as known. The cointegrating vectors and the loading matrix are again estimated.

Finally, in the FAVAR, the factors are estimated from the first differences of the data using the methods proposed by Stock and Watson (2002a, 2002b). Wherever the number of factors needs to be estimated, ie they are not imposed, the choice is based on the PC_2 criterion of Bai and Ng (2002).

9.4.2 *Results*

The results of the comparisons are reported in Tables 9.1 to 9.3 below. Each table contains, in its sub-panels, the results for each of the three equations (x_{2t}, x_{3t}, x_{4t}), the different methods, and the different combinations of N and T. Table 9.1 reports the results for DGP 1, where in panel A the number of factors is assumed known and is imposed while in panel B it is chosen according to Bai's (2004) IPC_2 information criterion when analysing data in levels and Bai and Ng's (2002) PC_2 criterion for data in differences. Since in practice correlation of the errors of the dynamic system is handled by including additional lags of the differenced dependent variable (labelled q) (see equation (9.8)), we report the results for this lag length fixed to 1 and 3, $q = 1$ and $q = 3$ respectively, and also where it is chosen by using the

Table 9.1. Results for DGP 1

		Ratios of Residual Variances											
		A: Number of factors imposed						B: Number of factors estimated					
		Equation 1		Equation 2		Equation 3		Equation 1		Equation 2		Equation 3	
	lags	FECM SW	FAVAR SW	FECM SW	FAVAR SW	FECM SW	FAVAR SW	FECM SW	FAVAR SW	FECM SW	FAVAR SW	FECM SW	FAVAR SW
T							N = 50						
50	q = 1	0.829	1.177	0.829	1.177	0.831	1.179	0.833	1.165	0.831	1.162	0.831	1.162
	q = 3	0.771	1.030	0.771	1.033	0.773	1.032	0.770	0.968	0.771	0.971	0.770	0.969
	HQ	0.841	1.019	0.838	1.026	0.839	1.018	0.839	0.967	0.839	0.965	0.838	0.969
100	q = 1	0.853	1.137	0.852	1.138	0.853	1.137	0.854	1.138	0.853	1.136	0.853	1.138
	q = 3	0.833	1.009	0.834	1.011	0.833	1.007	0.833	1.008	0.832	1.007	0.833	1.009
	HQ	0.840	0.979	0.841	0.982	0.841	0.980	0.845	0.981	0.842	0.978	0.841	0.976
200	q = 1	0.864	1.122	0.863	1.121	0.864	1.121	0.865	1.121	0.864	1.122	0.865	1.122
	q = 3	0.856	1.004	0.854	1.003	0.856	1.004	0.855	1.003	0.855	1.004	0.855	1.003
	HQ	0.846	0.946	0.847	0.943	0.846	0.945	0.848	0.946	0.848	0.946	0.849	0.947
500	q = 1	0.869	1.113	0.869	1.113	0.869	1.113	0.869	1.112	0.869	1.113	0.869	1.112
	q = 3	0.866	1.001	0.866	1.002	0.867	1.001	0.867	1.002	0.867	1.002	0.867	1.001
	HQ	0.861	0.942	0.860	0.943	0.861	0.943	0.859	0.942	0.860	0.942	0.860	0.943
T							N = 100						
50	q = 1	0.836	1.178	0.836	1.179	0.835	1.178	0.834	1.176	0.835	1.172	0.835	1.175
	q = 3	0.774	1.026	0.773	1.025	0.772	1.026	0.776	1.012	0.775	1.009	0.774	1.009
	HQ	0.841	1.019	0.842	1.031	0.843	1.024	0.845	1.003	0.845	1.001	0.846	0.999
100	q = 1	0.858	1.136	0.858	1.135	0.858	1.135	0.858	1.136	0.859	1.138	0.858	1.134
	q = 3	0.837	1.004	0.840	1.011	0.837	1.005	0.837	1.006	0.838	1.007	0.838	1.006
	HQ	0.847	0.981	0.847	0.980	0.846	0.979	0.850	0.980	0.849	0.981	0.849	0.977
200	q = 1	0.868	1.118	0.868	1.119	0.868	1.119	0.868	1.118	0.868	1.119	0.868	1.119
	q = 3	0.860	1.001	0.858	0.998	0.860	1.000	0.859	0.999	0.860	1.000	0.859	1.000
	HQ	0.852	0.941	0.853	0.945	0.852	0.942	0.852	0.941	0.852	0.942	0.853	0.944
500	p = 1	0.875	1.111	0.874	1.111	0.874	1.111	0.874	1.110	0.874	1.110	0.874	1.110
	p = 3	0.872	0.998	0.872	0.998	0.872	0.999	0.871	0.998	0.872	0.998	0.872	0.999
	HQ	0.864	0.938	0.864	0.938	0.865	0.939	0.865	0.939	0.865	0.939	0.865	0.939
T							N = 200						
50	q = 1	0.837	1.176	0.838	1.178	0.838	1.174	0.837	1.178	0.837	1.178	0.837	1.178
	q = 3	0.774	1.033	0.774	1.026	0.777	1.033	0.778	1.026	0.778	1.029	0.778	1.028
	HQ	0.846	1.022	0.846	1.012	0.843	1.014	0.843	1.013	0.845	1.013	0.844	1.012
100	q = 1	0.860	1.134	0.861	1.135	0.860	1.133	0.859	1.133	0.860	1.135	0.860	1.135
	q = 3	0.838	1.005	0.840	1.003	0.840	1.003	0.840	1.005	0.839	1.004	0.840	1.004
	HQ	0.848	0.974	0.848	0.976	0.847	0.973	0.848	0.974	0.848	0.973	0.850	0.977
200	q = 1	0.871	1.119	0.871	1.117	0.871	1.117	0.871	1.117	0.871	1.118	0.871	1.118
	q = 3	0.862	1.000	0.861	0.998	0.861	0.998	0.862	0.999	0.862	0.999	0.862	0.999
	HQ	0.855	0.943	0.856	0.941	0.855	0.941	0.852	0.940	0.852	0.939	0.852	0.938
500	q = 1	0.876	1.110	0.876	1.109	0.876	1.110	0.876	1.109	0.877	1.110	0.876	1.110
	q = 3	0.874	0.998	0.874	0.997	0.873	0.996	0.874	0.997	0.874	0.997	0.874	0.997
	HQ	0.867	0.938	0.867	0.938	0.867	0.937	0.868	0.938	0.868	0.939	0.868	0.938

k_estim

N = 50 T	FECM SW	FAVAR SW	N = 100 T	FECM SW	FAVAR SW	N = 200 T	FECM SW	FAVAR SW
50	1	1.595	50	1	1.188	50	1	1.008
100	1	1.001	100	1	1	100	1	1
200	1	1	200	1	1	200	1	1
500	1	1	500	1	1	500	1	1

Notes: Each cell of the table (ie for each equation, estimation method, and (N,T) configuration) in the panel labelled 'Ratios of Residual Variances' records the residual variance of the equation relative to the residual variance obtained from estimating, for the same configuration, the subset ECM consisting of (X_{2t}, X_{3t}, X_{4t}) only. The results are reported where the number of lagged differenced variables is fixed to 1 (q = 1), where it is fixed to 3 (q = 3) and where it is chosen by the HQ criterion (HQ). Equation 1 refers to the equation for X_{2t}, Equation 2 to X_{3t} and Equation 3 to X_{4t}. FECM-SW estimates the factor error-correction model with the factors extracted in levels according to Bai (2004). FAVAR-SW estimates factor augmented VAR models with factors extracted from differences of the data according to Stock and Watson (2002b).

The results are based on 10,000 replications for q = 1 and 2,000 replications for q = 3 and HQ.

The panel labelled k_estim records the (average) number (across replications) of estimated factors.

Table 9.2. Results for DGP 2

		Ratios of Residual Variances											
		A: Number of factors imposed						B: Number of factors estimated					
		Equation 1		Equation 2		Equation 3		Equation 1		Equation 2		Equation 3	
	lags	FECM SW	FAVAR SW	FECM SW	FAVAR SW	FECM SW	FAVAR SW	FECM SW	FAVAR SW	FECM SW	FAVAR SW	FECM SW	FAVAR SW
T							N = 50						
50	q = 1	0.893	1.206	0.867	1.071	0.867	1.067	0.894	1.190	0.868	1.050	0.868	1.049
	q = 3	0.832	1.077	0.806	0.991	0.808	0.995	0.829	1.012	0.801	0.934	0.802	0.932
	HQ	1.006	1.075	1.001	0.953	0.998	0.951	1.003	1.017	0.999	0.908	0.995	0.912
100	q = 1	0.921	1.172	0.892	1.036	0.892	1.037	0.921	1.173	0.892	1.036	0.891	1.036
	q = 3	0.902	1.065	0.871	0.975	0.871	0.974	0.900	1.063	0.871	0.975	0.870	0.973
	HQ	0.942	1.092	0.920	0.977	0.922	0.979	0.942	1.099	0.918	0.982	0.917	0.981
200	q = 1	0.932	1.160	0.902	1.026	0.902	1.025	0.932	1.160	0.902	1.026	0.902	1.026
	q = 3	0.924	1.061	0.895	0.972	0.894	0.974	0.924	1.062	0.895	0.973	0.894	0.973
	HQ	0.933	1.045	0.903	0.951	0.902	0.952	0.933	1.049	0.903	0.953	0.903	0.952
500	q = 1	0.938	1.153	0.907	1.020	0.907	1.020	0.938	1.154	0.907	1.021	0.907	1.020
	q = 3	0.936	1.062	0.906	0.974	0.906	0.974	0.937	1.062	0.906	0.974	0.906	0.973
	HQ	0.939	1.022	0.908	0.944	0.908	0.944	0.940	1.022	0.909	0.945	0.909	0.945
T							N = 100						
50	q = 1	0.897	1.208	0.873	1.068	0.872	1.066	0.897	1.201	0.873	1.063	0.872	1.062
	q = 3	0.834	1.074	0.808	0.993	0.807	0.989	0.834	1.055	0.808	0.973	0.808	0.972
	HQ	1.023	1.069	1.015	0.947	1.016	0.945	1.013	1.057	1.011	0.938	1.011	0.941
100	q = 1	0.925	1.173	0.898	1.036	0.898	1.036	0.923	1.171	0.897	1.035	0.896	1.035
	q = 3	0.903	1.062	0.875	0.972	0.876	0.973	0.903	1.062	0.876	0.973	0.876	0.973
	HQ	0.946	1.094	0.924	0.978	0.924	0.979	0.945	1.093	0.924	0.979	0.923	0.978
200	q = 1	0.936	1.159	0.908	1.023	0.908	1.025	0.937	1.160	0.908	1.025	0.908	1.025
	q = 3	0.929	1.063	0.900	0.971	0.900	0.971	0.927	1.060	0.899	0.971	0.899	0.972
	HQ	0.937	1.047	0.909	0.952	0.908	0.952	0.938	1.046	0.909	0.951	0.910	0.952
500	q = 1	0.943	1.153	0.914	1.020	0.914	1.020	0.943	1.154	0.913	1.020	0.913	1.019
	q = 3	0.941	1.061	0.912	0.972	0.912	0.972	0.940	1.060	0.912	0.972	0.912	0.973
	HQ	0.943	1.022	0.913	0.942	0.913	0.943	0.943	1.020	0.914	0.942	0.913	0.942
T							N = 200						
50	q = 1	0.900	1.212	0.874	1.067	0.874	1.068	0.900	1.206	0.876	1.067	0.875	1.067
	q = 3	0.834	1.075	0.814	0.994	0.814	0.992	0.836	1.075	0.810	0.990	0.810	0.990
	HQ	1.012	1.072	1.009	0.953	1.006	0.949	1.008	1.061	1.004	0.941	1.006	0.945
100	q = 1	0.926	1.174	0.900	1.035	0.900	1.034	0.926	1.172	0.900	1.035	0.900	1.036
	q = 3	0.904	1.060	0.875	0.967	0.876	0.972	0.905	1.062	0.879	0.973	0.879	0.972
	HQ	0.946	1.088	0.925	0.974	0.925	0.974	0.950	1.095	0.929	0.980	0.929	0.980
200	q = 1	0.938	1.158	0.910	1.024	0.911	1.024	0.938	1.159	0.911	1.024	0.911	1.025
	q = 3	0.930	1.059	0.903	0.971	0.903	0.970	0.929	1.060	0.902	0.970	0.903	0.971
	HQ	0.937	1.043	0.909	0.949	0.910	0.948	0.938	1.043	0.910	0.949	0.911	0.950
500	q = 1	0.945	1.154	0.917	1.019	0.917	1.019	0.944	1.152	0.916	1.019	0.916	1.019
	q = 3	0.942	1.060	0.915	0.971	0.916	0.972	0.942	1.061	0.915	0.972	0.916	0.972
	HQ	0.944	1.019	0.915	0.941	0.915	0.941	0.944	1.020	0.917	0.942	0.916	0.942

k_estim

N = 50 T	FECM SW	FAVAR SW	N = 100 T	FECM SW	FAVAR SW	N = 200 T	FECM SW	FAVAR SW
50	1	1.607	50	1	1.203	50	1	1.011
100	1	1.002	100	1	1	100	1	1
200	1	1	200	1	1	200	1	1
500	1	1	500	1	1	500	1	1

Notes: See notes to Table 9.1.

Table 9.3. Results for DGP 3

Ratios of Residual Variances

		A: Number of factors imposed						B: Number of factors estimated					
		Equation 1		Equation 2		Equation 3		Equation 1		Equation 2		Equation 3	
	lags	FECM SW	FAVAR SW	FECM SW	FAVAR SW	FECM SW	FAVAR SW	FECM SW	FAVAR SW	FECM SW	FAVAR SW	FECM SW	FAVAR SW
T						N = 50							
50	q = 1	0.850	1.027	0.919	1.103	0.934	1.125	0.814	0.964	0.881	1.006	0.914	1.010
	q = 3	0.825	1.009	0.858	1.029	0.865	1.041	0.717	0.798	0.749	0.802	0.760	0.802
	HQ	0.988	0.947	1.060	1.003	1.072	1.019	0.974	0.804	1.038	0.823	1.115	0.825
100	q = 1	0.860	0.999	0.944	1.076	0.962	1.096	0.850	0.966	0.920	1.007	0.965	1.008
	q = 3	0.894	0.991	0.934	1.022	0.945	1.038	0.844	0.905	0.883	0.910	0.900	0.911
	HQ	0.935	0.927	1.003	0.984	1.020	1.005	0.931	0.908	0.993	0.936	1.075	0.942
200	q = 1	0.880	0.994	0.956	1.070	0.975	1.087	0.877	0.971	0.952	1.001	0.977	1.001
	q = 3	0.919	0.991	0.961	1.024	0.972	1.037	0.911	0.943	0.953	0.941	0.966	0.939
	HQ	0.938	0.940	0.996	0.987	1.011	1.004	0.933	0.928	0.991	0.935	1.017	0.936
500	q = 1	0.887	0.992	0.963	1.068	0.983	1.084	0.887	0.975	0.963	0.981	0.983	0.975
	q = 3	0.932	0.991	0.974	1.026	0.985	1.039	0.932	0.964	0.975	0.947	0.985	0.936
	HQ	0.944	0.965	0.992	1.003	1.003	1.016	0.943	0.959	0.991	0.929	1.003	0.916
T						N = 100							
50	q = 1	0.856	1.028	0.922	1.104	0.936	1.126	0.831	0.971	0.896	1.014	0.926	1.017
	q = 3	0.823	1.006	0.859	1.040	0.865	1.054	0.743	0.811	0.774	0.809	0.784	0.812
	HQ	0.999	0.950	1.064	1.008	1.077	1.025	0.984	0.791	1.046	0.814	1.114	0.815
100	q = 1	0.875	1.001	0.945	1.080	0.963	1.100	0.871	0.972	0.942	1.017	0.964	1.019
	q = 3	0.898	0.988	0.935	1.025	0.944	1.040	0.888	0.908	0.925	0.915	0.937	0.918
	HQ	0.938	0.922	1.003	0.984	1.020	1.004	0.941	0.904	1.004	0.938	1.033	0.944
200	q = 1	0.885	0.995	0.957	1.077	0.976	1.094	0.886	0.978	0.957	1.020	0.976	1.020
	q = 3	0.923	0.986	0.961	1.025	0.972	1.041	0.924	0.948	0.962	0.954	0.972	0.956
	HQ	0.942	0.936	0.997	0.987	1.011	1.005	0.941	0.923	0.997	0.944	1.011	0.949
500	q = 1	0.892	0.993	0.965	1.074	0.984	1.091	0.892	0.981	0.964	1.008	0.984	1.005
	q = 3	0.937	0.988	0.976	1.027	0.986	1.042	0.938	0.967	0.976	0.963	0.986	0.959
	HQ	0.949	0.961	0.993	1.003	1.004	1.018	0.949	0.945	0.993	0.941	1.004	0.937
T						N = 200							
50	q = 1	0.857	1.030	0.921	1.108	0.934	1.131	0.855	0.981	0.919	1.027	0.934	1.038
	q = 3	0.828	1.007	0.860	1.038	0.867	1.057	0.813	0.842	0.844	0.851	0.851	0.855
	HQ	1.000	0.946	1.064	1.010	1.075	1.029	1.002	0.820	1.060	0.847	1.081	0.853
100	q = 1	0.875	1.000	0.945	1.083	0.962	1.104	0.876	0.977	0.946	1.030	0.963	1.035
	q = 3	0.902	0.987	0.937	1.026	0.946	1.044	0.899	0.917	0.935	0.930	0.944	0.935
	HQ	0.941	0.921	1.004	0.986	1.021	1.009	0.945	0.904	1.008	0.938	1.022	0.945
200	q = 1	0.887	0.995	0.958	1.079	0.976	1.097	0.888	0.981	0.958	1.028	0.976	1.028
	q = 3	0.925	0.984	0.962	1.024	0.972	1.042	0.925	0.948	0.962	0.956	0.972	0.958
	HQ	0.945	0.935	0.998	0.988	1.012	1.007	0.945	0.923	0.998	0.945	1.011	0.949
500	q = 1	0.895	0.993	0.966	1.077	0.984	1.094	0.894	0.984	0.965	1.024	0.984	1.022
	q = 3	0.940	0.986	0.977	1.027	0.986	1.044	0.939	0.968	0.977	0.973	0.986	0.973
	HQ	0.951	0.959	0.993	1.002	1.004	1.019	0.951	0.952	0.993	0.952	1.004	0.951

k_estim

N = 50 T	FECM SW	FAVAR SW	N = 100 T	FECM SW	FAVAR SW	N = 200 T	FECM SW	FAVAR SW
50	1.9952	3.046	50	1.8387	2.9871	50	1.1446	2.6085
100	1.9638	3	100	1.1969	2.995	100	1.0004	2.7457
200	1.1718	3	200	1	3	200	1	2.9752
500	1	3	500	1	3	500	1	3

Notes: See notes to Table 9.1.

Hannan–Quinn criterion, labelled *HQ* in the tables. We will refer to the two panels of Table 9.1 as Tables 9.1A and 9.1B. Tables 9.2A and 9.2B and Tables 9.3A and 9.3B report the corresponding results for DGP 2 and DGP 3 respectively. The average number of estimated factors (k_estim) is also reported in each table.

The results emerge with a great deal of clarity. For DGP 1, which is the simplest DGP, Table 9.1A indicates that FECM clearly dominates ECM and FAVAR, with gains typically in the range of 12% to 17%. In some cases the gain is even higher (in the order of 23%) especially where $T = 50$ (for almost all values of N) and the model includes 3 lags of the differenced dependent variable. FAVAR is often not better than ECM, except when T is large and selection of the lag length is by the Hannan–Quinn criterion which favours a lag-length selection of 3 or more in cases where the gains of FAVAR over ECM is the largest (for example where $T = 200$ or 500). The dominance of FECM however remains, and even when there are gains of FAVAR over ECM these are much smaller than those observed for FECM, ie in the neighbourhood of 5% in the best cases. Losing the long run, by estimating the model in differences, is a major loss for the fit of the equations which is a finding which matches quite precisely our predictions from the theory above. These results hold both when the number of factors is assumed to be known and when they are estimated (Table 9.1B), since, given that the data are generated with 1 factor imposed, the k_estim panel shows that the number of factors is chosen with high precision. When lag-length selection is undertaken using HQ, FECM and ECM are typically estimated without lags while FAVAR models include two or three lags. In this sense, by allowing for richer dynamics, HQ selection favours the FAVAR approach in comparison to the FECM, but is nevertheless insufficient to dilute the dominance of FECM.

For DGP 2, where the system for the first four variables is still self-contained (in the sense of there not being any extra cointegrating information coming from the rest of the system) but there is idiosyncratic cointegration, FECM continues to dominate FAVAR with the best results arising when q is set to 3. However, the gains are systematically smaller than for DGP 1. As in DGP 1, except when favoured by generous lag-length selection, FAVAR is again worse than ECM for a sizeable fraction of cases.

For DGP 3, where each model under comparison is misspecified and our theoretical analysis leads us to anticipate difficulties, there is an interesting dominance of FECM over the other models. However, the size of the gains from FECM depends on the equation estimated. These are noticeable particularly for equation 1, where the gains are seen to be as large as 28%, although gains around 15% are more typical. For equations 2 and 3, the gains are in the neighbourhood of 5% other than in exceptional cases. The comparison between FAVAR and ECM is generally much more ambiguous, with FAVAR occasionally performing approximately 10% worse than ECM, for example when lag-length is fixed at 1, while HQ as usual favours a greater lag length and hence improved performance of FAVAR in terms of fit. The panel labelled k_estim now shows much less precision concerning the estimation of the number of factors especially for FAVAR where the more complicated cointegrating information in the DGP leads to the choice of 3 (dynamic) factors. This is in marked contrast to the corresponding results for DGP 1 and 2 presented previously.

Overall, the simulation results suggest that the FECM provides an excellent modelling choice, even in difficult circumstances. However, the best test of its performance is with real economic data which we consider in the next section of the chapter.

9.5 Empirical Examples

In this section we present two empirical examples as illustrations of the theoretical and simulation results presented above. The first example analyses the relationships among US interest rates at different maturities, and among them and macroeconomic variables, an issue that is receiving increasing attention in the literature, see e.g. Diebold, Rudebusch, and Arouba (2006) and the references therein. The second example reconsiders the famous article by King *et al.* (1991) on stochastic trends and economic fluctuations in the US economy.

In both examples, the factors are estimated from a large set of 110 monthly US macroeconomic variables, extracted from the data set given in Stock and Watson (2005). The time span of the data series is 1959:1 to 2003:12, although for our examples we look only at a smaller interval, starting in 1985. We focus on the post-1985 period, both to consider a homogenous monetary policy regime and to avoid the potentially problematic effects of the great moderation on factor estimation. The data series as well as the transformations implemented are listed in Table 9.4.

The number of factors is estimated using the criteria in Bai (2004) for the I(1) case, and in Bai and Ng (2002) for the stationary case. Specifically, as in the simulations, we use their $IPC2$ and $PC2$ criteria respectively, which seem to have better finite sample properties.

Note that it is not the purpose of the estimation methodology proposed to identify the factors (which are incorporated in the FECM), since the estimated factors are not invariant to rotations of the space of factors. Instead, the factors proxy for and provide independent information on common trends, missing from both the standard ECM and the FAVAR. In particular, since the factors are orthogonal to each other they cannot be cointegrated—ie the additional cointegrating relations cannot simply be I(0) combinations of the factors being added, since such combinations are by construction impossible.

Table 9.4. Data set for the empirical examples

Code	Short Descrip.	Nom	Real	Fin	Tcode I(0) data set	Tcode I(1) data set
a0m052	PI	0	1	0	5	4
A0M051	PI less transfers	0	1	0	5	4
A0M224_R	Consumption	0	1	0	5	4
A0M057	M&T sales	0	1	0	5	4
A0M059	Retail sales	0	1	0	5	4
IPS10	IP: total	0	1	0	5	4
IPS11	IP: products	0	1	0	5	4
IPS299	IP: final prod	0	1	0	5	4
IPS12	IP: cons gds	0	1	0	5	4
IPS13	IP: cons dble	0	1	0	5	4
IPS18	IP: cons nondble	0	1	0	5	4
IPS25	IP: bus eqpt	0	1	0	5	4
IPS32	IP: matls	0	1	0	5	4
IPS34	IP: dble mats	0	1	0	5	4
IPS38	IP: nondble mats	0	1	0	5	4
IPS43	IP: mfg	0	1	0	5	4
IPS307	IP: res util	0	1	0	5	4
IPS306	IP: fuels	0	1	0	5	4
PMP	NAPM prodn	0	1	0	1	1
A0m082	Cap util	0	1	0	2	1
LHEL	Help wanted indx	0	1	0	2	1
LHELX	Help wanted/emp	0	1	0	2	1
LHEM	Emp CPS total	0	1	0	5	4
LHNAG	Emp CPS nonag	0	1	0	5	4
LHUR	U: all	0	1	0	2	1
LHU680	U: mean duration	0	1	0	2	1
LHU5	U < 5 wks	0	1	0	5	4
LHU14	U 5–14 wks	0	1	0	5	4
LHU15	U 15+ wks	0	1	0	5	4
LHU26	U 15–26 wks	0	1	0	5	4
LHU27	U 27+ wks	0	1	0	5	4
A0M005	UI claims	0	1	0	5	4
CES002	Emp: total	0	1	0	5	4
CES003	Emp: gds prod	0	1	0	5	4
CES006	Emp: mining	0	1	0	5	4
CES011	Emp: const	0	1	0	5	4
CES015	Emp: mfg	0	1	0	5	4
CES017	Emp: dble gds	0	1	0	5	4
CES033	Emp: nondbles	0	1	0	5	4
CES046	Emp: services	0	1	0	5	4
CES048	Emp: TTU	0	1	0	5	4
CES049	Emp: wholesale	0	1	0	5	4
CES053	Emp: retail	0	1	0	5	4
CES088	Emp: FIRE	0	1	0	5	4
CES140	Emp: Govt	0	1	0	5	4
A0M048	Emp-hrs nonag	0	1	0	5	4
CES151	Avg hrs	0	1	0	1	1
CES155	Overtime: mfg	0	1	0	2	1
aom001	Avg hrs: mfg	0	1	0	1	1
PMEMP	NAPM empl	0	1	0	1	1
HSFR	HStarts: Total	0	1	0	4	4
HSNE	HStarts: NE	0	1	0	4	4
HSMW	HStarts: MW	0	1	0	4	4
HSSOU	HStarts: South	0	1	0	4	4
HSWST	HStarts: West	0	1	0	4	4
HSBR	BP: total	0	1	0	4	4

Table 9.4. (*Continued*)

HSBNE	BP: NE	0	1	0	4	4
HSBMW	BP: MW	0	1	0	4	4
HSBSOU	BP: South	0	1	0	4	4
HSBWST	BP: West	0	1	0	4	4
PMI	PMI	0	1	0	1	1
PMNO	NAPM new orders	0	1	0	1	1
PMDEL	NAPM vendor del	0	1	0	1	1
PMNV	NAPM Invent	0	1	0	1	1
A0M008	Orders: cons gds	0	1	0	5	4
A0M007	Orders: dble gds	0	1	0	5	4
A0M027	Orders: cap gds	0	1	0	5	4
A1M092	Unf orders: dble	0	1	0	5	4
A0M070	M&T invent	0	1	0	5	4
A0M077	M&T invent/sales	0	1	0	2	1
FM1	M1	1	0	0	6	5
FM2	M2	1	0	0	6	5
FM3	M3	1	0	0	6	5
FM2DQ	M2 (real)	1	0	0	5	4
FMFBA	MB	1	0	0	6	5
FMRRA	Reserves tot	1	0	0	6	5
FMRNBA	Reserves nonbor	1	0	0	6	5
FCLNQ	C&I loans	1	0	0	6	5
FCLBMC	C&I loans	1	0	0	1	1
CCINRV	Cons credit	1	0	0	6	5
A0M095	Inst cred/PI	1	0	0	2	1
FYFF	FedFunds	0	0	1	2	1
FYGM3	3 mo T-bill	0	0	1	2	1
FYGT1	1 yr T-bond	0	0	1	2	1
FYGT10	10 yr T-bond	0	0	1	2	1
PWFSA	PPI: fin gds	1	0	0	6	5
PWFCSA	PPI: cons gds	1	0	0	6	5
PWIMSA	PPI: int mat'ls	1	0	0	6	5
PWCMSA	PPI: crude mat'ls	1	0	0	6	5
PSCCOM	Commod: spot price	1	0	0	6	5
PSM99Q	Sens mat'ls price	1	0	0	6	5
PMCP	NAPM com price	1	0	0	1	1
PUNEW	CPI-U: all	1	0	0	6	5
PU83	CPI-U: apparel	1	0	0	6	5
PU84	CPI-U: transp	1	0	0	6	5
PU85	CPI-U: medica	1	0	0	6	5
PUC	CPI-U: comm.	1	0	0	6	5
PUCD	CPI-U: dbles	1	0	0	6	5
PUS	CPI-U: service:	1	0	0	6	5
PUXF	CPI-U: ex food	1	0	0	6	5
PUXHS	CPI-U: ex shelter	1	0	0	6	5
PUXM	CPI-U: ex med	1	0	0	6	5
GMDC	PCE defl	1	0	0	6	5
GMDCD	PCE defl: dbles	1	0	0	6	5
GMDCN	PCE defl: nondble	1	0	0	6	5
GMDCS	PCE defl: services	1	0	0	6	5
CES275	AHE: goods	1	0	0	6	5
CES277	AHE: const	1	0	0	6	5
CES278	AHE: mfg	1	0	0	6	5
HHSNTN	Consumer expect	0	1	0	2	1

Notes: Transformation codes: 1 no transformation; 2 first difference; 3 second difference; 4 logarithm; 5 first difference of logarithm; 6 second difference of logarithm. Data set extracted from Stock and Watson (2005). Sample is 1985:1–2003:12.

For each model, we report the standard R^2, the adjusted R^2 and also the AIC and BIC criteria, in order to provide sufficient information for a comparison of the within-sample performance of each model. In addition, in order to assess the performance of these models in a forecasting context, we also report the MSFE and mean absolute error (MAE) for 1-step-ahead forecasts over the evaluation sample 1999:1–2003:12.

We provide a summary of the results in the two panels of Table 9.5, which will be called Tables 9.5A and 9.5B, with further details available from us upon request.

9.5.1 *Interest Rates at Different Maturities*

We focus on four interest rates: the fed-fund, the 3-month t-bill rate, and the 1- and 10-year bond rates. Thus, in the notation of section 9.2, $N_A = 4$. Over the sample under analysis, the variables tend to move closely together, with some more persistent deviations for the 10-year bond rate.

Empirically, the hypothesis of a unit root cannot be rejected for any series, using a standard ADF test with AIC or BIC lag-length selection. The interesting issue is whether and how many cointegrating relationships there are among the four rates. From a theoretical point of view, the expectational theory of the term structure implies the existence of 3 cointegrating vectors. However, when cointegration is tested with the Johansen (1988) trace statistic in a VAR with AIC or BIC lag-length selection, only two cointegrating vectors are detected (more formally, the hypothesis of at most one cointegrating vector is rejected), at the conventional 10% level. This result, $r_A = 2$ in the notation of section 9.2, does not change either with the addition of a lag in the VAR to capture possible serial correlation in the residuals, or when using the maximum eigenvalue version of the test.

The fit of the resulting ECM model, which corresponds to equation (9.9), is summarized in the first row of the first panel of Table 9.5A.

A possible rationale for the finding of two cointegrating vectors among the four rates is that the interest rate spreads are likely driven by the evolution of the economic fundamentals, and omitting these variables from the analysis can spuriously decrease the number of cointegrating vectors. To evaluate whether this is the case, we have enlarged the information set with the estimated factors from the nonstationary large data set (that includes the 110 variables less the 4 rates, i.e. $N = 110$ and $N_B = 106$), and jointly modelled the rates and the factors with a FECM, which corresponds to equation (9.8).

The Bai (2004) criterion suggests a single factor is sufficient to summarize the information in the whole data set, but since it instead indicates the need for four factors for the subset of real variables (one for the nominal variables), and omitting relevant variables in the FECM is problematic, we prefer to proceed with four factors. In this case, the AIC and BIC criteria for lag-length determination indicate either 3 or 1 lags in the VAR for the rates and the estimated factors, and again we prefer the less parsimonious specification to protect from omitted variable bias and serial correlation in the residuals.

For the FECM, the Johansen trace test indicates 4 cointegrating vectors. This is in line with the theoretical prediction of section 9.2 that we should find in the FECM a cointegrating rank equal to N_A. The fit of the resulting FECM is summarized in the second row of Table 9.5A. There is a systematic increase both in R^2 and in the adjusted R^2 with respect to the ECM and, interestingly, the gains increase with the maturity.

Finally, we evaluate a FAVAR model, where the changes in the variables are regressed on their own lags and on lags of estimated factors, using two lags of each regressor as suggested by the information criteria. More precisely, the $N_B = 106$ macroeconomic variables plus the $N_A = 4$ interest rates are assumed to depend on a set of common factors and on an idiosyncratic error. Each variable is properly transformed to achieve stationarity; in particular, the interest rates are first differenced. The factors are estimated as the principal components of the (stationary) variables, while we recall that the factors in the FECM are extracted from the variables in levels. The Bai and Ng (2002) criterion indicates six factors.

From the third row of Table 9.5A it may be seen that both the R^2 and the adjusted R^2 of the FAVAR are lower than those of the FECM for each of the four interest rates (even though the FECM uses only four factors). The strongest gains from the FECM arise from looking at the 10-year bond rate, which is in some sense an intuitive result given that long-run movements of the stock market are likely to be very relevant for this variable.

The second panel of Table 9.5A provides information on the computed AIC and BIC for the three models. The AIC ranking is very coherent with that reported in the first panel, while the BIC, which puts a stronger penalty on over-parametrization, prefers the more parsimonious ECM for 3-month and 10-year maturities.

The findings so far confirm empirically that it is important to take cointegration into account. Moreover, we recall that in the presence of cointegration the errors of the model for Δx_t are not invertible, so that they cannot be approximated by an AR process, as in the FAVAR, at least from a theoretical point of view.

The results reported in the third panel of Table 9.5A are, as expected, more ambiguous with respect to the efficacy of FECM models in a forecasting context. Comparisons of the (one-step ahead) MSFE and MAE criteria show that either the standard ECM and FECM provide better forecasts than FAVAR for each maturity. The comparison between the ECM and FECM is more mixed, attributable perhaps to the fact that the factor space is estimated and

Table 9.5. Empirical analyses

A - Alternative models for interest rates

	FF	3m	1y	10y	FF	3m	1y	10y
		R^2				Adjusted R^2		
ECM (1 lag, 2 coint.)	0.41	0.31	0.23	0.11	0.40	0.29	0.21	0.09
FECM (2 lags, 4 facs-lev, 4 coint.)	0.49	0.42	0.40	0.31	0.44	0.36	0.34	0.24
FAVAR (2 lags, 6 facs)	0.46	0.41	0.37	0.25	0.41	0.35	0.31	0.17
		AIC				BIC		
ECM (1 lag, 2 coint.)	−0.42	−0.52	0.09	0.14	−0.29	−0.39	0.22	0.27
FECM (2 lags, 4 facs-lev, 4 coint.)	−0.65	−0.65	−0.18	0.00	−0.33	−0.33	0.14	0.32
FAVAR (2 lags, 6 facs)	−0.59	−0.63	−0.14	0.09	−0.27	−0.32	0.18	0.41
		MSFE				MAE		
ECM (1 lag, 2 coint.)	0.016	0.031	0.043	0.069	0.098	0.135	0.162	0.211
FECM (2 lags, 4 facs-lev, 4 coint.)	0.033	0.023	0.037	0.101	0.146	0.119	0.155	0.249
FAVAR (2 lags, 6 facs)	0.024	0.032	0.046	0.087	0.133	0.143	0.171	0.239

Notes: FF is the federal fund rate while 3m, 1y, and 10y are, respectively, three month, 1 year, and 10 year treasury bill rates.
Information criteria are defined as minus log likelihood plus penalty function, hence should be minimized.
MSFE and MAE are for 1-step ahead forecasts (for interest rates in levels) over the sample 1999:1–2003:12.

B - Alternative models for the KPSW example

	C	PI	M	Ri	C	PI	M	Ri
		R^2				Adjusted R^2		
ECM (1 lag, 2 coint.)	0.16	0.13	0.32	0.38	0.13	0.10	0.30	0.36
FECM (2 lags, 4 facs-lev, 4 coint.)	0.28	0.18	0.50	0.47	0.21	0.10	0.45	0.41
FAVAR (2 lags, 6 facs)	0.26	0.18	0.40	0.37	0.19	0.10	0.34	0.31
		AIC				BIC		
ECM (1 lag, 2 coint.)	−7.78	−7.54	−8.65	4.33	−7.68	−7.43	−8.55	4.44
FECM (2 lags, 4 facs-lev, 4 coint.)	−7.81	−7.49	−8.85	4.31	−7.49	−7.17	−8.53	4.62
FAVAR (2 lags, 6 facs)	−7.79	−7.47	−8.66	4.47	−7.47	−7.15	−8.33	4.79
		MSFE				MAE		
ECM (1 lag, 2 coint.)	0.180	0.338	0.246	27.010	0.332	0.506	0.324	3.985
FECM (2 lags, 4 facs-lev, 4 coint.)	0.309	0.124	0.216	34.906	0.427	0.279	0.322	4.464
FAVAR (2 lags, 6 facs)	0.243	0.141	0.224	9.363	0.376	0.295	0.316	2.369

Notes: C is per capita real consumption, PI per capita real personal income, M real money, and Ri real interest rate.
Information criteria are defined as minus log likelihood plus penalty function, hence should be minimized.
MSFE and MAE are for 1-step ahead forecasts of growth in C, PI, M, and change in Ri over the sample 1999:1–2003:12.
MSFEs for C, PI, and M are multiplied by 10000, MAE by 100.

may thus be susceptible to the presence of structural breaks (which are of course important for forecasting and are not taken account of here). In future research it would be interesting to consider modifications of the FECM model to take account of structural breaks—along the lines of a differenced FECM model (DFECM) to correspond to the Hendry (2006) formulation of a DVECM model described briefly in the introduction, in order to allow for change in the cointegrating or equilibrium information that may have occurred.

9.5.2 *Stochastic Trends and Economic Fluctuations*

As a second example, we consider an updated and slightly simplified version of the model in King *et al.* (1991) henceforth KPSW. KPSW analysed a system with 6 variables at the quarterly frequency, over the period 1949–1988: per capita real consumption, per capita gross private fixed investment, per capita 'private' gross national product, money supply, inflation, and a short term interest rate. They detected three cointegrating vectors, which they identified as a money demand function (where real money depends on GNP and the interest rate), a consumption equation (where the ratio of consumption to GNP depends on the real interest rate), and an investment equation (where the ratio of investment to GNP depends on the real interest rate).

Since we have monthly time-series, we focus on four variables ($N_A = 4$): real consumption (C), real personal income (PI), real money (M), and real interest rate (Ri), where the first three variables are expressed in logs. We consider again the sample 1985–2003, and focus on three models: ECM, FECM, and FAVAR.[7]

The AIC and BIC criteria select 2 lags in the VAR, and in this case the Johansen trace test detects two cointegrating vectors, ie $r_A = 2$ (more formally, the hypothesis of at most one cointegrating vector is rejected), at the conventional 10% level. The cointegrating vectors are similar to the money demand and consumption equations of KPSW, except that personal income appears not to matter in the former. The fit of the resulting ECM model (the counterpart of the theoretical equation (9.9)) is summarized in the first row of the first panel of Table 9.5B.

We then enlarge the information set with the estimated factors from the nonstationary large data set (that includes the $N = 110$ variables less the $N_A = 4$ variables included in the ECM), and jointly model the four variables and the factors with a FECM (equation (9.8)). As in the previous example, and not surprisingly since the data are mostly the same, the Bai (2004) criterion suggests a single factor but it indicates four factors for the subset of real variables. Therefore, we proceed with four factors. In this case, the AIC and BIC criteria for lag-length determination indicate either 3 or 2 lags in the extended VAR and, as in the previous example, we prefer the less parsimonious specification to protect from omitted variable bias and serial correlation in the residuals. In this case, the Johansen trace test suggests 4 cointegrating vectors, two more than the standard ECM. This result is again in line with the theoretical prediction of rank equal to N_A. The fit of the resulting FECM is summarized in the second row of Table 9.5B.

As in the previous example, the performance of the FAVAR is slightly but systematically worse than that of the FECM, which also dominates the ECM

[7] Comparable results are obtained in a five variable system where the real interest rate is split into the nominal rate and the inflation rate.

in terms of fit.[8] This further reinforces the message that it is important to take cointegration between the variables and the factors explicitly into consideration.

The results reported in the second panel of Table 9.5B show that the ranking of the models is virtually unaltered according to the AIC, while, as in the case of the previous empirical example, the BIC prefers the more parsimonious ECM in most cases.

The final panel of Table 9.5B reports more mixed results when the models are used for one-step ahead forecasting. In particular, the FAVAR is best for the real interest rate, the ECM for real consumption, and the FECM for personal income and real money. Also in this case the mixed results could be related to the presence of structural breaks, and as above, research into robustifying the FECM to the presence of such breaks is an important element of our future research.

9.6 Conclusions

In this chapter we study modelling a large set of variables linked by cointegration relationships. This is a very important topic both from a theoretical point of view and for empirical applications. Early studies, such as Stock and Watson (1988), show that (the levels of) each cointegrated variable is driven by a limited number of common integrated trends plus an idiosyncratic stationary error term. Therefore, the variables in levels can be represented as a factor model, where orthogonality between the common and the idiosyncratic components is guaranteed by the fact that the former is integrated while the latter is stationary by construction.

A first result of this chapter is to notice that, in general, the factor structure is lost when the differences of the variables are modelled. In fact, even though the first differences of the factors are driving all the variables, they are no longer necessarily orthogonal to the 'idiosyncratic' errors. Moreover, even when the factors are orthogonal to the idiosyncratic errors, the latter are non-invertible processes. While this is not a problem for factor estimation, the presence of non-invertible errors does not allow autoregressive approximations of the factor model, FAVAR, which are instead commonly used in the literature.

The presence of the non-invertible errors in the model for the variables in differences is related to the omission of the error correction terms. Hence, we introduce the FECM which requires us to summarize the information in the (levels of the) large set of variables with a limited number of factors,

[8] The Bai and Ng (2002) criteria indicate again six factors (extracted from the 106 macroeconomic variables plus the four variables under analysis in this example, after a proper transformation of each variable to achieve stationarity).

and then to model jointly the factors and the variables of interest with a cointegrated VAR.

The FECM improves upon the standard small scale ECM by protecting from omitted variable bias both in the long run and in the short run. It also improves upon the FAVAR model by taking long-run restrictions into explicit account. However, the FECM remains an approximation, which is expected to work well only under certain conditions, in particular when the few variables of interest are influenced by a limited number of error correction terms.

Both Monte Carlo experiments and empirical analyses show that the FECM often performs better than ECM and FAVAR models.

To conclude, we believe that the FECM represents an interesting modelling approach, and a natural generalization of the FAVAR (to include long-run information) and the ECM (to include information from a large set of *cointegrated* variables). Because of this, the FECM is of potential use in a wide range of empirical analyses.

References

Bai, J. (2004). Estimating cross-section common stochastic trends in nonstationary panel data. *Journal of Econometrics*, **122**, 137–183.

——and Ng, S. (2002). Determining the number of factors in approximate factor models. *Econometrica*, **70**, 191–221.

————(2004). A PANIC attack on unit roots and cointegration. *Econometrica*, **72**, 1127–1177.

————(2006). Confidence intervals for diffusion index forecasts with a large number of predictors and inference for factor-augmented regressions. *Econometrica*, **74**, 1133–1150.

——Kao, C., and Ng, S. (2007). Panel cointegration with global stochastic trends. Center for Policy Research Working Paper No. 90, Syracuse University.

Banerjee, A. and Carrion-i-Silvestre, J. (2007). Cointegration in panel data with breaks and cross-section dependence. Mimeo.

——Marcellino, M., and Osbat, C. (2004). Some cautions on the use of panel methods for integrated series of macroeconomic data. *Econometrics Journal*, **7**, 322–340.

Bernanke, B. S., Boivin, J. and Eliasz, P. (2005). Measuring the effects of monetary policy: A factor-augmented vector autoregressive (FAVAR) approach. *Quarterly Journal of Economics*, **120**, 387–422.

Breitung, J. and Das, S. (2005). Panel unit root tests under cross-sectional dependence. *Statistica Neerlandica*, **59**, 414–433.

————(2008). Testing for unit roots in panels with a factor structure. *Econometric Theory*, **24**, 88–108.

Clements, M. P. and Hendry, D. F. (1995). Forecasting in cointegrated systems. *Journal of Applied Econometrics*, **10**, 127–146.

Davidson, J. E. H., Hendry, D. F., Srba, F., and Yeo, J. S. (1978). Econometric modelling of the aggregate time-series relationship between consumers' expenditure and income in the United Kingdom. *Economic Journal*, **88**, 661–692.

Diebold, F. X., Rudebusch, G., and Arouba, S. B. (2006). The macroeconomy and the yield curve: A dynamic latent variable approach. *Journal of Econometrics*, **131**, 309–338.

Engle, R. F. and Granger, C. W. (1987). Co-integration and error correction: Representation, estimation and testing. *Econometrica*, **55**, 257–276.

——and Kozicki, S. (1993). Testing for common features. *Journal of Business and Economic Statistics*, **11**, 369–390.

Favero, C., Marcellino, M., and Neglia, F. (2005). Principal components at work: The empirical analysis of monetary policy with large data sets. *Journal of Applied Econometrics*, **20**, 603–620.

Forni, M., Hallin, M., Lippi, M., and Reichlin, L. (2000). The generalized dynamic-factor model. *Review of Economics and Statistics*, **82**, 540–554.

————————(2005). The generalized dynamic factor model. *Journal of the American Statistical Association*, **100**, 830–840.

Hendry, D. F. (2006). Robustifying forecasts from equilibrium-correction systems. *Journal of Econometrics*, **135**, 399–426.

Johansen, S. (1988). Statistical analysis of cointegration vectors. *Journal of Economic Dynamics and Control*, **12**, 231–254.

——(1995). *Likelihood-Based Inference in Cointegrated Vector Autoregressive Models*. Oxford and New York: Oxford University Press.

King, R. G., Plosser, C. I., Stock, J. H. and Watson, M. W. (1991). Stochastic trends and economic fluctuations. *American Economic Review*, **81**, 819–840.

Pesaran, M. H. (2006). Estimation and inference in large heterogeneous panels with a multifactor error structure. *Econometrica*, **74**, 967–1012.

Stock, J. H. and Watson, M. W. (1998). Testing for common trends. *Journal of the American Statistical Association*, **83**, 1097–1107.

————(2002a). Forecasting using principal components from a large number of predictors. *Journal of the American Statistical Association*, **97**, 1167–1179.

————(2002b). Macroeconomic forecasting using diffusion indexes. *Journal of Business and Economic Statistics*, **20**, 147–162.

————(2005). Implication of dynamic factor models for VAR analysis. NBER Working Paper 11467.

10

In Praise of Pragmatics in Econometrics

Clive W. J. Granger

10.1 Some Initial Thoughts

A great deal of econometric literature, both textbooks and journal articles, start off with a set of formal assumptions, or axioms, and then derive theories and specific models. When these models are applied to actual economic data these models are often fitted without checking if the assumptions hold for the data. It is quite common to find problems with the model, possibly because of failure of the assumptions.

When the original model is inadequate, there are various *ad hoc* changes that can be considered to get to a model that is both acceptable and useful. This is the basic example of pragmatic econometrics, which is the topic of this discussion.

A definition of 'pragmatics' is just being 'concerned with practical consequences or values', according to the *Pocket Oxford Dictionary* (1995), whereas the *New Shorter Oxford Dictionary* states under the heading 'pragmatics': 'practical considerations as opposed to theoretical or idealistic ones'. Here the opposite of pragmatic will be taken to be 'dogmatic'. The theme in this chapter is to suggest that in many realistic situations, it is better for an econometrician to be pragmatic rather than dogmatic.

It will also be taken as being accepted that there is no overlap between the set of all dogmatic methods and the set of all purely pragmatic methods. However in practice the methods used can include a mixture of both and in fact such mixtures will usually be superior.

It is useful to start with a quote, from the very beginning of David Hendry's book *Dynamic Econometrics* (1995) taken from a paper by Joseph A. Schumpeter: 'The Common Sense of Econometrics', *Econometrica*, 1 (1933), p. 12:

1) The only way to a position in which our science might give positive advice on a large scale to politicians and business men, leads through quantitative work.
2) For as long as we are unable to put our arguments into figures, the voice of our science, although occasionally it may help to dispel gross errors, will never be heard by practical men.
3) They are, by instinct, econometricians all of them, in their distrust of anything not amenable to exact proof.

[Note: The original quotation has been broken into its three sentences, and they have been numbered, to make discussion easier.]

It is worth noting that this quotation comes from a paper that was published in the very first issue of the journal *Econometrica* which has since evolved into a journal that is tightly argued and is generally highly theoretical and non-practical.

In his book David Hendry, through the words of Schumpeter in the first two sentences, emphasizes the close links between empirical econometrics and practical decision makers, an important link that is too often forgotten.

The third sentence will also fit easily into my theme. If 'exact proof' is taken to mean some mathematical statement based either on asymptotics or a set of specific assumptions then that would not be 'pragmatic'. However if it was based on a careful and sound statistical analysis then it might be, as the original theoretical model may not fit the data adequately and may have to be adapted or even discarded in the light of the empirical discussion.

Some very simple examples of econometricians being pragmatic would include when they ignore the fact that the leap years in a data set have an extra day, and also the fact that not all months have the same number of days.

A further simple example is the use of 'dummy variables' when building a model, as discussed by Hendry (1995, p. 557). Dummies are used to capture the main features of a variety of situations where unclear effects occur, such as time-changing parameters, unspecific policy changes or 'breaks' in trends or seasonal components.

Many of the important procedures used for seasonal adjustment should be classified as being pragmatic as they are not based on any particular economic theory and there is a variety of alternatives to chose between.

A particularly pragmatic aspect of modelling is trend fitting. It is easy enough to give examples of a trend but it is very difficult to provide a comprehensive definition of one. There are a variety of methods to fit a trend including using moving averages or estimates of various monotonic functions of time. None of these approaches are based on a specific economic theory and there is little econometric reason to use one method rather than another other than the appearance of the data. This is almost the definition of pragmatic!

Whilst performing an econometric analysis it is quite usual to reach a point where there is a choice between the 'correct' but lengthy, and often expensive, procedure or a quick but sub-optimal 'pragmatic' method. If time or costs are of major importance the pragmatic method will be chosen but otherwise the lengthy, correct method will be used. The two methods could produce quite similar answers or the solutions may be quite different. When the two solutions are different it could be because the pragmatic solution is a poor approximation to the truth or because the theoretical solution is based on some assumptions that are unrealistic. When both of the solutions are available, the 'correct' and the 'pragmatic', their usefulness can be compared in the evaluation process, which ideally should always be undertaken.

Some common strategies that are used when an econometrician considers building a model are:

A. assume that a particular theory holds true and thus provides a fully specified model; or
B. start with a group of assumptions about the model, such that it is linear, dynamic, and with an error term having zero mean and which is multidimensionally Gaussian; or
C. start with some appropriate data and by using a careful statistical analysis, testing and comparisons, eventually reach a 'data-consistent' model.

Here [C] will be considered the 'pragmatic' approach, but the other two are not. However it might be noted that it is often useful to use a model suggested by theory as a starting point for the empirical investigation. If this model is correct then no further developments are required, but it is not sufficient merely to assume that the theory is correct. Considering [B] merely using some assumptions that are just convenient will not be considered pragmatic.

There is an appropriate discussion of the differences between a theory-based approach and a data-based approach on page 73 of David Hendry's 1993 book *Econometrics, Alchemy or Science*:

> ... with my earlier empirical studies the equation or model to be estimated was obtained from a theoretical derivation and was made stochastic by adding on an appropriately behaved 'error term'. The distributions of the dependent variables were then derived from those of the error terms and that generated the likelihood function for estimation, inference etc. It all seemed coherent implicitly; however, it still assumed omniscience. In a theory framework, the model obtained is a function of the assumptions made and as such is freely created by its proprietor.
>
> In an empirical framework, the **data** are given, and so the distributions of the dependent variables are already fixed by what the data generating process created them to be—I knew that from Monte Carlo. But I kept missing the obvious point until

Jean-Francois (Richard) drove it home: the consequence of given data and a given theory model is that *the error is the derived component* and one cannot make 'separate' assumptions about its properties. My model derivations were in essence back to front, and I had reversed the process and obtain error's distribution from that of the data distributions in empirical modelling.

These issues are further expanded in Hendry (1987).

It is useful here to include an early definition of Econometrics by three Nobel Prize Winners: Samuelson, Koopmans, and Stone (1954) as 'the quantitative analysis of actual economic phenomena based on the concurrent development of theory and observation, related by appropriate methods of inference'. (Quotation used by Hashem Pesaran in his article on 'Econometrics' in the 1987 version of *The New Palgrave Dictionary Of Economics*.)

10.2 An Initial and Obvious Example of Pragmatics

There are many ways to take the pragmatic approach; one of the most carefully developed is the model building procedure called PcGets by David Hendry and his co-workers at Oxford.

Here they start with a large data set, having a single variable to be modelled and possibly a large number of 'explanatory' variables, including lagged dependent variables. The program sorts through the many possibilities and suggests a few plausible 'feasible' models to be carried into a decision-making procedure. One may end either with a single model or with several alternatives, which should be worthy of further consideration. (A discussion of the boundaries and possible limitations of this procedure together with a brief discussion of its future developments can be found in Granger and Hendry, 2005.) The procedure is heavily based on data analysis and is fairly light on assumptions and the use of economic theory.

10.3 How Are Our Students Taught?

One way to consider the state of some concept in the literature is by looking at a sample of textbooks on Econometrics. Considering just those currently on my shelves they can roughly be classified as follows:

Class A: Basically Dogmatic

1. Jeff Wooldridge, *Introductory Econometrics* (1999). Discusses statistical models, such as various types of regressions, and only turns to applications in the final chapter.
2. Russell Davidson and James MacKinnon, *Estimation and Inference in Econometrics* (1993). Initially concentrates on theory and eventually discusses practical issues.

Class B: Mixture of dogmatic and Pragmatic

1. Fumio Hayashi, *Econometrics* (2000). Concentrates on the estimation of various models and on the properties of these estimates.
2. James Davidson, *Econometric Theory* (2000). Considers a variety of models, initially non-dynamic but later largely dynamic, and then discusses estimation and testing questions.
3. Aris Spanos, *Probability Theory and Statistical Inference* (1999). Starts with statistical and probability theory and then considers various theoretical and pragmatic applications.

Class C: Largely Pragmatic

1. Michio Hatanaka, *Time Series Based Econometrics* (1996).
2. James Stock and Mark Watson, *Introduction to Econometrics* (2007). Mixes examples of data analysis with the introduction of new models.
3. Ramu Ramanathan, *Introductory Econometrics* (1998). Every new model is associated with an empirical example.
4. William Greene, *Econometric Analysis* (2000). A variety of models are considered of increasing complexity. There are frequent mentions of applications and of practical problems concerning the data, often with pragmatic solutions.

It should be noted that these texts have been ranked only on their attitude towards pragmatism and may not agree with rankings on other qualities. Some econometrics texts, such as Greene, use a long list of topics according to type of data and then suggest appropriate model forms, which is pragmatic. Other texts, such as Wooldridge, always start with a theoretical construct and then, after development of its properties, later ask about the input of data. This is clearly not pragmatic. It seems that our students could face quite different accounts depending on which textbook is selected by the teacher in charge.

If one considers the question of how pragmatism should be taught it is difficult to think of anything better than just showing a number of good examples. Attempting to provide a systematic and complete survey of pragmatic procedures in econometrics would be quite contrary to the basic ideas of pragmatism.

It is tempting to teach pragmatism as a kind of 'theory of the second best', involving the methods to be used when the economic theory available is incomplete or the data inadequate in some way. However that would be the idealistic and unrealistic view of most actual economic problems, where the data is always insufficient and the theory is simplistic.

10.4 Some General Considerations on Pragmatism

As background it can be noted that there was some early discussion of pragmatism by several philosophers, in particular the Americans Charles Sanders Peirce, William James, and John Dewey, towards the start of the previous century. Pragmatism now seems to be a major topic in the area of philosophy and also more generally but no attempt will be made here to summarise this extensive work. It can be noted that Bertrand Russell has a well-known saying that pragmatism is a 'mere means to a better dinner', although many people would take this to be an endorsement rather than a criticism!

A review of the area finds the existence of *The Journal of Contemporary Pragmatism*, which covers many fields, (edited by John Snook), and which is affiliated to the International Pragmatic Society.

In Economics, there is the book *Explorations in Pragmatic Economics*, by George Akerlof (2005). The author won the Nobel Prize in Economics in 2001. The advertisement for the book states that 'following from his classical paper "The Market for Lemons" his work has changed the economics of information'. The book is a collection of his best known publications, but the book's index does not mention the topic 'pragmatics'.

10.5 Pragmatism in Practice

Pragmatism can include using quick and simple, easy and possibly sub-optimal solutions to a question. It is also involved with a variety of data problems, such as missing data points, shortage of data, outliers, and other problems with data quality as well as the usual residuals that are non-Gaussian, are not white noise and do not have constant variance.

Rather than attempt to use the optimal, theoretically best, and most efficient method (possibly based on unrealistic or un-testable assumptions) that are slow to find or even unobtainable in practice, it is often proposed to use a quicker, pragmatic method. These may be more robust as they are often based on fewer critical assumptions. In certain situations pragmatic methods may only approximate the best that are available but in other cases they actually could be the best.

If one is advising a decision maker pragmatics often has to be used as s/he needs to be told the likely costs and benefits of the alternatives in quite simple terms—such as 'build or do not build'—rather than giving the benefits in terms of a distribution function or the likelihood level achieved. What most matters is allowing the decision maker to make the better decision rather than making the econometrician feel good.

10.6 Some Further Specific Examples of Pragmatics in Econometrics and Associated Areas

A paper on this topic needs plenty of good examples of pragmatic approaches. Some cases could include the following:

a) In PcGets, when deciding if a variable should be retained in an equation, use *t*-statistics with a cut-off point of 1.5, say. Here the *t*-statistic is used merely as a useful criterion rather than as a formal test!

b) Using 'large-sample' approximations when the actual sample size is not very large but the relevant theory is not available for this size sample. For example, the sample size is 50 or 100, the statistics in the table for confidence intervals ends at $n = 25$, say, but it does give an asymptotic value.

c) Some earlier continuous time finance theory was used because one can get an elegant theory and results by also introducing a convenient assumption of Gaussianity. Although financial markets can be observed continuously, trades occur occasionally in time and prices are certainly not Gaussian. Current continuous time finance theory which rules out arbitrage assumes that prices follow semi-martingales, which allows for jumps and price changes at no regular times and does not need a Gaussian assumption, and so might be classified as pragmatic. It has been pointed out to me that it is not a lack of data which causes problems in this area, but the mis-match between the type of continuous time models that is often used and the structure of the data.

d) There is a growing literature about 'pragmatic Bayesian methods' which is based on the idea of 'model averaging' or Bayesian model combining. See for example, Strachan and van Dijk (2007) where the idea is applied to the Great Ratios and also to the risk of a liquidity trap. A referee points out that an issue is that the common sense exploratory analysis of the data may produce 'surprises', that are noted a priori in the model set, so that Bayesian learning is not applicable. Allowing an analysis of data to produce unexpected results is one of the main benefits of the pragmatic approach and should produce superior theories that can encompass such results.

e) Pragmatic testing could include the original 'quick and dirty' methods of statistics, which now include many non-parametric testing procedures. Several methods based on ranks or the range have subsequently been found to be both very robust and often powerful—in other words have been found to be equal to or even superior to classical parametric methods.

f) Granger-causality is based on a pragmatic definition although it is claimed that it does have some depth. The concept is easy to understand and also to use and consequently is more often applied as a basis for tests than are the alternatives! This topic is discussed in Granger (2007).

g) Pragmatics is probably found more in applied, numerical work than in theory. However a theory might make a hugely simplifying (and obviously incorrect) assumption to make progress. Representative agents provide an obvious example, as does consideration of a Robinson Crusoe economy.

It is worth noting that some pragmatic procedures can go wrong if they are based on simplifying assumptions that are NOT correct, for example that the shocks have mean zero, are Gaussian, or have a variance that is constant or is finite.

10.7 Forecasting and Pragmatics

The area of economic forecasting provides examples of both dogmatic and pragmatic techniques. An example of the dogmatic is the classical sequence, theory → model → forecast, so that a theory is used to form an empirical model and this provides forecasts.

However once these forecasts are evaluated they will often be found to be inadequate or suboptimal, and so then one moves to dogmatic → pragmatic, and the model is then re-specified.

As an example of the pragmatic, consider a variety of models → form alternative forecasts → then combine these forecasts.

A special form of combining is to use 'thick modelling' (as described by Granger and Jeon, 2004) where a decision maker is presented with several superior forecasts rather than the single 'best' forecast. This allows decision makers to base their decisions on more information.

The well-known statistically based forecasting method proposed by Box and Jenkins (1970) is clearly pragmatic as a variety of models are considered and one is chosen by analysis of the data.

10.8 Possible Advantages (and Disadvantages) of Being Pragmatic

What are the possible advantages of using a pragmatic approach?

i. It is possible to get an answer quickly. It is often the case that some reasonable answer that is available quickly is much better than a poor, constrained answer available on time or the best answer that is delivered too late!

ii. One can often consider a variety of alternative pragmatic approaches, and then compare the outcomes.
iii. This is useful for THICK decision making, where the decision maker is presented with the outputs of several good models rather than just from the 'best' single model, where the best model is found by using some imposed criterion which may not be relevant to the decision maker.
iv. The previous group of outputs could also include results from a non-pragmatic, fully optimizing method, if available.

What are the disadvantages?

i. It is often difficult to provide confidence intervals, either quickly or of a satisfactory quality, so we have to rely on statistical simulation.
ii. The final resulting model might be a long way from the best that could have been found.

10.9 The Purpose of a Model and Pragmatics

i. If the purpose of the model is to test the correctness of some theory, a situation that is fully discussed by Stigum (2003) in his book *Econometrics and the Philosophy of Economics* and in his previous articles in considerable detail and great clarity, then a pragmatic model may only be appropriate when discussing alternatives.
ii. If the purpose of the model is to directly help a decision maker to make a decision, then a pragmatic approach is likely to be helpful.
iii. The purpose of the model may be for forecasting. A present attitude towards forecasting considers building several alternative models, using each to produce forecasts and then using a THICK modelling approach in which just a few forecasts are presented to the decision maker or possibly a combination of the forecasts. In either case pragmatic models will be appropriate for inclusion in the set of models as they may use incomplete and/or very recent data.
iv. A referee raised the question of whether pragmatics can be important in short-run decision making but is likely to be less important for long-run decisions. It is correct to point out that long-run forecasting methods are less likely to be helpful in the long-run and so more weight should be given to economic theory. This is true only when the economic theory is correct, but this cannot safely be assumed as the rapidly expanding economics literature on 'puzzles' illustrates. One can only rely on a

dogmatic theory if the theory has been carefully evaluated in terms of the correctness of its forecasts, and this is difficult to do for the long-run.

10.10 Examples of Pragmatic and Dogmatic Models

A list of topics that are pragmatic, and so are not based on a theory, but build a model directly from data to explain some properties observed in practice could include:

a) *Cointegration*. Cointegration is a property of a group of stochastic variables and a data vector which may have it or may not.

b) *Error-correction models*. If series are cointegrated it follows that their generating mechanism will take this form, and so it has to be specified and estimated.

c) *ARCH models*. These models arise from the observation that volatility is often autocorrelated and ARCH is an example of a class of models that fit this observation.

d) *Logistic model*. Economic variables that are bounded in range clearly need a special class of non-linear models.

e) *ARIMA forecasting models*. This is a class of models proposed by Box and Jenkins as being pragmatically useful for forecasting.

f) *Time varying parameter models*. Linear models can be considered to have parameters that change in certain regimes or smoothly with time, as approximated by a Kalman filter.

g) *Long-memory models*. Examples are fractionally integrated models or those containing occasional breaks.

h) *Non-linear time-series models, including neural nets*. Most NL time-series models are considered because of inadequacies of linear models to explain all of the features of the data and are rarely derived from economic theory.

i) *Measuring risk*. When Harry Markowitz was inventing practical portfolio theory he was faced with a practical problem about how to measure risk. It was understood that risk relates to an unfortunate event occurring, so for an investment this corresponds to a low, or even negative, return. Thus getting returns in the lower tail of the return distribution constitutes this 'downside risk'. However, it is not easy to get a simple measure of this risk. The 'semi-variance', which is the variance measured over the distribution below some value (such as the median) is easy to define but is mathematically intractable. Because of these practical difficulties attention was turned to measuring risk by the variance. The obvious advantage is that it is easy to form and to manipulate statistically. The obvious problem is that it does not represent what is widely understood by risk, as it is influenced by the upper tail of the distribution as well as the lower tail. If your portfolio provides a surprisingly high return, this is not generally classified as a risk, but it will increase the variance. If you buy a lottery ticket, do you buy insurance in case you win? Markowitz's decision to use variance as a measure of risk was a pragmatic one and it was sensible given the state of computing at that time. Since then it would be possible to conduct portfolio selections based on semi-variance or other measures. Unfortunately everyone is so comfortable with using variance that except for some quantile measures there has been little consideration of measures of 'risk' other than variance. The pragmatic sub-optimal solution is so attractive that it is proving difficult to replace it.

The previous examples of pragmatics have all been about econometric models or techniques, whereas for risk the discussion now involved making a concept measurable. This illustrates the width of the use of pragmatics in our field.

Where exactly risk is, is a very personal matter and it follows that how it can be handled in practice is likely to be largely pragmatic. Examples of models that are (largely) based on a comprehensive theory, and so may be considered dogmatic include:

a) General equilibrium macroeconomic models.
b) Simultaneous equation stochastic econometric models, as developed by the Cowles Commission.

Some examples in between these two groups would include the partial equilibrium and rational expectations models.

10.11 Pragmatics and Diversification

A pragmatist should not be satisfied with a single model, method or theory—even if it is 'optimal' according to some criterion. Reference can be made to the paper by Paul Samuelson (1967) 'General proof that diversification pays', which considers cost functions other than least squares and also not necessarily just linear combinations of assets. It is worth noting that the cost function of the user of the output (such as maximizing profits) might be quite different from that being used by the econometrician (maximum likelihood, say).

Portfolio theory suggests that on occasions it is worthwhile including a method that performs badly by itself but is useful when added to the group. This suggests that pragmaticians should not ignore methods or models that perform badly but should consider them in a portfolio.

If several models are available, their outputs should be combined in some standard fashion. This means that if the group of models includes one that performs badly it will not be chosen by the decision maker.

10.12 Pragmatics in Practice

It is fairly common to meet a situation where a decision sequence reaches a case where two branches are equally likely or at least roughly so, for example:

a. Is a series I(0) or I(1)?
b. Are there two or three cointegrations, according to a test?
c. Should the autoregressive model use two or three lags?

In each and in hundreds of other possible examples, the test or criteria being used is not decisive and either answer is equally likely.

The dogmatic econometrician would bring any other information that is available to reach a decision, such as examples from previous studies, other numerical information and opinions, possibly as a Bayesian. Eventually the tie will be broken and a single model is fitted.

The pragmatic econometrician will conclude that the data cannot decide between the models at this moment and so BOTH models should be fitted and the analysis continued with them. As computing is now very inexpensive and quite easy there is little difficulty with this strategy, unless the basic model is extremely large, such as a global model or if the process of splitting occurs frequently as the model develops.

It is clear that this kind of a pragmatic approach will be more difficult to use with some panel models unless the highly unlikely, and ultra-pragmatic, assumption is made that all of the regions have the same time-series model!

10.13 Conclusions

The pragmatic attitude towards model building suggests that alternate models should be kept as viable options for as long as possible, so that a rich set of alternatives should be considered. The aim should be to obtain the most useful set of options for the decision maker rather than the single 'best' model.

References

Akerlof, G. (2005). *Explorations in Pragmatic Economics*. Oxford: Oxford University Press.
Box, G. E. P and Jenkins, G. M. (1970). *Time Series Analysis*. San Francisco: Holden Day.
Davidson, J. (2000). *Econometric Theory*. Oxford: Blackwell.
Davidson, R. and MacKinnon, J. (1993). *Estimation and Inference in Econometrics*. Oxford: Oxford University Press.

Granger, C. W. J. (2007). Causality in economics. Ch. 15 of Machamer and Wolters, *op. cit.*

——and Hendry, D. F. (2005). A dialogue concerning a new instrument for econometric modeling. *Econometric Theory*, **21**, 278–297.

——and Jeon, Y. (2004). Thick modelling. *Economic Modelling*, **21**, 323–343.

Greene, W. (2000). *Econometric Analysis*, 4th edition. New Jersey: Prentice Hall.

Hatanaka, M. (1996). *Time Series Based Econometrics*. Oxford: Oxford University Press.

Hayashi, F. (2000). *Econometrics*. Princeton: Princeton University Press.

Hendry, D. F. (1993). *Econometrics, Alchemy or Science?* Oxford: Blackwell.

——(1987). Econometric methodology: A personal perspective. In Bewley, T. F. (ed), *Advances in Econometrics*. Cambridge: Cambridge University Press.

——(1995). *Dynamic Econometrics*. Oxford: Oxford University Press.

Machamer, P. and Wolters, G. (2007). *Thinking about Causes. From Greek Philosophy to Modern Physics*. Pittsburgh: University of Pittsburgh Press.

Ramanathan, R. (1998). *Introductory Econometrics*, 4th edition. New York: Dryden.

Samuelson, P. A. (1967). General proof that diversification pays. *Journal of Financial and Quantitative Analysis*, **2**, 1–13.

——Koopmans, T. C., and Stone, J. R. N. (1954). Report of the evaluative committee for Econometrica. *Econometrica*, **22**, 141–146.

Schumpeter, J. (1933). The common sense of Econometrics. *Econometrica*, **1**.

Spanos, A. (1999). *Probability and Statistical Inference*. Cambridge: Cambridge University Press.

Stigum, B. P. (2003). *Econometrics and the Philosophy of Economics*. Princeton: Princeton University Press.

Stock, J. and Watson, M. (2007). *Introduction to Econometrics*, 2nd edition. Boston: Pearson Addison-Wesley.

Strachan, S. W. and van Dijk, H. K. (2007). Bayesian model averaging in vector autoregressive processes. Working Paper, Econometrics Institute, Erasmus University Rotterdam.

Wooldridge, J. (1999). *Introductory Econometrics*. Southwestern.

11

On Efficient Simulations in Dynamic Models

*Karim M. Abadir and Paolo Paruolo**

11.1 Introduction

Unit roots have become a central theme of modern econometrics. Numerous studies of the subject have used Monte Carlo (MC) techniques. Yet we do not know how these MC techniques, usually designed for stationary series, fare with nearly nonstationary ones.[1] An important aspect is the control of MC variability, which is shown here to increase with the sample size in nearly nonstationary series. For example, when simulating quantiles of AR statistics, this excess MC variation can be easily shown by using formula (10.29) of Kendall and Stuart (1977, p. 252) together with the thin long lower tails that are typical of AR densities.

The study of MC techniques in dynamic models lags behind other—admittedly more pressing—aspects of the subject. This chapter will attempt to partially redress this imbalance by presenting ideas on how to improve MC studies of autoregressive series, possibly with roots close to unity. More specifically, Variance Reduction Techniques (VRTs) will be suggested to cope with the problems of simulating dynamic models of this type.

VRTs are methods of combining different estimates obtained from using a single set of generated random numbers more than once. When successful, they reduce MC imprecision as explained in detail by Hendry (1984). Furthermore, unconventional uses for these VRTs can be found, as we will discuss later. In addition to MC, we use response surfaces and asymptotic results to compare the relative performance of various VRTs. Asymptotic methods are

* We thank David Hendry for being a continuing source of inspiration for us. We also thank Mario Cerrato and two anonymous referees for their comments. We gratefully acknowledge support from UK ESRC grant RES-062-23-0790 and Italian MUR Grant Cofin2006-13-1140.

[1] The term 'near nonstationarity' is used in this chapter to refer to autoregressive roots in the neighbourhood of unity, including a unit root.

employed in this context both in the econometrics and finance literature. Asymptotics for a large number of MC replicates are reported in Paruolo (2002), where VRTs are used to increase precision in test-power comparison. Ericsson (1991) employs small-σ asymptotics.[2] Finally, several other asymptotic methods are in use in finance; see eg Takahashi and Yoshida (2005) and references therein.

The outline of the chapter is as follows. First, the VRTs to be considered are defined in section 11.2. The new VRTs of this work will have to be compared to some benchmark. For this reason, existing VRTs will be briefly defined alongside the new ones. Next, section 11.3 compares these VRTs numerically and analytically (by response surfaces) in finite samples, placing special emphasis on typical nearly nonstationary conditions without excluding the possibility of stationarity from the study. In the response surface analysis, we show how to bridge the gap in the distribution theory that arises from stationary and nonstationary data by means of a simple function that will be given in (11.25).

The results show large efficiency gains (eg by an average factor of about 20 times) for a few of the VRTs, leading to the ability to conduct faster and more precise MC in the future. This is useful not just for academic econometricians. For example, in financial econometrics, a trader may wish to price an option (which is an expectation) precisely and quickly, in order to make a profitable trade that may otherwise be missed, and our VRTs can be used for this purpose; see eg Cerrato (2008).

Section 11.4 then describes encompassing formulations for these VRTs, and looks at some practical problems where they may be beneficially used. Some of these applications are nonstandard, including an illustration of how to use the results of earlier sections to devise a method of improving the efficiency of MC work on nearly nonstationary series. Other possible unconventional uses of these VRTs include the derivation of power functions of tests and numerical integration. It is worth stressing that all these benefits come at little programming cost. Typically, only 2 or 3 lines of code are required to program these VRTs, and they can be easily added to subroutines that generate random numbers.

In section 11.5, we use large-sample asymptotic results to analyse the variance-reduction factor of various VRTs. We employ functional central limit theorems to study the behaviour of relevant statistics for unstable autoregressions; for stable autoregressions we use standard central limit theorems together with covariance calculations. We are thus able to describe the correlation coefficient between antithetic variates as an explicit function of the autoregressive parameter, where this correlation is the key element in the

[2] For the problem considered in this chapter the statistics of interest is scale invariant, and small-σ asymptotics is not a viable option.

MC variance reduction formula. Moreover, these results allow us to discuss analytically the choice of a rotation parameter in some class of orthogonal antithetic variates.

Finally, concluding observations are made in section 11.6.

11.2 VRTs: New and Old

The two most prominent types of VRTs in econometrics will be considered in this work. They are Antithetic Variates (AVs) and Control Variates (CVs). The failing of known forms of AVs in dynamic models has been documented in Hendry (1984). Here, it will be shown analytically that conventional CVs also fail when the variables are nearly nonstationary. For reasons of simplicity, let the dynamic Data Generating Process (DGP) be

$$y_t = \alpha y_{t-1} + \varepsilon_t, \tag{11.1}$$

where $t = 1, \dots, T$, $y_0 = 0$, $\varepsilon_t \sim \mathrm{IN}(0,\sigma^2)$. The reason for choosing this DGP is that it is representative of the problems associated with the nearly nonstationary case. More general ARMA processes where the orders may even be unknown will give rise to similar results when treated as in Said and Dickey (1984), as long as deterministics are not included. Also, the study's emphasis on near nonstationarity means that the choice of distribution for ε_t in (11.1) is not crucial to the results, especially when T is not small; see Phillips (1987). So (11.1) was adopted to keep complexity of the exposition at a minimum.

A DGP with zero intercept and trend was chosen to retain the nonstandard results that arise in near nonstationarity with its associated unconventional problems. If any of these parameters were nonzero, normality of distributions would be restored to the usual statistics associated with (11.1) at the fast rates of $T^{3/2}$ and $T^{5/2}$, respectively. The choice of DGP (11.1) should not be seen as restricting the validity of the new VRTs defined below. Their general definition is independent of (11.1) in spite of being motivated by it, and can be used in a variety of frameworks other than (11.1).

Ordinary Least Squares (OLS) yields a consistent estimate of α in (11.1), and is given by

$$\hat{\alpha} := \sum_t y_t y_{t-1} \Big/ \sum_t y_{t-1}^2, \tag{11.2}$$

where $t = 1, \dots, T$ in the summation ($t = 1$ gives a zero term because $y_0 = 0$). VRTs have many uses, which we will illustrate with evaluating $\mathrm{E}(\hat{\alpha})$ when (α, σ^2) belongs to the parameter space $\{|\alpha| \leq 1, \sigma^2 > 0\}$ and $T \in \mathcal{T} \subset \mathbb{N}$. Here, the only difference with Hendry (1984) is in allowing $|\alpha| = 1$ within this parameter space.

A simple Monte Carlo technique would be to generate $n = 1, \dots, N$ replications of the series in DGP (11.1), and calculate N OLS estimates of α in (11.2).

By taking the average of these, one can estimate $\mathrm{E}(\hat{\alpha})$. This is called the 'crude MC estimator' and it is an unbiased estimator of $\mathrm{E}(\hat{\alpha})$, with MC variance given by $\mathrm{var}(\hat{\alpha})/N$. One can improve on the crude MC estimator by using VRTs. VRTs re-use the same set $\{\varepsilon_t\}$ once more, instead of simply using it once as the crude MC estimator.

The computational cost of VRTs is represented by the ratio, κ say, of the computing time required by the re-use of the set $\{\varepsilon_t\}$ relative to the computing time required by an additional replication of the crude MC estimator, which involves generating a new set of $\{\varepsilon_t\}$. The ratio κ depends on the hardware and software solutions used in the implementation; usually one has $\kappa < 1$ and often $\kappa \ll 1$. The benefits of VRTs are the ability to generate an estimator having the same expectation as $\hat{\alpha}$, but be less variable by a factor of 20 or so, as we will see in the next section; this is equivalent to having increased N by a factor of 20 in the ratio $\mathrm{var}(\hat{\alpha})/N$. A successful VRT can therefore lead to massive gains in terms of efficiency and speed.

In general, AVs transform the set $\{\varepsilon_t\}$ to an antithetic counterpart $\{\varepsilon_t^-\}$ that is used to generate another set of observations $\{y_t^-\}$ which is also called antithetic. Then, the same estimation method is applied to $\{y_t^-\}$, yielding a second estimate of α, denoted by $\hat{\alpha}^-$ and called the antithetic estimate. The antithetic transform is chosen so that $\hat{\alpha}$ and $\hat{\alpha}^-$ have the same expectation; this implies that the combined estimate

$$\widetilde{\alpha} := \frac{1}{2}\left(\hat{\alpha} + \hat{\alpha}^-\right) \tag{11.3}$$

has also the same expectation of $\hat{\alpha}$ and $\hat{\alpha}^-$ with variance

$$\mathrm{var}(\widetilde{\alpha}) = \frac{1}{4}\left(\mathrm{var}(\hat{\alpha}) + \mathrm{var}\left(\hat{\alpha}^-\right) + 2\mathrm{cov}(\hat{\alpha}, \hat{\alpha}^-)\right) \tag{11.4}$$

that is designed to be lower than the original $\mathrm{var}(\hat{\alpha})$. Following Hendry (1984), define the associated Efficiency Gain (EG) as

$$\mathrm{EGv} := \frac{\mathrm{var}\,(\hat{\alpha})}{\mathrm{var}\,(\widetilde{\alpha})}, \tag{11.5}$$

where v is the name of the VRT associated with $\widetilde{\alpha}$. When $\mathrm{var}(\hat{\alpha}) = \mathrm{var}(\hat{\alpha}^-) = \eta$, say, $\mathrm{var}(\widetilde{\alpha})$ simplifies to

$$\mathrm{var}(\widetilde{\alpha}) = \frac{\eta}{2}(1+\rho), \tag{11.6}$$

where $\rho := \mathrm{corr}(\hat{\alpha}, \hat{\alpha}^-)$. In this case

$$\mathrm{EGv} = \frac{2}{1+\rho}. \tag{11.7}$$

The conventional AV uses

$$\{\varepsilon_t^-\} := \{-\varepsilon_t\} \tag{11.8}$$

in an attempt to induce $\rho < 0$ which, if successful, would lead to $\mathrm{EG} > 2$.

Unfortunately in the case of (11.1), the conventional AV fails: $\hat{a}$ and $\hat{a}^-$ are identical, and the combined estimator is no better than either of its components since $\text{corr}(\hat{a},\hat{a}^-) = 1$ and $\text{var}(\hat{a}) = \text{var}(\hat{a}^-) = \text{var}(\tilde{a})$. One way out of this impasse is to use another type of estimator for $\hat{a}^-$. For example, let $\hat{a}^-$ be based on Instrumental Variable estimation rather than OLS. The two estimates of a would be numerically different but would be positively correlated (especially in large samples), so that the variance of the combined estimator given in (11.4) would be only marginally smaller than either $\hat{a}$ or $\hat{a}^-$. Because the expected efficiency gain is not likely to be large, one has to think of another alternative for generating $\{\varepsilon_t^-\}$ and hence $\hat{a}^-$.

The other direction that can be pursued in developing a different $\hat{a}^-$ is to reuse $\{\varepsilon_t\}$ differently. The general idea is to attempt to create a series $\{\varepsilon_t^-\}$ which leads to an $\hat{a}^-$ that is preferably negatively correlated with $\hat{a}$. Four general alternative techniques can now be suggested.

The first new AV, denoted henceforth by AV1, is based on transforming the pair ε_i and ε_j $(i \neq j)$ that were generated as $\text{IN}(0,\sigma^2)$ into

$$\varepsilon_i^- := \left(\pm\varepsilon_i \pm \varepsilon_j\right)/\sqrt{2} \quad \text{and} \quad \varepsilon_j^- := \left(\mp\varepsilon_i \pm \varepsilon_j\right)/\sqrt{2}, \tag{11.9}$$

which will also be $\text{IN}(0,\sigma^2)$. This can be checked by taking expectations of powers of ε in (11.9). If the estimator of interest is invariant to scale, as is the case here with $\hat{a}$, one can omit the $\sqrt{2}$ factors to speed up the calculations.

The signs in (11.9) mean that the new method can generate, for example, ε_i^- as either $\left(\varepsilon_i + \varepsilon_j\right)/\sqrt{2}$ or $-\left(\varepsilon_i + \varepsilon_j\right)/\sqrt{2}$. For now, only the upper signs from the general definition (11.9) will be considered, because one wishes to isolate the separate influences of combining innovations and of switching their signs. The sign-switching features of (11.9) will be temporarily ignored, as they will be considered separately by other explicit VRTs here. The encompassing generality of the formulation of (11.9) will be returned to later in section 11.4.

Definition (11.9) does not constrain the order of the variates i and j (except that $i \neq j$), though we shall also temporarily ignore this property to isolate the influence of combining two innovations as opposed to reordering them. Successive pairs will be selected so that $j = i + 1$. Again, we shall come back to these features in section 11.4 below.

Finally, we assume for simplicity that the sample size T is even. Otherwise, the last value of the antithetic set, ε_T^-, would need to be generated as if it were ε_{T+1}.

The second antithetic variate, AV2, is one way of resampling $\{\varepsilon_t\}$, and it consists of reversing the order of the original i.i.d. series to get

$$\{\varepsilon_t^-\} := \{\varepsilon_{T-t}\}. \tag{11.10}$$

It has the small disadvantage of requiring all the innovations $\{\varepsilon_t\}$ to be kept in storage, unlike the previous method which only requires storage space for two consecutive innovations at a time.

The third method, AV3, was mentioned but not tested by Hendry and Harrison (1974, p. 156). It is based on using

$$\{\varepsilon_t^-\} := \{(-1)^t \varepsilon_t\}, \tag{11.11}$$

which alters the sign of every other ε_t. This method should do best when α is close to 0 because the values assumed by $\{\varepsilon_t\}$ matter significantly less to the distribution of $\hat{\alpha}$ as $|\alpha| \to 1$ (see Phillips 1987), and because $\alpha = 0$ here gives deterministically

$$\widetilde{\alpha} \equiv \frac{1}{2}\left(\hat{\alpha} + \hat{\alpha}^-\right) = \frac{1}{2}\sum\nolimits_t \left(\varepsilon_t\varepsilon_{t-1} - \varepsilon_t\varepsilon_{t-1}\right) / \sum\nolimits_t \varepsilon_{t-1}^2 = 0 \tag{11.12}$$

as the combined estimator, hence providing an infinite variance reduction relative to the crude MC estimator. Note, however, that in this case $\widetilde{\alpha}$ is degenerate at 0, and it cannot be considered as a realization of an estimator (with the same expectation as $\hat{\alpha}$), which is a nondegenerate random variable. Hence, in the MC simulations concerning AV3, we will discard the case of $\alpha = 0$.

Finally, AV4 is a very intuitive and easily applicable new VRT. It is cheap on both programming and storage cost considerations. It relies on using exactly the same innovations

$$\{\varepsilon_t^-\} := \{\varepsilon_t\} \tag{11.13}$$

to generate $\{y_t\}$ through the same DGP as before but with parameter(s) of interest of the opposite sign, namely

$$y_t = -\alpha y_{t-1} + \varepsilon_t = \beta y_{t-1} + \varepsilon_t \tag{11.14}$$

with $\beta := -\alpha$. The new coefficient β is then estimated by OLS as in (11.2), and the negative of the resulting estimate, $-\hat{\beta}$, is the antithetic $\hat{\alpha}^-$ for the generic AV form in (11.3). When $\alpha = 0$, $\{y_t^-\} = \{y_t\}$ and $\hat{\alpha}^- \equiv -\hat{\beta} = -\hat{\alpha}$, which causes $\widetilde{\alpha}$ to be zero deterministically as in (11.12); a case which will be discarded in the MC simulations. Such an infinite variance reduction is not expected for any other value of α, and it is clear that, as α moves away from zero, the variance reduction will fall to finite levels both here and for AV3.

One can think of the last two methods as switching the sign of the effect on y_t of every other ε_t to obtain the antithetic set $\{y_t^-\}$. AV3 does it directly by changing the sign of every other ε_t, while AV4 does it indirectly by changing the sign of α through which lags of ε_t affect y_t. DGP (11.1) can be rewritten as

$$y_t = \sum_{j=0}^{t-1} \alpha^j \varepsilon_{t-j}, \tag{11.15}$$

where it is obvious that a change in the sign of α affects every other ε_{t-j} term. For autoregressive DGPs like (11.1), the two methods provide equal results since AV3 gives

$$y_t^- = (-1)^t \sum_{j=0}^{t-1} (-\alpha)^j \varepsilon_{t-j}, \tag{11.16}$$

while AV4 leads to

$$y_t^- = \sum_{j=0}^{t-1} (-\alpha)^j \varepsilon_{t-j}. \tag{11.17}$$

Given the respective definitions of $\hat{\alpha}^-$ for AV3 and AV4, (11.16) and (11.17) give the same combined estimator $\widetilde{\alpha}$ in the case of DGP (11.1). This equality is due to the choice of our dynamic DGP, and does not necessarily hold for all other DGPs. For example, a static DGP where the conventional AV works,

$$y_t = \alpha x_t + \varepsilon_t, \tag{11.18}$$

and where x_t is not a lagged value of y_t, causes AV3 and AV4 to be different. Static DGPs are not the focus of this study.

One should be careful to provide the proper justification for using AV4 to simulate moments of a certain order. In general, any AV is a statistically valid method of simulating the moment of order k of an econometric estimator η if and only if $\mathrm{E}(\hat{\eta}^k) = \mathrm{E}(\hat{\eta}^{k-})$, where $\hat{\eta}^{k-}$ is the k-th power of the antithetic estimator. For applying sign-switching AVs to DGP (11.1), this condition reduces to the requirement that $\mathrm{sgn}(\hat{\eta}^k) \times \mathrm{E}(\hat{\eta}^k)$ is an even function of η, so that changing the sign of η (directly or indirectly) in the DGP produces an antithetic variate $\hat{\eta}^{k-}$ with exactly the same expected value as $\hat{\eta}^k$.

For $k = 1$ and with DGP (11.1), this condition is violated for AV3 and AV4 when $\alpha = 0$ as we have seen before. However, when $\alpha \neq 0$, moment generating functions (White 1958, 1961; Abadir 1993b and references therein) show that the distribution of $\hat{\beta}$ is the mirror image of that of $\hat{\alpha}$, thus warranting the use of the technique of AV4 to simulate moments of any order or any other density-related properties such as quantiles. In addition, the other AVs considered in this work satisfy the condition for the first two moments. So, the optimal combination of an estimator and its antithetic counterpart is the simple (as opposed to weighted) average given in the generic form (11.3).

The condition detailed in the previous paragraph is also satisfied by the general ARMA models analysed by Cryer, Nankervis, and Savin (1989), who consider conditions for invariance and mirror image of estimators; see also Haldrup (1996) for mirror image properties in the case of time trends. The condition set here is not the same as the ones in Cryer *et al.* (1989) because of the different focus of the two papers: theirs considers whole distributions, whereas ours is only concerned with certain specific moments. Two different distributions may have the same mean, thus satisfying our condition for the first order moment, but not the one in Cryer *et al.* (1989). Their conditions are thus sufficient but not necessary for the present application.

As with AVs, CVs are meant to modify estimators like (11.2) so as to reduce MC variability. The CVs under consideration in this work will be extensions of Hendry's (1984, p. 953), which is denoted here by CV1. For CVs, the modified estimator of α takes the general form

$$\tilde{\alpha} := \hat{\alpha} - \frac{c}{h} \sum\nolimits_t \varepsilon_t y_{t-1}, \tag{11.19}$$

where h is a variant of

$$\mathrm{E}\left(\sum\nolimits_t y_{t-1}^2\right) = \begin{cases} \sigma^2 \frac{T}{2}(T-1) & (|\alpha| = 1), \\ \sigma^2 \frac{T(1-\alpha^2)+\alpha^{2T}-1}{(1-\alpha^2)^2} & (|\alpha| < 1). \end{cases} \tag{11.20}$$

For CV1, only the stationary case was analysed by Hendry (1984). The parameter c of (11.19) was set at 1 there and h was taken to be the asymptotically dominant term of (11.20) for the stationary case:

$$h = \sigma^2 T/(1 - \alpha^2). \tag{11.21}$$

Extending this definition to take account of near nonstationarity gives CV2 where $c = 1$ and h is given by (11.20). Finally, CV3 extends Hendry's CV a step further by estimating the minimum-variance version of (11.19). After generating all of the $\hat{\alpha}_n$ ($n = 1, \ldots, N$) replications of the MC experiment, let h be given by (11.20) and estimate the unrestricted regression

$$\hat{\alpha}_n = \text{constant} + \hat{c}\left(\sum\nolimits_t \varepsilon_t y_{t-1}/h\right)_n + r_n \tag{11.22}$$

so that

$$\tilde{\alpha}_n := \hat{\alpha}_n - \hat{c}\left(\sum\nolimits_t \varepsilon_t y_{t-1}/h\right)_n = \text{constant} + r_n,$$

where $\{r_n\}$ are the regression residuals and $\{\tilde{\alpha}_n\}$ are the N replications of the CV-modified estimator. This process gives rise to the optimal (minimum variance) CV as is described in Kleijnen (1974, pp. 138–159). Its only disadvantage in comparison with CV1 or CV2 is a minor computational requirement: a simple regression has to be run at the end of the simulation experiment.

The storage requirements for all three CVs are the same if the series of estimators generated in each replication are to be preserved for a study of moments other than just the mean. A last remark should be made about h. Since it does not vary from one replication to another, then its only purpose in CV3 is as a scale factor. It could be dropped from expression (11.22) for CV3 without affecting the final results in any way. We shall not do so here because it will be interesting to see how close the estimated c is, relative to the value of 1 which is assigned to c in the case of CV2. This analysis need not be repeated in practical MC studies.

The weakness of these CVs as $|\alpha|$ approaches 1 can now be established analytically for the first time by considering (11.19) and (11.20). The stabilizing normalization for $\sum_t \varepsilon_t y_{t-1}$ is $1/\sqrt{h}$. Therefore, because of the swift convergence of $\sum_t \varepsilon_t y_{t-1}/h = O_p(1/\sqrt{h})$ to zero as $|\alpha| \to 1$ and $T \to \infty$, CVs will fail under precisely these two conditions. In a way, CVs are paying the price for the fast convergence of $\hat{\alpha}$ to α in the case of α near the unit circle (eg see Evans and Savin 1981), and little can be done by means of CVs to improve the efficiency of the already super-consistent $\hat{\alpha}$. Note that the stochastic components of the CVs are essentially $\hat{\alpha} - \alpha \equiv \sum_t \varepsilon_t y_{t-1} / \sum_t y_{t-1}^2$ and $\sum_t \varepsilon_t y_{t-1}/h$, which differ only with respect to the type of normalization (stochastic vs. deterministic) that is chosen for $\sum_t \varepsilon_t y_{t-1}$.

11.3 Finite-Sample Results

DGP (11.1) was used with $\varepsilon_t \sim \text{IN}(0,1)$ to test the relative efficiency of the various VRTs suggested above. The parameters of the experiment were

$$\alpha = 0.00, 0.25, 0.50, 0.75, 0.80, 0.85, 0.90, 0.95, 0.99, 1.00;$$

$$T = 26, 50, 100, 200, 400; \qquad N = 10^4; \tag{11.23}$$

with α chosen to give more detail on (and more weight to) nearly nonstationary data, and where $T = 26$ was chosen as the first sample size to accommodate AV1 (for convenience only). There is no need to consider negative values of α for the purpose of this study where efficiency comparison is the only concern, because efficiency is independent of the sign of α; eg see Hendry (1984) or refer to the discussion of AV4 following (11.18) in section 11.2. Furthermore, considering changes in efficiency (variance) is tantamount to comparing mean squared errors because the biases of the modified estimators are the same as those of the original OLS. This follows from the discussion after (11.18) for the AVs, and from (11.19) for the CVs.

The results of the experiment are then summarized in two ways. First, descriptive statistics are reported for EGv as a crude means of comparing VRTs. Then, response surfaces are fitted to each EGv for an analytical explanation of how various VRTs fare as α and T change.

Tables 11.1–11.3 give some summary statistics on EGv as well as on $\hat{c}$, the OLS estimated value of the control coefficient of CV3 in (11.22). They cover different ranges of the parameter α because of the occasional distortions to the simple descriptive statistics introduced by the two extremes 0 and 1 of $|\alpha|$.[3] EGCV1 is absent from Tables 11.1 and 11.3 because it excludes $|\alpha| = 1$ by definition. AV4,3 excludes $\alpha = 0$ and so is absent from Tables 11.1 and 11.2.

[3] The response surfaces given below are more sophisticated, and do not share these distortions.

Table 11.1. Summary of MC results for the whole design

Variable	Mean	Minimum	Maximum
EGAV1	1.54	1.4	1.7
EGAV2	1.03	1.0	1.2
EGCV2	20.9	1.3	184
EGCV3	21.1	1.3	186
$\hat{c}$	0.99	0.83	1.20

Table 11.2. Summary of MC results excluding $|\alpha| = 1$.

Variable	Mean	Minimum	Maximum
EGAV1	1.53	1.4	1.7
EGAV2	1.01	1.0	1.1
EGCV1	23.2	1.1	185
EGCV2	23.0	1.4	184
EGCV3	23.3	1.4	186
$\hat{c}$	0.98	0.83	1.20

Table 11.3. Summary of MC results excluding $\alpha = 0$.

Variable	Mean	Minimum	Maximum
EGAV1	1.53	1.4	1.7
EGAV2	1.03	1.0	1.2
EGAV4,3	4.33	2.0	18
EGCV2	15.2	1.3	140
EGCV3	15.4	1.3	142
$\hat{c}$	0.99	0.83	1.20

On the whole, the following remarks can be made from the raw data (not listed here) and the summary tables:

Remark 11.1. AV2 is the weakest VRT, while AV1 is the second weakest.[4] They are the only ones to show a slightly better performance for $|\alpha| = 1$ than for $|\alpha| < 1$. All the others deteriorate (albeit from better initial levels) when $|\alpha| \to 1$, with AV1 performing better than CVs and almost as well as AV4,3 when $|\alpha| = 1$. On the other hand, the performance of AV2 is quite poor and declines as T increases, and has a relatively high memory cost. We would tend not to recommend methods that just reorder the innovations if the purpose is

[4] In this section, AV1 refers to the narrow definition where the residual-rearrangement and sign-switching features of the general definition of the method in (11.9) are temporarily ignored because they are covered by AV2 and AV3/AV4, respectively.

variance reduction in dynamic MC. Such methods are related to the Bootstrap which has nevertheless been successfully put to other uses.

Remark 11.2. Sign-switching AVs (AV3 and AV4) are extremely efficient and provide staggering efficiency gains. Their performance peaks at $\alpha = 0$ where EG is infinite, and declines exponentially to stabilize from $|\alpha| \approx 0.75$ onwards. Both are undoubtedly the best VRTs for unit roots where they provide an efficiency gain of 2; but CVs outperform them in the middle range of α, especially as T rises there. The average figure of 2 indicates by (11.4) and (11.5) that the two antithetics $\hat{a}^-$ of AV3 and $\hat{a}^-$ of AV4 are independent of $\hat{a}$ when $|\alpha| \approx 1$, a finding that will be established analytically in section 11.5.

Remark 11.3. CV2 is less volatile than CV1 because the latter performs better as $\alpha \to 0$ but is rather poor at the other extreme ($|\alpha| \to 1$) for understandable reasons (by construction). The reversal in ranking occurs at $|\alpha| \approx 0.8$ for $T < 100$, and at $|\alpha| \approx 0.9$ for $T \geq 100$. The higher $|\alpha|$ in the second case is explained by the smaller asymptotic relative difference between the normalization (h) of the two CVs; compare (11.20) with (11.21). As expected from the optimum estimation of c, CV3 is by definition the most efficient of all three CVs for each and every α, T. This property could be useful when N is small. In addition, it is more flexible than CV1 because it can cope with any value of α. A common feature of the CVs is that they suffer a marked deterioration of performance as $|\alpha| \to 1$ and T increases; a result in line with the analysis at the end of section 11.2.

Remark 11.4. The average value of $\hat{c}$ (the OLS estimator of the optimum control coefficient) is not statistically different from 1. The estimate of c is closest to 1 when $|\alpha| \approx 1$, CV2 and CV3 becoming almost identical. The gain (at little extra cost) from using CV3 instead of CV2 comes from $|\alpha| \ll 1$ where CV2 is even weaker than CV1; and it increases as T and/or N fall. The estimated $\hat{c}$ rises stochastically as α and T increase, albeit with increased volatility. This increased volatility is due to the problems of simulating near nonstationarity where values of N need to be larger than usual to achieve a given level of accuracy (eg see Lai and Siegmund, 1983, last column of their Table 2, for a related problem). This need for high N does not contradict the speedy convergence of unit-root distributions to their asymptotics. It just means that the price paid for faster convergence is increased volatility. To understand this, compare the standardization factors for $(\hat{a} - \alpha)$ when $|\alpha|$ goes from being a stable to a unit root: multiplying $(\hat{a} - \alpha)$ by T instead of $\sqrt{T}$ amplifies the variability of the resulting statistic from one replication to the other. The problem becomes very serious in explosive series with $|\alpha| > 1$ where the normalization factor is exponential (proportional to $|\alpha|^T$) *and* depends on the initial observation of the series (y_0). The lesson is that one should be careful in drawing conclusions from simulations of a system of series with significantly varying degrees of nonstationarity, especially if N is fixed at the same level for all the series that are being simulated.

The remainder of this section will be devoted to summarizing the features of each new VRT by means of a Response Surface (RS). The RS ascertains the average behaviour of efficiency gains as α and T change, so as to understand and predict the performance of the VRTs. Moreover as explained in Hendry (1984), a RS reduces the specificity of MC experiments. Letting $p_1 = 1, 2, \ldots$ and $p_2 = 0, 1, \ldots$, the explanatory variables are of the form $|\alpha|^{Tp_1}/T^{p_2/2}$, $\sinh(\alpha^2)/T^{p_1/2}$, and $\cosh(\alpha^2)/T^{p_1/2}$, with variables that are insignificant at the 5% level dropped from the RS. In the case of AVs, we also have the limiting EGs (that will be derived in section 11.5) as additional explanatory variables; whereas in the case of CVs, we add separate functions of $|\alpha|$ and T.

Hyperbolic functions can be defined as

$$\cosh(z) := \frac{1}{2}(e^z + e^{-z}) \quad \text{and} \quad \sinh(z) := \frac{1}{2}(e^z - e^{-z}). \tag{11.24}$$

Their appearance is in line with some analytical results on autoregressions; see Abadir (1993b). Powers of $|\alpha|^T$ can be thought of as dummies representing unit roots asymptotically and near nonstationarity when T is finite; since:

$$\begin{aligned} |\alpha|^T &= 1 \text{ for } |\alpha| = 1 \\ |\alpha|^T &\approx 1 \text{ for } |\alpha| \approx 1 \text{ and } T < \infty \\ |\alpha|^T &\approx 0 \text{ for } |\alpha| \ll 1, \text{ or for } |\alpha| < 1 \text{ and } T \to \infty. \end{aligned} \tag{11.25}$$

This takes care of the different nature of distributional results for the cases of $|\alpha| \approx 1$ and $|\alpha| \ll 1$. Such terms explain why there will be no evidence of structural breaks in the RSs when the root is near unity, in spite of the radically different asymptotic theories required by the two extremes 0 and 1 of $|\alpha|$. Powers of $|\alpha|^T$ could be used as weights in analytically solving the problem of finding closed forms for general finite-sample distributions whose range of applicability includes $|\alpha| \neq 1$ as well as $|\alpha| = 1$.[5] There is some evidence that this approach could bear fruit since finite-sample distributions are mixtures of the limiting normal and the distribution under $|\alpha| = 1$, with greater weight assigned to the latter for typical T. For example, compare Phillips' (1977, 1978a, and especially 1978b) finite sample approximations for the distributions when $|\alpha| < 1$ with the formulae in Abadir (1993a, 1995), or see the numerical results of Evans and Savin (1981). Abadir (1995) tackles this problem from a different angle (an asymptotic one): unit root distribution

[5] See Abadir (1992) for an asymptotic encompassing formula for the distributions of all statistics when $|\alpha| = 1$.

functions provide the general formulae that are encompassing generalizations of the standard normal which arises in the limit for the Studentized t statistic when $|\alpha| \neq 1$. The $|\alpha|^T$ term can also be interpreted as an exponential proxy for Hendry's (1984, p. 965) notion of 'effective sample size', extended to the case when $|\alpha| \geq 1$. Hendry's effective sample size, $T(1-\alpha^2)$, is only valid for $|\alpha| < 1$. For a different generalization of this term to include $|\alpha| \neq 1$, see Abadir (1993c). The disadvantage of the latter generalization is that it is discontinuous at $|\alpha| = 1$ and is useful only in asymptotic analysis, unlike the continuum provided by $|\alpha|^T$ throughout the range of α and T.

The RS of EGAV1 is

$$\log(\text{EGAV1}) = -\log(5+\alpha^2) + \underset{\substack{(0.005)\\ [0.004]}}{2.07} + \underset{\substack{(0.02)\\ [0.02]}}{0.21}\,|\alpha|^T - \underset{\substack{(0.19)\\ [0.19]}}{0.82}\,|\alpha|^T/\sqrt{T}$$

$$+ \underset{\substack{(0.07)\\ [0.06]}}{0.36}\,\sinh(\alpha^2)/\sqrt{T} \tag{11.26}$$

$$\bar{R}^2 = 0.83, \qquad S = 0.0218, \qquad CH(4,42) = 1.77,$$

where:

(.) = conventional standard errors,

[.] = White's (1980) heteroskedasticity-consistent standard errors,

$\bar{R}^2$ = the coefficient of determination after a degrees-of-freedom adjustment,

S = residual standard error,

CH(a,b) = Chow's (1960) test for structural break at $|\alpha| = 1$, with F(a,b) as reference distribution.

The first term of the RS is its asymptotic value when $|\alpha| < 1$, up to an additive constant. It is not estimated: the coefficient is restricted in accordance with the asymptotics of section 11.5.2 (notice that $\log 8 = 2.08$ which is approximately the constant term of (11.26)). There is no evidence of heteroskedasticity, as is seen from the small difference between the two types of standard errors. Furthermore, the 5% critical value for F(4,42) is 2.59, so there is no break at $|\alpha| = 1$. The fit is good, but it can be improved if one were to include more variables at the cost of interpretability and parsimony. Here, we can see that increasing $|\alpha|^T$ improves the efficiency gain (the gain increases with α, but declines with T especially when α is small), which was noted in Remark 11.1 above. The coefficient of the last term works in the same direction, while the impact of $|\alpha|^T/\sqrt{T}$ is smaller than the other terms because of the effect of a large T.

AV2 could be summarized by a RS similar to (11.26), but there is little point in doing so here because of the breakdown of this method when $T > 100$, and because of its relative cost; see (11.10) and the ensuing discussion.

The promising features of AV3 and AV4 can be described by the following RS, where the first term is again from the asymptotics of section 11.5.2:

$$\log(\text{EGAV4,3}) = \log(1+\alpha^{-2}) - \underset{\substack{(0.0051)\\ [0.0049]}}{0.0170} + \underset{\substack{(0.03)\\ [0.03]}}{0.28} \cosh(\alpha^2)/\sqrt{T} \tag{11.27}$$

$$\bar{R}^2 = 0.9998, \qquad S = 0.0163, \qquad CH(2,46) = 1.17,$$

where the five data points pertaining to $\alpha = 0$ have been replaced by five others that were generated under $|\alpha| = 0.1$, because $\alpha \to 0$ leads to an infinite EG which creates a precision problem for the regression. Notice that the figures for $\bar{R}^2$ are somewhat inflated by the large variation in the left-hand side, especially as $\alpha \to 0$. However, there is no break in this relation as $|\alpha| \to 1$, since the critical 5% value of F(2,46) is 3.20. Together, the asymptotics of section 11.5.2 and hyperbolic functions are seen here to dramatically explain a lot of what happens as α changes.

We now turn to CVs. The RS for all three are quite similar; to save space, only the RS of CV3 (which is superior to the other two) will be reported.

$$\begin{aligned}\log(\text{EGCV3}) &= \underset{\substack{(0.54)\\ [0.97]}}{10.63} - \underset{\substack{(6.05)\\ [5.75]}}{41.27}/\sqrt{T} - \underset{\substack{(0.37)\\ [0.64]}}{6.79} \cosh(\alpha^2) + \underset{\substack{(5.69)\\ [4.64]}}{33.47} \cosh(\alpha^2)/\sqrt{T} - \underset{\substack{(2.18)\\ [1.15]}}{7.68} \sinh(\alpha^2)/\sqrt{T}\\ &+ \underset{\substack{(0.030)\\ [0.031]}}{0.17} (1-|\alpha|)\log T - \underset{\substack{(0.11)\\ [0.08]}}{0.72} \left(1-|\alpha|^T\right) + \underset{\substack{(0.0065)\\ [0.0097]}}{0.079} \left(1-|\alpha|^T\right)\sqrt{T}\end{aligned} \tag{11.28}$$

$$\bar{R}^2 = 0.99, \qquad S = 0.107, \qquad CH(5,42) = 1.19.$$

Note that all the terms in the second line are zero when $\alpha = 1$. Note also that for $\alpha = 1$ and $T \to \infty$, one finds that log(EGCV3) is predicted to converge to the finite number $10.63 - 6.79\cosh(1) = 0.15$, ie (11.28) predicts that EGCV3 converges to 1.16. On the other hand, when $|\alpha| < 1$ (stationary case), the second line diverges as $T \to \infty$ and $\log(\text{EGCV3})/\sqrt{T} \to 0.079$, ie EGCV3 tends to ∞.

Here also, the fit is good and there is no evidence of either structural breaks at $|\alpha| = 1$ or heteroskedasticity. Though still small, S is higher in (11.28) than in any other RS presented in this work, due to the more volatile performance of CVs relative to the AVs considered above. The fit of (11.28) appears to be worse for α very close to 1, possibly due to the different behaviour for $|\alpha| = 1$ and $|\alpha| < 1$ as $T \to \infty$ discussed above; see also section 11.5.

11.4 Uses and Extensions of the VRTs

Caution should be exercised when employing VRTs in a dynamic context. There is a marked change in efficiency gains as $|\alpha|$ and T vary jointly. Contrary to what classical asymptotic theory suggests, doubling the sample size will have effects that are dependent on the *level* of T instead of just halving the variance of the modified estimator $\widetilde{\alpha}$. The RS of the previous section can be used to avoid such pitfalls by predicting how VRTs fare as $|\alpha|$ and T change.

For increased efficiency gains when $\alpha \neq 0$, one may combine more than one of the VRTs described above, depending on their correlation and on the specific problem at hand (eg magnitudes of α and T). The best method of doing so was detailed by Davidson and MacKinnon (1992) who show that the optimal combination of VRTs will be in the form of a regression run in the same spirit as (11.22). In order for the researcher not to waste valuable time generating VRTs that are not useful for the problem at hand, an a priori selection of VRTs should be made according to the criteria given earlier. These VRTs should then be the inputs of the aforementioned regression.

Combinations of VRTs of different *types* are likely to do best, when using the method of Davidson and MacKinnon (1992). This is an interesting area for future research. Given their relatively strong performance in dynamic DGPs, CV3 and one of AV3 or AV4 are the most prominent candidates. Moreover, because AV3 and AV4 have a good performance also for unit roots while CV3 does well for intermediate persistence, combining the two types of VRTs gives a smoother performance as persistence changes. Also, the exceptionally good performance of AV3 and AV4 when T is small should remedy the weakness of CV3 in small samples. In the more specific event of a nearly nonstationary DGP, the narrowly interpreted AV1—which is the only VRT (apart from the erratic AV2) to improve as $|\alpha|$ gets closer to 1—may also be added to the combination to yield even more efficiency gains.

The AVs presented earlier are special cases of what we can call an orthogonal-transform AV. In particular, AV1–AV3 are all special cases involving premultiplication of $\varepsilon := (\varepsilon_1, \ldots, \varepsilon_T)'$ by an orthogonal matrix; hence ε and its transformation have the same first two moments. These orthogonal matrices were, respectively:

1. $\boldsymbol{R} := \mathrm{diag}(\boldsymbol{Q}_1, \boldsymbol{Q}_2, \ldots)$, where $\boldsymbol{Q}_i := \boldsymbol{A}_{p_i}\boldsymbol{B}_{\omega_i}$ $(i = 1, \ldots, T/2)$ with

$$\boldsymbol{A}_p := \begin{pmatrix} (-1)^p & 0 \\ 0 & 1 \end{pmatrix}, \quad p \in \{0, 1\}; \quad \boldsymbol{B}_\omega := \begin{pmatrix} \cos\omega & \sin\omega \\ -\sin\omega & \cos\omega \end{pmatrix}, \quad \omega \in (0, 2\pi).$$

The 4 possible AV1s are obtained setting $p_i = p \in \{0, 1\}$ and $\omega_i = \omega \in \{\frac{1}{4}\pi, \frac{5}{4}\pi\}$.[6] The matrix $\boldsymbol{A}_p$ changes sign to the first innovation, while

[6] One could also vary p, ω with i, but we will not do so here.

$\boldsymbol{B}_\omega$ describes a rotation with angle ω. If $\boldsymbol{Q}_i = \boldsymbol{Q}_j$ for all i, j, then $\boldsymbol{R} = \boldsymbol{I}_{T/2} \otimes \boldsymbol{Q}_1$. This class contains many variants; a simple set of k distinct $\boldsymbol{R}$ matrices, denoted by $\boldsymbol{R}_1, \dots, \boldsymbol{R}_k$, can for instance be obtained by fixing $p_i = p \in \{0, 1\}$ and choosing angles $\omega_1 < \omega_2 < \dots < \omega_k$ in $(0, 2\pi)$.

2. $\boldsymbol{S} := (e_T, e_{T-1}, \dots, e_1)$, where e_i is the i-th column of the identity matrix $\boldsymbol{I}_T$. More generally, $\boldsymbol{S}$ can be chosen as any permutation of the columns of $\boldsymbol{I}_T$; i.e. a permutation matrix having exactly one element equal to 1 in any row (equivalent to sampling from ε without replacement). A simple set of k distinct $\boldsymbol{S}$ matrices, denoted $\boldsymbol{S}_1, \dots, \boldsymbol{S}_k$, can for instance be obtained by choosing k different permutations of the ordered set $\{1, 2, \dots T\}$.
3. $\boldsymbol{T} := \mathrm{diag}(-1, 1, -1, \dots)$, where the typical element of the diagonal is $(-1)^i$. This class contains many variants; a simple set of k distinct $\boldsymbol{T}$ matrices, denoted $\boldsymbol{T}_1, \dots, \boldsymbol{T}_k$, can for instance be obtained by setting $\boldsymbol{T}_i := \mathrm{diag}(-\boldsymbol{I}_i, \boldsymbol{I}_i, -\boldsymbol{I}_i, \dots)$, where the last block is possibly truncated so as to fit in a $T \times T$ matrix. (This corresponds to generating the AV $\{(-1)^{\kappa(t)}\varepsilon_t\}$, with $\kappa(t) = \lceil \frac{t}{i} \rceil$.) It is also possible to switch the sign randomly, but independently of ε, rather than do it deterministically.

Although VRTs were only mentioned so far in connection with estimating the moments of econometric estimators, it is possible to use them on a wider scale. For example, Rothery (1982) reduced the uncertainty in estimating the MC power of a test by using the known power of another as the control variate in a manner similar to CV1 and CV2 where c is fixed at 1.[7] Rothery's technique could be extended to allow for the estimation of $\hat{c}$ as in CV3. Another example is in Durbin and Koopman (1997, especially pp. 674–676), where independence properties of the normal distribution are exploited to generate a new class of AVs. CVs based on Taylor series are also given there.

VRTs can also be used to improve the accuracy of numerical integration routines (but see Fang, Wang, and Bentler, 1994) for an alternative approach). Using MC in numerical integration has become part of the Bayesian tool kit for analysing posterior densities since the seminal paper by Kloek and van Dijk (1978). Bayesian and other integration intensive applications stand to benefit from using the new VRTs.

Another illustration of the wide and not necessarily standard applicability of VRTs can be obtained by using the antithetic variates $\hat{\alpha}^-$ as if they were actual estimates $\hat{\alpha}$ from another replication, thus saving the time taken to generate half of the replications. This procedure can be used in any

[7] This method assumes that the distribution of the test used as CV can be calculated explicitly; see Paruolo (2002) on the influence of estimation of critical values in comparing test powers by simulation.

simulation work involving $\hat{a}$, such as estimating the distributions of *any* statistic associated with $\hat{a}$, under a null or under an alternative (e.g. power).

The dependence of $\hat{a}^-$ and $\hat{a}$ can be exploited as discussed above, see Davidson and MacKinnon (1992). When $\hat{a}^-$ and $\hat{a}$ happen to be independent, one can use them simply as different replicates; this is what happens for AV3 and AV4 in the case of near nonstationarity, for all values of T, since EGAV4,3 ≈ 2 by RS (11.27) or by Remark 11.2 on the results at the beginning of section 11.3; see also the following section 11.5 for an analytic proof.

11.5 Large-Sample Analytics

In this section, we study the asymptotic distribution of $(\hat{a},\hat{a}^-)$ when $T \to \infty$. We hence obtain the limiting EGs for the new AVs, see the discussion at the end of section 11.2. A similar analysis is also applied to study the limit behaviour of EGs for CVs. We discuss AVs in sections 11.5.1 and 11.5.2 for the nonstationary and the stationary cases, respectively; we treat CVs in section 11.5.3.

We start by introducting notation for AVs. Denote the initial sequence $\{\varepsilon_t\}$ as $\{\varepsilon_{1,t}\} := \{\varepsilon_t\}$, and we let $\{\varepsilon_{2,t}\} := \{\varepsilon_t^-\}$ indicate the AV innovations. Conformably, we indicate by $\{y_{1,t}\}$ and $\{y_{2,t}\}$ the corresponding values of y_t generated by the DGP (11.1). In order to emphasize the dependence on T, we indicate by $\hat{a}_{1,T}$ the crude MC estimate of a based on $\{y_{1,t}\}$ and by $\hat{a}_{2,T}$ the one obtained from $\{y_{2,t}\}$. The combined estimator is indicated by $\widetilde{a}_T := \frac{1}{2}(\hat{a}_{1,T} + \hat{a}_{2,T})$, where $\mathrm{E}(\hat{a}_{1,T}) = \mathrm{E}(\widetilde{a}_T) = \mathrm{E}(\hat{a}_{2,T})$.

In the light of the discussion of the last section, we extend the definition of AV1 to include all transformation of the type $\boldsymbol{B}_\omega$, excluding the sign-switching effect associated with $\boldsymbol{A}_1$.[8] Specifically, recall that T is even, and let $t = 1, \ldots, T$, and $m = 1, \ldots, T/2$. For AV1 we fix a given angle $\omega \in (0, 2\pi)$, and we employ the following pairs of definitions for t odd ($t = 2m - 1$) and t even ($t = 2m$):

$$\varepsilon_{2,2m-1} := \cos(\omega)\,\varepsilon_{1,2m-1} + \sin(\omega)\,\varepsilon_{1,2m}$$

$$\varepsilon_{2,2m} := -\sin(\omega)\,\varepsilon_{1,2m-1} + \cos(\omega)\,\varepsilon_{1,2m}.$$

Moreover, recall that in the present notation $\varepsilon_{2,t} := \varepsilon_{1,T-t}$ for AV2 and $\varepsilon_{2,t} := (-1)^t \varepsilon_{1,t}$ for AV3. AV4 is defined differently, but gives the same AV $\hat{a}_{2,T}$ as AV3, so we do not distinguish AV3 from AV4 in this section, and we refer to them as AV4,3.

We let $\hat{\theta}_T := (\hat{a}_{1,T}, \hat{a}_{2,T})'$ be the 2×1 vector of a estimates, so that $\widetilde{a}_T = \frac{1}{2}\boldsymbol{\imath}'\hat{\theta}_T$ where $\boldsymbol{\imath} := (1,1)'$ and consider limits as $T \to \infty$. Because of the consistency of estimators $\hat{a}_{i,T}$, ie plim $\hat{a}_{i,T} = a$, also plim $\widetilde{a}_T = a$. Moreover if $\hat{\theta}_T$ satisfies

[8] The effect of switching the sign is already investigated through the study of AV4,3.

some limit theorem of the type $\boldsymbol{a}_T := T^q(\hat{\theta}_T - \alpha\boldsymbol{\iota}) \overset{w}{\to} \boldsymbol{a}_\infty = O_p(1)$ (where $q = 1$ for $\alpha = 1$ and $q = \frac{1}{2}$ for $|\alpha| < 1$), then also $T^q(\widetilde{\alpha}_T - \alpha) \overset{w}{\to} \frac{1}{2}\boldsymbol{\iota}'\boldsymbol{a}_\infty = O_p(1)$, and the limit distribution of $\widetilde{\alpha}_T$ can be deduced from the one of $\hat{\theta}_T$. Hence, one can use the limit random vector $\boldsymbol{a}_\infty$ as an approximation to the distribution of $\hat{\theta}_T$ for finite T.

Let $\boldsymbol{m}_T := \mathrm{E}(\boldsymbol{a}_T)$, $\boldsymbol{V}_T := \mathrm{var}(\boldsymbol{a}_T)$, and note that $\mathrm{var}(\hat{\theta}_T) = T^{-2q}\boldsymbol{V}_T$. Substituting in (11.6) one finds

$$\mathrm{var}(\widetilde{\alpha}_T) = \frac{1}{4T^{2q}}\boldsymbol{\iota}'\boldsymbol{V}_T\boldsymbol{\iota}. \tag{11.29}$$

Let also $\boldsymbol{\Sigma} := \mathrm{var}(\boldsymbol{a}_\infty)$. Under regularity conditions, $\boldsymbol{V}_T$ converges to $\boldsymbol{\Sigma}$ as $\boldsymbol{a}_T \overset{w}{\to} \boldsymbol{a}_\infty$. If these conditions are met, then one can use $\boldsymbol{\Sigma}$ as guidance for $\boldsymbol{V}_T$ in (11.29).

Each AVj implies a different $\boldsymbol{V}_T$ and $\boldsymbol{\Sigma}$. We label $\boldsymbol{\Sigma}_j$ the limiting variance matrix for AVj and indicate by ρ_j the implied correlation coefficient. One can discuss which AV method is bound to give the highest variance reduction in (11.29) for large values of T by comparing

$$\boldsymbol{\iota}'\Sigma_j\boldsymbol{\iota} \tag{11.30}$$

for $j = 1, 2$, and 4, 3. This comparison can be based on values of the correlation ρ_j in the case of equal variances, see (11.7). In particular we indicate the limit value of EGv as

$$\mathrm{EGAV}j_\infty := \frac{2}{1+\rho_j}. \tag{11.31}$$

11.5.1 *AVs, Nonstationary Case*

Let $\alpha = 1$ and define the normalized partial sums for $i = 1, 2$

$$s_i(u) := \sigma^{-1}T^{-1/2}\sum_{t=1}^{\lfloor Tu \rfloor}\varepsilon_{it} = \sigma^{-1}T^{-1/2}y_{i,\lfloor Tu \rfloor},$$

and $\boldsymbol{s}(u) := (s_1(u), s_2(u))'$. In this case $q = 1$ in the normalization $\boldsymbol{a}_T := T^q(\hat{\theta}_T - \alpha\iota)$, where

$$a_{iT} := T(\hat{a}_{iT} - 1) = \frac{\sum_t s_i\left(\frac{t-1}{T}\right)\left(s_i\left(\frac{t}{T}\right) - s_i\left(\frac{t-1}{T}\right)\right)}{\frac{1}{T}\sum_t s_i\left(\frac{t-1}{T}\right)^2}$$
$$= \frac{\frac{1}{2}\left(s_i(1)^2 - \sum_t\left(s_i\left(\frac{t}{T}\right) - s_i\left(\frac{t-1}{T}\right)\right)^2\right)}{\frac{1}{T}\sum_t s_i\left(\frac{t-1}{T}\right)^2},$$

which is a functional of $s_i(u)$ for u in $U_T := \{\frac{t}{T}, t = 2, \ldots, T\}$. One has $a_{iT} = \psi(s_i) + o_p(1)$, where the functional ψ is defined as

$$\psi(x) := \frac{\frac{1}{2}\left(x^2(1) - 1\right)}{\int_0^1 x^2(\tau)\,\mathrm{d}\tau}$$

for any function $x(\tau)$ in the space $D[0,1]$ of cadlag functions on [0,1]. We notice that ψ is a continuous functional in the sup metric, provided the denominator is different from 0 a.s., which holds in the case of x equal to Brownian motions (BMs). Note that for the partial sums s_i, one has

$$\psi(s_i) = \frac{\frac{1}{2}\left(s_i(1)^2 - 1\right)}{\frac{1}{T}\sum_t s_i\left(\frac{t-1}{T}\right)^2}.$$

We also note that $\psi(x)$ is an even functional, in the sense that, given the function $x := x(\tau)$ and its reflection across the time axis $-x := -x(\tau)$, then $\psi(-x) = \psi(x)$, because $x(\tau)^2 = (-x(\tau))^2$, $0 \leq \tau \leq 1$, both in the numerator and denominator of ψ.

We wish to characterize the dependence between a_{1T} and a_{2T} for large T. In order to do this we study the weak limits of partial sums $s_1(u)$ and $s_2(u)$ in the following lemma. We denote by $W(u)$ a vector Brownian motion with variance $\boldsymbol{V}$, i.e. with $W(u) \sim \mathrm{N}(\mathbf{0}, u\boldsymbol{V})$ and by $B(u)$ a standard vector Brownian motion, ie $W(u)$ with $\boldsymbol{V} = \boldsymbol{I}_2$.

Lemma 11.1. *When $\alpha = 1$, the following holds, for various AVj.*

1. *For AV1, $\mathbf{s}(u) \overset{w}{\to} W(u)$ where $W(u)$ is a Brownian motion with*

$$\boldsymbol{V} = \begin{pmatrix} 1 & \cos(\omega) \\ \cos(\omega) & 1 \end{pmatrix}.$$

2. *For AV2,*

$$\begin{pmatrix} s_1(u) \\ s_2(u) \end{pmatrix} \overset{w}{\to} \begin{pmatrix} \int_0^u \mathrm{d}B_1(\tau) \\ \int_{1-u}^1 \mathrm{d}B_1(\tau) \end{pmatrix} = \begin{pmatrix} B_1(u) \\ B_1(1) - B_1(1-u) \end{pmatrix},$$

ie both $s_1(u)$ and $s_2(u)$ converge to a univariate standard Brownian motion, with the property that the second one, $B_1(1) - B_1(1-u)$, is the Brownian motion obtained by reversing the time of the first one, $B_1(u)$.

3. *For AV4,3,*

$$\mathbf{s}(u) \overset{w}{\to} B(u)$$

where $B(u)$ is a standard vector Brownian motion.

Proof: Cases AV1 and AV4,3: we apply a Cramér-Wold device. Consider real λ_i, $i = 1, 2$, $\lambda := (\lambda_1, \lambda_2)'$ and define

$$s_3(u) := \lambda' \mathbf{s}(u) = \sum_{i=1}^{2} \lambda_i s_i(u) = \sigma^{-1} T^{-1/2} \sum_{t=1}^{\lfloor Tu \rfloor} c_t \varepsilon_{1t},$$

where for AV1 one finds $c_{2m-1} = \lambda_1 + \lambda_2 (\cos(\omega) - \sin(\omega))$, $c_{2m} = \lambda_1 + \lambda_2 (\cos(\omega) + \sin(\omega))$, $m = 1, \ldots, T/2$, while for AV4,3 $c_t = \lambda_1 + (-1)^t \lambda_2$. Applying the univariate FCLT for martingale differences, see Brown (1971), one sees that

$$s_3(u) \overset{w}{\to} W_3(u) \qquad u = [0,1]$$

with $W_3(u)$ a Brownian motion with variance $v := \lim_{T\to\infty} T^{-1} \sum_{t=1}^{T} c_t^2$. For AV1,

$$\begin{aligned} v &= \frac{1}{2}\left((\lambda_1 + \lambda_2 (\cos(\omega) - \sin(\omega)))^2 + (\lambda_1 + \lambda_2 (\cos(\omega) + \sin(\omega)))^2 \right) \\ &= \lambda_1^2 + 2(\cos(\omega))\lambda_1\lambda_2 + \lambda_2^2 = \lambda' \boldsymbol{V} \lambda \end{aligned}$$

which implies the expression of $\boldsymbol{V}$ given in the statement of case 1. For AV4,3

$$v = \lambda_1^2 + \lambda_2^2 + 2\lambda_1\lambda_2 \lim_{T\to\infty} T^{-1} \sum_{t=1}^{T} (-1)^t = \lambda_1^2 + \lambda_2^2 = \lambda' \boldsymbol{I}_2 \lambda,$$

where we have used the fact that for integer p one has

$$\sum_{i=1}^{2p} (-1)^i = 0. \tag{11.32}$$

This shows convergence of the finite dimensional distributions of $\mathbf{s}(u)$ to $B(u)$. Tightness follows as in Brown (1971) Theorem 3.

Case AV2 follows as a direct application of time reversal of random walks and the associated limit BM.

Remark 11.5. AV1 generates correlated BMs. The correlation can be chosen to be positive or negative by choice of the angle ω. For instance $\omega = \pi/4$ gives a correlation of $\sqrt{2}/2$ while $\omega = 3\pi/4$ gives a correlation of $-\sqrt{2}/2$. In order to maximize correlations one can choose a small number δ and set $\omega = \delta$ for highly positive and $\omega = \pi - \delta$ for highly negative correlations.

Note, however, that the correlations generated by choice of ω may not help variance reduction for the functional ψ, because it is even. Note in fact, that if two univariate BMs W_1 and W_2 have correlation ρ, then W_1 and $-W_2$ have correlation $-\rho$. However, $\psi(W_2) = \psi(-W_2)$, so that generating BMs with positive or negative correlations will have the same effect on $\widetilde{\alpha}_T$ in the limit.

For the choice $\omega = \pi/4$ used in previous sections, we have estimated ρ_1 by simulating $\psi(s_1)$ and $\psi(s_2)$ for T = 1,000, 5,000, 10,000 and N = 10,000, and calculating the correlation between MC replications. We have obtained estimates of ρ_1 equal to 0.24, 0.23, 0.24 for the 3 values of T. We can hence infer that the large T value of ρ_1 is about 0.24. This gives $\text{EGAV1}_\infty = 2/1.24 = 1.61$, while the RS of section 11.3 gave essentially the same because $\exp(-\log(6) + 2.07 + 0.21) = 1.63$.

Remark 11.6. AV2 generates time-reversed BMs, B_1 and $B_1^{\hookleftarrow}$ say. Note that the functional $\psi(x)$ depends on the last value of the argument function x, which is equal for both BM, and on the area under the squared path of x, which is not equal for B_1 and $B_1^{\hookleftarrow}$. In fact by a simple change of variable $t = 1 - \tau$, one has

$$\int_0^1 B_1^{\hookleftarrow}(\tau)^2 \mathrm{d}\tau = \int_0^1 (B_1(1) - B_1(1-\tau))^2 \,\mathrm{d}\tau = \int_0^1 (B_1(1) - B_1(t))^2 \,\mathrm{d}t$$
$$= \int_0^1 B_1(t)^2 \mathrm{d}t + B_1(1)^2 - 2B_1(1) \int_0^1 B_1(t)\mathrm{d}t.$$

Hence one expects AV2 replicates $\hat{a}_{1,T}$, $\hat{a}_{2,T}$ to be correlated.

Also for AV2, we have estimated ρ_2 by simulating $\psi(s_1)$ and $\psi(s_2)$ for $T = 1{,}000$, 5,000, 10,000 and $N = 10{,}000$, and calculating the correlation between MC replications. We have obtained estimates of ρ_2 equal to 0.74 for all 3 values of T. We can hence infer that the large T value of ρ_2 is about 0.74. This gives $\text{EGAV2}_\infty = 2/1.74 = 1.15$.

Remark 11.7. AV4,3 generates independent BMs B_1 and B_2. Hence also $\psi(B_1)$ and $\psi(B_2)$ will be independent, and hence ρ_3 in (11.31) is null. This gives $\text{EGAV4,3}_\infty = 2$; while the RS of section 11.3 gave $\exp(\log(2) - 0.0170) = 1.97$.

The same remarks given above apply to AV4,3 when $(-1)^t$ is substituted by some other centred periodic function of t, eg like $(-1)^{\kappa(t)}$, $\kappa(t) = \lceil \frac{t}{i} \rceil$. In this case $2p$ needs to be replaced by ip in (11.32), where i is the period of the periodic function.

One can enquire how fast this independence is attained for AV4,3 in simulations with finite T. To this end, (11.32) above shows that $s_1(\frac{t}{T})$ and $s_2(\frac{t}{T})$ are independent under Gaussian ε_{1t} also for finite T, when t is even. When t is odd, $\mathrm{E}(s_1(\frac{t}{T})s_2(\frac{t}{T})) = \frac{1}{T}$.

11.5.2 *AVs, Stationary Case*

Let $|\alpha| < 1$, and set $q = \frac{1}{2}$ in the normalization of $\boldsymbol{a}_T := T^{1/2}(\hat{\theta}_T - \alpha\imath)$, where

$$a_{iT} := T^{1/2}(\hat{a}_{iT} - \alpha) := \frac{N_{iT}}{D_{iT}} := \frac{T^{-1/2}\sum_t y_{i,t-1}\varepsilon_{i,t}}{T^{-1}\sum_t y_{i,t-1}^2}.$$

In the case of $|\alpha| < 1$, y_t is stationary and ergodic, ie

$$D_{iT} := T^{-1}\sum_t y_{i,t-1}^2 \overset{a.s.}{\to} D_i := \mathrm{E}\left(y_{i,t}^2\right) = \frac{\sigma^2}{1-\alpha^2}.$$

It is hence natural to consider the approximation $a_{iT} = b_{iT} + o_p(1)$ with

$$b_{iT} := \frac{N_{iT}}{D_i} := \frac{T^{-1/2}\sum_t y_{i,t-1}\varepsilon_{i,t}}{\mathrm{E}\left(y_{i,t}^2\right)}.$$

Note that $\mathrm{E}(b_{i,T}) = 0$ and

$$\mathrm{var}\left(b_{i,T}\right) = \frac{\sigma^2}{TD_i^2}\sum\nolimits_t \mathrm{E}\left(y_{i,t-1}^2\right) \to \frac{\sigma^2}{D_i} = 1 - \alpha^2.$$

The following lemma summarizes results in the stationary case.

Lemma 11.2. *When $|\alpha| < 1$, $\boldsymbol{b}_T := (b_{1,T},\ b_{2,T})'$ is $O_p(1)$ for $T \to \infty$, and*

$$\mathrm{var}\left(\boldsymbol{b}_T\right) \to \Sigma := \left(1 - \alpha^2\right)\begin{pmatrix} 1 & \rho \\ \rho & 1 \end{pmatrix},$$

where the values of the correlation term ρ are given below for the various AVj, using the notation ρ_j for AVj:

$$\textit{for AV1, } \rho_1 = \frac{1+\alpha^2}{2}\cos^2\omega \textit{ and } \textit{EGAV1}_\infty = \frac{4}{2 + (1+\alpha^2)\cos^2\omega};$$

$$\textit{for AV2, } \rho_2 = 1 \textit{ and } \textit{EGAV2}_\infty = 1;$$

$$\textit{for AV4,3, } \rho_3 = -\frac{1-\alpha^2}{1+\alpha^2} \textit{ and } \textit{EGAV4,3}_\infty = 1 + \frac{1}{\alpha^2}.$$

Proof: The proof of this lemma is given in the Appendix.

The correlation terms ρ_j are continuous functions in α for $-1 < \alpha < 1$, but not all ρ_j are continuous as $|\alpha| \to 1$; see Figure 11.1. It is likely that these discontinuities could be bridged if a DGP with local-to-unity parameter is adopted; eg see Phillips (1987) for a definition of such a DGP and its relation to ours. For the current setup, we can note the following:

Remark 11.8. The *AV*1 correlation ρ_1 is always positive, and hence implies not-so-big variance reductions. It tends to $\cos^2\omega$ when $|\alpha| \to 1$ and to $\frac{1}{2}\cos^2\omega$ for $\alpha = 0$. For $\omega = \pi/4$, for instance $\rho_1 \to \frac{1}{2}$ for $|\alpha| \to 1$ and $\rho_1 = \frac{1}{4}$ for $\alpha = 0$. The correlation ρ_1 is discontinuous at $|\alpha| = 1$. From Remark 11.5 above, $\rho_1 = 0.24$ when $\alpha = 1$, $\omega = \pi/4$. Hence, $\lim_{\alpha\to 1}\rho_1 = \frac{1}{2} \neq 0.24$ and EG improves when $|\alpha|$ reaches 1.

Remark 11.9. The choice of ω influences the variance reduction properties of *AV*1. When $\omega \to 0$, the performance is worst, because $\cos^2\omega = 1$; for $\omega = \pi/2$ the performance is best, because in this case $\rho_1 = 0$ for all α. This is shown graphically in Figure 11.2 for $-1 < \alpha < 1$.

The case $\omega = \pi/2$ implies that the antithetic ε_{2t} is formed by interchanging consecutive ε_{1t} and changing the sign for odd t, ie $\varepsilon_{2,2m} = -\varepsilon_{1,2m-1}$, $\varepsilon_{2,2m-1} = \varepsilon_{1,2m}$. Comparing this to the effect of *AV*4,3, which just changes the sign for

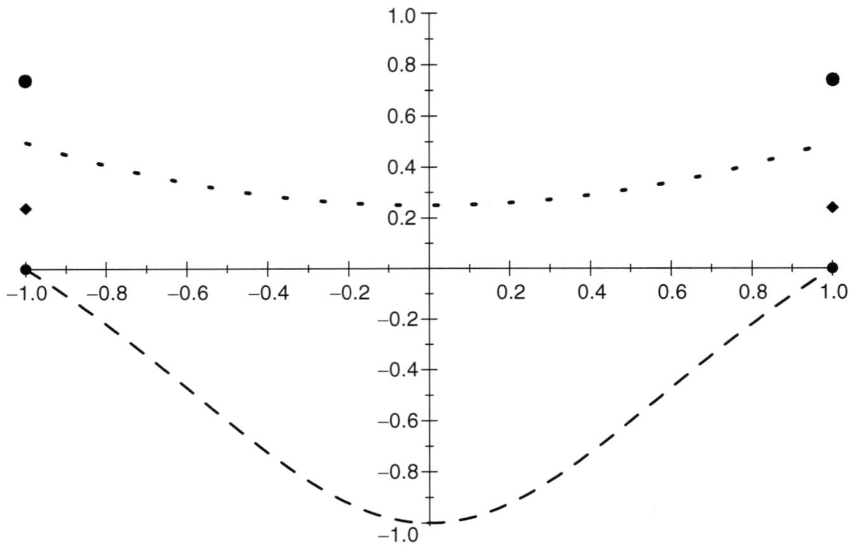

FIG. **11.1.** AV correlations as function of α: ρ_1 (dotted line and diamonds, $\omega = \frac{1}{4}\pi$), ρ_2 (solid line and filled dots) and ρ_3 (dashed line and filled dots).

odd t, we see that interchanging consecutive ε_{1t} has an adverse effect on variance reduction.

Remark 11.10. The *AV*2 correlation ρ_2 equals 1 for all $|\alpha| < 1$. Hence it gives no variance reduction. The correlation ρ_2 is discontinuous at $|\alpha| = 1$. From Remark 11.6 above, $\rho_2 = 0.74$ when $\alpha = 1$. Hence, $\lim_{\alpha \to 1} \rho_2 = 1 \neq 0.74$ and EG improves when $|\alpha|$ reaches 1.

Remark 11.11. The *AV*4,3 correlation ρ_3 equals 0 when $|\alpha| \to 1$ and equals -1 for $\alpha = 0$. It gives negative correlations for all $-1 < \alpha < 1$, and hence implies bigger variance reductions than *AV*1. The correlation ρ_3 is continuous at $\alpha = 1$. In fact $\lim_{\alpha \to 1} \rho_3 = 0$ where $\psi(s_1)$ and $\psi(s_2)$ are also independent thanks to Lemma 11.1, which implies $\rho_3 = 0$ when $\alpha = 1$. *AV*4,3 has the best performance in terms of EGv, and also presents a continuous behaviour as $|\alpha| \to 1$.

11.5.3 *CVs*

We next study the EG of control variates for large T. We consider the case of CV3 as a representative case; minor modifications apply for other CVs. Let $\hat{\alpha} - \alpha = N_T/D_T$, where $N_T := T^{-1/2} \sum_t y_{t-1}\varepsilon_t$ and $D_T := T^{-1} \sum_t y_{t-1}^2$ with a nota-

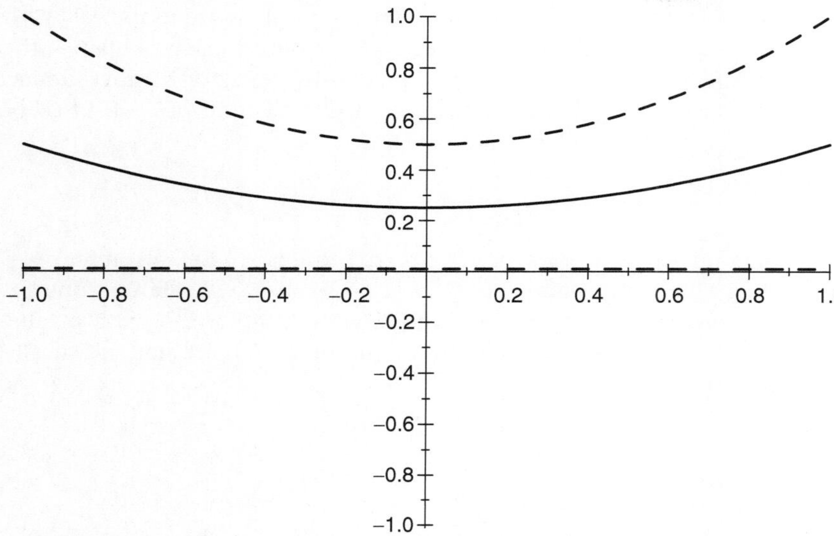

FIG. **11.2.** Influence of ω on ρ_1 as a function of α, $|\alpha| < 1$: upper dashed line $\omega = 0$, solid line $\omega = \frac{1}{4}\pi$, lower dashed line $\omega = \frac{1}{2}\pi$.

tion similar to the one in section 11.5.2. By properties of least squares, the fact that $\mathrm{E}(N_T) = 0$, and using the discussion in Davidson and MacKinnon (1992, bottom of page 206), one finds that

$$\mathrm{EGCV3}_T = \frac{1}{1-\xi_T^2}, \quad \text{where } \xi_T := \mathrm{corr}\left(\frac{N_T}{D_T}, \frac{N_T}{T^{-1/2}h}\right) = \mathrm{corr}\left(\frac{N_T}{D_T}, N_T\right). \tag{11.33}$$

Note that, being defined as a correlation coefficient, ξ_T is scale-invariant in both arguments; both can then be scaled appropriately and independently as T increases.

Equation (11.33) applies both for $\alpha = 1$ and for $|\alpha| < 1$. Under regularity conditions, when T grows large and $|\alpha| < 1$, $D_T \overset{a.s.}{\to} D$, a constant and hence ξ_T converges to $\mathrm{corr}(N_T/D, N_T) = \mathrm{corr}(N_T, N_T) = 1$. This implies that $\mathrm{EGCV3}_T \to \infty$ for $|\alpha| < 1$, in accordance with the prediction of (11.28).

When $\alpha = 1$ instead, N_T/D_T and N_T—when appropriately scaled—have the nondegenerate weak limits $\frac{1}{2}\left(B_1^2(1) - 1\right) / \int_0^1 B_1^2(\tau)\mathrm{d}\tau$ and $\frac{1}{2}\left(B_1^2(1) - 1\right)$ respectively, where B_1 is a standard Brownian motion, see section 11.5.1. Hence under regularity conditions ξ_T converges to

$$\xi := \mathrm{corr}\left(\frac{\frac{1}{2}\left(B_1^2(1) - 1\right)}{\int_0^1 B_1^2(\tau)\mathrm{d}\tau}, \frac{1}{2}\left(B_1^2(1) - 1\right)\right).$$

We have simulated ξ discretizing the Brownian motion as a random walk with T steps for $T = \{10^3, 10^4, 10^5, 5 \times 10^5\}$, using 10^5 replications; we obtained the following values for ξ: 0.5080, 0.5076, 0.5036, 0.4972. Regressing these values of ξ on a constant, $T^{-1/2}$, and T^{-1}, we get the prediction of $\xi = 0.4969$ for $T = \infty$. On the basis of this estimate, one finds

$$\log \mathrm{EGCV3}_{\infty} = \log \frac{1}{1-\xi^2} = \log \frac{1}{1-0.4969^2} = 0.28.$$

This prediction is similar to the prediction of formula (11.28). A test that $\gamma_1 + \gamma_3 \cosh(1) = 0.28$ in regression (11.28), where γ_1 and γ_3 indicate the constant and the coefficient of $\cosh(\alpha^2)$, gave an $F(1,47)$ statistic of 1.70 with p value of 0.198; hence the prediction of (11.28) and of (11.33) are not statistically different for $\alpha = 1$, $T = \infty$.

11.6 Conclusions

This chapter has investigated the effectiveness of a few VRTs in the context of dynamic DGPs. The best performers were new VRTs, with some providing staggering efficiency gains and thus potential for large time and/or precision gains. In general, the most efficient of all was AV4, a new VRT that relies on generating antithetic parameter estimates by inverting the sign of these parameters in the DGP. The resulting antithetic variate was always nonpositively correlated to the crude MC estimates, thereby reducing the variance of the combined estimator by large factors of 2 or more. Equally good but for the slower generation of estimators, AV3 was overall next best to AV4. AV3 relied on Hendry and Harrison's (1974) untried suggestion of changing the sign of every other residual.

This and many other methods that reformulate innovations were shown to be special cases of the new encompassing orthogonal-transform AV, which has a simple and convenient general formulation. Another special case of it was AV2 which applied some of the Jackknife/Bootstrap philosophy to variance reduction in dynamic MC. It seemed the least promising VRT for autoregressive series. Clearly however, this does not preclude the successful use of the Jackknife/Bootstrap philosophy in other areas and towards other ends.

Finally, the performance of CVs—as represented by the optimum CV3—was encouraging the closer α was to 0, in which case it improved with T. Large efficiency gains of 15 times were quite common, though AV3 and AV4 outperformed CVs whenever $|\alpha|$ was in the neighbourhood of 0 or 1, particularly when T was not large.

The invariance of the performance of AV3 and AV4 with respect to T, and their independence from $\hat{\alpha}$ when $|\alpha| \approx 1$ meant that they could be used for the fast generation of additional nearly nonstationary data for any sample size, thus reducing simulation times. This is a new and hitherto unknown general function that some VRTs may now serve in simulation under certain conditions.

The benefit derived from this unconventional application of VRTs was to allow the possibility of saving a significant amount of time in any future MC study of ARMA series with one autoregressive root near unity and stable/invertible remaining roots. The exact method for doing so was described in the latter part of section 11.4, and it shows that simulating nearly nonstationary series is not as uniquely problematic as it might have seemed earlier: in spite of the need for a larger number of replications to counteract the significant increase in MC volatility as $|\alpha|$ and T increase, AV3 and AV4 could be used unconventionally to compensate for such a requirement when $|\alpha| \approx 1$. Other VRTs can be used to fulfill such a function for cases when $|\alpha| > 1$. AV1 is one candidate, given its improved performance for α^2 close to 1.

In addition to summarizing the results, the response surfaces used in the chapter had the following benefits. First, they allowed for a smaller number of replications than would otherwise be needed because they reduce specificity. Second, they predict the range of beneficial application of a VRT by calculating the magnitude of the efficiency gain. Third, by comparing fitted and actual values, they detect features like increased MC volatility as $|\alpha|$ and T grow. The implication of this latter result for simulating Wiener processes is particularly important. These processes are typically generated by discrete random walks ($\alpha = 1$) with a large number of observations ($T \to \infty$). These are precisely the two ingredients that will increase MC variability, and one needs to be aware that a number of replications that is larger than usual is needed in that context. More generally, normalized Ornstein-Uhlenbeck processes are approximated by DGP (11.1), and their accuracy can now be controlled better.

It can be shown analytically that the results of this chapter are applicable to vector autoregressions and error-correction mechanisms. For technical details of the necessary matrix transformations, see Abadir, Hadri, and Tzavalis (1999). The magnitude of efficiency gains will depend on a mixture of the eigenvalues of an autoregressive matrix. Stable systems will behave like a stable AR, purely nonstationary systems like a random walk. Cointegrated systems will produce linear combinations that depend primarily on the extent of a rank-deficiency parameter.

Appendix

Proof of Lemma 11.2. For all AVs, we observe that $b_{1,T}$ and $b_{2,T}$ satisfy the central limit theorem for martingale differences, Brown (1971) Theorem 2; specifically $b_{1,T} \overset{w}{\to} \mathrm{N}(0, 1-\alpha^2)$. This implies that $\boldsymbol{b}_T := (b_{1,T}, b_{2,T})'$ is $O_p(1)$. In order to calculate var $(\boldsymbol{b}_T)$, we note that var $(b_{i,T}) \to 1 - \alpha^2$ and that

$$\operatorname{cov}(b_{1,T}, b_{2,T}) = \frac{1}{T}\frac{A}{D_1 D_2} \tag{11.34}$$

where $A = \sum_{s=2}^{T}\sum_{t=2}^{T} a_{st}$ and $a_{st} := \mathrm{E}\left(y_{1,s-1}\varepsilon_{1,s}y_{2,t-1}\varepsilon_{2,t}\right)$.

We compute A below in different subsections for each AV. Let $\mathrm{E}_t(\cdot)$ indicate expectations conditional on $\mathcal{F}_t := \sigma\{\varepsilon_{1,t-j}, j \geq 0\}$. We also define $\gamma_{12}(t) := \mathrm{E}\left(y_{1,t}y_{2,t}\right)$ and $\gamma_{12} := \lim_{t\to\infty}\gamma_{12}(t)$. In the following we only need that $\varepsilon_{1,t}$ has 0 third moment; this is implied by symmetry and existence of 3-rd absolute moments, as for the case of Gaussian $\varepsilon_{1,t}$.

AV1

Let $a := d := \cos\omega$, $b := -c = \sin\omega$. We note that $\varepsilon_{2,t}$ depends on $\varepsilon_{1,t-1}$, $\varepsilon_{1,t}$, for t even and on $\varepsilon_{1,t}$, $\varepsilon_{1,t+1}$ for t odd; hence $y_{2,t}$ is $\mathcal{F}_t$-measurable for t even and $\mathcal{F}_{t+1}$-measurable for t odd. More precisely for $t = 2m - 1$ (t odd) one has

$$\varepsilon_{2,t} = a\varepsilon_{1,t} + b\varepsilon_{1,t+1}, \qquad y_{2,t} = a\varepsilon_{1,t} + b\varepsilon_{1,t+1} + \alpha y_{2,t-1} \tag{11.35}$$

where $y_{2,t-1} \in \mathcal{F}_{t-1}$, whereas for $t = 2m$ (t even)

$$\varepsilon_{2,t} = c\varepsilon_{1,t-1} + d\varepsilon_{1,t}, \qquad y_{2,t} = g\varepsilon_{1,t} + h\varepsilon_{1,t-1} + \alpha^2 y_{2,t-2} \tag{11.36}$$

where $g := d + \alpha b$, $h := c + \alpha a$ and $y_{2,t-2}$ is $\mathcal{F}_{t-2}$-measurable. Sometimes in the following the observation that $y_{2,t}$ is $\mathcal{F}_t$-measurable for t even suffices.

We first prove that $a_{st} = 0$ for $t + 2 \leq s$ and $s \leq t - 2$, i.e.

$$A = \sum_{t=2}^{T}\sum_{s=t-1}^{t+1} a_{st} =: A_1 + A_2 + O(1). \tag{11.37}$$

where $A_1 := \sum_{m=1}^{T/2-1}\left(a_{2m-2,2m-1} + a_{2m-1,2m-1} + a_{2m,2m-1}\right)$ includes the terms for t odd and $A_2 := \sum_{m=1}^{T/2-2}\left(a_{2m-1,2m} + a_{2m-1,2m} + a_{2m+1,2m}\right)$ the one for t even. In fact for $t + 1 \leq s - 1$ one has that $y_{2,t-1}$ is $\mathcal{F}_t$-measurable, $\varepsilon_{2,t}$ is $\mathcal{F}_{t+1}$-measurable, and $\mathcal{F}_{t+1} \subseteq \mathcal{F}_{s-1}$ and hence

$$a_{st} = \mathrm{E}\left(y_{1,s-1}\varepsilon_{1,s}y_{2,t-1}\varepsilon_{2,t}\right) = \mathrm{E}\left(\mathrm{E}_{s-1}\left(\varepsilon_{1,s}\right)y_{1,s-1}y_{2,t-1}\varepsilon_{2,t}\right) = \mathrm{E}(0) = 0.$$

For $s = t - 2$ one has instead

$$a_{st} = \mathrm{E}\left(y_{1,s-1}\varepsilon_{1,s}y_{2,t-1}\varepsilon_{2,t}\right) = \mathrm{E}\left(y_{1,t-3}\varepsilon_{1,t-2}\mathrm{E}_{t-2}\left(y_{2,t-1}\varepsilon_{2,t}\right)\right) = 0$$

because $\mathrm{E}_{t-2}\left(y_{2,t-1}\varepsilon_{2,t}\right) = 0$; this follows from the fact that $\varepsilon_{2,t}$ is uncorrelated by construction with $y_{2,t-1}$ given the past, and because $\varepsilon_{2,t}$ (which depends on $\varepsilon_{1,t-1}$, $\varepsilon_{1,t}$, $\varepsilon_{1,t+1}$) is unaffected by conditioning on $\mathcal{F}_{t-2}$. The same argument holds when setting $s < t - 2$.

We next consider a_{st} for $t-1 \le s \le t+1$, distinguishing the cases of t odd or even. For $s = t-1$ and t even one finds

$$a_{st} = \mathrm{E}\left(y_{1,t-2}\varepsilon_{1,t-1}\left(a\varepsilon_{1,t-1} + b\varepsilon_{1,t} + \alpha y_{2,t-2}\right)\left(c\varepsilon_{1,t-1} + d\varepsilon_{1,t}\right)\right) = \alpha c\sigma^2\gamma_{12}\left(t-2\right).$$

Here we have used the fact that $\varepsilon_{1,t}$ has 0 third moment. For $s = t-1$ and t odd one finds $a_{st} = \mathrm{E}\left(y_{1,t-2}\varepsilon_{1,t-1}y_{2,t-1}\left(a\varepsilon_{1,t} + b\varepsilon_{1,t+1}\right)\right) = 0$ by conditioning on $\mathcal{F}_{t-1}$.

For $s = t$ and t even one finds

$$a_{st} = \sigma^4\left(ac + db\right) + \sigma^4\alpha^2 d\gamma_{12}\left(t-2\right) = \sigma^4\alpha^2 d\gamma_{12}\left(t-2\right)$$

because $ac + db = 0$, see (11.35), (11.36). Again here we have used the fact that $\varepsilon_{1,t}$ has 0 third moment. For $s = t$ and t odd one finds $a_{st} = a\sigma^2\gamma_{12}\left(t-1\right)$.

For $s = t+1$ and t even, one has $a_{st} = 0$, while for $s = t+1$ and t odd one finds $a_{st} = \alpha b\sigma^2\gamma_{12}\left(t-1\right)$. Summarizing

$$A_1 = \sum_{m=1}^{T/2-1}\left(a_{2m-1,2m-1} + a_{2m,2m-1}\right) = \sum_{m=1}^{T/2-1}\left(a + \alpha b\right)\sigma^2\gamma_{12}\left(2m-2\right),$$

$$A_2 = \sum_{m=1}^{T/2-2}\left(a_{2m-1,2m} + a_{2m,2m}\right) = \sum_{m=1}^{T/2-2}\left(\alpha c + \alpha^2 d\right)\sigma^2\gamma_{12}\left(2m-2\right),$$

$$A = \left(1+\alpha^2\right)\cos\left(\omega\right)\sigma^2\sum_{m=1}^{T/2-2}\gamma_{12}\left(2m-2\right) + O(1),$$

where $a + \alpha b + \alpha c + \alpha^2 d = \left(1+\alpha^2\right)\cos\omega$ and we note that the covariances $\gamma_{12}\left(t\right)$ are summed for t even.

In order to calculate $\gamma_{12}\left(t\right)$ for t even, write $y_{2,t} = \alpha^2 y_{2,t-2} + \eta_t$ where $\eta_t :=$ $g\varepsilon_{1,t} + h\varepsilon_{1,t-1}$, $g := d + \alpha b$, $h := c + \alpha a$ see (11.36). Next set $t = 2m$, write $y_{2,2m} =$ $\alpha^2 y_{2,2(m-1)} + \eta_{2m}$, and solve the recursions in m to find

$$y_{2,2m} = \sum_{i=0}^{m-1}\alpha^{2i}\left(g\varepsilon_{1,2(m-i)} + h\varepsilon_{1,2(m-i)-1}\right).$$

Represent $y_{1,t}$ in a similar way as

$$y_{1,2m} = \sum_{i=0}^{m-1}\alpha^{2i}\left(\varepsilon_{1,2(m-i)} + \alpha\varepsilon_{1,2(m-i)-1}\right).$$

Hence, because $b + c = 0$,

$$\gamma_{12}(2m) = \sum_{i=0}^{m-1} \mathrm{E}\left(\alpha^{2i}\left(\varepsilon_{1,2(m-i)} + \alpha\varepsilon_{1,2(m-i)-1}\right)\right)\left(\alpha^{2i}\left(g\varepsilon_{1,2(m-i)} + h\varepsilon_{1,2(m-i)-1}\right)\right)$$

$$= \sigma^2 g \sum_{i=0}^{m-1} \alpha^{4i} + \sigma^2 \alpha h \sum_{i=0}^{m-1} \alpha^{4i} = \sigma^2 (g + \alpha h) \frac{1 - \alpha^{4m}}{1 - \alpha^4} = \sigma^2 \cos\omega \frac{1 - \alpha^{4m}}{1 - \alpha^2}$$

Moreover for $T \to \infty$

$$\sum_{m=0}^{T/2-2} \gamma_{12}(2m) = \frac{\sigma^2 \cos\omega}{1 - \alpha^2}\left(\frac{T}{2} - 2 - \frac{1 - \alpha^{2T-4}}{1 - \alpha^4}\right) = \frac{T}{2}\frac{\sigma^2 \cos\omega}{1 - \alpha^2} + O(1) = \frac{T}{2}\gamma_{12} + O(1)$$

where $\gamma_{12} := \left(1 - \alpha^2\right)^{-1} \sigma^2 \cos\omega = \lim_{m\to\infty} \gamma_{12}(2m)$. Hence

$$T^{-1} A = \frac{1}{2}\left(1 + \alpha^2\right)\left(1 - \alpha^2\right)^{-1} \cos^2(\omega)\,\sigma^4 + o(1)$$

and substituting into (11.34)

$$\mathrm{cov}(b_{1,T}, b_{2,T}) = \frac{A}{TD_1 D_2} \to \frac{\cos^2(\omega)}{2}\left(1 + \alpha^2\right)\left(1 - \alpha^2\right).$$

AV2

Recall that for AV2 one has $\varepsilon_{2,t} = \varepsilon_{1,T-t}$; the following representations hold:

$$y_{1,s-1} = \sum_{j=0}^{s-2} \alpha^j \varepsilon_{1,s-1-j}, \qquad y_{2,t-1} = \sum_{i=0}^{t-2} \alpha^i \varepsilon_{2,t-1-i} = \sum_{i=0}^{t-2} \alpha^i \varepsilon_{1,T-t+1+i}$$

and hence

$$a_{st} := \mathrm{E}\left(y_{1,s-1}\varepsilon_{1,s} y_{2,t-1}\varepsilon_{2,t}\right) = \sum_{i=0}^{t-2}\sum_{j=0}^{s-2} \alpha^{i+j} \mathrm{E}\left(\varepsilon_{1,s-1-j}\varepsilon_{1,s}\varepsilon_{1,T-t+1+i}\varepsilon_{1,T-t}\right). \quad (11.38)$$

Indicate subscripts in the last term in (11.38) as follows: $n_1 := s - 1 - j$, $n_2 := s$, $n_3 := T - t + 1 + i$, $n_4 := T - t$. In order for the expectation on the r.h.s. of (11.38) to be nonzero, $n_1, \ldots, n_4$ must be equal in pairs. Note in fact that they cannot be all equal because of the presence of at least 1 lag between the terms that originate from t, $t - 1$, and s, $s - 1$. One has 2 cases: case 1, with $n_1 = n_3$, $n_2 = n_4$, and case 2, with $n_1 = n_4$, $n_2 = n_3$.

In case 1 one has $s - 1 - j = T - t + 1 + i$ and $s = T - t$; this implies $i = -(j + 2)$ which is outside the range of $i = 0, \ldots, t - 1$. This is because if $s = T - t$, then $y_{1,s-1}$ involves the past while $y_{2,t-1}$ involves the future, with no overlap. Hence case 1 gives 0 contribution to a_{st}.

Consider next case 2, with $s - 1 - j = T - t$ and $s = T - t + 1 + i$. This is equivalent to $i = j$ and $s - T + t - 1 = i$. Consider a given fixed t; then there are as many values of s as $i = 0, \ldots, t-2$ with $s \geq T-t+1$ for which $a_{st} = \alpha^{2i}\sigma^4$. Hence

$$T^{-1}A = \frac{\sigma^4}{T}\sum_{t=2}^{T}\sum_{i=0}^{t-2}\alpha^{2i} = \frac{\sigma^4}{T}\sum_{t=2}^{T}\frac{1-\alpha^{2(t-1)}}{1-\alpha^2} = \frac{\sigma^4}{1-\alpha^2} + o(1)$$

and thus

$$\mathrm{cov}(b_{1,T}, b_{2,T}) = \frac{1}{T}\frac{A}{D_1 D_2} \to \frac{\sigma^4}{1-\alpha^2}\frac{\left(1-\alpha^2\right)^2}{\sigma^4} = 1-\alpha^2.$$

AV4,3

We proceed as for AV1, recalling that for AV4,3 one has $\varepsilon_{2v,t} = (-1)^t\varepsilon_{1,t}$. In this case all terms

$$a_{st} := \mathrm{E}\left(y_{1,s-1}\varepsilon_{1,s}y_{2,t-1}\varepsilon_{2,t}\right)$$

are equal to 0 for $s < t$ by conditioning on $\mathcal{F}_{t-1}$. Symmetrically for $t < s$ one has $a_{st} = 0$ by conditioning on $\mathcal{F}_{s-1}$. Hence one is left with

$$a_t := a_{tt} = \mathrm{E}\left(y_{1,t-1}\varepsilon_{1,t}y_{2,t-1}(-1)^t\varepsilon_{1,t}\right) = (-1)^t\sigma^2\mathrm{E}\left(y_{1,t-1}y_{2,t-1}\right) = (-1)^t\sigma^2\gamma_{12}(t-1).$$

Moreover, one finds for $t = 2p$ (t even)

$$\gamma_{12}(t) = \mathrm{E}(y_{1,t}y_{2,t}) = \mathrm{E}\left(\sum_{i=0}^{t-1}\alpha^i\varepsilon_{1,t-i}\right)\left(\sum_{i=0}^{t-1}\alpha^i(-1)^{t-i}\varepsilon_{1,t-i}\right)$$

$$= \sum_{i=0}^{t-1}\alpha^{2i}(-1)^{t-i}\mathrm{E}(\varepsilon_{1,t-i}^2) = (-1)^t\sigma^2\sum_{i=0}^{t-1}\alpha^{2i}(-1)^i = \frac{1-\alpha^{2t}}{1+\alpha^2}\sigma^2,$$

where we have used the following fact, listing first the even and then the odd terms

$$\sum_{i=0}^{t-1}\alpha^{2i}(-1)^i = \sum_{m=0}^{p-1}\left(\alpha^{2\cdot 2m} - \alpha^{2\cdot(2m+1)}\right) = \left(1-\alpha^2\right)\frac{1-\alpha^{4p}}{1-\alpha^4} = \frac{1-\alpha^{4p}}{1+\alpha^2}.$$

When t is odd we use recursions and the previous expression to find

$$\gamma_{12}(t) = \mathrm{E}(y_{1,t}y_{2,t}) = \mathrm{E}\left(\left(\alpha y_{1,t-1} + \varepsilon_{1,t}\right)\left(\alpha y_{2,t-1} + (-1)^t\varepsilon_{1,t}\right)\right)$$

$$= \alpha^2\mathrm{E}\left(y_{1,t-1}y_{2,t-1}\right) - \sigma^2 = \left(\frac{1-\alpha^{2t-2}}{1+\alpha^2}\alpha^2 - 1\right)\sigma^2$$

$$= \frac{\alpha^2 - \alpha^{2t} - 1 - \alpha^2}{1+\alpha^2}\sigma^2 = -\frac{1+\alpha^{2t}}{1+\alpha^2}\sigma^2.$$

Hence substituting in a_t for t even ($t-1$ odd) one finds $a_t = \sigma^2\gamma_{12}(t-1) = -\sigma^4\frac{1+\alpha^{2t}}{1+\alpha^2}$, while for t odd ($t-1$ even) one has $a_t = -\sigma^2\gamma_{12}(t-1) = -\sigma^4\frac{1-\alpha^{2t}}{1+\alpha^2}$.

Hence, recalling that T is even

$$A = \sum_{t=2}^{T} a_t = \sum_{m=2}^{T/2} a_{2m-1} + \sum_{m=1}^{T/2} a_{2m} = -\frac{T}{2}\frac{\sigma^4}{1+\alpha^2} - \frac{T}{2}\frac{\sigma^4}{1+\alpha^2} + O(1).$$

Hence $T^{-1}A \to -\sigma^4\left(1+\alpha^2\right)^{-1}$ and therefore

$$\operatorname{cov}(b_{1,T}, b_{2,T}) = \frac{1}{T}\frac{A}{D_1 D_2} \to -\sigma^4 \frac{1}{1+\alpha^2}\frac{\left(1-\alpha^2\right)^2}{\sigma^4} = -\frac{1-\alpha^2}{1+\alpha^2}\left(1-\alpha^2\right).$$

References

Abadir, K. M. (1992). A distribution generating equation for unit-root statistics. *Oxford Bulletin of Economics and Statistics*, **54**, 305–323.

——(1993a). The limiting distribution of the autocorrelation coefficient under a unit root. *Annals of Statistics*, **21**, 1058–1070.

——(1993b). OLS bias in a nonstationary autoregression. *Econometric Theory*, **9**, 81–93.

——(1993c). On the asymptotic power of unit root tests. *Econometric Theory*, **9**, 187–219.

——(1995). The limiting distribution of the t ratio under a unit root. *Econometric Theory*, **11**, 775–793.

——Hadri, K., and Tzavalis, E. (1999). The influence of VAR dimensions on estimator biases. *Econometrica*, **67**, 163–181.

Brown, B. M. (1971). Martingale central limit theorems. *Annals of Mathematical Statistics*, **42**, 59–66.

Cerrato, M. (2008). Valuing American derivatives by least squares methods. Mimeo, Department of Economics, University of Glasgow.

Chow, G. C. (1960). Tests of equality between sets of coefficients in two linear regressions. *Econometrica*, **28**, 591–605.

Cryer, J. D., Nankervis, J. C., and Savin, N. E. (1989). Mirror-image and invariant distributions in ARMA models. *Econometric Theory*, **5**, 36–52.

Davidson, R. and MacKinnon, J. G. (1992). Regression-based methods for using control variates in Monte Carlo experiments. *Journal of Econometrics*, **54**, 203–222.

Durbin, J. and Koopman, S. J. (1997). Monte Carlo maximum likelihood estimation for non-Gaussian state space models. *Biometrika*, **84**, 669–684.

Ericsson, N. R. (1991). Monte Carlo methodology and the finite sample properties of instrumental variables statistics for testing nested and non-nested hypotheses. *Econometrica*, **59**, 1249–1277.

Evans, G. B. A. and Savin, N. E. (1981). Testing for unit roots: 1. *Econometrica*, **49**, 753–779.

Fang, K.-T., Wang, Y., and Bentler, P. M. (1994). Some applications of number-theoretic methods in statistics. *Statistical Science*, **9**, 416–428.

Haldrup, N. (1996). Mirror image distributions and the Dickey–Fuller regression with a maintained trend. *Journal of Econometrics*, **72**, 301–312.

Hendry, D. F. (1984). Monte Carlo experimentation in econometrics. In Griliches, Z. and Intriligator, M. D. (eds.), *Handbook of Econometrics*, vol. 2, Amsterdam: North-Holland.

——and Harrison, R. W. (1974). Monte Carlo methodology and the small sample behaviour of ordinary and two-stage least squares. *Journal of Econometrics*, **2**, 151–174.

Kendall, M. and Stuart, A. (1977). *The Advanced Theory of Statistics*, vol. 1. 4th edition. London: Charles Griffin & Co.

Kleijnen, J. P. C. (1974). *Statistical Techniques in Simulation*, part I. New York: Marcel Dekker.

Kloek, T. and van Dijk, H. K. (1978). Bayesian estimates of equation system parameters: An application of integration by Monte Carlo. *Econometrica*, **46**, 1–19.

Lai, T. L. and Siegmund, D. (1983). Fixed accuracy estimation of an autoregressive parameter. *Annals of Statistics*, **11**, 478–485.

Paruolo, P. (2002). On Monte Carlo estimation of relative power. *Econometrics Journal*, **5**, 65–75.

Phillips, P. C. B. (1977). Approximations to some finite sample distributions associated with a first-order stochastic difference equation. *Econometrica*, **45**, 463–485.

——(1978a). Edgeworth and saddlepoint approximations in the first-order noncircular autoregression. *Biometrika*, **65**, 91–98.

——(1978b). A note on the saddlepoint approximation in the first order non-circular autoregression. Cowles Foundation Discussion Paper No. 487, Yale University.

——(1987). Towards a unified asymptotic theory for autoregression. *Biometrika*, **74**, 535–547.

Rothery, P. (1982). The use of control variates in Monte Carlo estimation of power. *Applied Statistics*, **31**, 125–129.

Said, S. E. and Dickey, D. A. (1984). Testing for unit roots in autoregressive-moving average models of unknown order. *Biometrika*, **71**, 599–607.

Takahashi, A. and Yoshida, N. (2005). Monte Carlo simulation with asymptotic method. *Journal of Japanese Statistical Society*, **35**, 171–203.

White, H. (1980). A heteroskedastic-consistent covariance matrix estimator and a direct test for heteroskedasticity. *Econometrica*, **48**, 817–838.

White, J. S. (1958). The limiting distribution of the serial correlation coefficient in the explosive case. *Annals of Mathematical Statistics*, **29**, 1188–1197.

——(1961). Asymptotic expansions for the mean and variance of the serial correlation coefficient. *Biometrika*, **48**, 85–94.

12

Simple Wald Tests of the Fractional Integration Parameter: An Overview of New Results

*Juan J. Dolado, Jesus Gonzalo, and Laura Mayoral**

12.1 Introduction

A well-known feature of tests of $I(1)$ vs. $I(0)$—or $I(0)$ vs. $I(1)$—processes is that they reject their respective null hypotheses very occasionally when the true DGP for a time series $\{y_t\}_1^T$ is a fractionally integrated, $I(d)$, process. This is often the case for the Dickey–Fuller (DF)-type tests if $0.5 < d < 1$ and for the KPSS-type tests if $0 < d < 0.5$. Given that the microfoundations of $I(d)$ processes make them quite plausible in practice, this issue can have serious consequences when analysing the long-run properties of the variables of interest.[1] To mention only a few: (i) shocks could be identified as permanent when in fact they die out eventually, and (ii) two series could be considered as spuriously cointegrated when they are independent at all leads and lags (see, e.g., Gonzalo and Lee, 1998). These mistakes are more likely to occur in the presence of deterministic components like, eg, in the case of trending economic variables. Additionally, if the true DGP is an $I(0)$ process subject to structural breaks in its deterministic components, then it could be misinterpreted as a long-memory process, or vice versa.

* We are grateful to Carlos Velasco for many insightful comments. Financial support from the Spanish Ministry of Education through grants SEJ2006-00369 and SEJ2007-63098, and also from the Barcelona Economics Program of CREA is gratefully acknowledged. The usual disclaimer applies.

[1] For explanations of the origin of $I(d)$ processes based on aggregration of individual stationary series with heterogeneous persistence, see Robinson (1978) and Granger (1980), and for models which mimic some of the key properties of $I(d)$ processes based on the existence of shocks that die out at a certain probabilistic rate, see Parke (1999) and Diebold and Inoue (2001). For persuasive macroeconomic applications of these processes, see Michelacci and Zaffaroni (2000) and Lo and Haubrich (2001).

In view of these caveats, the goal of this chapter is four-fold. First, we illustrate the advantages, in terms of power under fixed alternatives, of recently proposed Wald tests of $I(d_0)$ vs. $I(d)$, $d \neq d_0$, with $d_0 = 1$ or $d_0 = 0$, relative to well-known LM and semiparametric tests; for simplicity, we do this in a setup when the time-series has i.i.d. error terms and is free of deterministic components. Second, we extend the previous procedures to allow for these components, possibly subject to structural breaks. Third, we derive new LM and Wald test statistics to test the null that a process is $I(d)$ with constant long-memory parameter, d, against the alternative of a break in d. Finally, the Wald tests are extended to account for autocorrelated disturbances in the DGP.

Specifically, we focus on a modification of the Fractional Dickey–Fuller (FDF) test by Dolado, Gonzalo, and Mayoral (2002; DGM hereafter) recently introduced by Lobato and Velasco (2007; LV hereafter) to achieve an improvement in efficiency over the former. Although this test—henceforth denoted as the EFDF (efficient FDF) test—was originally devised to extend the traditional DF test of $I(1)$ against $I(0)$ to the broader framework of $I(1)$ against $I(d)$ processes, with $d \in [0,1)$, we show that it can be easily generalized to cover the case of $I(0)$ vs. $I(d)$, with $d \in (0,1]$. This testing approach relies upon a simple regression model where both the regressand and the regressor are filtered to become $I(0)$ under the null and the alternative hypotheses, respectively.[2] The test is based on the t-ratio, t_{φ}, of the estimated slope, φ, of the regressor. Hence, when testing $I(1)$ vs. $I(d)$, Δy_t becomes the dependent variable. As regards the regressor, whereas DGM choose $\Delta^d y_{t-1}$, LV show that $z_{t-1}(d) = (1-d)^{-1}(\Delta^{d-1} - 1)\Delta y_t$ improves the efficiency of the test.[3] These tests belong to the Wald family because their underlying regression models are estimated under the alternative hypothesis. Thus, non-rejection of $H_0 : \varphi = 0$ against $H_1 : \varphi < 0$, implies that the process is $I(1)$ and, conversely, $I(d)$ when the null is rejected. As shown below, the EFDF test for testing $I(0)$ vs. $I(d)$ is based on an analogous t-ratio, t_{ψ}, this time in a regression of y_t on the regressor $s_{t-1}(d) = d^{-1}(1 - \Delta^d)y_t$.

To compute either version of the EFDF test, an input value for d is required. One could either consider a (known) simple alternative, $H_A : d = d_A < 1$

[2] In the DF setup, these filters are $\Delta = (1-L)$ and $\Delta^0 L = L$, so that the regressand and regressor are Δy_t and y_{t-1}, respectively.

[3] As explained in DGM (Appendix A; 2002), both regressors can be constructed by filtering the series $\{y_t\}_{t=1}^{T}$ with the truncated version at the origin (with pre-sample shocks set to 0) of the binomial expansion of $(1-L)^d$ in the lag operator L. Thus, $\Delta_+^d y_t = \Sigma_{i=0}^{t-1} \pi_i(d)\, y_{t-i}$, where $\pi_i(d)$ is the i-th coefficient in that expansion (for more details, see the end of this section). This 'deadstart' fractional process has been popularized, among others, by Robinson and Marinucci (2001), giving rise to Type-II fractional Brownian motion. Since the limit distributions of the EFDF tests discussed throughout this chapter are always Gaussian, none of the results depend on this choice. To simplify the notation, we will omit the truncation subscript in the sequel and refer to this filter simply as Δ^d.

(or $d_A > 0$) or, more realistically, a composite one, $H_1 : d < 1$ (or $d > 0$). We focus here on the latter case where LV (2007) have proved that the use of a T^{κ}-consistent estimate (with $\kappa > 0$) of the true d suffices to obtain a $N(0,1)$ limiting distribution of the resulting test.

Under a sequence of local alternatives approaching $H_0 : d = 1$ from below at a rate of $T^{-1/2}$, LV (2007, Theorem 1) prove that, under Gaussianity, the EFDF test of $I(1)$ vs. $I(d)$ is asymptotically equivalent to the uniformly most powerful invariant (UMPI) test, ie, the LM test introduced by Robinson (1991, 1994) and later adapted by Tanaka (1999) to the time domain. We show that this result also holds for the $I(0)$ vs. $I(d)$ case. Our first contribution here is to analyse the properties of Wald and LM tests in the case of fixed alternatives using the concept of Bahadur's *asymptotic relative efficiency* (ARE; see Gourieroux and Monfort 1995). Although both tests are consistent and diverge at the same rate under fixed alternatives, we find that the EFDF test fares better using Bahadur's ARE criterion in both setups. This is not surprising, given the well-known result about the better power properties of Wald tests in a wide range of models (see Engle 1984). Moreover, when compared to other tests of $I(1)$ or $I(0)$ vs. $I(d)$ which rely on direct inference about semiparametric estimators of d, the EFDF test also exhibits in general better power properties, under a correct specification of the stationary short-run dynamics of the error term in the auxiliary regression. This is due to the fact that the semiparametric estimation procedures often imply larger confidence intervals of the memory parameter, in exchange with less restrictive assumptions on the error term. By contrast, the combination of a wide range of semiparametric estimators for the input value of d with the auxiliary parametric regressions involved in the EFDF test, yields a parametric rate for the Wald tests.[4] Thus, in a sense, Wald tests combine the favourable features of both approaches in improving power while at the same time they reduce the danger of misspecifying short-run dynamics.

Following the development of unit-root tests in the past, we investigate how to implement Wald tests when some deterministic components are considered in the DGP, a case which is not treated in LV (2007). We first focus on the role of a *polynomial trend of known order* since many (macro) economic time-series exhibit this type of trending behaviour. Our main result is that, in contrast with the results for most tests for $I(1)$ against $I(0)$ or vice versa, the EFDF test remains efficient in the presence of deterministic components and maintains the same asymptotic distribution, insofar as they are correctly removed. This result mimics the one found for LM tests when these components are present; cf. Gil-Alaña and Robinson (1997). Next, we examine the cases where there are

[4] LV (2006, 2007) have shown that a Gaussian semiparametric estimator, such as the one proposed by Velasco (1999), suffices to achieve consistency and asymptotic normality in the analysed Wald tests (see sections 12.2 and 12.3 below) extending the results by DGM (2002) about parametric estimators.

structural breaks in the deterministic components, where we devise tests for $I(d)$ cum constant-parameter deterministic terms vs. $I(0)$ cum breaks in these components, or in the long-memory parameter, d, as well as other alternative time-varying schemes for d. Lastly, we show that the previous asymptotic results obtained for DGPs with i.i.d. disturbances remain valid when the error term is allowed to be parametrically autocorrelated, as in the (augmented) ADF setup. In particular, we propose a linear single-step estimation procedure to account for (parametric) AR disturbances which simplifies the two-step procedure proposed by LV (2007).

The rest of the chapter is structured as follows. Section 12.2 briefly overviews the properties of the EFDF tests when the process is either a driftless random walk or i.i.d. under the null, and derives new results about their power relative to the power of the LM test under fixed alternatives. Section 12.3 extends the previous results to processes containing trending deterministic components with constant parameters. Section 12.4 discusses tests to distinguish between $I(0)$ series whose deterministic terms may be subject to structural breaks and $I(d)$ processes with constant parameters. Section 12.5 deals with how to test for breaks in the long-memory parameter, d, as well as some other alternative time varying structures. Section 12.6 explains how to modify the previous tests when the error terms are autocorrelated. Lastly, section 12.7 concludes.

Proofs of the main results are in an Appendix, available as supplementary material to this chapter (see http://dolado-research.blogspot.com/).

In the sequel, the definition of an $I(d)$ process adopted here is the one proposed by Akonom and Gourieroux (1987) where a fractional process is initialized at the origin. This corresponds to Type-II fractional Brownian motion (see the previous discussion in footnote 3) and is similar to the definitions of an $I(d)$ process underlying the LM test proposed by Robinson (1994) and Tanaka (1999). Moreover, the following conventional notation is adopted throughout the chapter: $\Gamma(.)$ denotes the Gamma function, and $\{\pi_i(d)\}$, with $\pi_i(d) = \frac{\Gamma(i-d)}{\Gamma(-d)\Gamma(i+1)}$, represents the sequence of coefficients associated to the binomial expansion of $(1-L)^d$ in powers of L. The indicator function is denoted by $1_{\{.\}}$. Finally, $\xrightarrow{p}$ means convergence in probability, and $\xrightarrow{w}$ denotes weak convergence in $D[0,1]$ endowed with the Skorohod J_1 topology.

12.2 The EFDF Test

12.2.1 *I(1) vs. I(d)*

Following Robinson (1994), we consider an additive model for the process $\{y_t\}_1^T$ which is generated as the sum of a deterministic component, $\mu(t)$, and a stochastic component, u_t, that is

$$y_t = \mu(t) + u_t, \tag{12.1}$$

where $u_t = \Delta^{-d}\varepsilon_t 1_{\{t>0\}}$ is a purely stochastic $I(d)$ process, with $d \in [0,1]$, and ε_t is a zero-mean i.i.d. random variable.

When $\mu(t) \equiv 0$,[5] DGM (2002) developed a Wald-type (FDF) test for testing the null hypothesis $H_0 : d = 1$ against the composite alternative $H_1 : d \in [0,1)$, based on the t-ratio on ϕ to test $H_0 : \phi = 0$ in the OLS regression model

$$\Delta y_t = \phi \Delta^{d^*} y_{t-1} + v_t, \tag{12.2}$$

where $d^* \geq 0$ is an input value needed to perform the test. If d^* is chosen such that $d^* = \hat{d}_T$, where $\hat{d}_T$ is a T^{κ}-consistent estimator of d, with $\kappa > 0$, DGM (2002) and LV (2006) have shown that the asymptotic distribution of the resulting t-statistic, t_{ϕ}, is $N(0,1)$.

Recently, LV (2007) have proposed the EFDF test based on a modification of (12.2) that is more efficient while keeping the good finite-sample properties of Wald tests. Specifically, their proposal is to use the t-statistic, t_{φ}, associated to $H_0 : \varphi = 0$ in the OLS regression

$$\Delta y_t = \varphi z_{t-1}(d^*) + \varepsilon_t, \tag{12.3}$$

where $z_{t-1}(d^*)$ is defined as[6]

$$z_{t-1}(d^*) = \frac{\left(\Delta^{d^*-1} - 1\right)}{(1 - d^*)} \Delta y_t,$$

such that $\varphi = (d^* - 1)$ and $d^* > 0.5$ is an input value needed to implement the test. Note that, if d^* is the true integration order of the process, d, then $\varphi = 0$ under $H_0 : d = 1$ and the model becomes a random walk, ie, $\Delta y_t = \varepsilon_t$. By contrast, under $H_1 : d \in [0,1)$, it holds that $\varphi < 0$, and the model becomes a pure fractional process, ie, $\Delta^d y_t = \varepsilon_t$.

The insight for the higher efficiency of the EFDF test is as follows. Let $d^* = d$. Then under H_1, the regression model in (12.2) can be written as $\Delta y_t = \Delta^{1-d}\varepsilon_t = \varepsilon_t + (d-1)\varepsilon_{t-1} + 0.5d(d-1)\varepsilon_{t-2} + \ldots = \phi\Delta^d y_{t-1} + \varepsilon_t + 0.5d(d- \;\; 1)\varepsilon_{t-2} + \ldots$ with $\phi = d - 1$. Thus, the error term $v_t = \varepsilon_t + 0.5d(d-1)\varepsilon_{t-2} + \ldots$ in (12.2) is serially correlated. Although OLS provides a consistent estimator of ϕ, since v_t is orthogonal to the regressor $\Delta^d y_{t-1} = \varepsilon_{t-1}$, it is not the most efficient one. By contrast, the regression model used in the EFDF test does not suffer from this problem since, by construction, it yields an i.i.d. error term. In order to distinguish this test from the one proposed in the next subsection for

[5] Alternatively, $\mu(t)$ could be considered to be known. In this case, the same arguments go through after subtracting it from y_t to obtain a purely stochastic process.

[6] A similar model was first proposed by Granger (1986) in the more general context of testing for cointegration with multivariate series, a modification of which has been recently considered by Johansen (2005).

$H_0 : d = 0$, we denote it in the sequel as the EFDF(1) test. Finally, note that application of L'Hôpital rule to $z_{t-1}(d^*)$ in the limit case as $d^* \to 1$ leads to a regressor equal to $-ln(1-L)\Delta y_t = \Sigma_{j=1}^{\infty} j^{-1}\Delta y_{t-j}$, which is the one used in Robinson's LM test (see section 12.2.3).

Theorem 1 in LV (2007), which we reproduce below (as Theorem 12.1) for completeness, establishes the asymptotic properties of t_{φ}.

Theorem 12.1. *Under the assumption that the DGP is given by* $y_t = \Delta^{-d}\varepsilon_t 1_{\{t>0\}}$, *where* ε_t *is i.i.d. with finite fourth moment, the asymptotic properties of the t-statistic,* t_{φ}, *for testing* $\varphi = 0$ *in (12.3), where the input of* $z_{t-1}(\hat{d}_T)$ *is a* T^{κ}-*consistent estimator of* d^*, *for some* $d^* > 0.5$ *with* $\kappa > 0$, *are given by:*

a) Under the null hypothesis $(d = 1)$,

$$t_{\varphi}(\hat{d}_T) \overset{w}{\to} N(0,1).$$

b) Under local alternatives, $(d = 1 - \gamma/\sqrt{T})$,

$$t_{\varphi}(\hat{d}_T) \overset{w}{\to} N(-\gamma h(d^*), 1),$$

where $h(d^*) = \Sigma_{j=1}^{\infty} j^{-1}\pi_j(d^*-1)/\sqrt{\Sigma_{j=1}^{\infty}\pi_j(d^*-1)^2}$, $d^* > 0.5$, $d^* \neq 1$.

c) Under fixed alternatives $d \in [0,1)$, *the test based on* $t_{\varphi}(\hat{d}_T)$ *is consistent.*

LV (2007) have shown that the function $h(d^*)$ achieves a global maximum at 1 where $h(1) = \sqrt{\pi^2/6}$, and that $h(1)$ equals the noncentrality parameter of the locally optimal LM test (see subsection 12.2.2 below).[7] Thus, insofar as a T^{κ}-consistent estimator of d, with $\kappa > 0$, is used as an input of $z_{t-1}(d^*)$, the EFDF test is locally asymptotically equivalent to Robinson's LM test.

In practice, the obtained estimate of d could be smaller than 0.5. In these cases, the input value can be chosen according to the following rule: $\tilde{d}_{1T} = \max\{\hat{d}_T, 0.5 + \epsilon\}$, with $\epsilon > 0$, for which the test can be easily proved to diverge under H_1.

A power-rate consistent estimate of d can be easily obtained by applying some available semiparametric estimators. Among them, the estimators proposed by Abadir *et al.* (2005), Shimotsu (2006a), and Velasco (1999) provide appropriate choices since they also cover the case where deterministic components exist, as we do below.

12.2.2 *I(0) vs. I(d)*

Although the EFDF(1) test was originally derived for testing $I(1)$ vs. $I(d)$ processes, it can be easily extended to cover the case of $I(0)$ vs. $I(d)$, with

[7] DGM (2002, Theorem 3) in turn obtained that the corresponding distribution under local alternatives of the FDF test in (12.2) is $N(-\gamma, 1)$. Hence, the asymptotic efficiency of the FDF test relative to the EFDF(1) test is 0.78 ($\simeq \sqrt{6}/\pi$).

$d \in (0,1]$. This new test is labelled as the EFDF(0) test in the sequel. As before, the maintained hypothesis is taken to be (12.1), but now the null is $H_0 : d = 0$, and the composite alternative $H_1 : 0 < d \leq 1$.[8] We first focus on the simple case where $\mu(t) \equiv 0$. Adding and subtracting y_t to both sides of (12.1) and solving for y_t, yields

$$y_t = \psi s_{t-1}(d) + \varepsilon_t, \tag{12.4}$$

where

$$s_{t-1}(d) = \frac{1 - \Delta^d}{d} y_t,$$

such that $\psi = d$. Like in (12.3), $s_{t-1}(d)$ does not contain the current value of y_t since $(1 - \Delta^d) = (dL + \frac{1}{2}d(d-1)L^2 - \ldots)$. Under H_0, $\psi = 0$, while, under H_1, $0 < \psi \leq 1$. When $\psi = 0$, the model is $y_t = \varepsilon_t$ whereas it becomes $\Delta^d y_t = \varepsilon_t$ for $\psi = d \in (0,1]$. As in the $I(1)$ vs. $I(d)$ case, equation (12.4) motivates a test of $H_0 : \psi = 0$ based on the t-statistic of $\hat{\psi}$, t_{ψ}, computed in a regression of y_t on $s_{t-1}(d^*)$, where d^* is an input value needed to make the test feasible. Thus, the null is tested by means an upper-side test based on t_{ψ}. As with the EFDF(1) test, the limit case as $d^* \to 0$ implies that $s_{t-1}(d) \to -ln(1-L)y_t = \Sigma_{j=1}^{\infty} j^{-1} y_{t-j}$, which again corresponds to the regressor used in the LM test.

In this case, the following theory holds

Theorem 12.2. *Under the assumption that the DGP is given by $y_t = \Delta^{-d}\varepsilon_t 1_{\{t>0\}}$, where ε_t is i.i.d. with finite fourth moment, the asymptotic properties of the t-statistic, t_{ψ}, for testing $\psi = 0$ in (12.4) where the input of the regressor $s_{t-1}(\hat{d}_T)$ is a T^{κ}-consistent estimator of d^*, for some $d^* < 0.5$ with $\kappa > 0$, are given by:*

a) Under the null hypothesis ($d = 0$),

$$t_{\psi}(\hat{d}_T) \xrightarrow{w} N(0,1).$$

b) Under local alternatives, ($d = \gamma/\sqrt{T}$),

$$t_{\psi}(\hat{d}_T) \xrightarrow{w} N(\gamma g(d^*), 1),$$

where $g(d^*) = \Sigma_{j=1}^{\infty} j^{-1}\pi_j(d^*)/\sqrt{\Sigma_{j=1}^{\infty}\pi_j(d^*)^2}$, $d^* < 0.5$, $d^* \neq 0$.

c) Under fixed alternatives ($d \in (0,1)$), the test based on $t_{\psi}(\hat{d}_T)$ is consistent.

It is easy to show that the function $g(.)$ achieves an absolute maximum at 0, in which case $g(0)$ equals the noncentrality parameter of the locally optimal Robinson's LM test. Therefore, if the input of $s_{t-1}(.)$, $\hat{d}_T$, is a T^{κ}-consistent estimator of d with $\kappa > 0$, the test based on $t_{\psi}(\hat{d}_T)$ is locally optimal. In

[8] Note that if we were to take a null of $I(d_0)$, $d_0 \in (0,1]$, and an alternative of $I(0)$, the EFDF regression model would be $\Delta^{d_0} y_t = \rho[d_0^{-1}(\Delta^{-d_0} - 1)]\Delta^{d_0} y_t + \varepsilon_t$, with $\rho = -d_0$. In this case, under H_0, $\rho \neq 0$, whereas, under H_1, $\rho = 0$.

practice, to perform regression (12.4) the input value $\tilde{d}_{0T} = \min\{\hat{d}_T, 0.5 - \epsilon\}$, with $\epsilon > 0$, can be employed so that it is always strictly smaller than 0.5.

12.2.3 *Power Comparisons Under Fixed Alternatives*

As discussed before, the closer competitor to the EFDF test is the LM test proposed by Robinson (1991, 1994) in the frequency domain, subsequently extended by Tanaka (1999) to the time domain. In this section we discuss the power properties of the two competing tests under the case of fixed alternatives in Bahadur's ARE sense.[9]

We start with the LM test, henceforth denoted as LM_T, which considers $H_0 : \theta = 0$ against $H_1 : \theta \neq 0$ for the DGP $\Delta^{d_0+\theta} y_t = \varepsilon_t$. In line with the hypotheses considered in this chapter, we focus on the particular cases where $d_0 = 1$ and $-1 < \theta \leq 0$, and $d_0 = 0$ and $0 < \theta \leq 1$. Assuming that $\varepsilon_t \sim n.i.d.\ (0,\sigma^2)$, the score-LM test is computed as

$$LM_T = \sqrt{\frac{6}{\pi^2}}\, T^{1/2} \sum_{j=1}^{T-1} j^{-1} \hat{\rho}_j \overset{w}{\to} N(0,1), \tag{12.5}$$

where $\hat{\rho}_j = \Sigma_{t=j+1}^{T} \Delta^{d_0} y_t\, \Delta^{d_0} y_{t-j} / \Sigma_{t=1}^{T} (\Delta^{d_0} y_{t-j})^2$ (see Robinson, 1991 and Tanaka, 1999). Breitung and Hassler (2002) have shown that an alternative way to compute the LM test is as the t-ratio (t_λ) in the regression

$$\Delta^{d_0} y_t = \lambda x_{t-1}^* + e_t, \tag{12.6}$$

where $x_{t-1}^* = \Sigma_{j=1}^{t-1} j^{-1} \Delta^{d_0} y_{t-j}$.

Under a sequence of local alternatives of the type $\theta = 1 - T^{-1/2}\gamma$ with $\gamma > 0$ for $H_0 : d_0 = 1$, the LM_T (or t_λ) test is the UMPI test. However, as discussed earlier, the EFDF(1) is asymptotically equivalent to the UMPI test whenever an appropriate estimator of d, $\hat{d}_T$, is used since the limit case as $\hat{d}_T \to 1$ in the filter $(\Delta^{\hat{d}_T - 1} - 1)/(1 - \hat{d}_T)$ yields the linear filter used in the LM test. Similar arguments hold for the EFDF(0) test, where $H_0 : d_0 = 0$, and $\theta = T^{-1/2}\,\gamma$.

In the rest of this section, we analyse the case with fixed alternatives where, to our knowledge, results are new. In particular, we first derive the noncentrality parameters of two above-mentioned tests under an $I(d)$ alternative where the DGP is assumed to be $\Delta^d y_t = \varepsilon_t$. The permissible ranges of d in this analysis are $d \in [0,1)$ for the EFDF(1) test, and $d \in (0,0.5)$ for the EFDF(0) test.[10] In the

[9] The available results in the literature establish the consistency of the Wald and LM tests and derive their (identical) speed of divergence under fixed alternatives. However, they do not derive the noncentrality parameters as we do below which can be useful to characterize power differences for a *given* sample size.

[10] The intuition for why the two cases differ is that, under a fixed $I(d)$ alternative, the EFDF(1) test proceeds to first-difference the series, so that $\Delta y_t \sim I(d-1)$, and then, all the variables in regression (12.2) are stationary under the alternative hypothesis of $d < 1$. The EFDF(0) treats the series in levels so that $y_t \sim I(d)$ and then, for values of $d > 0.5$, regression

case of the EFDF(1) test, $H_0 : d = 1$ and, hence, $\Delta y_t = \Delta^{-b}\varepsilon_t$ where $b = d - 1 < 0$. Then, the following result holds.

Theorem 12.3. *If $\Delta^d y_t = \varepsilon_t$ with $d \in [0,1)$, the t-statistic, t_φ, associated to the EFDF(1) test satisfies*

$$T^{-1/2} t_\varphi \xrightarrow{p} -\left(\frac{\Gamma(3-2d)}{\Gamma^2(2-d)} - 1\right)^{1/2} := c_{1,EFDF}(d),$$

while, under the same DGP, the LM test defined in (12.5) *satisfies*

$$T^{-1/2} LM_T \xrightarrow{p} -\sqrt{\frac{6}{\pi^2}} \frac{\Gamma(2-d)}{(1-d)\Gamma(d-2)} \sum_{j=1}^{\infty} \frac{\Gamma(j+d-1)}{j\Gamma(j+2-d)} := c_{1,LM}(d), \qquad (12.7a)$$

where $c_{1,EFDF}(d)$ and $c_{1,LM}(d)$ denote the non-centrality parameters under the fixed alternative $H_1 : d \in [0,1)$ of the EFDF(1) and LM tests, respectively.

Secondly, for the EFDF(0) test, $H_0 : d = 0$, whereby now $y_t = \Delta^{-b}\varepsilon_t$ with $b = d$. Then

Theorem 12.4. *If $\Delta^d y_t = \varepsilon_t$ with $d \in (0,0.5)$, the t-statistic, t_ψ, associated to the EFDF(0) test satisfies,*

$$T^{-1/2} t_\psi \xrightarrow{p} \left(\frac{\Gamma(1-2d)}{\Gamma^2(1-d)} - 1\right)^{1/2} := c_{0,EFDF}(d),$$

while, under the same DGP, the LM test defined in (12.5) satisfies

$$T^{-1/2} LM_T \xrightarrow{p} \sqrt{\frac{6}{\pi^2}} \frac{\Gamma(1+d)}{\Gamma(-d)} \sum_{j=1}^{\infty} \frac{\Gamma(j-d)}{j\Gamma(j+d+1)} := c_{0,LM}(d), \qquad (12.7b)$$

where $c_{0,EFDF}(d)$, and $c_{0,LM}(d)$ denote the noncentrality parameters under the fixed alternative $H_1 : d \in (0,0.5)$ of the EFDF(0) and LM tests, respectively.

Figures 12.1 and 12.2 display the two noncentrality parameters of the LM and EFDF derived in Theorems 12.3 and 12.4. Their squares correspond to the approximate slopes in Bahadur's ARE so that the test with the greater slope is asymptotically more powerful. As expected, they behave similarly for values of d very close to the corresponding null hypotheses. However, despite being devised as the UIMP test for local alternatives, the LM test performs worse than the EFDF tests, for a given sample size, when the alternative is not local: $c_{1,EFDF}(d)$ ($c_{0,EFDF}(d)$) is much more negative (positive) than $c_{1,LM}(d)$ ($c_{0,LM}(d)$) when d departs from its respective nulls. Hence, the ARE ratio $c^2_{i,EFDF}(d)/c^2_{i,LM}(d)$ is larger than unity, favouring the Wald test. Extensive

(12.3) includes both stationary and nonstationary variables. As a result, the LLN can be applied on the EFDF(1) test for all $d < 1$ but only for values of $d < 0.5$ in the EFDF(0) case. If $d > 0.5$, the noncentrality parameter will converge to a random variable.

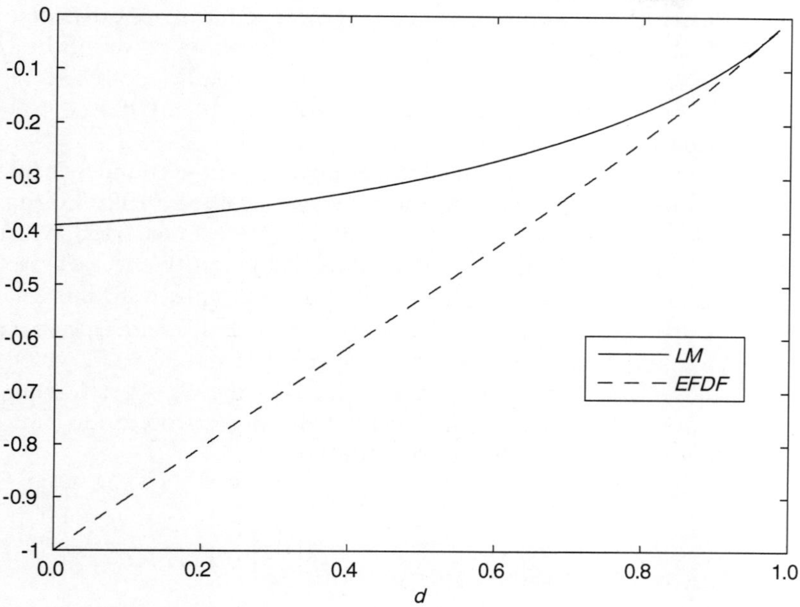

FIG. 12.1. Noncentrality parameters of EFDF(1) and LM tests.

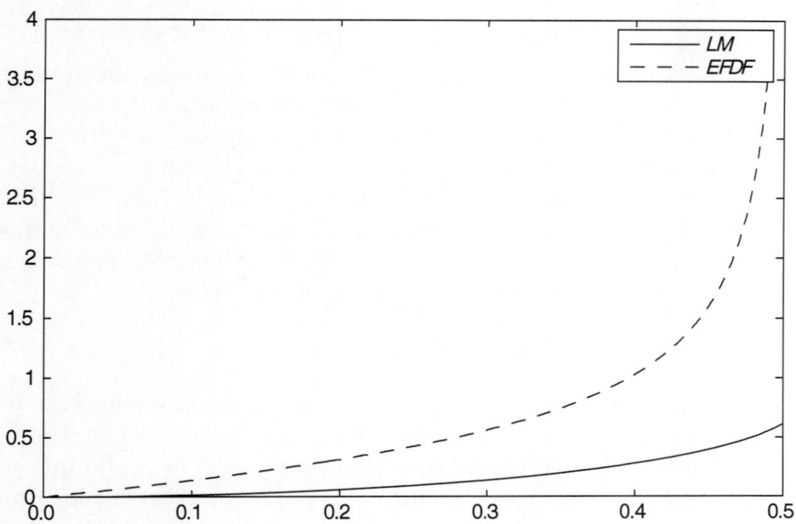

FIG. 12.2. Noncentrality parameters of EFDF(0) and LM tests.

Monte Carlo evidence supporting this better power performance can be found in LV (2007) and DGM (2008). The intuition for the worse power of the LM test is that there is no value for λ in (12.6) that makes e_t both i.i.d. and independent of the regressor for fixed alternatives, implying that x^*_{t-1} does not maximize the correlation with $\Delta^{d_0} y_t$.

As regards the power of semiparametric estimators, whose confidence intervals could be directly used for inference purposes, both the Fully Extended Local Whittle (FELW) (see Abadir *et al.*, 2005) and the Exact Local Whittle estimators (ELW) (see Shimotsu and Phillips, 2005) verify the asymptotic property: $\sqrt{m}(\hat{d}_T - d) \overset{w}{\to} N\left(0, \frac{1}{4}\right)$ for $m = o(T^{\frac{4}{5}})$. For example, test statistics for a unit root are based on $\tau_d = 2\sqrt{m}(\hat{d}_T - 1) \overset{w}{\to} N(0,1)$. Therefore, their rate of divergence under $H_1 : d < 1$ is the nonparametric rate $O_p(\sqrt{m})$ which is smaller than the $O_p(\sqrt{T})$ parametric rate achieved by the Wald test. Of course, this loss of power is just the counterpart of the higher robustness against misspecification achieved by semiparametric tests.

12.3 Deterministic Components without Breaks

In the case where $\mu(t) \neq 0$, DGM (2008) have derived the properties of the EFDF(1) test when the time-series is generated by (12.1) and $\mu(t)$ verifies the following condition.

Condition ET (Evolving trend): $\mu(t)$ is a polynomial in t of known order.

Under Condition *ET*, the DGP is allowed to contain trending regressors in the form of polynomials (of known order) of *t*. Hence, when the coefficients of $\mu(t)$ are unknown, the test described above is unfeasible. Nevertheless, it is still possible to obtain a feasible test with the same asymptotic properties as in Theorem 12.1 if a consistent estimate of $\mu(t)$ is removed from the original process. Indeed, under H_0, the relevant coefficients of $\mu(t)$ can be consistently estimated by OLS in a regression of Δy_t on $\Delta \mu(t)$. For instance, consider the case where the DGP contains a linear time trend, that is

$$y_t = \alpha + \beta t + \Delta^{-d} \varepsilon_t 1_{\{t>0\}}, \tag{12.8}$$

which, under $H_0 : d = 1$, leads to the popular case of a random walk with drift. Taking first differences, it follows that $\Delta y_t = \beta + \Delta^{1-d} \varepsilon_t 1_{\{t>0\}}$. Then, the OLS estimate of β, $\hat{\beta}$, (ie, the sample mean of Δy_t) is consistent under both H_0 and H_1. In effect, under H_0, $\hat{\beta}$ is a $T^{1/2}$-consistent estimator of β whereas, under H_1, it is $T^{3/2-d}$-consistent with $3/2 - d > 0.5$ (see Hosking, 1996, Theorem 8). Hence, if one uses the regression model

$$\widetilde{\Delta y_t} = \varphi \widetilde{z_{t-1}} \left(\hat{d}_T\right) + e_t, \tag{12.9}$$

where the input of $\widetilde{z_{t-1}}\left(\hat{d}_T\right)$ is a T^{κ}-consistent estimator of d with $\kappa > 0$, $\widetilde{\Delta y_t} = \Delta y_t - \Delta\hat{\mu}(t)$, $\widetilde{z_{t-1}}\left(\hat{d}_T\right) = \frac{\left(\Delta^{\hat{d}_T - 1} - 1\right)}{(1-\hat{d}_T)}(\Delta y_t - \Delta\hat{\mu}(t))$, and the coefficients of $\Delta\hat{\mu}(t)$ are estimated by an OLS regression of Δy_t on $\Delta\mu(t)$, then the asymptotic properties of the EFDF(1) test in (12.9) are identical to those stated in Theorem 12.1.

A similar result holds for the EFDF(0) test but this time using a T^{κ}-consistent estimator of d, for $d^* < 0.5$, with $\kappa > 0$. In this alternative setup of $I(0)$ vs. $I(d)$, the OLS estimators $\hat{\alpha}$ and $\hat{\beta}$ in the regression in levels of y_t on $\mu(t)$ are $T^{1/2-d}$ and $T^{3/2-d}$-consistent estimators of α and β, respectively. Consequently, the estimator of the trend slope, $\hat{\beta}$, is always consistent for $d \in (0,1]$ whereas the estimator of the intercept, $\hat{\alpha}$, is only consistent for $d \in (0,0.5)$, implying that the residuals from the OLS detrending procedure in levels are only valid for $d^* < 0.5$. Under fixed alternatives, since the true value of d could well exceed 0.5, one possibility in order to obtain consistent detrended series is to use Shimotsu's (2006a) detrending approach for $I(d)$ processes. This author notices that if one chooses the initial value of the series, y_1, as an estimator of α, then it holds that the deviations $y_1 - \alpha(= \Delta^{-d}\varepsilon_1 1_{t>0})$ are $O_p(1)$, implying that its variance is dominated by the exploding variance of y_t when $d \in (0.5,1]$. Thus, he recommends to use the above-mentioned FELW estimation procedure to the detrended series in levels $\tilde{y}_t = \dot{y}_t - \dot{\alpha}(d)$, where $\dot{y}_t = y_t - \hat{\alpha} - \hat{\beta}t$ are the OLS residuals and $\dot{\alpha}(d) = \omega(d)T^{-1}\Sigma\dot{y}_t + [1 - \omega(d)]\dot{y}_1$. Notice that $\dot{\alpha}(d)$ is a weighted average of the two alternative estimators of α earlier discussed with $\omega(d)$ being a smooth (twice continuously differentiable) weight function such that $\omega(d) = 1$ for $d \in (0,0.5)$.[11] Through this alternative detrending procedure, the difference between $\Delta^d\tilde{y}_t$ and ε_t becomes negligible for any value of $d \in (0,1]$. Therefore, if one considers the regression model

$$\widetilde{\Delta y_t} = \psi\widetilde{s_{t-1}}\left(\hat{d}_T\right) + e_t, \tag{12.10}$$

where the input of $\widetilde{s_{t-1}}(\hat{d}_T)$ is a T^{κ}-consistent estimator of d^*, for some $d^* < 0.5$ with $\kappa > 0$, having used as residuals $(\tilde{y}_t)$ the ones obtained from an OLS regression of y_t on $\mu(t)$, the asymptotic properties of the EFDF(0) test for testing $\psi = 0$ in (12.10) are identical to those stated in Theorem 12.2. Likewise, under fixed alternatives, a similar result holds for cases where $d \in (0.5,1)$, this time using Shimotsu's (2006a) residuals and $\tilde{d}_{0T}$, as an alternative estimator of the corresponding input value of the regressor $\widetilde{s_{t-1}}(.)$.

12.4 Deterministic Components with Breaks

Next we extend the EFDF tests to cover the case where the deterministic component, $\mu(t)$, of the time-series y_t in (12.1) is possibly subject to structural

[11] An example of $\omega(d)$ for $d \in (0.5,1)$ is $(1/2)[1 - \cos \pi d]$.

breaks, denoted hereafter as $\mu_B(t)$. One possibility is to consider breaks both under the null and the alternative hypotheses discussed in sections 12.2.1 and 12.2.2. In this case, similar two-stage procedures to those described in section 12.3 could be applied.[12] However, it is well known in the statistical literature that some features of long-range dependence (LRD) can be generated by either the process being $I(d)$ with smooth deterministic components or by an $I(0)$ process subject to breaks; see, eg, Bhattacharya *et al.* (1983), Mikosch and Starica (2004), and Berkes *et al.* (2006). Indeed, these studies show that conventional statistics designed to detect long range dependence behave similarly under weak dependence with change-points.[13]

For this reason we focus in the sequel on the pure distinction between these two *alternative* models that can account for the observed strong persistence of y_t: (i) u_t is an $I(d)$ process, with $d \in (0,1)$ and $\mu(t)$ is smooth, and (ii) u_t is a short-memory $I(0)$ process and $\mu(t)$ is subject to breaks. The EFDF approach, where one of the hypotheses encompasses the other, cannot directly accommodate these two types of models. This is so since the $I(d)$ hypothesis clearly nests the $I(0)$ one, but then the $\mu(t)$ component cannot nest $\mu_B(t)$ component at the same time. We therefore follow a comprehensive model approach, whereby non-nested models are tested within an artificially constructed general model that includes them as special cases. This approach was advocated by Atkinson (1970) and later taken up under a different guise by Davidson and MacKinnon (1981) in developing their J-test. In effect, let us think of two alternative models, denoted as $M1$ and $M2$, respectively, defined as follows

$$M1 : y_t = \mu_B^i(t) + \varepsilon_t, \tag{12.11}$$

and

$$M2 : y_t = \mu(t) + \Delta^{-d}\varepsilon_t 1_{t>0}, \text{ with } d \in (0,1), \tag{12.12}$$

where $\mu_B^i(t)$ is a linear deterministic trend function that may contain breaks at known or unknown dates (in principle, just a single break at date T_B would be considered) while $\mu(t)$ does not contain breaks. In line with Perron (1989),

[12] For tests of I(1) vs. I(0) with breaks under both the null and the alternative, see Banerjee and Urga (2005), and Kim and Perron (2006). Extensions of these tests to a fractional setup can be found in DGM (2005), Mayoral (2006), and Shimotsu (2006b).

[13] More recently, a similar issue has re-emerged in the econometric literature dealing with financial data. For example, Ding and Granger (1996), and Mikosch and Starica (2004) claim that the stochastic components of both the absolute and the squared returns of financial prices (bonds, exchange rates, options, etc.) are $I(0)$ and explain the evidence about LRD found in the data as spuriously induced by structural breaks in the parameters of the deterministic components over different subsamples due to significant events, such as the Great Depression of 1929 or the oil-price shocks in the 1970s. On the contrary, Lobato and Savin (1998) conclude that the LRD evidence found in the squared returns is genuine and, thus, not a spurious feature of structural breaks.

three definitions of $\mu_B^i(t)$, $i \in \{A, B, C\}$ will be considered,

$$Case\ A:\ \mu_B^A(t) = \mu_0 + (\mu_1 - \mu_0)DU_t(\omega_B)\,, \tag{12.13}$$

$$Case\ B:\ \mu_B^B(t) = \mu_0 + \beta_0 t + (\beta_1 - \beta_0)DT_t^*(\omega_B)\,, \tag{12.14}$$

$$Case\ C:\ \mu_B^C(t) = \mu_0 + \beta_0 t + (\mu_1 - \mu_0)DU_t(\omega_B) + (\beta_1 - \beta_0)DT_t(\omega_B)\,. \tag{12.15}$$

Case A corresponds to the *crash* hypothesis, case B to the *changing growth* hypothesis and case C to a combination of both. The dummy variables are defined as follows: $DU_t(\omega_B) = 1_{(T_B+1\leq t\leq T)}$, $DT_t^*(\omega_B) = (t - T_B)1_{(T_B+1\leq t\leq T)}$ and $DT_t(\omega_B) = t1_{(T_B+1\leq t\leq T)}$ where $\omega_B = T_B/T$ is a fixed value belonging to the subset of the interval (0,1) that describes the relative location of the break in the sample.

Then, noticing that $M2$ can be rewritten as

$$M2 : y_t = y_t - \Delta^d[y_t - \mu(t)] + \varepsilon_t, \tag{12.16}$$

one could follow Davidson and MacKinnon (1981) in considering the following linear combinations of $M1$ and $M2$

$$y_t = (1 - \zeta)\mu_B^i(t) + \zeta\{y_t - \Delta^d[y_t - \mu(t)]\} + \varepsilon_t, \tag{12.17}$$

or

$$y_t = (1 - \zeta)\{y_t - \Delta^d[y_t - \mu(t)]\} + \zeta\mu_B^i(t) + \varepsilon_t, \tag{12.18}$$

so that two J-tests can be applied, depending on whether $M1$ or $M2$ is considered to be the null hypothesis. In the case where $M1$ is taken to be H_0 and $M2$ to be H_1, the unknown parameters in $\{y_t - \Delta^d[y_t - \mu(t)]\}$ are not identified under H_0 since $\zeta = 0$. A solution of this problem is to replace the term $\{y_t - \Delta^d[y_t - \mu(t)]\}$ in (12.17) by $\{y_t - \Delta^{\hat{d}_T}[y_t - \hat{\mu}(t)]\}$, where $\hat{d}_T$ and $\hat{\mu}(t)$ are consistent under H_1, eg, using Shimotsu's (2006a) estimation procedure described in section 12.3. Hence, the following regression can be estimated

$$y_t = \mu_B^{*i}(t) + \zeta\widetilde{v_{t-1}} + \varepsilon_t, \tag{12.19}$$

where $\widetilde{v_{t-1}} = \{y_t - \Delta^{\hat{d}_T}[y_t - \mu(\hat{t})]\}$ and $\mu_B^{*i}(t) = (1 - \zeta)\mu_B^i(t)$. Under H_0, it follows that $\zeta = 0$, and this hypothesis can be tested using a t-test on the coefficient of $\widetilde{v_{t-1}}$, t_ζ. We will denote this test as the EFDF(B) test.

Conversely, if one chooses $M2$ to be H_0 and $M1$ to be H_1, the corresponding regression model becomes

$$\Delta^d y_t = \Delta^d\mu^*(t) - \zeta\widetilde{v_{t-1}}(d) + \varepsilon_t, \tag{12.20}$$

where now $\widetilde{v_{t-1}}(d) = \{y_t - \Delta^d y_t - \widehat{\mu_B^i}(t)\}$, $\mu^*(t) = (1 - \zeta)\mu(t)$ where d is taken to be knowns under the null, and $\widehat{\mu_B^i}(t)$ is estimated in a preliminary regression under the alternative of $I(0)$ cum breaks. Again, under H_0, we have that $\zeta = 0$, and a t-test, t_ζ, could be used to test for this hypothesis.

For simplicity, we have operated above as if the break dates were known in regressions (12.17) and (12.18). The more realistic case of unknown breaks when y_t is $I(0)$, are under current investigation following Bai's (1997) or Bai and Perron's (1998) procedures.

Finally, notice that, because non-nested hypothesis tests are designed as specification tests, rather than as procedures for choosing among competing models, it is not at all surprising that sometimes they do not lead us to choose one model over the other. If we would simply wish to choose the *best* model between M1 and M2, one could use some information criteria that help to discriminate between them. This approach is also in our current research agenda.

12.5 Breaks in the Long-Memory Parameter

Granger and Ding (1996) were the first to analyse the consequences of having a variable memory parameter d.[14] They consider two possible scenarios: (i) d_t is a stochastic process, e.g., an $AR(1)$ process with mean $\overline{d}$, and (ii) d_t switches between two regimes, e.g., $y_t = \lambda_t x_{1t} + (1-\lambda_t)x_{2t}$, with $x_{1t} \sim I(d_1)$, $x_{2t} \sim I(d_2)$ and λ_t following a 0–1 Markov switching process. Since this chapter is focused on testing, we consider a different setup. The memory parameter d can take two values, d_1 in a first given proportion of the sample and d_2 in the remaining proportion.

Both stationary and nonstationary fractional roots are considered. Although it is not difficult to generalize the analysis to allow for breaks in the deterministic components as well as short-term correlation in the disturbance terms, for simplicity we will focus in the sequel only on the case where the error terms are i.i.d. and no deterministic terms are present. More specifically, we assume that y_t is generated as

$$(1-L)^{d_0+\theta D_t(\omega_B)}\, y_t = \varepsilon_t 1_{t>0}, \tag{12.21}$$

so that y_t is a zero-mean integrated process (with an integer or fractional integration order), that can be either stationary or nonstationary. The order of integration of y_t is allowed to change along the sample at time T_B, with the dummy variable $D_t(\omega_B)$ taking a value equal to 1 if $\omega_B T < t$ and zero otherwise. Then, the process y_t is $I(d+\theta)$ until T_B and $I(d)$ after T_B, where θ can be either larger or smaller than zero.

Under H_0, no change in persistence occurs and therefore $H_0: \theta = 0$. By contrast, under H_1, a change in persistence occurs at time T_B, that is $H_1: \theta < 0$ or

[14] Detecting a change in the persistence of a process is usually tackled in the context of AR processes within the $I(0)/I(1)$ framework (see, e.g., Busetti and Taylor, 2004), later extended by Hassler and Scheithauer (2007) to $I(0)/I(d)$, $d > 0$. Nevertheless, as argued above, this framework can be too narrow in many empirical applications.

$H_1' : \theta > 0$, where the first (second) case corresponds to an increase (decrease) in persistence after T_B.

Since, to our knowledge, the LM tests have not been used so far to test this type of hypothesis, we start by deriving such a test in the present setup. Under Gaussianity, recall that Tanaka's (1999) time-domain version of the LM statistic for testing $H_0 : d = d_0$ vs. $H_1 : d \neq d_0$ uses the the log-likelihood

$$L\left(\theta,\sigma^2,\omega_B\right) = -\frac{T}{2}\log\left(2\pi\sigma^2\right) - \frac{1}{2\sigma^2}\sum_{t=1}^{T}\left\{(1-L)^{d_0+\theta D_t(\omega_B)}\,y_t\right\}^2 \tag{12.22}$$

Thus, an LM test for $H_0 : \theta = 0$ vs. $H_1 : \theta \neq 0$ rejects H_0 for large values of

$$LM_T = \left.\frac{\partial L\left(\theta,\sigma^2,\omega_B\right)}{\partial\theta}\right|_{H_0:\theta=0,\,\sigma^2=\hat{\sigma}^2} = -\frac{1}{\hat{\sigma}^2}\sum_{t=1}^{T}\left(\left\{\log(1-L)\times D_t(\omega_B)\,\Delta^{d_0}y_t\right\}\Delta^{d_0}y_t,\right.$$

where the estimated variance is $\hat{\sigma}^2 = T^{-1}\Sigma(\Delta^{d_0}y_t)^2$.

Since $log(1-L) = -\left(L + L^2/2 + L^3/3 + \ldots\right)$, and $D_t(\omega_B) = 0$ for $t > T_B$, then

$$LM_T = \frac{1}{\hat{\sigma}^2}\sum_{t=2}^{T_B}\left(\sum_{k=1}^{t-1}\frac{1}{k}\hat{\varepsilon}_{t-k}\right)\hat{\varepsilon}_t = T\sum_{t=2}^{T_B}\frac{\left(\sum_{k=1}^{t-1}\frac{1}{k}\hat{\varepsilon}_{t-k}\hat{\varepsilon}_t\right)}{\sum_{t=1}^{T}\hat{\varepsilon}_t^2} = T\sum_{k=1}^{T_B-1}\frac{1}{k}\hat{\rho}_k^*\left(\hat{\varepsilon}_t\right), \tag{12.23}$$

where $\hat{\rho}_k^*(\hat{\varepsilon}_t) = \sum_{t=k+1}^{T_B}\hat{\varepsilon}_{t-k}\hat{\varepsilon}_t/\sum_{t=1}^{T}\hat{\varepsilon}_t^2$. Notice that in finite samples $\hat{\rho}_k^*(\hat{\varepsilon}_t)$ is not identical to the k-th autocorrelation of residuals since in order to compute the numerator, only observations previous to the break are considered whereas all observations are employed to compute the denominator. This difference vanishes asymptotically. The following theorem describes the asymptotic properties of the test under local alternatives when the break date is known.

Theorem 12.5. *Under the hypothesis of $\theta = \delta/\sqrt{T}$, for a known value of T_B and a fixed δ it holds that, as $T \to \infty$,*

$$T^{-1/2}S_T(\omega_B) = \sqrt{T}\sum_{k=1}^{T_B-1}\frac{1}{k}\hat{\rho}_k^*\left(\hat{\varepsilon}_t\right) \xrightarrow{w} N\left(\frac{\pi^2}{6}\delta, \frac{\pi^2}{6}\omega_B\right). \tag{12.24}$$

Note that, since $\omega_B < 1$, the variance of this distribution is smaller than the variance in the case where no break occurs. This reflects the fact that only a fraction of the data is employed but the data is divided by $\sqrt{T}$. Along the lines of Tanaka (1999), it can also be shown that the test statistic proposed in (12.23) is locally optimal.

An EFDF test, denoted as EFDF(Bd), can also be constructed for this case. Following the derivations in section 12.2, one could consider the following maintained hypothesis

$$\Delta^{d_0}y_t = [1 - \Delta^{\theta D_t(\omega_B)}]\Delta^{d_0}y_t + \varepsilon_t, \tag{12.25}$$

which can be expressed in EFDF format as

$$\Delta^{d_0} y_t = \vartheta \left[\frac{1 - \Delta^{\theta}}{\theta} \right] \Delta^{d_0} y_t D_t(\omega_B) + \varepsilon_t, \tag{12.26}$$

where $\vartheta = \theta$. Thus, conditional upon the choice of ω_B, the EFDF(Bd) test would test $H_0 : \theta = 0$ against $H_1 : \theta \neq 0$ by means of a two-sided test based on the t-ratio, t_ϑ, which is estimated with observations $1, \ldots, T\omega_B$, and whose asymptotic distribution, under the null, would be $N(0,1)$ and, under local alternatives, satisfies Theorem 12.5. To construct the regressor in (12.26), the first step is to apply the 'deadstart' filter $\theta^{-1}[\Delta^{d_0} - \Delta^{d_0+\theta}]$ to $\{y_t\}_{t=1}^{T}$; next, the resulting filtered series is truncated to the first subsample by means of the dummy variable, $D_t(\omega_B)$. If θ is taken to be unknown, one could use a T^{κ}-consistent estimator of d from the first subsample and subtract it from d_0 using any of the estimation procedures discussed above.

This way of testing breaks in the long-memory parameter opens the possibility of testing a wide set of other alternative explanations for time varying long-memory behaviour. For instance, inspired by Granger and Ding (1996), the changes in d could be triggered by a strictly stationary and ergodic variable W_t that characterizes different regimes of the economy. More concretely, we are interested on testing $H_0 : y_t \sim I(d)$ versus $H_A : y_t \sim I(d)$ when $W_{t-1} \leq r$ and $I(d+\theta)$ when $W_{t-1} > r$. Substituting the structural break dummy $D_t(\omega_B)$ by the threshold dummy $I(W_{t-1} > r)$ in (12.26) and running the regression

$$\Delta^{d_0} y_t = \vartheta \left[\frac{1 - \Delta^{\theta}}{\theta} \right] \Delta^{d_0} y_t I(W_{t-1} > r) + \varepsilon_t, \tag{12.27}$$

where $\vartheta = \theta$, the corresponding EFDF test for threshold long memory, denoted by EFDF(Td), is a simple two-sided test based on the t-ratio, t_ϑ, whose asymptotic distribution, under the null, would be $N(0,1)$ assuming r is known (e.g., $r = 0$). Further issues stemming from an unknown r are beyond the scope of this chapter and are subject to current investigation by the authors.

12.6 Allowing for Serial Correlation

Lastly, we generalize the DGPs considered in section 12.2 to the case where u_t follows a stationary linear $AR(p)$ process, namely, $\Phi_p(L)u_t = \epsilon_t 1_{t>0}$ with $\Phi_p(L) = 1 - \phi_1 L - \ldots \phi_p L^p$ and $\Phi_p(z) \neq 0$ for $|z| \leq 1$. This motivates the following nonlinear regression model

$$\Delta^{d_0} y_t = \varphi[\Phi_p(L) x_{t-1}(d)] + \sum_{j=1}^{p} \phi_j \Delta^{d_0} y_{t-j} + \varepsilon_t, \tag{12.28}$$

where $x(.) = z(.)$ or $s(.)$, for the EFDF(1) and EFDF(0) test, respectively. The new model is similar to (12.3) and (12.4), except for the inclusion of the lags of $\Delta^{d_0} y_t$ and for the filter $\Phi_p(L)$ in the regressor $x_{t-1}(d)$. Estimation of this model is cumbersome due to the nonlinearity in the parameters φ and $\Phi = (\phi_1, \ldots, \phi_p)$. Compared with the i.i.d. case, LV (2007) claim that a practical problem arises because the vector Φ is unknown and therefore the regressor $[\Phi_p(L)x_{t-1}(d)]$ is unfeasible. For this reason, they recommend applying the following two-step procedure that allows one to obtain efficient tests also with autocorrelated errors.

Assuming, for simplicity, that $\mu(t) \equiv 0$ (or known),[15] in the first step, the coefficients of $\Phi_p(L)$ are estimated (under H_1) by OLS in the equation $\Delta^{\hat{d}_T} y_t = \sum_{t=1}^{p} \phi_j \Delta^{\hat{d}_T} y_{t-j} + a_t$, where $\hat{d}_T$ satisfies the conditions stated in Theorems 12.1 and 12.2. The estimator of $\Phi_p(L)$ is consistent with a convergence rate which depends on the rate κ. The second step consists of estimating by OLS the equation $\Delta^{d_0} y_t = \varphi[\hat{\Phi}_p(L)x_{t-1}(\hat{d}_T)] + \sum_{j=1}^{p} \phi_j \Delta^{d_0} y_{t-j} + v_t$, where $\hat{\Phi}_p(L)$ is the estimator from the first step, and $\hat{d}_T$ denotes the same estimated input used in that step as well. As LV (2007, Theorem 2) have shown, for the $I(1)$ vs. $I(d)$ case, the t_φ statistic in this augmented regression is still both normally distributed and locally optimal, but a similar argument applies to the $I(0)$ vs. $I(d)$ case. The tests will be denoted as AEFDF(i), $i = 1,0$, (augmented EFDF) tests in the sequel.

However, in DGM (2008) we claim that a feasible single-step procedure in the case of the AEFDF(1) test can also be applied with the same properties. In effect, under H_1, the process would be $\Phi_p(L)\Delta^d y_t = \varepsilon_t$, so that adding and subtracting the process under H_0, $\Phi_p(L)\Delta y_t$, it becomes

$$\Delta y_t = \varphi[\Phi_p(L)z_{t-1}(d)] + [1 - \Phi_p(L)]\Delta y_t + \varepsilon_t. \tag{12.29}$$

The one-step method we propose is based on the following decomposition of the lag polynomial $\Phi_p(L)$

$$\Phi_p(L) = \Phi_p(1) + \frac{1}{\Delta^{d-1} - 1}\Phi_p^*(L), \tag{12.30}$$

where the polynomial $\Phi_p^*(L)$ is defined by equating (12.30) to the standard polynomial decomposition

$$\Phi_p(L) = \Phi_p(1) + \Delta\tilde{\Phi}_p(L). \tag{12.31}$$

Hence

$$\Phi_p^*(L) = (\Delta^d - \Delta)\tilde{\Phi}_p(L) = \Delta^d\tilde{\Phi}_p(L) - [\Phi_p(L) - \Phi_p(1)]. \tag{12.32}$$

Substitution of (12.32) into (12.29), using (12.30) and noticing that $\varphi = d - 1$, $\Phi_p(1) + \tilde{\Phi}_p(0) = 1$ and $z_{t-1}(d) = \frac{\Delta^{d-1}-1}{1-d}\Delta y_t$, yields after some simple

[15] For the case where the coefficients of $\mu(t)$ are considered to be unknown, a similar procedure as that described in section 12.2.1 can be implemented and efficient tests will still be obtained.

algebra

$$\Delta y_t = \varphi[\Phi_p(1)]\ z_{t-1}(d) - \widetilde{\Phi}_p(L)[\Delta^d - 1]\ \Delta y_t - [\widetilde{\Phi}_p(L) - \widetilde{\Phi}_p(0)]\ \Delta y_t + \varepsilon_t. \quad (12.33)$$

where notice that the second and third regressors are predetermined since $(\Delta^d - 1)$ and $[\widetilde{\Phi}_p(L) - \widetilde{\Phi}_p(0)]$ do not include contemporaneous values of Δy_t. Hence, a one-step procedure can be implemented in a regression of Δy_t on $z_{t-1}(d)$, contemporaneous and lagged values of $[\Delta^d - 1]\ \Delta y_t$ and lags of Δy_t, by means of a t-test on the coefficient of $z_{t-1}(d)$. For example, in the case of an AR(1) disturbance, ie, $\Phi_1(L) = 1 - \phi L$, we have that $\Phi_1(1) = 1 - \phi$ and $\widetilde{\Phi}_1(L) = \widetilde{\Phi}_1(0) = \phi$, so that (12.33) becomes

$$\Delta y_t = \varphi(1-\phi) z_{t-1}(d) - \phi[\Delta^d - 1]\Delta y_t + \varepsilon_t. \quad (12.34)$$

A similar one-step testing procedure can be used for the AEFDF(0) test. In effect, adding and subtracting the process under H_0 to the process under H_1, yields

$$y_t = \psi[\Phi_p(L) s_{t-1}(d)] + [1 - \Phi_p(L)] y_t + \varepsilon_t. \quad (12.35)$$

Then, using the decompositions

$$\Phi_p(L) = \Phi_p(0) + \frac{1}{\Delta^d - 1}\Phi_p^*(L), \quad (12.36)$$

$$\Phi_p(L) = \Phi_p(0) + L\Phi_{p-1}(L), \quad (12.37)$$

and operating, yields

$$y_t = \psi s_{t-1}(d) - \frac{\Phi_{p-1}(L)}{\Phi_p(0)}\Delta^d y_{t-1} + \frac{1}{\Phi_p(0)}\varepsilon_t, \quad (12.38)$$

which for the illustrative case of an AR(1) disturbance, ie, $\Phi_1(L) = 1 - \phi L$, becomes

$$y_t = \psi s_{t-1}(d) + \phi\Delta^d y_{t-1} + \varepsilon_t. \quad (12.39)$$

Following LV (2007), one can show that the asymptotic properties of the two single-step AEFDF(i=1,2) tests above are identical to those in Theorems 12.1 and 12.2, except that, under local alternatives ($d = 1 - \gamma/\sqrt{T}$ for AEFDF(1) and $d = \gamma/\sqrt{T}$ for AEFDF(0), with $\gamma > 0$), we have that $t_\varphi(d) \xrightarrow{w} N(-\gamma\omega, 1)$ and $t_\psi(d) \xrightarrow{w} N(\gamma\omega, 1)$ where

$$\omega^2 = \frac{\pi^2}{6} - \varkappa'\Psi^{-1}\varkappa, \quad (12.40)$$

such that $\varkappa = (\varkappa_1, \ldots, \varkappa_p)'$ with $\varkappa_k = \sum_{j=k}^{\infty} j^{-1} c_{j-k}$, $k = 1, \ldots, p$, c_j's are the coefficients of L^j in the expansion of $1/\Phi(L)$, and $\Psi = [\Psi_{k,j}]$, $\Psi_{k,j} = \sum_{t=0}^{\infty} c_t c_{t+|k-j|}$, $k, j = 1, \ldots, p$, denotes the Fisher information matrix for $\Phi(L)$

under Gaussianity. Note that ω^2 is identical to the drift of the limiting distribution of the LM test under local alternatives (see Tanaka, 1999). The use of semiparametric estimators for d is very convenient here, since one can be agnostic about a parametric specification of the autocorrelation in the error terms when estimating the input value of d. Although it has not been proved yet, we conjecture that the single-step procedure can be generalized to deal with ARMA processes, rather than AR ones, by increasing the number of regressors in (12.33) or (12.38) at a certain rate, along the lines of DGM (2002, Theorem 7).

12.7 Concluding Remarks

Long-memory processes have become a very attractive research topic in econometrics during the last few years, due both to their flexibility and realistic microfoundations. Indeed, they received a lot of attention from the theoretical viewpoint but, in our opinion, so far this has not been sufficiently reflected in empirical work. There must be several reasons for this disconnection. We believe that one of them is that empirical researchers have found difficulties in implementing many of those theoretical results. Thus, our main goal in this chapter has been to frame the long-memory testing procedures in a setup somewhat equivalent to the nowadays familiar unit roots testing approach (à la Dickey–Fuller): t-statistics in simple time-domain regressions, with known conventional asymptotic distributions and easy to implement using standard econometrics softwares. Although our illustrations have focused on univariate processes, extensions to fully-fledged multivariate models should not be hard to derive. For example, a first try at applying the Wald test principles to the reduced-rank analysis in a system of $I(1)$ processes with fractional cointegrating relationships of order $(1 - b)$, $b \in [0,0.5)$, can be found in Avarucci and Velasco (2007).

References

Akonom, J. and Gourieroux, C. (1987). A functional limit theorem for fractional processes. CEPREMAP, Mimeo.

Abadir, K., Distaso, W., and Giraitis, L. (2005). Semiparametric estimation for trending I(d) and related processes. Imperial College, Mimeo.

Atkinson, A. (1970). A method for discriminating between models (with discussion). *Journal of the Royal Statistical Society*, B, B32, 323–353.

Avarucci, M. and Velasco, C. (2007). A Wald test for the cointegration rank in nonstationary fractional systems. Universidad Carlos III, Mimeo.

Bai, J. (1997). Estimation of a change point in multiple regression models. *Review of Economics and Statistics*, **79**, 551–563.

Bai, J. and Perron, P. (1998). Estimating and testing linear models with multiple structural changes. *Econometrica*, **66**, 47–78.

Banerjee, A. and Urga, G. (2005). Modelling structural breaks, long memory and stock market volatility: An overview. *Journal of Econometrics*, **129**, 1–34.

Berkes, I., Hovarth, L., Kokoszka, P., and Shao, Q-M. (2006). On discriminating between long-range dependence and changes in mean. *Annals of Statistics*, **34**, 1140–1165.

Bhattacharya, R. N, Gupta, V. K., and Waymire, E. (1983). The Hurst effect under trends. *Journal of Applied Probability*, **20**, 649–662.

Breitung, J. and Hassler, U. (2002). Inference on the cointegrated rank in fractionally integrated processes. *Journal of Econometrics*, **110**, 167–185.

Busetti, F. and Taylor, A. M. R. (2004). Tests of stationarity against a change in persistence. *Journal of Econometrics*, **123**, 33–66.

Davidson, R. and Mackinnon, J. G. (1981). Several tests for model specification in the presence of alternative hypothesis. *Econometrica*, **49**, 781–793.

Diebold, F. and Inoue, A. (2001). Long memory and regime switching. *Journal of Econometrics*, **105**, 131–159.

Ding, Z. and Granger, C. W. J. (1996). Varieties of long memory models. *Journal of Econometrics*, **73**, 61–77.

Dolado, J., Gonzalo, J., and Mayoral, L. (2002). A fractional Dickey–Fuller test for unit roots. *Econometrica*, **70**, 1963–2006.

———(2005). Structural breaks vs. long memory: What is what? Universidad Carlos III, Mimeo.

———(2008). Wald tests of I(1) against I(d) alternatives: Some new properties and an extension to processes with trending components. *Studies in Nonlinear Dynamics and Econometrics*, **12**(4), 1–32.

Engle, R. F. (1984). Wald, likelihood ratio and Lagrange multiplier tests in econometrics. In Griliches, Z. and Intrilligator, R. (eds.), *Handbook of Econometrics*, vol II, pp. 75–826. Amsterdam: North Holland.

Gil-Alaña, L. A. and Robinson, P. (1997). Testing unit roots and other statistical hypotheses in macroeconomic time series. *Journal of Econometrics*, **80**, 241–268.

Gonzalo, J. and Lee, T. (1998). Pitfalls in testing for long-run relationships. *Journal of Econometrics*, **86**, 129–154.

Gourieroux, C. and Monfort, A. (1995). *Statistics and Econometric Models*, Volume II. Cambridge: Cambridge University Press.

Granger, C. W. J. (1980). Long memory relationships and the aggregation of dynamic models. *Journal of Econometrics*, **14**, 227–238.

—(1986). Developments in the study of cointegrated economic variables. *Oxford Bulletin of Economics and Statistics*, **48**, 213–228.

—and Ding, Z. (1996). Varieties of long memory models. *Journal of Econometrics*, **73**, 61–77.

Hassler, U. and Scheithauer, J. (2007). Testing against a change from short to long memory. Mimeo.

Hosking, J. R. M. (1996). Asymptotic distributions of the sample mean, autocovariances, and autocorrelations of long-memory time series. *Journal of Econometrics*, **73**(1), 261–284.

Johansen, S. (2005). A representation theory for a class of vector autoregressive models for fractional processes. University of Copenhagen, Mimeo.

Kim, D. and Perron, P. (2006). Unit roots tests allowing for a break in the trend function at an unknown time under both the null and alternative hypotheses. Boston University, Mimeo.

Lo, A. W. and Haubrich, J. G. (2001). The sources and nature of long-term dependence in the business cycle. *Economic Review*, **37**, 15–30.

Lobato, I. and Savin, G. (1998). Real and spurious long memory properties of stock market data. *Journal of Business and Economic Statistics*, **16**, 261–268.

——and Velasco, C. (2006). Optimal fractional Dickey–Fuller tests for unit roots. *Econometrics Journal*, **9**, 492–510.

————(2007). Efficient Wald tests for fractional unit roots. *Econometrica*, **75**, 575–589.

Mayoral, L. (2006). Testing for fractional integration versus short memory with trends and structural breaks. Universitat Pompeu Fabra, Mimeo.

Michelacci, C. and Zaffaroni, P. (2000). Fractional beta convergence. *Journal of Monetary Economics*, **45**, 129–153.

Mikosch, T. and Starica, C. (2004). Nonstationarities in financial time series, long range dependence and the IGARCH model. *Review of Economics and Statistics*, **86**, 378–390.

Perron, P. (1989). The great crash, the oil price shock and the unit root hypothesis. *Econometrica*, **57**, 1361–1401.

Parke, W. R. (1999). What is fractional integration? *Review of Economics and Statistics*, **81**, 632–638.

Robinson, P. M. (1978). Statistical inference for a random coefficient autoregressive model. *Scandinavian Journal of Statistics*, **5**, 163–168.

——(1991). Testing for strong serial correlation and dynamic conditional heteroskedasticity in multiple regression. *Journal of Econometrics*, **47**, 67–84.

——(1994). Efficient tests of nonstationary hypotheses. *Journal of the American Statistical Association*, **89**, 1420–1437.

——and Marinucci, D. (2001). Narrow-band analysis of nonstationary processes. *Annals of Statistics*, **29**, 947–976.

Shimotsu, K. (2006a). Exact local Whittle estimation of fractional integration with unknown mean and time trend. Queen's Economics Dept. Working Paper 1061.

——(2006b), Simple (but effective) tests of long memory versus structural breaks, Queen's Economics Dept. Working Paper No. 1101.

——and Phillips, P. C. B. (2005). Exact local Whittle estimation of fractional integration. *Annals of Statistics*, **33**, 1890–1933.

Tanaka, K. (1999). The nonstationary fractional unit root. *Econometric Theory*, **15**, 249–264.

Velasco, C. (1999). Non-stationary log-periodogram regression. *Journal of Econometrics*, **91**, 325–371.

13

When is a Time-Series I(0)?

*James Davidson**

13.1 Introduction

Since the inception of integrated time-series modelling in econometrics, the question of what constitutes a 'nonintegrated' process has remained troublingly elusive. The inferential techniques developed for cointegration and related analyses require for their validity that the differences of the data series possess certain critical properties. These properties are nearly the same as those required for 'classical' asymptotics or, in other words, the application of the central limit theorem to approximate the distribution of regression coefficients and similar quantities. The project of doing time-series econometrics could hardly be viable, one would suppose, unless these properties could be both clearly delineated, and subject to verification.

Before the advent of cointegration these problems were often resolved willy-nilly, by an assumption of correct specification in the context of a fairly heroic conditioning exercise, whereby the explanatory variables in a model were held to be 'fixed in repeated samples'. The only stochastic components left to model (the disturbances) could then be treated as independently and identically distributed, and their treatment was elementary. However implausible these classical assumptions may always have been, they are manifestly inadequate to deal with cointegration models, because here it is not possible to hold the data conditionally fixed. It is the *observed series themselves*, not constructed disturbances, whose distributions must satisfy the critical regularity conditions.

* This chapter shares a title with the first version of a working paper that subsequently appeared as Davidson (2002). It further explores some themes that the earlier working paper broached rather briefly. I am glad of this excuse to revive a nice title, although there is in practice minimal overlap between the content of this chapter and its predecessor.

13.2 Defining I(0)

Early contributions to the cointegration literature tended to be fairly casual in their treatment of I(0), perhaps because this component of the theory was viewed as inherited from the pre-existing modelling methodology. The following definitions are culled from some widely cited articles and monographs.

1. 'Definition: A series with no deterministic component which has a stationary, invertible ARMA representation after differencing d times is said to be integrated of order d...' (Engle and Granger, 1987, p. 252).
2. 'It follows that [...] a short-memory series is I(0), as it needs differencing zero times' (Engle and Granger, 1991, p. 3).
3. '... if the series must be differenced exactly k times to achieve stationarity then the series is I(k), so that a stationary series is I(0)' (Banerjee, Dolado, Galbraith, and Hendry, 1993, p. 7).
4. 'A finite (non-zero) variance stochastic process which does not accumulate past errors is said to be integrated of order zero...' (Hendry, 1995, p. 43).
5. 'A stochastic process Y_t which satisfies $Y_t - E(Y_t) = \sum_{i=0}^{\infty} C_i \varepsilon_{t-i}$ is called I(0) if [$\sum_{i=0}^{\infty} C_i z^i$ converges for $|z| < 1$ and] $\sum_{i=0}^{\infty} C_i \neq 0$' (Johansen, 1995, pp. 34–35, the condition $\varepsilon_t \sim iid(0,\sigma^2)$ being understood).

Of these (chronologically ordered) quotations, 2, 3, and 4 can be thought of as informal and descriptive, while 1 and 5 are intended as more rigorous. Even so, it's interesting to note that they are by no means equivalent. The concepts of stationarity, short memory, and finite variance are each singled out as 'defining' descriptive characteristics, but it is not yet clear how these might be connected with one another. On the other hand, the more formal definitions restrict attention to a limited class of linear models, in which the three characteristics of stationarity, short memory, and (under Gaussianity) finite variance are united in a single parametric restriction. Note that in a more general framework it is easy to dispense with one while retaining another. The inclusion of deterministic components (eg 'trend stationarity') is only one of the many ways these models might be generalized.

Another approach to definition is the pragmatic one of simply specifying conditions under which the asymptotic theory is valid; see for example Stock (1994), Davidson (2002), and Müller (2008). These conditions are of course what motivate the technical and informal definitions just given, but in many ways it simplifies the analysis to state the desired properties directly, rather than conditions sufficient for them. Thus

Definition 13.1. *A time series $\{x_t\}_{t=1}^{\infty}$ is I(0) if the partial sum process X_T defined on the unit interval by*

$$X_T(\xi) = \omega_T^{-1} \sum_{t=1}^{[T\xi]} (x_t - Ex_t), 0 < \xi \leq 1 \tag{13.1}$$

where $\omega_T^2 = \mathrm{Var}(\sum_{t=1}^{T} x_t)$, converges weakly to standard Brownian motion B as $T \to \infty$.

This definition first makes it clear that I(0) is an attribute of an infinite stochastic sequence. In other words, it is not a well-defined concept for observed time-series except in the context of limit arguments as $T \to \infty$. Next, note that it implies the property $\omega_T^2 \sim T\omega^2$ for $0 < \omega^2 < \infty$, because otherwise the limit process cannot have the Brownian property $E(B(s) - B(r))^2) = s - r$ for $0 \leq r < s \leq 1$. For full applicability, it might need to be supplemented by the condition that a consistent estimator of ω^2 exists, which typically will be one of the class of kernel estimators; see Newey and West (1994) and Andrews (1991) *inter alia*. However, the best known sufficient conditions for these twin convergences, in distribution and probability, are in fact quite similar; see de Jong and Davidson (2000). It is quite possible that the best conditions actually coincide. Moreover, Kiefer, Vogelsang, and Bunzel (2002) have shown that valid inference is possible without consistent variance estimation, although as pointed out below, their results don't have application for testing the I(0) hypothesis, in particular.

What is clear is that a very wide class of processes satisfy these conditions, of which the cases cited by Engle and Granger (1987) and Johansen (1995), respectively, form only a small subset.

13.3 Conditions for I(0)

Davidson (2002 and 2006, section 5.5) provides a convenient summary of the technical conditions that ensure the property given in Definition 13.1 holds. A set of conditions is given for linear models that are effectively necessary for I(0), in the sense that convergence to a non-Brownian limit process (fractional Brownian motion) can be demonstrated in cases where they are violated.

Summability of the autocovariances (though not necessarily absolute summability) is the fundamental necessary condition for I(0), because on this condition depends the property $E(\omega_T^2) \sim T\omega^2$. Consider the class of covariance stationary moving average processes defined by

$$x_t = \sum_{j=0}^{\infty} a_j u_{t-j}, \quad \sum_{j=0}^{\infty} a_j^2 < \infty, \quad u_t \sim \mathrm{i.i.d.}(0, \sigma^2). \tag{13.2}$$

Since the mth order autocovariance is $\gamma_m = \sigma^2 \sum_{j=0}^{\infty} a_j a_{j+m}$, note that

$$\omega^2 = \sum_{m=-\infty}^{\infty} \gamma_m = \sigma^2 \left(\sum_{j=0}^{\infty} a_j \right)^2$$

so that summability of the autocovariances is equivalent to summability of the moving average coefficients. However, the conditions in (13.2) can be substantially relaxed by allowing dependence in the process $\{u_t\}$ itself, which can in its turn be weakly dependent with summable autocovariances. This can be illustrated by the obvious, though typically redundant, case where

$$u_t = \sum_{j=0}^{\infty} b_j \varepsilon_{t-j}, \quad \varepsilon_t \sim \text{i.i.d.}(0,\sigma^2).$$

Then we simply obtain

$$\omega^2 = \sigma^2 \left(\sum_{j=0}^{\infty} a_j \right)^2 \left(\sum_{j=0}^{\infty} b_j \right)^2$$

and this 'Russian doll' layering of the dependence structure could be iterated any finite number of times.

More pertinent are the cases where u_t exhibits some form of nonlinear dependence. In these cases, restrictions on the autocovariances may need to be supplemented by more general restrictions on dependence. The simplest is to let u_t be a stationary ergodic martingale difference. A variety of mixing conditions are also popular in the literature, although these have the drawback of non-transparency. Being restrictions on the entire joint distribution of the process at long range, they are difficult to test, either in an efficient manner, or at all. 'Geometric ergodicity' is a property of Markov chains which can be established for certain nonlinear difference equations (see, e.g. Tong, 1990). The condition of 'near-epoch dependence' links the distribution of an observed process to that of the near epoch of a specified underlying forcing process, which can for example be mixing. However, in a variety of nonlinear models driven by independent shocks, it is comparatively easy to specify testable (in principle) parametric restrictions which are sufficient for near-epoch dependence of specified 'size' (rate of memory decay) and in turn sufficient for I(0) in the sense of Definition 13.1. The cases of ARCH and GARCH models, bilinear models and SETAR models, among others, are analysed in Davidson (2002).

The obvious difficulty with Definition 13.1 is that it specifies an asymptotic property that cannot be verified in any finite sample. Summability of the autocovariances can never be resolved, one way or the other, from sample information. It is not unreasonable to ask whether sample autocorrelations 'look' summable, in the sense that they decline at such a rate as the lag increases that some implicit smoothness constraint must be violated, were they to behave differently at long range. However, a number of authors have examined difficult cases that place our ability to make this discrimination in doubt, even in large samples.

Leeb and Pötscher (2001) consider processes u_t that are covariance stationary, and for which there exists no covariance stationary process v_t such that $u_t = \Delta v_t$—in other words, are not over-differenced. They exhibit cases having these properties, yet lacking a spectral density (ie, the spectral distribution function is non-differentiable) which also lack the characteristic property (necessary for Brownian asymptotics) that the partial sum variance increases proportionately to sample size. Accordingly, such processes cannot be regarded as I(0). Their results emphasize the fact that attributes such as 'stationary' or 'short memory', cannot substitute for Definition 13.1.

Müller (2008), on the other hand, considers processes generated by expansions of the form

$$Y(s) = \frac{\sqrt{2}}{\pi} \sum_{k=1}^{\infty} g_k \sin(\pi s(k - \tfrac{1}{2}))\xi_k, \quad s \in [0,1] \tag{13.3}$$

where $\xi_k \sim$ i.i.d.N(0,1). Setting $g_k = 1/(k - \frac{1}{2})$ defines a Brownian motion (see Phillips, 1998) and sampling it at T points $s = 1/T, \ldots, 1$, yields a discrete integrated series. On the other hand, setting $g_k = 1$ yields, in the corresponding manner, a sample of Gaussian white noise. The interesting cases are found by setting $g_k = 1$ for $k = 1, \ldots, n$, for some $n < \infty$, and $g_k = 1/(k - \frac{1}{2})$ for $k > n$. For quite modest values of n, one can obtain a series that appears stationary, yet is also highly autocorrelated at long range. By letting n increase with T in just the right way, one can manufacture a series which is I(0) on Definition 13.1, yet the probability of rejection in any of a wide class of tests for (in effect) summable covariances converges to 1. This example is again artificial, but it illustrates the pitfalls that await those who seek to test the conditions embodied in the definition. As we show in more detail in the next section, there are always cases for which no sample is large enough to discriminate effectively.

13.4 Testing I(0)

Testing the hypothesis embodied in Definition 13.1 has been called an 'ill-posed' inference problem, and a number of recent research contributions have highlighted different aspects of the difficulty.

Consider three possible approaches to the testing problem. 1) perform a test in the context of a specified parametric or semiparametric model; 2) test a specific restriction on the sample distribution, such as the value of the spectrum at zero; 3) construct a nonparametric statistic whose null distribution depends directly on the conditions of Definition 13.1. In practice these approaches will to a large degree overlap, but it is instructive to consider the difficulties implicit in each. A fourth approach is to devise a consistent criterion for choosing between the specific alternatives of I(0) and I(1); see Stock (1994) and Corradi (1999). However, these latter methods have a rather specialized application, since they are predicated on the assumption that these two cases exhaust the possibilities. Given the existence of fractionally integrated processes in particular, this assumption appears unduly restrictive for our purposes.

13.4.1 *Parametric Hypotheses*

Start with the parametric framework. In an autoregressive or ARMA model, the null hypothesis takes the form 'the largest autoregressive root lies strictly inside the unit circle'.[1] The size control problems are immediately obvious, for the null hypothesis is defined by a non-compact set in the parameter space, say Ω_0, whose closure contains the leading case of the alternative (the unit root). If a test is consistent, then as sample size increases

$$\text{size} = \sup_{\omega \in \Omega_0} P_\omega(\text{test rejects}) \to 1.$$

One can certainly test the hypothesis that the largest autoregressive root lies in a specified stable region which does not have 1 as a boundary point. This approach has the virtue that a failure to reject the restricted hypothesis implies a failure to reject the I(0) hypothesis at at most the same significance level. However, it does not tell us how to interpret a rejection and hence it cannot be considered as a test of I(0) in the strict sense.

Another approach which has proved popular is to embed the I(0) case in the class of I(d) models, where d represents the fractional integration (long memory) parameter. Note that $d \neq 0$ is incompatible with Definition 13.1, since the limit of the normalized partial sum process is a fractional Brownian motion. The LM-type tests of Robinson (1991), Agiakloglou and Newbold (1994), Tanaka (1999), and Breitung and Hassler (2002) are all of this form. These tests are constructed, in effect, as functions of the sample autocovariances. One might also construct a confidence interval for the parameter d itself, using either a parametric or a semiparametric procedure—see Robinson (1994), Geweke and Porter-Hudak (1983), Moulines and Soulier (2000) *inter alia*. Being based on the periodogram, these estimators can again be thought of as functions of the sample autocovariances. The problem with all these tests is that autoregressive components, if present, assume the role of nuisance parameters. Local dependence is known to induce small sample bias in these

[1] There is also the parametrization which places stable roots outside the unit circle, but it is convenient for expository purposes to adopt the parametrization in which root and lag coefficient coincide in the AR(1) case.

estimators, so that conventional significance tests for d have to be treated with caution.[2] For correct asymptotic size, these tests require that autoregressive components be controlled for by some method of pre-whitening. A valid test of $d = 0$ requires that any such autoregressive roots are in the stable region. However, a unit root is, of course, observationally equivalent to the case $d = 1$. The previous problem of size control now re-emerges in a new form. If the prewhitening is done consistently, these tests must have power equal to size against the alternative of a unit root.

13.4.2 *'Ill-posed' Estimation Problems*

A number of authors including Blough (1992), Dufour (1997), Faust (1996, 1999), Pötscher (2002), and Müller (2005, 2008) have investigated a class of estimation problems in which testing of integration order (whether I(0) or I(1)) features prominently. As Dufour points out, there are two distinct cases that give rise to similar difficulties in practice. One is a failure of identification at points of the parameter space; in other words, the existence of observationally equivalent points. The second case is where the object of interest is a function of the underlying parameters, and the parameter space contains points of discontinuity of this function.

Of the various analyses offered in these papers, Faust (1996, 1999) demonstrates the second case neatly, as follows. Consider the class of processes in (13.2). For the purposes of the argument let the shocks be Gaussian, and since $a_0 = 1$ is not imposed there is no loss of generality in assuming $\varepsilon_t \sim NI(0,1)$. Define $A = \{a_0, a_1, a_2, \ldots\}$ to be a point in the space of square-summable sequences $\mathscr{A} \subset \mathbb{R}^\infty$. Let the distance $\|\cdot\|$ be defined on $\mathscr{A}$ such that

$$\|A_1 - A_2\| = \sqrt{\sum\nolimits_{j=0}^{\infty}(a_{1j} - a_{2j})^2}.$$

If $\{A_1, A_2, \ldots\}$ defines a sequence in $\mathscr{A}$ such that $\|A_k - A\| \to 0$, and the corresponding stochastic sequences are $\{X_{kt}\}$ such that

$$X_{kt} = \sum_{j=0}^{\infty} a_{kj}\varepsilon_{t-j}$$

then the distributions of the $\{X_{kt}\}$, say $\{P_{A_k}, k \geq 1\}$, converge weakly to P_A, the distribution of $\{X_t\}$. To demonstrate this, it is sufficient in view of the Gaussianity to show that the autocovariances of the processes converge. Given A, let $A^m = \{0, \ldots, 0, a_m, a_{m+1}, \ldots\} \in \mathscr{A}$, and note that $\|A_k^m - A^m\| \to 0$ if

[2] Davidson and Sibbertsen (2009) suggest a pre-test for bias.

$\|A_k - A\| \to 0$. Also note that if $\gamma_{km} = E(X_{kt}X_{k,t-m})$ then for each $m \geq 0$,

$$
\begin{aligned}
|\gamma_{km} - \gamma_m| &= \left|\sum_{j=0}^{\infty} a_{kj}a_{k,j+m} - \sum_{j=0}^{\infty} a_j a_{j+m}\right| \\
&= \left|\sum_{j=0}^{\infty} a_{kj}(a_{k,j+m} - a_{j+m}) + \sum_{j=0}^{\infty} a_{j+m}(a_{kj} - a_j)\right| \\
&\leq \left\|A_k^m - A^m\right\| \|A_k\| + \|A_k - A\| \|A^m\| \to 0 \quad \text{as} \quad k \to \infty,
\end{aligned}
$$

using the triangle and Schwarz inequalities. In other words, if $\|A_k - A\|$ is small then the difference between the distributions of $\{X_{kt}\}$ and $\{X_t\}$ is correspondingly small. Now consider the sequence $A_k = \{a_1, a_2, \ldots a_k, 0, 0, \ldots\}$, such that $A_k \to A \in \mathcal{A}$ but suppose $\sum_{j=0}^{\infty} a_j = \infty$. The sums $\sum_{m=0}^{\infty} \gamma_{km}$ are accordingly diverging as $k \to \infty$. $\{X_{kt}\}$ is an I(0) sequence for each k, but the limit is not I(0) in spite of lying arbitrarily close in distribution to I(0) sequences.

The implications for tests of the I(0) hypothesis should be clear. Supposing we seek to construct a confidence interval of level α for the spectral density at 0, say $f(0) = \pi^{-1}(\frac{1}{2}\gamma_0 + \sum_{m=1}^{\infty} \gamma_m)$. Let $(\Omega, \mathcal{F}, \mu)$ represent the probability space generating the process innovations, and also let $\mathcal{B}$ represent the Borel sets of the real line. An α-level confidence interval depending on a sample $\{X_1, \ldots, X_T\}$ is a measurable mapping $C_T(\alpha) : \mathcal{A} \times \Omega \longmapsto \mathcal{B}$ such that

$$
\inf_{\mathcal{A}} P_A\left(f_A(0) \in C_T(\alpha)\right) \geq 1 - \alpha.
$$

In words, a valid $C_T(\alpha)$ needs to contain $f_A(0)$ with probability at least $1 - \alpha$, no matter how the data are generated. It is evident that for any $\alpha > 0$, $C_T(\alpha)$ is unbounded. More alarmingly, this is also the case if attention is confined just to the subset $\mathcal{A}_0 = \{A \in \mathcal{A} : f_A(0) < \infty\}$, since this set is not compact, as demonstrated. Note that $\mathcal{A} \subset \overline{\mathcal{A}_0}$ (the closure of $\mathcal{A}_0$). *Every* non-summable element of $\mathcal{A}$ can be constructed as the limit of a sequence of summable elements, and $\overline{\mathcal{A}} = \overline{\mathcal{A}_0}$. The closure of the set of square-summable sequences contains the non-square-summable sequences.

This property of confidence intervals holds for any finite T. A standard kernel estimator of $f_A(0)$ should tend in distribution to the normal, with variance shrinking at the rate K_T/T where K_T is the bandwidth. However, the implied approximate confidence interval is an arbitrarily poor approximation to the true confidence interval. There exist data generation processes arbitrarily close to A for which the kernel estimate is diverging at the rate K_T, and has no well defined limiting distribution.

A closely related analysis considers the distribution of the difference processes $x_t = \Delta X_t$, having the representation

$$x_t = \sum_{j=0}^{\infty} a_j^* \varepsilon_{t-j}$$

where $a_0^* = a_0$ and $a_j^* = a_j - a_{j-1}$ for $j \geq 1$. Denote the generic sequence constructed in this way from an element A of $\mathscr{A}$ by $A^* \in \mathscr{A}$. If $A \in \mathscr{A}_0$ then $A^* \in \mathscr{A}_0^*$, where $\mathscr{A}_0^*$ is the subset of $\mathscr{A}$ having the property $\sum_{j=0}^{\infty} a_j = 0$. If attention is restricted to exponential lag decay processes, having the property $\sum_{j=m}^{\infty} a_j = O(a_m)$, we may further say that $\{X_t\}$ is I(0) if and only if the difference process belongs to $\mathscr{A}_0^*$. Evidently, sequences of elements of $\mathscr{A} - \mathscr{A}_0^*$ can be constructed whose limits lie in $\mathscr{A}_0^*$. In other words, there exist sequences of non-I(0) processes whose weak limits are I(0).

Pötscher (2002) points out that the existence of such points implies that consistent estimation is not a *uniform* property with respect to the parameter space. In other words, letting $\hat{\theta}_T$ denote an estimator of $f(0)$ the quantity $\sup_{A \in \mathscr{A}} E_A |\hat{\theta}_T - f_A(0)|^2$ is infinite, for every $T \geq 1$. A more subtle implication of the Faust–Pötscher analysis is that $\mathscr{A} - \mathscr{A}_0$ is dense in $\mathscr{A}$. *Every* model A with $f_A(0) < \infty$ is arbitrarily close to a case A' with $f_{A'}(0) = \infty$. Now, it might be thought that this result depends on the parameter space being explicitly infinite dimensional. Parametric representations of linear processes, such as the ARMA(p, q), are defined by subspaces of $\mathscr{A}$, (the images of mappings from $\Theta \subset \mathbb{R}^{p+q+1}$ to $\mathscr{A}$) which, it might be hoped, exclude most problematic regions. However, Pötscher shows that even the ARMA(1, 1) class contains problematic points such that the uniform consistency criterion fails. Hence it also fails for every superset thereof.

13.4.3 *The ARMA(1,1) Process*

Consider the element of $\mathscr{A}$ defined by

$$(1 - \phi L)X_t = \sigma(1 - \psi L)\varepsilon_t$$

so that $a_0 = \sigma$ and $a_j = \sigma(\phi - \psi)\phi^{j-1}$ for $j \geq 1$. Consider initially just the AR(1), by fixing $\psi = 0$, and note that the sequence A_k defined by setting $\phi = \phi_k$ for $\phi_k = 1 - 1/k$ lies in $\mathscr{A}_0$, with limit $A \in \overline{\mathscr{A}} - \mathscr{A}_0$. In this case $A \notin \mathscr{A}$, and there is also a failure of the weak convergence of the distributions. The discontinuity in the space of probability measures at the stationarity boundary is a familiar feature of this class. However, as noted previously, the null hypothesis of I(0) is represented by the open set $\Omega_0 = \{\phi : |\phi| < 1\}$, such that the leading case of the alternative $\phi = 1$ lies in its closure. It follows that if a test of I(0) is defined by a statistic s_T and a critical region W_T, such that the hypothesis of I(0) is rejected if $s_T \in W_T$, then for any $T \geq 1$ the power of the test against the alternative $\phi = 1$ can never exceed the size defined as $\sup_{A \in \Omega_0} P_A(s_T \in W_T)$.

A special feature of the ARMA(1,1) class, closely related to the present problem although distinct from it, is the existence of the set of unidentified structures with $\phi = \psi$. Having the same likelihood corresponding to the case $\phi = \psi = 0$, all these structures represent i.i.d. data, although the case $\phi = \psi = 1$ is arbitrarily close in model space to I(1) cases with $\phi = 1$, $\psi < 1$. Pötscher (2002) considers the following example. Construct a sequence of coefficient pairs, $\{\phi_k, \psi_k\}$ such that the sequence of spectral densities is

$$f_k(\omega) = \frac{\sigma^2}{2\pi}\frac{1 + \psi_k^2 - 2\psi_k \cos\omega}{1 + \phi_k^2 - 2\phi_k \cos\omega}.$$

Choose $M \geq 0$, and set $0 < \phi_k < 1$ and $\psi_k = 1 - M(1 - \phi_k)$, also requiring $\phi_k > (M-1)/M$ in the cases with $M > 1$ so that $\psi_k > 0$. Otherwise, $\{\phi_k\}$ can be an arbitrary sequence converging to 1. Note that $\psi_k \uparrow 1$ as $\phi_k \uparrow 1$, and also that along these sequences, $f_k(0) = \frac{1}{2}\pi^{-1}M^2\sigma^2$ for every k. Except at the limit point, the sequences of models have $\phi_k \neq \psi_k$ and hence they are technically identified, but depending on the path chosen they can have effectively any non-negative spectral density at 0, in spite of being arbitrarily close to one another as the limit is approached.

As in the examples of the previous section, a confidence interval for $f(0)$ must be either unbounded, or have level zero. For a more familiar insight into this issue, consider the one parameter IMA(1, 1) class of models, defined by the MA parameter ψ. This has nonsummable lag coefficients for every $\psi \in (-1, 1)$, yet the case $\psi = 1$, lying in closure of this set, defines the i.i.d. case. Be careful to note that the fact this point is unidentified in the ARMA(1,1) class is irrelevant, for it is perfectly well identified in the IMA class. This problem is related strictly to the discontinuity of $f(0)$ as a function of ψ.

13.4.4 *Nonparametric Tests*

The most popular procedures for checking I(0) involve computing statistics that address the question of summability of the autocovariances directly. Among tests in this class are the modified R/S test (Lo, 1991), the KPSS test (Kwiatkowski *et al.*, 1992), the LM test of Lobato and Robinson (1998), the V/S test of Giraitis *et al.* (2003), the 'remote autocorrelations' test of Harris *et al.* (2008), and the increment ratio test of Surgailis *et al.* (2008). Except for the last, these tests all depend on an estimator of the long run variance of the process, which is assumed finite under the null hypothesis. In fact, it is true to say that the properties of the tests are completely defined by the properties of these variance estimators. It is necessary to specify the null by specifying a finite lag, beyond which the sum of the autocovariances is either exactly zero or arbitrarily close to zero. Different choices of truncation point effectively define different null hypotheses, all of which are strictly contained in the 'I(0) hypothesis' proper.

The force of this point is nicely illustrated by the fact that the KPSS statistic, if constructed using the Bartlett kernel with bandwidth set equal to sample size, has a degenerate distribution with value $\frac{1}{2}$ (see Kiefer and Vogelsang, 2002). In other words the KPSS test can be viewed as comparing two variance estimators, respectively imposing and not imposing a truncation point smaller than sample size. The problem is there are $T-1$ such comparisons that can be made in a sample of size T, and no formal constraints on the proper choice. Since the null hypothesis imposes no finite truncation point, as such, the test is bound to be oversized for any finite truncation; equivalently, there is always a valid truncation point which sets power equal to size.[3]

13.5 Fingerprinting I(0)

The literature surveyed in this chapter may appear to place a question mark over large areas of econometric practice. If there are serious problems in discriminating between I(0) models and alternatives, what is the future for methods of analysis which depend critically on making this assessment reliably at the outset? Indeed, some authors have evidenced a certain satisfaction at pouring cold water on the efforts of time-series analysts in this area.

Before going too far in this pessimistic direction, however, we do well to remind ourselves of the actual question usually being posed. In almost every application, this is: 'Will asymptotic distribution results based on the assumption of I(0) provide more accurate approximate inferences than alternatives, in my sample?' Call this Question 1. It is clearly a different question from the following, which we will call Question 2: 'Will the distributions obtained by extending my sample indefinitely match the asymptotic distributions implied by the I(0) hypothesis?' It is Question 2 that has proved to be difficult to answer in the conventional manner. However, this is of little concern if there is no actual prospect of extending the sample indefinitely, and if there were then the difficulties would resolve themselves by the same token. As to Question 1 it is, arguably, reasonable to be guided by the popular adage: 'If it walks like a duck, and quacks like a duck, then (let's assume) it's a duck.'

The problem is to find an independent yardstick by which to judge, in a simulation experiment for example, whether the answer to Question 1 is affirmative. Linking back to Definition 13.1, this is essentially the question of whether the partial sums of the process approximate to Brownian motion in a sufficiently large sample. A natural approach to answering this question is to formulate a real-valued statistic whose limiting distribution corresponds to a unique functional of Brownian motion. Unfortunately, most statistics

[3] Interestingly, $\frac{1}{2}$ actually exceeds the 5% critical value of the limiting KPSS null distribution, so there always exists a truncation to guarantee rejection under both null and alternative at the nominal 5% level.

known to converge to pivotal Brownian functionals (for example, the Dickey–Fuller statistic and variants) are dependent on unknown scale factors, and embody estimates of the long-run variances. As previously noted, invoking these would tend to make the problem circular.

There is one nice exception, however. Consider the statistic $T^{-1}\hat{\varrho}_T$ where

$$\hat{\varrho}_T = \frac{\sum_{t=1}^T U_t^2}{T\sum_{t=1}^T u_t^2}$$

where $U_t = u_1 + \cdots + u_t$, and either $u_t = x_t - \bar{x}$ with $\bar{x}$ denoting the sample mean, or $u_t = x_t - \hat{\delta}' z_t$ where z_t is a vector of deterministic regressors, such as intercept and time trend. For simplicity we consider only the former case, but the extension is very easily handled. Note that $\hat{\varrho}_T$ is similar to the KPSS statistic, except that the variance estimate is not autocorrelation-corrected. This statistic is proposed by Breitung (2002) as a nonparametric test of I(1). Suppose that $v_t \sim \mathrm{I}(0)$ with mean 0 and long-run variance $\sigma^2 < \infty$, and $x_t = \sum_{s=1}^t v_s$. Then (by definition)

$$T^{-1/2}x_{[T\cdot]} \xrightarrow{d} \sigma W(\cdot)$$

where W is standard Brownian motion, and accordingly, by the continuous mapping theorem, $T^{-1}\hat{\varrho}_T \xrightarrow{d} \Xi_0$ where

$$\Xi_0 = \frac{\int_0^1 \left(\int_0^\tau W(s)ds - \tau\int_0^1 W(s)ds\right)^2 d\tau}{\int_0^1 W(\tau)^2 d\tau - \left(\int_0^1 W(\tau)d\tau\right)^2}. \tag{13.4}$$

Breitung points out that under the alternative hypothesis $u_t \sim \mathrm{I}(0)$, $T^{-1}\hat{\varrho}_T = O_p(T^{-1})$, and hence, using the lower tail as a rejection region yields a consistent test of I(1) against the alternative of I(0).

The test does not provide a consistent test against the alternative of $\mathrm{I}(1+d)$ for $d > 0$ (and hence by implication a test of I(0) applied to the partial sums) because the distribution of $T^{-1}\hat{\varrho}_T$ has bounded support. In fact, it never exceeds $1/\pi^2$ regardless of the distribution of $\{x_t\}$ (see Davidson, Magnus, and Wiegerinck, 2008). However, consider the case where v_t is $I(d)$ for $d > 0$. If $d < \frac{1}{2}$, then under mild assumptions on the increments (see for example Davidson and de Jong, 2000) we have the result

$$T^{-d-1/2}\sum_{s=1}^{[T\tau]} v_s \xrightarrow{d} \sigma W_d(\tau)$$

where σ is the long-run variance of the fractional differences $(1-L)^d v_t$, and W_d is fractional Brownian motion as defined by Mandelbrot and Van Ness

(1968) for $-\frac{1}{2} < d < \frac{1}{2}$. The Breitung statistic then has the limit

$$\Xi_d = \frac{\int_0^1 \left(\int_0^\tau W_d(\zeta)d\zeta - \tau \int_0^1 W_d(s)ds\right)^2 d\tau}{\int_0^1 W_d(\tau)^2 d\tau - \left(\int_0^1 W_d(\tau)d\tau\right)^2}. \tag{13.5}$$

On the other hand, if $\frac{1}{2} < d < \frac{3}{2}$ then

$$T^{-d-1/2}\sum_{s=1}^{[T\tau]} \upsilon_s \xrightarrow{d} \int_0^\tau W_{d-1}(\zeta)d\zeta, \qquad 0 \le \tau \le 1$$

and

$$\Xi_d = \frac{\int_0^1 \left(\int_0^\tau \int_0^\alpha W_{d-1}(\zeta)d\zeta d\alpha - \tau \int_0^1 \int_0^\alpha W_{d-1}(\zeta)d\zeta d\alpha\right)^2 d\tau}{\int_0^1 \left(\int_0^\tau W_{d-1}(\zeta)d\zeta\right)^2 d\tau - \left(\int_0^1 \int_0^\tau W_{d-1}(\zeta)d\zeta d\tau\right)^2}. \tag{13.6}$$

Be careful to note how the extra normalization factors T^{-2d} cancel in the ratio, as does σ, so that these distributions remain $O_p(1)$ and free of nuisance parameters other than d. These distributions have been tabulated by simulation for four values of d, using 1,000 NID(0,1) drawings to represent the υ_s (see Figure 13.1). While any I(0) process υ_s must yield (13.4) in the limit, it is

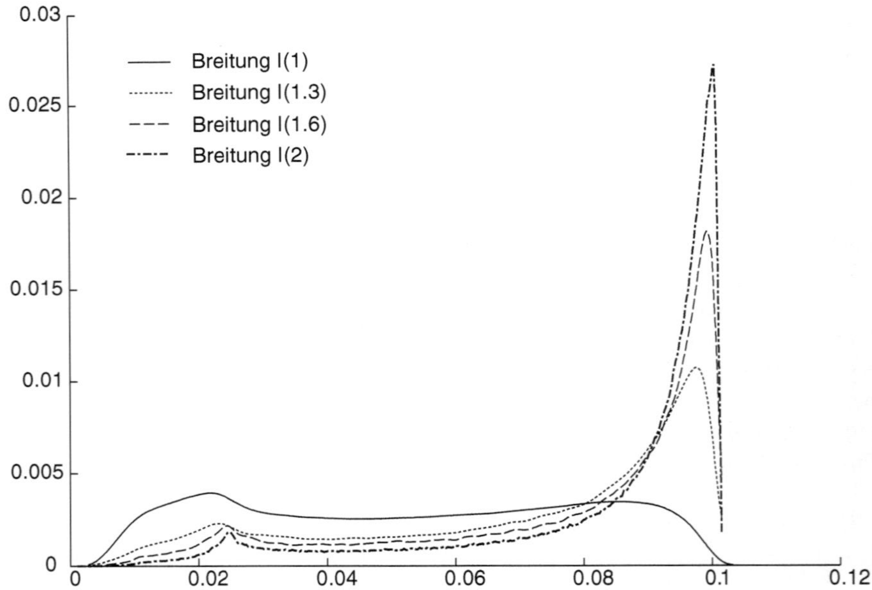

FIG. 13.1. Breitung (2002) statistic with cumulated I(d) increments. The case I(1) is Breitung's null distribution. (Kernel density plots from 1 million replications.)

Table 13.1. KPSS rejections in Gaussian AR(1) models with parameter ϕ, in 100,000 replications. The last row shows the Kolmogorov–Smirnov statistic for comparison of partial sums with the Breitung distribution

	T	50				100			200	
	ϕ	0.3	0.5	0.7	0.9	0.5	0.7	0.9	0.7	0.9
KPSS:	Bw = 4	0.062	0.087	0.145	0.270	0.095	0.172	0.403	0.189	0.509
	Bw = 12	0.043	0.043	0.051	0.080	0.055	0.077	0.174	0.087	0.236
	Andrews	0.044	0.029	0.011	0.028	0.041	0.026	0.003	0.043	0.010
	N–W	0.060	0.077	0.112	0.212	0.073	0.114	0.264	0.115	0.316
K–S	for $T^{-1}\hat{\varrho}_T$	0.727	**1.486**	**2.786**	**6.790**	0.737	**1.434**	**4.404**	0.802	**2.401**

clear that the passage to the limit may be substantially different, depending on the strength of dependence. Thus, the distribution of $T^{-1}\hat{\varrho}_T$ where v_t is an autoregressive process, with a root close to unity, is likely to resemble Ξ_1 more closely than Ξ_0 in samples of moderate size.

The idea to be explored here is to use the null distribution of Breitung's statistic to fingerprint (the partial sums of) an I(0) process. If the latter distribution cannot be distinguished from the former, in a sample of given size, it is a reasonable conjecture that the dependence in the process is innocuous from the point of view of applying asymptotic inference. Of course, this is by no means the only statistic that might be used for this purpose, but it does have two notable advantages, independence of scale parameters and bounded support. The latter is a particularly convenient feature for implementing a comparison of distributions.

In Table 13.1, data have been simulated from five I(0) processes, the Gaussian AR(1) with coefficients $\phi = 0, 0.3, 0.5, 0.7$, and 0.9, and three sample sizes, $T = 50$, 100, and 200. In all these cases the correct answer to Question 2 is affirmative. The KPSS test has been computed for these series with HAC variance estimator computed using the Bartlett kernel and four choices of bandwidth, two fixed, and two selected by data-based 'plug-in' methods as proposed by, respectively, Andrews (1991) and Newey and West (1994) (denoted N–W in the table).[4] To provide critical values, 1.5 million Gaussian i.i.d. samples were used to construct tabulations for each choice of T, so ensuring that all features of the data and test procedure, except the dependence, are correctly modelled. Viewed as attempts to answer Question 2, all of these procedures appear to represent an unsatisfactory compromise. Only

[4] The plug-in formulae have the form bandwidth = $1.447(\alpha T)^{1/3}$ where $\alpha = \alpha_A$ and $\alpha = \alpha_{NW}$, respectively, and $\alpha_A = 4\hat{\rho}^2/(1-\hat{\rho})^2(1+\hat{\rho})^2$ where $\hat{\rho}$ is the first-order autocorrelation coefficient, and $\alpha_{NW} = [2\sum_{j=1}^{[n_T]} j\hat{\gamma}_j/(\hat{\gamma}_0 + 2\sum_{j=1}^{[n_T]}\hat{\gamma}_j)]^2$ where $\hat{\gamma}_j$ is the jth order sample autocovariance. Here, [.] is the floor function, and $n_T = 3(T/100)^{2/9}$ so that $[n_{50}] = 2$, and $[n_{100}] = [n_{200}] = 3$. Newey and West advocate a pre-whitening step using an autoregression before applying their kernel estimator, but this step has been omitted here.

the Andrews method is never over-sized, but its power against a unit root alternative appears in doubt.

The last row of the table shows the Kolmogorov–Smirnov tests of the Breitung distributions generated from the Monte Carlo replications for each case, using the tabulations from the i.i.d. data to provide the benchmark distributions. Those cases exceeding the asymptotic 5% critical value, of 1.35, are shown in boldface in the table.[5] Suppose we take rejection on this test as a negative answer to Question 1. On this criterion, only the case $\phi = 0.3$ is included in the null hypothesis in a sample of size 50. In a sample of size 100, $\phi = 0.5$ enters the acceptance region, and in a sample of 200, so does $\phi = 0.7$. The point to be emphasized here is that the KPSS tests are even less satisfactory as a means for answering Question 1 than for answering Question 2. Except for the Andrews method, which has no power, the rejection rates for a given ϕ all *increase* with sample size, whereas on the criterion of Question 1, as indicated by the last row, we should like them to decrease. It is, manifestly, the evidence contained in the last row of Table 13.1 that we should most like to possess, when evaluating Question 1. The next section attempts to operationalize this insight.

13.6 A Bootstrap Test of I(0)

A test of I(0) in the sense of Question 1, based directly on the comparison of fingerprinting distributions, might be implemented by the following steps.

1. Formulate and fit a model of the data generation process.
2. Use this estimate to simulate the series many times and tabulate the Breitung statistic $T^{-1}\hat{\varrho}_T$ for the partial sums.
3. Use the Kolmogorov–Smirnov test to compare the distribution of this statistic with the benchmark case based on independent increments.

Given an implementation of Step 1, which we discuss in detail below, Step 2 might be performed using a Gaussian random number generator, or by bootstrap draws from the Step 1 residuals. In the latter case it is very important to generate the benchmark distribution from the same sample as the test distribution, to avoid a spurious difference. The drawings are recoloured by the estimated filter to create the test distribution, and used unfiltered to create the benchmark. Note that differences in the variances of the two draws are unimportant, since scale effects cancel in the construction of the Breitung statistic. For Step 3, the benchmark distribution should preferably be estimated in parallel with matching sample size, and compared by the

[5] For clarity the table shows only the most extreme cases of the null hypothesis, as indicated by the K–S statistic.

two-sided Kolmogorov–Smirnov test. This is to ensure that it is exclusively the dependence that influences the test outcome, not the accuracy of the asymptotic approximation.

Estimation of the DGP is clearly the trickiest step, in effect the counterpart of the bandwidth selection problem in conventional tests, although the constraints it imposes are different and generally more favourable. Note that nonparametric methods for bootstrapping under dependence, such as the block bootstrap or Fourier bootstrap, are not attractive in this context because of the problem of matching the distributions under the null hypothesis. Given a suitable estimator of the autocovariance function, it would be feasible to simulate using the Choleski method or the circulant embedding algorithm (Davies and Harte, 1987). However, this estimation problem is precisely the source of the difficulties described in section 13.4.2. Therefore, parametric modelling as in Step 1 appears the most promising approach.

For power against unit and near-unit root autoregressive alternatives, an autoregressive model naturally suggests itself. However, this is a less attractive option from the point of view of detecting fractional alternatives, since unrestricted estimation of a hyperbolic AR(∞) lag structure poses obvious efficiency problems. Therefore it seems important that the autocorrelation model contain a fractional integration component. One possibility is to fit an ARFIMA model to the data, although there are well-known identification and numerical problems involved in simultaneously fitting an autoregressive root and fractional d parameter. Multi-modal and poorly conditioned likelihoods are commonly encountered in these models. For the purposes of a Monte Carlo study, where a routine of model checking and evaluation at each replication is not feasible, three options have been compared. The first is a sieve autoregression, using the Akaike criterion to select the AR order from the set $0, \ldots, [0.6T^{1/3}]$. The second is to fit an ARFI(1,d) two-parameter model by nonlinear least squares. The third alternative considered is to fit a truncated fractional model, of the form

$$x_t = -\sum_{j=1}^{\min(\tau,t-1)} b_j x_{t-j} + e_t$$

where $b_j = (j - d - 1)b_{j-1}/j$, with $b_0 = 1$, and the fitted parameters are d and τ. Think of this as a restricted version of the sieve autoregression, parsimoniously approximating either a low-order autoregressive alternative with τ small, or a fractional alternative with τ large.

Table 13.2 shows the results of replicating these three test procedures, using 500 bootstrap draws to generate the test distributions at Step 2. For four sample sizes, $T = 50$, 100, 200, and 500, the rows of the table show the results for these three estimation methods augmented by the 'True' model, where the known data generation process has been used to create the bootstrap

Table 13.2. Bootstrap I(0) test: Rejection rates for the Kolmogorov–Smirnov test of Breitung's statistic in 5000 replications

T	Test	Size (Nominal 5% Test)	Power						
			AR(1): ϕ				FI: *d*		
			0.3	0.5	0.7	0.9	0.3	0.5	0.7
50	True	0.050	0.206	0.682	0.997	1	1	1	1
	Sieve AR	0.068	0.164	0.492	0.828	0.975	0.293	0.672	0.924
	ARFI(1,*d*)	0.174	0.064	0.092	0.305	0.797	0.383	0.622	0.861
	Trunc. FI	0.129	0.135	0.366	0.730	0.964	0.458	0.733	0.926
100	True	0.050	0.085	0.207	0.673	1	1	1	1
	Sieve AR	0.054	0.086	0.204	0.557	0.962	0.105	0.479	0.846
	ARFI(1,*d*)	0.153	0.073	0.092	0.193	0.810	0.554	0.758	0.730
	Trunc. FI	0.095	0.112	0.168	0.473	0.953	0.548	0.761	0.877
200	True	0.050	0.069	0.098	0.261	0.986	1	1	1
	Sieve AR	0.050	0.071	0.096	0.249	0.867	0.197	0.516	0.857
	ARFI(1,*d*)	0.165	0.080	0.096	0.155	0.602	0.842	0.914	0.855
	Trunc. FI	0.094	0.077	0.063	0.139	0.818	0.750	0.862	0.884
500	True	0.050	0.050	0.056	0.075	0.381	1	1	1
	Sieve AR	0.050	0.050	0.056	0.074	0.344	0.070	0.208	0.755
	ARFI(1,*d*)	0.143	0.083	0.109	0.159	0.369	0.960	0.975	0.928
	Trunc. FI	0.081	0.044	0.035	0.045	0.283	0.890	0.967	0.985

replications. This test is of course infeasible in practice, but it provides a yardstick against which to gauge the effectiveness of the alternative feasible methods.

The table entries show the proportion of rejections in the Kolmogorov–Smirnov test comparing the distribution of Breitung's statistic constructed from the re-coloured data with that of the statistic constructed from the same number of i.i.d. bootstrap drawings. Each statistic was first tabulated under the null hypothesis from 10,000 replications using i.i.d. normal drawings, so as to provide correct critical values for each sample size. Taking the critical values for the 5%-level 'True' test as the yardstick (so that these table entries are 0.05 by construction, note) the first column of the table shows the estimated sizes of the nominal 5% tests. The remaining columns show estimates of the true powers (using the null tabulations to provide critical values) against seven alternatives, based on 5,000 replications of each case. The cases are four AR(1) processes with parameter ϕ and three ARFIMA(0,d,0) processes, with i.i.d. Gaussian shocks and zero start-up values in each case.

Some important points of interpretation need to be borne in mind, in studying this table. In the limiting case as $T \to \infty$, we should expect to find power = size for each of the four cases of the I(0) hypothesis, and power = 1 for each of the three cases of the I(d) alternative. In finite samples, however, rejection in the I(0) cases is not an incorrect outcome. The issue is whether the autocorrelation is strong enough to put asymptotic inference criteria into question. The infeasible 'True' cases represent the ideal outcomes from this point of view, against which the feasible tests can be judged. If this test were to be adopted as a pre-test before a conventional inference procedure, we can even see it as a means of discriminating between data sets which (by chance) tend to satisfy our validity criteria, from those which violate it. Failure to reject can be conjectured to indicate that subsequent tests with these data may not be too badly sized.

In the event, the truncated fractional model appears to have the best all-round performance. The sieve AR method performs generally closest to the infeasible test in the I(0) cases, but has poor power properties against the fractional alternatives. The ARFI method suffers the worst from spurious rejection and so diverges furthest from the 'True' benchmark under I(0), while the truncated fractional method appears to offer the best compromise in both cases. Of course, this is chiefly due to the fact that it gives a good approximation to both the AR(1) and FI alternatives tested. To determine how it performs in a more general setting calls for more experiments. In practical implementations (as opposed to a Monte Carlo experiment) the test should be performed following the specification and estimation of a time-series model by the investigator, and so tailored more accurately to the data set in question.

13.7 Concluding Remarks

The hypothesis that a time-series is I(0) has been justly described as an 'ill-posed' problem for statistical investigation. A number of studies have shown that this question, as conventionally posed, is unsuited to standard methods of inference. This chapter suggests that there are more suitable hypotheses to test, relating directly to the implications of the distribution of the data for asymptotic (ie, approximate) inference. A convenient asymptotically pivotal statistic is used as a yardstick, to assess how far data features such as local dependence affect the distribution, in a sample of given size. The null hypothesis under test is not 'I(0)' in the strict sense, but the arguably more useful hypothesis that the assumption of I(0) is innocuous from the point of view of the asymptotic approximation of test distributions.

It's important to emphasize that this test is strictly of the properties of a *model* (or DGP), not a direct test on an observed series, as such. The link between the model and the data has to be supplied by the explicit modelling exercise, which is accordingly the key component of the procedure. The reported Monte Carlo results, which show simple models fitted mechanically to series with a known simple structure, need to be interpreted with care in this light. Whereas reproducing the observed autcorrelation structure of the data is a key requirement, don't overlook the fact that (for example) an uncorrelated IGARCH process is a case of the alternative. Power against such cases depends on a suitable choice of model. In view of the cited result of

Müller (2008), there are bound to be cases which defy the ability of popular time-series models to capture the dependence structure, although being non-causal it is questionable whether processes of the type (13.3) can feature in observed economic time-series. It will be useful to compare the performance of the test in alternative DGPs, especially with nonlinear dynamics, and also to calibrate the performance of conventional tests, such as the Dickey–Fuller, in conjunction with bootstrap 'pre-testing'. Among other important questions is whether the Breitung statistic is the best candidate for comparison, or whether a range of benchmarks might be implemented. Such exercises must however be left for future work.

References

Agiakloglou, Ch. and Newbold, P. (1994). Lagrange multiplier tests for fractional difference. *Journal of Time Series Analysis*, **15**, 253–262.

Andrews, D. W. K. (1991). Heteroskedasticity and autocorrelation consistent covariance matrix estimation. *Econometrica*, **59**(3), 817–858.

——and Monahan, J. C. (1992). An improved heteroskedasticity and autocorrelation consistent covariance matrix estimator. *Econometrica*, **60**(4), 953–966.

Banerjee, A., Dolado, J. J., Galbraith, J. W., and Hendry, D. F. (1993). *Co-integration, Error Correction and the Econometric Analysis of Non-Stationary Data*. Oxford: Oxford University Press.

Blough, S. R. (1992). The relationship between power and level for generic unit root tests infinite samples. *Journal of Applied Econometrics*, **7**, 295–308.

Breitung, J. (2002). Nonparametric tests for unit roots and cointegration. *Journal of Econometrics*, **108**, 343–363.

——and Hassler, U. (2002). Inference on the cointegration rank in fractionally integrated processes. *Journal of Econometrics*, **110**, 167–185.

——and Taylor, A. M. R. (2003). Corrigendum to 'Nonparametric tests for unit roots and cointegration'. *Journal of Econometrics*, **117**, 401–404.

Busetti, F. and Taylor, A. M. R. (2004). Tests of stationarity against a change in persistence. *Journal of Econometrics*, **123**, 33–66.

Cavaliere, G. and Taylor, A. M. R. (2005). Stationarity tests under time-varying second moments. *Econometric Theory*, **21**, 1112–1129.

Corradi, V. (1999). Deciding between I(0) and I(1) via Flil-based bounds. *Econometric Theory*, **15**(5), 643–663.

Davidson, J. (2002). Establishing conditions for the functional central limit theorem in nonlinear and semiparametric time series processes. *Journal of Econometrics*, **106**, 243–269.

——(2006). Asymptotic Methods and Functional Central Limit Theorems. Ch. 5 of Mills, T. C. and Patterson, K. (eds.), *Palgrave Handbook of Econometrics: Vol. 1 Econometric Theory*. Palgrave Macmillan.

——and de Jong, R. M. (2000). Consistency of kernel estimators of heteroscedastic and autocorrelated covariance matrices. *Econometrica*, **68**(2), 407–424

——and Sibbertsen, P. (2009). Tests of bias in log-periodogram regression. Forthcoming in *Economics Letters*.

Davidson, J., Magnus, J., and Wiegerinck, J. (2008). A general bound for the limiting distribution of Breitung's statistic. Econometric Theory, **24**(5), 1443–1455.

Davies, R. B. and Harte, D. S. (1987). Tests for Hurst effect. *Biometrika*, **74**, 95–102.

de Jong, R. M. and Davidson, J. (2000). The functional central limit theorem and weak convergence to stochastic integrals I: Weakly dependent processes. *Econometric Theory*, **16**, 621–42.

Den Haan, W. J. and Levin, A. (1997). A practitioner's guide to robust covariance matrix estimation. Ch. 12 of Maddala, G. S. and Rao, C. R. (eds.), *Handbook of Statistics 15: Robust Inference*, pp. 291–341. Elsevier.

Dufour, J.-M. (1997). Some impossibility theorems in econometrics with applications to structural and dynamic models. *Econometrica*, **65**(6), 1365–1387.

Engle, R. F. and Granger, C. W. J. (1987). Co-integration and error correction: Representation, estimation and testing. *Econometrica*, **35**, 251–276.

————(1991). *Long-run Economic Relationships: Readings in Cointegration*. Oxford: Oxford University Press.

Faust, J. (1996). Near observational equivalence and theoretical size problems with unit root tests. *Econometric Theory*, **12**(4), 724–731.

——(1999). Conventional confidence intervals for points on spectrum have confidence level zero. *Econometrica*, **67**(3), 629–637.

Geweke, J. and Porter-Hudak, S. (1983). The estimation and application of long-memory time series models. *Journal of Time Series Analysis*, **4**, 221–237.

Giraitis, L., Kokoszka, P., Leipus, R., and Teyssiere, G. (2003). Rescaled variance and related tests for long memory in volatility and levels. *Journal of Econometrics*, **112**, 265–294.

Harris, D., McCabe, B. M., and Leybourne, S. (2008). Testing for long memory. *Econometric Theory*, **24**(1), 143–175.

Hendry, D. F. (1995). *Dynamic Econometrics*. Oxford: Oxford University Press.

Hurvich, C. M., Deo, R., and Brodsky, J. (1998). The mean squared error of Geweke and Porter-Hudak's estimator of a long memory time series. *Journal of Time Series Analysis*, **19**, 19–46

Johansen, S. (1995). *Likelihood-based Inference in Cointegrated Vector Autoregressive Models*. Oxford: Oxford University Press

Kiefer, N. M., Vogelsang, T. J. and Bunzel, H. (2000). Simple robust testing of regression hypotheses. *Econometrica*, **68**(3), 695–714.

————(2002). Heteroskedasticity-autocorrelation robust standard errors using the Bartlett kernel without truncation. *Econometrica*, **70**(5), 2093–2095.

Kwiatkowski, D., Phillips, P. C. B., Schmidt, P., and Shin, Y. (1992). Testing the null hypothesis of stationarity against the alternative of a unit root. *Journal of Econometrics*, **54**, 159–178.

Leeb, H. and Pötscher, B. M. (2001). The variance of an integrated process need not diverge to infinity, and related results on partial sums of stationary processes. *Econometric Theory*, **17**(4), 671–685.

Lo, A. W. (1991). Long-term memory in stock market prices. *Econometrica*, **59**(5), 1279–1313.

Lobato, I. N. and Robinson, P. M. (1998). A Nonparametric Test for I(0). *Review of Economic Studies*, **65**(3), 475–495.

Mandelbrot, B. B. and van Ness, J. W. (1968). Fractional Brownian motions, fractional noises and applications. *SIAM Review*, **10**, 442–437.

Moulines, E. and Soulier, P. (1999). Broad ban log-periodogram estimation of time series with long-range dependence. *Annals of Statistics*, **27**, 1415–1439.

Müller, U. K. (2005). Size and power of tests of stationarity in highly autocorrelated time series. *Journal of Econometrics*, **128**, 195–213.

——(2008). The impossibility of consistent discrimination between I(0) and I(1) processes. *Econometric Theory*, **24**, 616–630.

Newey, W. K. and West, K. D. (1987). A simple, positive semi-definite, heteroskedasticity and autocorrelation consistent covariance matrix. *Econometrica*, **55**, 703–708.

————(1994). Automatic lag selection in covariance matrix estimation. *Review of Economic Studies*, **61**, 631–654.

Phillips, P. C. B. (1998). New tools for understanding spurious regression. *Econometrica*, **66**, 1299–1325.

Pötscher, B. M. (2002). Lower risk bounds and properties of confidence sets for ill-posed estimation problems with applications to spectral density and persistence estimation, unit roots and estimation of long memory parameters. *Econometrica*, **70**(3), 1035–1065.

Robinson, P. M. (1991). Testing for strong serial correlation and dynamic conditional heteroskedasticity in multiple regressions. *Journal of Econometrics*, **47**, 67–84.

——(1994). Efficient tests of nonstationary hypotheses. *Journal of the American Statistical Association*, **89**, 1420–1437.

Stock, J. H. (1994). Deciding between I(1) and I(0). *Journal of Econometrics*, **63**, 105–131.

Surgailis, D., Teyssiere, G., and Vaiciulis, M. (2008). The increment ratio statistic. *Journal of Multivariate Analysis*, **99**, 510–541.

Tanaka, K. (1999). The nonstationary fractional unit root. *Econometric Theory*, **15**, 549–582

Tong, H. (1990). *Non-linear Time Series*. Oxford: Oxford University Press.

14

Model Identification and Nonunique Structure

*David F. Hendry, Maozu Lu, and Grayham E. Mizon**

14.1 Introduction

Economists often address issues such as examining the efficacy of alternative economic policies, assessing the lasting effects of EU membership on transition economies, forecasting the future values of key economic variables (eg the rate of inflation), or discriminating between alternative economic theories. In analysing these and similar issues, econometric models are frequently used, and if they are to provide relevant, reliable, and robust information, empirical models must be subjected to rigorous evaluation (Bontemps and Mizon, 2003). Assessing the coherence of a model with the sources of information including economic theory, empirical observation (congruence), and alternative models (encompassing), is a powerful way to evaluate the model's credentials: see Hendry (1995a) and Mizon (1995). It is desirable that the inferences drawn from any model are unambiguous, and an important ingredient in this is requiring the model's parameters to be identified. In this chapter, we analyse the interpretation and role of identification in model development and discrimination, and illustrate that the standard textbook approach to identification is inadequate relative to the more comprehensive approach we propose.

The literature on identification is vast, and it may be thought to be definitive. Important contributions to this literature include Wright (1915), Working (1927), Frisch (1934, 1938), Marschak (1942), Haavelmo (1944), Koopmans (1949), Koopmans and Reiersøl (1950), Fisher (1966), Rothenberg (1971), Bowden (1973), Hatanaka (1975), Sargan (1983), and Hsiao (1983).

* Financial support from the UK Economic and Social Research Council under grant L138251009 is gratefully acknowledged.

The history of these developments is documented by Qin (1989) and Aldrich (1994). A critical view of this literature is presented by Liu (1960) (echoed by Sims, 1980) and responded to by Fisher (1961). Much of this literature has concerned simultaneous equations models, but an equally large body of work has addressed dynamic systems—see, *inter alia*, Phillips (1956), Deistler (1976), Deistler and Seifert (1978), Deistler, Ploberger, and Pötscher (1982), and Hannan and Deistler (1988). Rather than develop new technical results, or generalizations thereof, we argue in this chapter that some interpretations of the available results on identification are less well based than might be thought (see e.g., Faust and Whiteman, 1997). For example, we seek to clarify what can, and cannot, be deduced from finding that a given model is 'uniquely identified'. A particular example of this would be a uniquely identified simultaneous equations model with non-rejected over-identifying restrictions. In this case, standard textbook approaches usually claim that the model is a good representation of the underlying structure of that part of the economy related to the phenomena of interest. We argue that this is not necessarily the case, and often will not be true. In fact, there are a number of key questions that remain unanswered. With respect to which information set is the model unique? Is the model really a structural model? Does the model correspond to the unknown process that generated the observations on the phenomena of interest? Has the model been correctly interpreted?

In practice, the meaning of 'identified' can be ambiguous as in 'Have you identified the parameters of the money demand function?' Indeed identification has many meanings. In the time-series literature it means 'match the model to the evidence' ie, discover a representation accurate up to a white-noise error (see e.g., Box and Jenkins, 1976, and Kalman, 1982). In the econometric literature generally, but especially in standard textbook descriptions, it relates to the uniqueness of the parametrization that generated the observed data.[1] In contrast, we adopt the approach in Hendry (1995a) who follows the notions first discerned by Wright (1915), and so consider three aspects of identification: 'uniqueness', 'correspondence to the desired entity', and 'satisfying the assumed interpretation (usually of a theory model)' (see Hendry and Morgan, 1995, p. 23). As an analogy, a regression of quantity on price delivers a unique function of the data second moments, but need not correspond to any underlying economic behaviour, and may be incorrectly interpreted as a supply schedule due to a positive sign on price. The first sense of identification was used by the Cowles Commission (Koopmans, Rubin, and Leipnik, 1950) who formalized conditions for the

[1] Such problems also arise in the time-series literature in relation to ARMA models, where 'redundant' dynamic common factors can occur.

uniqueness of coefficients in simultaneous systems, and this is often the sense intended in econometrics. Conditions for the correct interpretation of parameters in the light of a theory model are not so easily specified in general because they depend on subject-matter considerations. Equally, the correspondences between parameters of models and those of the underlying data generation processes (DGPs) are also often hidden, but merit careful appraisal.

Thus, we consider each of these three attributes, and discuss those issues which we do not find fully clear in many presentations. Specifically, we show that uniqueness (as determined by the rank condition, say) holds only within specifications, and that several distinct yet valid over-identified representations can coexist, each satisfying its own rank condition. Thus, the famous Cowles' Commission rank condition uniquely specifies a model only subject to the given restrictions, and does not preclude other distinct, but conflicting, over-identified models. The algebraic result underlying this point is known in the literature, but its significance in econometric modelling is rarely appreciated so we provide an illustration of it.[2] Second, we consider 'correspondence to the desired entity' in a non-stationary world, where models that do not correspond can be eliminated, thereby facilitating unique identification. We also address the identification of 'structure'. Third, we briefly discuss failures of interpretation. Hence the approach that we adopt by requiring all three conditions to be satisfied encompasses other approaches such as the one commonly presented in econometrics textbooks.

The chapter is organized as follows. Section 14.2 discusses the concepts of identification and observational equivalence for the DGP and models thereof. Section 14.3 illustrates that a model may be uniquely identified but not correspond to reality, or be interpretable. Section 14.4 considers observational equivalence and mutual encompassing, and illustrates models being indistinguishable in a sample due to weak evidence. Sections 14.5 and 14.6 describe in turn nonunique just- and over-identified representations, relating the former to multivariate cointegration analysis and illustrating the latter by four distinct over-identified simultaneous-equations models that are nevertheless fully consistent with the reduced form. Section 14.7 investigates the next attribute of identification, namely correspondence to reality, and notes that structure might be inherently unidentifiable in a stationary world. However, section 14.8 argues that nonstationarities, specifically structural breaks, can help discriminate nonstructural from structural representations. Finally, section 14.9 concludes.

[2] In an earlier discussion related to our approach, Preston (1978) distinguishes between identification of structures and models.

14.2 Identification: Concepts and Definitions

The concepts of identification and observational equivalence apply separately to the DGP and to models thereof. The parameters of the DGP could be identified when those of a model were non-unique, or conversely, the model may have a unique parametrization, but the parameters of interest from the DGP may be unobtainable. We now summarize the essential concepts and definitions underlying the subsequent argument. More details can be found in *inter alia* Hendry (1995a).

Let $\mathbf{x}_t$ be the vector of n variables to be modelled, chosen on the basis of economic considerations related to the phenomena of interest and their statistical properties. From the theory of reduction (see *inter alia,* Hendry, 1995a, and Mizon, 1995), there exists a local DGP (LDGP) for these chosen variables $\mathbf{x}_t$ conditional on their history $\mathbf{X}_{t-1} = (\mathbf{X}_0, \mathbf{X}^1_{t-1})$ when $\mathbf{X}_0$ are initial conditions and $\mathbf{X}^1_{t-1} = (\mathbf{x}_1, \mathbf{x}_2, \ldots \mathbf{x}_{t-1})$:[3]

$$\mathsf{D_X}\left(\mathbf{x}_t \mid \mathbf{X}_{t-1}, \boldsymbol{\phi}\right) \quad \text{where } \boldsymbol{\phi} \in \boldsymbol{\Phi} \subseteq \mathbb{R}^s. \tag{14.1}$$

Let $\boldsymbol{\phi}_1 \in \boldsymbol{\Phi}$ and $\boldsymbol{\phi}_2 \in \boldsymbol{\Phi}$ be two distinct values of the s-dimensional parameter vector $\boldsymbol{\phi}$. When there exist observations $\mathbf{x}_t$ for which $\mathsf{D_X}\left(\mathbf{x}_t|\mathbf{X}_{t-1},\boldsymbol{\phi}_1\right) \neq \mathsf{D_X}\left(\mathbf{x}_t|\mathbf{X}_{t-1},\boldsymbol{\phi}_2\right)$ implies that $\boldsymbol{\phi}_1 \neq \boldsymbol{\phi}_2$, then $\boldsymbol{\phi}$ is a sufficient parameter (see Madansky, 1976). If $\boldsymbol{\phi}_1 \neq \boldsymbol{\phi}_2$ implies that there are observations $\mathbf{x}_t$ for which $\mathsf{D_X}\left(\mathbf{x}_t|\mathbf{X}_{t-1},\boldsymbol{\phi}_1\right) \neq \mathsf{D_X}\left(\mathbf{x}_t|\mathbf{X}_{t-1},\boldsymbol{\phi}_2\right)$, then $\boldsymbol{\phi}$ is (uniquely) identifiable. Thus it is possible to uniquely identify which parameter value generated the data only when different parameter values lead to different event probabilities. This property applies globally, $\forall\boldsymbol{\phi} \in \boldsymbol{\Phi}$. Alternatively, if there exists a neighbourhood $\mathcal{N}(\boldsymbol{\phi}_1)$ of $\boldsymbol{\phi}_1$ such that $\boldsymbol{\phi}_2 \neq \boldsymbol{\phi}_1$ implies that $\mathsf{D_X}\left(\mathbf{x}_t|\mathbf{X}_{t-1},\boldsymbol{\phi}_1\right) =$ / $\mathsf{D_X}\left(\mathbf{x}_t|\mathbf{X}_{t-1},\boldsymbol{\phi}_2\right)$ $\forall\boldsymbol{\phi}_2 \in \mathcal{N}(\boldsymbol{\phi}_1)$ then $\boldsymbol{\phi}_1$ is locally uniquely identifiable. When the LDGP is uniquely identified, let the value of $\boldsymbol{\phi}$ that generated the sample data $\mathbf{X}^1_T = (\mathbf{x}_1, \mathbf{x}_2, \ldots \mathbf{x}_T)$ be the 'true' value $\boldsymbol{\phi}_0$. Further, note that any 1–1 transformation of $\boldsymbol{\phi}$, $\boldsymbol{\psi} = \mathbf{f}(\boldsymbol{\phi}) \in \boldsymbol{\Psi}$, also constitutes a valid parametrization.

In general, the LDGP is unknown and so models of it are developed in order to make inferences that are intended to be relevant for the LDGP. Let $\mathcal{M}_1$ be an econometric model of the process generating $\mathbf{x}_t$ denoted by:

$$\mathcal{M}_1 = \{\mathsf{f}_1(\mathbf{x}_t \mid \mathbf{X}_{t-1}, \boldsymbol{\theta}) \text{ for } t = 1, 20, \ldots T \text{ where } \boldsymbol{\theta} \in \boldsymbol{\Theta} \subseteq \mathbb{R}^p\} \tag{14.2}$$

when $\mathsf{f}_1(\mathbf{x}_t|\mathbf{X}_{t-1},\boldsymbol{\theta})$ is the postulated sequential joint density at time t, and $p < s$ (usually). If $\mathcal{M}_1$ were correctly specified, then the identifiability of $\boldsymbol{\theta}$ could be defined as for that of $\boldsymbol{\phi}$ in the LDGP above. In particular, $\boldsymbol{\theta}$ is uniquely identifiable if $\boldsymbol{\theta}_1 \neq \boldsymbol{\theta}_2$ implies that $\mathsf{f}_1(\mathbf{x}_t|\mathbf{X}_{t-1},\boldsymbol{\theta}_1) \neq \mathsf{f}_1(\mathbf{x}_t|\mathbf{X}_{t-1},\boldsymbol{\theta}_2)$. However, correct

[3] Local refers to the DGP being the joint density for $\mathbf{x}_t$ (conditional on its history) alone, recognizing that $\mathbf{x}_t$ is usually a subset of the variables that fully characterize an economy which itself might be local or global.

specification is rare and so the identifiability of parameters (in all three senses), and the properties of statistics in mis-specified models, must be considered. Confining attention to cases in which the LDGP is uniquely identified, with the 'true' value of $\boldsymbol{\phi}$ for $\mathbf{X}_T^1$ being $\boldsymbol{\phi}_0$, then assuming identifiable uniqueness on $\boldsymbol{\Theta}$ ensures that $\boldsymbol{\theta}$ is uniquely identified (see eg, Gallant and White, 1988; and White, 1994). Indeed, under these conditions, the maximum likelihood estimator $\hat{\boldsymbol{\theta}}_T$ of $\boldsymbol{\theta}$ tends in probability to its pseudo-true value $\boldsymbol{\theta}_0 = \boldsymbol{\theta}(\boldsymbol{\phi}_0)$ which is given by

$$\boldsymbol{\theta}(\boldsymbol{\phi}_0) = \underset{\boldsymbol{\theta}\in\boldsymbol{\Theta}}{\operatorname{argmax}}\, \mathsf{E}_{LDGP}\left[L_T(\boldsymbol{\theta})\right] \tag{14.3}$$

when:

$$L_T(\boldsymbol{\theta}) = \sum_{t=1}^{T} \log \mathsf{f}_1\left(\mathbf{x}_t \mid \mathbf{X}_{t-1},\boldsymbol{\theta}\right). \tag{14.4}$$

When $L_T(\boldsymbol{\theta})$ has a maximizer $\hat{\boldsymbol{\theta}}_T \in \boldsymbol{\Theta}$ for each T then, requiring the sequence $\{\hat{\boldsymbol{\theta}}_T\}$ to be identifiable uniquely on $\boldsymbol{\Theta}$ rules out the possibility that $L_T(\boldsymbol{\theta})$ becomes flatter in a neighbourhood of $\hat{\boldsymbol{\theta}}_T$ as $T \to \infty$, and precludes that there are other sequences of estimators $\{\tilde{\boldsymbol{\theta}}_T\}$ which are such that $\{L_T(\tilde{\boldsymbol{\theta}}_T)\}$ approaches arbitrarily closely the almost sure limit of $L_T(\boldsymbol{\theta})$ as $T \to \infty$. Thus the identification of the model parameter $\boldsymbol{\theta}$ is equivalent to the uniqueness of the pseudo-true value $\boldsymbol{\theta}_0 = \boldsymbol{\theta}(\boldsymbol{\phi}_0)$.

$\mathcal{M}_1$ with $\boldsymbol{\theta} = \boldsymbol{\theta}_0$ provides the best approximation to the LDGP $\mathsf{D}_\mathsf{X}\left(\mathbf{x}_t|\mathbf{X}_{t-1},\boldsymbol{\phi}_0\right)$ in the sense that the Kullback–Leibler information criterion (KLIC)

$$\mathcal{I}\left(\boldsymbol{\phi}_0,\boldsymbol{\theta}\right) = \int \log \frac{\mathsf{D}_\mathsf{X}\left(\mathbf{x}_t|\mathbf{X}_{t-1},\boldsymbol{\phi}_0\right)}{\mathsf{f}_1\left(\mathbf{x}_t|\mathbf{X}_{t-1},\boldsymbol{\theta}\right)} \mathsf{D}_\mathsf{X}\left(\mathbf{x}_t \mid \mathbf{X}_{t-1},\boldsymbol{\phi}_0\right) d\mathbf{x}_t \tag{14.5}$$

is minimized by $\boldsymbol{\theta} = \boldsymbol{\theta}_0$. In general $\mathcal{I}\left(\boldsymbol{\phi}_0,\boldsymbol{\theta}\right) \geq 0$, with $\mathcal{I}\left(\boldsymbol{\phi}_0,\boldsymbol{\theta}\right) = 0$ if and only if $\mathsf{f}_1\left(\mathbf{x}_t|\mathbf{X}_{t-1},\boldsymbol{\theta}_0\right) = \mathsf{D}_\mathsf{X}\left(\mathbf{x}_t|\mathbf{X}_{t-1},\boldsymbol{\phi}_0\right)$ with probability one (see Kullback and Leibler, 1951). Note that if $\boldsymbol{\theta}_0$ is to be the unique solution to (14.3), then it is required that

$$\mathsf{E}_{LDGP}\left[\frac{\partial L_T(\boldsymbol{\theta})}{\partial \boldsymbol{\theta}}\right] = \mathbf{0} \tag{14.6}$$

if and only if $\boldsymbol{\theta} = \boldsymbol{\theta}(\boldsymbol{\phi}_0)$. Despite being the best KLIC-approximation to the LDGP, $\mathcal{M}_1$ with $\boldsymbol{\theta} = \boldsymbol{\theta}_0$ may only be locally identified, as opposed to a correctly specified $\mathcal{M}$ which is globally identified. Equally, a uniquely identified model may not reflect completely the LDGP, or alternatively even if it does reflect the LDGP, it may not be interpretable. We now illustrate that the standard textbook approach to identification, by only requiring the parameters of a model to be uniquely identified, does not guarantee that a particular parmeterization is capable of yielding relevant and reliable inferences on the phenomena of interest.

14.3 Limitations of the Textbook Approach to Identification

We first illustrate that a mis-specified model can be uniquely identified but not reflect the LDGP parameters.

Suppose all a priori information suggests that the following model provides the best description of the data $(x_1, x_2, \ldots x_T)$:

$$f(\theta) = \begin{cases} \theta x^{\theta-1} & x \in [0,1] \\ 0 & \text{otherwise} \end{cases}, \quad \theta > 0$$

when in fact the LDGP is a uniform distribution on $[0, 1+\delta]$, $\delta > 0$. Then, the expectation of the log-density $\log f(\theta)$ under the LDGP is given by

$$\begin{aligned} \mathsf{E}_{LDGP}\left[\log\ f(\theta)\right] &= \frac{1}{1+\delta}\int_0^{1+\delta} \log f(\theta)\, dx \\ &= \frac{1}{1+\delta}\left\{\int_0^1 \left[\log\theta + (\theta-1)\log x\right] dx + \int_1^{\delta} 0 dx\right\} \\ &= \frac{1}{1+\delta}\left\{\log\theta - (\theta-1)\right\}, \end{aligned}$$

which attains its maximum at

$$\theta^*(\delta) = \underset{\theta>0}{\operatorname{argmax}}\left\{\frac{1}{1+\delta}\left[\log\theta - (\theta-1)\right]\right\} = 1.$$

Hence, the pseudo-true value $\theta^*(\delta) = 1$ is uniquely determined, implying that θ is identified. However, $\theta^*(\delta)$ does not depend on the LDGP parameter δ, and so any change in δ (with $\delta > 0$) will leave $\theta^*(\delta)$ unaffected at unity. In particular, though $f(\theta^*(\delta))$ is a uniform distribution, it is defined on a different interval from that of the LDGP: observations outside the interval [0,1] would of course reveal that mis-specification. Equally, each quasi log-likelihood function

$$\log L_T(\theta) = T\log\theta + (\theta-1)\sum_{t=1}^{T}\log x_t,$$

has a well defined maximum at

$$\theta_T^* = \frac{-T}{\sum_{t=1}^{T}\log x_t},$$

the existence and uniqueness of which does not depend on δ in the LDGP.

We next illustrate that a model which does reflect the LDGP parameters may nonetheless be a worse description than the previous model of the uniform

LDGP. Let $\delta < 0$ in the LDGP, hence

$$\begin{aligned}\int \log f(\theta) h(\delta) &= \frac{1}{1+\delta}\int_0^{1+\delta} \log f(\theta)\, dx \\ &= \frac{1}{1+\delta}\left\{\int_0^{1+\delta} \left[\log\theta + (\theta-1)\log x\right] dx\right\} \\ &= \log\theta + (\theta-1)\left\{\log(1+\delta) - 1\right\},\end{aligned}$$

implies that the pseudo-true value is given by

$$\begin{aligned}\theta^*(\delta) &= \underset{\theta>0}{\operatorname{argmax}}\left\{\log\theta + (\theta-1)\left[\log(1+\delta)-1\right]\right\} \\ &= \frac{1}{1-\log(1+\delta)}.\end{aligned} \tag{14.7}$$

Monotonicity of the logarithmic function then guarantees that $\theta^*(\delta)$ is uniquely determined for $-1 < \delta < 0$. Thus the model parameter θ is uniquely identified and does reflect the LDGP, but the model is not a uniform distribution.

Finally, it is possible for a model to be uniquely identified and reflect the LDGP parameters, but not be interpretable—also see section 14.5. The 'classic' example is regression estimation of an unidentifiable supply–demand model in price (p_t) and quantity (q_t)

$$\begin{aligned}p_t &= \mu_{11} q_t + v_{1,t} \\ q_t &= \mu_{21} p_t + v_{2,t}\end{aligned}$$

with

$$\begin{pmatrix} v_{1,t} \\ v_{2,t} \end{pmatrix} \sim \mathsf{IN}_2\left[\begin{pmatrix} \alpha_1 \\ \alpha_2 \end{pmatrix}, \begin{pmatrix} \sigma_{11} & \sigma_{12} \\ \sigma_{12} & \sigma_{22} \end{pmatrix}\right],$$

which nevertheless delivers a unique function of the LDGP parameters and the error (co)variances

$$\begin{pmatrix} p_t \\ q_t \end{pmatrix} \sim \mathsf{IN}_2\left[\begin{pmatrix} \lambda_1 \\ \lambda_2 \end{pmatrix}, \begin{pmatrix} \omega_{11} & \omega_{12} \\ \omega_{12} & \omega_{22} \end{pmatrix}\right].$$

In particular, the OLS estimator $\hat{\mu}_{11}$ of μ_{11} converges to

$$\operatorname*{plim}_{T\to\infty} \hat{\mu}_{11} = \frac{\omega_{12} + \lambda_1\lambda_2}{\omega_{22} + \lambda_2^2},$$

which could have either sign (but the same sign as $\operatorname{plim}_{T\to\infty} \hat{\mu}_{21}$).

14.4 Observational Equivalence, Identification, and Mutual Encompassing

When two models always generate identical outcomes, they are observationally equivalent and data alone cannot distinguish between them. A sufficient condition is that all their parameters be unidentifiable, but this is not necessary, and identified models can be observationally equivalent as is illustrated in sections 14.5 and 14.6. Observational equivalence arises whenever there is an unidentified model, and there is an equivalence set of models that impose just-identifying restrictions. As an example consider the following bivariate regression model

$$y_t = \alpha + \beta x_t + u_t \text{ with } u_t \sim \mathsf{IN}\left[\mu, \sigma^2\right] \tag{14.8}$$

in which μ and α are not uniquely identified. However, the set of models that imposes a single restriction on μ and α (eg, $\mu = 0$ or $\alpha = \alpha^*$) forms a set of models that cannot be distinguished from each other on the basis of observations. More generally at the level of the LDGP, since $\mathsf{D}_\mathsf{X}\left(\mathbf{x}_t|\mathbf{X}_{t-1}, \boldsymbol{\phi}\right)$ is unchanged under 1–1 transformations of the parameter $\boldsymbol{\phi}$ to $\boldsymbol{\psi} = \boldsymbol{\psi}\left(\boldsymbol{\phi}\right) \in \boldsymbol{\Psi}$ then $\mathsf{D}_\mathsf{X}\left(\mathbf{x}_t|\mathbf{X}_{t-1}, \boldsymbol{\phi}\right)$ and $\mathsf{D}_\mathsf{X}\left(\mathbf{x}_t|\mathbf{X}_{t-1}, \boldsymbol{\psi}\right)$ are observationally equivalent and hence isomorphic. If $\boldsymbol{\psi} = \boldsymbol{\psi}\left(\boldsymbol{\phi}\right)$ but is not 1–1 (eg, as a result of setting some irrelevant parameters at their population values of zero), the processes are said to be equivalent.

Observationally equivalent models are KLIC-equivalent, in that the relevant version of the criterion in (14.5) will be zero. Equally, since encompassing is the ability of one model to account for the salient features of another model, observationally-equivalent models will encompass each other, that is, be mutually encompassing (see Mizon, 1984; Mizon and Richard, 1986; and Hendry, 1995a). In analysing the relationships between observational equivalence, KLIC equivalence, and encompassing, Lu and Mizon (1997) showed that models are KLIC-equivalent if and only if they are mutually encompassing with respect to their complete parameter vectors (complete parametric encompassing) and their log sequential densities (Cox encompassing). Further, Bontemps and Mizon (2003) defined a congruent model to be one that parsimoniously encompasses the LDGP, and showed that congruence of a nesting model is sufficient for it to encompass models nested within it. Therefore, an example of mutual encompassing arises whenever a nesting model is both congruent and parsimoniously encompassed by a nested model.

A distinction can be drawn between population and sample mutual encompassing. Mutual encompassing in the population is observational equivalence. For example, there might exist an equivalence set of representations of the LDGP, in which the representations are usually re-parametrizations of each other, though not necessarily having parameter spaces of the same dimension. However, mutual encompassing in the sample can arise from observational equivalence, or from weak evidence resulting in the models being indistinguishable on the basis of the available information.

14.4.1 *An Example*

Consider the congruent representation of the LDGP for y_t given in $\mathcal{M}_2$

$$\mathcal{M}_2\colon\ y_t = \mu + \epsilon_t + \theta\epsilon_{t-1} \tag{14.9}$$

when $\epsilon_t \sim \mathsf{IN}\,[0,1]$ and $|\theta| < 1$. An alternative, and observationally equivalent, representation of the LDGP is given by $\mathcal{M}_3$

$$\mathcal{M}_3\colon\ y_t = \frac{\mu}{1+\theta} + \sum_{i=1}^{\infty}(-\theta)^i y_{t-i} + \epsilon_t. \tag{14.10}$$

In this simple example, $\mathcal{M}_2$ and $\mathcal{M}_3$ are mutually encompassing, both congruent, and observationally equivalent. However, $\mathcal{M}_3$ is only relevant in the population, since only a finite-order autoregression can be estimated using sample data. In fact, since $|\theta| < 1$, a finite-order autoregression

$$\mathcal{M}_4\colon\ y_t = \alpha + \sum_{i=1}^{m}\beta_i y_{t-i} + u_t \tag{14.11}$$

will give a good approximation to (14.10) when only sample data are available. Indeed, $\mathcal{M}_4$ with $m = 3$ is likely to be indistinguishable from $\mathcal{M}_2$ empirically, so both $\mathcal{M}_2$ and $\mathcal{M}_4$ would be empirically congruent even though only the former is congruent. Bontemps and Mizon (2003) contains a more detailed analysis of a related example.

The next two sections discuss examples of models that are observationally equivalent even though they are just-identified and over-identified respectively. These examples illustrate the fact that models can be identified within their own chosen specification and satisfy that specification's interpretation, but nonetheless not be unique or structural.

14.5 Nonunique Just-identified Representations

A well-known example of identified models forming an equivalence set arises in the just-identified simultaneous equations model (SEM). Consider a closed vector autoregression (VAR)

$$\mathbf{x}_t = \sum_{i=1}^{k}\mathbf{D}_i\mathbf{x}_{t-i} + \boldsymbol{\delta} + \boldsymbol{\varepsilon}_t \quad \text{with } \boldsymbol{\varepsilon}_t \sim \mathsf{IN}_n\left[\mathbf{0},\boldsymbol{\Omega}\right] \tag{14.12}$$

which can be written alternatively as a vector equilibrium-correction model (VEqCM)

$$\Delta \mathbf{x}_t = \sum_{i=1}^{k-1} \boldsymbol{\Gamma}_i \Delta \mathbf{x}_{t-i} + \boldsymbol{\pi} x_{t-1} + \delta + \varepsilon_t \quad \text{with } \boldsymbol{\varepsilon}_t \sim \mathsf{IN}_n\left[\mathbf{0},\boldsymbol{\Omega}\right]. \tag{14.13}$$

When $\boldsymbol{\pi}$ has full rank n, the variables $\mathbf{x}_t$ are $\mathsf{I}(0)$, and the parameters $(\boldsymbol{\Gamma}_1,\boldsymbol{\Gamma}_2,\ldots,\boldsymbol{\Gamma}_{k-1},\boldsymbol{\pi},\delta,\boldsymbol{\Omega})$ or $(\mathbf{D}_1,\mathbf{D}_2,\ldots,\mathbf{D}_k,\delta,\boldsymbol{\Omega})$ are all identified, in that their maximum likelihood estimators are unique, and obtained by multivariate least squares. Indeed, the VAR and the VEqCM are both just-identified and observationally-equivalent models. The set of observationally-equivalent just-identified models, though, includes far more than these two models. The parameters of interest for many investigators are those of a SEM such as

$$\mathbf{A}_0\mathbf{x}_t = \sum_{i=1}^{k} \mathbf{A}_i\mathbf{x}_{t-i} + \mathbf{c} + \mathbf{v}_t \quad \text{with } \mathbf{v}_t \sim \mathsf{IN}_n\left[\mathbf{0},\boldsymbol{\Sigma}\right] \tag{14.14}$$

rather than the VAR or the VEqCM. Without further information, the parameters of (14.14) are unidentified as is well known, and this leads to the traditional analysis of identification in simultaneous equations models—see *inter alia* Spanos (1986) and Greene (2000). All the SEMs resulting from sets of a priori restrictions on $(\mathbf{A}_0,\mathbf{A}_1,\ldots,\mathbf{A}_k,\mathbf{c},\boldsymbol{\Sigma})$ that achieve just-identification are observationally equivalent, and thus observationally equivalent to the VAR and the VEqCM in (14.12) and (14.13) respectively.

A further identification issue arises when rank $(\boldsymbol{\pi}) = r < n$, in which case $\mathbf{x}_t \sim \mathsf{I}(1)$, but there are r cointegrating vectors $\boldsymbol{\beta}'\mathbf{x}_t \sim \mathsf{I}(0)$. In this case, (14.13) becomes

$$\Delta \mathbf{x}_t = \sum_{i=1}^{k-1} \boldsymbol{\Gamma}_i \Delta \mathbf{x}_{t-i} + \boldsymbol{\alpha}\boldsymbol{\beta}'\mathbf{x}_{t-1} + \delta + \boldsymbol{\varepsilon}_t \quad \text{with } \boldsymbol{\varepsilon}_t \sim \mathsf{IN}_n\left[\mathbf{0},\boldsymbol{\Omega}\right],$$

where $\boldsymbol{\alpha}$ and $\boldsymbol{\beta}$ are $n \times r$ matrices of rank r. It is well known that $\boldsymbol{\alpha}$ and $\boldsymbol{\beta}$ are not identified without further restrictions. Nevertheless, the Johansen procedure (see eg, Johansen, 1995) for empirically determining the value of r, produces unique estimates of $\boldsymbol{\alpha}$ and $\boldsymbol{\beta}$ as a result of requiring $\boldsymbol{\beta}$ to be orthogonal and normalized (see eg, Johansen and Juselius, 1994). This estimate of $\boldsymbol{\beta}$, for a given value of r, spans the space of just-identified cointegrating vectors, and is observationally equivalent to any other just-identified estimate of $\boldsymbol{\beta}$. The fact that the just-identified estimate of $\boldsymbol{\beta}$ provided by the Johansen procedure may not have an economic interpretation is usually unimportant, since this estimate is only used to provide a value for the unrestricted log likelihood function to be compared with the value of the log-likelihood function corresponding to sets of over-identifying restrictions on $\boldsymbol{\beta}$ which do have an economic interpretation. When $r = 1$, of course, $\boldsymbol{\beta}$ should have an economic interpretation, perhaps subject to eliminating irrelevant coefficients. When $r > 1$ β may, or may not, have an economic interpretation.

In both cases, mis-interpretation of β can occur. One illustration is when an equation normalized on (say) money, is interpreted as a 'long-run money–demand relation' because $\gamma > 0$

$$m - p - y = -\gamma (R_l - R_s), \tag{14.15}$$

(where m is nominal money, p is the price deflator of real income y, and R_l and R_s are long- and short-term interest rates), but actually is an 'interest-rate spread' equation, as in

$$R_l = R_s + \gamma^{-1} \upsilon,$$

where $\upsilon = p + y - m$ is the velocity of circulation. The values of the α_{ij} can help discrimination—if there were no feedback from (14.15) onto money (interest rates), one might question the first (second) interpretation respectively (see e.g., Hendry and Juselius, 2001, for an exposition).

14.6 Nonunique Over-identified Representations

A related class of model where the common interpretation of the available results on identification may not always be well founded is that of over-identified simultaneous equations models. Though this analysis applies for closed versions of linear dynamic models, such as the VAR and VEqCM in (14.12) and (14.13), we use a notation that usually is associated with static SEMs[4]

$$\mathbf{B}\mathbf{y}_t + \mathbf{C}\mathbf{z}_t = \mathbf{u}_t \text{ with } \mathbf{u}_t \sim \mathsf{IN}_q\left[\mathbf{0}, \boldsymbol{\Sigma}\right]. \tag{14.16}$$

Several models of $(\mathbf{y}_t, \mathbf{z}_t)$ can be over-identified, satisfy the rank condition, and not fail over-identification tests empirically, even when such models conflict theoretically (see Hendry and Mizon, 1993). Thus, the Cowles' rank condition is insufficient for the three attributes, although it is sufficient for uniqueness within theories, thus achieving uniqueness for a given interpretation as we now show.

Consider all linear transforms $\mathbf{R}$ of $(\mathbf{B} : \mathbf{C})$ to establish whether the uniquely admissible $\mathbf{R}$ is $\mathbf{R} = \mathbf{I}_q$. When $(\mathbf{B} : \mathbf{C})$ are unconstrained, $(\mathbf{RB} : \mathbf{RC})$ comprise all linear systems. However, when $(\mathbf{B} : \mathbf{C})$ are restricted, admissible $\mathbf{R}$s are only relative to the restrictions on the given choice, so no longer span all relevant linear models. Thus

$$\mathbf{B}\mathbf{y}_t + \mathbf{C}\mathbf{z}_t = \mathbf{u}_t \text{ and } \mathbf{B}^*\mathbf{y}_t + \mathbf{C}^*\mathbf{z}_t = \mathbf{u}_t^*,$$

[4] This is not a limitation since the $k \times 1$ vector $\mathbf{z}_t$ in (14.16) could be defined to include lagged values of the $q \times 1$ vector $\mathbf{y}_t$.

can generate the same $\{\mathbf{y}_t\}$, so long as

$$\mathbf{B}^{-1}\mathbf{C} = (\mathbf{B}^{*})^{-1}\,\mathbf{C}^{*} = -\Pi,$$

and

$$\mathbf{B}^{-1}\Sigma B^{-1\prime} = (\mathbf{B}^{*})^{-1}\,\Sigma^{*}(\mathbf{B}^{*})^{-1\prime}.$$

The equivalence class is

$$\mathbf{C}^{*} = \mathbf{B}^{*}\mathbf{B}^{-1}\mathbf{C}, \tag{14.17}$$

or any $\mathbf{S}$ such that $\mathbf{B}^{*} = \mathbf{SB}$ at the same time as $\mathbf{C}^{*} = \mathbf{SC}$, even though within their own restriction sets, $(\mathbf{B} : \mathbf{C})$ and $(\mathbf{B}^{*} : \mathbf{C}^{*})$ are both uniquely identified. This matches Hsiao (1983), who proves that observational equivalence requires such an $\mathbf{S}$ since, from (14.17) we then have

$$\mathbf{C}^{*} = \mathbf{B}^{*}\mathbf{B}^{-1}\mathbf{C} = \mathbf{SBB}^{-1}\mathbf{C} = \mathbf{SC},$$

consistent with his claim. Therefore, all examples must satisfy this restriction.

How does this relate to the analysis of the Cowles Commission researchers? They sought $\mathbf{R}$ such that for *restricted* $\mathbf{B}$ and $\mathbf{C}$, the only admissible $\mathbf{R}$ is $\mathbf{R} = \mathbf{I}_q$ where

$$(\mathbf{RB} : \mathbf{RC}) = (\mathbf{B}^{*} : \mathbf{C}^{*})\,.$$

Such an $\mathbf{R}$ must satisfy the a priori constraints on the $(\mathbf{B} : \mathbf{C})$ matrix. It is clear that the (unrestricted) Π matrix in

$$\mathbf{y}_t + \Pi z_t = \mathbf{v}_t \;\text{ with }\; \mathbf{v}_t \sim \mathsf{IN}_q\left[\mathbf{0},\Omega\right],$$

is always identified because

$$\left(\mathbf{DI}_q : \mathbf{D}\Pi\right) = \left(\mathbf{I}_q : \Pi\right),$$

enforces $\mathbf{D} = \mathbf{I}_q$: that result holds true independently of the correctness (or otherwise) of the model specification, and the interpretability of its coefficients. The Cowles' rank condition ensures the same for $(\mathbf{B} : \mathbf{C})$—but it does not preclude the possibility of a differently restricted $(\mathbf{B}^{*} : \mathbf{C}^{*})$ that also satisfies the rank condition, such that

$$(\mathbf{B}^{*} : \mathbf{C}^{*}) = (\mathbf{SB} : \mathbf{SC})\,,$$

which is thus a member of the equivalence set.

Although the algebra in this section is clear, its significance for econometric modelling appears not to be fully appreciated. Hence in the next section, we present theoretical models to illustrate the implications of the algebraic result.

14.6.1 *An Example*

We consider an example in which there are four alternative observationally-equivalent representations, each of which is over-identified and has (potentially at least) an economic interpretation. The system ('reduced form') itself is restricted, as in the following LDGP for a set of two endogenous variables ($y_{1,t}$, $y_{2,t}$) conditional on four super strong exogenous regressors ($z_{1,t}$, $z_{2,t}$, $z_{3,t}$, $z_{4,t}$) (see Engle, Hendry, and Richard, 1983)

$$\begin{pmatrix} y_{1,t} \\ y_{2,t} \end{pmatrix} = \begin{pmatrix} \pi_{11} & \pi_{12} & \pi_{13} & 0 \\ \pi_{21} & 0 & \pi_{23} & \pi_{24} \end{pmatrix} \begin{pmatrix} z_{1,t} \\ z_{2,t} \\ z_{3,t} \\ z_{4,t} \end{pmatrix} + \begin{pmatrix} \epsilon_{1,t} \\ \epsilon_{2,t} \end{pmatrix}. \tag{14.18}$$

The reduced-form coefficient matrix Π in this case has six free elements, and imposes two restrictions. Notice that any linear restrictions can be re-parametrized to zero restrictions. Consequently, one of the over-identified representations is (14.18). Two other over-identified representations follow.

14.6.1.1 SIMULTANEOUS REPRESENTATION 1

Consider the simultaneous-equations representation given in (14.19)

$$\begin{pmatrix} 1 & b_{12} \\ 0 & 1 \end{pmatrix} \begin{pmatrix} y_{1,t} \\ y_{2,t} \end{pmatrix} = \begin{pmatrix} c_{11} & c_{12} & 0 & c_{14} \\ c_{21} & 0 & c_{23} & c_{24} \end{pmatrix} \begin{pmatrix} z_{1,t} \\ z_{2,t} \\ z_{3,t} \\ z_{4,t} \end{pmatrix} + \begin{pmatrix} u_{1,t} \\ u_{2,t} \end{pmatrix}, \tag{14.19}$$

where

$$\begin{aligned} \Pi &= \begin{pmatrix} 1 & b_{12} \\ 0 & 1 \end{pmatrix}^{-1} \begin{pmatrix} c_{11} & c_{12} & 0 & c_{14} \\ c_{21} & 0 & c_{23} & c_{24} \end{pmatrix} \\ &= \begin{pmatrix} c_{11} - b_{12}c_{21} & c_{12} & -b_{12}c_{23} & c_{14} - b_{12}c_{24} \\ c_{21} & 0 & c_{23} & c_{24} \end{pmatrix} \\ &= \begin{pmatrix} c_{11} - b_{12}c_{21} & c_{12} & -b_{12}c_{23} & 0 \\ c_{21} & 0 & c_{23} & c_{24} \end{pmatrix}. \end{aligned}$$

Comparison with (14.18) shows that the population values must satisfy $c_{14} = b_{12}c_{24}$: clearly, it is necessary that $c_{24} \neq 0$ otherwise $z_{4,t}$ becomes an irrelevant variable. This representation will be valid if and only if $b_{12} = -\pi_{13}/\pi_{23}$ with $\pi_{23} \neq 0$, which defines b_{12}. The second equation is over-identified, and hence so is the system although the first is just identified (imposing $c_{14} = b_{12}c_{24}$ would ensure both equations were over-identified).

14.6.1.2 SIMULTANEOUS REPRESENTATION 2

A second over-identified formulation consistent with (14.18) is given by

$$\begin{pmatrix} 1 & 0 \\ b_{21} & 1 \end{pmatrix} \begin{pmatrix} y_{1,t} \\ y_{2,t} \end{pmatrix} = \begin{pmatrix} d_{11} & d_{12} & d_{13} & 0 \\ 0 & d_{22} & d_{23} & d_{24} \end{pmatrix} \begin{pmatrix} z_{1,t} \\ z_{2,t} \\ z_{3,t} \\ z_{4,t} \end{pmatrix} + \begin{pmatrix} e_{1,t} \\ e_{2,t} \end{pmatrix}, \qquad (14.20)$$

where now

$$\Pi = \begin{pmatrix} d_{11} & d_{12} & d_{13} & 0 \\ -b_{21}d_{11} & 0 & d_{23} - b_{21}d_{13} & d_{24} \end{pmatrix},$$

so this system requires $d_{22} = b_{21}d_{12}$ and imposes $b_{21} = -\pi_{21}/\pi_{11}$ which defines b_{21}.

Thus, all three over-identified models are observationally equivalent. To satisfy that requirement, we must have

$$\Pi = \begin{pmatrix} \pi_{11} & \pi_{12} & -b_{12}\pi_{23} & 0 \\ -b_{21}\pi_{11} & 0 & \pi_{23} & \pi_{24} \end{pmatrix},$$

where b_{12} and b_{21} are defined above. Such a Π has six free elements as required, and satisfies the two restrictions in (14.18). The matrix $\mathbf{S}$ above that links the two simultaneous-equations representations is

$$\mathbf{S} = \begin{pmatrix} 1 - b_{12}b_{21} & b_{12} \\ -b_{21} & 1 \end{pmatrix},$$

where $|\mathbf{S}| = 1$.

14.6.1.3 SIMULTANEOUS REPRESENTATION 3

The final over-identified formulation consistent with (14.18) combines the two 'simultaneous' relations

$$\begin{pmatrix} 1 & b_{12} \\ b_{21} & 1 \end{pmatrix} \begin{pmatrix} y_{1,t} \\ y_{2,t} \end{pmatrix} = \begin{pmatrix} f_{11} & f_{12} & 0 & f_{14} \\ 0 & f_{22} & f_{23} & f_{24} \end{pmatrix} \begin{pmatrix} z_{1,t} \\ z_{2,t} \\ z_{3,t} \\ z_{4,t} \end{pmatrix} + \begin{pmatrix} u_{1,t} \\ u_{2,t} \end{pmatrix}, \qquad (14.21)$$

where $b_{12}b_{21} \neq 1$ and

$$\Pi = \frac{1}{1 - b_{12}b_{21}} \begin{pmatrix} f_{11} & (1 - b_{12}b_{21})\, f_{12} & -b_{12}\, f_{23} & 0 \\ -b_{21}\, f_{11} & 0 & f_{23} & (1 - b_{21}b_{12})\, f_{24} \end{pmatrix},$$

which implies that $b_{21} = -\pi_{21}/\pi_{11}$ and $b_{12} = -\pi_{13}/\pi_{23}$ (both scaled by the determinant $\pi_{23}\pi_{11}/(\pi_{23}\pi_{11} - \pi_{13}\pi_{21})$): enforcing $f_{22} = b_{21}\, f_{12}$ and $f_{14} = b_{12}\, f_{24}$ would ensure both equations were over-identified.

Consequently, demonstrating that a given model is over-identified and that all the over-identifying restrictions are valid (even asymptotically) is insufficient to demonstrate that it is a unique representation. Hence satisfying the assumed interpretation, usually of an economic theory model, does not ensure that the representation is unique or that it is structural.

14.7 Identifying Structure

We turn to the next attribute of identification, namely 'correspondence to reality'. This notion shares features with the time-series concept of identification. Historically, Frisch (1938) thought that structure was inherently unidentifiable (see the commentary offered in Hendry and Morgan, 1995). It is easy to construct examples of unidentified structures, where a nonstructural sub-system is identified. Consider the system

$$m_t - \rho y_t - \lambda p_t = \boldsymbol{\delta}_1' \mathbf{z}_t + v_{1,t} \tag{14.22}$$

$$y_t - \phi p_t = \boldsymbol{\delta}_2' \mathbf{z}_t + v_{2,t} \tag{14.23}$$

$$p_t = \boldsymbol{\delta}_3' \mathbf{z}_t + v_{3,t}. \tag{14.24}$$

Here the $\mathbf{z}_t$ are strongly exogenous, and the $v_{i,t}$ are i.i.d. errors. When there are no restrictions on $\boldsymbol{\delta}_1$, then (14.22) is not identifiable.

However, consider a setting where y_t is both unobserved, and its relevance is not realized, so analyses only consider the nonstructural sub-system

$$m_t - (\lambda + \rho\phi)\, p_t = \left(\boldsymbol{\delta}_1' + \rho\boldsymbol{\delta}_2'\right) \mathbf{z}_t + v_{1,t} + \rho v_{2,t} \tag{14.25}$$

$$p_t = \boldsymbol{\delta}_3' \mathbf{z}_t + v_{3,t}. \tag{14.26}$$

When a theory correctly specifies that sufficient elements of $\boldsymbol{\delta}_1' + \rho\boldsymbol{\delta}_2'$ are zero, (14.25) can be identifiable on the conventional rank condition in this bivariate process. Equation (14.25) may even be interpretable (eg, as a money-demand equation when $\lambda + \rho\phi = 1$), but it obviously does not correspond to the structure.

Thus, conventional notions of identification are indeed limited to 'uniqueness', despite the sometimes ambiguous use of the phrase noted in the introduction. In the next section, we consider whether 'structural change' in an economy can help to discriminate between structural and non-structural representations of the LDGP.

14.8 Structural Change

We define structure as the set of invariant features of the economic mechanism (see Frisch, 1934; Haavelmo, 1944; Wold and Juréen, 1953; and Hendry,

1995b). More precisely, $\theta \in \Theta$ defines a structure if θ directly characterizes the relations of the economy and is invariant over time, to extensions of the information set, and to policy interventions. The last three attributes are empirically testable, although the first is not, as with the corresponding attribute of identification. Consequently, although all four representations considered in the example of section 14.6.1 are well defined and observationally equivalent in a constant-parameter world, at most one representation of each equation can be invariant to changes and hence be structural (see Hendry and Mizon, 1993, and Hendry, 1995a).

Clearly, no parametrization $\theta \in \Theta$ can be invariant to all change, so structure is relative—atomic war would radically alter the economies of all participants. Thus, the class of 'admissible' interventions must be delineated. In their analyses of the sources of forecast errors, Clements and Hendry (1998, 1999) find that shifts in deterministic terms (intercepts and deterministic trends etc.) are the primary empirical cause of forecast failure, a result corroborated by the Monte Carlo results in Hendry (2000) where other forms of structural break (eg, in other parameters) did not induce forecast failure. Consequently, invariance to deterministic shifts in unmodelled variables seems one essential (but insufficient) requirement of structure. Indeed, the concept of identification in Working (1927) and Frisch (1938) is close to using 'shifts' to isolate the invariant structure.

14.8.1 *External Change*

In terms of the example in section 14.6.1, all four representations are equally structural to external changes, such as shifts in the distributions of the $z_{k,t}$, precisely because they all correspond to the same system (reduced form) which is itself invariant to such shifts.

Nevertheless, consider a model of the first equation of (14.18) that also—or incorrectly—included $z_{4,t}$ when its long-run mean (ie, $\mathsf{E}[z_{4,t}] = \mu_4$ say) changed: then that equation would forecast a shift in $y_{1,t}$ which did not materialize, hence fail to be structural on the grounds of a lack of invariance. As argued in Hendry and Mizon (1993), such 'spurious' structures can often be detected using structural breaks induced by natural experiments and policy changes. Some of the simulation experiments in Clements and Hendry (2002) illustrate this situation. Thus, mis-specification (or serious mis-estimation) can be revealed by external structural change, but alternative, correctly-specified, mutually-encompassing, representations all survive.

However, the issue is complicated by the possibility of 'extended constancy' (see Hendry, 1996, and Ericsson, Hendry, and Prestwich, 1998). A model may fail on forecasts because of a deterministic shift, and so be extended to incorporate the variable that changed, as well as being reparametrized to link that variable into an already included regressor (as in an interest-rate differential, say). As a result the model finishes with precisely the same parameters on the same number of variables as initially, but with one variable re-defined (or, more precisely, re-measured). The example in section 14.8.3 illustrates this phenomenon.

14.8.2 *Internal Change*

Now we allow for one of the π_{ij} in each equation to shift, so neither equation in the 'reduced form' (14.18) can be structural, nor can either of the corresponding equations in (14.19) or (14.20). However, for shifts for which $\pi_{13} = b_{21}\pi_{23}$ then b_{12} remains constant, as do all the other parameters of the first equation, so it is structural in (14.19) and (14.21); equivalently for the second equation when $\pi_{21} = b_{12}\pi_{11}$ (say). However, if both π_{11} and π_{23} shift, neither equation in (14.21) remains constant, and the matching equation in (14.19) or (14.20) only remains constant if other parameters also shift (eg, π_{21} offsets the change in π_{11} for (14.19) to remain constant).

The first example can be made a special case of the second by endogenizing all the variables, in which case, shifts in some variables' distributions preclude them from being structural, albeit that the same shifts might highlight the structurality of other equations.

An interesting re-interpretation of identification follows when the internal break is discovered and correctly modelled. Consider (14.19) when $\pi_{13} = b_{12}\pi_{23}$ but π_{23} shifts at time T_1 to $\pi_{23} + \eta$. Let $1_{\{t \geq T_1\}}$ denote the indicator for this event, and consider the augmented system

$$\begin{pmatrix} 1 & b_{12} \\ 0 & 1 \end{pmatrix}\begin{pmatrix} y_{1,t} \\ y_{2,t} \end{pmatrix} = \begin{pmatrix} c_{11} & c_{12} & 0 & c_{14} & 0 \\ c_{21} & 0 & c_{23} & c_{24} & \eta \end{pmatrix}\begin{pmatrix} z_{1,t} \\ z_{2,t} \\ z_{3,t} \\ z_{4,t} \\ 1_{\{t \geq T_1\}} z_{3,t} \end{pmatrix} + \begin{pmatrix} u_{1,t} \\ u_{2,t} \end{pmatrix}. \quad (14.27)$$

Then (14.27) has constant parameters, but the first equation has a higher degree of over-identification than that in (14.19), confirming the identifying role of 'shifts' first discussed by Wright (1915).

14.8.3 *An Example*

The Banking Act of 1984 in the UK, which permitted interest payments on current accounts in exchange for all interest payments being after the deduction of 'standard rate' tax, provided a natural experiment that illustrates the role of structural breaks in isolating structure. Following this legislative change, previously estimated models of the demand for narrow money (M1) (such as Hendry and Mizon, 1993) suffered serious forecast failure. This is shown in the first column of graphs in Figure 14.1 for which the model used the competitive rate of interest R_c as a measure of the opportunity cost of

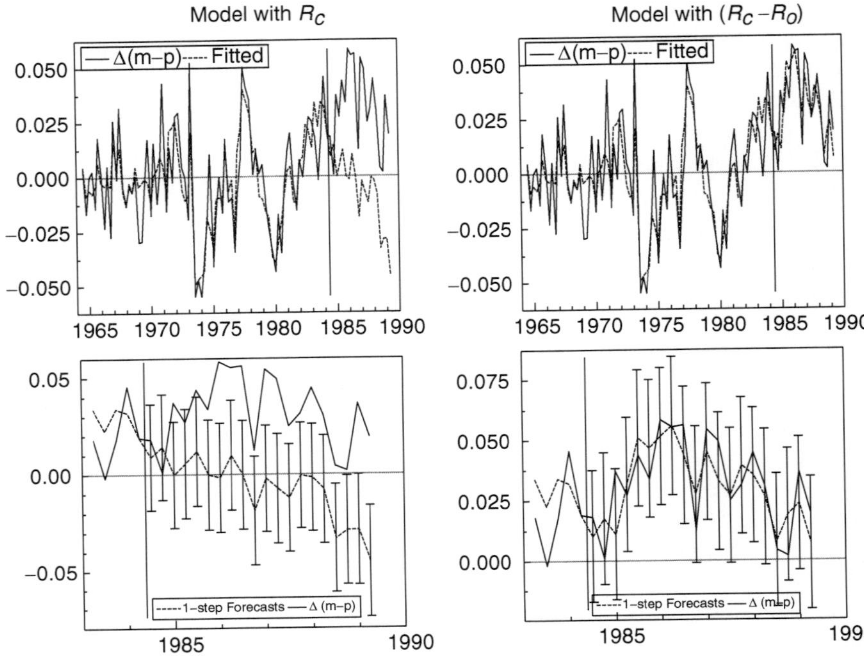

FIG. **14.1.** The effects of a change in the opportunity cost of holding money.

holding money. In fact, the own rate of interest (R_o) changed from zero to near the value of the competitive rate (R_c: about 12% per annum at the time) within 18 months, inducing very large inflows to M1. The effect was a large shift in the opportunity cost of holding money, namely a deterministic shift from R_c to $(R_c - R_o)$. Models that correctly re-measured the opportunity cost by $(R_c - R_o)$ continued to forecast well, once the break was observed—see the second column of graphs in Figure 14.1. Moreover, these models had the same estimated parameter values after the break as before. Thus, the forecast failure of models using R_c as a proxy for the opportunity cost was instrumental in the recognition that, once a more appropriate measure of opportunity cost was used, there was no change in structure for the money demand equation, although there clearly was for the opportunity cost equation (or both equations for R_c and R_o).

14.9 Conclusions

If identification were no more than the uniqueness of a parametrization, it could be achieved by imposing sufficient arbitrary restrictions. We suspect that was not what Cowles Commission researchers envisaged, nor does it correspond to the normal use of language: few would accept the 'identification' of an approaching 'Mini' as a Rolls-Royce by false claims as to its size, shape, composition, and form. Rather, the attributes of correct interpretation and correspondence to an actual entity are also important. Thus, we reconsidered these three attributes, as well as the potential identification of 'structure', defined as invariance under extensions of the information set.

First, for uniqueness, both local and global identification of the parameters of the local data generation process (LDGP) and of a model were considered. The converse of uniqueness is observational equivalence, which arises whenever, in the population, models are mutually encompassing. In sample, though, mutual encompassing can arise from the available information being unable to discriminate between distinct models.

Next, we showed that Cowles Commission rank conditions for simultaneous equations models (SEMs) only ensure uniqueness within a theory—there can be other over-identified (and interpretable) models that are observationally equivalent under constant parameters. Forecast failure and structural change can be valuable in discriminating nonstructural (but uniquely over-identified) representations, from those which potentially contain structure. However, there is no guarantee that structure can be identified. Finally, interpretation remains in the eye of the beholder, usually dependent on a theoretical framework. However, rejection of the relevant theory-based identifying restrictions, or violation of theory-derived constancy requirements, would preclude such interpretations.

References

Aldrich, J. (1994). Haavelmo's identification theory. *Econometric Theory*, **10**, 198–219.

Bontemps, C. and Mizon, G. E. (2003). Congruence and encompassing. In Stigum, B. (ed.), *Econometrics and the Philosophy of Economics*, pp. 354–378. Princeton: Princeton University Press.

Bowden, R. (1973). The theory of parametric identification. *Econometrica*, **41**, 1069–1074.

Box, G. E. P. and Jenkins, G. M. (1976). *Time Series Analysis, Forecasting and Control*. San Francisco: Holden-Day. First published, 1970.

Clements, M. P. and Hendry, D. F. (1998). *Forecasting Economic Time Series*. Cambridge: Cambridge University Press.

———(1999). *Forecasting Non-stationary Economic Time Series*. Cambridge, Mass.: MIT Press.

———(2002). Modelling methodology and forecast failure. *Econometrics Journal*, **5**, 319–344.

Deistler, M. (1976). The identifiability of linear econometric models with autocorrelated errors. *International Economic Review*, **17**, 26–45.

Deistler, M. and Seifert, H. (1978). Identifiability and consistent estimability in econometric models. *Econometrica*, **46**, 969–980.

——Ploberger, W., and Pötscher, B. M. (1982). Identifiability and inference in ARMA systems. In Anderson, O. (ed.), *Time Series Analysis: Theory and Practice 2*, pp. 43–60. Amsterdam: North-Holland.

Engle, R. F., Hendry, D. F., and Richard, J.-F. (1983). Exogeneity. *Econometrica*, **51**, 277–304.

Ericsson, N. R., Hendry, D. F., and Prestwich, K. M. (1998). The demand for broad money in the United Kingdom, 1878–1993. *Scandinavian Journal of Economics*, **100**, 289–324.

Faust, J. and Whiteman, C. H. (1997). General-to-specific procedures for fitting a data-admissible, theory-inspired, congruent, parsimonious, encompassing, weakly-exogenous, identified, structural model of the DGP: A translation and critique. *Carnegie–Rochester Conference Series on Public Policy*, **47**, 121–161.

Fisher, F. M. (1961). On the cost of approximate specification in simultaneous equation estimation. *Econometrica*, **29**, 139–170.

——(1966). *The Identification Problem in Econometrics*. New York: McGraw Hill.

Frisch, R. (1934). *Statistical Confluence Analysis by Means of Complete Regression Systems*. Oslo: University Institute of Economics.

——(1938). Statistical versus theoretical relations in economic macrodynamics. Mimeograph dated 17 July 1938, League of Nations Memorandum. Reproduced by University of Oslo in 1948 with Tinbergen's comments. Contained in Memorandum 'Autonomy of Economic Relations', 6 November 1948, Oslo, Universitets Økonomiske Institutt. Reprinted in Hendry, D. F. and Morgan, M. S. (1995), *op.cit.*

Gallant, A. R. and White, H. (1988). *A Unified Theory of Estimation and Inference for Nonlinear Dynamic Models*. Oxford: Blackwell.

Greene, W. H. (2000). *Econometric Analysis*, 4th edition. New Jersey: Prentice-Hall.

Haavelmo, T. (1944). The probability approach in econometrics. *Econometrica*, **12**, 1–118. Supplement.

Hannan, E. J. and Deistler, M. (1988). *The Statistical Theory of Linear Systems*. New York: John Wiley & Sons.

Hatanaka, M. (1975). On the global identification of the dynamic simultaneous equations model with stationary disturbances. *International Economic Review*, **16**, 545–554.

Hendry, D. F. (1995a). *Dynamic Econometrics*. Oxford: Oxford University Press.

——(1995b). Econometrics and business cycle empirics. *Economic Journal*, **105**, 1622–1636.

——(1996). On the constancy of time-series econometric equations. *Economic and Social Review*, **27**, 401–422.

——(2000). On detectable and non-detectable structural change. *Structural Change and Economic Dynamics*, **11**, 45–65. Reprinted in The Economics of Structural Change. Hagemann, H., Landesman, M., and Scazzieri (eds.), Cheltenham: Edward Elgar, 2002.

——and Juselius, K. (2001). Explaining cointegration analysis: Part II. *Energy Journal*, **22**, 75–120.

——and Mizon, G. E. (1993). Evaluating dynamic econometric models by encompassing the VAR. In Phillips, P. C. B. (ed.), *Models, Methods and Applications of Econometrics*, pp. 272–300. Oxford: Basil Blackwell.

——and Morgan, M. S. (1995). *The Foundations of Econometric Analysis.* Cambridge: Cambridge University Press.

Hsiao, C. (1983). Identification. In Griliches, Z. and Intriligator, M. D. (eds.), *Handbook of Econometrics,* Vol. 1, Ch. 4. Amsterdam: North-Holland.

Johansen, S. (1995). *Likelihood-based Inference in Cointegrated Vector Autoregressive Models.* Oxford: Oxford University Press.

——and Juselius, K. (1994). Identification of the long-run and the short-run structure: An application to the ISLM model. *Journal of Econometrics,* **63**, 7–36.

Kalman, R. E. (1982). Identification from real data. In Hazewinkel, M. and Rinrooy Kan, A. H. G. (eds.), *Current Developments in the Interface: Economics, Econometrics, Mathematics,* pp. 161–196. Dordrecht: D. Reidel.

Koopmans, T. C. (1949). Identification problems in economic model construction. *Econometrica,* **17**, 125–144.

——and Reiersøl, O. (1950). The identification of structural characteristics. *The Annals of Mathematical Statistics,* **21**, 165–181.

——Rubin, H., and Leipnik, R. B. (1950). Measuring the equation systems of dynamic economics. In Koopmans, T. C. (ed.), *Statistical Inference in Dynamic Economic Models,* No. 10 in Cowles Commission Monograph. New York: John Wiley & Sons.

Kullback, S. and Leibler, R. A. (1951). On information and sufficiency. *Annals of Mathematical Statistics,* **22**, 79–86.

Liu, T. C. (1960). Underidentification, structural estimation, and forecasting. *Econometrica,* **28**, 855–865.

Lu, M. and Mizon, G. E. (1997). Mutual encompassing and model equivalence. Discussion Papers in *Economics and Econometrics,* No. 9702, Economics Department, University of Southampton.

Madansky, A. (1976). *Foundations of Econometrics.* Amsterdam: North-Holland.

Marschak, J. (1942). Economic interdependence and statistical analysis. In Lange, I. *et al.* (eds.), *Studies in Mathematical Economics and Econometrics—In Memory of Henry Schultz,* pp. 125–150. Chicago: University of Chicago Press.

Mizon, G. E. (1984). The encompassing approach in econometrics. In Hendry, D. F. and Wallis, K. F. (eds.), *Econometrics and Quantitative Economics,* pp. 135–172. Oxford: Basil Blackwell.

——(1995). Progressive modelling of macroeconomic time series: the LSE methodology. In Hoover, K. D. (ed.), *Macroeconometrics: Developments, Tensions and Prospects,* pp. 107–169. Dordrecht: Kluwer Academic Press.

——and Richard, J.-F. (1986). The encompassing principle and its application to non-nested hypothesis tests. *Econometrica,* **54**, 657–678.

Phillips, A. W. H. (1956). Some notes on the estimation of time-forms of reactions in interdependent dynamic systems. *Economica,* **23**, 99–113.

Preston, A. J. (1978). Concepts of structure and model identifiability for econometric systems. In Bergstrom, A. R., Catt, A. J. L., Peston, M. H., and Silverstone, B. D. J. (eds.), *Stability and Inflation,* Ch. 16. New York: Wiley.

Qin, D. (1989). Formalisation of identification theory. *Oxford Economic Papers,* **41**, 73–79.

Rothenberg, T. J. (1971). Identification in parametric models. *Econometrica,* **39**, 577–592.

Sargan, J. D. (1983). Identification and lack of identification. *Econometrica*, **51**, 1605–1633.

Sims, C. A. (1980). Macroeconomics and reality. *Econometrica*, **48**, 1–48. Reprinted in Granger, C. W. J. (ed.) (1990), *Modelling Economic Series*. Oxford: Clarendon Press.

Spanos, A. (1986). *Statistical Foundations of Econometric Modelling*. Cambridge: Cambridge University Press.

White, H. (1994). *Estimation, Inference and Specification Analysis*. Cambridge: Cambridge University Press.

Wold, H. O. A. and Juréen, L. (1953). *Demand Analysis: A Study in Econometrics*, 2nd edition. New York: John Wiley.

Working, E. J. (1927). What do statistical demand curves show? *Quarterly Journal of Economics*, **41**, 212–235.

Wright, P. G. (1915). Review of Moore, 'Economic Cycles' (1915). *Quarterly Journal of Economics*, **29**, 631–641.

15

Does it Matter How to Measure Aggregates? The Case of Monetary Transmission Mechanisms in the Euro Area

*Andreas Beyer and Katarina Juselius**

15.1 Introduction

A wide range of empirical macro models for the Euro zone including, eg, the area wide models by Fagan, Henry, and Mestre (2005, henceforth FHM), Artis and Beyer (2004), and Smets and Wouters (2003) are based on aggregated Euro zone data. However, for annual or quarterly econometric time-series models the post monetary union sample after 1999 is still too short to allow for meaningful parameter estimates and hypothesis testing. Therefore, a key issue in empirical studies for the Euro zone is the creation of aggregated data for the period prior to the single currency. Because member countries previously had separate currencies susceptible to revaluations and devaluations, aggregate time-series data for the Euro area do not exist, and have to be created from the individual countries' records.[1]

There are four main aggregation methods in common use: summing the levels data or the growth rates by using either fixed or variable weights, in any combination. Beyer, Doornik, and Hendry (2000, 2001), (henceforth BDH),

* The views expressed in this chapter are those of the authors and do not necessarily represent those of the ECB. We thank Gabriel Fagan, Jérôme Henry, Ricardo Mestre, Chiara Osbat, and Bernd Schnatz for helpful comments on earlier versions of this chapter.

[1] It can be mentioned that the European System of National and Regional Accounts (ESA) defines the accounting rules that allow for mutual and consistent comparison between economic time-series across EU countries, see ESA (1995). These are based on the System of National Accounts (SNA), see SNA (1993).

show analytically that three out of the four methods might yield problematic results in a situation when exchange rate shifts induce relative-price changes between individual countries in the Euro area. The least problematic method was found to be the variable weight method of growth rates considering the following two criteria. First, any method deserving serious consideration for aggregating across exchange-rate changes must work accurately when such exchange rate induced changes of relative prices do *not* occur. Second, if a variable measured in national currency increases (decreases) in every member state, then the aggregate should not move in the opposite direction. Although these may seem to be minimal requirements, BDH showed that levels aggregators need not perform appropriately in this respect when large currency changes occur: measured aggregates (of GDP say) can fall purely because of an exchange-rate change even though every country's GDP increases. Since fixed-weight methods deliver the same aggregates when applied to levels or changes, aggregating growth rates with flexible weights is left as the only method that survives both criteria.

Despite its superiority, the BDH method may, nevertheless, face a non-trivial decision problem when applied to real data. This is because the real GDP weights needed for the aggregation of variables can be sensitive to the choice of base year for the implicit GDP price deflators. The chapter shows that the time-series of weights for the individual countries may deviate quite significantly in *absolute* value when different base years are chosen but that the mean corrected series are quite similar. However, this problem is shown to disappear altogether by choosing nominal rather than real GDP weights.

Because the mean-corrected relative BDH weights series seem fairly robust to the choice of base year, it is of some interest to investigate whether this choice is very important in practice. The second part of this chapter tries to shed some light on this issue by checking whether the main empirical conclusions from a VAR analysis of the Euro area monetary transmission mechanisms reported in Coenen and Vega (2001), (henceforth CV), are robust to the choice of aggregation method. The robustness check is based on a variety of tests and estimates from a VAR analysis using the same core variables as in CV aggregated by the FHM fixed and the BDH flexible real and nominal weights methods.

The organization of the chapter is as follows: section 15.2 first gives a brief review of the fixed FHM and flexible BDH aggregation methods, then provides an analytical expression for the base year effect on the flexible real GDP weights and demonstrates that nominal GDP weights are immune to the base year problem. Section 15.3 illustrates the various aggregation method effect with a stylized example. Section 15.4 compares the real GDP and the implicit GDP price deflator aggregated by the fixed FHM weights and flexible real and nominal BDH weights methods. Section 15.5 re-estimates the VAR analysis of the Euro area monetary transmission mechanisms reported in CV using flexible weights aggregates and compares the results. Section 15.6 concludes.

15.2 Constructing Aggregates: Fixed versus Variable Weights

The fixed weights (FHM) and flexible weights (BDH) methods are first briefly introduced. We then demonstrate why the BDH method based on real GDP weights is sensitive to the choice of base year for a price index and show that the BDH method based on nominal GDP weights is immune to this problem.

15.2.1 *Log-level Aggregation Using Fixed Weights*

The data for the ECB's area wide model in Fagan, Henry, and Mestre (2005) has been aggregated by fixed weights of log-levels of national variables:

$$x_t = \sum_{i=1}^{n} x_{i,t} w_i, \tag{15.1}$$

where $x_{i,t} = \log(X_{i,t})$ in country i at time t and the weights are fixed over time, for example 30.5% for Germany, 21.0% for France, and 20.3% for Italy.

Compared to the 'naïve' level method where variables in levels are first converted into a common currency and then aggregated, the above method has the advantage of avoiding distortions due to the influence of currency appreciations or devaluations. The disadvantage of any fixed weight approach remains: the choice of the fixed weights is to some extent arbitrary and fixed weights rule out that the constructed aggregates reflect the evolvement of countries' comparative competitiveness over time. See BDH for a discussion.

15.2.2 *The BDH Method Based on Flexible Real GDP Weights*

Instead of aggregating log levels of a variable, x_t, BDH proposed to aggregate growth rates, Δx_t, with variable weights, so that the aggregated growth rate becomes a weighted average of the n individual country growth rates according to the formula:

$$\Delta x_t = \sum_{i=1}^{n} \Delta x_{i,t} w_{i,t-1}, \quad t = 1, \ldots, T \tag{15.2}$$

where the weights $w_{i,t-1}$ for country i at time t are constructed as

$$w_{i,t-1} = \frac{E_{i.c,t-1} Y^r_{i,t-1}}{\sum_{i=1}^{n} E_{i.c,t-1} Y^r_{i,t-1}} \tag{15.3}$$

and $y^r_{i,t}$ is the real income of country i at time t, and $E_{i.c,t}$ is the exchange rate of country i at time t vis-a-vis a common currency, c.

The level of the aggregate can be recovered from the formula

$$x_t = \Delta x_t + x_{t-1} \text{ for } t = 1, \dots, \text{ and } x_0 \text{ given.} \tag{15.4}$$

When using (15.2)–(15.4) to construct aggregate nominal GDP, y^n_t, and real GDP, y^r_t, as well as the GDP price deflator, $p_{y,t}$, BDH showed that the constructed GDP deflator, $p_{y,t}$, coincides with the implied deflator, $y^n_t - y^r_t$. While this is an important advantage compared to the FHM method, the former is shown to be sensitive to the choice of a common base year for the price indices.

15.2.3 *Real GDP Weights: Prices versus a Price Index*

We shall focus on two cases: (1) the absolute prices of a basket of goods are known, (2) only a price index is known such as the CPI or the implicit GDP price deflator. As an illustration of why the choice of the base year matters for the real GDP weights in (15.3), we construct the aggregate real GDP for three countries, Germany, France, and Italy assuming that Germany is the reference country. Table 15.1 provides the data.

Case 1:. We know the absolute prices of a basket of goods, $P_{i,t}$, for each country $i = 1,2,3$. The weight for Germany, say, would be calculated as:

$$\omega^r_{1,t} = \frac{(Y^n_{1,t}/P_{1,t})}{(Y^n_{1,t}/P_{1,t}) + (Y^n_{2,t}/P_{2,t})E^{-1}_{2.1,t} + (Y^n_{3,t}/P_{3,t})E^{-1}_{3.1,t}} \tag{15.5}$$

or equivalently

$$\omega^r_{1,t} = \frac{Y^n_{1,t}}{Y^n_{1,t} + Y^n_{2,t}\left(\frac{P_{1,t}}{P_{2,t}}\right)E^{-1}_{2.1,t} + Y^n_{3,t}\left(\frac{P_{1,t}}{P_{3,t}}\right)E^{-1}_{3.1,t}}. \tag{15.6}$$

It appears from (15.6) that using real income weighted by nominal exchange rates is the same as using nominal income weighted by real exchange rates. Because $(\frac{P_{1,t}}{P_{j,t}})\ E^{-1}_{j.1,t} \simeq 1$, the country-specific nominal income is not transformed into a common currency in this case. Hence, the weights should be calculated from nominal income weighted by nominal exchange rates if

Table 15.1. Constructing weights: A three country example

	Germany	France	Italy
Nom. GDP	$Y^n_{1,t}$	$Y^n_{2,t}$	$Y^n_{3,t}$
Price Index =	$PI_{1,t} = P_{1,t}/P_{1,t_0}$	$PI_{2,t} = P_{2,t}/P_{2,t_0}$	$PI_{3,t} = P_{3,t}/P_{3,t_0}$
Nom. exchange	$E_{1.1,t}(Dmk/Dmk)$	$E_{2.1,t}(Fr/Dmk)$	$E_{3.1,t}(Lir/Dmk)$

they are flexible or, alternatively, by relative prices translated into a common currency if nominal exchange rates are fixed.

Case 2:. We know the prices relative to a base year. For example, we measure prices by a commodity price index, such as CPI, $PI_{i,t} = P_{i,t}/P_{i,t_0}$, where P_{i,t_0} is the price of country i in the base year or we measure prices by an implicit price deflator, such as the implicit GDP deflator, $PI_{i,t}$, with base year t_0. The weights become

$$\tilde{\omega}^r_{1,t} = \frac{Y^n_{1,t}}{Y^n_{1,t} + Y^n_{2,t}\frac{P_{1,t}}{P_{2,t}}E^{-1}_{2.1,t}\left(\frac{P_{2,t_0}}{P_{1,t_0}}\right) + Y^n_{3,t}\frac{P_{1,t}}{P_{3,t}}E^{-1}_{3.1,t}\left(\frac{P_{3,t_0}}{P_{1,t_0}}\right)}. \tag{15.7}$$

From (15.7) it is easy to see that the choice of base year will influence the calculated weights. To illustrate the base year impact, it is useful first to express the nominal exchange rate at time t as $E_{j.i,t} = E_{j.i,t_0} + \delta^E_{ji,t}$ and then transform it into a growth factor

$$E_{j.i,t} = \left(1 + \frac{\delta^E_{i.j,t}}{E_{j.i,t_0}}\right)E_{j.i,t_0} = g^E_{i.j,t}E_{j.i,t_0}. \tag{15.8}$$

Similarly, relative prices can be formulated as:

$$\left(\frac{P_{i,t}}{P_{j,t}}\right)\left(\frac{P_{j,t_0}}{P_{i,t_0}}\right) = \left(1 + \frac{\delta^P_{ij,t}}{100}\right) = g^P_{i.j,t}. \tag{15.9}$$

When an implicit deflator is used, real and nominal GDP are identical in the base year, so that $PI_{i,t_0} = 100$ and relative prices indices measure directly the relative price change from the base year for the two countries

$$\frac{PI_{i,t}}{PI_{j,t}} = \left(1 + \frac{\delta^P_{i.j,t}}{100}\right) = g^P_{i.j,t}.$$

Using (15.8) and (15.9), (15.7) can be rewritten as

$$\tilde{\omega}^r_{1,t} = \frac{Y^n_{1,t}}{Y^n_{1,t} + Y^n_{2,t}g^P_{2.1,t}g^E_{1.2,t}E_{1.2,t_0} + Y^n_{3,t}g^P_{3.1,t}g^E_{1.3,t}E_{1.3,t_0}}. \tag{15.10}$$

If nominal exchange rates correctly reflect relative price changes compared to the base period, then $g^P_{i.j,t}g^E_{j.i,t} \approx 1$ and the individual nominal incomes will be translated into the common currency using the nominal exchange rate of the base year. But this will not in general correctly reflect the relative strength of the two countries. For example, if at time t two countries i and j had experienced vastly different inflation rates compared to the base period and the nominal exchange rate had correctly reflected this development, then the nominal exchange rate at t_0 would no longer be representative for the economic strength of country i and j at time t.

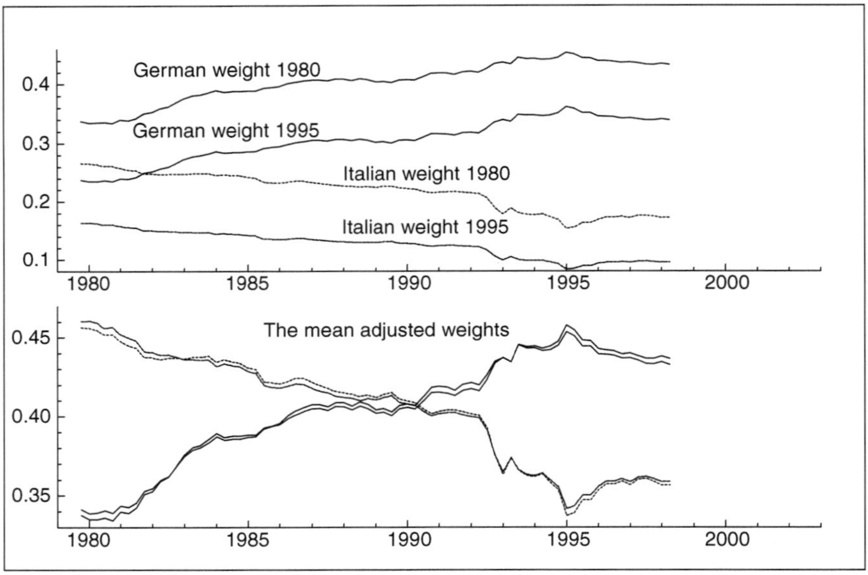

FIG. 15.1. Weights for Italy and Germany, created on real GDP with base year 1980 and 1995 (upper graph) and adjusted for mean (lower graph).

In a fixed exchange rate regime, the weights would, instead, be based on relative price indices which implies that weights become

$$\tilde{\omega}^n_{1,t} = \frac{Y^n_{1,t}}{Y^n_{1,t} + Y^n_{2,t} g^P_{1.2,t} E_{1.2} + Y^n_{3,t} g^P_{1.3,t} E_{1.3}}. \tag{15.11}$$

Because the relative price growth factor $g^P_{i.j,t}$ is not invariant to the choice of base year, the weights $\tilde{\omega}^n_{i.j,t}$ will differ depending on this choice. However, it seems quite likely that the time profile of the weights will be similar for different choice of base year, even though the absolute level of weights will differ.

This is illustrated by Figure 15.1. The graphs in the upper panel show that the absolute size of the real GDP weights for Germany and Italy, respectively, differ a lot depending on the chosen base year, whereas the mean-adjusted graphs in the lower panel suggest that the dynamic evolvement of the weights for the two countries over time is nearly unaffected. Thus, even in a case where the nominal exchange rate have exhibited substantial variation, the weight profiles are quite similar.

Nevertheless, the calculated weight of an individual country at time t using the weights (15.10) or (15.11) may in some cases give a somewhat wrong impression of its *absolute* economic strength vis-a-vis other countries in the aggregate. For example, in 1980 comparing Germany's weight of 22% (when the base year is 1995) with Italy's weight of almost 30% (when the base year is 1980 instead), does not seem meaningful.

15.2.4 *Proposing a Solution*

The ultimate task is to construct aggregation weights that adequately reflect the economic strength of the individual countries in the aggregate. In the ideal case, the weights should properly reflect a 'true' purchasing power parity between two countries, for example measured by the absolute prices of a basket of commodities, say, in one country relative to the corresponding price in the other country, both expressed in a common currency.

Under flexible exchange rates and prices measured by a price index such as the implicit GDP deflator, there is, however, no information on absolute prices in the domestic currency. The only information we have is the nominal exchange rate that provides information on the absolute price of one unit of the currency of country i in terms of a common currency j at time t. Therefore, we propose to use nominal exchange rates as a measure of the relative price development between two countries. Expressed in terms of (15.3) it amounts to using nominal rather than real GDP in the calculation of the BDH weights

$$\omega^n_{1,t} = \frac{Y^n_{1,t}}{Y^n_{1,t} + Y^n_{2,t}E_{1.2,t} + Y^n_{3,t}E_{1.3,t}}. \tag{15.12}$$

It is easy to see that the weights are now invariant to the choice of base year, as this is no longer an issue. In a world where purchasing power parity is satisfied in every period $E_{i.j,t} = P_{j,t}/P_{i,t}$ and the weights would indeed adequately reflect the economic strength of each country over time. However, it is well known that real exchange rates often deviate from purchasing power parity for extended periods of time (see eg Rogoff, 1996). Unfortunately, (15.12) does not solve this problem, unless there is reliable information on the real depreciation/appreciation rate of country i relative to country j, $q_{i.j,t}$, at each period t. With such information, the appropriate weights would become

$$\omega^n_{1,t} = \frac{Y^n_{1,t}}{Y^n_{1,t} + Y^n_{2,t}E_{1.2,t}q_{2.1,t} + Y^n_{3,t}E_{1.3,t}q_{3.1,t}}. \tag{15.13}$$

Under fixed exchange rates with known absolute prices, we propose to use the ratio of the absolute prices in one country relative to the corresponding price in the common currency, ie $P_{j,t}/P_{i,t}$. If prices are measured by a price index it becomes important to choose the base year such that it approximately corresponds to a period when purchasing power parity holds between the countries. Even though it is highly unlikely that such a period has existed jointly for all member states it should, nevertheless, be possible to calculate an optimal aggregate in the following way:

1. Find a base period when PPP holds for two countries, for example Germany and France, and construct a two country aggregate for GDP, $y_t^a(G+F)$, in a common currency (for example, DM) using the flexible weights method.
2. Find a new base period when PPP holds for Germany and another country, say Italy, and construct a new GDP aggregate, $y_t^a(G+F+I)$, by combining $y_t^a(G+F)$ and $y_t(I)$ using the flexible weights.
3. Continue until all relevant countries have been included in the aggregate, $y_t^a(EU)$.

15.3 A Simple Example

The two-country example in Table 15.2 illustrates how the real GDP weights in (15.2) are affected by the choice of different base years assuming either fixed or flexible exchange rates. These results are compared with the case when the weights are based on nominal rather than real GDP. To see the effect of exchange rate misalignments for the nominal GDP weights, we have calculated the weights for the case when purchasing power parity holds and when it does not. For simplicity, only three annual observations, $t = 0,1,2$, are used as this is sufficient to calculate GDP growth rates for two periods ie at $t = 1$ and $t = 2$. For this stylized two-country economy we assume that:

1. output and prices remain constant in country 2;
2. nominal income in country 1 is constant in the first year (from $t = 0$ to $t = 1$) and doubles in the second year;
3. the price in country 1 doubles in the first year, and remains constant thereafter;
4. by consequence of assumption 3, real income in country 1 is reduced by 50% in the first year and returns back to its starting level in the subsequent year;
5. nominal exchange rate is either fixed or flexible; in the latter case it either reflects PPP or it deviates from PPP.

The upper part of Table 15.2 reports the economic facts about the two countries. The big price increase in country 1 serves the purpose of illustrating the effect of choosing different base years.[2] Nominal income is given in absolute values, while the BDH aggregation formula (15.2) is based on logarithmic values. The real income growth rate is, therefore, calculated as a percentage change in the table. Comparing the corresponding GDP weights for country 1

[2] This stylized example is in no way realistic. In a real world economy, the exchange rate would, of course, not remain constant after such a dramatic price change.

Table 15.2. A stylized example of BDH aggregation of two countries over three periods

	Base year: $t = 0$			Base year: $t = 2$		
	$t = 0$	$t = 1$	$t = 2$	$t = 0$	$t = 1$	$t = 2$
$Y^n_{1,t}$	1.0	1.0	2.0	1.0	1.0	2.0
$PI_{1,t}$	100	200	200	50	100	100
$Y^r_{1,t}$	1.0	0.5	1.0	2.0	1.0	2.0
$\Delta Y^r_{1,t}$ *in* %		−50%	100%		−50%	100%
$Y^n_{2,t}$	1.0	1.0	1.0	1.0	1.0	1.0
$PI_{2,t}$	100	100	100	100	100	100
$Y^r_{2,t}$	1.0	1.0	1.0	1.0	1.0	1.0
$\Delta y^r_{2,t}$ *in* %		0%	0%		0%	0%
$PI_{1,t}/PI_{2,t}$	1.0	2.0	2.0	1/2	1.0	1.0
$E_{1.2,t}$*(fixed exch.)*	1.0	1.0	1.0	1.0	1.0	1.0
$E_{1.2,t}$*(flex.exch.PPP)*	1.0	2.0	2.0	1.0	2.0	2.0
$E_{1.2,t}$*(flex.exch.NoPPP)*	1.0	1.5	1.5	1.0	1.5	1.5
Real GDP weights						
$w^{real.y}_{1,t}$*(fixed exch.)*	**0.50**	**0.33**	**0.50**	0.67	0.50	0.67
$w^{real.y}_{1,t}$*(flex.exch.PPP)*	0.50	0.50	0.67	0.67	0.33	0.80
Nominal GDP weights						
$w^{nom.y}_{1,t}$*(PPP holds)*	**0.50**	**0.33**	**0.50**	**0.50**	**0.33**	**0.50**
$w^{nom.y}_{1,t}$*(NoPPP)*	0.50	0.50	0.40	0.50	0.50	0.59
y^r_t aggregated with						
$w^{real.y}_{1,t}$*(fixed exch.)*	**1.00**	**0.75**	**1.00**	1.50	1.00	1.50
$w^{real.y}_{1,t}$*(flex.exch.PPP)*	1.00	0.75	1.12	1.50	1.00	1.33
$w^{nom.y}_{1,t}$*(PPP holds)*	**1.00**	**0.75**	**1.00**	**1.50**	**1.13**	**1.50**
$w^{nom.y}_{1,t}$*(NoPPP)*	1.00	0.75	1.12	1.50	1.13	1.70
Δy^r_t in %						
$w^{real.y}_{1,t}$*(fixed exch.)*	—	**−25%**	**33%**	—	−33%	50%
$w^{real.y}_{1,t}$*(flex.exch.PPP)*	—	−25%	50%	—	−33%	33%
$w^{nom.y}_{1,t}$*(PPP holds)*	—	**−25%**	**33%**	—	**−25%**	**33%**
$w^{nom.y}_{1,t}$*(NoPPP)*	—	−25%	50%	—	−25%	50%

and 2 shows that the choice of base year for the price index matters: for base year $t = 0$ both countries would have an identical real GDP in year 0, whereas for base year $t = 2$ the real GDP of country 1 is twice the size of country 2 in year 0 and 2, but identical in year 1. The latter is a good illustration of the base year effect: for base year $t = 2$, the price levels are identically 100 by construction even though prices have doubled in country 1. In both cases the change in real GDP is correctly calculated: from $t = 0$ to $t = 1$ the GDP of country 1 drops by 50%, whereas the one of country 2 is unchanged.

The previous section demonstrated that the base year problem is not only associated with prices but also with exchange rates and whether these are adequately reflecting purchasing power parity or not. The exchange rates have been constructed such that for base year $t = 0$ purchasing power parity holds both when the exchange rates are fixed and flexible.

According to (15.4) real aggregate GDP is constructed by cumulating real growth rates from an initial value. The latter has been calculated as a weighted average of the two real incomes with equal weights. Based on this, Table 15.2 shows that the constructed real aggregate incomes based on the BDH real GDP weights and fixed exchange rates are identical at $t = 0$, 2 and drop by 25% at $t = 1$. However, the absolute level of real income is higher for base year $t = 2$. When comparing the aggregate growth rates we note that they evolve proportionally for the two base years, but the calculated growth rates are at a higher level for base year $t = 2$. With flexible exchange rates, the real GDP weights perform less well, as predicted by (15.10). For base year $t = 0$, it overestimates real aggregate income at $t = 2$, and for base year $t = 2$, it underestimates its value. Furthermore, the growth rates do not evolve proportionally. This can now explain the development of the weights in Figure 15.1, where the relatively higher Italian weights for base year 1981 is likely to be the result of the high inflation rate in Italy relative to Germany in that period.

Based on these facts, a method that adequately accounts for the economic development assumed for country 1 (and with no change in country 2) should produce a measure of real *aggregate* income which is equal for $t = 0,2$ and which declines by 25% at $t = 1$. The entries in the table that satisfy this criterion are in bold face.

The BDH method based on nominal GDP weights performs well both in terms of the real aggregate income levels and their percentage growth rates when PPP is satisfied. When PPP is not satisfied because of a real appreciation in period 1 and 2, the aggregate becomes over-valued. Thus, if nominal GDP weights are used, one should account for any deviation of the real exchange rate from its equilibrium value according to (15.13).

15.4 Conversion with Fixed and Flexible Weights: A Comparison

The previous section demonstrated that the choice of base year matters for the BDH method when real GDP aggregation weights are used. The purpose of this section is therefore to investigate graphically how the various aggregation methods affect aggregated E11 prices, real income, and interest rates in levels and changes. We have constructed aggregates based on the flexible BDH real GDP weights method with base year 1981 and 1995 (hereafter Flex81 and Flex95), the flexible BDH nominal GDP weights method (FlexNom) and the fixed FHM real GDP weights of 1995 (Fix95). Because the year 1995 was

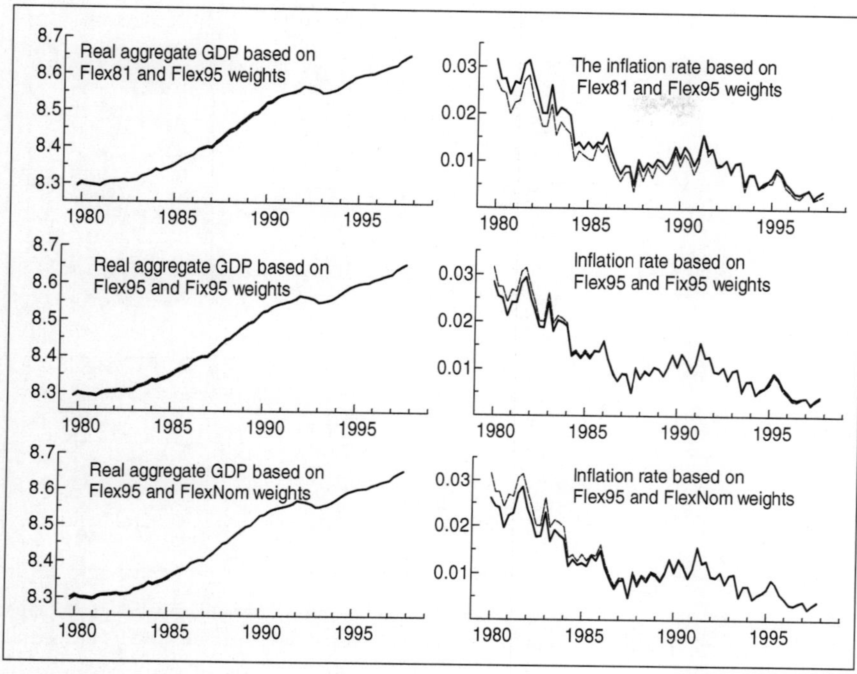

FIG. 15.2. Comparing aggregate real GDP (left hand side) and inflation rate (right hand side) based on different aggregation weights.

used to calculate the Euro-area aggregates in FHM used by CV, it has been considered a reference year for the comparisons. The year 1981 represents a period when the member states were far from a common European PPP level, and has been chosen to illustrate the base year effect of the BDH method for a no-PPP period as compared to 1995 which was much closer to a PPP period.

Figure 15.2 shows real GDP based on Flex81 and Flex95 (upper l.h.s. panel), Flex95 and Fix95 (middle l.h.s. panel), and Flex95 and FlexNom (lower l.h.s. panel). Similar graphs are shown for inflation rates. Consistent with the results in the previous section, the absolute deviations between aggregate real GDP based on the different methods are generally small and hardly discernible in the graphs, whereas those of the inflation rate seem more significant. Generally, the first six years seem more affected than the more recent part of the sample period. Also, Flex95 seems to underestimate inflation rate compared to Flex81 and FlexNom.

Even though the aggregation methods produced very similar aggregates in absolute values, the deviations can be highly persistent as shown below and,

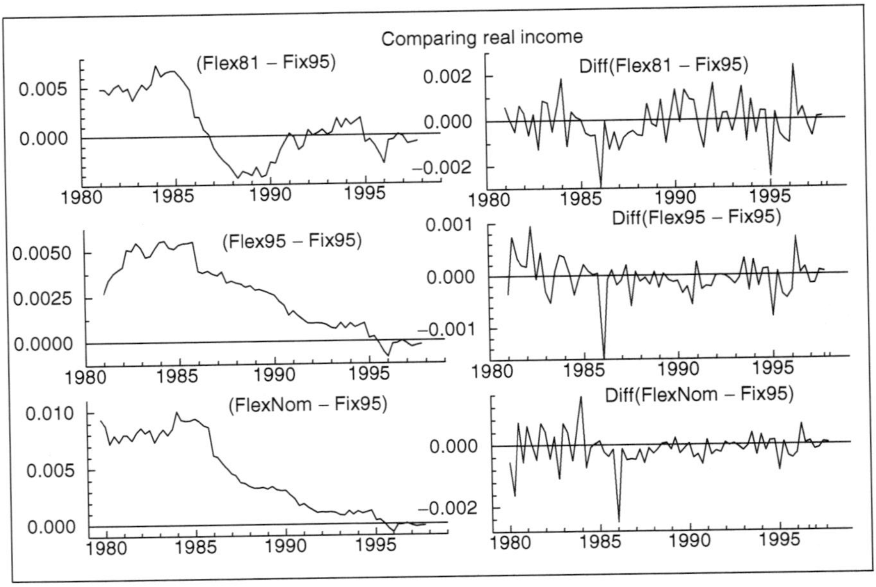

FIG. **15.3.** The differential between aggregate real income based on 1981, 1985, and 1995 flexible weights relative to the fixed 1995 weights (left hand side) and its difference (right hand side).

therefore, may very well influence the cointegration properties of empirical models. To illustrate the persistency aspect, Figures 15.3–15.5 show the deviations of aggregate real GDP, prices, and the short-term interest rate[3] based on Flex81, Flex95, and FlexNom compared to Fix95. Obviously, all these tiny differentials are highly persistent. The real GDP differentials in the left hand side of Figure 15.3 are likely to be approximately I(1) as their differences in the right hand side of the figure look reasonably mean-reverting. The price differentials, on the other hand, in the left hand side of Figure 15.4 exhibit pronounced persistent behaviour typical of I(2) variables. This is consistent with the I(1) behaviour of the inflation rate differentials in the right hand side of the figure. We note that the fixed weights method overestimates price inflation compared to Flex81 and FlexNom. The short-term interest rate differentials shown in the left hand side of Figure 15.5 seem to exhibit I(1) behaviour consistent with the mean reverting behaviour of their differences.

Whatever the case, the aggregation differentials are definitely not stationary and the choice of aggregation method might, therefore, have a significant

[3] CV used aggregates of income, inflation, and a short and long interest rate based on fixed GDP weights to estimate a structure of three cointegration relations. To economize on space, the comparison of long-term interest rate differentials is not reported as it is very similar to the short rates.

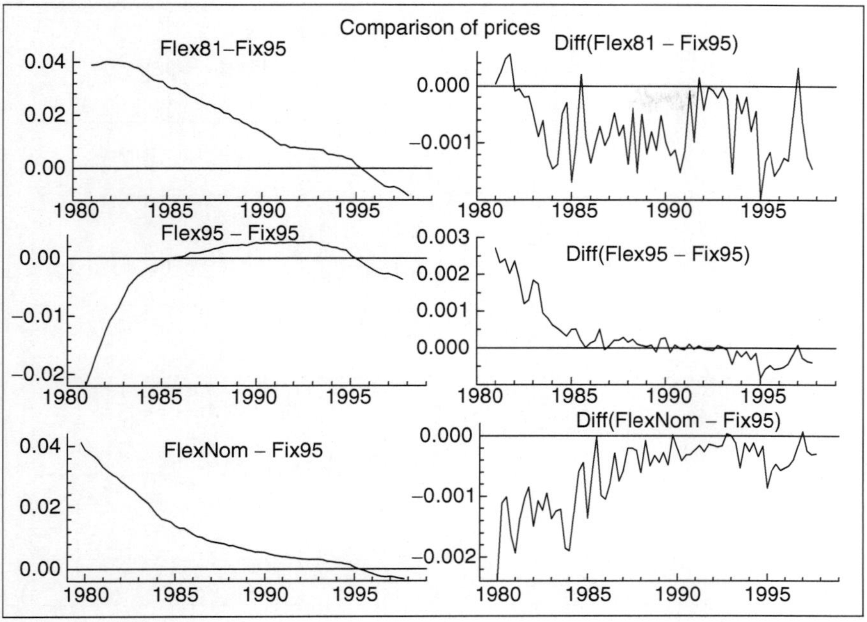

FIG. **15.4.** The differential between the implicit price deflator of aggregate GDP based on 1981, 1985, and 1995 flexible weights and the fixed 1995 weights (left hand side) and its difference (right hand side).

effect on the cointegration properties in empirical models. The following example illustrates such effects. Under the assumption that real GDP is unit root nonstationary, ie $y_t^r = (y_t^n - p_t) \sim I(1)$, we would expect $\{y_t^n, p_t\} \sim I(2)$ and, thus, $\{y_t^n, p_t\}$ to be cointegrated $CI(2,1)$ with cointegration vector $[1, -1]$. As discussed in Juselius (2006, Chapters 2, 16, and 18) this would be the case when the nominal variables satisfy long-run price homogeneity, a desirable property from an economic point of view. The empirical verification of price homogeneity is, however, likely to be sensitive to measurement errors unless these errors are stationary, or at most $I(1)$. Because the price differentials $(p^{Flex} - p^{Fix})$ in Figure 15.4 look approximately $I(2)$, the choice of aggregation method might have an impact on the long-run price homogeneity tests.

As an illustration, assume that the flexible weights aggregation method is correct and that long-run price homogeneity is satisfied, so that $(y_t^{n,Flex} - p^{Flex}) \sim I(1)$. If, instead, the fixed weights method is used to construct the aggregates, $y_t^{n,Fix}$ and p^{Fix}, and $(y_t^{n,Flex} - y_t^{n,Fix})$ and $(p^{Flex} - p^{Fix})$ are $I(2)$ then:

$$y_t^{r,Fix} = \underbrace{y_t^{n,Flex} - p_t^{Flex}}_{I(1)} - \underbrace{(y_t^{n,Flex} - y_t^{n,Fix})}_{I(2)} + \underbrace{(p^{Flex} - p^{Fix})}_{I(2)}. \tag{15.14}$$

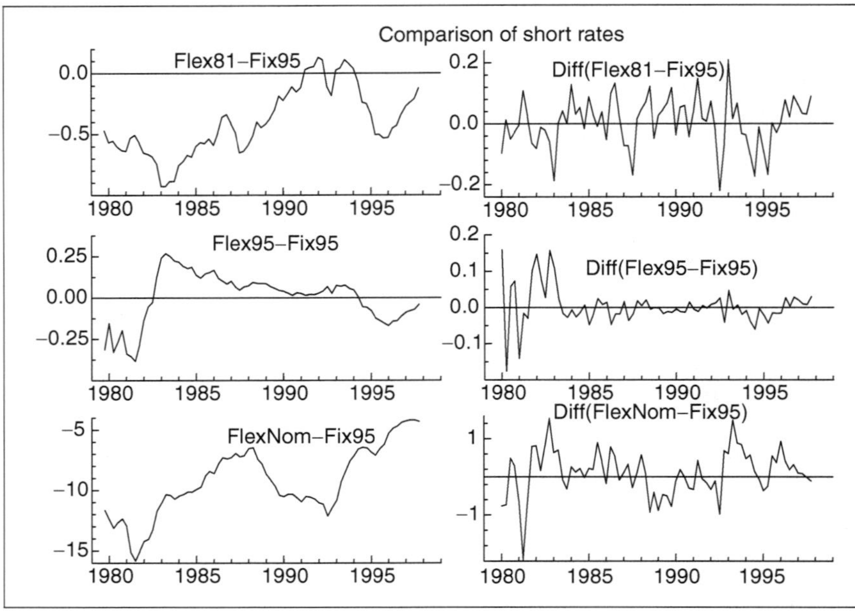

FIG. 15.5. The differential between short-term E11 interest rate based on flexible and fixed weights (left hand side) and its difference (right hand side).

Thus, $y_t^{r,Fix}$ would generally be I(2) unless the two $I(2)$ differentials in (15.14) are cointegrating $CI(2,1)$ or $C\,I\,(2,\,2)$.

In the comparison above, most differentials, while persistent, were tiny in absolute value. The question is whether the test for long-run price homogeneity has sufficient power to reject the null hypothesis of long-run price homogeneity when real income contains such a tiny I(2) aggregation error. In a similar set-up, Jørgensen (1998) showed by simulation experiments that such I(2) errors may not be easily detectable if they are small relative to the I(1) component. Kongsted (2005) demonstrated that even though the small I(2) component may not be found significant by testing, the trace test for cointegration rank and other inference in the cointegrated VAR model can, nevertheless, be affected in often inexplicable ways.

Thus, it is of some interest to investigate whether these tiny, but highly persistent, aggregation differentials have a significant influence on the cointegration properties of aggregate Euro area models, ie whether the choice of aggregation method is likely to have implications for the estimated long-run relations. In the next section we shall, therefore, take a look at the cointegration properties of the Euro area model in CV using aggregates based on the four different aggregation methods discussed above.

15.5 The CV Model with Flexible and Fixed Weights

The small monetary model in CV, one of the first empirical studies on monetary transmission mechanisms in the Euro zone, is based on aggregated fixed 1995 weights data. The paper discusses a cointegrated VAR analysis of the vector

$$x_t' = [m3_t, y_t, \Delta p_t, R_t^s, R_t^l], \quad t = 1981.1, \ldots, 1997.4,$$

where $m3$ is the log of real aggregate M3, y, is the log of real aggregate GDP, Δp is the difference of log GDP price, R^s is the short-term interest rate, R^l is the long-term government bond rate. The data are aggregated over the E11 member states. Here we shall compare the results of the CV model based on fixed 1995 weights with those obtained with flexible weights. Among the latter, we estimate the model for real GDP weights data with base year 1981 and 1995 and for nominal GDP weights. The sample covers most of the transition period from the beginning of the EMS to the start of the EMU but, as in CV, the first two years have been left out as they seem to generate instability in the VAR model. The reason why we use pre-EMU data is to exclude any influence of 'proper' post EMU data on the results.

Our study follows the CV model specification, two lags, an unrestricted constant term, and no trend in the cointegration relations. The last assumption was first checked, as one should in principle allow for a trend both in the stationary (β) and the nonstationary ($\beta_\perp$) directions when data are trending (Nielsen and Rahbek, 2000). The trend was found to be significant in the long-run relations, but the main conclusions of CV seemed reasonably robust to this change in the model. Thus, even though the VAR model with a trend was preferable on statistical grounds, we decided to continue with the CV model specification to preserve the comparative aspects of the study.

In the empirical analysis we examine some of the more important aspects of the VAR model: (1) the determination of cointegration rank based on the trace test, the roots in the characteristic polynomial, the largest t-ratio of α_r in the rth cointegration relation, (2) some general properties of the model describing the pulling and pushing forces by testing a zero row in α and a unit vector in α, (3) the long-run β structure described by the estimates and the p-value of the CV long-run structure, as well as the combined long-run relation of the money and inflation equation, respectively, and (4) the long-run impact of shocks on inflation and real income.

15.5.1 *The Determination of Cointegration Rank*

The choice of rank is a crucial step in the analysis as all subsequent results are conditional on this choice. Before using the I(1) trace tests we checked whether the model showed evidence of I(2). No such evidence was detected

Table 15.3. Some indicator statistics for rank determination

r	$r = 2$			$r = 3$		
	λ_r	$\rho_r^{\max}$	$t_{\alpha_r}^{\max}$	λ_r	$\rho_r^{\max}$	$t_{\alpha_r}^{\max}$
Fix95	0.29	0.76	3.04	0.24	0.94	3.07
Flex95	0.30	0.87	4.09	0.22	0.94	3.55
Flex81	0.29	0.66	3.54	0.16	0.76	2.23
FlexNom	0.28	0.67	3.50	0.19	0.90	3.33

and, following the recommendations in Juselius (2006), we report the rth eigenvalue, λ_r, the largest unrestricted characteristic root, $\rho_r^{\max}$, for a given r, and the largest t value of α_r. Based on the results reported in Table 15.3 for $r = 3$ (the CV choice) and, the closest alternative, $r = 2$ it appears that the former choice leaves a fairly large unrestricted root in the model for all methods except Flex81. A large unrestricted root means that at least one of the cointegration relations is likely to exhibit a fair degree of persistence. A graphical analysis shows that it is the short–long interest rate spread, the third relation in the CV structure, that looks rather nonstationary. Whether one should classify it as stationary can, therefore, be questioned.

Table 15.3 shows that all five aggregation methods give reasonably similar conclusions, possibly with the exception of Flex81, which was sticking out to some extent. Altogether, $r = 2$ seems preferable based on statistical grounds, but $r = 3$ could also be defendable. Again, to preserve comparability with the CV results we continue with $r = 3$.

15.5.2 *Pulling and Pushing Forces*

The test of a zero row in α, ie no levels feed-back, and a unit vector in α, ie pure adjustment, (see Juselius, 2006) are useful as a check of whether the general dynamic properties of the model have changed as a result of the aggregation method. The results reported in Table 15.4 show that, for the short rate, the zero row in α was acceptable with fairly high p-values for all aggregation methods, implying absence of levels feed-back from the other variables on the short rate. In addition, the zero row hypothesis was also accepted for the long-term bond rate except in the case of Flex81. This seems to indicate that it is the cumulated empirical shocks to the two interest rates that have broadly been pushing this system. Nonetheless, the joint hypothesis of a zero row for both interest rates was (borderline) rejected[4] and it was not possible to decompose the variables of the system into three pulling and two pushing

[4] If accepted, it would have been inconsistent with the CV assumption that the interest rate spread is a cointegration relation.

Table 15.4. Pulling and pushing forces in the model

	m^r	y^r	Δp	R_s	R_l
Zero row in α $(r = 3)$					
Fix95	20.50 [0.00]	8.27 [0.04]	6.89 [0.08]	**4.71** [0.19]	**4.77** [0.19]
Flex95	25.29 [0.00]	7.60 [0.06]	7.35 [0.06]	**4.29** [0.23]	**4.82** [0.19]
Flex81	7.26 [0.06]	13.68 [0.00]	12.47 [0.01]	**0.74** [0.86]	7.58 [0.06]
FlexNom	10.02 [0.02]	13.22 [0.00]	7.80 [0.05]	**1.53** [0.68]	**5.89** [0.12]
Unit vector in α $(r = 3)$					
Fix95	**3.75** [0.15]	**2.87** [0.24]	**3.54** [0.17]	8.26 [0.02]	6.42 [0.04]
Flex95	**4.08** [0.13]	**1.22** [0.54]	**3.26** [0.20]	8.35 [0.02]	4.88 [0.09]
Flex81	**3.39** [0.18]	4.81 [0.09]	**1.16** [0.56]	4.41 [0.11]	**1.59** [0.45]
FlexNom	**1.48** [0.48]	**2.59** [0.27]	**2.58** [0.28]	6.37 [0.04]	**3.49** [0.17]

Entries with a p-value > 0.10 in bold face.

variables. Consistent with the above results, the hypothesis of a unit vector in α seemed generally acceptable for money stock and inflation rate, and for real income. Altogether the Fix95, Flex95, and FlexNom methods seem to generate quite robust conclusions, whereas Flex 81 differed to some extent.

15.5.3 *The Long-run β Structure*

The three long-run relations identified in CV consisted of:

(1) A money demand relation: $m^r - \beta_{11}y^r + \beta_{12}R_s$;

(2) The real long–term interest rate: $R_l - \Delta p$;

(3) The short–long interest rate spread: $R_s - R_l$.

Since only the first relation, the money demand relation, contains free parameters to be estimated, Table 15.5 reports the estimates of the latter and, in the last column, the p-value for the fully identified structure. The restrictions of the CV structure were accepted for all methods, but the p-values were much higher for Fix95 and FlexNom than for the Flex95 and Flex81 methods. The estimated coefficient to the short rate was positive for all methods, though insignificant for Flex95. A similar result was found in Bosker (2006).

We note that the interest coefficient implies a negative short-term interest rate effect on money holdings. A priori this seems surprising as R_s is likely to be strongly correlated with the interest rate on the interest yielding part of money stock. To check this finding, we also report the combined effects of all three relations given by the first row of the $\Pi = \alpha\beta'$ matrix for $r = 3$.[5] Because the CV model is a study of monetary transmission mechanism, we also report the combined effect for the inflation equation. To improve comparability, we have normalized on money (inflation rate) and report the overall adjustment

[5] No restrictions are imposed on α and β in this case.

Table 15.5. Comparison of the estimated long-run structure

	m^r	y^r	Δp	R_s	R_l	p-value
Money demand relation						
Fix95	1.0	−1.32 [−47.25]	—	2.89 [5.82]	—	0.30 [0.99]
Flex95	1.0	−1.34 [−63.39]	—	0.61 [1.61]	—	7.96 [0.09]
Flex81	1.0	−1.45 [−65.21]	—	2.90 [7.29]	—	7.75 [0.10]
FlexNom	1.00 [*NA*]	−1.37 [−59.39]		2.59 [6.66]		3.05 [0.55]
Combined effects: Money equation						$\pi_{m,m}$
Fix95	**1.0**	**−1.34** [−6.45]	1.88 [1.25]	**−4.65** [−4.29]	**5.58** [3.24]	**−0.26** [−6.46]
Flex95	**1.0**	**−1.32** [−6.99]	0.45 [0.41]	**−4.00** [−4.79]	**4.61** [3.50]	**−0.31** [−7.06]
Flex81	**1.0**	**−1.46** [−2.66]	**7.20** [2.31]	**−7.60** [−2.78]	**3.80** [1.05]	**−0.15** [−2.84]
FlexNom	**1.0**	**−1.35** [4.95]	2.50 [−1.42]	**−5.27** [4.02]	**5.82** [−3.16]	**−0.26** [−4.97]
Combined effects: Inflation equation						$\pi_{\Delta p,\Delta p}$
Fix95	−0.01 [−0.14]	0.02 [0.39]	**1.00**	0.10 [0.55]	**−1.05** [−3.60]	**−0.58** [−3.94]
Flex95	−0.04 [−1.11]	0.06 [1.40]	**1.00**	0.24 [1.25]	**−1.22** [−4.01]	**−0.54** [−3.96]
Flex81	−0.00 [−0.13]	0.02 [0.53]	**1.00**	−0.03 [−0.14]	**−0.63** [−2.04]	**−0.59** [−3.85]
FlexNom	0.02 [−0.31]	−0.01 [0.14]	**1.00**	0.09 [−0.35]	**−0.97** [3.06]	**−0.58** [−3.59]

Coefficients with t-values > 2.0 in bold face.

coefficient measured by the diagonal element in the PI-matrix of money (inflation) in the last column of the table.

The combined effects in the money stock equation now suggest that money demand is in fact positively related to the short rate and negatively to the long-term interest rate. The estimated coefficients to the interest rates and the real income seem quite robust, whereas those to the inflation rate less so, in particular for Flex81. The coefficients to the interest rates are similar with opposite sign, suggesting that the interest rate spread, rather than the short rate, is an appropriate measure of the alternative cost of holding money. In addition, money stock is negatively related to the inflation rate, but not very significantly so, except for Flex81.

Altogether, the finding that the demand for M3 is primarily a function of the cost of holding money relative to bonds and real assets seems quite robust in the five aggregation methods and the basic conclusions would remain almost unchanged independently of the aggregation method.

The combined effects of the inflation rate equation are also quite similar between the models: inflation rate is essentially only related to the long-term interest rate in an approximately one to minus one relationship (except for Flex81, where the coefficient is lower); it is not significantly related to excess money, nor to the short-term interest rate.

Altogether, the comparison seems to indicate that the main conclusions are reasonably robust, but that the estimated coefficients vary to some extent. The largest variation was found between the Flex81, the no-PPP base year method, and the other methods.

15.5.4 *The Long-run Impact of Empirical Shocks*

The CV analysis contained a structural VAR analysis which distinguished between two permanent shocks, labelled shocks to monetary policy objective and shocks to aggregate supply, and three transitory shocks, labelled shocks to money demand, aggregate demand, and an interest rate shock. Since the credibility of the labels is difficult to assess without reporting several 5×5 matrices, jeopardizing the comparative aspect of this study, we have followed a slightly different route.

The two major policy goal variables are inflation and income. The CV study (as most structural VAR analyses) is essentially consistent with the following assumptions:

1. an aggregate supply shock, $u_{r,t}$, has no long-run impact on inflation rate;
2. an aggregate demand shock, $u_{n,t}$, has no long-run impact on real income.

The first assumption is the equivalent of saying that the inflation row of the C matrix is an estimator of a nominal shock, ie $u_{n,t} = \iota'_{\Delta p} C \varepsilon_t$, where ι_x is a unit vector picking out the xth variable. The second assumption that the real income row is an estimator of a real shock would then correspond to $u_{r,t} = \iota'_{y^r} C \varepsilon_t$ (Johansen, 2009). Table 15.6 reports these two estimates for each of the four models.

The estimates in the upper part of the table suggest that the stochastic trend in real income was positively associated with empirical shocks to real money stock (all models, but FlexNom less significantly so), negatively with empirical shocks to the short-term and positively to the long-term interest rate (all models except the Flex81 model), and positively, but not very significantly so to empirical shocks to inflation rate (all models except the Flex81 model).

Table 15.6. Comparison of the long-run impact of shocks on inflation and real income

	$\varepsilon(m^r)$	$\varepsilon(y^r)$	$\varepsilon(\Delta p)$	$\varepsilon(R_s)$	$\varepsilon(R_l)$
The real income row in the long-run impact matrix C					
Fix95	**0.51** [2.61]	**1.38** [2.51]	1.66 [1.85]	**−6.03** [−2.29]	**5.92** [2.16]
Flex95	**0.46** [3.14]	0.50 [1.38]	0.78 [1.38]	**−5.80** [−3.29]	**2.74** [1.93]
Flex81	**0.51** [3.83]	**0.69** [2.22]	−0.65 [−1.09]	−0.82 [−0.61]	−1.33 [−0.78]
FlexNom	0.33 [1.74]	0.49 [1.54]	1.00 [1.76]	**−5.71** [−3.34]	2.55 [1.71]
The inflation row in the long-run impact matrix C					
Fix95	0.04 [1.19]	0.08 [0.83]	**0.51** [3.10]	−0.36 [−0.74]	**1.52** [3.01]
Flex95	0.05 [1.76]	0.03 [0.36]	**0.37** [3.14]	−0.48 [−1.30]	**1.41** [4.74]
Flex81	**0.03** [1.90]	0.03 [0.63]	−0.01 [−0.18]	**0.43** [2.30]	0.21 [0.89]
FlexNom	0.02 [0.66]	−0.01 [−0.09]	**0.37** [3.38]	−0.57 [−1.73]	**1.22** [4.25]

Coefficients with a t-value > 1.9 in bold face.

The estimates in the lower half of the table suggest that the stochastic trend in inflation rate was positively associated with the residuals to the long-term interest rate and negatively (though not significantly so) to the short-term interest rate residuals. This was the case for all models except the Flex81 model for which the long-term interest rate residual became insignificant while the short-term interest rate became significantly positive. The residuals to real money and real income do not seem to have any significant effect on the stochastic trend in the inflation rate in all five models.

Altogether, the estimates are fairly similar and the conclusions quite robust for all aggregation models with the exception of the Flex81 model. A tentative conclusion might be that the differentials between the aggregation methods are sufficiently tiny (though persistent) not to significantly change the empirical results. However, the less satisfactory performance of Flex81, suggests that this may hold as long as the base year for the fixed real GDP weights is not too far from a purchasing power parity year.

15.6 Summarizing the Results

This chapter has demonstrated that the flexible real GDP weights proposed by Beyer, Doornik, and Hendry (2001) needed for the aggregation of variables is sensitive to the choice of base year for prices and that the time-series of weights for the individual countries may deviate quite significantly in *absolute* value for different base years while the mean corrected series are likely to be more similar. The chapter shows that this problem disappears altogether when nominal rather than real GDP weights are used.

A comparision of aggregates calculated with fixed and flexible weights methods, showed that the differences between the methods are not large for the aggregates in absolute value but, nevertheless, highly persistent. Thus, the choice of aggregation method might affect the cointegration properties in empirical models. Recalculating the monetary model in Coenen and Vega (2001) for the various aggregation methods tentatively suggests that the effect on the statistical inference in the VAR model is not dramatic. The only exception was for the flexible BDH method in the case when the base year represented a period when purchasing power in the member states deviated very significantly from parity, suggesting that some caution is needed in the choice of base year. But, on the whole, most conclusions remained relatively unchanged. This is more or less in line with the conclusions in Kongsted (2005), and Jørgensen (1998) who studied a similar question.

References

Artis, M. and Beyer, A. (2004). Issues in money demand: The case of Europe. *Journal of Common Market Studies*, **42**, 717–736.

Beyer, A., Doornik, J. and Hendry, D. (2000). Reconstructuring aggregate Euro-zone data. *Journal of Common Market Studies*, **38**(4), 613–624.

———— (2001). Reconstructuring historical Euro-zone data. *Economic Journal*, **111**, 308–327.

Bosker, E. (2006). On the aggregation of Eurozone data. *Economics Letters*, **90**, 260–265.

Coenen, G. and Vega, J-L. (2001). The demand for M3 in the euro area. *Journal of Applied Econometrics*, **16**(6), 727–748.

Dennis, J., Johansen, S. and Juselius, K. (2005). *CATS for RATS: Manual to Cointegration Analysis of Time Series*. Illinois: Estima.

ESA (1995). *European System of National and Regional Accounts*. Luxembourg: Office for Official Publications of the European Communities.

Fagan, G., Henry, J. and Mestre, R. (2005). An area-wide model (AWM) for the euro area. *Economic Modelling*, **22**(1), 39–59.

Jørgensen, C. (1998). A simulation study of tests in the cointegrated VAR model. Ph.D. thesis, Department of Economics, University of Copenhagen.

Johansen, S. (2009). Some identification problems in the cointegrated VAR model. Forthcoming in the *Journal of Econometrics*.

Juselius, K. (2006). *The Cointegrated VAR Model: Methodology and Applications*. Oxford: Oxford University Press.

Kongsted, H. C. (2005). Testing the nominal-to-real transformation. *Journal of Econometrics*, **124**(2), 205–225.

Nielsen, B. and Rahbek, A. (2000). Similarity issues in cointegration analysis. *Oxford Bulletin of Economics and Statistics*, **62**(1), 5–22.

Rogoff, K. (1996). The purchasing power parity puzzle. *Journal of Economic Literature*, **34**, 647–68.

Smets, F. and Wouters, R. (2003). An estimated stochastic dynamic general equilibrium model of the euro area. *Journal of European Economic Association*, **1**(5), 1123–1175.

SNA (1993). System of National Accounts. Brussels/Luxembourg: Commission of the European Communities; Washington, D.C.: International Monetary Fund; Paris: Organisation for Economic Co-operation and Development; New York: United Nations; Washington, D.C.: World Bank.

16

US Natural Rate Dynamics Reconsidered

*Gunnar Bårdsen and Ragnar Nymoen**

16.1 Introduction

There is little doubt that the natural rate of unemployment counts as one of the most successful concepts in the history of macroeconomics. Governments and international organizations customarily refer to the natural rate, or to the related concept of the 'non-accelerating inflation rate of unemployment', NAIRU, calculations in their discussions of employment and inflation prospects,[1] and the existence of a natural rate is also used to rationalize current monetary policy.[2] In the US in particular, the empirical wage Phillips curve provides the operational method for estimation of the natural rate, see Fuhrer (1995), Gordon (1997), and Blanchard and Katz (1999).[3] Thus, the empirical wage Phillips curve is also the basis of the consensus view that the US natural rate of unemployment fell during the last decade of the previous century, see eg, Blanchard (2005, pp. 177–178). In this chapter we analyse the US natural rate from different methodological angles.

The crux of the natural rate hypothesis is that there is only one unemployment rate which can be reconciled with nominal stability of the economy, and that the natural rate equilibrium is asymptotically stable. This leads to several important questions that can only be answered by modelling the rate of unemployment, and thereby its steady state, as a system property. In particular we need to know the economic mechanisms which stabilize the

* The numerical results in the chapter were produced by GiveWin 2 and PcGive 10, see Doornik and Hendry (2001b) and Doornik and Hendry (2001a). This research is supported by The Research Council of Norway. Thanks to Alfred Stiglbauer for giving access to the data set compiled for the OeNB Summer University at the Joint Vienna Institute, 29 August–2 September 2005.

[1] See Elmeskov and MacFarlan (1993), Scarpetta (1996), and OECD (1997, Ch. 1) for examples, and e.g., Bårdsen *et al.* (2005, Ch. 1.3) for discussion of the concepts.

[2] See the discussion in King (1998) for a central banker's views.

[3] In this chapter, the asymptotically stable equilibrium rate of unemployment can correspond to a natural rate, independently of the foreign steady state rate of inflation, or to a NAIRU, which depends on such an inflation rate, see 16.2.1 and 16.2.2, but often we will simply use the term natural rate for brevity.

actual unemployment rate around its mean, and what kind of shocks to the system are likely to change the long-run mean.

We present two models which are often contrasted in the way economists think about the natural rate: the standard North-American model of the natural rate with a wage Phillips curve, PCM, and a model with wage equilibrium correction, WECM. We then show that whether the PCM and the WECM really are the polar cases in terms of natural rate dynamics that for example Blanchard and Katz (1999) make them out to be, depends on the specification of other parts of the macroeconomic model.

At a general level it stands to reason that the degree of mean reversion of the rate of unemployment is system dependent, rather than being strongly conditioned by a small set of restrictions on a single (wage) equation. Other essential features of dynamics, like cointegration and equilibrium correction, are known to be system properties, as stressed by Hendry (1995, Ch. 8.6), and unemployment dynamics can be seen as a special case. From this starting point, we show in section 16.2 that equilibrium correction elsewhere in the model, for example in price setting, implies that the dynamic properties of the PCM and WECM are qualitatively similar, in particular for the rate of unemployment. We refer to this result as *extended equilibrium correction* since it shows that the issue about mean reverting behaviour of the rate of unemployment is just as much a question about equilibrium correction elsewhere in the system as in the wage equation. In section 16.3 these points are illustrated empirically by dynamic simulation of different econometric models of the US rate of unemployment and its determinants.

The econometric test results do not reject the view that extended equilibrium correction is a feature to be reckoned with. We demonstrate that the effect of choosing a Phillips curve equation or an equilibrium correction equation for wages on the natural rate dynamics may have become overstated by the earlier literature. Only if the extended equilibrium correction mechanisms are omitted, which statistical tests indicate that they should not be, does the sharp distinction between the PCM and the WECM come into full play.

In a wider interpretation, the econometric models allow a larger role for aggregate demand than in the standard model of the US natural rate. For example, the results are consistent with the view that persistent demand shocks may affect the rate of unemployment beyond the period of the business cycle. In the light of our empirical results, the comparative stability of the US natural rate is the joint outcome of demand effects and the flexibility of the US labour market. That said, our model includes proxies for institutional developments and regime shifts, ie, changes which also standard theory predicts should have an effect on the equilibrium rate. In section 16.5, we discuss the stability of the natural rate in the period from 1990 to 2004. As noted above, the received view is that the natural rate was significantly reduced in the period. Our results confirm that a reduction may have taken place, but that estimated reduction is smaller than in existing studies. According to the model, unusual low worker bargaining power is one of the explanations for the lower natural rate. Section 16.6 concludes.

16.2 A Stylized Dynamic System

The main variables (in logarithms) in a linearized model of natural rate are the following: wages per hour, denoted w_t, a price level variable, p_t, labour productivity, z_t, and a rate of unemployment, u_t. The PCM and the WECM are consistent with the following two assumptions about the temporal data properties:

A1. Nonstationarity: w_t has a stochastic trend, while $\Delta w_t = w_t - w_{t-1}$ has no trend. Hence $w_t \sim \mathsf{I}(1)$, reading *integrated of degree 1*. Likewise $p_t \sim \mathsf{I}(1)$ and $z_t \sim \mathsf{I}(1)$ as well.

A2. Cointegration: $w_t - p_t - \iota z_t - \mu_w \sim \mathsf{I}(0)$, with $0 \leq \iota \leq 1$, and $u_t - \mu_u \sim \mathsf{I}(0)$, possibly after removal of shifts in the respective means μ_w and μ_u.

The first assumption, A1, is essentially an assumption of local, or stochastic, trends in wages, prices, and productivity variables. Hence, expected growth rate of eg productivity is a constant parameter, while the actual growth rate is stochastic. The alternative assumption would be a global or deterministic trend, which is less appealing on the grounds of realism. A variable trend assumption is tantamount to assuming that the variables become stationary after differentiation, and A1 states that the analysis is based on the premise that it is sufficient to difference w_t, p_t, and z_t once to obtain stationarity.

Economic theory implies cointegration. In A2 above, there are two cointegration relationships. The first asserts the stationarity of the productivity corrected real wage. The second assumption in A2, $u_t - \mu_u \sim \mathsf{I}(0)$, says that the rate of unemployment is stationary with a constant mean. However, in our interpretation, the mean can be conditional on regime shifts which can be represented by either deterministic variables or by strongly exogenous stochastic forcing variables. A2 is also consistent with a 'wage-curve' between the real wage, the rate of unemployment (and productivity), see Blanchflower and Oswald (1994).

Given the assumption that $u_t - \mu_u \sim \mathsf{I}(0)$ after removal of structural breaks, there exists a time-series model of u_t which is asymptotically stable.[4] As pointed out above, the natural rate hypothesis implies only one

[4] Formally, the solution of the linear difference equation of u_t is unique when it has no roots on the unit circle, and the mean of u_t is thus also unique and time independent. Hence

unemployment rate which can be reconciled with nominal stability of the economy, and that the natural rate equilibrium is asymptotically stable. Hence μ_u can be interpreted as the mean of the rate of unemployment, in other words, the equilibrium value which the rate of unemployment returns to asymptotically after a shock. To know the economic mechanisms which stabilize the actual unemployment rate around its mean, and what kind of shocks to the system are likely to change the mean, we therefore model the rate of unemployment, and thereby its mean, as a system property.

The two theories are consistent with a restricted cointegration vector where $\iota = 1$ so that $w_t - p_t - z_t - \mu_w \sim \mathrm{I}(0)$. A stylized model which encompasses both theories is:

$$\Delta w_t = \beta_{w0} - \beta_{w1} u_t + \beta_{w2} \Delta z_t + \beta_{w3} \Delta p_t - \underset{<1}{\theta_w} (w - p - z)_{t-1} + \varepsilon_{w,t}, \quad (16.1)$$

$$u_t = \beta_{u0} + \underset{<1}{\beta_{u1}} u_{t-1} + \underset{\geq 0}{\beta_{u2}} (w - p - z)_{t-1} - \beta_{u3} x_{u,t} + \varepsilon_{u,t}, \quad (16.2)$$

$$\Delta p_t = \zeta (\Delta w_t - \Delta z_t) + (1 - \zeta) \Delta pi_t + \varepsilon_{p,t}, \quad (16.3)$$

$$\Delta z_t = g_z + \varepsilon_{z,t}, \quad (16.4)$$

$$\Delta pi_t = g_{pi} + \varepsilon_{pi,t}, \quad (16.5)$$

where imported price growth Δpi_t is in terms of domestic currency. With $\theta_w = 0$, equation (16.1) is the wage Phillips curve which is typically found to represent the relationship between aggregate (annual) wage inflation, and unemployment in the US, see for example Blanchard and Katz (1999). The role of inflation in the wage setting process is an important issue. Often Δp_t is replaced by expected inflation, Δp_t^e or Δp_{t+1}^e, which are in turn approximated by, or instrumented by Δp_{t-1}, but the simultaneous equations specification in (16.1) is convenient for our purpose. Δz_t represents a possible effect of labour productivity on wage growth. $\varepsilon_{w,t}$ denotes a disturbance term, which is assumed to be normally distributed with a constant standard deviation, and (for simplicity) also uncorrelated with the other disturbances of the model ($\varepsilon_{u,t}$, $\varepsilon_{p,t}$, $\varepsilon_{z,t}$, and $\varepsilon_{pi,t}$).

Wage bargaining models imply equilibrating mechanism whereby wages are directly influenced by profits, see Forslund *et al.* (2008), in addition to the indirect channel through the unemployment rate. This implies $0 < \theta_w < 1$ and $\beta_{w1} > 0$ in (16.1).[5] Equilibrium correction models for wages and prices have a long history in econometrics. Sargan (1964, 1980) coined the term, and saw the formulation as an extension of the original Phillips curve. Later, it has

the model of (linear) hysteresis of Blanchard and Summers (1986) is inconsistent with A1 and A2.

[5] We abstract from negative (but stable) values of θ_w with reference to nominal wage rigidity.

been established that there is also a close correspondence between modelling wages in terms of cointegration and equilibrium correction, and a theoretical framework of the wage bargaining type, see Nymoen (1989, 1991) and Bårdsen *et al.* (2005, Chs. 4–6).

The rate of unemployment is modelled in (16.2) as rising when real wages are high relative to productivity, corresponding to standard microeconomic predictions of firm behaviour. The 'catch-all' variable $x_{u,t}$ represents (a vector) of other factors than wages which affect the rate of unemployment. It might contain conventional demand side variables (foreign demand, changes in the domestic savings rate, and policy instruments), but also shocks that affect the supply of labour at the going real wage (for example demographic changes).

The three last equations of the PCM are even more stylized than the first two. Equation (16.3) gives price inflation as determined by the growth rate of domestic unit labour costs and of import prices (in dollars). Equations (16.4) and (16.5) specify productivity and import prices as random walks with expected growth rates g_z and g_{pi}. Imported price growth Δpi_t is in terms of domestic currency and the formulation in (16.5) is consistent with assuming that there is no pricing-to-market.

16.2.1 *Phillips Curve Dynamics*

The PCM is defined by setting $\theta_w = 0$, thus omitting wage equilibrium correction. Nevertheless, the PCM is an equilibrium correction system. To clarify the implication of this, use equation (16.3) to substitute out the Δp_t term in the wage PCM, giving a semi-reduced form equation for wage growth:

$$\Delta w_t = b_{w0} - b_{w1} u_t + b_{w2} \Delta z_t + b_{w4} \Delta pi_t + \varepsilon'_{w,t}, \tag{16.6}$$

where $b_{w1} = \beta_{w1}/(1 - \beta_{w3}\zeta)$, $b_{w2} = (\beta_{w2} - \beta_{w3}\zeta)/(1 - \beta_{w3}\zeta)$, and $b_{w4} = \beta_{w3}(1 - \zeta)/(1 - \beta_{w3}\zeta)$. Next, substitute u_t in (16.6) by the right hand side of equation (16.2), and note that the equilibrium correction coefficient of the lagged wage level term in the Δw_t equation becomes $-\beta'_{w1}\beta_{u2}$. Hence, as long as the PCM *system* displays both an effect from unemployment on wage growth, $-\beta_{w1} < 0$, *and* an effect of the wage level on unemployment, $\beta_{u2} > 0$, the dynamics of wages and unemployment are of the equilibrium correction type. Since equilibrium correction implies cointegration, and since cointegration corresponds to dynamic stability, it follows that a sufficient condition for dynamic stability is that $-\beta_{w1} < 0$ and $\beta_{u2} > 0$ hold *jointly*.

Formal dynamic analysis of (16.1)–(16.5) confirms that, subject to $\theta_w = 0$, $-\beta_{w1} < 0$ and $\beta_{u2} > 0$ the PCM system has two stable roots and three unit roots. The unit roots represent the I(1)-ness of the price level index p_t, productivity z_t, and the import price index, pi_t. Consistent with A2, the two equilibrium values, corresponding to the means of the wage-share and unemployment are given by

$$\mu_{u,PCM} = \frac{\beta_{w0}}{\beta_{w1}} + \frac{(\beta_{w2}-1)}{\beta_{w1}}g_z + \frac{(\beta_{w3}-1)}{\beta_{w1}}g_{pi}, \text{and} \qquad (16.7)$$

$$\mu_{w,PCM} = -\frac{\beta_{u0}}{\beta_{u2}} + \frac{(1-\beta_{u1})}{\beta_{u2}}\mu_u + \frac{\beta_{u3}}{\beta_{u2}}x_u, \qquad (16.8)$$

where we have added the PCM acronym to the subscript of the two means. The case of the vertical long-run Phillips curve is represented by $\beta_{w3} = 1$, and implies that $\mu_{u,PCM}$ is independent of inflation, ie, the usual implication of dynamic homogeneity of the wage Phillips curve. With $\beta_{w3} = 1$ imposed, the steady state unemployment rate coincides with the expression for the natural rate of unemployment that most economists would write down when asked.

It remains one of the great appeals of the PCM that the NAIRU, $\mu_{u,PCM}$ only depends on the parameters of one of the equations of the system. Estimation of a wage (or price) Phillips curve is the dominant strategy for estimation of the natural rate, and Staiger *et al.* (1997) is an important contribution.[6] However, the standard approach does not address another important question: whether the estimated natural rate corresponds to an asymptotically stable equilibrium, see Bårdsen *et al.* (2005, Ch. 4.2).

16.2.2 *Wage Equilibrium Correction Dynamics*

Wage equilibrium correction, $0 < \theta_w < 1$ represents an adjustment mechanism which stabilizes wages at any given rate of unemployment. The two equilibrating mechanisms supporting the cointegration properties of $w_t - p_t - z_t - \mu_w \sim \mathsf{I}(0)$ and $u_t - \mu_u \sim \mathsf{I}(0)$ mean that the speed of adjustment will be faster in the case of the WECM than in the PCM case. Hence, if the PCM system is dynamically stable, then the WECM system is also stable, *a fortiori*. Another difference from the PCM is that the natural rate is a genuine system property in WECM—it can no longer be retrieved from the wage equation alone. Solving for the steady-state rate of unemployment gives

$$\mu_{u,WECM} = \frac{\theta_w\{\beta_{uo} + \beta_{u3}x_u\} + \beta_{u2}\{\beta_{w0} + (\beta_{w2}-1)g_z + (\beta_{w3}-1)g_{pi}\}}{\theta_w(1-\beta_{u1}) + \beta_{w1}\beta_{u2}}. \qquad (16.9)$$

Note that a permanent change in the exogenous variable x_u (a shock which does not disappear) has an impact on the equilibrium rate of unemployment in this model, while it does not affect the PCM natural rate. Dynamic

[6] Blanchard and Katz (1997) review the standard model of the natural rate in the following way (p. 60): 'U.S. macroeconometric models ... determine the natural rate through two equations, a "price equation" ... and a "wage equation".' The 'wage equation' specified in Blanchard and Katz is identical to our equation (16.1), albeit without the productivity term, and the 'price equation' is the same as (16.3) but without the productivity and import price terms.

homogeneity, $\beta_3 = 1$, also in the WECM case removes imported inflation g_{pi} from the expression of the steady state rate of unemployment. The implication that permanent changes on the 'demand side' of the economy (in a parameter like β_{uo} or in the variable x_u) affects steady-state employment is robust to the dynamic homogeneity restriction though.

The appearance of the labour demand shift variable x_u in the WECM equilibrium unemployment rate fits the idea that relatively permanent changes in unemployment might be due to structural breaks that occur intermittently, in line with our maintained view of the rate of unemployment as I(0) but subject to (infrequent) structural breaks. The PCM, while not inconsistent with this view, nevertheless would attribute the mean-shifting capability only to those structural changes which occur distinctly on the supply side (through shifts in the Phillips curve intercept β_{w0}). The difference between the PCM and WECM is thus one of degree, not of principle. The WECM might be said to allow the longer list of candidates for regime shifts—from different sectors of the macro economy. For example, if we associate the equations for wage, prices, and productivity with the supply side of the macroeconomy and (16.2) with the demand side, then (16.9) allows permanent demand shocks to affect the equilibrium rate through x_u.

16.2.3 *Extended Equilibrium Correction Dynamics*

Both the PCM and the WECM are equilibrium correction models of the natural rate. The difference is that the PCM implies a more restrictive stabilization process than the WECM. In the PCM, equilibrium correction takes place in the unemployment equation alone. The WECM has an additional stabilization mechanism in the wage equation itself. Moreover, the PCM is a special case of the WECM, and $\theta_w = 0$ implies, $\mu_{u,WECM} = \mu_{u,PCM}$.

In the two models, the price setting equation has been kept deliberately simple, in so-called differenced form. As pointed out by Hendry *et al.* (1984), an equation in differenced form implies that the variable in question, the price level in our case, is always on its steady-state trajectory. This is unrealistic, goes against theory (eg, Blanchard 1987), and is an unnecessary constraint on an empirical model. Modern models of the wage–price inflation spiral instead model *both* wage and price inflation as influenced by past equilibria, see eg, Nymoen (1991). We refer to such models as systems with extended equilibrium correction dynamics relative to the standard PCM and WECM models above.

Bårdsen and Nymoen (2003) show that extended equilibrium correction generally makes the wage–price process become dynamically stable also in the theoretical case where the rate of unemployment is exogenous and fixed.[7]

[7] See also the analysis of the conditional wage–price system in Bårdsen *et al.* (2005, Ch. 6.4).

As a corollary, we now state that if there is equilibrium correction in price setting and/or productivity, the restriction $\theta_w = 0$ no longer guarantees that the dynamic system has the properties of the PCM. Hence, even if there is a wage Phillips curve in the system, the expression for the natural rate of unemployment in (16.7) may not correspond to the true steady state implied by the extended equilibrium correction system. The presence of equilibrium correction in price setting is due to mark-up pricing, while efficiency wage theory predicts that worker productivity depends on real wages, see Stiglitz (1986), which can give rise to a lagged wage share term in a dynamic representation.[8] At the system level, extended equilibrium correction adds extra stability to the rate of unemployment. In other words, with extended equilibrium correction, the natural rate is no longer determined by the parameters of the wage Phillips curve alone.

Extended equilibrium correction dynamics in wage- and price-setting models has a realistic ring to it, and the surveys of the literature in Kolsrud and Nymoen (1998) and Bårdsen and Nymoen (2003) indicate that there may have been an over-emphasis on the differences in wage dynamics. Specifically, even if there is a well defined empirical wage Phillips curve in the US, it does not imply that $\mu_{u,PCM}$ defined by that Phillips curve is a relevant parameter for the US natural rate of unemployment. This is because there may be equilibrium correction elsewhere in the wage–price–productivity system which dominate the wage Phillips curve, so that the implied mean of the rate of unemployment becomes a system property, more in line with $\mu_{u,WECM}$ above.

In the next section, where we consider an empirical PCM for the US economy, we will see an instance of how price setting equilibrium correction influences the behaviour of the system—and the rate of unemployment in particular.

16.3 Inflation–Unemployment Dynamics in the US

In this section we specify econometric models with different equations for wage dynamics, and investigate their impact on natural rate dynamics. Based on the discussion above, we expect to find that the specification of the wage equation has a large impact on the natural rate and its dynamics if there is little equilibrium correction elsewhere in the completing macroeconomic model. Conversely, with extended equilibrium correction in the system as a whole, the consequences of choosing between a Phillips curve and a wage equilibrium correction model are less important.

[8] Stiglitz (1986) lists five different theories for the relationship between wages and productivity.

16.3.1 *Data and Empirical Framework*

Our operational measure of the rate of unemployment is the civilian unemployment rate, which is the commonly used unemployment variable in wage studies. The operational measure of the wage variable is the hourly manufacturing compensation rate, w_t, and productivity is defined as value added per hour worked, and is denoted z_t, see the Appendix for details. In parallel to the theoretical model, we also include an import price index in the data set, it is denoted pi_t. The theoretical section abstracted from the difference between 'consumer' and 'producer' prices. In the empirical model we include both a consumer price index, p_t, and a deflator of manufacturing value added, q_t. This affects the econometric specification of the two hypotheses of wage setting.

The Phillips curve model (PCM). In this case, the hypothesis A2 carries over directly, but notably for the producer real wage. Hence $w_t - q_t - z_t - \mu_w \sim \text{I}(0)$, which is the same as claiming that the wage share is stationary; and $u_t - \mu_u \sim \text{I}(0)$. The implied equilibrium correction dynamics is that Δw_t adjusts with respect to $u_{t-1} - \mu_u$, and that Δu_t adjusts with respect to $w_{t-1} - q_{t-1} - z_{t-1} - \mu_w$.

The wage equilibrium model (WECM). Workers' utility is linked to the consumer real wage, $w_t - p_t$, while firms care about the producer real wage, $w_t - q_t$. Theory nevertheless implies that, as long as unions have a strong bargaining power, the settled nominal wage will mainly reflect q_t and z_t. Empirical tests on data from the Scandinavian small open economies lend support to this view. For the US case, where unions are different in character and bargaining is more fragmented, a better hypothesis may be that the productivity corrected *consumer real wage* is stationary, hence $w_t - p_t - \iota z_t - \mu_w \sim \text{I}(0)$, with $0 \leq \iota < 1$. The idea is that rather weak and uncoordinated unions manage to achieve a degree of compensation for increases in costs of living, but that workers only manage to extract a fraction of the productivity gains. Also in this case $u_t - \mu_u \sim \text{I}(0)$, and in the equilibrium correction model, Δu_t adjusts with respect to $w_{t-1} - q_{t-1} - z_{t-1} - \mu_w$, but wage setting is different from the PCM case and Δw_t is assumed to adjust with respect to $w_{t-1} - p_{t-1} - \iota z_{t-1} - \mu_w$.

The empirical wage Phillips curve is well established on US data, so we start with this model. We first test the two PCM cointegration propositions, ie, $w_t - q_t - z_t - \mu_w \sim \text{I}(0)$ and $u_t - \mu_u \sim \text{I}(0)$, and as a second step we specify a simultaneous equations model using the PCM equilibrium correcting mechanism as identifying restrictions. The methodology is discussed in detail in Bårdsen *et al.* (2005, Chs. 4–6).

16.3.2 *An Empirical PCM*

Given the assumption of I(1)-ness of wages, prices, and productivity, logical consistency of the Phillips curve model of the natural rate requires that wages, producer prices, and productivity are cointegrated. In this subsection we first show that cointegration is supported by formal tests, and second estimate a dynamic model which is an extension of the standard model of section 16.2.1.

16.3.2.1 COINTEGRATION ANALYSIS

To test the null hypotheses of no cointegration, ie, $w_t - q_t - z_t - \mu_w \sim \mathsf{I}(1)$ and $u_t - \mu_u \sim \mathsf{I}(1)$ we estimate a 2nd order VAR for the three endogenous variables w_t, q_t, and u_t. The test is conditional on productivity, z_t.[9] The sample period is 1962–2004. Formally, the Johansen (1995) approach to cointegration analysis suggests one or two cointegrating vectors. Our interpretation of this result is that $w_t - q_t - z_t - \mu_w \sim \mathsf{I}(0)$ holds strongly in the data, while $u_t - \mu_u \sim \mathsf{I}(0)$ is a weaker empirical cointegrating relationship. On this basis the cointegration rank is set to 2, and we proceed to test the 4 implied over-identifying restrictions. The likelihood ratio test statistic is $\chi^2(4) = 5.75$, with a p-value of 0.22 showing that the PCM restrictions on the cointegrating vectors are statistically acceptable.

These conclusions are supported by Dickey–Fuller tests. For the rate of unemployment in particular, a 2nd order Dickey–Fuller regression, augmented by three dummies for structural breaks (namely ken_t, $oil_{1,t}$, and pow_t which are explained below) is a statistically adequate model for inference, following the principles of Andreou and Spanos (2003). The Dickey–Fuller statistics of this model, calculated sequentially over the period from 1975–2004 are never lower (in absolute value) than 2.5 and the average of the sequence is much higher. The end of sample value is 4.7. Although the exact critical value is unknown in this case (because of the inclusion of dummies), these values of the Dickey–Fuller statistic are highly suggestive that a formal test would reject the null hypothesis of a unit root.[10] The estimated mean μ_u is also stable, using the 1961–1975 sample we obtain $\exp(\hat{\mu}_u) = 5.3\%$, and using the full sample 1962–2004 the estimated mean of the unemployment rate is $\exp(\hat{\mu}_u) = 5.6\%$. Hence, both the VAR cointegrating analysis and the Dickey–Fuller tests corroborate the validity of the modelling assumptions of $w_t - q_t - z_t - \mu_w \sim \mathsf{I}(0)$ and $u_t - \mu_u \sim \mathsf{I}(0)$ stated in section 16.2.

16.3.2.2 ECONOMETRIC PCM MODEL

The next stage is to specify and estimate a PCM, with the lagged wage share and the lagged unemployment rate included as equilibrium correction terms. At this point in the analysis, we first estimate an unrestricted equilibrium correction model, which we dub p-ecm and second we attempt to encompass

[9] The weak exogeneity of z_t may not hold in the data (in fact this would be an example of extended equilibrium correction), and in that case we lose statistical efficiency but this must be balanced against the gain in degrees of freedom.

[10] Already, Perron (1989) showed that the inclusion or omission of dummy variables is important for the outcome of unit root tests.

the unrestricted system by an econometric model which has a wage Phillips curve as its core. This empirical model is an extension of the stylized model in equations (16.1)–(16.5) above. The notable extensions of the theoretical model are:

1. Two price indices: Since there are two domestic price indices, the econometric PCM contains equations for both Δq_t (producer prices) and Δp_t (consumption price index).
2. Extended equilibrium correction: The cointegration analysis of the system made up of w_t, q_t, and u_t shows evidence of equilibrium correction of q_t with respect to the wage-share, so we expect to find such a relationship also in the simultaneous equations model. Moreover, since p_t was not included in the VAR, equilibrium correction behaviour in Δp_t may yet be revealed at this stage. Hence, the relationship in differences (16.3) in the standard PCM, is replaced by two equilibrium correction equations for Δq_t and Δp_t. Finally, and as noted above, equilibrium correction may affect Δz_t as well, in which case the random walk equation (16.4) in the standard model is replaced by an equation in equilibrium correction form.
3. Structural breaks: Variables representing shocks and intermittent structural breaks are included. First, we include a dummy (*ken*) which captures the Kennedy–Johnson administration policy to reduce unemployment. Second, there are two oil-price dummies, for 1974 and 1980 ($oil_{1,t}$ and $oil_{2,t}$) and in addition the annual rate of change of the oil price itself ($\Delta poil_t$) is an explanatory variable in the model. Third, a dummy representing periods of unusually high/low productivity growth, the 1990s in particular ($prod_t$). Fourth, a dummy (pow_t) representing the hypothesis that worker's ability to take benefit of the industrial prosperity was significantly lower in the 1990s than in earlier US booms. This hypothesis has been influential, also in the policy process. For example, Pollin (2002) argues that in the mid 1990s, the leadership of the Federal Reserve was convinced that the decline in bargaining power was a prime cause of the surprisingly low inflationary pressure.[11]

The p-ecm column of Table 16.1 shows the estimated standard errors (denoted $\hat{\sigma}_{\Delta_w}$, $\hat{\sigma}_{\Delta_u}$, $\hat{\sigma}_{\Delta_p}$, $\hat{\sigma}_{\Delta_q}$, $\hat{\sigma}_{\Delta_z}$) of the 5 endogenous variables in the unrestricted equilibrium correction model. Below the estimated residual standard errors of each variable, the table shows two diagnostic tests based on the residual vector, for 1st order residual autocorrelation ($\mathsf{F}_{\mathsf{AR}(1-1)}$), and departure from normality ($\chi^2_{\mathsf{normality}}$). The tests are vector versions of the well known single equation

[11] See for example (Greenspan), http://www.bog.frb.us.boarddocs/hh/1997/July/Testimony.htm, and (Yellen, then member of the Fed Board of Governors), http://www.federalreserve.gov/FOCM/Transcripts/1996/19960294Meeting.pdf, p21.

Table 16.1. Diagnostics for VAR and identified econometric models

	p-ecm	gen-ecm	Table 16.2 Identified PCM	Table 16.3 Identified WECM
$\hat{\sigma}_{\Delta w}$	0.78%	0.79%	0.59%	0.56%
$\hat{\sigma}_{\Delta u}$	8.64%	8.80%	8.14%	8.12%
$\hat{\sigma}_{\Delta p}$	0.67%	0.61%	0.62%	0.61%
$\hat{\sigma}_{\Delta z}$	1.17%	1.12%	1.15%	1.13%
$\hat{\sigma}_{\Delta q}$	1.70%	1.68%	2.28%	2.29%
$F_{AR(1-1)}$	0.72[0.81]	0.87[0.64]	0.87[0.65]	1.16[0.30]
$\chi^2_{normality}$	14.57[0.15]	20.62[0.02]	10.846[0.37]	22.5[0.01]
$\chi^2_{enc,p-ecm}$			50.316[0.38] 48 restrictions	
$\chi^2_{enc,gen-ecm}$			82.11[0.006] 53 restrictions	60.76[0.22] 53 restrictions

The numbers in [ ] are p-values. The sample is 1962–2004.

diagnostics, see Doornik and Hendry (2001a). The respective p-values are in brackets, and clearly we can proceed on the basis that the disturbances are normally distributed, and test relevant restrictions on the p-ecm, with the aim of obtaining an identified simultaneous equations PCM model.

The column labelled Table 16.2 shows diagnostics for the identified PCM, consisting of the estimated equations shown in Table 16.2 below. The model, estimated by FIML, corresponds to a set of restrictions on the p-ecm. Without any restrictions the model structure is unidentified, but the model in Table 16.2 is over-identified, and we are particularly interested in whether this model is a valid parsimonious representation of the p-ecm—ie, whether it is an encompassing model. A natural test statistic is the likelihood ratio test of the over-identifying restrictions, see Hendry *et al.* (1988). This test statistic is denoted $\chi^2_{enc,p-ecm}$ in Table 16.1, and it shows that the 48 restrictions separating the unrestricted system from the identified PCM are jointly statistically acceptable, with a rather high p-value (columns 3 and 5 of Table 16.1 are relevant for the discussion of the bargaining model below).

The first equation is the wage Phillips curve. Augmentation is in terms of consumer price growth Δp_t, producer price growth Δq_t, and productivity in the form of the two year growth rate $\Delta_2 z_t$. The latter variable is consistent with the idea that it is the persistent productivity changes that lead to increased wage growth.[12] Note that the vertical long run Phillips curve restriction is imposed, ie, the coefficients of Δp_t and Δq_t sum to unity. Both the change in unemployment and the lagged rate u_{t-2} are significant at conventional levels of significance.

[12] Staiger *et al.* (2002) report that without inclusion of productivity growth, their estimated real wage Phillips curve equations have unstable parameters. Our model is consistent with this observation.

Table 16.2. The econometric PCM

$$\begin{aligned}
\Delta w_t = {} & \underset{(0.0083)}{0.0229} + \underset{(0.0891)}{0.8855}\,\Delta p_t + \underset{(--)}{0.1145}\,\Delta q_t + \underset{(0.0408)}{0.3238}\,\Delta_2 z_t - \underset{(0.00859)}{0.02818}\,\Delta u_t - \underset{(0.00409)}{0.01731}\,u_{t-2} \\
& - \underset{(0.00236)}{0.01188}\,\Delta^2 poil_t + \underset{(0.00689)}{0.0237}\,oil_{2,t} + \underset{(0.00286)}{0.0129}\,pow_t \\
\Delta u_t = {} & \underset{(2.25)}{9.17} + \underset{(0.407)}{1.572}\,(w-q-z)_{t-1} - \underset{(0.0712)}{0.3565}\,u_{t-1} + \underset{(0.666)}{3.331}\,\Delta p_{t-1} + \underset{(0.12)}{0.2097}\,(p-pi)_{t-1} \\
& - \underset{(0.0426)}{0.1764}\,ken_t \\
\Delta p_t = {} & \underset{(0.0108)}{0.02507} + \underset{(0.0636)}{0.6097}\,\Delta p_{t-1} + \underset{(0.0205)}{0.152}\,\Delta pi_t + \underset{(0.00523)}{0.01938}\,\Delta poil_t - \underset{(0.0102)}{0.02385}\,(p-pi)_{t-1} \\
& - \underset{(0.00777)}{0.01907}\,\Delta u_{t-1} - \underset{(0.00572)}{0.009358}\,u_{t-1} - \underset{(0.00755)}{0.02462}\,oil_{1,t} \\
\Delta z_t = {} & \underset{(0.283)}{0.6106} + \underset{(0.0515)}{0.1113}\,(w-q-z)_{t-1} + \underset{(0.00921)}{0.04003}\,\Delta u_{t-1} + \underset{(0.00745)}{0.02039}\,u_{t-2} + \underset{(0.0102)}{0.04525}\,(p-pi)_{t-1} \\
& + \underset{(0.00293)}{0.0123}\,prod_t \\
\Delta q_t = {} & \underset{(0.54)}{1.089} + \underset{(0.0403)}{0.9744}\,\Delta(w-z)_t + \underset{(0.0982)}{0.1975}\,(w-q-z)_{t-1} + \underset{(---)}{0.02562}\,\Delta pi_t - \underset{(0.0169)}{0.06179}\,oil_{2,t}
\end{aligned}$$

Notes: The sample is 1962 to 2004. Estimation is by FIML.
Standard errors are in parentheses below the parameter estimates.
See Table 16.1 for residual standard errors, diagnostic tests, and encompassing tests.

In addition to the conventional augmentation, the Phillips curve specification contains three variables representing the effects on wages of stochastic shocks and structural breaks: The stochastic shock is the double difference in oil prices, showing that oil price shocks wage growth. The OPEC-II oil price hike was of course special, and the positive and significant coefficient of $oil_{2,t}$ shows that there was a one-off compensation for that event. Finally, the estimation results confirm the hypothesis of low worker ability to push for higher wages in the 1990s: pow_t is a significant explanatory variable, and it is zero or negative for most of the last decade of the previous century—see the Appendix.

The second equation in Table 16.1 shows the empirical counterpart of equation (16.2) in the theoretical model. The lagged wage share $\beta_{u2}(w-q-z)_{t-1}$ appears strongly in the estimated equation with a coefficient of 1.57 for β_{u2}. The effect of the lagged unemployment rate is important for the stability of the system, and the fact that the coefficient corresponding to β_{u1} in equation (16.2) is found to be precisely estimated (with a value of –0.36) is thus corroborating the cointegration results in support of $u_t - \mu_u \sim \mathrm{I}(0)$ and $w_t - q_t - z_t - \mu_w \sim \mathrm{I}(0)$.

In addition to the crucial significance of $(w-q-z)_{t-1}$ in the unemployment equation, we identify a positive effect of the rate of lagged inflation, Δp_{t-1}, which we interpret as an effect of economic policy: higher inflation typically leads to a tightening of monetary policy and the rate of unemployment of course represents an important transmission mechanism. It is perhaps more surprising that we also estimate a positive effect of the lagged real exchange rate $(p - pi)_{t-1}$. Hence, despite the vastness of the domestic US economy, its rate of unemployment does not appear to be completely sheltered from sustained loss of international competitiveness.

In the theoretical PCM model, the third equation is a 'consumer price equation' cast in differenced form, as explained above. In Table 16.2 there is a separate equilibrium correction model for Δp_t. It would represent a price Phillips curve if it was not for the inclusion of $(p - pi)_{t-1}$ albeit with a small coefficient (below, we will present robustness tests of its impact on the dynamic behaviour of the system). This is the first encounter of extended equilibrium correction dynamics.

There is evidence of other extensions of equilibrium correction in the two last equations of the model. Productivity Δz_t equilibrium corrects to the lagged wage share, corresponding to predictions from efficiency wage theories (it was assumed exogenous in the theoretical PCM model (16.1)–(16.5)), and it also depends on the lagged change and rate of unemployment. The last equation in Table 16.2 shows the estimated manufacturing producer price equation. As can be seen from the specification, Δq_t is simultaneously determined with Δw_t through the change in unit labour costs. There is a small effect of the change in import prices as well, but a quite large equilibrium correction coefficient with respect to the lagged wage share.

In sum, the empirical PCM contains the kind of extended equilibrium correction which, according to the analysis in section 16.2, may cause natural rate dynamics to behave significantly differently from the conventional Phillips curve dynamics. In section 16.4 we illustrate the dynamics of the empirical PCM by dynamic simulation. Before that, we consider whether an alternative to the wage Phillips curve can be formulated on this data set.

16.3.3 *An Empirical WECM*

The previous sections showed that the two hypotheses of $w_t - q_t - z_t - \mu_w \sim \mathrm{I}(0)$ and $u_t - \mu_u \sim \mathrm{I}(0)$ are supported by cointegration analysis, and that a corresponding dynamic PCM with desirable statistical properties—for example encompassing the p-ecm—can be specified. Moreover, adding $(w - q - z - \mu_w)_{t-1}$ to the wage Phillips curve gives an insignificant coefficient (the 't-value' is 0.01). These findings are quite different from results on for example Scandinavian data, where the lagged wage share is typically found to be a significant equilibrium correction term in manufacturing sector wage equations, see e.g., Nymoen and Rødseth (2003).[13]

[13] In Bårdsen *et al.* (1998), the equilibrium correction framework is used to explain aggregate wage and price setting in Norway and the United Kingdom, with comparable and similar results for the two economies.

However, as explained in section 16.3.1, there are other possible equilibrium correction specifications to consider. For example with weak and poorly organized unions, wages may be set by firms in the light of the reference wage ($\bar{w}_t$) and worker's probability of getting a job elsewhere. The job probability can be approximated by the unemployment rate, while at the aggregate level $\bar{w}_t$ is probably linked to the general price level of the economy and to productivity. Hence we have the following alternative to $(w - q - z - \mu_w)_{t-1}$ as a predictor of Δw_t in an economy dominated by wage setting at the individual level or with weak unions:

$$w_t - p_t - \iota z_t - \lambda u_t - \mu_{wp} \sim \mathsf{I}(0), 0 \leq \iota < 1, \lambda \geq 0, \tag{16.10}$$

which can be viewed as a linear combination of the two I(0) variables $w_t - p_t - \iota z_t \sim \mathsf{I}(0)$ and $u_t \sim \mathsf{I}(0)$.

Analysis of a VAR consisting of w_t, p_t, and z_t, keeping u_t as non-modelled, does not yield very strong results, but setting $\iota = 0.2$ and $\lambda = 0.1$ gives an equilibrium correction variable which at least has some stationary traits. Importantly, when the equilibrium correction variable is added to the unrestricted equilibrium correction system, to form a generalized unrestricted reduced form, gen-ecm, the PCM of Table 16.2 is no longer an encompassing model: the p-value of the encompassing test falls from 0.38 to 0.006, cf. the entry for $\chi^2_{\text{enc,gen-ecm}}$ in the bottom row of Table 16.1. Hence, there is need for a different structural model to account for the force of $w_{t-1} - p_{t-1} - 0.2z_{t-1} + 0.1u_{t-1}$ in gen-ecm.

In terms of specification, the only difference between the econometric PCM and WECM is the wage equation. But in order to check how the point estimates of the coefficients of other equations in Table 16.2 are affected, all 5 of the WECM equations are reported in Table 16.3. The equilibrium correction wage equation includes $(w - p - 0.2z + 0.1u)_{t-1}$, and although the equilibrium correction coefficient is quite small numerically, its 't-value' is still significant (−5.9).

The coefficients of the other explanatory variables in the wage equation change very little compared to the PCM case, which indicates that the equilibrium correction term is relatively orthogonal with respect to the variables of the Phillips curve. The coefficient of the bargaining power dummy is an exception. The estimated coefficient halved, probably because the equilibrium correction term itself is related to bargaining power.[14] With the wage equation in place, the econometric WECM easily encompasses the gen-ecm, as shown by the value of $\chi^2_{\text{enc,gen-ecm}}$ in the right column of Table 16.1. Direct inspection of the other structural equations confirms that their estimated coefficients

[14] The other main difference between the two wage equations is the presence of $\Delta^2 u_t$ in the WECM, but that difference is due to the specification of the error correction term, with u_{t-1} rather than u_{t-2} as Table 16.2 would suggest.

change very little compared to the PCM case, hence any differences in the dynamic behaviour of the two models can be directly related to the different specifications of the wage equations.

16.4 Natural Rate Dynamics

The last section discussed two dynamic models of the US natural rate. The only difference between the two models is the specification of the wage equation. It is a wage Phillips curve in the PCM in Table 16.2, and an equilibrium correction wage equation in the model in Table 16.3. According to a view shared by most economists, this difference is essential and should have important implications for the dynamics of the equilibrium wage, see Blanchard and Katz (1999).

However, we have hypothesized that extended equilibrium correction may come to dominate unemployment dynamics even though the structural wage equation is a Phillips curve. In this section we illustrate the empirical relevance of these ideas using the estimation results of the previous section.

The PCM and WECM solutions for wage growth and unemployment are easily found by dynamic simulation of the two models in Table 16.2 (PCM) and Table 16.3 (WECM). Figure 16.1, panel (a) and (b) show the solution for Δw_t and u_t in the WECM. The model's solution is seen to fit the data rather well. For Δw_t some of the good fit at the end of the period is of course due to inclusion of the two dummies: pow_t because it is an explanatory variable in the wage equation itself, and $prod_t$ because that dummy helps keep the

Table 16.3. The econometric model with a wage equilibrium correction equation, WECM

$$\begin{aligned}
\Delta w_t = & -\underset{(0.0199)}{0.1198} + \underset{(0.0665)}{0.8053}\,\Delta p_t + \underset{(--)}{0.1947}\,\Delta q_t + \underset{(0.0338)}{0.2955}\,\Delta_2 z_t - \underset{(0.0017)}{0.0094}\,\Delta^2 poil_t \\
& + \underset{(0.00607)}{0.02627}\,oil_{2,t} + \underset{(0.00219)}{0.006145}\,pow_t - \underset{(0.0048)}{0.02229}\,\Delta^2 u_t - \underset{(0.012)}{0.0712}\,(w - p - 0.2z + 0.1u)_{t-1} \\[1ex]
\Delta u_t = & \underset{(2.23)}{8.951} - \underset{(0.0429)}{0.1721}\,ken_t - \underset{(0.072)}{0.3456}\,u_{t-1} + \underset{(0.673)}{3.369}\,\Delta p_{t-1} + \underset{(0.404)}{1.537}\,(w - q - z)_{t-1} \\
& + \underset{(0.121)}{0.2097}\,(p - pi)_{t-1} \\[1ex]
\Delta p_t = & \underset{(0.0106)}{0.02443} + \underset{(0.0637)}{0.6231}\,\Delta p_{t-1} + \underset{(0.0211)}{0.1594}\,\Delta pi_t + \underset{(0.00533)}{0.0177}\,\Delta poil_t - \underset{(0.0103)}{0.02021}\,(p - pi)_{t-1} \\
& - \underset{(0.00785)}{0.02366}\,\Delta u_{t-1} - \underset{(0.00556)}{0.00918}\,u_{t-1} - \underset{(0.00778)}{0.02721}\,oil_{1,t} \\[1ex]
\Delta z_t = & \underset{(0.28)}{0.6404} + \underset{(0.051)}{0.1173}\,(w - q - z)_{t-1} + \underset{(0.00906)}{0.04593}\,(p - pi)_{t-1} + \underset{(0.00933)}{0.04517}\,\Delta u_{t-1} \\
& + \underset{(0.00625)}{0.0223}\,u_{t-2} + \underset{(0.00253)}{0.01221}\,prod_t \\[1ex]
\Delta q_t = & \underset{(0.495)}{1.016} + \underset{(0.0319)}{0.9664}\,\Delta(w - z)_t + \underset{(0.0901)}{0.1843}\,(w - q - z)_{t-1} + \underset{(--)}{0.03361}\,\Delta pi_t - \underset{(0.0168)}{0.06224}\,oil_{2,t}
\end{aligned}$$

Notes: See Table 16.2.

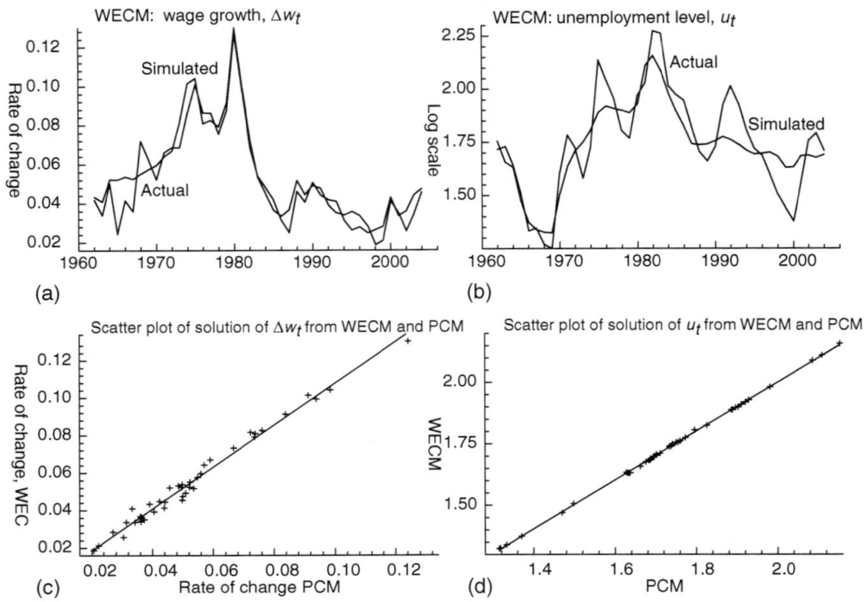

FIG. **16.1.** Dynamic simulation of the WECM and PCM for the period 1962–2004. Panel (a) shows the WECM solution for Δw_t together with the actual value, and panel (b) is the same graph for u_t. Panel (c) shows the scatter plot of the simulated Δw_t values of the WECM and PCM models, with regression line drawn. Panel (d) shows the similar graph for the rate of unemployment.

solution for Δz_t on track, and productivity growth in turn affects wages in the model, as we have seen.

The solution for the rate of unemployment shown in panel (b) tracks the reduction in actual unemployment to 3.5%, corresponding to 1.25 on the log scale of panel (b). This is mainly due to the ken_t dummy variable in the model. The solution also tracks the tendency in the unemployment changes in the period from the mid 1970s to the late 1980s. For the last 15 years of the period, the solution for the unemployment rate is relatively constant though. The 'lack of fit' in the 1990s is however not a sign of model failure, but reflects that by starting the simulation in 1962 the simulated values for 1990–2004 are quite close to the model's steady state.[15] According to the model, the explanatory variables with most influence on the steady state, are the bargaining and power productivity dummies, pow_t and $prod_t$, though these two variables affect the solution for the rate of unemployment

[15] This is confirmed by starting the simulation 10 years later, in 1974. For Δw_t and u_t in particular, the solution of the 1990s is not much affected. There are some large roots in the solution though. In the WEM the nontrivial roots are 0.98, 0.94, 0.8 and 0.7 (a complex pair) and in the PCM: 0.94, 0.79, 0.67 and 0.31 (a complex pair).

only indirectly, through their effect on the solution for the wage-share. The solution in panel (b), therefore shows that the two main structural breaks during the last 15 years of the sample have affected the steady state rate of unemployment rather weakly.

Having looked at the solution of the WECM, we next turn to the differences between the solution of that model and of the PCM. As explained above, the consensus view is that the difference is likely to be large, because there are fundamental differences in wage setting in the two models. However, panels (c) and (d) of Figure 16.1, showing the scatter plots of the simulated values of Δw_t and u_t of the two models, tell a different story: the solutions of the PCM and the WECM are nearly identical. However, this paradox is resolved by remembering the appearance of extended equilibrium correction effects in the two models, which dominates the effects of the different specifications of the wage equation.

In order to specify a PCM which behaves distinctively different from the WECM, and more in line with the textbook case of a vertical long run Phillips curve, the equilibrating mechanisms of the model must be restricted much more than in Table 16.2. Hence we consider a *restricted* econometric PCM which corresponds to the theoretical PCM of section 16.2.1, where there are no extended equilibrium correction in the Δp_t or Δz_t equations. Therefore, in the restricted PCM, the coefficients of $p_{t-1} - pi_{t-1}$ in the Δp_t and Δz_t equations are set to zero, along with for example the coefficient of the lagged wage share in the Δq_t equation. It should come as no surprise to find that these additional restrictions are statistically rejected, with a value of the test statistic $\chi^2_{\text{enc,p-ecm}} = 128$ (cf. Table 16.1), which is highly significant with 57 degrees of freedom. Hence, unlike the econometric PCM and WECM, which encompass their respective unrestricted equilibrium correction systems, the restricted PCM is firmly rejected by the statistical tests.

Figure 16.2 shows how the three different models respond to a permanent and exogenous shock to unemployment. Thus we consider a counterfactual experiment which corresponds to a reduction in the parameter β_{u0} in equation (16.2) of the theory model. The shock has been calibrated to correspond to a reduction from 5% to 4.5% in the unemployment rate. In Figure 16.2, panel (a), the graph for the econometric PCM shows the most vigorous wage response, corresponding to a lowering of the annual rate from 5% to 4.4% in the third year after the shock. There is less marked difference between the responses of the WECM and the PCM in panel (b), which shows the inflation response, which is due to the direct effect of the rate of unemployment in the Δp_t equation of both models.

The differences between the three models are also apparent in panels (c) and (d), showing the cumulated multipliers for unemployment and the wage share. For the WECM and the PCM, there is a sharp and lasting increase in the rate of unemployment. This kind of response cannot be reconciled with the stylized Phillips curve model of section 16.2.1, which only allows

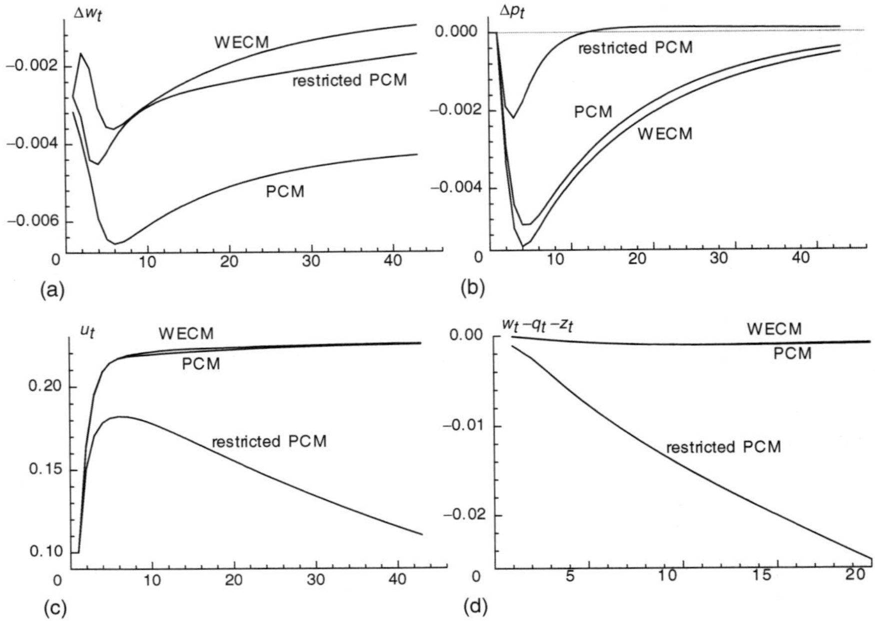

FIG. **16.2.** Dynamic multipliers of the econometric models PCM, WECM, and the restricted PCM, to a permanent exogenous 0.5 reduction in the unemployment percentage.

shocks that arise in the Phillips curve equation to affect the steady state unemployment rate—cf. that the parameter β_{u0} that we have increased in the experiment does not appear in the expression for the theoretical PCM steady state unemployment rate in equation (16.7). Nevertheless, the responses in Figure 16.2 happen for perfectly logical reasons since the *econometric* WECM and PCM are in fact quite similar due to extended equilibrium correction.

The graph for the restricted econometric PCM in panel (c) shows the response pattern that corresponds to the model of Section 16.2.1, and of the theoretical PCM steady state unemployment rate in equation (16.7) of the vertical Phillips curve. Since the steady state unemployment rate of this specification of the model only depends on the parameters of the wage Phillips curve, the shock to the unemployment rate has to be reversed completely before a new equilibrium can be restored. The single equilibrating mechanism of the model is the response of Δu_t to the lagged wage share, which therefore has to fall to a new steady state level. As can be seen in panels (c) and (d), the speed of adjustment is very low. For practical purposes it is as if the level of unemployment never returns to its initial and natural value. Thus, in the *restricted* PCM, corresponding to the standard natural rate Phillips curve model of section 16.2.1, the single equilibrating mechanism is extremely weak, making stationarity of u_t more of a formality than an important system property.

16.5 Stability of the Natural Rate

Frisch (1936) anticipated the day when it would become common among economists to define (and measure) 'normal' or natural values of economic variables by the values of the variables in a stationary state. As pointed out above, there has been little development in that direction in the estimation of the natural rate of unemployment. The dominant strategy has been to estimate the natural rate from partial models, as in the case of the wage Phillips curve. While econometrically sophisticated, as in Staiger *et al.* (1997), these studies do not address the important issue of dynamic stability of the rate of unemployment around the estimated natural rate. Moreover, completely ad hoc methods for measuring the natural rate have also gained currency, see eg, Holden and Nymoen (2002) for an appreciation of one of the OECD's methods.

As pointed out by Fair (2005), part of the explanation for the slow progress in the direction that Frisch foresaw lies in the low confidence in the steady-state properties of estimated macroeconometric models. In this chapter we have illustrated at least one feature of econometric models of the natural rate of unemployment which is crucial for the evaluation of steady-state properties, namely the specification of equilibrium correction mechanisms. We regard this mainly as a methodological contribution, and the detailed specification of the models can of course be contested. We do believe, however, that the main picture of extended equilibrium correction dominating the standard Phillips curve will prove to be a robust feature.

In none of the models considered above is the natural rate a completely constant and invariant entity. However, there is a difference between our framework and the *time varying NAIRU* model of Gordon (1997). In the time varying natural rate model, *all* shocks, small and large, influence the estimated natural rate. However, small and random shocks, by their very nature, either vanish or are counteracted by other shocks, usually after only a short while. Thus, a method which feeds such disturbances into the estimated natural rate may induce too much volatility in the estimated natural rate. It is a different matter with intermittent and large shocks, and with events which are usually recognized as important in contemporary economic analysis and debate. Our modelling framework allows such structural changes to affect the estimated natural rate.

As we have seen, the empirical PCM and the WECM, but not the *restricted* PCM, appear to be dynamically stable. On this basis, following Frisch's suggestion, we may interpret the values obtained by dynamic simulation, as reasonably good approximations to the models' implied natural rate, for example $\mu_{u,WECM}$ in the notation of section 16.2.

However, there is still the issue about the credibility of using simulated values to represent the natural rate. For one thing, even if one accepts our method in principle, there is a question whether the simulated values actually correspond to the steady state or whether they are influenced by the initial conditions, or by other factors which should not, by our definition, influence the natural rate. Above we showed that the initial conditions do not have much impact on the simulated values in Figure 16.1, panel (b). However, the simulated values of other variables of the model may nevertheless have an influence on the solution of the rate of unemployment in the 1989–2004 period.

In order to check the robustness of the model solution qua natural rate we have calculated a natural rate estimate based on the semi-reduced form for the rate of unemployment. The resulting estimated equation is similar to the augmented Dickey–Fuller regression of section 16.3.2.1, but with the lagged values of the wage share and the real exchange rate as additional variables. The natural rate estimate of this model is obtained by setting the explanatory variables equal to their average values. In this way, we 'cut off' the link between the reduced form of the rate of unemployment and the rest of the model.[16]

Figure 16.3 shows the actual rate of unemployment as the dotted line. The estimate from the semi-reduced form, denoted *'Frisch natural rate'* in the graphs, is shown as a thick line, and we have added the associated 95% confidence interval of the mean, denoted as $\pm 2se$ in the graph. The *'Frisch natural rate'* has been estimated recursively, hence the starting point of the lines are based on the 29 observations from 1961 to 1989. The end-point of the curve shows the results for the full sample from 1961 to 2004. The impression is that this estimate is very stable over the 16 year period from 1989–2004. Figure 16.3 also shows the simulated values of WECM, ie, the same solution as shown in Figure 16.1 (panel b), but transformed to percentages. As argued above, due to asymptotic stability of the model, these simulated values approximate the implied natural rate of the full model, $\hat{\mu}_{u,WECM}$.

As explained above, the estimated WECM includes two of the most cited candidates for a reduction of the 'natural rate' in the 1990s: the reduction of workers' bargaining power and the unusually high productivity growth. The two factors have statistically and numerically significant effects on wage growth in our estimated model, and logically they are part of the explanation

[16] This can be seen as a variant of the procedure proposed in Frisch (1936), as an alternative to the full steady state, for estimation of natural values of variables by modifying structural macroeconomic models, see Fair (2005).

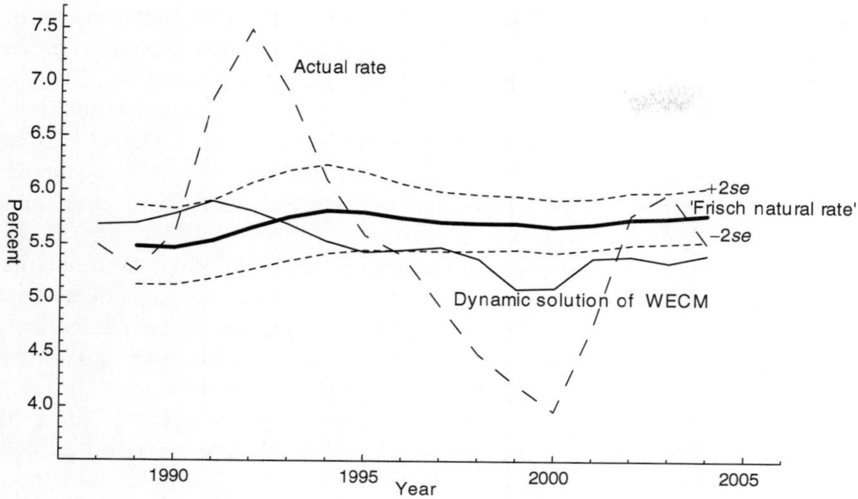

FIG. 16.3. The civilian unemployment rate together with two measures of the natural unemployment rate: the solution of the estimated WECM, see panel (b) of Figure 16.1, and the mean unemployment rate from a semi-reduced form from WECM, with ±2 standard errors, denoted ±2*se* in the graph.

why the line for the dynamic solution of WECM lies below the line of *'Frisch natural rate'* after 1993. The highest $\hat{\mu}_{u,WECM}$ is 5.9% (in 1991), and the lowest is 5.1% (in 1999). This is however a smaller estimated reduction in the natural rate than the best evidence based on estimation of Phillips curves, Staiger *et al.* (2002), which suggests a 1.5 percentage point reduction between 1992 and 2000. Moreover, while the graphs of Staiger *et al.* (2002) indicate a continued fall in the natural rate also after 2002, our estimate suggests that the natural rate might have been stabilized in the course of the period 2000–2004.

16.6 Conclusions

This chapter has discussed methodological and substantive issues relating to the empirical assessment of the US natural rate, starting by noting that the methodology underlying the consensus view is based on a highly restrictive model of wages, prices, and the rate of unemployment, dubbed PCM above. Another model, called WECM, with equilibrium correction in wage setting is an alternative hypothesis to the wage Phillips curve. The consensus view is that the PCM and WECM are polar cases, but we show that this is only true if one abstracts from equilibrium correction behaviour elsewhere in the system, in price setting in particular. We dub this system 'feature extended equilibrium correction'. Thus, even if the wage Phillips curve is the preferred model of US wage dynamics, it does not follow that the natural rate can be estimated from the empirical wage Phillips curve alone. Due to extended equilibrium correction, the PCM dynamics might become almost indistinguishable from the dynamics of the WECM. Our econometric versions of PCM and WECM confirm this feature, and only in the case where we tailor the PCM dynamics by imposing restriction that are rejected by statistical tests, do the dynamics correspond to the standard analysis.

It is a widely held view that differences in wage dynamics between the USA and Europe go a long way towards explaining the different behaviour of the unemployment rates on the two sides of the Atlantic. Hence research has focused on the specification of wage equations. One belief shared by a majority of economists is that the relatively swift adjustment of the US unemployment rate, and its apparent insulation from shocks originating in the demand sector of the economy, is due to supply side behaviour which is represented by a wage Phillips curve. While not wanting to downplay the importance of wage dynamics for the comparative macroeconomic performance of different economies, our results show that the wage Phillips curve and the error correcting wage equation may not be the polar cases that the standard framework will have us believe. In our analysis, equilibrium correction elsewhere in the system may be (almost) as important for natural rate dynamics as wage setting dynamics. Thus, the comparative stability of the US natural rate may be less of a Phillips curve property, and more of a system property than the conventional analysis suggests. Specifically, the natural rate may have stayed constant because demand shocks have had a tendency to disappear in this vast economy, sometimes with the aid of good economic policies. Unlike the incumbent model of the US natural rate, our empirical results do not rule out the possibility that a sufficiently large and persistent demand shock, may have long lasting effects on US unemployment.

16.7 Data Definitions

Economic time-series

A main data source has been the AMECO (Annual Macro-Economic) database of the European Commisions's Directorate General for Economic and Financial Affairs (DG ECFIN). The other main sources are EcoWin and Economagic.

W_t– Compensation of employees, manufacturing industry, nominal USD. AMECO code: HMCMW. The AMECO series was spliced by the Bureau of Labor Statistics Employment cost index, manufacturing, private industry. Source: Economagic.

P_t– Consumer price index. 1995=100. AMECO code ZCPIN.

Q_t– Price deflator of gross value added, manufacturing industry, 1995=100. AMECO code PVGM.
Z_t– Labour productivity, output per hours worked, manufacturing. EcoWin code ew:usa09102.
PI_t– Price deflator on imports of goods and services. 1995=100. AMECO code PMGS.
U_t– Unemployment rate, in percent. Civilian unemployment, Source: Economagic, St.Louis Fed.
$POIL_t$– Price of West Texas Intermediate Crude, USD Per Barrel. Source: Economagic.

As explained in the text, lower case letters refer to the logarithm of the original variables above, $u_t = \log(U_t)$ for example.

Dummies
pow_t– Bargaining power dummy, see section 16.3.2 for motivation. It is 1 in 1962 and 1964; −0.5 in 1995; −1 in 1996 and 1997; −0.5 in the years 1998-2001; and −0.5 in 2003. Otherwise zero.
$prod_t$– Dummy for unanticipated high or low productivity growth. It is −1 in 1974, 1979, 1980 and 1989; and 1 in the period 1995–2003.
oil_{1t}– 1 in 1974, otherwise zero.
oil_{2t}– 1 in 1980, otherwise zero.
ken_t– 1 Kennedy-Johnson dummy, 1 in the period 1965–1969, zero elsewhere.

References

Andreou, E. and Spanos, A. (2003). Statistical adequacy and the testing of trend versus difference stationarity. *Econometric Reviews*, **22**, 217–237.

Bårdsen, G., Eitrheim, Ø, Jansen, E. S. and Nymoen, R. (2005). *The Econometrics of Macroeconomic Modelling*. Oxford: Oxford University Press.

——Fisher, P. G. and Nymoen, R. (1998). Business cycles: real facts or fallacies? In Strøm, S. (ed.), *Econometrics and Economic Theory in the 20th Century: The Ragnar Frisch Centennial Symposium*, no. 32 in Econometric Society Monograph Series, ch. 16, pp. 499–527. Cambridge: Cambridge University Press. Econometric Society Monographs No. 31.

——and Nymoen, R. (2003). Testing steady-state implications for the NAIRU. *Review of Economics and Statistics*, **85**, 1070–1075.

Blanchard, O. J. (1987). The wage price spiral. *Quarterly Journal of Economics*, **101**, 543–565.

——(2005). *Macroeconomics*, 4th edition. New Jersey: Pearson Prentice Hall.

——and Katz, L. (1997). What do we know and do not know about the natural rate of unemployment? *Journal of Economic Perspectives*, **11**, 51–72.

————(1999). Wage dynamics: reconciling theory and evidence. *American Economic Review*, **89**(2), 69–74. Papers and Proceedings (May, 1999).

——and Summers, L. H. (1986). Hysteresis and the European Unemployment Problem. *NBER Macroeconomics Manual*, **1**, 15–78.

Blanchflower, D. G. and Oswald, A. J. (1994). *The Wage Curve*. Cambridge, Mass. MIT Press.

Doornik, J. A. and Hendry, D. F. (2001a). *Empirical Econometric Modelling Using PcGive 10. Volume 1*. London: Timberlake Consultants.

——(2001b). *GiveWin. An Interface to Empirical Modelling*. London: Timberlake Consultants.

Elmeskov, J. and MacFarlan, M. (1993). Unemployment persistence. *OECD Economic Studies*, **21**, 59–88.

Fair, R. (2005). *Natural Concepts in Macroeconomics*. Cowles Commision. International Centre for Finance, Yale University.

Forslund, A., Gottfries, N., and Westermark, A. (2008). Real and nominal wage adjustment in open economies. *Scandinavian Journal of Economics*, **110**(1), 169–195.

Frisch, R. (1936). On the notion of equilibrium and disequilibrium. *The Review of Economic Studies*, **3**, 100–105.

Fuhrer, J. C. (1995). The Phillips Curve is alive and well. *New England Economic Review*, 41–56.

Gordon, R. J. (1997). The time-varying NAIRU and its implications for economic policy. *Journal of Economic Perspectives*, **11**(1), 11–32.

Hendry, D., Pagan, A., and Sargan, J. (1984). Dynamic specification. In Griliches, Z. and Intriligator, M. (eds.), *Handbook of Econometrics*, vol. II, ch. 18. Amsterdam: Elsevier.

Hendry, D. F. (1995). Econometrics and business cycle empirics. *The Economic Journal*, **105**, 1622–1636.

——Neale, A. J. and Srba, F. (1988). Econometric analysis of small linear systems. *Journal of Econometrics*, **38**, 203–226.

Holden, S. and Nymoen, R. (2002). Measuring structural unemployment: NAWRU estimates in the Nordic countries. *The Scandinavian Journal of Economics*, **104**(1), 87–104.

Johansen, S. (1995). Identifying restrictions of linear equations with applications to simultaneous equations and cointegration. *Journal of Econometrics*, **69**, 111–132.

King, M. (1998). Mr King explores lessons from the UK labour market. *BIS Review*, **103**.

Kolsrud, D. and Nymoen, R. (1998). Unemployment and the open economy wage-price spiral. *Journal of Economic Studies*, **25**, 450–467.

Nymoen, R. (1989). Modelling wages in the small open economy: an error-correction model of Norwegian manufacturing wages. *Oxford Bulletin of Economics and Statistics*, **51**, 239–258.

——(1991). A small linear model of wage- and price-inflation in the Norwegian economy. *Journal of Applied Econometrics*, **6**, 255–269.

——and Rødseth, A. (2003). Explaining unemployment: Some lessons from Nordic wage formation. *Labour Economics*, **10**, 1–29.

OECD (1997). *Employment Outlook*. Paris: OECD. July 1997.

Perron, P. (1989). The Great Crash, the Oil Price Shock, and the unit root hypothesis. *Econometrica*, **57**, 1361–1401.

Pollin, R. (2002). Wage bargaining and the U.S. Phillips Curve: Was Greenspan right about 'traumatized workers' in the 1990s? Paper presented at the AEA/URPE session

'Recessions, Inflation and the Prospects of Equitable Growth', ASSE meeting Washington D.C., 3 January, 2003.

Sargan, J. D. (1964). Wages and prices in the United Kingdom: A study of econometric methodology. In Hart, P. E., Mills, G., and Whitaker, J. K. (eds.), *Econometric Analysis for National Economic Planning*, pp. 25–63. London: Butterworth Co.

——(1980). A model of wage-price inflation. *Review of Economic Studies*, **47**, 113–135.

Scarpetta, S. (1996). Assessing the role of labour markets policies and institutional settings on unemployment: A cross-country study. *OECD Economic Studies*, **26**, 43–98.

Staiger, D., Stock, J. H., and Watson, M. W. (1997). The NAIRU, unemployment and monetary policy. *Journal of Economic Perspectives*, **11**, 33–49.

——(2002). Prices, wages and the U.S. NAIRU in the 1990s. In Kruger, A. and Solow, R. (eds.), *The Roaring Nineties*, ch. 1, pp. 3–60. New York: Russell Sage Foundation.

Stiglitz, J. E. (1986). Theories of wage rigidity. In Butkiewicz, J. L., Koford, K., and Miller, J. B. (eds.), *Keynes' Economic Legacy: Contemporary Economic Theories*, pp. 153–206. New York: Praeger Publishers.

17

Constructive Data Mining: Modelling Argentine Broad Money Demand

*Neil R. Ericsson and Steven B. Kamin**

17.1 Introduction

We are delighted to contribute to this Festschrift in honor of David F. Hendry. As discussed in Ericsson (2004), David has contributed to numerous areas of econometrics and economics, including:

- money demand,
- error correction models and cointegration,
- exogeneity,
- model development and design,
- econometric software,
- economic policy,
- consumers' expenditure,
- Monte Carlo methodology,
- the history of econometrics, and
- the theory of economic forecasting.

We draw on David's contributions to the first six topics to assess and improve upon Kamin and Ericsson's (1993) model of Argentine broad money demand,

* The views in this chapter are solely the responsibility of the authors and should not be interpreted as reflecting the views of the Board of Governors of the Federal Reserve System or of any other person associated with the Federal Reserve System. The authors are grateful to Julia Campos, Jurgen Doornik, Dale Henderson, David Hendry, Katarina Juselius, Jaime Marquez, Bent Nielsen, and Anders Rahbek for helpful comments. All numerical results were obtained using PcGive Version 12.00, Autometrics Version 1.5, and PcGets Version 1.02: see Doornik and Hendry (2007), Doornik (2009), and Hendry and Krolzig (2001).

focusing on model design and cointegration analysis. Recent developments by David and co-authors in computer-automated model selection help us obtain a more parsimonious, empirically constant, data-coherent, error correction model for broad money demand in Argentina. Cointegration between money, inflation, the interest rate, and exchange rate depreciation depends on the inclusion of a 'ratchet' variable that captures irreversible effects of inflation.

To better understand money demand and currency substitution in a hyperinflationary economy, Kamin and Ericsson (1993) develop an empirical model of broad money (M3) in Argentina for monthly data over 1978–1993, a period including hyperinflation and a subsequent decline in inflation to a rate close to contemporary US and European levels. Kamin and Ericsson's underlying economic theory is a standard money demand model, augmented by short-run nonlinear dynamics and a ratchet effect from inflation. Their empirical model clarifies the relative importance of factors determining money demand and currency holdings. Also, the structure of broad money demand in Argentina does not appear to have changed over the 1980s and 1990s. Rather, the fall in demand during the late 1980s and into the 1990s is explained by changes in the determinants of money demand itself.

That said, the analysis in Kamin and Ericsson (1993) has three notable shortcomings. First, their cointegration analysis excludes a trend, which may have affected inferences. Second, in their single equation modelling of Argentine money demand, Kamin and Ericsson augment the data from the cointegration analysis with an impulse dummy (for a known asset freeze from the Plan Bonex) and an asymmetric term in price acceleration. While both variables are stationary in principle, their exclusion from the cointegration analysis could have affected the results obtained. Third, an alternative single equation model might have been obtained if a different model search path had been followed.

Following the approach in Ericsson (2009, Chs. 9 and 10), the current chapter addresses these issues, as follows. Cointegration is re-analysed, including the impulse dummy, the asymmetric inflation term, and a trend. The cointegrating vector in this expanded framework is similar to the one obtained by Kamin and Ericsson (1993). Path dependence in model selection is examined by using two model selection algorithms: David Hendry and Hans-Martin Krolzig's (2001) PcGets, and Jurgen Doornik and David Hendry's (2007) Autometrics. Kamin and Ericsson's (1993) analysis is robust to multi-path searches by both algorithms; at the same time, Autometrics finds an even more parsimonious specification. The details of the model improvement highlight the strengths and the limitations of computer-automated model selection. Our approach thus illustrates new techniques, which shed light on existing results. And, re-examination of an existing data set with new techniques is very much in the spirit of other work in this area, including Hendry and Mizon (1978),

Engle and Hendry (1993), Doornik, Hendry, and Nielsen (1998), and Hendry (2006).

This chapter is organized as follows. Section 17.2 briefly describes the economic theory and the data. Section 17.3 summarizes the cointegration analysis and error correction model for Argentine money demand in Kamin and Ericsson (1993). Section 17.4 re-analyses the long-run properties of Argentine money demand on the expanded data set. Section 17.5 then designs a single equation model of money demand, using the algorithms for computer-automated model selection in PcGets and Autometrics. Depending upon the modelling strategy, pre-search testing, choice of required regressors, and representation and choice of the initial general model, PcGets and Autometrics obtain several distinct—albeit similar—final models in their general-to-specific selection processes. Additional analysis of those models obtains a final specification that is similar to—but more parsimonious than—the one in Kamin and Ericsson (1993). That final specification appears well-specified with empirically constant coefficients; and its economic interpretation is straightforward. Section 17.6 concludes.

For expositional convenience, two conventions are adopted. First, 'domestic' means Argentine. Second, Argentine currency is always denominated in pesos (the Argentine currency at the end of the sample) although historically other currencies were used.

17.2 Economic Theory and the Data

This section first discusses the theory of money demand (section 17.2.1) and then considers the data themselves (section 17.2.2).

17.2.1 *Economic Theory*

The standard theory of money demand posits

$$M^d/P = q(Y, \mathbf{R}), \tag{17.1}$$

where M^d is nominal money demanded, P is the price level, Y is a scale variable, and $\mathbf{R}$ (in bold) is a vector of returns on various assets. The function $q(\cdot, \cdot)$ is increasing in Y, decreasing in those elements of $\mathbf{R}$ associated with assets excluded from M, and increasing in those elements of $\mathbf{R}$ for assets included in M.

Three assets for Argentine residents are considered: broad money (M3), domestic goods, and dollars. Their nominal returns are denoted R, Δp, and Δe, where E is the exchange rate (domestic/foreign), variables in lowercase are in logarithms, and Δ is the difference operator. This choice of assets and returns seems reasonable. Relatively few peso instruments outside of M3 were held in significant quantities during most of the sample period. Also, the interest rate on dollar deposits was small and unvarying relative to Δe, so it was excluded in calculating the return on dollar-denominated assets.

Empirical models below employ (17.1) in its standard log-linear form, with two modifications. First, the scale variable is omitted, as in Cagan's (1956) money demand model for hyperinflationary economies.[1] Second, following Enzler, Johnson, and Paulus (1976), Simpson and Porter (1980), Piterman (1988), Melnick (1990), Ahumada (1992), and Uribe (1997) *inter alia*, the money demand equation includes a ratchet variable, which is the maximum inflation rate to date, denoted Δp^{max}. Higher inflation rates may induce innovations to economize on the use of domestic money balances. Once inflation subsides, these innovations are unlikely to disappear immediately (if at all), leading to a long-lived negative effect of inflation on money demand. Hence, Δp^{max} may proxy for financial innovation, be it a shift toward dollar usage or toward other forms of economizing on domestic money holdings.

With these two modifications, equation (17.1) has the following form

$$m - p \;=\; \gamma_0 + \gamma_1 R + \gamma_2 \Delta p + \gamma_3 \Delta e + \gamma_4 \Delta p^{max} . \qquad (17.2)$$

Anticipated signs of coefficients are $\gamma_1 > 0$, $\gamma_2 < 0$, $\gamma_3 < 0$, and $\gamma_4 \leq 0$. Broad money is composed primarily of interest-bearing deposits, so the interest rate R should exert a positive effect on money demand. The coefficients on Δp and Δe should be negative: goods and dollars are alternatives to holding money. Because Δp^{max} increases monotonically throughout the sample, a strictly negative γ_4 implies irreversible reductions in money demand due to historically higher rates of inflation.

If R, Δp, and Δe enter equation (17.2) only as relative rates of return, then $\gamma_2 + \gamma_3 = -\gamma_1$, and equation (17.2) can be rewritten as

$$m - p \;=\; \gamma_0 - \gamma_2(R - \Delta p) - \gamma_3(R - \Delta e) + \gamma_4 \Delta p^{max} . \qquad (17.3)$$

Equation (17.3) links real money demand to two opportunity costs and the ratchet effect. This representation is particularly useful when interpreting empirical error correction models in the context of multiple markets influencing money demand.

17.2.2 *The Data*

This subsection describes the data available and considers some of their basic properties. The data are a broad measure of money (M3), as measured by

[1] A preliminary investigation found little role for Y in the cointegration analysis or in error correction modelling. This is consistent with Ahumada's (1992) evidence on currency demand, and may be due to the relatively stationary nature of real GDP in Argentina over the sample period.

all peso-denominated currency and domestic bank deposits (M, millions of pesos); the domestic consumer price index (P, 1968 = 1.00); the interest rate on domestic peso-denominated 30-day fixed-term bank deposits (R, fraction at a monthly rate); and the free-market exchange rate (E, in pesos per dollar). Also, p is transformed to the variable $\max(0, \Delta^2 p)$ [denoted $\Delta^2 p^{pos}$] to measure the differential effect of positive (rather than negative) accelerations in prices, as in Ahumada (1992). The variable $\Delta^2 p^{pos}$ is interpretable as allowing asymmetric short-run effects of inflation, similar to Δp^{max} allowing asymmetric long-run effects. All data are monthly and seasonally unadjusted, over January 1977–January 1993. Allowing for lags and transformations, estimation is over February 1978–January 1993 ($T = 180$) unless otherwise noted. Two dummy variables are also used: B, an impulse dummy for the beginning of the Plan Bonex (January 1990); and S, the seasonal dummy. Kamin and Ericsson (1993, Appendix) provide further details on the data.

Figure 17.1a plots the logarithms of nominal money and prices (m and p), which are notable by spanning orders of magnitude. Sharp increases in both series are visible around 1985 and 1989. While M is the variable of central interest in this study, its evolution is most easily understood in light of the various rates of return. Figure 17.1b plots the (monthly) inflation rate Δp, along with the generated ratchet variable Δp^{max}. Figure 17.1c plots Δp and the interest rate R, which move closely together, albeit with inflation being more volatile on a month-to-month basis. Figure 17.1d graphs R and the depreciation in the nominal exchange rate Δe, which also move closely together, with exchange rate depreciation being highly volatile. That said, real ex post *monthly* returns are commonly in excess of (plus-or-minus) 2%, in large part owing to the high variability in the inflation rate.

The overall behaviour of inflation (and so of R and Δe) can be characterized by periods of increasing inflation, followed by government 'plans' to rein in inflation. The acceleration of prices during the early 1980s was sharply reversed in mid-1985 by the Plan Austral, which combined wage, price, and exchange rate freezes with some fiscal adjustment. Reductions in the fiscal deficit were not sufficient to eliminate inflationary pressures, which resumed in earnest by 1987. The August 1988 Plan Primavera ('Spring Plan') followed, and it aimed to limit the growth of prices and the official exchange rate to 4% per month. While inflation fell temporarily, the real exchange rate appreciated and the fiscal situation deteriorated. In February 1989, the Central Bank floated the exchange rate for financial transactions, which promptly depreciated sharply; and inflation rapidly increased to a record 197% per month in July 1989.

Under newly elected President Menem, the authorities announced a new program similar to the Plan Austral. Initially, inflation fell dramatically; but appreciation of the real exchange rate forced the Central Bank to float the

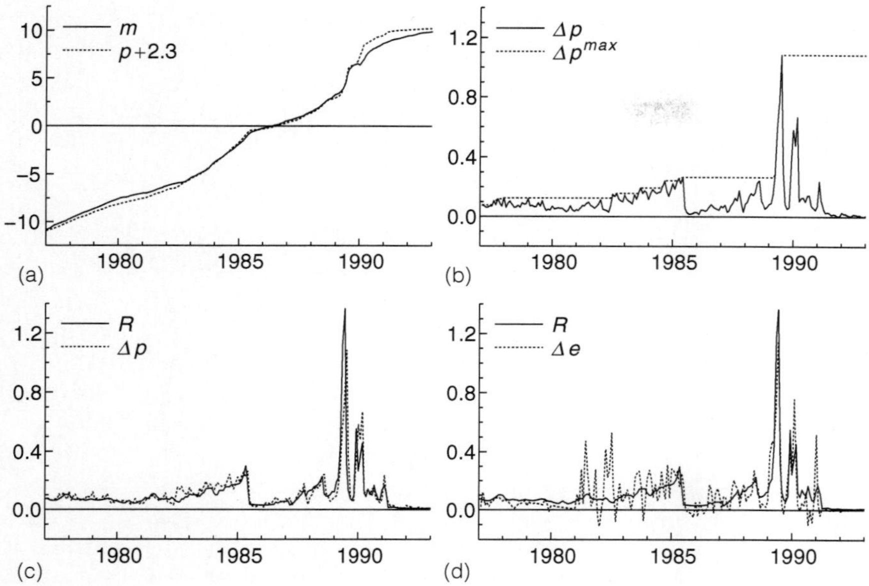

FIG. **17.1.** The logarithms of nominal money and prices (m and p), inflation Δp and maximal inflation Δp^{max}, R and Δp, and R and Δe.

commercial exchange rate, which quickly depreciated in value and spurred price inflation. In January 1990, the authorities attempted to restrain inflation by freezing most domestic peso-denominated bank time deposits and converting them to 10-year dollar-denominated bonds known as Bonex. The so-called Plan Bonex had little immediate effect upon inflation, but it did further reduce the Argentine public's faith in their financial system. By March 1990, when inflation reached 95.5% per month, broad money reached a record low of 3.1% of GDP.

Subsequently, inflation declined to single-digit levels due to a reduction in monetary emission made possible by concerted efforts to achieve fiscal adjustment. The fiscal deficit declined from over 20% of GDP in 1989 to about 3% in 1990 and 2% in 1991. In March 1991, the government announced the 'Convertibility Program', which fixed the exchange rate against the dollar and required the Central Bank to hold international reserves equivalent to the monetary base. Subsequently, the inflation rate fell to under 1% per month.

Figure 17.2 graphs the log of real money ($m - p$) and the negative of the ratchet variable Δp^{max}. Real money initially increases gradually, then falls abruptly by 20% in 1982. After continuing to fall through 1984, real money increases until the hyperinflation in 1989, when it plummets to

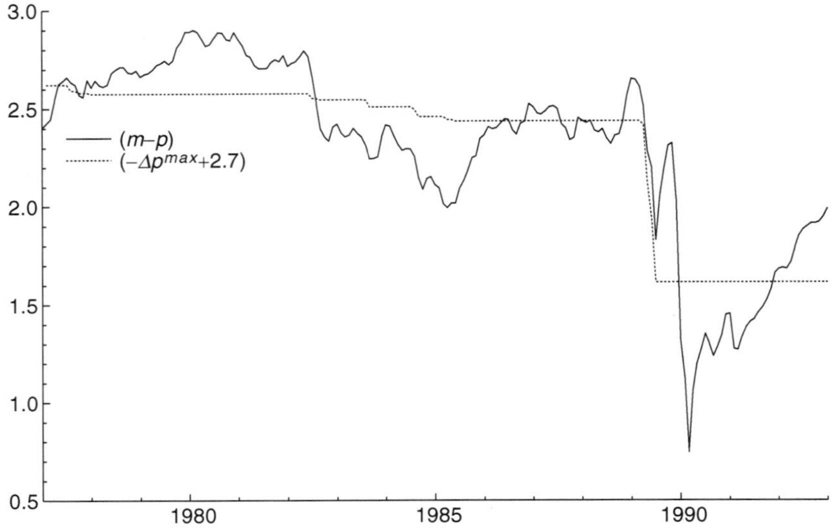

FIG. 17.2. The logarithm of real money $(m - p)$ and the negative of the maximal inflation rate (Δp^{max}), adjusted for means.

approximately half its 'pre-hyper' level. Even after very low inflation in subsequent years, real money did not return to its level of early 1989. Declines in real money are closely correlated with increases in the ratchet variable, although the stability of a relation between these variables may be an issue, noting the remaining large deviations between them.[2]

17.3 Previous Results

This section summarizes the model of Argentine money demand developed by Kamin and Ericsson (1993).

Kamin and Ericsson (1993) test for and find cointegration between real money, the interest rate, the inflation rate, exchange rate depreciation, and the ratchet variable; and the ratchet variable is key to finding cointegration. While the interest rate and the exchange rate do not appear to be weakly exogenous, there are only minor differences between system estimates of the cointegrating vector and the solved long-run coefficients from a conditional single-equation autoregressive distributed lag (ADL) model. So, Kamin and

[2] For further analytical and empirical discussion of the Argentine economy, see Howard (1987), the World Bank (1990), Kamin (1991), Kiguel (1991), Manzetti (1991), Beckerman (1992), Kamin and Ericsson (1993), and Helkie and Howard (1994). See Dominguez and Tesar (2007) for a history of the post-1990 period.

Ericsson (1993) model broad money as a single-equation conditional error correction model (ECM).

In their single equation modelling, Kamin and Ericsson (1993) start with a seventh-order ADL that has 63 coefficients and simplify it to a more restricted 'intermediate' ADL with only 30 coefficients. Kamin and Ericsson (1993) then further simplify to obtain the following 16-coefficient model, which is their equation (6).

$$
\begin{aligned}
\Delta\widehat{(m-p)}_t = {} & \underset{\substack{(0.028)\\ [0.035]}}{0.264}\ \Delta(m-p)_{t-1} + \underset{\substack{(0.031)\\ [0.032]}}{0.091}\ \Delta^2(m-p)_{t-5} - \underset{\substack{(0.040)\\ [0.041]}}{0.740}\ \Delta^2 p_t \\
& + \underset{\substack{(0.040)\\ [0.054]}}{0.101}\ \Delta^2 p_{t-5} - \underset{\substack{(0.078)\\ [0.089]}}{0.594}\ \Delta^2 p_t^{pos} + \underset{\substack{(0.018)\\ [0.021]}}{0.059}\ \Delta\Delta_6 p_t \\
& + \underset{\substack{(0.022)\\ [0.018]}}{0.182}\ \Delta^2 R_t + \underset{\substack{(0.044)\\ [0.045]}}{0.536}\ (R-\Delta p)_{t-1} + \underset{\substack{(0.022)\\ [0.022]}}{0.103} \\
& - \underset{\substack{(0.0078)\\ [0.0080]}}{0.0337}\ (m-p)_{t-1} - \underset{\substack{(0.017)\\ [0.019]}}{0.069}\ \Delta e_{t-1} - \underset{\substack{(0.010)\\ [0.010]}}{0.028}\ \Delta p_{t-1}^{max} \\
& - \underset{\substack{(0.038)\\ [0.039]}}{0.216}\ B_t + \underset{\substack{(0.032)\\ [0.020]}}{0.179}\ B_{t-3} + \underset{\substack{(0.64)\\ [0.43]}}{2.45}\ S_{t-6} + \underset{\substack{(0.62)\\ [0.74]}}{5.09}\ S_{t-12}
\end{aligned}
\tag{17.4}
$$

$T = 180$ [1978(2)–1993(1)] $\quad R^2 = 0.9489 \quad \hat{\sigma} = 2.192\% \quad dw = 2.08$

$Inn_1 : F(47, 117) = 1.47^{+} \quad Inn_2 : F(14, 150) = 1.46 \quad AR : F(7, 157) = 0.61$

$ARCH : F(7, 150) = 2.75^{*} \quad Normality : \chi^2(2) = 0.59 \quad RESET : F(1, 163) = 0.43$

$Hetero : F(26, 137) = 0.99 \quad Form : F(102, 61) = 0.71 \quad Chow : F(33, 131) = 0.76,$

where a circumflex ^ on the dependent variable denotes its fitted value, the subscript t is the time index, $\Delta\Delta_6 p_t = \Delta(p_t - p_{t-6})$, R^2 is the squared multiple correlation coefficient, and $\hat{\sigma}$ is the estimated residual standard error. The long-run solution to (17.4) is

$$m - p = 3.05 + 15.93(R - \Delta p) - 2.04\Delta e - 0.84\Delta p^{max}. \tag{17.5}$$

Kamin and Ericsson (1993) show that equation (17.4) has a straightforward economic interpretation and is statistically satisfactory. Economically, the long-run coefficients in (17.5) satisfy sign restrictions that are consonant with a money demand function. The short-run variables and coefficients in (17.4) are also easily understood. Each short-run variable enters as a second difference (an acceleration), which is a natural transformation to stationarity for a potentially I(2) variable. The coefficient on $\Delta^2 p_t$ is close to -1, implying that, in the short run, agents are in essence adjusting nominal (and not real) money.[3] The lag lengths on $\Delta^2(m-p)_{t-5}$, $\Delta^2 p_{t-5}$, and $\Delta\Delta_6 p_t$ are consistent with agents' adjustments for seasonality in the data. The variable $\Delta\Delta_6 p_t$ is also consistent with a natural data-based predictor of future (seasonal) inflation, extending the theoretical and empirical developments on such predictors in Flemming (1976), Hendry and Ericsson (1991), and Campos and Ericsson (1999). And, the coefficient on $\Delta^2 p_t^{pos}$ is very negative and statistically significant, implying stronger reactions to rising inflation than to falling inflation.

The estimated money demand function also sheds light on the dollarization of the Argentine economy. Kamin and Ericsson (2003) reinterpret the ratchet effect in light of data measuring the extent of dollarization. Specifically, the reduction in peso money demand attributable to the ratchet effect is comparable in magnitude to the estimated stock of total dollar assets held domestically by Argentine residents, where those assets are estimated from US Treasury data. This suggests that secular reductions in the demand for pesos reflect substitution into dollars rather than mere economizing on peso balances (or other forms of financial innovation). Thus, the ratchet may proxy for dollar holdings, which relaxes the draconian assumption of true irreversibility.

Statistically, Kamin and Ericsson (1993) show that equation (17.4) is parsimonious and empirically constant and satisfies a variety of diagnostic tests. Equation (17.4) and the regressions below report diagnostic statistics for testing against various alternative hypotheses: residual autocorrelation (*dw* and *AR*), skewness and excess kurtosis (*Normality*), autoregressive conditional heteroscedasticity (*ARCH*), RESET (*RESET*), heteroscedasticity (*Hetero* and *Form*), non-innovation errors relative to a more general model (*Inn*), and predictive failure (*Chow*, Chow's prediction interval statistic). The asymptotic null distribution is designated by $\chi^2(\cdot)$ or $F(\cdot,\cdot)$, where the degrees of freedom fill the parentheses. Estimated standard errors are in parentheses $(\cdot)$, below coefficient estimates; heteroscedasticity-consistent standard errors are in brackets $[\cdot]$. See Doornik and Hendry (2007) for details and references.

In spite of the apparent robustness of equation (17.4), its design has shortcomings. The associated cointegration analysis excludes $\Delta^2 p^{pos}$, a linear trend, and an impulse dummy for the Plan Bonex. And, equation (17.4) may depend

[3] Hendry and Ericsson (1991, p. 853) and Baba, Hendry, and Starr (1992) find similar results for narrow money demand in the United Kingdom and the United States. Also, in keeping with this observation about $\Delta^2 p_t$, Kamin and Ericsson (1993) simplify the restricted intermediate ADL to obtain an alternative ECM where that ECM has Δm_t as the dependent variable.

on the path taken for model selection. The remainder of the current chapter addresses these issues.

17.4 Integration and Cointegration

This section presents unit root tests for the variables of interest (section 17.4.1). Then, Johansen's maximum likelihood procedure is applied to test for cointegration among real money, inflation, the interest rate, exchange rate depreciation, $\Delta^2 p^{pos}$, the ratchet variable, and a linear trend (section 17.4.2). Coefficient restrictions and the adjustment mechanism are examined in the Johansen framework.

17.4.1 *Integration*

Table 17.1 lists augmented Dickey–Fuller (ADF) statistics and related calculations for the data. In order to test whether a given series is I(0), I(1), I(2), or I(3), Table 17.1 calculates unit root tests for the original variables, for their changes, and for the changes of the changes. This permits testing the order of integration, albeit by testing adjacent orders of integration in a pairwise fashion. The largest estimated root ($\hat{\rho}$) is listed adjacent to each ADF statistic: this root should be approximately unity if the null hypothesis is correct. The lag length of the reported ADF regression is based on minimizing the AIC, starting with a maximum of twelve lags.

Nominal money, prices, and the exchange rate appear to be I(2). Real money, the nominal interest rate, inflation, and the inflation ratchet variable appear to be I(1). The ex post real interest rate and $R - \Delta e$ appear stationary.

17.4.2 *Cointegration*

Cointegration analysis helps clarify the long-run relationships between integrated variables. A brief review leads to the current analysis and places the latter in context.

Johansen's (1988, 1991) procedure is maximum likelihood for finite-order vector autoregressions (VARs) with variables that are integrated of order one [I(1)], and it is easily calculated for such systems. Various approaches exist for modelling possibly cointegrated I(2) variables. Johansen (1992b) proposes and implements a unified (vector autoregressive) system approach for the entire testing sequence going from I(2) to I(1) to I(0). His empirical application uses data on UK narrow money demand, which appear to have the same orders of integration as the Argentine series above. For the UK data, Johansen (1992b) tests for and finds that nominal money and prices (which are I(2)) cointegrate with a (+1 : −1) cointegrating vector to give real money, which is I(1). He then

Table 17.1. ADF statistics for testing a unit root in various time series

Variable[a,b]	lag ℓ	$t_{ADF(\ell)}$	$\hat{\rho}$	$\hat{\sigma}$ (%)	t-prob (%)	F-prob (%)	AIC
m	8	−2.81	0.988	5.318	2.1	52.1	−5.75
p	12	−2.95	0.984	7.741	17.8	—	−4.98
e	8	−3.07	0.970	12.63	0.1	43.7	−4.02
$m-p$	11	−3.08	0.934	6.912	2.9	47.1	−5.22
R	12	−2.06	0.821	9.208	8.2	—	−4.64
Δp^{max}	10	−1.74	0.983	2.631	5.7	62.9	−7.15
$R-\Delta p$	5	−4.64**	0.079	9.300	0.1	12.4	−4.65
$R-\Delta e$	1	−9.72**	0.069	10.65	1.4	24.2	−4.40
Δm	8	−2.28	0.849	5.431	15.8	48.6	−5.71
Δp	12	−2.45	0.810	7.905	8.1	—	−4.94
Δe	8	−2.76	0.703	12.96	13.7	84.6	−3.97
$\Delta(m-p)$	7	−3.95*	0.380	7.118	14.0	67.5	−5.18
ΔR	11	−5.46**	−1.952	9.334	2.4	43.5	−4.61
$\Delta(\Delta p^{max})$	9	−4.27**	0.487	2.657	3.0	76.4	−7.14
$\Delta(R-\Delta p)$	11	−6.16**	−5.268	9.670	1.1	81.7	−4.54
$\Delta(R-\Delta e)$	12	−7.49**	−7.758	10.71	9.1	—	−4.33
$\Delta^2 m$	6	−9.12**	−1.348	5.520	1.7	40.8	−5.69
$\Delta^2 p$	10	−4.96**	−1.517	8.072	11.7	43.9	−4.91
$\Delta^2 e$	6	−9.36**	−2.257	13.26	0.0	66.7	−3.94
$\Delta^2(m-p)$	9	−7.56**	−3.759	7.323	1.2	46.0	−5.11
$\Delta^2 R$	12	−7.87**	−11.81	9.888	4.1	—	−4.49
$\Delta^2(\Delta p^{max})$	10	−6.09**	−2.108	2.778	11.6	78.5	−7.04
$\Delta^2(R-\Delta p)$	11	−7.67**	−17.68	10.65	2.3	86.0	−4.35
$\Delta^2(R-\Delta e)$	12	−8.49**	−19.20	12.19	0.2	—	−4.07
$\Delta^2 p^{pos}$	5	−3.17+	0.643	4.188	0.7	76.7	−6.24

Notes:

a. Twelfth-order ADF regressions were initially estimated, and the final lag length was selected to minimize the Akaike Information Criterion (AIC). The columns report the name of the variable examined, the selected lag length ℓ, the ADF statistic on the simplified regression ($t_{ADF(\ell)}$), the estimated coefficient on the lagged level that is being tested for a unit value ($\hat{\rho}$), the regression's residual standard error ($\hat{\sigma}$, in %), the tail probability of the t-statistic on the longest lag of the final regression (t-prob, in %), the tail probability of the F-statistic for the lags dropped (F-prob, in %), and the AIC.

b. All of the ADF regressions include an intercept, monthly dummies, and a linear trend. MacKinnon's (1991) approximate finite-sample critical values for the corresponding ADF statistics are −3.14 (10%), −3.44 (5%), and −4.01 (1%) for $T = 177$. In this table, and in the other results reported herein, rejection of the indicated null hypothesis is denoted by +, *, and ** for the 10%, 5%, and 1% levels. Samples sizes are $T = 179$, $T = 178$, and $T = 177$ respectively for the three null hypotheses.

tests for and finds that real money, inflation, real income, and interest rates (all of which are I(1)) cointegrate. Because the I(2) Argentine variables m and p appear to cointegrate as the I(1) variable $m-p$, the cointegration analysis here *begins* with the variables $m-p$, Δp, R, Δp^{max}, Δe, $\Delta^2 p^{pos}$, and a linear trend.

Empirically, the lag order of the VAR is not known a priori, so some testing of lag order may be fruitful in order to ensure reasonable power of the Johansen procedure. Given the number of variables, the number of observations, and the data's periodicity, the largest system considered is a seventh-order VAR of $m-p$, Δp, R, Δp^{max}, Δe, and $\Delta^2 p^{pos}$. In that VAR, the linear trend is restricted to lie in the cointegration space; and an intercept,

Table 17.2. A cointegration analysis of the Argentine money demand data

Rank r	$r=0$	$r \le 1$	$r \le 2$	$r \le 3$	$r \le 4$	$r \le 5$	$r \le 6$
Log-likelihood	2497.21	2528.69	2551.50	2563.38	2571.45	2576.82	2578.52
Eigenvalue λ_r	—	0.295	0.224	0.124	0.086	0.058	0.019

Null hypothesis	$r=0$	$r \le 1$	$r \le 2$	$r \le 3$	$r \le 4$	$r \le 5$
λ_{max}	62.98**	45.61**	23.77	16.13	10.75	3.38
λ^a_{max}	48.28*	34.97	18.22	12.37	8.24	2.59
95% c.v.	43.97	37.52	31.46	25.54	18.96	12.25
λ_{trace}	162.6**	99.64**	54.03	30.26	14.13	3.38
λ^a_{trace}	124.7*	76.39	41.42	23.20	10.83	2.59
95% c.v.	114.9	87.31	62.99	42.44	25.32	12.25

Eigenvectors β' Variable	$m-p$	Δp	R	Δp^{max}	Δe	$\Delta^2 p^{pos}$	*trend*
	1	10.89	−17.53	1.20	6.17	62.69	−0.0028
	0.08	1	−0.78	0.04	−0.30	0.50	0.0003
	−0.25	−2.40	1	−0.29	−0.49	4.66	−0.0002
	−0.61	−8.49	47.66	1	−17.90	−5.39	−0.0062
	−1.43	15.50	−18.97	−0.38	1	7.94	−0.0092
	−0.63	0.34	−2.35	−1.27	0.35	1	0.0058

Variable	Adjustment coefficients α					
$m-p$	−0.020	0.265	0.083	0.002	0.010	0.010
Δp	0.015	−0.365	0.015	−0.002	−0.013	−0.002
R	0.034	0.085	−0.067	0.002	−0.020	0.015
Δp^{max}	0.016	−0.137	−0.005	0.002	−0.004	0.002
Δe	−0.048	0.877	0.093	0.011	−0.034	−0.012
$\Delta^2 p^{pos}$	0.005	−0.344	−0.052	0.000	−0.009	0.001

Weak exogeneity test statistics	$m-p$	Δp	R	Δp^{max}	Δe	$\Delta^2 p^{pos}$
$\chi^2(1)$	6.57*	3.70^{+}	9.89**	12.6**	4.58*	0.59

Statistics for testing the significance of a given variable in $\beta' x$	$m-p$	Δp	R	Δp^{max}	Δe	$\Delta^2 p^{pos}$	*trend*
$\chi^2(1)$	2.71^{+}	2.79^{+}	7.65**	3.89*	7.44**	16.7**	1.31

Multivariate statistics for testing trend stationarity	$m-p$	Δp	R	Δp^{max}	Δe	$\Delta^2 p^{pos}$
$\chi^2(5)$	48.4**	45.7**	43.7**	56.6**	30.6**	24.2**

seasonal dummies, and the Plan Bonex dummy B (and three of its lags) enter freely. Empirically, the seventh lag may be statistically insignificant, but no further lag restrictions appear feasible, so inferences below are for the seventh-order VAR.

Table 17.2 reports the standard statistics, 95% critical values (c.v.'s), and estimates for Johansen's procedure applied to this seventh-order VAR. The maximal eigenvalue and trace eigenvalue statistics (λ_{max} and λ_{trace}) strongly reject the null of no cointegration in favour of at least one cointegrating relationship, and likely in favour of two cointegrating relationships. However, parallel statistics with a degrees-of-freedom adjustment (λ^a_{max} and λ^a_{trace}) suggest only one cointegrating relationship. Because the VAR for Table 17.2 uses a large number of degrees of freedom in estimation, inferences are based on the adjusted eigenvalue statistics.

Table 17.2 also reports the standardized eigenvectors and adjustment coefficients, denoted β' and α in a common notation. The first row of β' is the estimated cointegrating vector, which can be written in the form of (17.2)

$$\begin{aligned} m - p \;=\; & \text{intercept} \;-\; \underset{(3.72)}{10.89}\,\Delta p \;+\; \underset{(4.48)}{17.53}\,R \;-\; \underset{(0.32)}{1.20}\,\Delta p^{max} \\ & -\; \underset{(1.55)}{6.17}\,\Delta e \;-\; \underset{(10.68)}{62.69}\,\Delta^2 p^{pos} \;+\; \underset{(0.0020)}{0.0028}\,t. \end{aligned} \qquad (17.6)$$

All coefficients have their anticipated signs. Also, the trend t appears to be statistically insignificant: $\chi^2(1) = 1.31$ [0.252], where the asymptotic p-value is in square brackets. And, the hypothesis of 'relative rates of return' in (17.3) appears acceptable. Numerically, the sum of the coefficients on Δp and Δe (−17.06) is approximately equal to minus the coefficient on R (17.53). Statistically, that restriction cannot be rejected: $\chi^2(1) = 0.04$ [0.850]. Jointly, the restrictions on the trend and rates of return also appear acceptable: $\chi^2(2) = 1.39$ [0.498].

Table 17.3 reports the estimated values of α and β when estimated unrestrictedly, and when estimated with a zero coefficient on the trend imposed, with the hypothesis of 'relative rates of return' imposed, and with both of those restrictions imposed. The similarity of coefficient estimates across the various restrictions points to the robustness of the results and is partial evidence in favour of those restrictions.

Thus, the nominal interest rate and inflation enter the long-run money demand function as the ex post real rate, with a semi-elasticity of about eleven, which is about unity at annual rates. The nominal interest rate relative to the exchange-rate depreciation has about half that effect on money demand. Money demand is highly sensitive to the movement of inflation, both through $\Delta^2 p^{pos}$ and through the ratchet variable Δp^{max}. In particular, for each additional percent in the maximal monthly inflation rate over the relative past, the coefficient on Δp^{max} implies approximately one percent lower money holdings.

Figure 17.3 plots key aspects of equation (17.6)—namely, the relationship between $(m - p)$, Δp^{max}, and $(R - \Delta p)$. Real money holdings fall as Δp^{max} increases and as the return on money relative to goods $(R - \Delta p)$ declines.

Returning to Table 17.2, the coefficients in the first column of α measure the feedback effects of the (lagged) disequilibrium in the cointegrating relation on the variables in the vector autoregression. Specifically, −0.020 is the estimated feedback coefficient for the money equation. The negative coefficient implies

Table 17.3. Just-identified and over-identified estimates of β and α, with corresponding estimated standard errors, from a cointegration analysis of Argentine money demand

Variable corresponding to an element of β' or α'						
$m-p$	Δp	R	Δp^{max}	Δe	$\Delta^2 p^{pos}$	*trend*
Estimate of β' (just-identified)						
1	10.89	−17.53	1.20	6.17	62.69	−0.0028
	(3.72)	(4.48)	(0.32)	(1.55)	(10.68)	(0.0020)
Estimate of β' (zero coefficient on trend imposed)						
1	10.45	−14.49	0.92	3.51	45.28	0
	(2.71)	(3.27)	(0.14)	(1.07)	(7.75)	
Estimate of β' (rates-of-return restriction imposed)						
1	10.64	−16.60	1.21	5.96	58.67	−0.0027
	(3.55)	(3.87)	(0.27)	(1.46)	(8.14)	(0.0019)
Estimate of β' (trend and rates-of-return restrictions imposed)						
1	10.19	−13.58	0.94	3.38	41.48	0
	(2.56)	(2.76)	(0.12)	(1.01)	(5.51)	
Estimate of α' (just-identified)						
−0.020	0.015	0.034	0.016	−0.048	0.005	
(0.007)	(0.007)	(0.012)	(0.004)	(0.021)	(0.005)	
Estimate of α' (zero coefficient on trend imposed)						
−0.024	0.016	0.050	0.020	−0.051	0.003	
(0.010)	(0.009)	(0.016)	(0.005)	(0.029)	(0.007)	
Estimate of α' (rates-of-return restriction imposed)						
−0.021	0.015	0.036	0.017	−0.050	0.005	
(0.008)	(0.007)	(0.012)	(0.004)	(0.022)	(0.005)	
Estimate of α' (trend and rates-of-return restrictions imposed)						
−0.026	0.017	0.054	0.022	−0.054	0.004	
(0.011)	(0.010)	(0.017)	(0.006)	(0.031)	(0.007)	

that lagged excess money induces smaller holdings of current money. The coefficient's numerical value implies slow adjustment to remaining disequilibrium. The estimated coefficient is numerically smaller than those for quarterly broad money demand (e.g., −0.26, −0.15, and −0.20 in Taylor, 1986) and monthly currency demand (e.g., −0.14 for Argentina in Ahumada, 1992). However, smaller adjustment coefficients are plausible with high-frequency data for a broad aggregate.

The third block from the bottom of Table 17.2 reports values of the statistic for testing weak exogeneity of a given variable for the cointegrating vector. Equivalently, the statistic tests whether or not the corresponding row of α is zero; see Johansen (1992a, 1992b). If the row of α is zero, disequilibrium in the cointegrating relationship does not feed back onto that variable. Surprisingly, inflation (including in its form $\Delta^2 p^{pos}$) may be weakly exogenous. However, the interest rate, the exchange rate, and the ratchet variable are not weakly exogenous, justifying a systems approach to analysing cointegration.

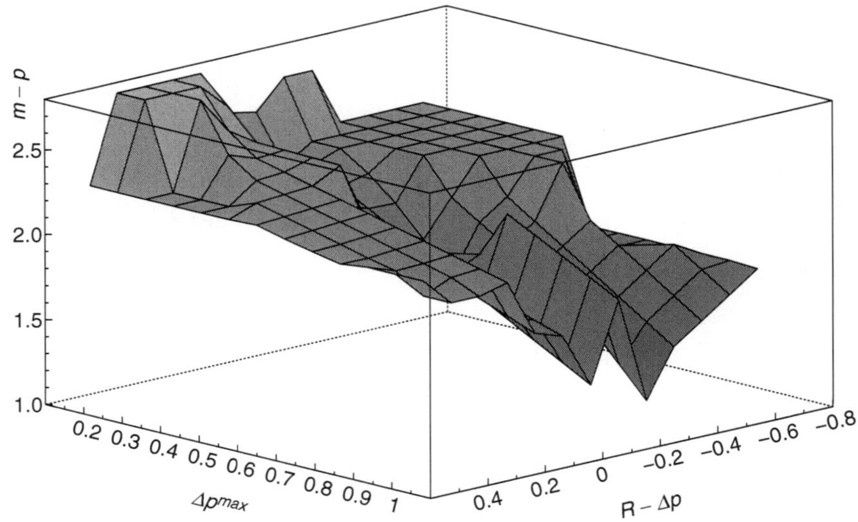

FIG. **17.3.** The logarithm of real money $(m - p)$, plotted against the maximal inflation rate (Δp^{max}) and the real interest rate $(R - \Delta p)$.

The penultimate block in Table 17.2 reports statistics for testing the significance of individual variables in the cointegrating vector. Each variable is significant, except the linear trend.

The final block in Table 17.2 reports values of a multivariate statistic for testing the trend stationarity of a given variable. Specifically, this statistic tests the restriction that the cointegrating vector contains all zeros except for a unity corresponding to the designated variable and an unrestricted coefficient on the trend, with the test being conditional on the presence of exactly one cointegrating vector; see Johansen (1995, p. 74). For instance, the null hypothesis of trend-stationary real money implies that the cointegrating vector is $(1\ 0\ 0\ 0\ 0\ 0\ *)'$, where '$*$' represents an unrestricted coefficient on the linear trend. Empirically, all of the stationarity tests reject with p-values less than 0.1%. By being multivariate, these statistics may have higher power than their univariate counterparts. Also, the null hypothesis is the stationarity of a given variable rather than the nonstationarity thereof, and stationarity may be a more appealing null hypothesis. That said, these rejections of stationarity are in line with the *inability* in Table 17.1 to reject the null hypothesis of a unit root in each of $m - p$, Δp, R, Δp^{max}, and Δe.

Because R, Δp^{max}, and Δe are not weakly exogenous for the cointegrating vector, inferences in a single equation for broad money could be hazardous if the cointegrating vector is estimated jointly with the equation's dynamics; see Hendry (1995). One solution is to model a sub-system. A second solution is to construct an error correction term from the system estimates and then develop a single equation ECM that uses that system-based error correction term. A third solution—adopted below—is to develop a single equation ECM from the single equation ADL, noting that the system estimate of the cointegrating relationship is numerically close to the ADL's long-run solution. See Hendry and Doornik (1994) and Juselius (1992) for paradigms of the first two approaches.

17.5 Computer-automated Model Selection

This section first describes the model selection algorithms in PcGets and Autometrics (section 17.5.1) and then applies these algorithms to an ECM representation of an ADL for Argentine money demand (section 17.5.2).

17.5.1 *The Algorithms in PcGets and Autometrics*

Hendry and Krolzig (2001) developed a computer program PcGets, which extends and improves upon Hoover and Perez's (1999) automated model-selection algorithm; see also Hendry and Krolzig (1999, 2003, 2005) and Krolzig and Hendry (2001). Doornik and Hendry (2007) implemented a third-generation algorithm called Autometrics, which is part of PcGive version 12. PcGets and Autometrics utilize one-step and multi-step simplifications along multiple paths, diagnostic tests as additional checks on the simplified models, and encompassing tests to resolve multiple terminal models. Both analytical and Monte Carlo evidence show that the resulting model selection is relatively nondistortionary for Type I errors. At an intuitive level, PcGets and Autometrics function as a series of sieves that aim to retain parsimonious congruent models while discarding both noncongruent models and over-parametrized congruent models. This feature of the algorithms is eminently sensible, noting that the data generation process itself is congruent and is as parsimonious as feasible.

The remainder of the current subsection summarizes PcGets and Autometrics as automated model-selection algorithms, thereby providing the necessary background for interpreting their application in section 17.5.2. For ease of reference, the algorithm in PcGets is divided into four 'stages', denoted Stage 0, Stage 1, Stage 2, and Stage 3. For full details of PcGets's algorithm, see Hendry and Krolzig (2001, Appendix A1). Hendry and Krolzig (2003) describe the relationship of the general-to-specific approach to other modelling approaches in the literature, and Hoover and Perez (2004) extend the general-to-specific approach to cross-section regressions.

Stage 0: the general model and F pre-search tests. Stage 0 involves two parts: the estimation and evaluation of the general model, and some pre-search tests aimed at simplifying the general model before instigating formal multi-path searches.

First, the general model is estimated, and diagnostic statistics are calculated for it. If any of those diagnostic statistics are unsatisfactory, the modeller must decide what to do next—whether to 'go back to the drawing board' and develop another general model, or whether to continue with the simplification procedure, perhaps ignoring the offending diagnostic statistic or statistics.

Second, PcGets attempts to drop various sets of potentially insignificant variables. PcGets does so by dropping all variables at a given lag, starting with the longest lag. PcGets also does so by ordering the variables by the magnitude of their t-ratios and either dropping a group of individually insignificant variables or (alternatively) retaining a group of individually statistically significant variables. In effect, an F pre-search test for a group of variables is a single test for multiple simplification paths, a characteristic that helps control the costs of search. If these tests result in a statistically satisfactory reduction of the general model, then that new model is the starting point for Stage 1. Otherwise, the general model itself is the starting point for Stage 1.

Stage 1: a multi-path encompassing search. Stage 1 tries to simplify the model from Stage 0 by searching along multiple paths, all the while ensuring that the diagnostic tests are not rejected. If all variables are individually statistically significant, then the initial model in Stage 1 is the final model. If some variables are statistically insignificant, then PcGets tries deleting those variables to obtain a simpler model. PcGets proceeds down a given simplification path only if the models along that path have satisfactory diagnostic statistics. If a simplification is rejected or if a diagnostic statistic fails, PcGets backtracks along that simplification path to the most recent previous acceptable model and then tries a different simplification path. A terminal model results if the model's diagnostic statistics are satisfactory and if no remaining regressors can be deleted.

If PcGets obtains only one terminal model, then that model is the final model, and PcGets proceeds to Stage 3. However, because PcGets pursues multiple simplification paths in Stage 1, PcGets may obtain multiple terminal models. To resolve such a situation, PcGets creates a union model from those terminal models and tests each terminal model against that union model. PcGets then creates a new union model, which nests all of the surviving terminal models; and that union model is passed on to Stage 2.

Stage 2: another multi-path encompassing search. Stage 2 in effect repeats Stage 1, applying the simplification procedures from Stage 1 to the union model obtained at the end of Stage 1. The resulting model is the final model. If Stage 2 obtains more than one terminal model after applying encompassing tests, then the final model is selected by using the Akaike, Schwarz, and Hannan–Quinn information criteria. See Akaike (1973, 1981), Schwarz (1978), and Hannan and Quinn (1979) for the design of these information criteria, and Atkinson (1981) for the relationships between them.

Stage 3: subsample evaluation. Stage 3 re-estimates the final model over two subsamples and reports the results. If a variable is statistically significant in the full sample and in both subsamples, then the inclusion of that variable in the final model is regarded as '100% reliable'. If a variable is statistically insignificant in one or both subsamples or in the full sample, then its measure of reliability is reduced. A variable that is statistically insignificant in both subsamples and in the full sample is regarded as being '0% reliable'. The modeller is left to decide what action, if any, to take in light of the degree of reliability assigned to each of the regressors.

PcGets thus has two components:

1. Estimation and diagnostic testing of the general unrestricted model (Stage 0); and
2. Selection of the final model by
   (a) pre-search simplification of the general unrestricted model (Stage 0),
   (b) multi-path (and possibly iterative) selection of the final model (Stages 1 and 2), and
   (c) post-search evaluation of the final model (Stage 3).

This subsection's description of these four stages summarizes the algorithm in PcGets. Below, section 17.5.2 summarizes the actual simplifications found by PcGets in practice, thereby providing additional insight into PcGets's algorithm.

PcGets requires the modeller to choose which tests are calculated and to specify the critical values for those tests. In PcGets, the modeller can choose the test statistics and their critical values directly, although doing so is tedious because of the number of statistics involved. To simplify matters, PcGets offers two options with pre-designated selections of test statistics and critical values. These two options are called 'liberal' and 'conservative' model selection strategies. The liberal strategy errs on the side of keeping some variables, even though they may not actually matter. The conservative strategy keeps only variables that are clearly significant statistically, erring in the direction of excluding some variables, even though those variables may matter. Which strategy is preferable depends in part on the data themselves and in part on the objectives of the modelling exercise, although (as below) the two approaches may generate similar or identical results.

The algorithm in PcGets is general-to-specifc, multi-path, iterative, and encompassing, with diagnostic tests providing additional assessments of statistical adequacy, and with options for pre-search simplification. The algorithm in Autometrics shares these characteristics with the algorithm in PcGets; hence, many of the remarks above about PcGets apply directly to

Autometrics. However, Autometrics (unlike PcGets) uses a tree search method, with refinements on pre-search simplification and on the objective function. See Doornik and Hendry (2007) and Doornik (2009) for details.

17.5.2 *Modelling of Argentine Money Demand Revisited*

Using PcGets and Autometrics, the current subsection assesses the possible path dependence of equation (17.4). The initial general model is estimated; and the algorithms simplify that general model under each of the 24 permutations implied by the list of choices below. While the algorithms do obtain multiple distinct final models, equation (17.4)—or simple variants of it—appears statistically sensible; and one variant obtained by Autometrics is even more parsimonious than (17.4). These results bolster the model design in Kamin and Ericsson (1993) and offer an improvement on it.

The multi-path searches in PcGets and Autometrics allow investigation of equation (17.4)'s robustness and examination of the empirical properties of the two algorithms themselves. In addition, four choices within the model selection process permit further insights. In PcGets, these choices concern the following.

1. Model strategy: either liberal (L) or conservative (C).
2. Pre-search testing (Stage 0): either switched on (Yes) or off (No).
3. The representation of the initial general ECM (three options): either the representation as tabulated, or either of two representations that explicitly nest equation (17.4). The latter two representations are distinguished by whether the variables from (17.4) are 'free' or 'fixed'. Fixed variables are forced to always be included in regression, whereas free variables may be deleted by the algorithm.
4. The choice of the general model: either the unrestricted ADL, or the *intermediate* ADL described in section 17.3.

For model strategy (choice #1), the options in Autometrics do not correspond precisely to PcGets's liberal and conservative strategies. Instead, Autometrics allows the user to select a 'target size', which is meant to equal 'the proportion of irrelevant variables that survives the [simplification] process' (Doornik, 2009). In the analysis below, Autometrics's target size is either 5% or 1%, which appear to approximate liberal and conservative strategies in PcGets. For pre-search testing (choice #2), the selected option in Autometrics is either pre-search for both variable reduction and lag reduction, or no pre-search for either—in order to match PcGets as closely as possible. The third choice above is identical for PcGets and Autometrics, as is the fourth choice.

For both PcGets and Autometrics, the third choice (the representation of the initial general ECM) can affect the final model selected. In simplifying the initial model, PcGets and Autometrics impose only 'zero restrictions',

Table 17.4. An unrestricted error correction representation for real money conditional on inflation, the interest rate, and the change in the exchange rate

Variable[a,b,c]	Lag j							
	0	1	2	3	4	5	6	7
$\Delta(m-p)_{t-j}$	−1 (–)	0.270 (0.088)	0.154 (0.093)	−0.019 (0.094)	0.029 (0.079)	0.204 (0.079)	−0.125 (0.072)	
Δp_{t-j}	−0.768 (0.101)	0.177 (0.149)	−0.041 (0.140)	0.144 (0.136)	0.121 (0.117)	0.168 (0.119)	−0.275 (0.122)	−0.053 (0.079)
ΔR_{t-j}	0.222 (0.053)	0.031 (0.159)	0.172 (0.149)	0.140 (0.143)	−0.039 (0.128)	0.002 (0.096)	−0.131 (0.090)	
$\Delta(\Delta p_{t-j}^{max})$	−0.223 (0.155)	−0.169 (0.184)	0.327 (0.281)	0.599 (0.297)	−0.104 (0.268)	−0.211 (0.264)	0.132 (0.317)	
$\Delta^2 p_{t-j}^{pos}$	−0.406 (0.162)	−0.049 (0.154)	0.180 (0.161)	−0.114 (0.156)	−0.168 (0.133)	0.003 (0.137)	0.181 (0.130)	−0.017 (0.112)
Δe_{t-j}	−0.004 (0.020)	−0.040 (0.022)	−0.014 (0.023)	0.025 (0.022)	−0.040 (0.022)	0.011 (0.023)	0.032 (0.023)	−0.032 (0.022)
$(m-p)_{t-j}$		−0.053 (0.015)						
R_{t-j}		0.441 (0.158)						
Δp_{t-j}^{max}		−0.055 (0.019)						
B_{t-j}	−0.353 (0.139)	0.178 (0.078)	0.058 (0.073)	0.286 (0.084)				
S_{t-j}	0.160 (0.047)		−1.62 (1.20)	−0.08 (1.21)	0.41 (1.10)	−0.21 (1.16)	2.81 (1.02)	
S_{t-j-6}		0.06 (0.97)	0.10 (1.03)	−0.55 (1.01)	0.86 (1.03)	0.20 (1.02)	4.35 (1.02)	

$T = 180$ [1978(2)–1993(1)] $R^2 = 0.968$ $\hat{\sigma} = 2.058\%$ $dw = 2.02$ $AR: F(7, 110) = 0.67$ [0.695] $LM_p: F(1, 116) = 0.08$ [0.773][d]

$ARCH: F(7, 103) = 0.92$ [0.491] $Normality: \chi^2(2) = 0.77$ [0.682] $Hetero: F(109, 7) = 0.08$ [1.000] $RESET: F(1, 116) = 1.89$ [0.171]

Notes:
[a] The dependent variable is $\Delta(m-p)_t$. Even so, the equation is in levels, not in differences, noting the inclusion of the regressor $(m-p)_{t-1}$. Estimated standard errors are in parentheses, beside coefficient estimates. [b] The variables $\{S_{t-j}\}$ are the seasonal dummies, except that S_0 is the intercept. February is S_{t-2}, March is S_{t-3}, etc. For readability, the coefficients and estimated standard errors for the seasonal dummies have been multiplied by 100. [c] The 33 coefficients that are 'boxed in' are set equal to zero in the partially restricted intermediate error correction representation denoted Table 17.4*. [d] The statistic LM_p is the Lagrange multiplier statistic for testing the imposed restriction of long-run price homogeneity.

Table 17.5. Statistics on computer-automated model selection by PcGets of models for Argentine money demand, categorized according to model strategy, pre-search testing, representation of the general model, and choice of general model

Model strategy	Pre-search?	Representation?	k_1	k_f	Number of paths	Number of terminal models	$\hat{\sigma}$ (%)
		The general model is Table 17.4 or equivalent.					
L	No	Table 17.4	63, 31	19	55, 7	13, 1	2.132
L	No	Nested	63, 31, 26	24	56, 18, 9	9, 3, 5	1.952
L	No	Fixed	63, 25	22	53, 10	6, 3	1.954
L	Yes	Table 17.4	26	21	10	3	2.078
L	Yes	Nested	28	23	11	3	1.989
L	Yes	Fixed	23	22	6	2	1.986
C	No	Table 17.4	63, 32, 31	23	61, 21, 20	10, 5, 4	2.015
C	No	Nested	63, 31	21	61, 22	9, 5	2.007
C	No	Fixed	63, 24	21	55, 9	6, 3	1.988
C	Yes	Table 17.4	21	21	1	1	2.139
C	Yes	Nested	22, 21	21	10, 8	2, 1	2.073
C	Yes	Fixed	24, 18	18	11, 3	1, 1	2.137
		The general model is Table 17.4* or equivalent.					
L	No	Table 17.4*	30	20	18	1	2.149
L	No	Nested	30	18	20	1	2.137
L	No	Fixed	30	18	20	1	2.137
L	Yes	Table 17.4*	20	20	1	1	2.149
L	Yes	Nested	18	18	1	1	2.137
L	Yes	Fixed	18	18	1	1	2.137
C	No	Table 17.4*	30, 20	20	19, 3	1, 1	2.149
C	No	Nested	30, 18	18	22, 3	2, 1	2.137
C	No	Fixed	30, 18	18	22, 3	2, 1	2.137
C	Yes	Table 17.4*	20, 20	20	3, 3	1, 1	2.149
C	Yes	Nested	18, 18	18	3, 3	1, 1	2.137
C	Yes	Fixed	18, 18	18	3, 3	1, 1	2.137

ie, the algorithms can set coefficients to be equal only to zero. Although a linear model is invariant to nonsingular linear transformations of its data, the coefficients of that model are *not* invariant to such transformations. For example, a model with regressors x_t and x_{t-1} is invariant to including the regressors Δx_t and x_{t-1} instead; but the deletion of x_{t-1} results in two different simplifications, depending on the representation. See Campos and Ericsson (1999) for additional discussion.

Table 17.4 lists the estimates and standard errors for the ECM representation of the unrestricted seventh-order ADL model of $m - p$, Δp, R, Δp^{max}, Δe, and $\Delta^2 p^{pos}$. The standard diagnostic statistics do not reject. The implied coefficient on the error correction term appears to be highly significant statistically, with a t-ratio of -3.53. The intermediate ADL (in ECM representation) is Table 17.4, but re-estimated with the 'boxed-in' coefficients in Table 17.4

Table 17.6. Statistics on computer-automated model selection by Autometrics of models for Argentine money demand, categorized according to target size, pre-search testing, representation of the general model, and choice of general model

Target size	Pre-search?	Representation?	k_1	k_f	Number of models estimated	Number of terminal models	$\hat{\sigma}$ (%)
		The general model is Table 17.4 or equivalent.					
5%	No	Table 17.4	63, 41	23	706	10, 17	1.997
5%	No	Nested	63, 36	21	378	8, 13	1.978
5%	No	Fixed	63, 31	20	306	6, 7	2.003
5%	Yes	Table 17.4	57, 37	22	470	6, 12	2.008
5%	Yes	Nested	50, 32	22	371	6, 7	1.972
5%	Yes	Fixed	45, 30	22	255	8, 8	1.986
1%	No	Table 17.4	63, 37	19	751	10, 20	2.095
1%	No	Nested	63, 29	21	501	8, 10	1.978
1%	No	Fixed	63, 22	18	497	2, 2	2.096
1%	Yes	Table 17.4	41, 35	20	677	10, 20	2.072
1%	Yes	Nested	39, 26	20	394	5, 5	2.014
1%	Yes	Fixed	30, 23	19	168	4, 4	2.078
		The general model is Table 17.4* or equivalent.					
5%	No	Table 17.4*	30, 20	20	46	1, 1	2.149
5%	No	Nested	30, 18	18	65	1, 1	2.137
5%	No	Fixed	30, 18	18	65	1, 1	2.137
5%	Yes	Table 17.4*	25, 20	20	36	1, 1	2.149
5%	Yes	Nested	23, 18	18	40	1, 1	2.137
5%	Yes	Fixed	23, 18	18	43	1, 1	2.137
1%	No	Table 17.4*	30, 18	18	77	1, 1	2.211
1%	No	Nested	30, 14	14	139	1, 1	2.236
1%	No	Fixed	30, 16	16	2	1	2.192
1%	Yes	Table 17.4*	21, 20	20	30	1, 1	2.149
1%	Yes	Nested	19, 17	17	36	1, 1	2.168
1%	Yes	Fixed	19, 17	17	38	1, 1	2.168

set to zero. Kamin and Ericsson (1993) show that the estimated coefficients in this intermediate model are close to those in the unrestricted ECM in Table 17.4; and the intermediate ADL is a statistically acceptable reduction of Table 17.4, with $Inn: F(33, 117) = 1.42$ [0.091]. For ease of reference, the intermediate ADL is denoted Table 17.4*.

Table 17.5 summarizes PcGets's model simplifications under the 24 different scenarios described above; Table 17.6 does likewise for Autometrics. In these tables, k_1 is the number of regressors in the general model for multi-path searches, k_f is the number of coefficients in the final specific model for multi-path searches, the 'number of paths' is the number of different simplification paths considered in a multi-path search, the 'number of terminal models' is the number of distinct terminal specifications after a multi-path search, and $\hat{\sigma}$ is the residual standard error of the final specific model. If multi-path searches are iterated, the table lists values for each iteration, where appropriate. The 'number of models estimated' is the total number of distinct models estimated in the multi-path search.

Several features of the simplifications in Tables 17.5 and 17.6 are notable. First, pre-search testing typically reduces the number of paths that need to be searched in Stage 1, and often markedly so. As a consequence, pre-search testing frequently reduces the number of multiple terminal models and, in some instances, obtains the final model. Second, if the initial general model is the intermediate ECM (Table 17.4*, rather than the general ECM in Table 17.4), that choice is in effect a pre-search, albeit an informal one. That choice also typically obtains a single terminal model on the initial multi-path search. Third, a conservative strategy generally obtains a more parsimonious model than a liberal strategy, as expected. Fourth, Kamin and Ericsson's (1993) model results from a conservative-like strategy, as is apparent from examining the specifications of the final models in Tables 17.5 and 17.6. Fifth, the 5% and 1% target sizes in Autometrics appear closely comparable to the liberal and conservative strategies in PcGets. That said, in several instances, Autometrics dominates PcGets by obtaining a more parsimonious model with a better fit (in terms of $\hat{\sigma}$), whereas PcGets never dominates Autometrics in that sense. This outcome reflects differences in the algorithms' details. Finally, data transformations through the 'nesting' approach permit a final representation that is more highly parsimonious than previously obtained; see the boxed-in result for Autometrics on Table 17.6.

The corresponding model, which improves on equation (17.4), is as follows.

$$
\begin{aligned}
\widehat{\Delta(m-p)_t} = \; & \underset{\substack{(0.025)\\ [0.024]}}{0.281}\; \Delta(m-p)_{t-1} - \underset{\substack{(0.041)\\ [0.040]}}{0.759}\; \Delta^2 p_t - \underset{\substack{(0.078)\\ [0.090]}}{0.564}\; \Delta^2 p_t^{pos} \\
& + \underset{\substack{(0.017)\\ [0.022]}}{0.040}\; \Delta\Delta_6 p_t + \underset{\substack{(0.022)\\ [0.019]}}{0.180}\; \Delta^2 R_t + \underset{\substack{(0.044)\\ [0.041]}}{0.543}\; (R-\Delta p)_{t-1} \\
& + \underset{\substack{(0.022)\\ [0.025]}}{0.093} - \underset{\substack{(0.0078)\\ [0.0088]}}{0.0300}\; (m-p)_{t-1} - \underset{\substack{(0.018)\\ [0.019]}}{0.060}\; \Delta e_{t-1} \\
& - \underset{\substack{(0.010)\\ [0.011]}}{0.025}\; \Delta p_{t-1}^{max} - \underset{\substack{(0.034)\\ [0.030]}}{0.253}\; B_t + \underset{\substack{(0.032)\\ [0.023]}}{0.170}\; B_{t-3} \\
& + \underset{\substack{(0.62)\\ [0.37]}}{1.97} S_{t-6} + \underset{\substack{(0.62)\\ [0.74]}}{4.78}\; S_{t-12} \qquad (17.7)
\end{aligned}
$$

$T = 180$ [1978(2)–1993(1)] $R^2 = 0.9462$ $\hat{\sigma} = 2.236\%$ $dw = 2.10$
$Inn_3 : F(49, 117) = 1.61^*$ $Inn_4 : F(16, 150) = 1.85^*$ $AR : F(7, 159) = 1.65$
$ARCH : F(7, 152) = 2.73^*$ $Normality : \chi^2(2) = 0.44$ $RESET : F(1, 165) = 1.60$
$Hetero : F(22, 143) = 1.08$ $Form : F(75, 90) = 0.92$ $Chow : F(33, 133) = 0.86$

The coefficients in equation (17.7) are little changed from the corresponding ones in equation (17.4), except that the coefficients for $\Delta^2(m-p)_{t-5}$ and $\Delta^2 p_{t-5}$ are restricted to be zero. No tests reject at the 1% level (an implication of choices made in the algorithm's parameters), although some do at the 5% level. Equation (17.7) has virtually the same economic interpretation as equation (17.4), and it is more parsimonious than (17.4). PcGets and Autometrics thus verify the robustness of equation (17.4)'s specification, and Autometrics improves upon that specification.

17.6 Conclusions

Computer-automated model selection with the software packages PcGets and Autometrics demonstrates the robustness of Kamin and Ericsson's (1993) final error correction model and improves on it by using multi-path searches that would be tedious and prohibitively time-consuming with standard econometrics packages. Long-run money demand is driven by a negative ratchet effect from inflation, and by the opportunity cost of holding peso-denominated financial assets rather than Argentine goods or US dollars. Short-run dynamics are consistent with an *Ss*-type inventory model that is interpretable as having either real or nominal short-run bounds.

Several general remarks are germane, and each suggests extensions to the current analysis. First, improvements to the model selection algorithms may and do obtain an improved model specification. Computer-automated model-selection algorithms are still in their youth—if not in their infancy—and considerable analytical, Monte Carlo, and empirical research is ongoing; see Hendry and Krolzig (1999, 2003, 2005), Krolzig and Hendry (2001), Hoover and Perez (2004), Doornik (2009), Hendry, Johansen, and Santos (2008), Hoover, Demiralp, and Perez (2009), Hoover, Johansen, and Juselius (2008), and Johansen and Nielsen (2009).

Second, insights by other researchers may improve the current model in a progressive research strategy. For example, Nielsen (2008), building on Hendry and von Ungern-Sternberg (1981), proposes an alternative measure of the opportunity cost of holding money that may better capture agents' behaviour in a hyperinflationary environment. Preliminary tests for that alternative measure as an omitted variable in Table 17.4 do not reveal an improved specification, however. For instance, for a variable X in levels, define

∇X_t as $(X_t - X_{t-1})/(X_{t-1})$, which is X's percentage change, measured as a fraction. Omitted variables tests include $F(8, 109) = 1.23$ [0.290] for $\{\nabla P_{t-i};\ i = 0, \ldots, 7\}$, $F(24, 93) = 1.10$ [0.363] for $\{\nabla P_{t-i}, \nabla P^{max}_{t-i}, \Delta\nabla P^{pos}_{t-i}; i = 0, \ldots, 7\}$, and $F(32, 85) = 1.01$ [0.474] for $\{\nabla P_{t-i}, \nabla P^{max}_{t-i}, \Delta\nabla P^{pos}_{t-i}, \nabla E_{t-i}; i = 0, \ldots, 7\}$. None of these tests reject at standard levels. Still, Table 17.4 is a relatively unrestricted model, so further investigation is merited, particularly because Δp_t differs substantially from ∇P_t at high inflation rates and hence the interpretation of Δp_t may be affected.

Third, Kongsted (2005) develops a procedure for testing the nominal-to-real transformation, which is only informally investigated herein for money by using the ADF statistics. Fourth, in the VAR, the variables Δp^{max} and $\Delta^2 p^{pos}$ are transformations of Δp , so further consideration of their joint distributional properties is desirable. Fifth, data observations after 1993 may be informative. Even so, mechanistic extensions of the existing data may not be sufficient, as when data definitions change, the array of available assets alters, and underlying economic conditions shift; see Ericsson, Hendry, and Prestwich (1998).

References

Ahumada, H. (1992). A dynamic model of the demand for currency: Argentina 1977–1988. *Journal of Policy Modeling*, **14**(3), 335–361.

Akaike, H. (1973). Information theory and an extension of the maximum likelihood principle. In Petrov, B. N. and Csáki, F. (eds.), *Second International Symposium on Information Theory*, pp. 267–281. Budapest: Akadémiai Kiadó.

——(1981). Likelihood of a model and information criteria. *Journal of Econometrics*, **16**(1), 3–14.

Atkinson, A. C. (1981). Likelihood ratios, posterior odds and information criteria. *Journal of Econometrics*, **16**(1), 15–20.

Baba, Y., Hendry, D. F., and Starr, R. M. (1992). The demand for M1 in the U.S.A., 1960–1988. *Review of Economic Studies*, **59**(1), 25–61.

Beckerman, P. (1992). *The Economics of High Inflation*. New York: St. Martin's Press.

Cagan, P. (1956). The monetary dynamics of hyperinflation. Ch. 2 in Friedman, M. (ed.), *Studies in the Quantity Theory of Money*, pp. 23–117. Chicago: University of Chicago Press.

Campos, J. and Ericsson, N. R. (1999). Constructive data mining: Modeling consumers' expenditure in Venezuela. *Econometrics Journal*, **2**(2), 226–240.

Dominguez, K. M. E. and Tesar, L. L. (2007). International borrowing and macroeconomic performance in Argentina. Ch. 7 in Edwards, S. (ed.), *Capital Controls and Capital Flows in Emerging Economies: Policies, Practices, and Consequences*, pp. 297–342 (with discussion). Chicago: University of Chicago Press.

Doornik, J. A. (2009). Autometrics. In Castle, J. L. and Shephard, N. (eds.), *The Methodology and Practice of Econometrics: A Festschrift in Honour of David F. Hendry*. Oxford: Oxford University Press, this volume.

Doornik, J. A. and Hendry, D. F. (2007). *PcGive 12*. London: Timberlake Consultants Ltd (4 volumes).

——— and Nielsen, B. (1998). Inference in cointegrating models: UK M1 revisited. *Journal of Economic Surveys*, **12**(5), 533–572.

Engle, R. F. and Hendry, D. F. (1993). Testing super exogeneity and invariance in regression models. *Journal of Econometrics*, **56**(1/2), 119–139.

Enzler, J., Johnson, L., and Paulus, J. (1976). Some problems of money demand. *Brookings Papers on Economic Activity*, **1976**(1), 261–280 (with discussion).

Ericsson, N. R. (2004). The *ET* interview: Professor David F. Hendry. *Econometric Theory*, **20**(4), 743–804.

—— (2009). *Empirical Modeling of Economic Time Series*, in preparation.

—— Hendry, D. F., and Prestwich, K. M. (1998). The demand for broad money in the United Kingdom, 1878–1993. *Scandinavian Journal of Economics*, **100**(1), 289–324 (with discussion).

Flemming, J. S. (1976). *Inflation*. Oxford: Oxford University Press.

Hannan, E. J. and Quinn, B. G. (1979). The determination of the order of an autoregression. *Journal of the Royal Statistical Society, Series B*, **41**(2), 190–195.

Helkie, W. L. and Howard, D. H. (1994). External adjustment in selected developing countries in the 1990s. *Journal of Policy Modeling*, **16**(4), 353–393.

Hendry, D. F. (1995). On the interactions of unit roots and exogeneity. *Econometric Reviews*, **14**(4), 383–419.

—— (2006). Robustifying forecasts from equilibrium-correction systems. *Journal of Econometrics*, **135**(1–2), 399–426.

—— and Doornik, J. A. (1994). Modelling linear dynamic econometric systems. *Scottish Journal of Political Economy*, **41**(1), 1–33.

—— and Ericsson, N. R. (1991). Modeling the demand for narrow money in the United Kingdom and the United States. *European Economic Review*, **35**(4), 833–881 (with discussion).

—— Johansen, S., and Santos, C. (2008). Automatic selection of indicators in a fully saturated regression. *Computational Statistics*, **23**(2), 317–335, 337–339.

—— and Krolzig, H.-M. (1999). Improving on 'Data mining reconsidered' by K. D. Hoover and S. J. Perez. *Econometrics Journal*, **2**(2), 202–219.

——— (2001) *Automatic Econometric Model Selection Using PcGets 1.0*. London: Timberlake Consultants Press.

——— (2003). New developments in automatic general-to-specific modeling. Ch. 16 in Stigum, B. P. (ed.), *Econometrics and the Philosophy of Economics: Theory-Data Confrontations in Economics*, pp. 379–419. Princeton: Princeton University Press.

——— (2005). The properties of automatic *Gets* modelling. *Economic Journal*, **115**(502), C32–C61.

—— and Mizon, G. E. (1978). Serial correlation as a convenient simplification, not a nuisance: A comment on a study of the demand for money by the Bank of England. *Economic Journal*, **88**(351), 549–563.

—— and von Ungern-Sternberg, T. (1981). Liquidity and inflation effects on consumers' expenditure. Ch. 9 in Deaton, A. S. (ed.), *Essays in the Theory and Measurement of Consumer Behaviour: In Honour of Sir Richard Stone*, pp. 237–260. Cambridge: Cambridge University Press.

Hoover, K. D., Demiralp, S., and Perez, S. J. (2009). Empirical identification of the vector autoregression: The causes and effects of US M2. In Castle, J. L. and Shephard, N. (eds.), *The Methodology and Practice of Econometrics: A Festschrift in Honour of David F. Hendry*. Oxford: Oxford University Press, this volume.

——Johansen, S., and Juselius, K. (2008). Allowing the data to speak freely: The macro-econometrics of the cointegrated vector autoregression. *American Economic Review*, **98**(2), 251–255.

——and Perez, S. J. (1999). Data mining reconsidered: Encompassing and the general-to-specific approach to specification search. *Econometrics Journal*, **2**(2), 167–191 (with discussion).

————(2004). Truth and robustness in cross-country growth regressions. *Oxford Bulletin of Economics and Statistics*, **66**(5), 765–798.

Howard, D. H. (1987). Exchange rate regimes and macroeconomic stabilization in a developing country. International Finance Discussion Paper No. 314, Board of Governors of the Federal Reserve System, Washington, D.C., November.

Johansen, S. (1988). Statistical analysis of cointegration vectors. *Journal of Economic Dynamics and Control*, **12**(2/3), 231–254.

——(1991). Estimation and hypothesis testing of cointegration vectors in Gaussian vector autoregressive models. *Econometrica*, **59**(6), 1551–1580.

——(1992a). Cointegration in partial systems and the efficiency of single-equation analysis. *Journal of Econometrics*, **52**(3), 389–402.

——(1992b). Testing weak exogeneity and the order of cointegration in UK money demand data. *Journal of Policy Modeling*, **14**(3), 313–334.

——(1995). *Likelihood-based Inference in Cointegrated Vector Autoregressive Models*. Oxford: Oxford University Press.

——and Nielsen, B. (2009). An analysis of the indicator saturation estimator as a robust regression estimator. In Castle, J. L. and Shephard, N. (eds.), *The Methodology and Practice of Econometrics: A Festschrift in Honour of David F. Hendry*. Oxford: Oxford University Press, this volume.

Juselius, K. (1992). Domestic and foreign effects on prices in an open economy: The case of Denmark. *Journal of Policy Modeling*, **14**(4), 401–428.

Kamin, S. B. (1991). Argentina's experience with parallel exchange markets: 1981–1990. International Finance Discussion Paper No. 407, Board of Governors of the Federal Reserve System, Washington, D.C., August.

——and Ericsson, N. R. (1993). Dollarization in Argentina. International Finance Discussion Paper No. 460, Board of Governors of the Federal Reserve System, Washington, D.C., November.

————(2003). Dollarization in post-hyperinflationary Argentina. *Journal of International Money and Finance*, **22**(2), 185–211.

Kiguel, M. A. (1991). Inflation in Argentina: Stop and go since the Austral plan. *World Development*, **19**(8), 969–986.

Kongsted, H. C. (2005). Testing the nominal-to-real transformation. *Journal of Econometrics*, **124**(2), 205–225.

Krolzig, H.-M. and Hendry, D. F. (2001). Computer automation of general-to-specific model selection procedures. *Journal of Economic Dynamics and Control*, **25**(6–7), 831–866.

MacKinnon, J. G. (1991). Critical values for cointegration tests. Ch. 13 in Engle, R. F. and Granger, C. W. J. (eds.), *Long-run Economic Relationships: Readings in Cointegration*, pp. 267–276. Oxford: Oxford University Press.

Manzetti, L. (1991). *The International Monetary Fund and Economic Stabilization: The Argentine Case*. New York: Praeger.

Melnick, R. (1990). The demand for money in Argentina 1978–1987: Before and after the Austral program. *Journal of Business and Economic Statistics*, **8**(4), 427–434.

Nielsen, B. (2008). On the explosive nature of hyper-inflation data. *Economics: The Open-Access, Open-Assessment E-Journal*, **2**, 2008–21.

Piterman, S. (1988). The irreversibility of the relationship between inflation and real balances. *Bank of Israel Economic Review*, **60**, January, 72–83.

Schwarz, G. (1978). Estimating the dimension of a model. *Annals of Statistics*, **6**(2), 461–464.

Simpson, T. D. and Porter, R. D. (1980). Some issues involving the definition and interpretation of the monetary aggregates. In Federal Reserve Bank of Boston (ed.), *Controlling Monetary Aggregates III*, Boston: Federal Reserve Bank of Boston, *Conference Series No. 23*, 161–234 (with discussion).

Taylor, M. P. (1986). From the general to the specific: The demand for M2 in three European countries. *Empirical Economics*, **11**(4), 243–261.

Uribe, M. (1997). Hysteresis in a simple model of currency substitution. *Journal of Monetary Economics*, **40**(1), 185–202.

World Bank (1990). *Argentina: Reforms for Price Stability and Growth*. Washington, D.C.: World Bank.

Index

Note: page numbers in *italics* refer to Figures and Tables.

Index

Index

Printed and bound by CPI Group (UK) Ltd, Croydon, CR0 4YY